The **Rough Guide** to

Korea

written and researched by

Norbert Paxton

ROUGH GUIDES

NEW YORK • LONDON • DELHI

www.roughguides.com

Contents

◀◀ Chokseongnu pavilion, Jinju ◀ Seoraksan National Park, Gangwon

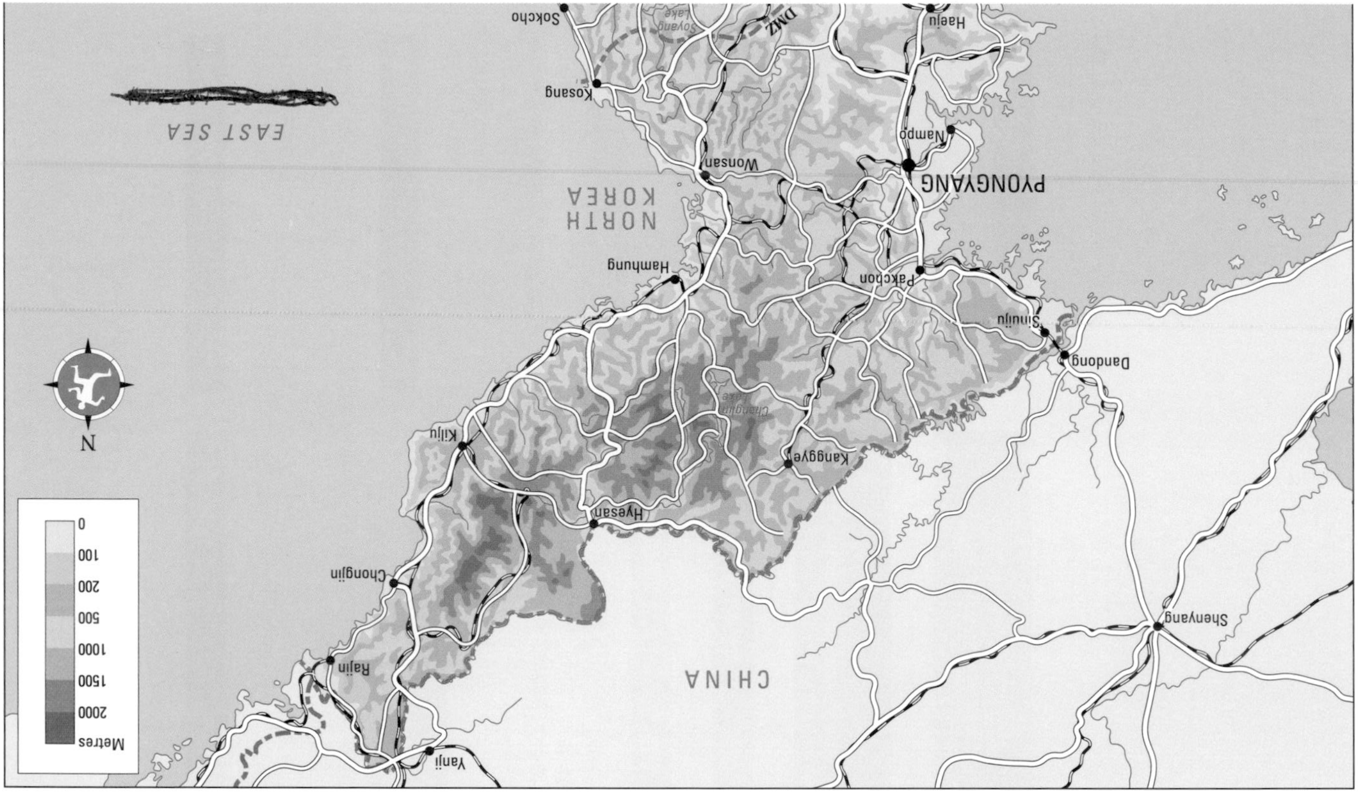
Metres
2000
1500
1000
500
200
100
0
N
EAST SEA
NORTH KOREA
CHINA
Yanji
Rajin
Chongjin
Kilju
Hyesan
Hamhung
Kanggye
Changjin Lake
Wonsan
Kosang
Sokcho
Soyang Lake
DMZ
Pakchon
PYONGYANG
Nampo
Haeju
Sinuiju
Dandong
Shenyang

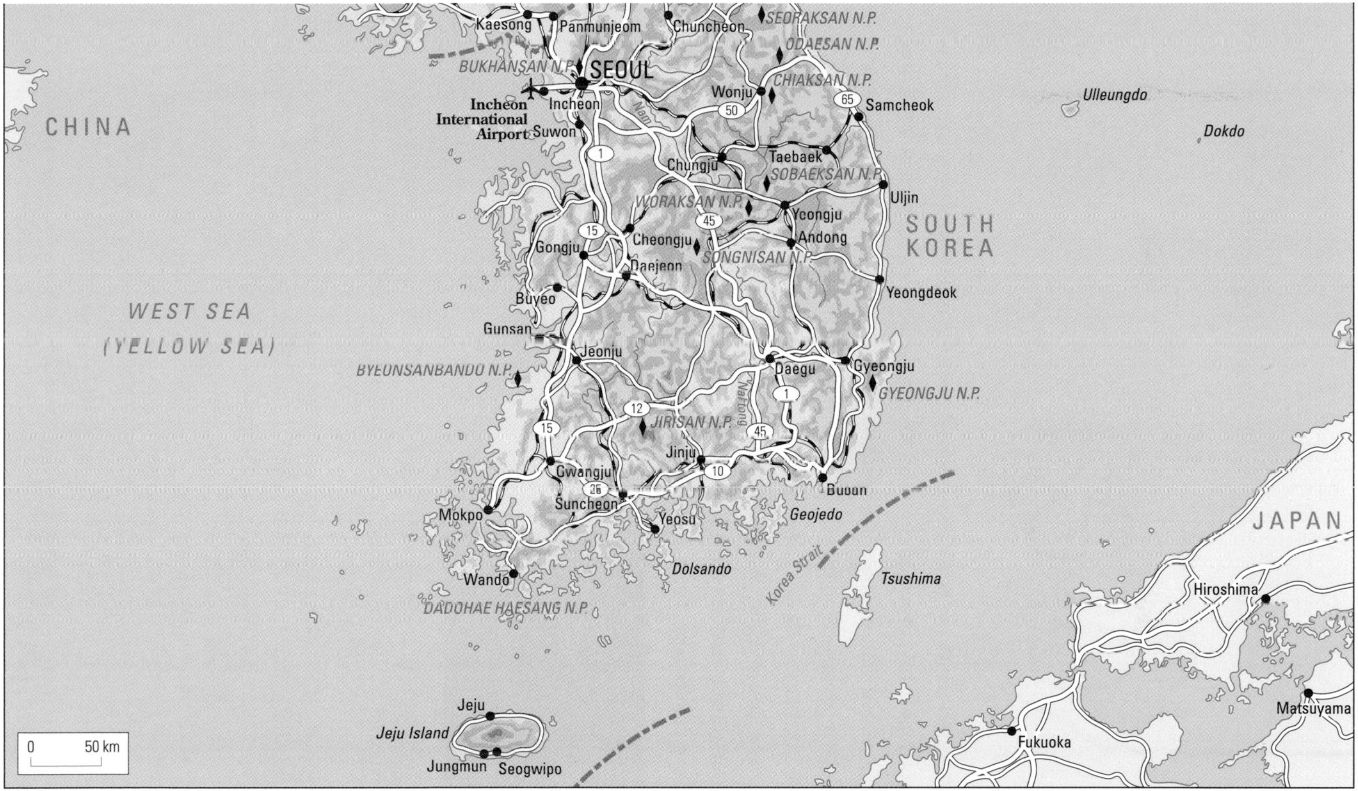
Kaesong
Panmunjeom
Chuncheon
SEORAKSAN N.P.
ODAESAN N.P.
BUKHANSAN N.P.
SEOUL
CHIAKSAN N.P.
Wonju
Incheon International Airport
Incheon
Samcheok
Ulleungdo
Dokdo
CHINA
Suwon
Taebaek
Chungju
SOBAEKSAN N.P.
Uljin
WORAKSAN N.P.
Yeongju
SOUTH KOREA
Gongju
Cheongju
Andong
SONGNISAN N.P.
Daejeon
Buyeo
Yeongdeok
WEST SEA (YELLOW SEA)
Gunsan
Jeonju
Daegu
Gyeongju
BYEONSANBANDO N.P.
GYEONGJU N.P.
Naktong
JIRISAN N.P.
Jinju
Gwangju
Busan
Suncheon
Mokpo
Yeosu
Geojedo
JAPAN
Korea Strait
Dolsando
Tsushima
Wando
Hiroshima
DADOHAE HAESANG N.P.
Jeju
Jeju Island
Matsuyama
0 50 km
Fukuoka
Jungmun
Seogwipo
Nam
1
50
65
15
45
12
45
10
26

Introduction to Korea

A pine-clad land of mountains, misty archipelagos and rice paddies of emerald green, Korea is something of a mystery to many travellers, but that it exists at all is little short of miraculous. Surrounded by three of the greatest powers in history – China, Russia and Japan – it spent much of its past as an East Asian punchbag, yet has somehow not only survived, but has done so with its culture and customs largely intact.

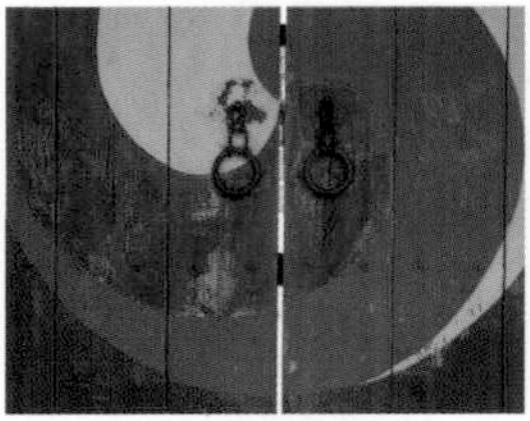

Not surprisingly, Koreans have a keen sense of national identity: the peninsula plays host to two of the most **distinctive societies** on earth, now cleaved into North and South Korea by the spiky twin frontiers of the Demilitarized Zone. The two countries went their separate ways in 1953 after the catastrophic **Korean War** – essentially a civil war, but one largely brought about by external forces – which left millions dead, and flattened almost the whole peninsula. **North Korea** has since armed itself to the teeth, stagnated in its pursuit of a local brand of **communism** and become one of the least accessible countries in the world. Unbelievably, many foreigners seem to expect something similar of **South Korea**, which shows just how well kept a secret it really is – beyond Seoul, *gimchi*, dog meat and taekwondo, little is known about the country on the outside.

The South gradually embraced democracy and has since gone on to become a powerful and dynamic economy, its **cities** a pulsating feast of eye-searing neon, incessant activity and round-the-clock business. Here you can shop 'til you drop at markets that never close, feast on eye-wateringly spicy food, get giddy on a bottle or two of *soju*, then sweat out the day's exertions at a night-time sauna. However, set foot outside the main cities and your mere presence will cause quite a stir – in the remote **rural areas** life continues much as it did before the "Economic Miracle" of the 1980s, and pockets of **islands** exist where no foreigner has ever set foot.

For all its newfound prosperity, though, the South remains a land steeped in **tradition**. An unbroken line of more than one hundred kings stretches back almost two thousand years before being abruptly choked off by the Japanese occupation in 1910 – their grassy burial mounds have yielded thousands of golden relics – and even the capital, Seoul, has a number of **palaces** dating back to the fourteenth century. The wooden *hanok* housing of decades gone by may have largely given way to rows of apartment blocks, but you'll never be more than a walk away from an immaculately

▲ Mural of the Great Leader

Fact file

- The Korean peninsula is split in two by the four-kilometre-wide Demilitarized Zone (DMZ), sharing borders with China and – for about 20km near Vladivostok – Russia. These frontiers form a northern boundary with **North Korea** – the "Democratic People's Republic of Korea" – whose population of around 23 million live in an area half the size of the United Kingdom. Slightly smaller **South Korea**, also known as the "Republic of Korea", has a population of 49 million, making it the world's 26th most populous country.
- Ethnic Koreans dominate the populations of both countries, making them two of the most **ethnically homogenous** societies on earth. Before splitting both were traditionally Buddhist nations – though deeply steeped in Confucianism and shamanistic ritual. Since then the North has followed Juche, a local brand of communism, while in the South Christianity has become the most popular religion.
- Before the Japanese occupation in 1910, the Silla, Goryeo and Joseon dynasties were ruled over by an unbroken run of **116 monarchs**, dating back to 57 BC.
- The economies of South and North Korea were almost equal in size until the mid-1970s. The "Economic Miracle" that followed in the South has made it the world's eleventh largest economy, while the North languishes in 92nd place.

Grandmother techno

While modern K-pop has swept across continental Asia, there's another strain of music that you're just as likely to come across on your way around Korea: "**Trot**" songs – best described as a kind of **grandmother techno** – are fast-paced ballads, set to odd synthesized rhythms and crooned out in a semi-compulsory warbly voice. The songs have changed over the years but the style has been around since the 1930s and remains hugely popular with Korea's older set, as anyone who's seen a clutch of grannies getting down to the beats will testify. However, *Trot* is not the sole preserve of the elderly, and is unlikely to go out of fashion for some time – you'll find university students belting hits out in *noraebang* (Korean karaoke dens) and kids listening to them on tape, while young artists such as Jang Yoon-jeong have scored big by crossing the genre with the ballads that younger Koreans tend to prefer. Ubiquitous cabaret shows mean that *Trot* is rarely off the television, and the highway service stations you'll call in at on long-distance bus journeys are filled with *Trot* tapes – at just W1000 each, they make fantastic souvenirs.

▼ Sangwonsa temple, Odaesan National Park

painted **Buddhist temple**, while some mountains still host shamanist rituals, and Confucian-style formal ceremonies continue to play an important part in local life.

The **Korean people** themselves are a real highlight: fiercely proud, and with a character almost as spicy as their food, they're markedly eager to please foreigners who come to live or holiday in their country. Within hours of arriving, you'll probably find yourself racing up a mountainside – new friends in tow – lunching over a delicious barbequed *galbi*, throwing back *dongdongju* until dawn, or singing the night away at a *noraebang*. Few travellers leave without tales of the kindness of Korean strangers, and almost all wonder why the country isn't a more popular stop on the international travel circuit. Tourist numbers are, however, rising, so come quickly – the secret is well and truly out.

Where to go

Korea is still something of an unknown territory, and more than half of all its visitors get no further than **Seoul**. One of the largest and most technically advanced cities in the world, the capital regularly confounds expectations by proving itself steeped in history. Here, fourteenth-century palaces, imperial gardens, teeming markets and secluded tearooms continue to exude charm among a maze of skyscrapers and shopping malls. From Seoul, anywhere in the country is reachable within a day, but the best day-trip by far is to the **DMZ**, the strip of land that separates the two Koreas from coast to coast.

Gyeonggi-do, the province that surrounds Seoul, is a largely unappealing area dissected by the roads and railways that snake their way into the capital, though two of its cities deserve a visit: **Suwon**, home to a wonderful fortress dating from the late eighteenth century; and cosmopolitan **Incheon**, where you can eat some of the best food in the country before making your way to the **islands** of the West Sea. By contrast, the neighbouring province of **Gangwon-do** is unspoilt and stuffed full of attractions – in addition to a number of national parks, of which craggy **Seoraksan** is the most visited, you can head to the unspoilt beaches and colossal caves that surround the small city of **Samcheok**, or race along a disused countryside train line on a rail bike from **Aruaji**.

The peninsula plays host to two of the most distinctive societies on earth.

▼ Wolchulsan National Park, Jeolla

The Taegeukki

South Korea's national flag – the *Taegeukki* – is one of the most distinctive around, and is heavily imbued with philsophical meaning. The design itself has changed a little since its first unveiling in the 1880s, though its fundamental elements remain the same: a red-and-blue circle surrounded by four black trigams, all set on a white background. The puritanical connotations of the white are obvious, whereas the circle and trigrams offer greater food for thought. The four trigams make up half of the eight used in the *I Ching*, an ancient Chinese book of divination. Each can represent a number of different concepts: moving clockwise from the top-left of the flag, these may be read as spring, winter, summer and autumn; heaven, moon, earth and sun; father, son, mother and daughter; as well as many more besides. The circle is split into the "Yin–Yang" shape, its two halves representing opposites such as light and dark, male and female, day and night. Though coincidental, connections with the divided Korean peninsula are easy to find with two opposing halves forming part of the same whole, the red half is even on top.

Stretching down from Gangwon to the South Sea lie the markedly traditional **Gyeongsang** provinces, home to some of the peninsula's most popular attractions. Foremost among these is gorgeous **Gyeongju**, capital of the Silla dynasty for almost a thousand years, and extremely laid-back

▼ Changing of the guard, Gyeongbokgung

▲ Tea fields in Boseong

by Korean standards, it's spotted with the grassy burial tombs of the many kings and queens who ruled here. There's enough in the surrounding area to fill at least a week of sightseeing, most notably **Namsan**, a hill peppered with some intriguing highlights, and the sumptuously decorated **Bulguksa** temple. **Andong** is almost as relaxed as Gyeongju, and a great base from

Titles and transliteration

The Korean peninsula is split into the Republic of Korea (South Korea) and the Democratic People's Republic of Korea (North Korea). Most of this book is about the former, which is referred to throughout as "**Korea**"; this is how locals refer to their nation when talking to outsiders, though in Korean they use the term "*Hanguk*". North Korea has, where necessary, been referred to as such, or as "the **DPRK**"; North Koreans' own word for both country and peninsula is "*Choson*".

Also note that a uniform system of **transliteration** is used throughout. It's the best and most recent one, but as older generations have been schooled with different systems you may well spot a few varieties of the same word on your travels – see the Language section on p.453 for more information.

which to access **Dosan Seowon**, a remote Confucian academy, and the charmingly dusty village of **Hahoe**, a functioning showcase of traditional Korean life. The region's rustic charm is actually best appreciated offshore on the windswept island of **Ulleungdo**, an extinct volcanic cone that rises precipitously from the East Sea, and where tiny fishing settlements cling barnacle-like to its coast. Thrills of a more urban bent can be had in **Busan**, Korea's second city, which has an atmosphere markedly different from Seoul; as well as the most raucous nightlife outside the capital, it has the best fish market in the country, and a number of excellent beaches on its fringes.

Even more characterful are the **Jeolla** provinces, which make up the southwest of the peninsula. Left to stagnate by the government while Korea's economy kicked into gear, they have long played the role of the renegade; however, this energy is now being re-channelled. Violent

▼ Hanok village, Jeonju

▲ Haeundae beach, Busan

political protests took place in regional capital **Gwangju** as recently as 1980, though the city has reinvented itself to become one of the artiest and most business-savvy in the land. **Jeonju** has a similar feel and a delightful district of traditional *hanok* housing, and is justly famed for its wonderful cuisine. Earthy **Mokpo** is the hub for ferry trips to a mind-boggling number of **West Sea islands**, dotted with fishing communities where life has changed little in decades, while inland there are a number of excellent national parks.

The **Chungcheong** provinces at the centre of the country are bypassed by many travellers, but contain some of its finest sights. The old Baekje capitals of **Gongju** and **Buyeo** provide glimpses of a dynasty long dead, **Daecheon beach** hosts an annual mud festival that ranks as Korea's most enjoyable event, and there are temples galore – the gigantic golden Buddha at **Beopjusa** is surrounded by thousand-metre-high peaks, while the meandering trails and lurid paint schemes at **Guinsa** make it the most visually stimulating temple in the land.

Lying within a ferry ride of the mainland's southern shore is the island of **Jeju**. A popular honeymoon destination for Koreans, anyone who has climbed the volcanic cone of **Hallasan**, walked through the lava tubes of **Manjanggul** or watched the sun go down from **Yakcheonsa** temple will tell you the trip is worthwhile.

From Seoul, anywhere in the country is reachable within a day, but the best day-trip by far is to the DMZ.

Finally, of course, there's **North Korea**. A visit to one of the world's most feared countries will instantly earn you kudos – even experienced travellers routinely put the DPRK at the top of their "most interesting" list. Visits don't come cheap and can only be made as part of a guided tour, but the country's inaccessibility brings an epic quality to its few officially sanctioned sights.

When to go

Korea's year is split into **four distinct seasons**. **Spring** generally lasts from April to June, and is one of the best times of the year to visit: flowers are in bloom, and a fluffy cloak of cherry blossom washes a brief wave of pinkish white from south to north. Locals head for the hills, making use of the country's many national parks, and the effects of the change in weather can also be seen in a number of interesting festivals.

Korea's **summer** can be unbearably muggy, and you may find yourself leaping from one air-conditioned sanctuary to the next. You'll wonder how Koreans can persist with their uniformly fiery food at this time, but be grateful for the ubiquitous water fountains. It's best to avoid the **monsoon** season: more than half of the country's annual rain falls from early July to late August. In a neat reversal of history, Japan and China protect Korea from most of the area's typhoons, but one or two manage to get through the gap each year.

The best time of the year to visit is **autumn** (Sept–Nov), when temperatures are mild, rainfall is generally low and festivals are easy to

▼ Daegu

come across. Korea's mountains erupt in a magnificent array of reds, yellows and oranges, and locals flock to national parks to picnic under their fiery tones. T-shirt weather can continue long into October, though you're likely to need some extra layers by then.

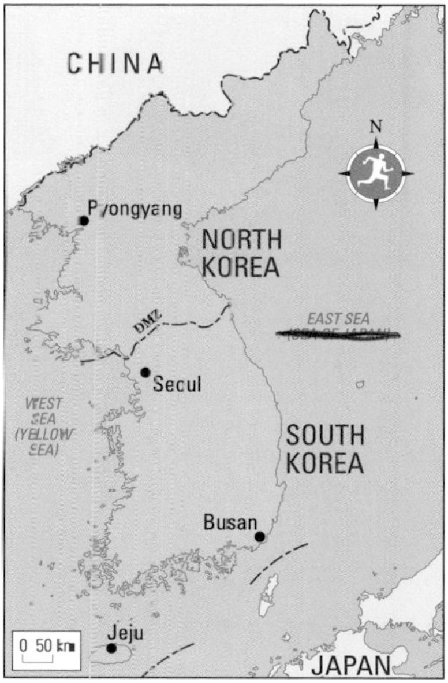

The Korean **winter** is long and cold, with the effects of the Siberian weather system more pronounced the further north you go. However, travel at this time is far from impossible – there's almost no change to public transport, underfloor *ondol* heating systems are cranked up, and the lack of rain creates photogenic contrasts between powdery snow, crisp blue skies, off-black pine trees and the earthy yellow of dead grass.

Average temperatures (in °C) and rainfall (in mm)

	Jan	Feb	Mar	Apr	May	Jun	Jul	Aug	Sep	Oct	Nov	Dec
Busan												
Max	6	7	12	17	21	24	27	29	26	21	15	9
Min	-2	-1	3	8	13	17	22	23	18	12	6	1
Rainfall	43	36	69	140	132	201	295	130	173	74	41	31
Jeju City												
Max	10	12	15	19	23	26	28	29	27	23	17	13
Min	5	6	8	10	14	18	23	24	20	14	8	6
Rainfall	84	89	94	176	171	205	356	243	184	95	93	82
Pyongyang												
Max	-3	1	7	16	22	26	29	29	24	18	9	0
Min	-13	-10	-4	3	9	15	20	20	14	6	-2	-10
Rainfall	15	11	25	46	67	76	237	228	112	45	41	21
Seoul												
Max	0	3	8	17	22	27	29	31	26	19	11	3
Min	-9	-7	-2	5	11	16	21	22	15	7	0	-7
Rainfall	31	20	38	76	81	130	376	267	119	41	46	25

25 things not to miss

It's not possible to see everything that Korea has to offer on a short trip – and we don't suggest you try. What follows is a selective taste of the city's highlights: fascinating museums, spectacular buildings and a few ways just to indulge yourself. They're arranged in five colour-coded categories, which you can browse through to find the very best things to see and experience. All highlights have a page reference to take you straight into the guide, where you can find out more.

01 **Ilchulbong** Page **362** • Wake up early to catch the day's first rays at "Sunrise Peak", a verdant green caldera on the eastern tip of beautiful island of Jeju.

02 Gyeongju Page **201** • This former capital of Silla is the most traditional city in Korea, and should be on every visitor's itinerary.

03 Dongdaemun Market Page **104** • A 24-hour market in a city that never sleeps, Dongdaemun is a Seoul institution, with sights and smells redolent of decades gone by.

04 Galbi see ***Korean cuisine* colour section** A fire at the centre of your table and a plateful of raw meat to throw on it – could this be the world's most fun-to-eat dish?

05 Hongdae Page **109** • There's no better place to party than Hongdae, Seoul's most happening nightlife district.

06 Boryeong Mud Festival Page **324** • Korea's dirtiest, most enjoyable festival takes place each July on the west coast – don't forget your soap.

07 West Sea Islands Page **274** • Over three thousand islands sprinkled like confetti around Korea's western coast; Mokpo is the best point of access.

08 Beopjusa Page **335** • A 33-metre-high golden Buddha stands over this wonderful temple, surrounded by the peaks of Songnisan National Park.

09 The DMZ Page **159** • Take a step inside the 4km-wide Demilitarized Zone, separating North and South Korea, the world's frostiest remnant of the Cold War.

10 Noraebang Page **108** • A near-mandatory part of a Korean night out is a trip to a "singing room", the local take on Japan's karaoke bars.

11 Buyeo Fortress Page **321** • Korea's most charming and historic fortress by far – this is where the Baekje dynasty met its end, literally toppling to extinction into the adjacent river.

12 Guinsa Page **343** • The most distinctive temple complex in the country, Guinsa's paths wind snake-like routes up a tight, remote valley in Korea's heartland.

13 Jagalchi Fish Market Page **245** • Your food may be so fresh that it's still wriggling on your plate at this highly atmospheric Busan fish market.

14 Seoraksan National Park Page **178** • Bald, rocky peaks jut out from the pines at what the locals claim to be the country's most magnificent park.

15 Jeongdongjin Page **188** • Korea's most surreal village has a train station on the beach, a ship-hotel atop a cliff, an American warship and an equally real North Korean spy submarine.

16 Dosan Seowon Page **230** • The wonderfully unspoilt countryside surrounding the city of Andong is studded with gems, but this former Confucian academy is one of the best.

17 Dongdongju Page **45** & ***Korean cuisine* colour section**
Consumed by students all over Korea and often served in rustic wooden bowls, drinking this creamy rice wine is the most traditional way to guarantee a banging hangover.

18 Jeonju Hanok Village Page **293** • Here you can sleep in a traditional wooden *hanok* house heated from underneath by gentle flames, in one of Korea's most agreeable cities.

19 Biwon Page **99** • Relax by the lake as kings once did at this secluded "Secret Garden", which nestles at the back of a UNESCO-listed palace in central Seoul.

20 Jeju Teddy Bear Museum Page **371** • The epitome of kitsch, most notable for its diorama room portraying twentieth-century events such as teddies tearing down the Berlin Wall, landing on the moon and going down with the *Titanic*.

21 Insa-dong Page **85** • Immerse yourself in wholesome traditional activities on Seoul's most popular street, one peppered with art galleries, tearooms and rustic restaurants.

22 Paekdusan Page **415** • The legendary birthplace of the Korean nation, this dormant volcano – the highest peak on the peninsula – rises up through the Chinese–North Korean border, its crater lake a preternatural blue when not frozen over.

23 Socialist Realist Art Page **390** • What has become an ironic style in Eastern Europe remains iconic in the DPRK, with colourful murals found all across the country – send one home on a postcard.

24 Pyongyang Page **399** • The world's least-visited capital is a rhapsody of brutalist architecture, many buildings topped with red Hangeul slogans extolling the virtues of the government and its leaders.

25 Arirang Mass Games Page **410** • Performers outnumber spectators at this feast of synchronized dance, one of the biggest and most spectacular festivals you're ever likely to see.

Basics

Basics

Getting there

South Korea is effectively an island in international travel terms, with its only land border the spiky frontier of the Demilitarized Zone (DMZ), which keeps its northern neighbour at arms length. The military deadlock is unlikely to be broken any time soon; the only current routes into South Korea are by air or sea, with the vast majority of travellers arriving at the modern Incheon international airport, located on an island west of Seoul. For North Korea travel basics, see p.385.

Korean Air and Asiana are the two big Korean **airlines**, operating direct flights from a number of destinations around the world. Seoul increasingly features as a stopover on round-the-world trips, and the country is well served by dozens of international carriers.

Fares increase for travel in the summer months and at Christmas time. A **departure tax** applies when leaving Korea, but will almost certainly be factored in to your ticket price.

Incheon itself is served by a number of Chinese **ferry** ports, and there are services from several destinations in Japan to Busan. Those arriving by ferry will be rewarded with a pretty introduction to the country – the Korean coastline around Incheon melts into countless islands, though the port area itself has been ravaged by industry, as have some nearby islands. Yet more interesting would be to arrive by **train** through North Korea, but though the country's relationship with the outside world has so far prevented Seoul-bound trains from making the journey from Beijing, lines across the DMZ have been upgraded in anticipation of a political thaw on the peninsula – keep your eyes peeled.

Flights from the UK and Ireland

Korean Air and Asiana have **direct** connections from London Heathrow to Incheon – Korean Air has a daily service, while Asiana has five per week. The journey takes eleven hours, with fares costing around £550; this can sail over £700 during summer and at Christmas, when it's common for all flights to be fully booked weeks in advance. Many travellers save money by taking a **transit flight** – ticket prices for flying with Emirates via Dubai often dip below £400 during low season, though they add several hours to the total flight-time, while Qatar Airways takes marginally less time but you'll usually pay a little more. It's also worth checking deals with KLM and Air France, whose routes are as close to direct as possible.

There are no direct flights to Korea from **Ireland** so transit flights are your only option.

Flights from the US and Canada

If you are coming from the **US** you have a number of options available to you: there are direct flights to Incheon from New York, Dallas, Las Vegas, Los Angeles, San Francisco, Seattle, Chicago, Atlanta and Washington; carriers include Delta Airlines, Northwest Airlines and United Airlines, as well as Asiana and Korean Air. Sample low season fares are $1400 from New York (a journey of around fourteen hours), $1200 from Chicago (fourteen hours) and $1150 from Los Angeles (thirteen hours). In all cases you may save up to a couple of hundred dollars by taking a transit flight – San Francisco and Seattle being popular hubs. Fares on many routes can almost double during summer and Christmas time.

Korean Air has direct flights from Incheon from two **Canadian** cities, Vancouver and Toronto, but these can be very expensive when demand is high (over C$3000). Again, you're likely to save money by taking a transit flight, in which case C$1700 would be a typical low season fare from both cities.

Fly less – stay longer! Travel and climate change

Climate change is the single biggest issue facing our planet. It is caused by a build-up in the atmosphere of carbon dioxide and other greenhouse gases, which are emitted by many sources – including planes. Already, flights account for around 3–4 percent of human-induced global warming: that figure may sound small, but it is rising year on year and threatens to counteract the progress made by reducing greenhouse emissions in other areas.

Rough Guides regard travel, overall, as a global benefit, and feel strongly that the advantages to developing economies are important, as are the opportunities for greater contact and awareness among peoples. But we all have a responsibility to limit our personal "carbon footprint". That means giving thought to how often we fly and what we can do to redress the harm that our trips create.

Flying and climate change

Pretty much every form of motorized travel generates CO_2, but planes are particularly bad offenders, releasing large volumes of greenhouse gases at altitudes where their impact is far more harmful. Flying also allows us to travel much further than we would contemplate doing by road or rail, so the emissions attributable to each passenger become truly shocking. For example, one person taking a return flight between Europe and California produces the equivalent impact of 2.5 tonnes of CO_2 – similar to the yearly output of the average UK car.

Less harmful planes may evolve but it will be decades before they replace the current fleet – which could be too late for avoiding climate chaos. In the meantime, there are limited options for concerned travellers: to reduce the amount we travel by air (take fewer trips, stay longer!), to avoid night flights (when plane contrails trap heat from Earth but can't reflect sunlight back to space), and to make the trips we do take "climate neutral" via a carbon offset scheme.

Carbon offset schemes

Offset schemes run by **climatecare.org**, **carbonneutral.com** and others allow you to "neutralize" the greenhouse gases that you are responsible for releasing. Their websites have simple calculators that let you work out the impact of any flight. Once that's done, you can pay to fund projects that will reduce future carbon emissions by an equivalent amount (such as the distribution of low-energy lightbulbs and cooking stoves in developing countries). Please take the time to visit our website and make your trip climate neutral.

www.roughguides.com/climatechange

Flights from Australia, New Zealand and South Africa

From **Australia**, the only two cities with direct connections to Korea are Sydney (ten hours), which has a couple of flights per day, and Brisbane (nine hours), which has five per week; there are sometimes direct flights from Cairns during the Korean winter, and a connection to Melbourne was being established at the time of writing. The number of Koreans going to Australia mean that bargain flights are few and far between, but Qantas usually prices its direct services competitively – return fares start at around A$1500, while the Korean carriers may ask for almost double that. It's worth checking around for flights that transit in a Southeast Asian hub; prices can often drop close to A$1000. Likewise, if travelling from **New Zealand** – keep your fingers crossed for a NZ$1400 fare, but assume you'll pay around NZ$1900. There are also direct flights from Auckland (twelve hours), and a few from Christchurch.

At the time of writing, there were no direct flights from **South Africa**.

Flights from Japan and China

If you're travelling from elsewhere in Asia – particularly from **Japan** or **China**'s eastern seaboard – it may be worth checking for a connection to another Korean international airport. In decreasing order of importance, these include Busan's Gimhae airport, Jeju, Daegu and Gwangju; those at Yangyang (near Sokcho) and Cheongju are also equipped to handle international flights, though don't always get the opportunity. There's also a handy, and extremely regular, connection between Seoul's Gimpo airport and Tokyo Haneda, both of which are closer to the centre of their respective capitals than the larger hubs, Incheon and Narita.

Stopovers, open-jaws and round-the-world tickets

If you have the time and money to visit Korea as part of a longer trip, a **round-the-world** (RTW) ticket may be the most practical way to go. Airlines or travel agents will be able to create a customized tour, though it's usually far cheaper to get an "off the shelf" route with set destinations. These are more likely to include Tokyo or Beijing than Seoul, though a growing number of people are popping to Korea on a side-trip from either of the two. Those with slightly tighter travel plans in mind can check out the cheaper Asian or Circle Pacific passes provided by some travel agents or major airlines, which most commonly offer a maximum mileage or number of connections in a predefined period.

Airlines, agents and operators

Online booking

www.expedia.co.uk (in UK) **www.expedia.com** (in US) **www.expedia.ca** (in Canada)
www.lastminute.com (in UK)
www.opodo.co.uk (in UK)
www.orbitz.com (in US)
www.travelocity.co.uk (in UK) **www.travelocity.com** (in US) **www.travelocity.ca** (in Canada)
www.zuji.com.au (in Australia) **www.zuji.co.nz** (in New Zealand)

Airlines

Aeroflot UK 020/7355 2233, US 1-888 340-6400, Canada 1-416-642-1653, Australia 02/9262-2233, www.aeroflot.co.uk, www.aeroflot.com

Air Canada Canada 1-888/247-2262, UK 0871/220 1111, Republic of Ireland 01/679 3958, Australia 1300/655 767, New Zealand 0508/747 767, www.aircanada.com.

Air China UK 020/7744 0800, Australia 02/9232 7277, US 212-371-9898, Canada 416-581-8833, www.air-china.co.uk, www.airchina.com.cn.

Air France UK 0870/142 4343, US 1-800/237-2747, Canada 1-800/667-2747, Australia 1300/390 190, South Africa 0861/340 340, www.airfrance.com.

Air India UK 020/8560 9996 or 8745 1000, US 1-800/223-7776, Canada 416-865-1033, Australia 02/9283 4020, New Zealand 09/631 5651, www.airindia.com.

Alitalia UK 0870/544 8259, Republic of Ireland 01/677 5171, US 1-800/223-5730, Canada 1-800/361-8336, New Zealand 09/308 3357, South Africa 11/721 4500, www.alitalia.com.

All Nippon Airways (ANA) UK 0870/837 8866, Republic of Ireland 1850/200 058, US & Canada 1-800/235-9262, www.anaskyweb.com.

American Airlines UK 0845/778 9789, Republic of Ireland 01/602 0550, US 1-800/433-7300, Australia 1300/650 747, New Zealand 0800/887 997, www.aa.com.

Asiana Airlines UK 020/7514 0201/8, US 1-800/227-4262, Australia 02/9767 4343, www.flyasiana.com.

British Airways UK 0870/850 9850, Republic of Ireland 1890/626 747, US & Canada 1-800/AIRWAYS, Australia 1300/767 177, New Zealand 09/966 9777, www.ba.com.

Cathay Pacific UK 020/8834 8888, US 1-800/233-2742, Australia 131747, New Zealand 09/379 0861, www.cathaypacific.com.

China Airlines UK 020/7436 9001, US 1-917/368-2003, Australia 02/9231 5588, New Zealand 09/308 3364, www.china-airlines.com.

China Eastern Airlines UK 0870/760 6232, Australia 02/9290 1148, www.chinaeastern.co.uk.

China Southern Airlines US 1-888/338-8988, Australia 02/9231 1988, www.cs-air.com.

Continental Airlines UK 0845/607 6760, Republic of Ireland 1890/925 252, US & Canada 1-800/523-3273, Australia 02/9244 2242, New Zealand 09/308 3350, International 1800/231 0856, www.continental.com.

CSA (Czech Airlines) UK 0870/444 3747, Republic of Ireland 0818/200 014,

US ⓣ 1-800/223-2365, Canada ⓣ 416/363-3174, ⓦ www.czechairlines.co.uk.
Delta UK ⓣ 0845/600 0950, Republic of Ireland ⓣ 1850/882 031 or 01/407 3165, US & Canada ⓣ 1-800/221-1212, Australia ⓣ 1300/302 849, New Zealand ⓣ 09/379 3370, ⓦ www.delta.com.
EgyptAir UK ⓣ 020/7734 2343, US ⓣ 1-800/334-6787 or ⓣ 1-212/315-0900, Canada ⓣ 1-416/960-0009, Australia ⓣ 1300/309 767, South Africa ⓣ 11/3804 1267/8/9, ⓦ www.egyptair.com.eg.
Emirates UK ⓣ 0870/243 2222, US ⓣ 1-800/777-3999, Australia ⓣ 02/9290 9700, New Zealand ⓣ 09/968 2200, ⓦ www.emirates.com.
EVA Air UK ⓣ 020/7380 8300, US & Canada ⓣ 1-800/695-1188, Australia ⓣ 02/8338 0419, New Zealand ⓣ 09/358 8300, ⓦ www.evaair.com.
Garuda Indonesia UK ⓣ 020/7467 8600, US ⓣ 1-212/279-0756, Australia ⓣ 1300/365 330 or 02/9334 9944, New Zealand ⓣ 09/366 1862 ⓦ www.garuda-indonesia.com.
IranAir UK ⓣ 020/7491 3656 or 020/7499 7186, Canada ⓣ 1-905/882-2244, ⓦ www.iranair.com.
JAL (Japan Air Lines) UK ⓣ 0845/774 7700, Republic of Ireland ⓣ 01/408 3757, US & Canada ⓣ 1-800/525-3663, Australia ⓣ 02/9272 1111 New Zealand ⓣ 09/379 9906, ⓦ www.ar.jal.com.
Kenya Airways UK ⓣ 01784/888 222, US ⓣ 1-866/536-9224, Australia ⓣ 02/9767 4303, South Africa ⓣ 11/881 9795, ⓦ www.kenya-airways.com.
KLM (Royal Dutch Airlines) See Northwest/KLM. UK ⓣ 0870/507 4074, Republic of Ireland ⓣ 1850/747 400, US ⓣ 1-800/225-2525, Australia ⓣ 1300/303 747, New Zealand ⓣ 09/921 6040, South Africa ⓣ 11/961 6767, ⓦ www.klm.com.
Korean Air UK ⓣ 0800/413 000, Republic of Ireland ⓣ 01/799 7990, US & Canada ⓣ 1-800/438-5000, Australia ⓣ 02/9262 6000, New Zealand ⓣ 09/914 2000, ⓦ www.koreanair.com.
Lufthansa UK ⓣ 0870/837 7747, Republic of Ireland ⓣ 01/844 5544, US ⓣ 1-800/645-3880, Canada ⓣ 1-800/563-5954, Australia ⓣ 1300/655 727, South Africa ⓣ 0861/842 538, ⓦ www.lufthansa.com.
Malaysia Airlines UK ⓣ 0870/607 9090, Republic of Ireland ⓣ 01/676 2131, US ⓣ 1-212/697-8994, Australia ⓣ 132627, New Zealand ⓣ 0800/777 747, ⓦ www.malaysia-airlines.com.
MIAT (Mongolian Airlines) ⓦ www.miat.com.
Northwest/KLM UK ⓣ 0870/507 4074, US ⓣ 1-800/225-2525, Australia ⓣ 1300/767 310, ⓦ www.nwa.com.
Philippine Airlines UK ⓣ 01293/596 680 US ⓣ 1-800/FLY-PAL, Australia ⓣ 1300/888 PAL, New Zealand ⓣ 09/308 5206, ⓦ www.philippineairlines.com.
Qantas Airways UK ⓣ 0845/774 7767, Republic of Ireland ⓣ 01/407 3278, US & Canada ⓣ 1-800/227-4500, Australia ⓣ 131313, New Zealand ⓣ 0800/808 767 or 09/357 8900, South Africa ⓣ 11/441 8550, ⓦ www.qantas.com.
Qatar Airways UK ⓣ 020/7896 3636, US ⓣ 1-877/777-2827, Canada ⓣ 1-888/366-5666, Australia ⓣ 386/054 855, South Africa ⓣ 11/523 2928, ⓦ www.qatarairways.com.
Royal Brunei UK ⓣ 020/7584 6660, Australia ⓣ 1300/721 271, New Zealand ⓣ 09/977 2209, ⓦ www.bruneiair.com.
SAS (Scandinavian Airlines) UK ⓣ 0870/6072 7727, Republic of Ireland ⓣ 01/844 5440, US & Canada ⓣ 1-800/221-2350, Australia ⓣ 1300/727 707, ⓦ www.scandinavian.net.
Singapore Airlines UK ⓣ 0844/800 2380, Republic of Ireland ⓣ 01/671 0722, US ⓣ 1-800/742-3333, Canada ⓣ 1-800/663-3046, Australia ⓣ 131011, New Zealand ⓣ 0800/808 909, South Africa ⓣ 11/880 8560 or 11/880 8566, ⓦ www.singaporeair.com.
South African Airways UK ⓣ 0870/747 1111, US & Canada ⓣ 1-800/722-9675, Australia ⓣ 1800/221 699, New Zealand ⓣ 09/977 2237, South Africa ⓣ 11/978 1111, ⓦ www.flysaa.com.
Thai Airways UK ⓣ 0870/606 0911, US ⓣ 1-212/949-8424, Canada ⓣ 1-416/971-5181, Australia ⓣ 1300/651 960, New Zealand ⓣ 09/377 3886; ⓦ www.thaiair.com.
Turkish Airlines UK ⓣ 020/7766 9300, Republic of Ireland ⓣ 1/844 7920, US ⓣ 1-800/874-8875, Canada ⓣ 1-866/435-9849, Australia ⓣ 02/9299 8400, ⓦ www.thy.com.
United Airlines UK ⓣ 0845/844 4777, US ⓣ 1-800/UNITED-1, Australia ⓣ 131777, ⓦ www.united.com.
US Airways UK ⓣ 0845/600 3300, Republic of Ireland ⓣ 1890/925 065, US & Canada ⓣ 1-800/428-4322, ⓦ www.usair.com.
Vietnam Airlines UK ⓣ 0870/224 0211, US ⓣ 1-415/677-0888, Canada ⓣ 1-416/599-6555, Australia ⓣ 02/9283 1355, ⓦ www.vietnamairlines.com.

Agents and operators

ebookers UK ⓣ 0800/082 3000, Republic of Ireland ⓣ 01/488 3507, ⓦ www.ebookers.com. Low fares on an extensive selection of scheduled flights and package deals.
North South Travel UK ⓣ 01245/608 291, ⓦ www.northsouthtravel.co.uk. Friendly, competitive travel agency, offering discounted fares worldwide. Profits are used to support projects in the developing world, especially the promotion of sustainable tourism.

On the Go Tours UK ⓣ020/7371 1113, ⓦwww.onthegotours.com. Runs group and tailor-made tours to Egypt, India, Sri Lanka, Africa, Jordan, Russia, China and Turkey.
STA Travel US ⓣ1-800/781-4040, Canada ⓣ1-888/427-5639, UK ⓣ0870/163 0026, Australia ⓣ1300/733 035, New Zealand ⓣ0508/782 872, SA ⓣ0861/781 781, ⓦwww.statravel.com. Worldwide specialists in independent travel; also student IDs, travel insurance, car rental, rail passes, and more. Good discounts for students and under-26s.
Trailfinders UK ⓣ0845/058 5858, Republic of Ireland ⓣ01/677 7888, Australia ⓣ1300/780 212, ⓦwww.trailfinders.com. One of the best-informed and most efficient agents for independent travellers.

Local tour operators

Aju Tours ⓦwww.ajutours.co.kr. Has a few interesting additions to the regular Seoul tours and DMZ trips, including bird-watching, oriental health or a tour of shamanistic sites.
Grace Travel ⓦwww.triptokorea.com. A user-friendly website – click on "Customised Tours", select your time window, then choose from a range of interesting options.
Rye Tour ⓦwww.ryetour.com. In addition to a few Korea-only itineraries, they also offer week-long tours which combine Seoul and Busan with Beijing, Shanghai or Tokyo.
TIK Tour Service ⓦwww.tiktourservice.com. Offers affordable tours including skiing holidays, temple tours and trips around Jeju Island.

Getting to Korea by train and ferry

Despite the fact that South Korea is part of the Eurasian landmass, and technically connected to the rest of it by rail, the DMZ and North Korean red tape means that the country is currently **inaccessible by land**. This may well change – two old lines across the DMZ have been renovated and 2007 saw trains rumble across the border as part of a peace ceremony. However, overnight trains from Beijing remain a distant prospect. Until then, surface-based access from the continent takes the form of **ferries** from Japan, China or Russia via a ride on the Trans-Siberian Railway (see box below). Note that if you're heading to or from China or Japan, you can make use of a **combined rail and ferry ticket** that gives substantial discounts on what you'd pay separately – see ⓦwww.korail.com for details.

Ferries from Russia

From Zarubino, a **Russian** port settlement near Vladivostok, there are twice-weekly **ferries** to the Korean east-coast city of Sokcho (see p.172), though the vagaries of Russian visa applications mean that it's hard to get to Korea on this route. The journey takes eighteen hours and one-way prices start at around W168,000 – Korean-speakers can call ⓣ033/638-2100, or visit ⓦwww.dongchunferry.co.kr for more information. It's worth noting that this route is commonly used by Korean travellers wishing to head to **Paekdusan** (see p.415), a beautiful mountain on the border of China and North Korea, and the highest on the peninsula – it's possible to book a package tour once you're in Korea, though far more affordable to do it yourself if you're passing through China.

The Trans-Siberian train

Although you can't actually reach South Korea by train, if you're coming from or via Europe you may wish to consider one of the world's best overland trips – a **train-ride across Russia**. There are three main routes from Moscow, the main one a week-long, 9288km journey ending in Vladivostok on the East Sea. The Trans-Manchurian and Trans-Mongolian are slightly shorter rides ending in Beijing. The most popular cities to stop at – other than the termini of Moscow, Vladivostok and Beijing – are Irkutsk, next to beautiful Lake Baikal in Russian Siberia, and Ulaan Baatar, the idiosyncratic capital of Mongolia. Prices from Moscow to Vladivostok, including visas and a couple of nights' accommodation at each end, start at around £550/U$1100/A$1300; trips ending in Beijing will be slightly more expensive once the additional visa or visas have been factored in, and you can do the lot yourself for around half the price. For more information go to ⓦwww.seat61.com.

Ferry connections from China and Japan

Chinese ports	Departure days and times	Journey times
Dalian	Mon, Wed & Fri at 3.30pm	17 hours
Dandong	Tues, Thurs & Sun at 3pm	16 hours
Lianyungang	Mon at 11pm, Thurs at 1pm	24 hours
Qingdao	Mon, Wed & Fri at 4pm	15 hours
Qinhuangdao	Wed & Sun at 1pm	23 hours
Shidao	Tues, Thurs & Sun at 6pm	14 hours
Tanggu (Tianjin)	Thurs & Sun at 11am	24 hours
Weihai	Tues, Thurs & Sun at 6pm	14 hours
Yantai	Mon, Wed & Fri at 5pm	14 hours
Yingkou	Mon & Thurs at 11am	24 hours

Ferries from Japan and China

There are several ferry routes from **China**'s eastern coast, almost all of which head to Incheon's international termini. The route from Shanghai to Mokpo had been discontinued at the time of writing, though may well reappear in the future, but for now the most popular connections include sailings from Dalian, Dandong and Qingdao, while Tianjin's port in Tanggu is the most convenient for those wanting to head to or from Beijing. See box above for more information on these routes.

Services from **Japan** depart from Fukuoka and Shimonoseki to Busan (see p.241), reasonably close to the train station, so you can be heading to other Korean destinations in no time. There are, in fact, two different services to and from Fukuoka – one a regular ferry, departing Busan every day except Sunday (15 hours; ¥9000), or a faster jetfoil with at least five services per day (3 hours; ¥13,000). Daily ferries from Shimonoseki (14 hours; ¥8500) leave from a port near the train station, but as times, dates and prices for all sailings have been inconsistent for years, it's best to check with a Japanese tourist office for up-to-date information.

Getting around

Travelling around the country is simple – even if the train won't take you where you want to go, there's almost always a bus that will; should you have a choice, it's usually faster but more expensive to take the train. Travel prices are also reasonable by First World standards, even if you choose to hop on one of the surprisingly numerous domestic flights. Korea is surrounded by islands, and should you make a ferry-trip to one of these, it may well be the most pleasurable part of your visit to the country. Inner-city transport should hold no great fears, either – all cities have comprehensive (if slightly incomprehensible) bus networks, and many now have subway lines; if all else fails, taxis are remarkably good value, and even feasible ways of travelling from city to city.

Wherever you are, it's wise to avoid **peak travel seasons** if possible. During the two biggest holidays (Seollal and Chuseok; see pp.49–50) it can often feel as if the whole

Distance in kilometres

	Sokcho	Jeonju	Gyeongju	Chuncheon
Seoul	239	221	347	89
Busan	431	325	71	431
Gwangju	488	105	289	401
Daejeon	361	97	211	257
Daegu	385	295	68	288
Chuncheon	176	303	339	–
Gyeongju	359	325	–	339
Jeonju	382	–	325	303
Sokcho	–	382	359	176

country is on the move, as people rush to their home towns and back again – there's gridlock on the roads, it's hard to find a seat on trains or buses, and many shops and businesses (including some hotels) close down. Weekend or rush-hour train tickets can also be hard to come by throughout the year. For **travel information**, it's best to ask at a tourist office, or call the English-speaking information line on ⓣ1330.

By plane

For such a small country, Korea is surprisingly well served by **domestic flights**. The two national carriers, Korean Air and Asiana, have near-identical services – with near-identical fares – linking over a dozen airports across the nation, with the two main hubs being Gimpo in Seoul, and the holiday mecca of Jeju Island. However, the country is so well covered by train and bus that only a trip to Jeju would see the average traveller need to use a domestic flight. Prices are reasonable – around W85,000 from Gimpo to Jeju, for example – which is hardly surprising given that few trips take longer than an hour; when check-in and transport to the airport are taken into account, it's often much faster to go by train. Don't forget your **passport**, as you're likely to need it for identification purposes.

By ferry

With several thousand islands sprinkled around Korea's western and southern shores, no trip to Korea would be complete without a **ferry ride**. Several towns and cities have connections, though the main ports of entry to Korea's offshore kingdom are Incheon, Mokpo, Wando, Yeosu and Busan, all of which embrace sizeable island communities. The choice from Mokpo, in particular, is incredible – some travellers have inadvertently made trailblazers of themselves, finding their way onto islands that had never seen a foreign face. Popular **Jeju Island** is quite the opposite, and although the vast majority of Koreans travel here by plane, it has ferry connections to a number of south-coast mainland cities (see p.353 for details).

Moving on from Incheon Airport

Connections to Seoul from Incheon Airport are good; most choose to take the limousine buses that run from the airport on a variety of routes to the capital, but in 2007 a dedicated new train line opened, connecting the airport to Seoul by rail. At the time of writing, this only ran as far as Gimpo airport to the west of Seoul on subway line 5 (the arrival point for most domestic flights), but work was underway to connect it to Seoul station in the very centre of the city; see p.73 for more information. There are also express buses that dash to all of the country's major cities at pleasingly regular intervals, with price dependent on the distance travelled. Wherever you're going, useful signs help point the way, or you can ask at the information desk to find the most suitable route.

Daegu	Daejeon	Gwangju	Busan	Seoul
283	155	231	385	–
128	253	249	–	385
222	178	–	249	231
149	–	178	253	155
–	149	222	128	283
288	257	401	431	89
68	211	289	71	347
295	97	105	325	221
385	361	488	431	239

Fares, on the whole, are reasonable – short hops may cost as little as W5000, but for return fares to outlying islands such as Jeju, Hongdo, Ulleungdo or Dokdo you'll probably have to shell out at least ten times that price. Only tickets to these destinations will be in much danger of selling out, and even then, only in high season; at these times, it's best to head to a Korean travel agent.

By rail

A fleet of excellent **trains** ply the mainland provinces – sleek, affordable and punctual to a fault. Being a mountainous nation that has only in recent decades had the riches to embark on extensive tunnel-building projects, Korea doesn't have as many lines as it probably needs, but given the choice, it's best to take the train; there are two main lines from Seoul, one running to Busan in the southeast, the other to Mokpo in the southwest. The highest of four main classes of train is the **KTX** – these high-speed machines entered service in 2004, and occasionally reach speeds of over 300km/h. The Gyeongbu line runs from Seoul to Busan and connects the cities in under two hours (W47,900); trains heading to Gwangju or Mokpo branch off in Daejeon. The KTX has taken over from the previous lord of the tracks, the **Saemaeul**; though slower (Seoul to Busan takes over four hours), travelling on this class cuts KTX costs by around a third (W39,300 Seoul to Busan), and the greater legroom usually makes for a more comfortable journey. A third cheaper again is the network's third class of train, the **Mugunghwa**, which was forced to cede most of its schedule space to the KTX – a good thing, since the Seoul to Busan journey (W26,500) is now a haul of nearly six hours. Last of all are the dirt-cheap **commuter class** trains (*tonggeun*), which largely cater for rural communities – only a handful of lines use them, and you're unlikely to see or need one. All non-commuter trains have **toilets**, and folk pushing trolleys of beer, peanuts, chocolate and *kimbap* for sale down the carriages with almost disturbing frequency.

Tickets and passes

Almost all stations have English-language signs where necessary, and schedules can also be checked online. When buying your **tickets**, the bigger stations have special lanes for foreigners, though it doesn't really matter which one you use, as the ticketing system is computerized and buying one is easy. Simply state your destination and the class you require, and the cashier will swing a computer screen in your direction, showing the price and seat availability. If she's pointing at a zero and looking apologetic, you'll probably need another train; additional allocations of standing tickets are available on Mugunghwa class once all seats are sold out, and with these you'll be able to use any empty ones that become available. For higher classes you'll be given a carriage and seat number: take your seat and not someone else's, otherwise it throws the seating system into disarray and causes many a disgruntled passenger. As trains are far less numerous than buses, they're far more likely to sell out quickly – on holidays or weekends, you'll need fortune on your side to walk into a station and find KTX tickets for the main routes. **Advance reservations** are highly recommended – tickets for all classes go on sale a month ahead of travel, and can be bought at any station. Also, quite sensibly, a **return ticket** costs the same as two single ones.

Though getting across the country is fairly cheap by international standards, a **KR Pass** may cut costs further for those who will be travelling extensively. These are for foreigners only, and they are only available outside the country – STA Travel is the usual conduit. Passes are valid for three days (US$76), five days ($114), seven days (US$144) or ten days (US$166); discounts are available for people under 25 years of age, or those travelling in couples or groups – see Korail's website (p.39) for up-to-date details.

Subway trains

Six Korean cities now have **underground** networks – Busan, Daegu, Daejeon and Gwangju have independent systems, while Incheon's lines are linked to the marauding Seoul network; all are continuing to grow, and new networks are likely to be born in other cities. Prices start at about W1000 for a short hop (or from one end to the other on the single lines in Daejeon and Gwangju), and increase with distance in the bigger cities, though even the full run through Seoul from Soyosan to Cheonan – about one-third of the country, and one of the longest metro routes in the world at three hours plus – will only set you back W3100. Signs are dual-language, and station maps easy to read.

By bus

There are a staggering number of **long-distance buses** in Korea – during rush hour, some scheduled services can run as often as every two minutes, with all departing on time. They come in two types – express (*gosok*) and intercity (*si-oe*, pronounced "shee-way"). Although the express services are more expensive and tend to be used for longer journeys, they are likely to run in tandem with intercity buses on many routes; allied to this, the two bus types use **separate stations** in most cities, and even the locals don't always know which one to go to, or which one they'll be arriving at – a very frustrating arrangement, though some cities are starting to see sense and group both into one building (Gwangju, for example). Some cities have even more than two, so all in all it pays to keep a loose schedule when using buses, even more so if the highways are full.

Longer journeys are broken at **service stations**, housing fast-food bars and snack shops, resonating to the sound of the "throat" (a Korean word for warbly grand-mother techno; see p.8) tapes on sale outside. You typically get fifteen minutes to make your purchases and use the **toilets** (there aren't any on the buses), but many a traveller has come a cropper after exiting the building to be confronted by forty near-identical vehicles, of which half-a-dozen may be heading to the same destination – your bus won't wait for you, so make sure that you know where it's parked.

Buses are so frequent that it's rare for them to sell out, though the last service of the day between major cities tends to be quite full. This can be surprisingly early: many services make their last trips at 7pm, though some have overnight connections. **Prices** are reasonable and usually lower than the trains, with intercity services slightly cheaper than express if the two coexist – Seoul to Busan is around W20,000 (5hr) on the former, W30,000 (4hr 30min) on the latter. Journeys take longer than the fastest trains, and are more prone to delays. Tickets are often checked at the start of the journey, but also at the end, so if possible try to avoid losing your ticket, lest the driver refuse to release you from his bus (which does happen).

City buses

With little English language on the signs or vehicles, Korea's **city bus** networks can be more than a little confusing for the first-time visitor, and some of Seoul's route numbers look more like postcodes. Once familiar with a route, city buses can be a good way of getting around – they're pleasingly frequent, and very affordable at around W1000 per ride. Throw your money into the collection box next to the driver; change will be spat out just below – make sure that you've an ample supply of coins or W1000 notes with you, as higher-value bills are unlikely to be accepted (though foreigners in such situations may be waved on with a grin). The bigger cities have started to avoid these problems by introducing **pre-paid cards**; these work out cheaper per journey than paying by cash, and some are also valid on subway networks or longer-distance buses. They last for as long as you have credit, and can be topped up in increments of W5000 at kiosks or ticket booths.

By car or motorbike

There are good reasons for the relative reluctance of travellers to **hire a car** in Korea. The main one is the country's excellent public transport infrastructure, another the threat posed by Korean drivers. Korean **road fatality rates** are often cited as the highest in the world, with most estimates putting the figures above 30 per 100,000 people per year – five times higher than the UK, for example. If you do decide to drive, you will inevitably get snarled up in the traffic that blights the cities and highways, with exceptions being Jeju Island and rural Gangwon province in the northeast, where the roads are relatively calm and free of traffic.

To hire a car you will need an international driving licence, and to be at least 21 years of age. Rental offices can be found at all airports and many train stations, as well as around the cities. Prices usually start at W35,000 per day, though as insurance is compulsory, you should budget on a little extra. Vehicles usually drive on the right-hand-side of the road (though not all the time; the pavement can be just as popular in some city areas).

Car rental agencies

Avis UK ⓣ0870/606 0100, Republic of Ireland ⓣ021/428 1111, US ⓣ1-800/230-4898, Canada ⓣ1-800/272-5871, Australia ⓣ136333 or 02/9353 9000, New Zealand ⓣ09/526 2847 or 0800/655 111, ⓦwww.avis.com.
Budget US ⓣ1-800/527-0700, Canada ⓣ1-800/268-8900, UK ⓣ0870/156 5656, Australia ⓣ1300/362 848, New Zealand ⓣ0800/283 438, ⓦwww.budget.com.
Hertz US & Canada ⓣ1-800/654-3131, UK ⓣ020/7026 0077, Republic of Ireland ⓣ01/870 5777, New Zealand ⓣ0800/654 321, ⓦwww.hertz.com.
National US ⓣ1-800/CAR-RENT, UK ⓣ0870/400 4581, Australia ⓣ0870/600 6666, New Zealand ⓣ03/366 5574, ⓦwww.nationalcar.com.

Taxis

Korean **taxis** are pleasingly cheap for a developed country, and in any city you shouldn't have to wait long to spot one. Look for cars with illuminated blocks on top, usually something resembling a plastic pyramid. Those whose blocks aren't illuminated are taken or on call; others can be **waved down** from the roadside, though to make sure of being understood you'll have to do it the Korean way – arm out, palm to the ground, fingers dangling underneath. Yellow taxis, for some reason, are said to be lucky. As few drivers speak English, it's a good idea to have your destination **written down**, if possible – even the cheapest motels should have business cards with their address on. **Rates** will vary slightly from city to city though they should start at under W2000 – over short distances, cab rides may work out cheaper than taking buses if you're in a group. All taxis are **metered** and though dishonesty is rarely an issue, when you start moving, check that the numbers are doing likewise. The only time that you may have to negotiate a fee is if you're using a *chong-al* – or "bullet" – taxi. Piloted by death-wish drivers, these hover like vultures around train and bus stations when tickets have sold out, or daily services have finished. Rides in such vehicles are not recommended for those of a nervous disposition, while others may find it quite a thrill.

Motorbikes

You'll be hard pushed to find two-wheeled vehicles above 125cc in the country, as the vast majority of Oriental superbikes are exported for use in Europe or America. Despite this, though, a sizeable number of expats still don leather during their Korean stint. One good place to hunt for information or cycle partners is *Yongsan Motorcycle Club*, whose website (ⓦwww.roaddragons.com) features a calendar of forthcoming trips and events.

Korean addresses

First, the good news – almost all Korean road signs are dual-language in nature, spelling the *hangeul* out in Roman characters for ease of use. The bad news is that there are very few street signs – most streets don't even have names. Instead, addresses point to a numbered section of a *dong* (city district), which could be helpful if the numbers always ran sequentially, which they rarely do as they're usually doled out in chronological order when the buildings are made. As you can imagine, this patchwork system leads to all sorts of problems; it's common for hotels and restaurants to include a small map on their business cards. With all this in mind, almost all of the accommodation listed in this guidebook is either mapped or easy to find. The local tourist office may be able to contact hotels and get them to fax you through a map, or you could take your chances in a taxi. Drivers will know the location of each city *dong*, but not necessarily the exact road or address, so don't worry if they pull in at a police station – it's quite common for cabbies to consult police maps for exact directions.

Despite the general confusion, addresses fit into a very rigid system; unlike the Western world, components are usually listed from largest to smallest when writing an address. The country (*–guk*) is split into nine *–do*, or provinces. In these you'll find cities (*–si*, pronounced shee), towns (*–eup*) and villages (*–ri* or *–li*), with the larger cities split into a number of *–gu*, or wards. The number of *–gu* will vary with the city's size – Seoul, for example, has 25 such sections – and these are further subdivided into *–dong* districts. Large roads are signified by a *–no*, *–ro* or *–lo* suffix, with the very meatiest divided into numbered *–ga* sections. Smaller roads come with a *–gil* suffix; anything else will be a number in its local *–dong* city section, which is itself part of a larger *–gu*. Therefore Tapgol Park in *Seoul-si* sits at the end of *Insadong-gil* in *Insa-dong*, part of *Jongno-gu*, at the confluence of *Samillo* and *Jongno 2-ga*. Happy hunting!

Cycling

There are nowhere near as many **bikes** on the roads of South Korea as there are in other Asian countries, the chief reason being that Korean roads are dangerous places to be whatever vehicle you're in or on. Not that you're much safer away from the street; cars regularly glide along the pavements looking for a place to park, and half of the country's road fatalities are **pedestrians** – an unusually high proportion. There are, however, a few pleasant areas to cycle along rural roads; particular recommendations are the sparsely populated provinces of Gangwon and Jeju Island. Rides circumnavigating the latter take around four days at a steady pace, and are becoming more and more commonplace. Those confined to a city will usually be able to go for a ride on a riverbank, with bikes available for hire at the most popular places; details have been included in the Guide where appropriate.

Hitching

Foreigners who attempt to cover long distances by **hitching rides** in Korea generally have a hard time of things. Even with your destination on a handwritten sign, and even after having confirmed to the smiling driver where it is that you want to go, you're likely to be dropped at the nearest bus or train station. After all, to Koreans, this is the only sensible way to travel if you don't have a vehicle of your own – hitching is almost unheard of as a money-saving device. **Short-distance** rides are a different proposition altogether; although the scope of Korea's public transport system means that you'd be very unfortunate to find yourself stuck without a bus or train, it can happen, and in such circumstances hitching a ride can be as easy as flagging down the first car that you see. Of course, accepting lifts with strangers isn't devoid of risk anywhere on earth, but if you're ever determined to give it a try, there can be few easier and safer places to do it than the Korean countryside.

Online travel resources

Incheon International Airport Ⓦwww.airport.or.kr. Information on flights into and out of Korea's main airport.

Korail Ⓦwww.korail.go.kr. Information on train times and passes, including discounted combined train and ferry tickets to Japan.

Korean Airports Corporation Ⓦwww.airport.co.kr. Almost identical to the Incheon site, this has details of domestic and international flights for the smaller Korean airports.

Seoul Metropolitan Rapid Transport (SMRT) Ⓦwww.smrt.co.kr. Timetables, and a useful best-route subway map.

Tour2Korea Ⓦenglish.tour2korea.com. Good for bus connections between major cities, and has cursory information on trains and ferries.

Accommodation

Accommodation is likely to form a large chunk of your travel budget, especially for those who favour Western-style luxuries, but for adventurous travellers there are ways to keep costs to a minimum. Finding a place is less likely to be a problem – Korea has an incredible number of places to stay, and one would be forgiven for thinking that there are actually more beds than there are people in the country. Do note, however, that most of these are on the cheaper side – only a few places around the country have top-drawer hotel facilities.

At the top end, luxury hotels can be found in all cities and major tourist areas, as well as a number of specially dedicated tourist hotels, though with space at such a premium, rooms are generally on the small side. Dropping down the price scale, budget travellers can choose from thousands of motels and guesthouses – many of which have nicer rooms than the dedicated tourist hotels at far lower prices – or even sleep in a *jjimjilbang* (a Korean sauna; see box p.41). At these levels, there's so much choice that reservations are almost unheard of. English is spoken with varying degrees of ability in all top hotels, but elsewhere it pays to know a few keywords in Korean (or to have good miming skills).

Hotels

The big **hotel** chains have dipped their toes into the Korean market, and there's at least one five-star option in every major city. Prices are generally constant year-round; you're most likely to pay full rack rates in July or August, though high-season at national parks and ski resorts will be autumn and winter respectively. Standards are high, by and large, though it's hard to find rooms of a decent size.

Korean hotels are split by **class**; from top to bottom, these are super deluxe, deluxe,

Accommodation price codes

All the accommodation listed in this book has been categorized into one of nine **price codes**, as set out below. These represent the cost of the **cheapest** room in **high season**; in the case of dorms in hostels, we give the price of a bed in won.

- ❶ up to W20,000
- ❷ W21,000–30,000
- ❸ W31,000–40,000
- ❹ W41,000–60,000
- ❺ W61,000–100,000
- ❻ W101,000–150,000
- ❼ W151,000–250,000
- ❽ W251,000–400,000
- ❾ W401,000 and above

first-class, second-class and third-class. Categories are marked by a plaque at the front showing a number of flowers – five for super-deluxe down to one for third-class. Many **tourist hotels** were built as Korea was getting rich in the 1980s, and now offer questionable value; stained carpets, tiny bathrooms and curious smells have become the norm, and few have staff with English language skills. Indeed, some of the most recently built motels offer better rooms, and at much lower prices. Most hotels have "Western" or "Korean" rooms; there are no beds in the latter, though the replacement sandwich of blankets on a heated *ondol* floor represents the traditional Korean way to sleep, and prices for both styles are about the same.

When booking, bear in mind that the 11 percent **tax** levied on hotel rooms is not always factored into the quoted prices; in higher-end establishments, you're also likely to be hit with an additional 10 percent service charge.

Motels

Bearing little resemblance to their American counterparts, **motels** are usually found near highway exits or clustered around long-distance bus terminals. Most offer fairly uniform en-suite doubles for W25,000 to W40,000, and standard facilities include shampoo and shower gel, hairdryers, televisions, a water fountain and free cans of beer, coffee or "vitamin juice". Extortion of foreigners is extremely rare, and you shouldn't be afraid to haggle the price down if you're travelling alone, especially outside summer.

It must be said that motels won't appeal to everybody, as they're generally used as a much-needed source of privacy by young couples (or those who need to keep their relationship secret). A few would be more honestly described as "love hotels" – pink neon and Cinderella turrets are the most apparent giveaways, while the interior may feature heart-shaped beds, condom machines and more mirrors than you can shake a stick at. That said, the majority of establishments are quite tame, any seaminess is kept behind closed doors, and even for lone women most make acceptable places to stay – indeed those that can put up with the decor will find them Korea's best-value accommodation option. The motels that have gone up since the turn of the century, in particular, often have cleaner rooms than the average tourist hotel.

Guesthouses

Yeogwan are older, smaller, less polished versions of the motel experience. Slightly cheaper, but often a little grubby, they once formed the backbone of Korea's budget travel accommodation, and can still be found in teams around bus and train stations. With whole streets full of them, it's easy to hunt around for the best deal – a double room usually costs W20,000–W35,000, though prices are higher in Seoul, and tend to rise in high season. Single rooms do not exist, but almost all have en-suite bathrooms.

Minbak rooms are usually rented-out parts of a residential property, and are less likely to have private bathrooms. These are most commonly found on islands and by popular beaches or national parks, and though the prices are comparable to *yeogwan* rates for much of the year they can quadruple if there's enough demand – summer is peak season for the beaches and islands, spring and autumn for the parks.

Even cheaper rooms can be found at a **yeoinsuk** – around W10,000 per night. Although they're slowly disappearing from the accommodation scene, these are a noisier, more spartan variation of the *yeogwan*, which are invariably found in older areas of town, with rooms containing nothing more than a couple of blankets, a television and a heated linoleum *ondol* floor to sleep on. Such wipe-clean minimalism generally makes for clean rooms, though some have a cockroach problem, and the communal toilets and showers can be quite off-putting.

Hostels

Aside from a smattering of backpacker dens in Seoul, Korean **hostels** differ greatly from those that Western travellers might be used to – created for and primarily used by the nation's youth, the atmosphere is more boarding school than Bohemian. Generally found in the countryside, most hostels are large, well-appointed places with private rooms of various sizes, and a few dormitories;

Staying at a jjimjilbang

For travellers willing to take the plunge and bare all in front of curious strangers, saunas (known locally as **jjimjilbang**) are one of the cheapest and most uniquely Korean places to get a night's sleep. Almost entirely devoid of the seedy reputations that may dog similar facilities abroad, *jjimjilbang* are large, round-the-clock establishments primarily used by families escaping their homes for the night, businessmen who've worked or partied beyond their last trains, or teenage groups having a safe night out together. They can be found in any Korean city, typically costing W5000–8000, and consist of a shower and pool area, a sauna or steam room, and a large playschool-style quiet room or two for communal napping; most also have snack bars and Internet terminals. Upon entry, guests are given a locker key and matching t-shirts and shorts to change into – outside clothes are not allowed to be worn inside the complex, though it's okay to wear underwear beneath your robe. All must be sacrificed on entry to the pools, which are segregated by gender. The common rooms are uniformly clean but vary in style; some have televisions and hi-tech recliner chairs, others invite you to roll out a mini-mattress, but all will have a floorful of snoring Koreans.

dorm beds go for W8000–10,000, and private rooms for W20,000–W100,000.

Camping and mountain huts

Most national parks have at least one **campsite** to cater for the swarms of Korean hikers who spend their weekends in the mountains. Most are free, but those that charge (typically under W5000) have excellent toilet and shower facilities. Jirisan and Seoraksan, two of the largest parks, have well-signposted **shelters** (*daepiso*) or **huts** (*sanjang*) dotted around the hiking trails; these cost under W8000 per person, though they may only open from summer until autumn, and you're advised to book ahead – check the national park website at ⓦenglish.knps.or.kr. At both campsites and shelters, drinking water should always be available, and though simple snacks may also be on offer, it's best to bring your own food.

Alternative places to stay

Saunas are Korea's cheapest places to sleep under a roof, and can make for a memorable travel experience (see box above). Another unusual option is to stay in a 24-hour **DVD room** (*DVD-bang*); most commonly used by young couples, they offer a large television, a comfy sofa and much-needed privacy for W8000 per film. They're a cheap option if you only need a few hours' rest – just rent out *The Godfather* and turn down the volume. They're easy to find usually in areas where there is an abundance of bars and clubs.

If you're looking for a more traditional experience, you could try staying at a **temple**. Though temples with sufficient room are pretty much obliged to take in needy travellers for the night, many offer interesting, prearranged programmes for around W50,000 per night, some with the capacity for English-language translation – see ⓦeng.templestay.com for more details. There's usually meditation, grounds-sweeping, a tea ceremony and a meal or two on the agenda, but be prepared for spartan sleeping arrangements and a pre-dawn wake-up call. Those who'd like something traditional but without the routine can try hunting down a **hanok** – these are traditional Korean buildings, replete with wooden frames, sliding doors and a woodfired underfloor heating system. Few such buildings cater for travellers, though some can be found at the traditional villages scattered around the country (Hahoe near Andong is the best; see p.229), and there are dedicated districts in Seoul (see box, p.85) and Jeonju (p.293); many offer tea ceremonies and other activities such as *gimchi*-making as part of the price.

Online accommodation resources

ⓦeng.templestay.com Information on the various templestay programmes around the country.

ⓦ **english.knps.or.kr** Korea National Park service site detailing available shelters.
ⓦ **www.asiarooms.com** An excellent discount site with interesting reviews of the hotel rooms on offer.
ⓦ **www.hostelworld.com** Good listings of Seoul's budget accommodation, and a few more choices from around the country.
ⓦ **www.hotelwide.com** See just how much you're saving by comparing quotes with rack rates.
ⓦ **www.khrc.com** Website for the Korea Hotel Reservation Centre and worth a look for occasional special deals.
ⓦ **www.koreahotels.net** A well-presented site with a wealth of choice.

Food and drink

Korean cuisine deserves greater international attention. A thrillingly spicy mishmash of simple but invariably healthy ingredients, it's prepared with consummate attention, then doled out in hearty portions at more restaurants than you could possibly count – even if every single person in the country suddenly decided to go out for dinner, there would probably still be some free tables. Most are open from early morning until late at night, and a full 24 hours a day in many cases. You can usually find a restaurant to suit your budget, and there will always be an affordable option close by, a fact attested by the great number of foreigners that live here quite happily for weeks, months or even years on end without doing a single bit of cooking for themselves.

Though Korean cuisine is one of the most distinctive around, few Westerners arrive with knowledge of anything other than **gimchi** (fermented vegetables) and **dog meat**. To say that the former is ubiquitous is a severe understatement, as it's served as a side dish with pretty much everything you order (for more information about popular Korean dishes see the *Korean Cuisine* colour insert), but rest assured that the latter will not be part of your diet unless you go to a dedicated restaurant (see box, p.46). One common problem for visitors is the **spice** level of the food, an issue that has given Korea one of the world's highest rates of stomach cancer. It's not so much the spiciness of the individual dishes that causes problems (English travellers trained on curry, for example, rarely have any problems adjusting to Korean spice) but the fact that there's little respite from it – red pepper paste (*gochujang*) is a component of almost every meal. Another common complaint by foreign visitors is the lack of attention paid to **vegetarians**, as such folk are extremely rare in Korea. Despite the high vegetable content of many meals, almost all have at least a little meat, and very few are cooked in meat-free environments. Most resort to asking for *bibimbap* without the meat, eating *ramyeon* (instant noodles), or poking the bits of ham out of *gimbap* with a chopstick.

When eating with locals, it's polite to observe Korean **culinary etiquette** (see p.55 for a few pointers). Many meals are eaten with flattened stainless-steel **chopsticks**; those unable to use them may have to rely on a combination of fork and spoon, as knives are rarely used.

Korean eating establishments are somewhat hard to pigeonhole. The lines between bar, restaurant, snack-shop and even home are often blurry to say the least, and some places cover all bases: in provincial towns, you may well see children tucked up for the night under empty tables. The more traditional eateries will see diners sitting on floor-cushions, their legs folded under low tables in a modified lotus position which can play merry hell on Western knees and ankles.

Many dishes are for **sharing**, a fantastic arrangement that fosters togetherness and increases mealtime variety, though this has adverse implications for single travellers – Koreans don't like to eat alone, and are likely to fret about those who do. One other point worth mentioning is the incredible number of foodstuffs that are claimed to be "good for **sexual stamina**"; at times it feels as if food is an augmenter of male potency first, and a necessary means of sustenance second. Raw fish and dog meat, in particular, are said to be good for this.

Drinking in Korea can be just as much fun as eating: while *soju* is the national hooch, there are several other alcoholic drinks unique to the country, as well as a local range of beers. Those who want to stay off the juice can take advantage of some of the excellent **tearooms** still found in Seoul or at national parks.

Korean staples

Those who eat out in Korea will quickly become aware of the mind-boggling number of meals on offer, so knowledge of a few basic dishes is highly important; the following are available around the country, and few will cost more than W5000. Many meals involve **rice** in various forms: one that proves a hit with many foreigners is **bibimbap**, a mixture of shoots, leaves and vegetables on a bed of rice, flecked with meat, then topped with an egg and spicy *gochujang* pepper sauce. The dish can cost as little as W3500, though there are sometimes a few varieties to choose from. See the *Korean cuisine* colour section for more details on this classic dish. Other dishes to be served on a bed of rice include beef (*bulgogi deop-bap*), highly spicy squid (*ojingeo deop-bap*) or a mixture of the two (*obul deop-bap*), as well as *donkasseu*, a breaded pork cutlet dish imported from Japan that's particularly popular with those who want to avoid spice. Also fulfilling this need are rolls of **gimbap**: *gim* means seaweed laver, *bap* means rice, and the former is rolled around the latter, which itself surrounds strips of egg, ham and pickled radish; the resulting tube is then cut into segments with a sharp knife to make the dish chopstick-friendly. The basic dish is filling and only costs W1000 or so, but for a little more you'll usually have a variety of fillings to choose from, including tuna (*chamchi*), minced beef (*sogogi*), processed cheese (*chi-jeu*) and *gimchi*; some places also serve *chungmu gimbap*, a rustic tray of *gimchi*, spicy squid and seaweed-rolled rice that originates from the Tongyeong area.

Noodles are also used as a base in many dishes, and one of the cheapest dishes to eat – a bowl of **ramyeon** can go for just W1000. This is a block of instant noodles boiled up in a spicy red pepper soup, and usually mixed in with an egg and some onion. For double the price you can have dumplings (*mandu*), rice-cake (*ddeok*) or processed cheese thrown in. Those travelling in the sticky Korean summer will find it hard to throw back a bowl of hot, spicy soup – a better choice may be **naengmyeon**, bowls of grey buckwheat noodles served with a boiled egg and vegetable slices in a cold soup (though still spicy – this is Korea, after all).

Soups are also available without noodles; the names of these dishes usually end with *-tang* or *-guk*, though special mention must be made of the spicy **jjigae** broths. These are bargain meals that cost W3500 and up, and come with rice and a range of vegetable side dishes; the red pepper broth contains chopped-up vegetables, as well as a choice of tofu (*sundubu*), tuna, soybean paste (*doen-jang*) or *gimchi*. Many foreigners find themselves going for the more familiar **dumpling** (*mandu*) options; again, these can cost as little as W1000 for a dish, and you can have them with meat (*gogi*) or *gimchi* fillings. Most are steamed, though it's sometimes possible to have them flash-fried.

All of the above can be found at **fast-food chains** around the country; two of the largest are *Gimbap Cheonguk* and *Gimbap Nara*, and as long as you're in an urban environment, there'll probably be one within walking distance. It's also possible to find these meals in the **food courts** of department stores, or simple eateries in train or bus stations. All of these places are good for single travellers, as "proper" restaurants require at least two people for most of their meals.

Restaurant food

The traditional Korean **restaurant** is filled with low tables in such instances, diners are required to remove their footwear and sit on floor-cushions. There are a number of rules of restaurant **etiquette** to observe (see p.55 for details) but a substantial amount of custom also surrounds the food itself; while what often appears to be a culinary free-for-all can draw gasps from foreign observers (eat the meal; boil off the soup; throw in some rice to fry up with the scraps; add some noodles), Korea's great on conformity, and you may well provoke chuckles of derision by performing actions that you deem quite sensible – it's best just to follow the Korean lead.

Restaurant meals usually consist of communal servings of **meat** or **fish** around which are placed a bewildering assortment of **side dishes** (*banchan*). Often, these are the best part of the meal – a range of fish, meat, vegetables and steamed egg broth, they're included in the price of the meal, and there may be as many as twenty on the table; when your favourite is finished, waitresses will scoot around with a free refill. Two of the most popular meat dishes are **galbi** and **samgyeopsal**, which are almost always cooked by the diners themselves in the centre of the table. *Galbi* is rib-meat, most often beef (*so-galbi*) but sometimes pork (*dwaeji-galbi*); see the *Korean cuisine* colour section for more details. **Samgyeopsal** is strips of rather fatty pork belly. Prices vary but figure on around W7000 per portion for beef and a little less for pork; a minimum of two diners is usually required. Better for single travellers may be the **hanjeongsik**; this is a traditional Korean banquet meal centred on a bowl of rice and a spicy *jjigae* stew, which are surrounded by side dishes – a full belly of healthy, lovingly prepared food can be yours for just W6000 or so. **Ssambap** meals are similarly good-value collections of rice and vegetable side dishes, though here the array is far greater – often filling the whole table – and is supposed to be wrapped up in leaves before it enters the mouth; figure on W8000 per person, and a total failure to clear everything that's in front of you.

Snack food

Though the most common variety of Korean **snack food** is *gimbap* there are many more options available. One is a dish called **ddeokbokki**, a mix of rice-cake and processed fish boiled up in a highly spicy red-pepper sauce; this typically costs around W2000 per potion, and is doled out in bowls by street vendors and small roadside booths. The same places usually serve **twiggim**, which are flash-fried pieces of squid, potato, seaweed-covered noodle-roll or stuffed chilli pepper, to name but a few ingredients. The price varies but is usually around W2000 for six pieces – make your selection from the display, and they'll

Royal cuisine

Being such an important part of daily Korean life, it's inevitable that food should wend its way into traditional events. The hundredth day of a child's life is marked with a feast of colourful rice-cake, while a simpler variety is served in a soup (*ddeokguk*) to celebrate Lunar New Year. More interesting by far, however, is **royal court cuisine**: a remnant of the Joseon dynasty, which ruled over the Korean peninsula from 1392 to 1910, this was once served to Korean rulers and associated nobility. The exact ingredients and styles vary and go by several different names, but usually rice, soup and a charcoal-fired casserole form the centre of the banquets, and are then surrounded by a team of perfectly prepared dishes; twelve was once the royal number of dishes and banned to the peasant class, but now anyone can indulge as long as they have the money – such meals can go for as much as W300,000 per person. The aim of the combination is to harmonize culinary opposites such as spicy and mild, solid and liquid, rough and smooth; a balance of colour and texture is thereby achieved – the yin-yang principle in edible form – with the end result every bit as well prepared and aesthetically pleasing as the more famous styles found across the sea in Japan.

Some of the best places to try this kind of food are *Korea House* (p.122) and *Sanchon* in Seoul (p.124), or *Naebang* in Busan (p.249).

be re-fried in front of you. You can have the resulting dish smothered in *ddeokbokki* sauce for no extra charge – delicious.

Convenience stores are usually good places to grab some food, as all sell sandwiches, rolls and triangles of *gimbap*, and instant noodles; boiling water will always be available for the latter, as well as a bench or table to eat it from, an activity that will mark you down in locals' eyes as an honorary Korean. A less appealing practice, but one that will endear you to Koreans more than anything else can, is the eating of *beondegi* – boiled silkworm larvae. You'll smell them before you see them, the acrid stench emanating from booths that spring up on pavements and riverbanks in colder months.

Those with a **sweet tooth** will be able to find ice cream in any convenience store, where prices can be as low as W500; if you want to keep your selection as Korean as possible, go for those flavoured with green tea (*nok-cha*), melon, or red-bean paste. An even more distinctively local variety, available from specialist snack bars, is *patbingsu*, a strange concoction of fruit, cream, shaved ice and red-bean paste. Also keep an eye out in colder months for a *hoddeok* stand – these press out little fried pancakes of rice-mix filled with brown sugar and cinnamon for just W500 per piece, and are extremely popular with foreigners.

Seafood, market fare and mountain food

Some Korean eateries exude an essence little changed for decades; these include raw fish stalls around the coast, city-centre market-places and mountain restaurants, and are your best options for that traditional feeling.

Korean **seafood** is a bit of a maze for most foreigners, and much more expensive than other meals, though it's worth persevering. Some is served raw, while other dishes are boiled up in a spicy soup. Jagalchi market (p.248) in Busan deserves a special mention, but in small coastal villages – particularly on the islands of the West and South seas – there's little other industry to speak of; battered fishing flotillas yo-yo in and out with the tide, and you may be able to buy fish that's straight off the boat. This may seem as fresh as seafood can possibly be, but octopus is often served live (*sannakji*), its severed tentacles still squirming as they head down your throat. Be warned: several people die each year when their prey decides to make a last futile stab at survival, so you may wish to wait until it has stopped moving, or at least kill the nerves with a few powerful bites. **Pojangmacha** are some of Korea's most atmospheric places to eat – these are tent-like stalls, usually covered with orange tarpaulin, that are set up on pavements and riverbanks around the country. While the choice is bewildering, there's a simple route to take – make it clear how much you'd like to spend (W20,000 per person should buy plenty), and point to the creatures you desire to eat. A far simpler choice is *hoe deop-bap*, a widely available dish similar to *bibimbap*, but with sliced raw fish in place of egg and meat.

Korean **markets** offer similar opportunities for culinary exploration. Here you're also likely to spot seafood on sale, but added to this are fruits, vegetables, grilled or boiled meats and an assortment of snacks. Many of the options available have been listed under snack food (see opposite), but one favourite almost unique to the market is *sundae*, a kind of sausage made with intestinal lining and noodles, and absolutely nothing to do with ice cream. Sokcho on the Gangwon coast is the best place to sample this dish (see p.175).

Those doing a bit of hiking in one of Korea's wonderful **national parks** will doubtless take the opportunity to make use of the teams of restaurants that surround a number of main park entrances. One of the most popular hiker dishes is *sanchae bibimbap*, a variety of the Korean staple made with roots, shoots and vegetables from the surrounding countryside – knowing that everything passing your gums is sourced locally somehow makes the dish taste better. Most popular, though, are *pajeon*; locals may refer to these as "Korean pizza", but they're more similar to a savoury pancake. They usually contain strips of spring onion and seafood (*haemul pajeon*), though other varieties are likely to be available; it's usually washed down with a bowl or three of *dongdongju*, a milky rice wine.

Dog meat

Korea's consumption of **dog meat** became global knowledge during the country's hosting of the 1988 Olympics, at which time the government kowtowed to Western mores and attempted to sweep the issue under the carpet. Foreigners looking for it on the menu or in their hamburgers are likely to be relieved, as it's almost nowhere to be seen. For those who wish to know, it's a slightly stringy meat somewhere between duck and beef in texture, and is generally agreed to taste better than it smells. The most popular dish featuring dog meat is *yeongyangtang*, a soup that can be hunted down in specialist restaurants.

Today, the consumption of dog meat amounts to a shameful national secret. Should the issue be raised, even with a Korean who you know well, it's likely that they'll laugh and tell you that they don't eat dog, and that the practice only takes place behind closed doors, if at all. This is manifestly not the case; *yeongyangtang*, for one, is still a popular dish due to its purported health-giving properties, though is becoming less and less so as you drop down the age demographic. However, any fears of Koreans chowing down on an Alsatian or Border Collie should be quelled; almost all dog meat comes from a scraggly mongrel breed colloquially known as the *ddong-gae*, or "shit-dog", an animal apparently named for its tendency to eat whatever it finds on the floor. Even so, the poor conditions that the animals are often kept in, and the continuing – and occasionally verified – stories of dogs being clubbed to death to tenderize the meat, are good reasons to avoid this kind of meal.

International cuisine

While many visitors fall head over heels for Korean food, it's not to everybody's taste, and after a while the near-permanent spicy tang of red-pepper paste can wear down even the most tolerant taste buds. One problem concerns **breakfast**, a meal that, to most Koreans, is simply another time-window for the intake of *gimchi* and rice. This is too heavy for many Westerners, but though a fry-up or smörgåsbord will be hard to find outside the major hotels, you may find some solace in the buns, cakes and pastries of major bakery chains such as *Tous Les Jours* and *Paris Baguette*, or the mayonnaise-heavy sandwiches of the convenience stores.

International food is getting easier to come by in Korea, though only Seoul can be said to have a truly cosmopolitan range (and a thinly spread one, at that). **American-style fast food**, however, can be found pretty much everywhere – *McDonald's* and *Burger King* are joined by *Lotteria*, a local chain, and there are also a great number of fried chicken joints scattered around. Traditional **Japanese food** has made serious inroads into the Korean scene, and the obligatory red lanterns of *izakaya*-style bar-restaurants are especially easy to spot in student areas. **Italian food** has long been popular with Koreans, though they've added their own twists to pizzas and pasta – almost every single meal will be served with a small tub of pickled gherkin, an addition that locals assume to be *de rigeur* in the restaurants of Napoli or Palermo. **Chinese restaurants** are equally numerous, though they too deserve no awards for authenticity: even in the many cases where the restaurateurs themselves are Chinese, the Korean palette is only accepting of a limited number of flavours. One recommendation, however, is *bokkeumbap* – this is fried rice mixed with cubes of ham and vegetable, topped with a fried egg and black bean sauce, and served with deliciously spicy seafood broth; the whole thing will cost about W4000, and is, therefore, a great way to fill up on the cheap.

Drink

Finding a place to drink in Korea is no hard task, particularly if it's alcohol you're after. A potato wine named **soju** is the national drink – a cheap, clear Korean version of vodka that you'll either love or hate (or love, then hate the next morning) – but there's a pleasing variety of grog to choose from. The country also has a wealth of excellent tea on offer, though coffee is increasingly winning the urban caffeine battles.

Alcoholic drinks

Though the staccato imbibing of *soju* is *de rigeur* at restaurants of an evening, the two main breeds of drinking den are bars and "hofs"; there are a quite incredible number of both in the cities, though the majority can be surprisingly empty, even at weekends – you may wonder how most of them stay in business. **Hofs**, pronounced more like "hop", are bright, booth-filled places serving **beer** (*maekju*) by the bucketload. The main brands are Cass, OB and Hite; prices are more or less equal, starting at about W2500 for a 500cc glass, and you'll soon find your favourite. Quite fascinating are the three- or five-litre plastic jug of draught beer (*saeng-maekju*), which often come billowing dry ice and illuminated with flashing lights. The downside of such places is that customers are pretty much obliged to eat as well as drink; you'll be given free snacks, but you are expected to order something from the menu.

Bars are almost invariably dark yet neon-strewn dens; unlike in *hofs*, customers are not usually expected to eat and tend to take roost in an extensive cocktail menu; beer will still be available, in draught or bottled form. Each city has one or more main "going out" district, with the most raucous to be found outside the rear entrances of the **universities** (which maintain a veneer of respectability by keeping their main entrances free of such revelry). Most cities have at least one resident **expat bar**; these are usually the best places for foreigners to meet fellow *waeguk-in* or new Korean friends.

One extremely popular Korean drink is **makkeolli** (pronounced "ma-ko-li"), a sweet, typically milky rice wine. Specialist *makkeolli* halls have taken root in student areas, recognizable by the alcohol-fuelled hubbub and calligraphic wallpaper, as well as the bruised golden pots that the drink is served in. Be warned – *makkeolli* is dangerous stuff, and though it may taste sweet and smooth, it's common for first-timers to hit the wall after a pot or two before waking up to a colossal hangover. Many foreigners take to starting a night out outside a **convenience store**; all sell alcohol, and they make particularly good meeting points in warmer months, when they're often surrounded by tables and chairs. Some owners have even built wooden verandas to cater for their foreign customer base. Though you may need to fend off swarms of insects, such stores can be surprisingly good places to meet people, and drinks are, of course, much cheaper than at a bar or *hof*. Beer and *soju* are the obvious choices, though special mention must be made of Jinro House Wine: this curiously pink liquid, which may or may not be derived from grapes, costs about W2000 per bottle and can only be described as "comedy wine" as it tends to give people the giggles. More serious are *insamju*, a ginseng liquor, and *baekseju*, a nutty, whisky-coloured rice wine costing about W3500 for a small bottle; Koreans love to mix the latter with *soju*, a potent combination known as *o-shipseju*. Connoiseurs can hunt down a number of special local brands, including *baem soju* – regular *soju*, but sharing its bottle with a dead snake (it's apparently quite good for your back).

Tea and coffee

Tea is big business in Korea. Unfortunately, most of the drinking takes place at home or work, though Insa-dong in Seoul has dozens of interesting tearooms (see p.123), and there are some gems outside national parks and in Jeonju's *hanok* district (p.296). Green tea, or *nok-cha*, is by far the most popular across the country by consumption, though those who find their way to a specialist tearoom should take the opportunity to try something more special.

Korean tea varieties

Daechu-cha Jujube tea
Gukhwa-cha Chrysanthemum tea
Gyepi-cha Cinnamon tea
Gyulsam-cha Honey ginseng tea
Insam-cha Ginseng tea
Ma-cha Wild herb tea
Maesil-cha Plum tea
Nok-cha Green tea
Omija-cha Five Flavours tea
Saenggang-cha Ginger tea
Yak-cha Medicinal herb tea
Yuja-cha Citron tea
Yulmu-cha "Job's Tears" tea.

Café culture has gradually found its way into the lives of Korean youth, and though you shouldn't have to look too hard to find a *Starbucks*, local clones are cheaper and even more numerous. Only recently foreign visitors were forced to stomach weak, expensive coffee concoctions at bars, more often than not given a chemical zing of hazelnut. In addition to coffee, modern cafés usually serve delicious **green tea latte** (*nok-cha latte*), with some of the more adventurous throwing in ginseng or sweet potato varieties for good measure. Worth mentioning are the cold coffees on sale in convenience stores, though these are certainly not for purists. Here, cans or cartons of "*keo-pi uyu*" (coffee milk) can provide a morning pick-me-up for just W500, or for W1000 you can choose from flavours such as mocha, caramel, double espresso and maple. Those who stay in the country a while will doubtless come into regular contact with instant-coffee brands such as Maxim and Tasters' Choice; free sugary shots are often offered after restaurant meals, and sachets can sometimes be found next to water dispensers in shops.

The media

Korean media has come a long way since bursting out of the dictatorial strait-jacket of the 1970s and 1980s, but with the country's relatively small number of foreigners and low level of English language skills, most of it remains inaccessible to all but those versed in Korean.

The two big English-language **newspapers** are the *Korea Times* (Ⓦwww.koreatimes.co.kr) and *Korean Herald* (Ⓦwww.koreanherald.co.kr), near-identical dailies with near-identical addictions to news agency output and dull business statistics. Neither paper has got the hang of graphic illustration, both usually opting to trot out their parade of cold, hard facts in paragraph form. This said, both have decent listings sections in their Saturday editions, which detail events around the country, as well as the goings-on in Seoul's restaurant, film and club scenes. The *International Herald Tribune* is pretty easy to track down in top hotels, with copies containing the eight-page *Joongang Daily* (Ⓦjoongangdaily.joins.com), an interesting local news supplement. You should also be able to hunt down the previous week's *Time*, *Newsweek* or *Economist* in most Korean cities – try the book section of a large department store. An interesting source of information is *Ohmy News* (Ⓦenglish.ohmynews.com), a large online compendium of articles written by members of the public that has long been a quirky bee in the bonnet of local politicians and "proper" journalists.

Korean **television** often reveals itself to be exactly what people would expect of Japanese television – a gaudy feast of madcap game shows and soppy period dramas. Foreign viewers are likely to be baffled by most of the output, but there are few more accessible windows into the true nature of Korean society. **Arirang** (Ⓦwww.arirang.co.kr) is a 24-hour English-language television network based in Seoul, which promotes the country with occasionally interesting documentaries, and has regular news bulletins. Arirang TV is free-to-air throughout much of the world, and though not free in Korea itself, it comes as part of most cable packages.

Festivals

Koreans love to have a good time, and on even a short trip around the country you're more than likely to stumble across a special event of some sort. Many are religious in nature, with Buddhist celebrations supplemented by Confucian and even animist events. Most festivals are concentrated around spring and autumn, but a whole host are spread throughout the year. If you're heading to one, don't be shy – the locals love to see foreigners joining in with traditional Korean events, and those who dare to get stuck in may finish the day with a whole troupe of new friends.

It must be said that a large proportion of **Korean festivals** are quite unappealing: many are brazenly commercial in nature, making no bones about being held to "promote the salted seafood industry", for example. Other festivals include those dedicated to agricultural utensils, clean peppers and the "Joy of Rolled Laver" – you'll easily be able to spot the duds. The most interesting events are highlighted below, though bear in mind that celebrations for two of the big national festivals – *Seollal* the Lunar New Year, and a Korean version of Thanksgiving named *Chuseok* – are family affairs that generally take place behind closed doors.

January–March

Sinjeong (New Year's Day) **January 1** Korea celebrates New Year in much the same fashion as Western countries; if you don't want to party at a club of some sort, good places to be include Ilchulbong, a peak in Jeju Island (p.362), and Hyangiram, a hermitage south of Yeosu (p.290).

Seollal (Lunar New Year) **Usually early February** One of the most important holidays on the calendar, Lunar New Year sees Koreans flock to their home towns for a three-day holiday of relaxed celebration, and many businesses close up.

April–June

Cherry blossom festivals Usually early April Heralding the arrival of spring, soft blossom wafts through the air across the country, a cue for all good Koreans to lay down blankets at parks or riverbanks, barbeque some meat and throw back the *soju*.

Jeonju International Film Festival Last week of April Smaller and more underground than the biggie in Busan, JIFF focuses on the arty, independent side of the movie industry (p.291).

Children's Day May 5 Koreans make an even bigger fuss over their kids than usual on this national holiday – expect parks, zoos and amusement parks to be jam-packed.

Buddha's Birthday Late May A public holiday during which temples across the land are adorned with colourful paper lanterns; there's an even more vibrant night parade in Seoul (see box, p.132).

International Mime Festival May Held in the Gangwonese capital of Chuncheon, this foreigner-friendly event is a showcase of soundless talent (p.167).

Dano Usually June A shamanist festival held on the fifth day of the fifth lunar month, featuring circus acts, *ssireum* wrestling, mask dramas and a whole lot more. The city of Gangneung (p.183) is host to the biggest displays.

Korean Queer Culture Festival Early June Still the only pride event in the country, this takes place over a fortnight at locations across Seoul, and features a film festival (once banned by the police), forums, exhibitions and a street parade – see ⓦwww.kqcf.org for more details.

July–September

Boryeong Mud Festival Late July This annual expat favourite pulls mud-happy hordes to Daecheon Beach (p.324) for all kinds of muck-related fun.

Independence Day August 15 The country becomes a sea of Korean flags on this holiday celebrating the end of Japanese rule in 1945.

International Puppet Festival August Puppets and their masters come from around the world to flaunt their skills in Chuncheon (p.167), a city in Gangwon province.

Firefly Festival August Glow worms are the tiny stars of the show at this modest night-time event, which takes place over a weekend near Muju (p.298).

One unexpected treat is the chance to don a firefly costume.

Gwangju Biennale September to November A wide-ranging, two-month-long festival of contemporary art, the biennale usually takes place on alternate autumns, though in the past has also been held in the spring.

Andong Mask Dance Festival Late September or early October Legend has it that if a person fails to attend a mask festival in their lifetime, they cannot get into heaven, so if you're in Korea in the autumn you might as well have a crack at salvation in the form of participating in one of the country's most popular events – a week of anonymous dancing, performed by the best troupes in the land (p.226).

Chuseok (Harvest Moon Festival) Late September or early October One of the biggest events on the Korean calendar is this three-day national holiday, similar to Thanksgiving; families head to their home towns for a spot of ancestor worship, and the eating of a special crescent-shaped rice-cake.

October–December

Pusan International Film Festival Usually October One of Asia's biggest such events, PIFF draws in big-shots and hangers-on for a week of cinematic fun. Haeundae beach is the hub of activity, though screens around the city spool out an increasingly diverse range of film. English-speakers are well catered for (see box, p.242).

National Foundation Day October 3 A national holiday celebrating the 2333 BC birth of Dangun, the legendary founder of the Korean nation. Shamanist celebrations take place around the country, with the most important in Taebaeksan National Park (p.193).

Baekje Festival Early October This annual event commemorating the Baekje dynasty is held alternately in the old Baekje capitals of Gongju and Buyeo (even-numbered years in Buyeo, odd ones in Gongju).

World Martial Arts Festival Usually October A week-long series of international fisticuff action, held each year in Chungju (p.338).

Gimchi Festival Late October Gimchi – you either love it or hate it. Held in Gwangju, you'll be able to see, smell and taste dozens of varieties of the spicy stuff, and there's even a *gimchi*-making contest for foreigners keen to show off.

Pepero Day November 11 A crass marketing ploy, but an amusing one nonetheless – like Pocky, their Japanese cousins, Pepero are thin sticks of chocolate-coated biscuit, and on this date in the year when it looks as if four of them are standing together, millions of Koreans say "I love you" by giving a box to their sweethearts, friends, parents or pets.

Christmas Day December 25 Every evening looks like Christmas in neon-drenched Korea, but on this occasion Santa Haraboji (Grandpa Santa) comes to throw his gifts around.

Sports and outdoor activities

The 1988 Seoul Olympics did much to thrust Korea into the international spotlight, a trick repeated with the even more successful 2002 FIFA World Cup, an event co-hosted with Japan. But sport here is less about watching than doing, a fact evident in the well-trodden trails of the national parks, and the svelte proportions of the average Korean.

Many people come to Korea to practise a martial art such as taekwondo, *hapkido* or *geomdo*, but those seeking more Western sports such as football, baseball or basketball will not have far to look. The most popular activity is **hiking**, the national pastime owing to the country's abundance of mountains and national parks – see the *Hiking in Korea* colour section for more details.

Spectator sports

The two most popular spectator sports in the country are **football** and **baseball**. Koreans tend to follow one or the other, though football has been in the ascendancy of late, particularly with females and the younger generations. Those looking for something authentically Korean should try to hunt down a *ssireum* wrestling tournament.

Football

Soccer, or *chuk-gu*, rode the crest of the 2002 World Cup wave to become the most popular sport in the country. The ten gleaming new *gyeonggi-jang* built for the World Cup were swiftly moved into by teams from the national K-League (see below), but the high attendances that the tournament spawned dropped sharply as spectators realized that their local boys weren't really better than Argentina – swathes of empty seats mean that you'll always be able to get a ticket at the door. Since the turn of the century, the club Seongnam has ruled the domestic roost, though Pohang and Suwon have been more successful in the Asian Champions League; Suwon and Daejeon are said to have the rowdiest fans. Other teams are listed below, though note that most teams operate as American-style "franchises" that can move lock, stock and barrel to more profitable locations at the drop of a hat. The reason for this cold commerce is that most teams are tied to Korea's huge conglomerates, the *jaebeol*, though exceptions include the community-owned Daejeon Citizen, and Gwangju Phoenix, a military outfit. A few locals have escaped the K-League for more lucrative pastures, and Koreans are immensely proud of their sporting diaspora; as a foreigner you're very likely to be quizzed about players such as Park Ji-sung, who made it to Manchester United via Holland, and Ahn Jung-hwan, a success in Italy until being sacked by his club for daring to knock the Italian national team out of the World Cup.

K-League teams

Busan I'Park Asiad Main Stadium, Busan
Chunnam Dragons Gwangyang Stadium, Gwangyang
Daegu FC World Cup Stadium, Daegu
Daejeon Citizen World Cup Stadium, Daejeon
FC Seoul World Cup Stadium Seoul
Gwangju Phoenix Guus Hiddink Stadium, Gwangju
Gyeongnam FC Civil Stadium, Changwon
Incheon United Munhak Stadium, Incheon
Jeju United FC World Cup Stadium, Seogwipo
Jeonbuk Motors World Cup Stadium, Jeonju
Pohang Steelers Steelyard Stadium, Pohang
Seongnam Chunma Seongnam Stadium, Seongnam
Suwon Bluewings Big Bird Stadium, Suwon
Ulsan Tigers Munsu Cup Stadium, Ulsan

The 2002 World Cup

The first World Cup to be held in Asia took place in South Korea in 2002, throwing the country into the international spotlight. Originally bidding against Japan, the two nations chose to do a bit of bridge-building by co-hosting the tournament. The global media devoted most of its attention to Japan in the pre-tournament build-up, but the focus shifted to Korea as the tournament progessed, thanks in no small part to the "Red Devils", South Korea's noisy, colourful supporter base. Though both countries held an equal number of games, the Koreans saw nearly twenty goals more than the Japanese, as well as most of the matches that went down as "classics" – including Senegal's win over then-champions France and Brazil's sensational 5–2 win over Costa Rica.

Despite the wealth of global talent on display, most fuss was given to the South Korean team themselves, led by Dutch manager Guus Hiddink. Without a single victory in their fourteen previous World Cup games, victory in the opener against Poland was the cue for wild celebrations across the country. Followed by a draw with USA and a gritty win over Portugal, the minnows of South Korea amazingly went through to the knockout phase as group winners. Korean games were beamed live to huge screens across the country, each surrounded by a sea of red and a cacophony of noise, and to everyone's surprise the team shrugged off European giants Italy and Spain to become the first Asian team to reach the semi-finals. With a final against Brazil in sight, a narrow 1–0 defeat to Germany finally killed the dream, but the nation's footballers and vibrant support were the stories of the tournament.

Baseball

Until 2002, **baseball** (*yagu*) was the spectator sport of choice. Though its popularity has waned, you'll see a lot of games on Korean television, or attend one yourself by heading to see a professional team at one of the *yagu-jang* listed below; seasons run from April to October, with a break at the height of summer. Though the fielding, in particular, isn't quite up to the level that American fans will be used to (and neither is the atmosphere at the ballpark), several Korean players have made their way into the Major League, including pitchers Kim Byung-hyun and Park Chan-ho. The Gwangju-based Tigers were the team to watch in the 1980s and 1990s, though since the turn of the century the Unicorns and Lions, from Suwon and Daegu respectively, have shared the limelight. Bear in mind that the team names listed below are subject to regular change, thanks to the franchise system in operation.

KBO teams

Doosan Bears Jamsil Baseball Stadium, Seoul
Hanhwa Eagles Baseball Stadium, Daejeon
Hyundai Unicorns Baseball Stadium, Suwon
Kia Tigers Moodeung Stadium, Gwangju
LG Twins Jamsil Baseball Stadium, Seoul
Lotte Giants Sajik Baseball Stadium, Busan
Samsung Lions Baseball Stadium, Daegu
SK Wyverns Munhak Baseball Stadium, Incheon

Ssireum

Though inevitably compared to *sumo*, this Korean form of wrestling bears more resemblance to Mongolian styles – the wrestlers are chunky, rather than gargantuan, and they rely on grabs and throws, rather than slaps and pushes. As with *sumo*, the object of the wrestlers is to force their opponents to the floor, but in **ssireum** the fights start with both fighters interlocked. The sport is markedly less popular than its Japanese counterpart; few Koreans will be able to point you in the right direction if you wish to see a tournament, and even if you hunt one down the atmosphere will usually be low-key. The best place to catch a fight will be as part of a traditional festival, notably the early summer Dano in Gangneung (see p.183), or one of the Chuseok events that take place around the country.

Participatory sports

In addition to being a nation of compulsive hikers (see the *Hiking* colour section), all Koreans are taught at school to exercise as a matter of course. Martial arts such as taekwondo are among the nation's most famed exports, but Western activities such as golf and skiing have caught on in recent decades. Even rugby players will be able to get some practise in – see p.134 for details of male and female clubs in Seoul.

Martial arts

Most Korean martial arts are variations of those that originated in China or Japan. **Taekwondo** is the best known – developed in Tang-dynasty China, it was given a Korean twist during the Three Kingdoms period, since going on to become one of the country's most famed exports, and an Olympic sport to boot. The predominantly kick-based style is taught at schools, and forms the backbone of compulsory military service for the nation's men. There are dozens of less common local styles to choose from; these include *hapkido*, better known in the West as *aikido*, its Japanese counterpart; *geomdo*, a form in which participants get to bonk each other with wooden poles and likewise known to the world as *kendo*; and *teukgong-musul*, created by the South Korean Special Forces. See p.134 for information about taekwondo classes in Seoul.

Golf

The success of professional Korean golfers, mainly females such as LPGA champ Park Se-ri, has tempted many into taking up the game. Over a hundred **courses** dot the country, mainly surrounding Seoul or on Jeju Island; most are members-only clubs, however, and those that aren't are pretty dear – the fact that Korean golfers often go to Japan to save money says it all. If you come in with clubs, don't forget to **declare** them on arrival at the airport. Tourist offices will have information about nearby courses, though the average traveller will have to stick to the **driving ranges** dotted around the cities – scan the urban horizon for tower blocks topped by a large green net.

Skiing

With sub-zero winters and mountainous terrain, it's hardly surprising that **skiing** is big business in Korea, a country that came agonizingly close to being selected as the host of the 2010 and 2014 Winter Olympics. Non-Olympians looking to ski or snowboard in Korea should have few problems – there are a number of resorts, mainly in the northern provinces of Gyeonggi and Gangwon; most of these have ample accommodation facilities, though prices soar in the ski season (usually December to February). Other than Yongpyeong ski resort (p.187), the hub of the Olympic bid, other interesting venues include Muju in Jeolla province (p.298) and Sajo Village near Suanbo in Chungcheong province (p.338). Clothes and ski equipment are available for hire, and many resorts have English-speaking instructors; **prices** vary from place to place, but expect lift passes to cost around W60,000 per day, with ski or snowboard rental another W30,000 on top of that.

Football and rugby

Football is played across the country by young males, mostly in the form of kick-abouts that would gladly absorb a foreign player or two. The best places to look are riverside flood plains, often wide enough to accommodate the odd pitch, or university campuses. There's also the **foreigners' football league**, a highly competitive affair; ask at your local expat bar for details, or try your luck on @ssflkorea.com. Also see p.134 for details of Seoul **rugby** teams.

Culture and etiquette

You may have mastered the art of the polite bow, worked out how to use the tricky steel chopsticks, and learnt a few words of the Korean language, but beware, you may upset new friends by accepting gifts with your hand in the wrong place. While even seasoned expats receive heartfelt congratulations for getting the easy bits right (some are even surprised when foreigners are able to use Korean money), there are still innumerable ways to offend the locals, and unfortunately it's the things that are hardest to guess that are most likely to see you come a cropper.

Korea is often said to be the world's most **Confucian** nation, a fact stemming from a centuries-long following of the creed that ended just a few generations ago – the Joseon dynasty, which ran from 1392 to 1910, represents the world's longest-running example of Confucian rule, though much of the theoretical structure was actually in place long before Joseon times. Under this system, everyone was born into a hierarchical position governed by the ruling *yangban* scholars, with aspects such as gender, age and family background placing strict guidelines on everything from what clothes people wore to the dimensions of their house, as well as limiting the scope of what any individual could seek to achieve. Today, it's still basically true that anyone older, richer or more important than you – or just male as opposed to female – is simply "better" and deserving of more respect, a fact that becomes sorely clear to many working in Korea. Perhaps most evident to foreigners will be what amounts to a national obsession with **age** – you're likely to be asked how old you are soon after your first meeting with any Korean, and any similarity of birth years is likely to be greeted with a genuine whoop of delight (note that Koreans count years differently from Westerners – children are already

1 when they're born, and gain another digit at Lunar New Year, meaning that they could already be 2 years old two days after their birth). **Foreigners** are largely exempt from the code of conduct that would be required of both parties following their knowledge of age, employment and background, and little is expected of them in such terms, but this does have its drawbacks – in such an ethnically homogenous society, those that aren't Korean will always remain "outsiders", even if they speak the language fluently or have actually spent their whole lives in the country. Korea's social workings frustrate many foreigners that come to live here, but it's advisable to let things ride as much as possible and remember why you came in the first place – getting angry won't change the way that the country functions, and the chance to see the machinations of such a highly distinctive society, logical or otherwise, is one that genuine travellers should relish.

Conduct

The East Asian concept of "face" is highly important in Korea, and known here as *gibun*; the main goal is to avoid the **embarrassment** of self or others. Great lengths are usually taken to smooth out awkward situations, and foreigners getting unnecessarily angry are unlikely to invoke much sympathy. This occasionally happens as the result of an embarrassed smile, the traditional Korean retort to an uncomfortable question or incident; remember that they're not laughing at you (even if they've just dropped something on your head), merely trying to show empathy or move the topic onto safer ground. Foreigners may also see Koreans as disrespectful: nobody's going to thank you for holding open a door, while most locals will be more than happy to barge you out of the way to get where they're going. Again, this is a cultural difference – they haven't been introduced to you, and simply don't know where to fit you in on the grand Confucian scheme of things. **Dressing well** has long been important, but though pretty much anything goes for local girls these days, foreign women may be assumed to be brazen hussies (or, as often happens, Russian prostitutes) if they wear revealing clothing.

Meeting and greeting

Foreigners will see notice Koreans **bowing** all the time, even during telephone conversations. Though doing likewise will do much to endear you to locals, don't go overboard – a full, right-angled bow would only be appropriate for meeting royalty (and the monarchy ended in 1910). Generally, a short bow with eyes closed and the head directed downwards will do just fine, but it's best to observe the Koreans themselves, and the action will become quite natural after a short time; many visitors find themselves inadvertently maintaining the habit long after they've left. The method of **attracting attention** is also different from what most foreigners are used to – beckoning is done with fingers fluttering beneath a downward-facing palm, rather than with index fingers protruding hook-like from an upturned one.

Koreans are great lovers of **business cards**, and these are exchanged in all meetings that have even a whiff of commerce about them. The humble rectangles garner far greater respect than they do in the West, and folding or stuffing one into a pocket or wallet is a huge *faux-pas* – accept your card with profuse thanks, leave it on the table for the duration of the meeting, and file it away with respect (a card-holder is an essential purchase for anyone here on business). Also note that it's seen as incredibly rude to write someone's name in red ink – this colour is reserved for names of those who have died, a practice that most Koreans seem to think goes on all around the world.

If you're lucky enough to be invited to a Korean home, try to bring a **gift** – fruit, chocolates and flowers go down well. The offering is likely to be refused at first, and probably on the second attempt too – persevere and it will eventually be accepted with thanks. The manner of receiving is also important – your receiving hand should be held from underneath by the non-receiving one, the distance up or down the arm dependent on exactly how polite you want to be. This will only come with experience and will not be expected of most foreigners, but you will be expected to take your **shoes off** once inside the house or apartment, so try to ensure that your socks are devoid of muck or holes.

Dining

Korea's Confucian legacy can often be a great boon to foreigners, as it has long been customary for hosts (usually "betters") to **pay** – many English teachers get taken out for regular slap-up meals by their bosses, and don't have to pay a dime. Koreans also tend to make a big show of trying to pay, with the bill passing rapidly from hand to hand until the right person coughs up. Nowadays things are changing slowly – "going Dutch" is increasingly common as a payment method, where it would have been unthinkable before – but there are still innumerable codes of conduct to follow; Koreans will usually guide foreign inductees through the various dos and don'ts. Many surround the use of **chopsticks** – don't use these to point at people or pick your teeth, and try not to spear food with them unless your skills are really poor. It's also bad form, as natural as it may seem, to leave your chopsticks in the bowl: this is said to resemble incense sticks used after a death, but to most Koreans it just looks wrong (just as many Westerners obey unwritten and seemingly meaningless rules governing cutlery positions). Just leave the sticks balanced on the rim of the bowl.

Many Korean meals are group affairs, and this has given rise to a number of rules surrounding who **serves the food** from the communal trays to the individual ones – it's usually the youngest woman on the table. Foreign women finding themselves in this position will be able to mop up a great deal of respect for performing the duty, though as there are particular ways to serve each kind of food, it's probably best to watch first. The **serving of drinks** is a little less formal, though again the minutae of recommended conduct could fill a small book – basically, you should never refill your own cup or glass, and should endeavour to keep topped up those belonging to others. The position of the hands is important – watch to see how the Koreans are doing it (both the pourer and the recipient), and you'll be increasing your "face" value in no time.

One big no-no is to **blow your nose** during the meal – preposterously unfair, given the spice level of pretty much every Korean dish. Should you need to do so, make your excuses and head to the toilets. It's also proper form to wait for the **head of the table** – the one who is paying, in other words – to sit down first, as well as to allow them to be the first to stand at the end of the meal. The latter can be quite tricky as many Korean restaurants are sit-on-the-floor affairs that play havoc on the knees and backs of foreigners unaccustomed to the practice.

All in all, Koreans will tolerate anything viewed as a "mistake" on the part of the foreigner, and offer great encouragement to those who are at least attempting to get things right. This can sometimes go a little too far – you're likely to be praised for your chopstick-handling abilities however long you've been around, and it's almost impossible to avoid the Korean Catch-22: locals love to ask foreigners questions during a meal, but anyone stopping to answer will likely fail to keep pace with the fast-eating Koreans, who will then assume that your dish is not disappearing quickly because you don't like it.

Living and working in Korea

There are two main types of foreigner in Korea: English teachers and American soldiers. Other jobs are hard to come by, though today's Korea is becoming ever more prominent in global business, with the resulting foreign contingent gradually permeating Seoul's army of suits. It's still fairly easy to land a teaching job, though to do this legally a degree certificate is nigh-on essential; wages are good, and Korea is a popular port of call for those wishing to pay off their student loan quickly while seeing a bit of the world. The cost of living, though rising, is still below that in most English-speaking countries, and many teachers are able to put financial considerations out of their mind for the duration of their stay – many slowly realize that they've inadvertently been saving sixty or seventy percent of their salary.

With the number of **teaching jobs** on offer, it's quite possible to handpick a city or province of your choice. Seoul is an obvious target and the easiest place from which to escape into Western pleasures if necessary, but those who head to provincial cities such as Daejeon, Mokpo or Busan generally seem to have a better time of things, and emerge with a truer appreciation of the country. There are also those who arrive with a specific purpose in mind – surfers dig Jeju and the east coast, for example, and others choose to find the true essence of Korea by staying in the smallest possible town. As well as teaching, some come to **study**. Korea has given a number of martial arts to the world, and continues to draw in students keen to learn directly from the horse's mouth; others choose to learn the local language.

Teaching English

Uncomplicated entry requirements, low tax and decent pay cheques make Korea one of the most popular stops on the **English-teaching** circuit. Demand for native speakers is high and still growing; English-teaching qualifications are far from essential, and all that is usually required is a degree certificate, and a copy of your passport – many people have been taken on by a Korean school without so much as a telephone interview. Most new entrants start off by teaching kids at a language school (*hagwon*). Some of the bigger companies are ECC, YBM and Pagoda, and most pay around W2,000,000 per month, though even for people doing the same job at the same school this may vary depending on nationality and gender – Canadian women usually get the most, British gents the least. After a year or two, many teachers are sick of kids and puny holiday allowances, and make their way to a university teaching post; pay is usually lower and responsibilities higher than at a *hagwon*, though the holiday allowances are hard to resist, often as much as five months per year. It's also possible to teach adults in business or government schools, or you could volunteer for a couple of hours a week at one of the country's many orphanages. Most teachers give their bank balance a nudge in the right direction by offering **private lessons** on the side – an illegal practice, but largely tolerated unless you start organizing them for others. To land a full-time job from outside Korea you'll have to go online, and it's still the best option if you're already in Korea – popular sites include Dave's ESL Café (Ⓦwww.eslcafe.com), ESL Hub (Ⓦwww.eslhub.com) and HiTeacher (Ⓦhiteacher.com), though a thorough web search will yield more.

One of the most regular *hagwon*-related **complaints** heard in expat bars is the long hours many teachers have to work – figure on up to 30 per week. This may include Saturdays, or be spread quite liberally across the day from 9am to 9pm – try to find jobs with "no split shift" if possible. Questionable school policies also come in for stick; for example, teachers are often expected to be present at the school for show even if they have no lessons on. Real scare stories are ten-a-penny, too – every teacher knows an unfortunate fellow-foreigner whose school suddenly closed, the manager having ridden off into the sunset with a pay cheque or two. This said, most schools are reputable; you can typically expect them to organize **free accommodation**, and to do the legwork with your **visa** application. Some countries operate Working Holiday visa schemes with Korea, but others will need a full working visa to be legally employed; those unable to collect this in their home country are usually given a plane ticket and directions for a quick visa-run to Japan (the closest embassy is in Fukuoka).

Studying in Korea

Korea has long been a popular place for the study of **martial arts**, while the country's ever-stronger ties with global business is also prompting many to gain a competitive advantage by studying the Korean language. It's also one of the world's great **archery** hotbeds, though courses here are not for amateurs and teachers demand substantial time and effort from their charges – if you're interested in studying this sport in Korea, look into it through your home country's archery federation.

Language

Those looking to study **Korean** have a full range of options to choose from, depending on what linguistic depth they require and how long they have to attain it. Students desiring fluency may consider attending one of the institutes run by many of the larger **universities**, though even these vary in terms of price, study time, skill level and accommodation. Most of the year-long courses are in Seoul and start in March – apply in good time. There's a good list at Ⓦenglish.tour2korea.com, while information on study visas and how to apply for them can be found on the Ministry of Education's website (Ⓦwww.studyinkorea.go.kr). There are **private institutes** dotted around Seoul and other major cities – Ⓦenglish.seoul.go.kr has a list of safe recommendations in the capital, while other official city websites are the best places to look for institutes elsewhere in the country. Those who find themselves working in Korea may have no time for intensive study; in these cases it's worth looking into the **government-funded courses** run by a few major cities, some of which are so cheap that their price is barely an issue. Many opt for an even higher degree of informality and take language lessons from friends or colleagues, but with so few English speakers around, just living in Korea can be all the practice you need.

Martial arts classes

Finding classes for the most popular styles (including **taekwondo**, *hapkido* and *geomdo*) isn't hard, but very few classes cater for foreigners – it's best to go hunting on the expat circuit. The obvious exception is Seoul; here, popular introductory taekwondo courses take place at Gyeonghuigung palace. Those looking for something more advanced should seek advice from their home country's own taekwondo federation.

Buddhist teachings

Many **temples** around the country offer teaching and templestay programmes for around W50,000 per night – a wonderful opportunity to see the "Land of Morning Calm" at its most serene (as long as you can stand the early mornings). Some temples are able to provide English-language instruction, and some not – see Ⓦeng.templestay.com for more details.

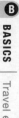

Travel essentials

Costs

Some people come to Korea expecting it to be a budget destination on par with the Southeast Asian countries, while others arrive with expectations of Japanese-style levels. The truth is somewhere on the latter side of the scale – those staying at five-star hotels and eating at Western-style restaurants will spend almost as much as they would in other developed countries, though there are numerous ways for budget travellers to make their trip a cheap one. Your biggest outlay is likely to be **accommodation** – Seoul has some grand places to stay for W400,000 (£215/US$420/€310) and up, though most cities have dedicated tourist hotels for around W100,000 (£55/US$105/€75). Though they're not to everyone's taste, motels usually make acceptable places to stay; costing around W30,000 (£16/US$31/€23), and often double that in Seoul. The capital does, however, have a few backpacker flophouses which can cost anything from motel levels to W10,000 (£5/US$10/€8), while real scrimpers can stay at a *jjimjilbang* (see box, p.41) for a few bucks.

Because of the country's small size, **transport** is unlikely to make too much of a dent in your wallet – even a high-speed KTX train from Seoul in the northwest to Busan in the southeast will only set you back W45,000 (£24/US$48/€35), and you can cut that price in half by taking a slower service. Inner-city transport is also good value, with most journeys costing W1000 or thereabouts, and **admission charges** to temples, museums and the like are similarly unlikely to cause your wallet discomfort.

By staying in motels or guesthouses and eating at reasonably cheap restaurants, you should be able to survive easily on a daily budget of W40,000 (£22/US$42/€31), or even half this if seriously pushed. After you've added in transport costs and a few entry tickets, a realistic daily figure may be W60,000 (£32/US$63/€46).

Tipping plays almost no part in Korean transactions – try not to leave unwanted change in the hands of a cashier, lest they feel forced to abandon their duties and chase you down the street with it. Exceptions are tourist hotels, most of which tack a ten percent service charge onto the room bill; these are also among the few places in the country to omit **tax** – levied at eleven percent – from their quoted prices.

Crime and personal safety

Korea is one of those countries in which you're far more likely to see someone running towards you with a dropped wallet than away with a stolen one – tales abound about travellers who have left a valuable possession on a restaurant table or park bench and returned hours later to find it in the same place. Though you'd be very unlucky to fall victim to a crime, it's prudent to take a few simple precautions. One involves the country's awful **road safety** record, the gruesome statistics heightened by the number of vehicles that use pavements as shortcuts or parking spaces. Caution should also be exercised around any **street fights** that you may have the misfortune to come across, since Korean men practice taekwondo to a fairly high level during their compulsory national service, Korea is not a great place to get caught in a scuffle. The most common source of foreigner-related fisticuffs is the "theft" – or apparent theft – of a Korean girl by a foreign man. Though feelings of resentment in these instances are quite widespread among Korean men, most remain bubbling beneath the surface until the consumption of alcohol.

Electricity

The electrical **current** runs at 220v, 60Hz throughout the country, and requires European-style plugs with two round pins, though some older buildings, including many *yeogwan* and *yeoinsuk*, may still take flat-pinned plugs at 110v.

Entry requirements

Citizens of almost any Western nation can enter Korea visa-free with an onward ticket, though the duration of the permit varies. Most West European nationals qualify for a three-month visa exemption, as do citizens of New Zealand and Australia; Italians and Portuguese are allowed sixty days, Americans and South Africans just thirty, and Canadians a full six months. If you need more than this, apply before entering Korea. **Overstaying** your visa will result in a large fine (up to W500,000 per day), with exceptions only being made in emergencies such as illness or loss of passport. Getting a new passport is time-consuming and troublesome, though the process will be simplified if your passport has been registered with your embassy in Seoul, or if you can prove your existence with a birth certificate or copy of your old passport.

Work visas, valid for one year and extendable for at least one more, can be applied for before or after entering Korea. Applications can take up to a month to be processed by Korean embassies, but once inside the country it can take as little as a week. Your **employer** will do all the hard work with the authorities then provide you with a visa confirmation slip; the visa must be picked up outside Korea (the nearest consulate is in Fukuoka, Japan; visas here can be issued on the day of application). Visas with the same employer can be extended without leaving Korea. An **alien card** must be applied for at the local immigration office within 90 days of arrival – again, this is usually taken care of by the employer. Work visas are forfeited on leaving Korea, though re-entry visas can be applied for at your provincial immigration office, W30,000 for single entry, W50,000 for multiple. Australians, Canadians and New Zealanders can apply for a **working holiday** visa at their local South Korean embassy.

South Korean embassies and consulates abroad

Australia 113 Empire Circuit, Yarralumla, ACT 2600 ⓣ02/6270 4100, ⓦwww.korea.org.au; Level 13, 111 Elisabeth St, Sydney NSW 2000 ⓣ02/9210 0200.

Canada 150 Boteler St, Ottawa, Ontario K1N 5A6 ⓣ613/244-5010; 555 Avenue Rd, Toronto, Ontario M4V 2J7 ⓣ416/920-3809; 1002 Sherbrooke St West Suite 2500, Montreal, Quebec H3A 3L6 ⓣ514/845-3243; 191 Yale Ave, Winnipeg, Manitoba R3M 0L2 ⓣ203/477-0490; 1600–090 West Georgia, Vancouver, BC V6E 3V7 ⓣ604/681-9581; Field Atkinson Perraton, 1900 First Canadian Centre 350–7th Ave SW, Calgary, Alberta T2P 3N8 ⓣ403/260-3500.

China No 3 4th Avenue East, Sanlitun, Chaoyang District, Beijing 100600 ⓣ10/6532 0290; 4th Floor Shanghai Int'l Trade Center, 2200 Yan An Rd (W), Shanghai ⓣ21/6219 6417.

Ireland 20 Clyde Rd, Ballsbridge, Dublin 4, ⓣ01/660 8800.

Japan 1-1-3 Jigyohoma, Chuo-ku, Fukuoka 810 ⓣ092/771 0464; 1-2-5 Minami-Azabu, 1-chome, Minato-ku, Tokyo 106 ⓣ03/3452 7611.

New Zealand 11th Floor, ASB Bank Tower, 2 Hunter St, Wellington ⓣ04/473 9073, ⓦwww.koreanembassy.org.nz; 10th Floor, 396 Queen St, Auckland ⓣ09/379 0818.

Singapore 47 Scotts Rd #08-00 Goldbell Towers, Singapore 228233 ⓣ6256 1188, ⓦwww.koreaembassy.org.sg.

South Africa Green Park Estates, Building 3, 27 George Storrar Drive, Groenkloof, Pretoria, ⓣ012/460 2508.

Thailand 23 Thiam-Ruammit Rd, Ratchadapisek, Huay Kwang, Bangkok 10320 ⓣ02/247 7537.

UK 60 Buckingham Gate, London SW1E 6AJ ⓣ020/7227 5500, ⓦwww.koreanembassy.org.uk.

USA 2450 Massachusetts Ave NW, Washington, DC 20008 ⓣ202/939-5600, ⓦwww.koreaembassyusa.org; 229 Peachtree St, International Tower Atlanta GA 30303 ⓣ404/522-1611; One Gateway Center 2nd Floor, Boston, MA 02458 ⓣ617/641-2830; #2700 NBC Tower, 455 Cityfront Drive, Chicago, IL 60611 ⓣ312/822-9485; 2756 Pali Highway, Honolulu, HI 96817 ⓣ808/595-3046; 1990 Post Oak Blvd, #1250, Houston, TX 77056 ⓣ713/961-0186; 3243 Wiltshire Blvd, Los Angeles, CA 90010 ⓣ213/385-9300; 460 Park Ave, 5th Floor, New York, NY 10022 ⓣ212/752-1700; 3500 Clay St, San Francisco, CA 94118 ⓣ415/921-2251; 2033, 6th Ave, #1125, Seattle WA 98121 ⓣ206/441-1011.

Gay and lesbian travellers

Despite Goryeo-era evidence suggesting that undisguised homosexuality was common in Royal and Buddhist circles, the **gay scene** in today's Korea forms a small, alienated section of society. Indeed, many locals genuinely seem to believe that Korean homosexuality simply does not exist, regarding it instead as a "foreign disease" that instantly gives people AIDS. The prevalent Confucian attitudes, together with the lack of a decent gay scene, have been the bane of many a queer expat's life in the country. For Korean homosexuals, the problems are more serious – although the law makes no explicit reference to the legality of sexual intercourse between adults of the same sex, this is less a tacit nod of consent than a refusal of officialdom to discuss such matters, and gay activities may be punishable as sexual harassment, or even, shockingly, "mutual rape" if it takes place in the military. In the early 1990s, the first few gay and lesbian websites were cracked down on by a government that, during the course of the subsequent appeal, made it clear that human rights did not fully apply to homosexuals – all the more reason for the "different people" (*iban-in*), already fearful of losing their jobs, friends and family, to lock themselves firmly in the closet.

Korean society is, however, slowly but surely becoming more liberal. With more and more high-profile homosexuals coming out, a critical mass has been reached, and younger generations are markedly less prejudiced against – and more willing to discuss – the pink issue. Gay clubs, bars and saunas, while still generally low-key outside "Homo Hill" in Seoul's Itaewon district (see p.110), can be found in every major city, and lobbyists have been making inroads into the Korean parliament. Still the only pride event in the country, the **Korean Queer Culture Festival** takes place over a fortnight in early June at locations across Seoul, see box, p.132 for more information.

Gay information sources

Buddy Ⓦ buddy79.com/htm/foreign-1.htm. A popular gay and lesbian lifestyle magazine.

Chingusai Ⓦ chingusai.net. Loosely meaning "Among Friends", Chingusai's trailblazing magazine is available at many gay bars in the capital; though mainly in Korean, the site has some English-language information.

Happy & Safe Most useful for its gay scene city maps, you may come across the odd copy of this little guide on your way around Seoul's bars.

Utopia Asia Ⓦ www.utopia-asia.com/tipskor.htm. Site containing useful information about bars, clubs and saunas, much of which goes into their book, *The Utopia Guide to Japan, Korea* and *Taiwan*.

Health

South Korea is pretty high up in the world rankings as far as **healthcare** goes, and there are no compulsory vaccinations or diseases worth getting too worried about. Hospitals are clean and well staffed, and most doctors can speak English, so the main health concerns for foreign travellers are likely to be financial – without adequate insurance cover, a large bill may rub salt into your healing wounds if you end up in hospital (see opposite). Though no **vaccinations** are legally required, get medical advice ahead of your trip, particularly regarding Hepatitis A and B, typhoid and Japanese B Encephalitis (which are all rare in Korea but it's better to err on the side of caution), and make sure you're up to date with the usual boosters. It's also wise to bring along any medicines that you might need, especially for drugs that need to be prescribed – bring a copy of your prescription, as well as the generic name of the drug in question, as brand names may vary from country to country.

Despite the swarms of mosquitoes that blanket the country in warmer months, **malaria** is not prevalent in Korea. However, infected mosquitoes breed in the DMZ, so those planning to hang around the rural north of the Gyeonggi or Gangwon provinces should take extra precautions to prevent getting bitten. All travellers should get up-to-date malarial advice from their GP before arriving in Korea, and wherever you are in the country during the monsoon season in late summer, it's also a good idea to slap on some repellent before going out.

Drinking Korean **tap water** is a poor idea, and with free drinking fountains in every restaurant, hotel, supermarket, police station, department store and PC bar in the country, there really should be no need. Those about to take a train or bus ride will be able to buy water at the station – usually W500 for a small bottle. Restaurant food will almost always be prepared and cooked adequately (and all necessary precautions taken with raw fish), however bad it looks, though it's worth bearing in mind that the incredible amount of red pepper paste consumed by the average Korean has made stomach cancer the country's number one killer.

In an **emergency**, you should first try to ask a local to call for an ambulance. Should you need to do so yourself, the number is ⓣ119, though it's possible that no English-speaker will be available to take your call. Alternatively, try the tourist information line on ⓣ1330, or if all else fails dial English directory assistance on ⓣ080/211-0114. If you're in a major city and the problem isn't life-threatening, the local tourist office should be able to point you in the direction of the most suitable doctor or hospital. Once there, you may find it surprisingly hard to get information about what's wrong with you – as in much of East Asia, patients are expected to trust doctors to do their jobs properly, and any sign that this trust is not in place results in a loss of face for the practitioner.

For minor complaints or medical advice, there are **pharmacies** all over the place, usually distinguished by the Korean character "*yak*" at the entrance, though English-speakers are few and far between. Travellers can also visit a practitioner of **oriental medicine**, who use acupuncture and pressure-point massage, among other techniques, to combat the problems that Western medicine cannot reach. If you have Korean friends, ask around for a personal recommendation in order to find a reputable practitioner.

Medical resources for travellers

Australia, New Zealand and South Africa

Travellers' Medical and Vaccination Centre ⓦwww.tmvc.com.au, ⓣ1300-658844. Lists travel clinics in Australia, New Zealand and South Africa.

UK and Ireland

British Airways Travel Clinics ⓣ0845/600 2236, ⓦwww.britishairways.com/travel/healthclinintro/public/en_gb for nearest clinic.

Hospital for Tropical Diseases Travel Clinic ⓣ0845/155 5000 or ⓣ020/7387 4411, ⓦwww.thehtd.org.

MASTA (Medical Advisory Service for Travellers Abroad) ⓦwww.masta.org or ⓣ0113/238 7575 for the nearest clinic.

Tropical Medical Bureau Republic of Ireland ⓣ1850/487674, ⓦwww.tmb.ie. Has a list of clinics in the Republic of Ireland.

US and Canada

CDC ⓣ1-877-394-8747, ⓦwww.cdc.gov/travel. Official US government travel health site.

International Society for Travel Medicine ⓣ1-770-736-7060, ⓦwww.istm.org. Has a full list of travel health clinics.

Canadian Society for International Health ⓦwww.csih.org. Extensive list of travel health centres.

Insurance

The price of hospital treatment in Korea can be quite high and, therefore, it's advisable to take out a decent **travel insurance** policy before you go. Bear in mind that most policies exclude "dangerous activities"; this term may well cover activities as seemingly benign as hiking or skiing, and if you plan to bungee or raft you'll probably be paying a premium. Keep the emergency number of your insurance company handy in the event of an accident and, as in any country, if you have anything stolen make sure to obtain a copy of the police report, as you will need this to make a claim.

Internet

You should have no problem getting online in South Korea, possibly the most connected

Rough Guides travel insurance

Rough Guides has teamed up with Columbus Direct to offer you **travel insurance** that can be tailored to suit your needs. Products include a low-cost **backpacker** option for long stays; a **short break** option for city getaways; a typical **holiday package** option; and others. There are also annual **multi-trip** policies for those who travel regularly. Different sports and activities (trekking, skiing, etc) can be usually be covered if required.

See our website (www.roughguides.com/website/shop) for eligibility and purchasing options. Alternatively, UK residents should call ⓣ0870/033 9988; Australians should call ⓣ1300-669999 and New Zealanders should call ⓣ0800-559911. All other nationalities should call ⓣ+44 870/890 2843.

nation on the planet. It's a national addiction – **PC rooms** (pronounced *"pishi-bang"*) are everywhere, and in any urban area the same rule applies: look around, and you'll see one. These noisy, air-conditioned shrines to the latest computing equipment hide behind neon-lit street signs (the PC in Roman characters; the *bang*, meaning room, in Korean text), and despite their ubiquity can be full to the brim with gamers – you're likely to be the only one checking your mails. These cafés have charged the same price since the dawn of the Internet age: an almost uniform W1000 per hour, with a one-hour minimum charge (though it's far more expensive in hotels, and usually free in post offices). Most will have snacks and instant noodles for sale behind the counter – customers need occasional nutrition – and some will offer you a free tea or coffee when you sit down, topping you up every few hours.

Laundry

Almost all tourist hotels provide a **laundry** service, and some of the Seoul backpacker hostels will wash your smalls for free, but with public laundries so thin on the ground those staying elsewhere may have to resort to a spot of DIY cleaning. All motels have 24-hour hot water, as well as soap, body lotion and/or shampoo in the bathrooms, and in the winter clothes dry in no time on the heated *ondol* floors. Summer is a different story, with the humidity making it very hard to dry clothes in a hurry.

Mail

The Korean postal system is cheap and trustworthy, and there are **post offices** in even the smallest town. Most are open Monday to Friday 9am–6pm; all should be able to handle international mail, and the larger ones offer free Internet access. The main problem facing many travellers is the relative dearth of **postcards** for sale, though if you do track some down postal rates are cheap, at around W400 per card. Letters will cost a little more, though as with **parcels** the tariff will vary depending on their destination – the largest box you can send (20kg) will cost about W150,000 to mail to the UK or USA, though this price drops to about W50,000 if you post via **surface mail**, a process that can take up to three months. All post offices have the necessary boxes for sale, and will even do your packing for a small fee.

Maps

Almost the whole country seems to have been rendered in map form, and **free maps** – many of which are available in English – can be picked up at any tourist office or higher-end hotel, as well as most travel terminals. The main drawback with them is that distances and exact street patterns are hard to gauge, though it's a complaint the powers that be are slowly taking on board. Mercifully, the **national park** maps are excellent and drawn to scale, and can be bought for W1000 at the ticket booths.

Money

The **Korean currency** is the won (W), which comes in notes of W1000, W5000 and W10,000, and coins of W10, W50, W100 and W500. The highest-value note is of little relative worth by international standards, and it's still possible to see Koreans paying for expensive household goods with foot-high wads of cash. In 2006 the Korean government unleashed plans to release W50,000 and W100,000 banknotes, these notes are expected to be in circulation by 2009. At the time of writing the **exchange rate** was approximately W1850 to £1, W1300 to €1, and W950 to US$1.

Travellers occasionally encounter difficulties when attempting to withdraw money from **ATMs** (there are several different systems in operation, even within the same banking chains), but most should be able to withdraw cash using an international debit or credit card. The official advice is to head to an ATM marked "Global"; don't go looking for these in a bank, as they're much more commonplace in the ubiquitous 24-hour convenience stores such as Family Mart, 7-Eleven or LG25. Most machines capable of dealing with foreign cards are able to switch to English-language mode, but it's common for ATMs to shut down at night. Bear in mind that smaller towns may not have such facilities – stock up on cash in larger cities.

Despite its place at the forefront of the technological age, few transactions in Korea are made by card, and **cash** is manifestly still the way to go. Foreign **credit cards** are however, being accepted in more and more hotels, restaurants and shops. It shouldn't be too hard to **exchange** foreign notes or traveller's cheques for Korean cash once in the country; banks are all over the place, and the only likely problem when dealing in dollars, pounds or euros is time – some places simply won't have exchanged money before, forcing staff into procedure manual consultations. **Leaving Korea** with local currency is not advisable, as it's hard to exchange outside the country – get it changed before you head to the airport if you want a good rate.

Opening hours and public holidays

Until recently, the country was one of the few in the world to have a **six-day working week**; though this has been officially realigned to five, the changes won't filter through to all workers, and Korea's place at the top of the world's "average hours worked per year" table is unlikely to be affected. The number of **national holidays** has fallen, however, in an attempt to make up the slack, and as most of the country's population is forced to take their holiday at the same times, there can be chaos on the roads and rails. Three of the biggest holidays – Lunar New Year, Buddha's birthday and *Chuseok* – are based on the Lunar calendar, and have no fixed dates. See pp.49–50 for further details on the more interesting national holidays.

South Korean public holidays

Sinjeong (New Year's Day) January 1
Seollal (Lunar New Year) Usually early February.
Independence Movement Day March 1.
Children's Day May 5.
Buddha's Birthday Usually late May
Memorial Day June 6.
Constitution Day July 17.
Independence Day August 15.
Chuseok (Thanksgiving) Usually September or October.
National Foundation Day October 3.
Christmas Day December 25.

Korea is one of the world's truest 24-hour societies – **opening hours** are such that almost everything you need is likely to be available when you require it. Most shops and almost all restaurants are open seven days a week, often until late, as are tourist information offices. Post offices keep more sensible hours (Mon–Fri 9am–6pm), and banks generally open Monday to Friday 9.30am to 4pm. A quite incredible number of establishments are open 24/7, including convenience stores, saunas, Internet cafés and some of the busier shops and restaurants.

Phones

With Korea one of the world's most important fonts of **mobile phone** technology, what may qualify as cutting-edge elsewhere may be viewed as passe by Koreans. Getting hold of a phone while you're in the country is easy – there are 24-hour rental booths at Incheon Airport, and some top-class hotels have free-to-hire mobile phones in their rooms. Those who will be in Korea for a while may care to purchase a second-hand mobile phone – these can be as cheap as W15,000, and the pace of change means that even high-quality units may be available for knock-down prices; the best places to look are shopping districts, electrical stores or underground malls – just look for a glassed-off bank of phones. After purchase you'll need to register with a major service provider – KTF and SK Telecom are two of the biggest chains, and so ubiquitous are their stores that the nearest is likely to be within walking distance. Registration is free (bring your passport), and you can top up pay-as-you-go accounts in increments of W10,000. Despite the prevalence of mobile phones, you'll still see **payphones** on every major street; these aging units only take W10, W50 and W100 coins, so you'll have to pump in change at a furious pace to avoid the deafening squawks that signal the end of your call-time.

Photography

Photography is a national obsession in Korea – at tourist sights around the country, locals feed their cameras as they would hungry pets, with many of the resulting stash of

Calling home from abroad

Note that the **initial zero is omitted** from the area code when dialing the UK, Ireland, Australia and New Zealand from abroad. Dial 001 to get an international connection.

Australia International access code + 61 + city code.

New Zealand International access code + 64 + city code.

Republic of Ireland International access code + 353 + city code.

South Africa International access code + 27 + city code.

UK International access code + 44 + city code.

US and Canada International access code + 1 + area code.

Calling Korea from abroad

Korea's international dialling code is ⓣ82; when dialling from abroad, omit the initial zero from the area codes, which read as follows (note that some cities have their own dedicated code):

Busan ⓣ051	Gwangju ⓣ062	Jeonbuk ⓣ063
Chungbuk ⓣ043	Gyeongbuk ⓣ054	Jeonnam ⓣ061
Chungnam ⓣ041	Gyeonggi ⓣ031	Seoul ⓣ02
Daegu ⓣ053	Gyeongnam ⓣ055	Ulsan ⓣ052
Daejeon ⓣ042	Incheon ⓣ032	
Gangwon ⓣ033	Jeju Island ⓣ064	

images ending up on personal homepages. Though the digital revolution has scaled back sales of **film**, the regular brands are still available around the country, and getting it processed is cheap and efficient – expect a developing fee of W2000, plus a few hundred won per picture. Most **Internet cafés** are kitted out for the transfer of digital images from memory cards.

A mountainous country with four distinct seasons, pulsating cities and a temple around every corner, Korea should keep your camera-finger busy; if you want a personal shot, few locals will mind being photographed, though of course it's polite to ask first. One serious no-no is to go snap-happy on a tour of the DMZ (see p.159) – this can, and has, landed tourists in trouble. You may also see temple-keepers and monks poised at the ready to admonish would-be photographers of sacrosanct areas.

Shopping

Most visitors who want to splash their cash do so in **Seoul**, which has some fantastic shopping opportunities, including the trinket shops on Insadong-gil, the underground EXPO mall, the brand-name flagship stores in Apgujeong, and the colossal markets of Dongdaemun and Namdaemun; see "Shopping" in Seoul on pp.134–136 for more information.

Time

The Korean peninsula shares a **time zone** with Japan – one hour ahead of China, nine hours ahead of Greenwich Mean Time, seven hours ahead of South Africa, fourteen hours ahead of Eastern Standard Time in the US or Montreal in Canada, and one hour behind Sydney. Bear in mind that daylight saving hours are not observed, so though noon in London will be 9pm in Seoul for much of the year, the difference drops to eight hours during British Summer Time.

Tourist information

The Korean tourist authorities churn out a commendable number of English-language maps, pamphlets and books, most of which are handed out at **information booths** – you'll be able to find one in every city, usually outside the train or bus stations. Not all of these are staffed with an English-speaker, but you'll be able to get 24-hour assistance and advice on the dedicated **tourist information line** – dial ⓣ1330 and you'll be put through to helpful call-centre staff who speak a number of languages and can advise on transport, sights, accommodation and much more. If calling from a mobile phone or abroad, you'll also need to put in a regional prefix – to reach Seoul, for example, dial ⓣ02/1330. The official **Korean tourist website** (ⓦenglish.tour2korea.com) is quite useful, and most cities and provinces have sites of their own.

Tourist offices and government sites

Australian Department of Foreign Affairs ⓦwww.dfat.gov.au, ⓦwww.smartraveller.gov.au.
British Foreign & Commonwealth Office ⓦwww.fco.gov.uk.
Canadian Department of Foreign Affairs ⓦwww.dfait-maeci.gc.ca.
Irish Department of Foreign Affairs ⓦwww.foreignaffairs.gov.ie.
New Zealand Ministry of Foreign Affairs ⓦwww.mft.govt.nz.
South African Department of Foreign Affairs ⓦwww.dfa.gov.za.
US State Department ⓦwww.travel.state.gov.

Travelling with children

Korea is a country with high standards of **health and hygiene**, low levels of crime and plenty to see and do – bringing children of any age should pose no special problems. **Changing facilities** are most common in Seoul – department stores are good places to head – though few restaurants have highchairs, and baby food labelled in English is almost non-existent. A few hotels provide a **babysitting service**, though those in need can ask their concierge for a newspaper with babysitter adverts. Every city has cinemas, theme parks and a zoo or two to keep children amused; Everland (p.148) and Seoul Land (p.117) are the two most popular escapes from Seoul, while there are a number of interesting museums in the capital itself. Note that some of the restaurants listed in this guide – especially those serving *galbi*, a self-barbecued meat – have hot-plates or charcoal in the centre of the table, which poses an obvious danger to little hands, and in a country where it's perfectly normal for cars to drive on the pavements, you may want to exercise a little more caution than normal when walking around town.

Travellers with disabilities

Despite its First World status, South Korea can be filed under "developing countries" as far as **disabled accessibility** is concerned, and with rushing traffic and crowded streets, it's never going to be the easiest destination to get around. Until recently, very little attention was paid to those with disabilities, but things are changing fast. Streets are being made more wheelchair-friendly, and many subway and train stations have been fitted with lifts. Almost all motels and tourist hotels have these, too, though occasionally you'll come across an entrance that hasn't been built with wheelchairs in mind. Some museums and tourist attractions will be able to provide a helper if necessary, but wherever you are, willing Koreans will jump at the chance to help travellers in obvious need of assistance.

Guide

Guide

1 Seoul

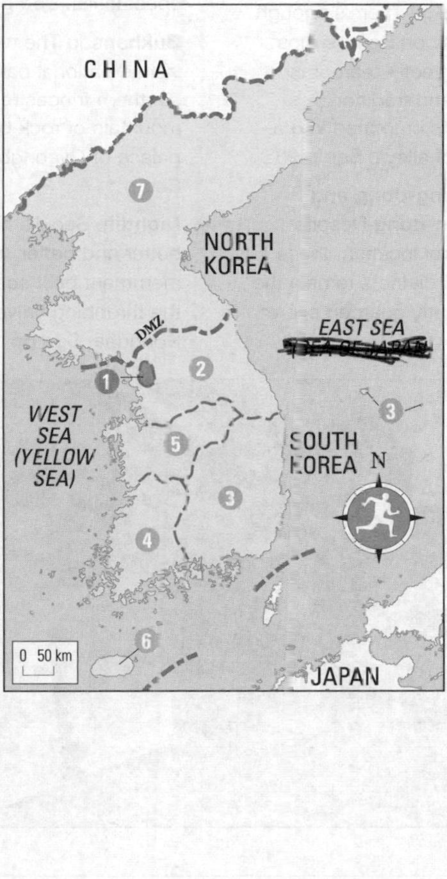
CHINA
NORTH KOREA
DMZ
EAST SEA
WEST SEA (YELLOW SEA)
SOUTH KOREA
N
JAPAN
0 50 km
1
2
3
3
4
5
6
7

CHAPTER 1

Highlights

* **Hanok guesthouses** Stay a night in a *hanok* – a wooden building kept warm in the winter by underfloor fires – an authentically Korean experience. See p.85
* **Confucian palaces** Five beautiful palaces remain from Seoul's time as capital of the Joseon dynasty, each with its own merits. See p.88
* **Insadong-gil** There's enough to fill a day on Seoul's most popular street – tearooms, galleries and traditional restaurants crammed into a network of alleys. See p.93
* **Samcheong-dong and Bukcheon-dong** Despite their central location, these traditional districts remain the locals' tightly guarded secret. See p.96
* **Dongdaemun** Head to this huge market, which never sleeps and is at its most atmospheric around midnight, for an assault on the senses. See p.104
* **Namsan at sunset** Make sure you're at the top of Seoul's mountain for sunset, when the city's transition from grey to neon is nothing short of spectacular. See p.105
* **Bukhansan** The world's most visited national park, whose southern fringes rear up in a mountain of rock behind the palace of Gyeongbokgung. See p.117
* **Nightlife** Seoul's nightlife gets better and better, with the merriment best soaked up in the throbbing university area of Hongdae. See pp.128–131

▲ Insa-dong street

1

Seoul

The terms "24-hour city" and "place of contrasts" are much bandied descriptions of Asian megalopolises, but enigmatic **SEOUL** is thoroughly deserving of either cliché. A whirring, purring maelstrom of high-rise, neon-saturated streets and pulsating commerce, its twenty-million-plus souls, packed sardine-like into a metropolitan area smaller than Luxembourg, make it one of the most densely populated places on the planet. Here you can eat at restaurants at any time of day or night, shop at gargantuan markets and underground shopping malls, or drink, dance and sing the night away in one of the high-energy student zones. But for all its non-stop consumption, Seoul is also a place of considerable tradition and history. **Joseon-dynasty palaces**, displayed like medals in the centre of the city, proclaim its status as a seat of regal power from as far back as 1392; the tiled roofs of wooden *hanok* houses gently fish-scale their way towards the ash-coloured granite crags of **Bukhansan**, the world's most-visited national park; the ancient songs and dances of farmhands and court performers are still clashed out in a whirligig of sound and colour along Insadong-gil. A city with a hyper-efficient transport system, a negligible rate of crime, locals eager to please foreign guests and an almost astonishing wealth of locally produced modern art: it's little wonder that so many who visit Seoul come away hugely impressed.

Top of most tourists' agendas are the half-a-dozen sumptuous **palaces** dating from the late fourteenth century that surround the city centre; these include **Gyeongbokgung** and **Changdeokgung**, together with the nearby ancestral shrine of **Jongmyo**. Situated in the middle is **Insa-dong**; by far the most popular part of the city with tourists, its warren of tight streets is littered with traditional restaurants, quaint tearooms, art galleries and trinket shops, and makes for a great wander; **Samcheong-dong** and **Bukcheon-dong** are two areas offering similar delights, though with fewer tourists. The amount of art on display in all three areas can come as quite a surprise – contemporary Korean work receives a fraction of the international press devoted to art from Japan or China, but it's just as creative. Also offering a modern-day fusion of Korea old and new are the colossal markets of **Dongdaemun** and **Namdaemun**, in whose sprawling reaches you'll find anything from pig intestines to clip-on ties. The more modern facets of the city can be seen in the shoppers' paradise of **Myeong-dong** or achingly fashionable **Apgujeong**, while the number of American soldiers hanging out in cosmopolitan **Itaewon** hint at Seoul's proximity to North Korea – it's even possible to take a day-trip to the border.

It's not just Seoul's sights that provide pleasure to visitors – simply walking down the streets is an assault on the senses, and will give you a concentrated dose of what makes Korea so special and unique. Consumption in all its forms is what makes Seoul tick, with some of the idiosyncratic offerings including 24-hour saunas, rooms for singing or watching DVDs with friends, restaurants serving chicken feet, and tearooms filled with birds. With all this in a city that many in the western world wouldn't be able to locate on a map, another cliché may be in order – "well-kept secret".

Some history

Quite contrary to the expectations of many a visitor, Seoul possesses a long and interesting past; after first rising to prominence at the beginning of the **Three Kingdoms** period, it was then ruled over by almost every major power in Korean history. In 18 AD, then named Wiryeseong, it became the first capital of the **Baekje** kingdom (see box, p.317); the exact location is believed to be a site just east of present-day Seoul, but this was to change several times. The kings and clans were forced far south to Gongju in 475, having been squeezed out by the rival **Goguryeo** kingdom; less than a century later, the city completed a Three Kingdoms clean-sweep when King Jinheung expanded the domain of his **Silla** kingdom (see p.199) far to the north, absorbing Seoul – then known as Hanseong – on the way. By 668, Silla forces held control of the whole peninsula, but having chosen Gyeongju as their capital, Seoul faded into the background. In the tenth century, Silla was usurped by the nascent **Goryeo** kingdom – they chose Kaesong, in modern-day North Korea, as the seat of their power, though Seoul was close enough to become an important trading hub, and soon earned yet another name, Namgyeong, meaning "Southern Capital".

It was not until the end of the Goryeo dynasty that Seoul really came into its own. In 1392, the "Hermit Kingdom" of **Joseon** kicked off over five centuries of power; after running the rule over a few prospective candidates, **King Taejo** – the inaugurator of the dynasty – chose Seoul as his new capital, impressed by its auspicious location. He immediately set about reorganizing the city: both the sumptuous palace of Gyeongbokgung (p.88) and the ancestral shrine complex of Jongmyo (p.99) were built with startling speed in the first few years of his reign, as was a city wall erected to surround and protect them, one studded with fabulous "Great Gates", some of which still stand today. Exactly two hundred years after its birth, Joseon was invaded by **Japanese** forces from 1592 to 1598 under the control of warlord Hideyoshi; Seoul was pillaged in the course of the battles, and many of its most beautiful buildings lay in ruins. Though the country survived this particular struggle, mainly thanks to the heroic Admiral Yi (see box, p.289), the Japanese proved more obdurate on their return in the late nineteenth century. After making tame inroads with a series of trade treaties, an escalating series of events – including the assassination of Queen Min in Gyeongbokgung – culminated in outright **annexation** of the peninsula in 1910, which lasted until the end of World War II, and closed the long chapters of Korean regal rule. During this time, Japan tried their best to erase any sense of Korean nationality; part of this was a drive to wipe out the Korean language, and earned Seoul yet another name – Keijo, which roughly translates as "Walled-off Capital". The city was to suffer greater indignity when its beloved palaces were modified in an attempt to make them "more Japanese"; a few of these alterations are still visible today. After the war, peninsular infighting and global shifts in power and ideology resulted in the **Korean War** (1950–53). Seoul's position in the centre of the peninsula, as well as its obvious importance as the long-time Korean capital, meant that it changed hands four times, coming under North Korean control twice before being wrested back. Seoul finally ended up under South Korean control, though most of the city lay in ruins, but despite – or perhaps, because of – all these setbacks, there has been no stopping it since then. The economic reforms inaugurated by president **Park Chung-hee** in the 1970s brought it global attention as a financial dynamo, and Seoul's population has ballooned to over ten million, more than double this if the whole metropolitan area is taken into account.

Arrival, information and orientation

The majority of international planes to Korea touch down at **Incheon International Airport**, which sits in curvy, chrome-and-glass splendour on an island about 50km west of central Seoul. With this distance easy to cover on public transport, Seoul is the first and last Korean city that most foreign visitors see. Arriving from elsewhere in the country, your choices will mainly be bus or train; the **bus** system is the more comprehensive, and its services usually cheaper, though **trains** arrive at more convenient locations in the centre of Seoul, their services more impervious to the heavy traffic.

By plane

Most people take the bus from Incheon Airport to Seoul, but following the completion of a **train line** between Incheon and Gimpo airports (the terminus for most domestic flights, and a few short-haul international services), Incheon Airport is now connected to the Seoul underground network: take an AREX train to Gimpo Airport, then change for subway line 5 to central Seoul. Trains take about thirty minutes to get to Gimpo station and cost W3100, though this price is likely to rise in order to cover costs for an AREX line extension to Seoul Station – this is due for completion in 2010, when central Seoul will be less than an hour away. For now, it's around thirty minutes from Gimpo to central Seoul by regular subway train.

You may still find it more efficient to take the **bus** from Incheon Airport, which will also take about an hour to Seoul, depending on your destination. There are no fewer than fifteen routes heading to the capital (W7000–8000), while more expensive limousine buses head straight to many of the top hotels (W12,000). Alternatively you can take a **taxi**, which will take around thirty minutes to get to central Seoul and cost about W45,000; the black "deluxe" taxis are more costly.

Seoul arrival

Airports	
Incheon Airport	인천 공항
Gimpo Airport	김포 공항
Tourist office	관광 안내소
Train stations	
Cheongnyangni	청량리
Seoul	서울
Yongsan	용산
Bus terminals	
Dong-Seoul Terminal	동서울 버스 터미널
Express Bus Terminal	고속 버스 터미널
Nambu Bus Terminal	남부 버스 터미널

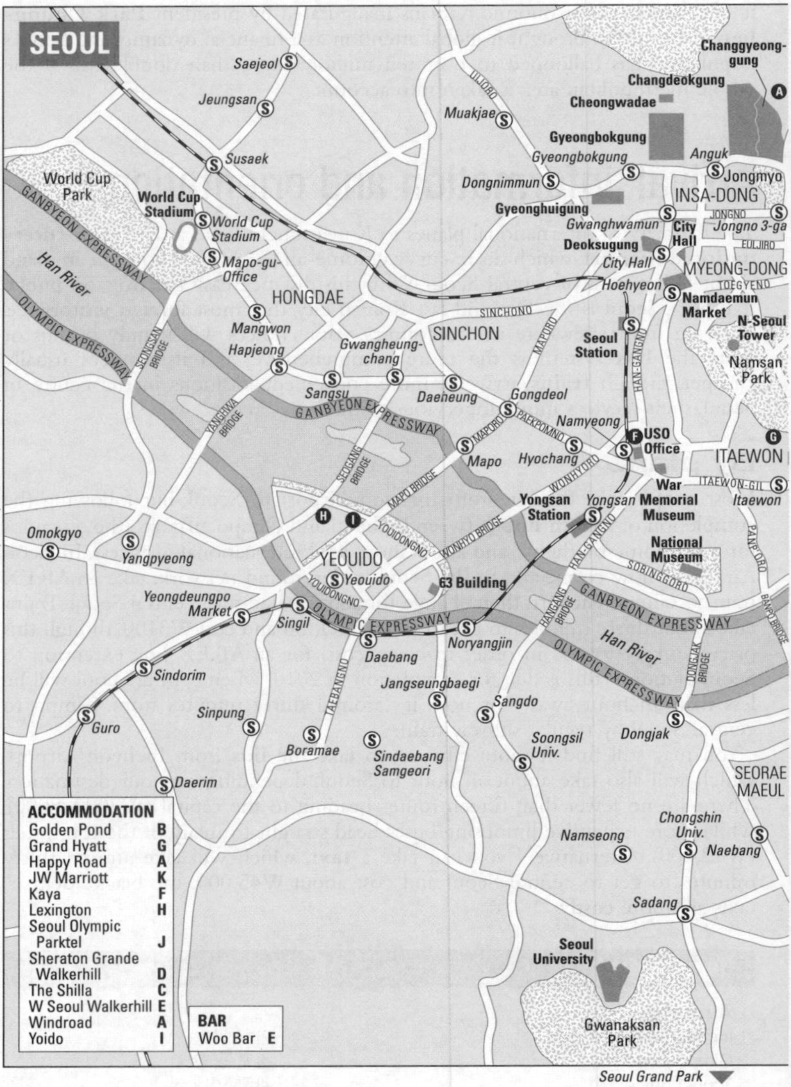

By train and bus

There are three major **train** stations in Seoul – most services arrive at either Seoul or Yongsan stations, both on subway line 1 in the city centre, but those coming from Gangwon province will arrive at the comparatively decrepit Chongnyangni station a short way to the east.

When travelling from other Korean cities by **bus**, you have a choice of Seoul terminals to choose from: most head to either the express bus terminal on the south side of the river (subway lines 3 and 7), or Dong-Seoul terminal to the east of town on line 2.

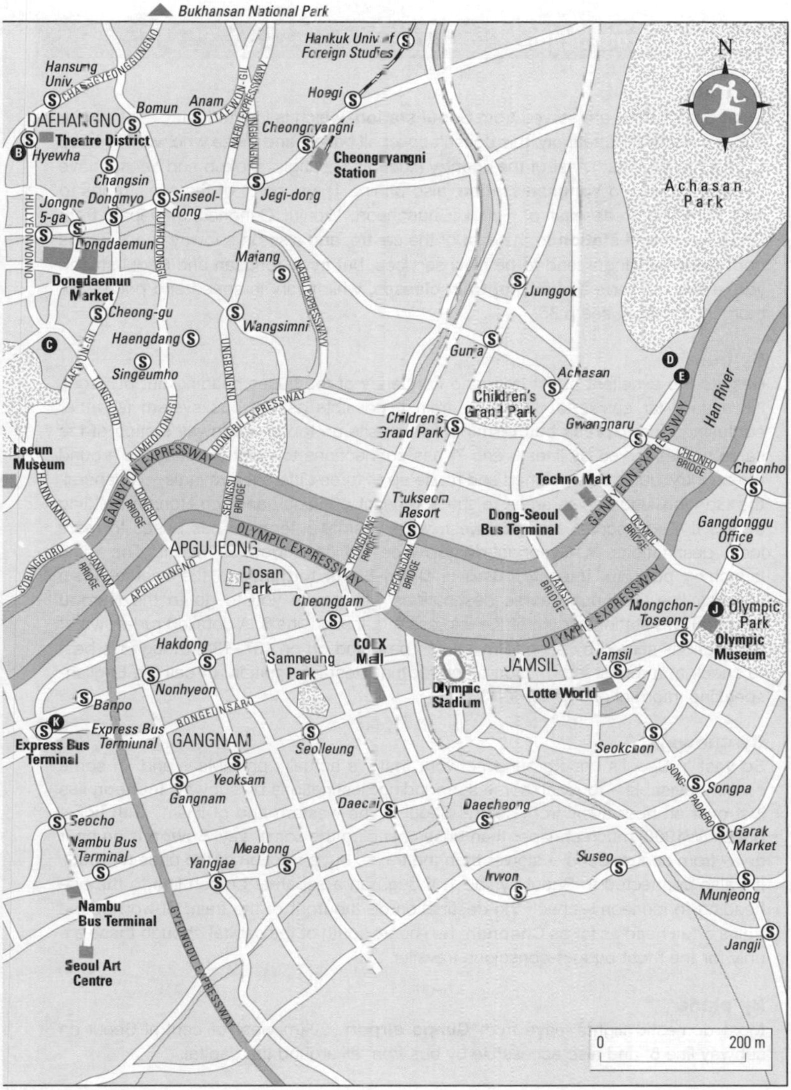

Information

Seoul is dotted with **information booths**, all of which dole out maps of the city, can advise on accommodation and help out with any transportation enquiries. The largest and most info-packed is the main **KTO office** (daily 9am–8pm; ⓣ02/729-9497), which fills the basement level of a tall tower that overlooks the Chonggyecheon, a stream just south of Jonggak subway station – take exit five, cross the bridge and turn right. Other useful information points include those in Seoul station, Itaewon subway station, City Hall, Dongdaemun Stadium and three on and around Insadong-gil.

Moving on from Seoul

By train

Most destinations are served from **Seoul station**, which is located fairly centrally on subway line 1. Frustratingly, this doesn't cover all bases, and those who want to head to cities to the southwest of the country (such as Gwangju, Mokpo and Yeosu) have to head instead to **Yongsan station** (also on line 1) just north of the river. Trains to and from the areas east of Seoul (Chuncheon, Wonju, Gangneung) depart from **Cheongnyangni station** to the east of the centre, and also on subway line 1. Trains from Cheongnyangni tend to be slow services, but from Yongsan and Seoul station you're likely to have a choice of **train classes**, which vary in speed and price – for more information, see p.35.

By bus

Despite the excellent punctuality and frequency of the buses heading out of Seoul, it's usually far easier to depart by train if possible as the bus system is rather confusing. The **express bus terminal** (which sits on top of a subway station of the same name, served by lines 3 and 7) has connections to most destinations around the country, but is badly signed and made up of three different terminals – in general, the Gongbu side serves areas to the southeast of Seoul, and the Honam building across the way serves the southwest, while a smaller terminal has buses to more local destinations in Gyeonggi-do province, which surrounds Seoul. The main launching point for intercity buses is **Dong-Seoul terminal** to the east of town (subway line 2), though some destinations will require you to go to the **Nambu terminal** two stations south of the express terminal on line 3. A detailed run-down of destinations served by each terminal can be found on pp.137–138, though it's best to check at a tourist information office for the latest information, or call the English-speaking information line on ⓣ1330.

By subway

So vast is Seoul's underground network that it's actually possible – and, in some cases, advisable – to reach some surrounding destinations by subway. **Incheon** lies just over an hour away from central Seoul at the western end of line 1, with ticket prices (W1900) much cheaper than buses heading the same way. **Suwon** is an hour away from central Seoul – slower than the trains, but a fraction of the price (W1600). It's also connected to Seoul by line 1, though on a separate branch line to the one heading to Incheon – check the destination on the front of the train. Suwon-bound trains often head as far as **Cheonan**, two hours south of the capital, though these are only for the most budget-conscious traveller.

By plane

Most domestic flights leave from **Gimpo airport**, 20km west of central Seoul on subway line 5, and also accessible by bus from all around the capital.

Wherever you are in Korea, as long as you've got access to a telephone, you'll be able to make use of a supremely useful **dedicated foreigners' helpline** – just dial ⓣ1330. Helpful call-centre staff provide 24-hour information in a number of languages, and are able to hunt down train times, bus routes, hotel recommendations, theatre ticket prices or pretty much any information that you need. Note that if dialling from a mobile phone, you'll need to add an area code; to reach the Seoul centre, for example, dial ⓣ02/1330. It's also possible to call from abroad – just ditch the zero from the area code.

One interesting way to see the city is under the wing of a **Goodwill Guide**. These are volunteers (usually students seeking to improve their language skills) on hand to assist foreign travellers, able to translate, advise, inform and escort. The service is free (Ⓦwww.goodwillguide.com), though you'd be expected to pay your guide's way – this includes transport, entry prices at tourist sights, and meals or accommodation where necessary.

There are a number of English-language **magazines** detailing life in the capital. Options are more than a little dry – quirky publications pop up from time to time, though few survive more than a couple of print-runs – *K Scene* has endured longer than most, a free fortnightly publication focusing on art and entertainment. Far easier to find is *Seoul*, an entertaining free monthly magazine.

Orientation

Seoul is nothing short of colossal, its metropolitan area stretching far and wide in a confusion of concrete and cleaved in two by the **Han**, a wide river much crossed by bridges. But despite its size, a very definite city centre – just small enough to be traversed by foot – has been in place north of the Han River since the late fourteenth century, and bounded by the five **grand palaces**. Sitting in the middle of these is **Insa-dong**, Seoul's tourist hub. A short walk north are **Samcheong-dong** and **Bukchon-dong**, two quirky zones that offer similar delights – though less touristed – to Insa-dong. This whole area is hemmed in to the north by the muscular granite peaks of **Bukhansan**, a wonderful backdrop to Gyeongbokgung and Changdeokgung, the most northerly – and popular – of the five palaces.

South of Insadong are the busy parallel roads of Jongno and Euljiro, two of Seoul's most important thoroughfares. These sit either side of **Cheonggyecheon**, a recently gentrified stream that lies beneath street level. A walk east along this stream will bring you to **Dongdaemun**, once the eastern gate to the city, but now a traffic-heavy focal point of the colossal 24-hour market that blankets the area. Walking west instead to Cheonggyecheon's "source" – the point at which the subterranean stream becomes open-air – will land you near **City Hall**; surrounded by skyscrapers, it's flanked on one side by Deoksugung – another of the five palaces – and on the other by a maze of five-star hotels. These segue into **Myeong-dong**, the busiest shopping area in the country, packed with clothes stores and restaurants. Just west of Myeong-dong is **Namdaemun** – a market almost as big as Dongdaemun, and similarly named after a city gate – while heading south will bring you to the slopes of **Namsan**, Seoul's very own mountain, which affords fantastic views of the city centre and beyond.

South of Namsan is **Itaewon**, long the hub of foreign activity in the city; a curious mix of the sleazy and the cosmopolitan, it's home to some of Seoul's best restaurants, bars and clubs, but also most of its brothels. However, even Itaewon's nightlife is nothing compared with that found in happening **Hongdae**. This is a university area west of central Seoul, and possesses by far the most rocking nightlife in the country, a neon-drenched maze of hip-hop clubs, live music venues and trendy subterranean bars.

A number of interesting city districts lie south of the Han River. Starting in the west is the islet of **Yeouido**, Seouls main centre of business and politics, and a rather uninteresting place. Further east are **Gangnam**, a shop- and restaurant-filled south-bank alternative to Myeong-dong, and ultra-trendy **Apgujeong**, where numerous boutique stores and some of the best restaurants in the city can be found. East again is **Jamsil**, home to the COEX Mall, a gigantic underground shopping complex, and Lotte World, one of the country's most popular theme parks. Also in the area is Olympic Park, where Seoul's Summer Games were held in 1988.

Seoul on the web

Korea Times ⓦwww.koreatimes.co.kr. The online version of an English-language newspaper, it's worth checking out for its job listings, though the news itself is insipid.

Seoul Searching ⓦwww.seoulsearching.com. Helpful advice for Seoul's expat population, including listings of restaurants for food from around the globe.

Seoul Style ⓦwww.seoulstyle.com. A pleasingly fresh source of Seoul information, this site is most useful for its well-informed, up-to-date listings of restaurants, bars and nightclubs.

The Seoul Times ⓦwww.theseoultimes.com. Though the news itself is stale to say the least, the site has good job listings and is a useful place to hunt for flatmates.

Tour2Korea ⓦenglish.tour2korea.com. The official site of the Korea Tourism Organisation, this provides quality information on sightseeing, transport, culture and everything from TV dramas to taekwondo.

Visit Seoul ⓦwww.visitseoul.net. This is the official tourist site of Seoul's city government; its offerings are basically a capital-focused version of *Tour2Korea*'s pages.

City transport

With Seoul's hectic streets making car hire almost tantamount to suicide, and bicycle riding even more so, it's lucky that the city is covered by a cheap, clean and highly comprehensive **public transport** system – the subway network is one of the best developed in the world, not least because of the sheer number of workers it has to speed from A to B. Buses dash around the city every which way, and even taxis are cheap enough to be viable for many routes. Those staying in the city for more than a few days should invest in a **transport card** such as T-money or Upass, available for W2000 at all subway stations and some street-level kiosks. You'll have to load them with at least W5000 credit, but you'll save W100 on each subway or bus journey (not to mention time waiting in ticket queues), and any remaining balance can be refunded at the end of your stay. These cards occasionally make it possible to switch at no extra cost from bus to subway – or vice versa – should a combination be needed to complete your journey; you'll otherwise need two separate tickets.

Busy roads and noxious emissions mean that **walking** through Seoul is rarely pleasurable, though Insadong-gil is closed to traffic on Sundays; the shopping district of Myeong-dong and club-heavy Hongdae are so swamped with people that vehicles tend to avoid these areas; and there are innumerable malls and underground shopping arcades around the city. Riding a **bike** is only really advisable on a specially designed route along the Han River; see p.112 for further details.

The subway

With eight lines and well over two hundred stations, Seoul's **subway system** is one of the most comprehensive on earth – in the area bounded by the circular 2 line, you'll never be more than a short taxi ride from the nearest station, while line 1 runs for a whole third of the country's length, stretching well over 100km from Soyosan in the north to Cheonan in the south. It's also possible to get to Suwon or Incheon by subway, and a special extension line finally connected the network to Incheon Airport in 2007; see p.73 for more information. **Fares** are extremely reasonable, starting at W1000 for rides of less than 10km, and very rarely costing more than W2000, less if you use one of the transport cards listed above. The system is also very user-friendly – **network maps** are conveniently located around the stations, which are made easily navigable by multi-language signage. You'll be able to find maps of the surrounding area on walls near the station exits, though be warned that north only faces upwards about quarter of the time. Also beware of occasionally inconsistent line colours – line 7's official olive frequently veers into line 6's brown or even mint green, while line 6 itself sometimes turns orange, much to the annoyance of line 3. Trains are extremely frequent but are packed to bursting at rush hour, and often livened up by hawkers selling anything from hand cream to folk music.

Buses

In comparison with the almost idiot-proof subway system, Seoul's **bus network** often proves too complicated for foreign guests – English-language signage is rare, and some of the route numbers would look more at home in a telephone directory (for instance, the #9009-1 to City Hall), the result of a somewhat misguided system "overhaul" in 2004. The buses are split into four coloured categories – **blue** buses travel long distances along major arterial roads, **green** buses are for shorter hops, **red** ones travel to the suburbs and **yellow** ones travel tight loop routes. These are marked on the side and the rear by a big letter B for blue, R for red and so on. **Fares** start at W900 for blue and green, W1500 for red and W550 for yellow buses, with prices increasing by distance on longer journeys; cash is still accepted on the bus, alternatively see opposite for details about travel cards. For more information on routes go to Ⓦbus.seoul.go.kr, or call Ⓣ1330.

Taxis

As in every Korean city, Seoul's taxis are **cheap** and ubiquitous. A W1900 fare covers the first 2km, and goes up in W100 increments every 144 metres – given that bus and subway fares start at W1000, it often works out cheaper for groups of three or four to travel short distances by cab rather than public transport. Note that a 20 percent **surcharge** is added between midnight and 4am. There are also deluxe *mobeom* cabs, which are black with a yellow stripe; these usually congregate around expensive hotels, charging W4500 for the first 3km and W200 for each additional 164 metres. You should never have to wait long for a cab. Drivers do not expect tips, but it's also unlikely that they'll speak any **English** – having your destination written in *hangeul* is the easiest way to get the information across, though many drivers will be willing to call an interpreter on their phone.

Accommodation

Seoul has by far the best range of **accommodation** in the country, with everything from five-star hotels to backpacker flophouses. Rooms in the capital are around fifty percent more **expensive** than similar accommodation elsewhere, though prices decrease the further you head away from the main centres of entertainment, transport or business. Those seeking high-quality accommodation have a great wealth of places to choose from, particularly

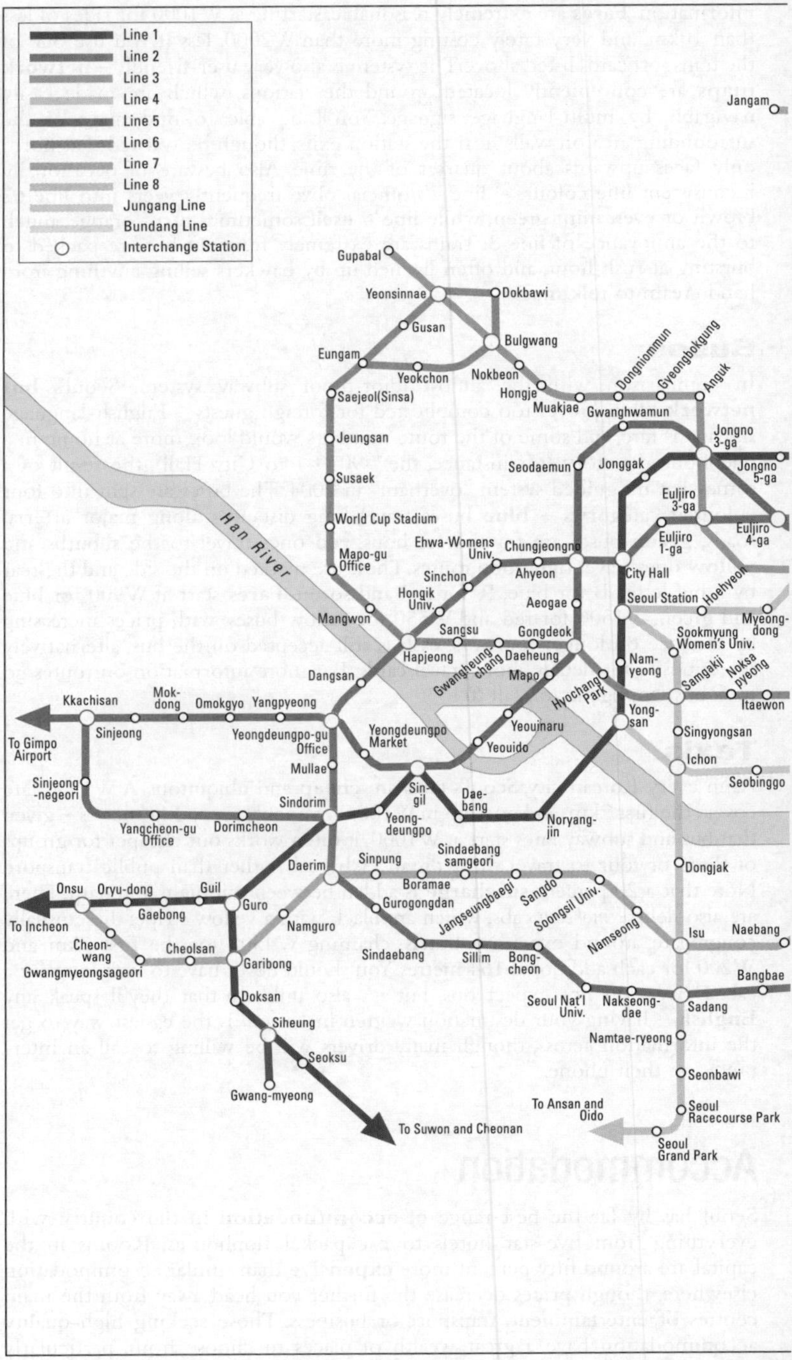
Line 1
Line 2
Line 3
Line 4
Line 5
Line 6
Line 7
Line 8
Jungang Line
Bundang Line
Interchange Station
Jangam
Gupabal
Yeonsinnae
Dokbawi
Gusan
Bulgwang
Eungam
Yeokchon
Nokbeon
Dongnimmun
Gyeongbokgung
Anguk
Hongje
Muakjae
Gwanghwamun
Saejeol(Sinsa)
Jeungsan
Jongno 3-ga
Seodaemun
Jonggak
Jongno 5-ga
Susaek
Euljiro 3-ga
World Cup Stadium
Han River
Euljiro 4-ga
Euljiro 1-ga
Ehwa-Womens Univ.
Chungjeongno
Mapo-gu Office
Sinchon
Ahyeon
City Hall
Hoehyeon
Hongik Univ.
Aeogae
Seoul Station
Mangwon
Myeong-dong
Sangsu
Gongdeok
Sookmyung Women's Univ.
Hapjeong
Gwangheung-chang
Daeheung
Nam-yeong
Mapo
Noksa pyeong
Dangsan
Hyochang Park
Samgakji
Mok-dong
Kkachisan
Omokgyo
Yangpyeong
Itaewon
Yong-san
Sinjeong
Yeouinaru
Yeongdeungpo-gu Office
Yeongdeungpo Market
Singyongsan
To Gimpo Airport
Yeouido
Ichon
Mullae
Sin-gil
Seobinggo
Sinjeong-negeori
Dae-bang
Sindorim
Yeong-deungpo
Noryang-jin
Yangcheon-gu Office
Dorimcheon
Sindaebang samgeori
Dongjak
Sinpung
Daerim
Onsu
Oryu-dong
Boramae
Guil
Sangdo
Soongsil Univ.
Jangseungbaegi
Guro
Gaebong
Gurogongdan
To Incheon
Namseong
Namguro
Isu
Naebang
Cheon-wang
Cheolsan
Sindaebang
Sillim
Bong-cheon
Garibong
Gwangmyeongsageori
Bangbae
Doksan
Seoul Nat'l Univ.
Nakseong-dae
Sadang
Siheung
Namtae-ryeong
Seoksu
Seonbawi
Gwang-myeong
To Ansan and Oido
Seoul Racecourse Park
To Suwon and Cheonan
Seoul Grand Park

SEOUL SUBWAY

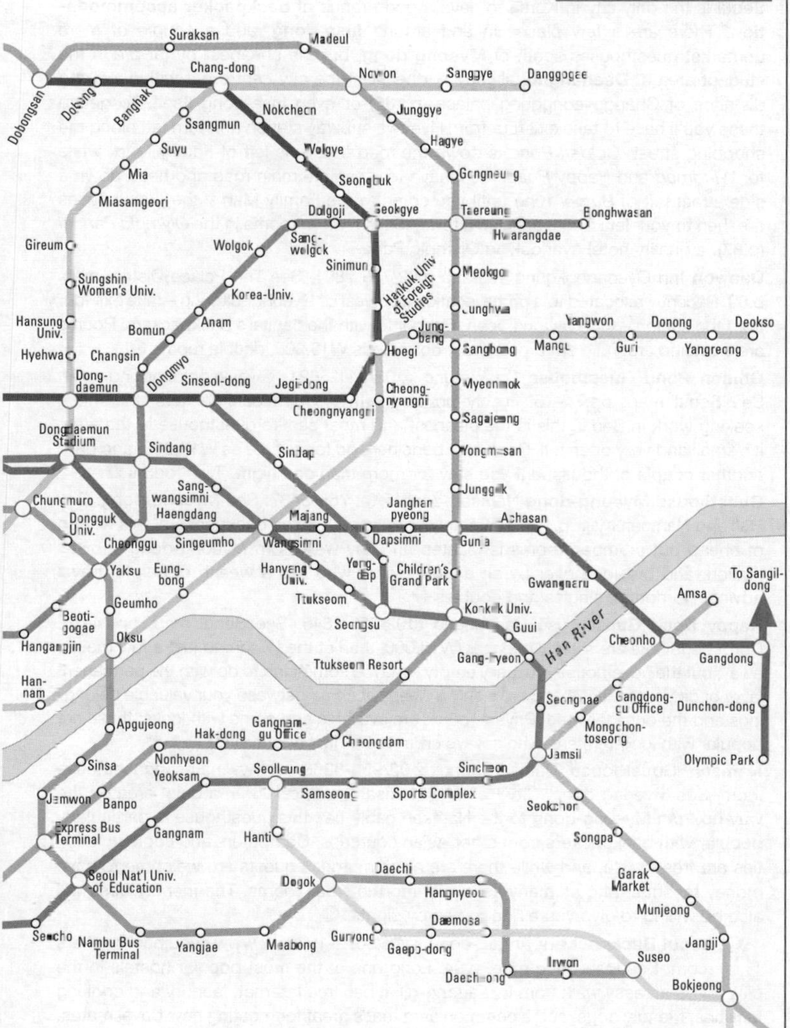

Backpacker guesthouses

Seoul is the only city in Korea to have a good range of **backpacker accommodation**. There are a few places in and around **Insa-dong**, and a couple of more upmarket guesthouses south of **Myeong-dong**, but the cheapest by far are in the student area of **Daehangno**, slightly northeast of the city centre but within walking distance of Changgyeonggung palace (p.100) or even Insa-dong itself. To get to these you'll have to take exit four from Hyehwa subway station and turn left along the shopping street; *Golden Pond* is down the road that runs left of Family Mart, while for *Windroad* and *Happy Road* you'll have to cross the main road and head down a side street left of *Burger King* until you come to the Family Mart – the guesthouses are then to your left. There are also a few excellent dorm rooms in the *Olympic Parktel* (p.87), a quality hotel overlooking Olympic Park.

Daewon Inn Gyeongbokgung Yeok-ap ⓣ02/735-7891. See The Palace District map, p.89. Recently relocated to a prime location just west of Gyeongbokgung – take exit four from the station – this has long been a favourite with the capital's backpackers. Rooms are clustered around a small courtyard; dorm beds W19,000, double rooms ❸.

Golden Pond Guesthouse Daehangno ⓣ02/741-5621, ⓦwww.goldenpond.co.kr. See Seoul map, pp.74–75. Highly popular with western backpackers and those seeking work in Seoul, this is the cleanest and most secure guesthouse in the area; it's small and very often full. Dormitory beds here go for as little as W13,000, and drop another couple of thousand if you stay for more than one night. Twin rooms ❸.

Guesthouse Myeong-dong Namsan-dong ⓣ02/755-5437. See Myeong-dong, City Hall and Namsan map, p.106. Extremely popular with Asian backpackers, this warren of cheap but cramped rooms is located an easy walk from Myeong-dong subway station, and presided over by an affable owner who has a wealth of helpful travel advice. No dorms; singles and doubles ❸.

Happy Road Guesthouse Daehangno ⓣ02/703-2845. See Seoul map, pp.74–75. Dorm beds here are slightly cheaper (W13,000) than at the *Windroad* just a few metres away, but the guesthouse is usually empty – maybe something to do with the permanent layer of dirt, or the fact that there's only a sleepy *ajumma* between your valuable belongings and the outside world. Private rooms are available and come with locks; these are popular with long-termers, who always claim to be "just about to move out".

Namsan Guesthouse Namsan-dong ⓣ02/953-8368, ⓦwww.namsanguesthouse.com. See Myeong-dong, City Hall and Namsan map, p.106. In a quiet area on the way up from Myeong-dong to the Namsan cable car, this guesthouse is particularly popular with backpackers from other Asian countries. Computers and cooking facilities are free to use, and while there are no dormitories guests are welcome to save money by squeezing as many as will fit into the small rooms. The friendly boss will also be willing to give you a ride to nearby sights. ❸

Seoul Backpackers Anguk-dong ⓣ02/3672-1972, ⓦwww.seoulbackpackers.com. See Insa-dong map, p.94. Long one of the most popular hostels in the city, this is an easy walk from Insaadong-gil; it has free Internet, laundry and cooking facilities, friendly dogs, and a common area that's great for meeting new travel mates. Dorms cost W18,000 (double rooms ❸), and there's bread and jam to tuck into in the morning, as well as free tea and coffee throughout the day. Take exit four from Anguk subway station, head straight past the palace and turn left, then right at the crossroads; if it's full, there's a sister hostel around the corner.

Windroad Guesthouse Daehangno ⓣ02/6407-2012, ⓦwww.backpackerkorea.net. See Seoul map, pp.74–75. You're guaranteed to find some party mates at this amiable lair (also known as *Windflower* for reasons best known to the boss). Dorms are scruffy and cramped but acceptable for the price, which starts at W13,000 but goes down a couple of thousand after your first night. You can even stay for free if you put in a few hours a day of volunteer work at the desk. Twin rooms ❸.

around Myeong-dong and City Hall on the north of the river, and Gangnam to the south; at the lower end are Seoul's popular collection of **backbacker guesthouses** (see box opposite). Almost every room in the top-end places will have an Internet connection, and some even provide computers; some do so for free, while others charge over W20,000 per day – be sure to check beforehand. It's also important to ascertain whether tax and service charges – around ten percent each – are factored into the quoted prices. Official tourist hotels are graded from two to five stars. Those at the higher levels usually have on-site restaurants, fitness and business centres, currency exchange and cafés, but many foreign guests are disappointed by the small size and impersonal nature of the rooms.

One interesting cheaper option, which is popular with foreign travellers, is the range of **traditional wooden guesthouses** north of Anguk station (see box, p.85 for details). At around the same price, though different in character, **motels** form a cheap alternative to official tourist hotels, sometimes having rooms of almost comparable size and quality; see Basics, p.29 for more information. Note that two of the most popular nightlife areas – Itaewon and Hongdae – have a shockingly poor range of motel accommodation.

City Hall

A number of five-star hotels congregate around Seoul Plaza and City Hall, near Deoksugung palace; it's also convenient for the Myeong-dong shopping area. All the places listed below are marked on the Myeong-Dong, City Hall and Namsan map on p.106.

Koreana Hotel Taepyeong-no ⓣ02/2171-7000, ⓦwww.koreanahotel.com. Half the price of some of its competitors, but with similar rooms and service standards. It's worth paying a little extra for the larger "Prestige" rooms – try to nab one from the eleventh to the fifteenth floors, which have been renovated. ❼

Lotte Hotel Sogone-dong ⓣ02/771-1000, ⓦwww.lottehotel.co.kr. Like others in the chain, the *Lotte* sits on top of a busy shopping mall. The hotel has two wings – the older one, though cheaper, is truly dire, with rooms no better than the average motel, but while those in the new wing are far bigger, they're still of questionable value. ❾

Metro Hotel Euljiro 2-ga ⓣ02/752-1112, ⓦwww.metrohotel.co.kr. A modern, squeaky-clean hotel away from the main Myeong-dong riff-raff, where the staff are friendly and the breakfast comes free. Rooms are fresh and have free Internet connections, though views are generally poor – ask to see a few. Come out of Euljiro 1-ga subway station, turn right off the main road then right again. ❻

Seoul Plaza Hotel City Hall ⓣ02/771-2200, ⓕ02/755-8897. Directly facing City Hall, adjacent to Deoksugung and within easy reach of some of Seoul's main banks and embassies, you could hardly wish for a more central location. Such convenience comes at a price, but it's almost worth it just for the Manhattan-like views from the north-facing upper rooms, where skyscrapers tower over City Hall. ❾

Westin Chosun Sogong-dong ⓣ02/771-0500, ⓦwww.echosunhotel.com. Serious effort has been put into making this the most appealing hotel in central Seoul – an energetic group of knowledgeable staff preside over rooms that eschew the typical Korean concrete blockiness for splashes of lime, plush carpets and curved sofas. Even the bathrooms are graced with modern art, and a free mobile phone will be yours for the duration of your stay. Prices are high but often fall to W250,000 off-season. ❾

Myeong-dong

Seoul's busy shopping area has a wide range of accommodation, from flophouses to five-star. Unless otherwise stated, all the places listed below are on the Myeong-dong, City Hall and Namsan map on p.106.

Astoria Hotel Namhak-dong Ⓣ02/2268-7111, Ⓕ02/2274-3187. Set away from the bustle of central Myeong-dong (though still on a main road), the gently decaying *Astoria* has rooms that are acceptable but totally devoid of frills; try to nab one with a view of Namsan to the south. 5

Pacific Hotel Namsan-dong Ⓣ02/752-5101, Ⓕ02/755-5582. Excellent value when off-season discounts kick in, this hotel tries its best to look like a five-star, with a wide range of on-site services including a tailor and bakery. Some rooms have views of Namsan or central Myeong-dong. 7

Seoul accommodation

Anguk Guesthouse	안국 게스트하우스
Astoria Hotel	아스토리아 호텔
Bukchon Guesthouse	북촌 게스트하우스
COEX Intercontinental	코엑스 인터콘티넨탈 호텔
Daewon Inn	대원 여관
Dongam Motel	동암 모텔
Geumseong-jang	금성장
Golden Pond	골덴 폰드
Grand Hyatt	그랜드 하얏트
Grand Intercontinental	그랜드 인터콘티넨탈 호텔
Guesthouse Myeong-dong	게스트하우스 명동
Hamilton Hotel	해밀튼 호텔
Happy Road	해피 로드
Hotel Kaya	가야 관광 호텔
Hotel Richmond	호텔 리취몬드
Hotel Riviera	호텔 리베라
Hotel Saerim	호텔 새림
Hotel Samjung	호텔 삼정
Hotel Yoido	호텔 여의도
Itaewon Hotel	이태원 호텔
Jelly Hotel	젤리 호텔
JW Marriott	매리어트 호텔
Koreana Hotel	코레아나 호텔
Kwanghwa Hotel	광화 호텔
Lexington Hotel	렉싱턴 호텔
Lotte Hotel	롯데 호텔
Metro Hotel	메트로 호텔
Namsan Guesthouse	남산 게스트하우스
Novotel Ambassador	노보텔
Pacific Hotel	파시픽 호텔
Ritz-Carlton	리즈 칼튼 호텔
Sejong Hotel	세종 호텔
Seoul Backpackers	서울 백팩크스
Seoul Guesthouse	사울 게스트하우스
Seoul Olympic Parktel	사울 올림픽 파크텔
Seoul Plaza Hotel	사울 프라자 호텔
Seoul Royal Hotel	사울 로얄 호텔
Sheraton Grande Walkerhill	쉐라톤 그란드 워커힐
The Shilla	신라 호텔
Sunbee	모텔 선비
Tea Guesthouse	티 게스트하우스
Tomgi	톰기
W Seoul Walkerhill W	더블유 서울 워커힐
Westin Chosun	웨스틴 조선 호텔
Windroad	윈드로드

Sejong Hotel Chungmu-ro ⓣ02/77-6000, ⓦwww.sejong.co.kr. This large but expensive Myeong-dong landmark seems to attract most of the city's Japanese tourists, and is extremely busy for much of the year. Some rooms have great views of Namsan and its tower, and access to the hotel is easy as there's an airport limousine bus stop right outside the entrance. ❽

Seoul Royal Hotel Myeong-dong ⓣ02/756-1112, ⓦwww.seoulroyal.co.kr. Golden hues and comfy beds are on the menu at this towering hotel, which rises near the cathedral at the centre of Myeong-dong's sprawling shopping district. Rooms are cosy, the grill and buffet bars on the 21st floor are good, and there are free shuttle buses to and from the airport. ❽

The Shilla Namsan-dong ⓣ02/2233-3310, ⓦwww.shilla.net. See Seoul map, pp.74–75. Hiding away in a quiet area on the eastern access road to Namsan, this hotel is characterized by the traditional style of its exterior. The lobby and restaurants are a luscious shade of brown, as if they've been dunked in tea, though the common areas can often be a little busy – this is one of Seoul's most popular conference venues. The rooms themselves are fine, if a little overpriced. ❾

Insa-dong and around

Despite Insa-dong's status as a tourist magnet, accommodation here is only at the cheaper end of the scale – the nearest places with decent tourist facilities are around City Hall. The three most useful subway stations are Anguk, Jonggak and Jongno 3-ga. Unless otherwise stated, all the places listed below are on the Insa-dong map on p.94.

Traditional guesthouses

In the surprisingly tranquil city sector north of Anguk subway station lie some of Seoul's most interesting places to stay – here you can spend the night in traditional Korean housing known as **hanok**. Highly beautiful, these are wooden buildings with tiled roofs, set around a dirt courtyard – a style that once blanketed the nation, but rarely seen in today's high-rise Korea. The generally bed-less rooms – you'll be sleeping Korean-style in a sandwich of blankets – are kept deliberately rustic and heated in the winter with the underfloor *ondol* system; all, however, provide modern day indoor toilets and Internet access. The places listed below are marked on the Palace District map, p.89.

Anguk Guesthouse Anguk-dong ⓣ02/736-3304, ⓦwww.anguk-house.com. There are just five rooms at this tiny guesthouse, all coming with free breakfast. The owner speaks excellent English and is full of information about the area; though his place is tucked away down some small side-alleys, the website has good directions. ❸

Bukchon Guesthouse Gye-dong ⓣ02/743-8530, ⓕ02/743-8531. A pleasing courtyard setting, within easy walking distance of two palaces and Insadong-gil. The owners are friendly, and will even pick you up at nearby Anguk subway station if you ring them from the telephones inside; if you feel like walking, take exit three and continue straight up the main road, then take the first left, and the guesthouse will be on your left after five minutes or so. ❹

Seoul Guesthouse Gye-dong ⓣ02/745-0057, ⓦwww.seoul110.com. Seoul by name but not by nature – for somewhere so close to the centre, the atmosphere here is astonishingly farm-like. There are no beds though the simple rooms do come with Wi-Fi Internet connections. ❸

Tea Guesthouse Bukchon-dong ⓣ02/3675-9877, ⓦwww.teaguesthouse.com. More expensive than the other traditional guesthouses in the area, but *Tea*'s owners put in a lot of effort introducing Korean traditions to their guests – if there are enough people around, you may find yourself making (and eating) *kimchi* or *pajeon*. The boss also has an endearing habit of chalking up information, such as the day's weather, on a tiny blackboard. ❺

Dongnam Motel Jongno-dong. Though often used by amorous couples, this is a cheap and acceptable motel within sniffing distance of Insadong-gil and its delights – take exit three from Jongno 3-ga subway station, and the motel entrance is right there. Rooms have comfy beds and a/c, and free sachets of coffee for the morning pick-me-up. ❸

Kwanghwa Hotel Dangju-dong ⓣ02/738-0751. See the Palace District map, p.89. While not in Insa-dong itself, this is a dirt-cheap motel within walking distance of some of Seoul's best sights. It's a little above the usual motel standard – note the Miró copy in the stairwell – and some rooms have huge TVs. ❸

Hotel Saerim Gwanhun-dong ⓣ02/739-3377, ⓕ02/734-3333. Whatever its titular claims, this is a motel through and through. Some rooms have huge televisions and Internet making it extremely good value for the area. ❹

Sunbee Gwanhun-dong ⓣ02/730-3451, ⓕ02/737-8857. Tucked into a side street near Insadong-gil, rooms here are moderately sized, quirkily designed and good value; all have Internet and large televisions, and staff will bring you free toast in the morning. ❺

Tomgi Nagwon-dong ⓣ02/742-6660, ⓕ02/742-6659. Rooms at this pleasantly seedy love motel are excellent value for the area, and come in a variety of fresh styles, some of which include whirlpool baths. Just choose from the panel at reception: those not illuminated are taken (or just "busy"). Take exit four from Jongno 3-ga subway station. ❹

Itaewon

Given the area's popularity with foreigners, there aren't that many places to stay in Itaewon. All the places listed below are marked on the Itaewon map on p.109.

Geumseong-jang Yeogwan Itaewon-dong. A grubby but cheap place for Itaewon party-goers to crash, a short walk south of the subway station from the main crossroads. Though the rooms are small, there's enough space for contraceptive vending machines on the walls. ❶

Grand Hyatt Hannam-dong ⓣ02/797-1234, ⓦwww.seoul.grand.hyatt.com. See also Seoul map, pp.74–75. A favourite of visiting dignitaries, this is one of Seoul's top hotels in more ways than one – perched on a hill overlooking Itaewon, almost every room has a fantastic view through floor-to-ceiling windows. There's also a fitness centre, an ice rink and squash courts, as well as swimming pools, indoors and out. ❼

Hamilton Hotel Itaewon-dong ⓣ02/794-0171, ⓦwww.hamilton.co.kr. More of an Itaewon landmark than a decent place to stay, but countless foreigners do regardless. Despite dated rooms and patchy service, this remains the best place to stay on the strip, and guests can make use of an outdoor pool in warmer months. ❼

Itaewon Hotel Hannam-dong ⓣ02/792-3111, ⓕ02/795-3126. A 5min walk east of Itaewon subway station, this hotel is less popular than the *Hamilton*, though just as old-fashioned, and usually much cheaper. The ceilings are surprisingly low and staff are unlikely to speak English, but it's an acceptable back-up option. ❻

Hotel Kaya Galwol-dong ⓣ02/798-5101, ⓦwww.kayahotel.net. See also Seoul map, pp.74–75. Far more professional and less seedy than your average motel, this is as close as you'll get to the USO base if you're going on one of their early-starting tours of the DMZ. Try to get a room at the back if possible – the views aren't great, but at least you'll get some light. ❹

Yeouido

Yeouido has a few hotels to cater to its population of travelling businessmen; they're not near the subway line, but cabs will cost less than W3000 from Yeouinaru station. The places listed below are marked on the Seoul map, pp.74–75.

Lexington Hotel Yeouido-dong ⓣ02/6670-7000, ⓦwww.thelexington.co.kr. By far the best hotel on Yeouido island, with stylish communal areas, immaculate rooms and an airport limousine bus stop directly outside. Discounts of thirty percent are not uncommon, and it's easy to wangle free breakfast at all but the busiest times. ❼

Hotel Yoido Yeouido-dong ⓣ02/782-0121, ⓕ02/785-2510. Eschews the usual Korean tourist hotel decor for frosted glass in the lobby, zebra-print carpets in the corridors and airy rooms, all of which have computer terminals; some of the doubles have pretty views over the Han. Staff are extremely amiable, and breakfast is free. ❻

Gangnam, Apgujeong and Jamsil

There are a great number of places to stay in Gangnam, mostly lining Bongeunsaro, the road one kilometre north of Gangnam subway station, though there are a number of motels closer to the station exits. Apgujeong, Seoul's fashion capital, has surprisingly few places to stay, while there are motels and hotels sprinkled around the wide Jamsil area. Unless otherwise stated, all the places listed below are on the Gangnam and Apgujeong map on p.113.

COEX Intercontinental COEX complex ⓣ02/3452-2500, ⓦwww.seoul.intercontinental.com. One of a pair sitting at opposite ends of the COEX mall, this is newer, cheaper and less inviting than the *Grand*, though still has high service standards and admirable restaurants. ❽

Grand Intercontinental COEX complex ⓣ02/555-5656, ⓦwww.seoul.intercontinental.com. Designed with an attention to detail often lacking in Korea, this hotel belies its age by keeping up to date with regular overhauls. Rooms are fresh and tastefully decorated in pleasing tones, with modern furniture. Some of Seoul's best restaurants can be found on the lower floors (see p.126). Guests can also make use of a gym and indoor swimming pool. ❾

Jelly Hotel Yeoksam-dong ⓣ02/553-4737, ⓦwww.jellyhotel.com. A hip and extremely interesting love hotel that has achieved cult status with young Seoulites, some of whom come to couple up (a "rest" is half the price of a night's stay), others to party with a group of friends. The hotel is possibly home to the weirdest rooms in the city – some contain pool tables, Jacuzzis or karaoke systems. ❺

JW Marriott Hotel Banpo-dong ⓣ02/6282-6262, ⓦwww.marriott.com. See Seoul map pp.74–75. Though the hotel towers over the express bus terminal, confusing signs make access a little problematic. It proudly claims to have the biggest bathrooms in Korea, though the rooms are otherwise bland, and occasionally patchy service means that they're not really worth the money unless you're doing business around Jamsil, or in cities accessible from the bus terminal. ❽

Novotel Ambassador Yeoksam-dong ⓣ02/567-1101, ⓦwww.ambatel.com. More of a base for business travellers than tourists, rooms here are accordingly more practical than aesthetically pleasing. There's a health club on site, as well as a buffet restaurant, and the friendly staff will be more than happy to give travel advice. ❽

Hotel Richmond Yeoksam-dong ⓣ02/562-2151, ⓦwww.hotel-richmond.co.kr. A fantastic budget option if you don't mind not having valet parking or other five-star facilities. Rooms here come with free Internet access and large TVs, and the more expensive ones are at least as big as those in the nearby *Ritz*. ❹

Ritz-Carlton Yeoksam-dong ⓣ02/3451-8000, ⓦwww.ritzcarltonseoul.com. Service here is as professional as you'd expect from the chain, and no effort has been spared to make this one of Seoul's top hotels. The on-site restaurants are excellent (including a leafy outdoor area for warmer months), but though the rooms aren't terribly spacious, there are wonderful views from those that face north. ❾

Hotel Riviera Cheongdam-dong ⓣ02/541-3111, ⓦwww.riviera.co.kr. Very convenient for Apgujeong's upper-class shopping strip, though the main road outside has twelve lanes and is a conduit for traffic rampaging over the Han. Ask to be placed in the newer building, which has bigger and airier rooms than those in the old block; some doubles have great views over the river. ❽

Hotel Samjung Yeoksam-dong ⓣ02/557-1121. Aimed at Korean tourists rather than foreigners, this hotel is substantially cheaper than most of its neighbours, though utterly lacking in atmosphere. ❼

Seoul Olympic Parktel Bangi-dong ⓣ02/410-2114. See Seoul map, pp.74–75. A reasonable hotel overlooking Olympic Park, this may be of particular interest to those carrying a youth hostel card – a few rooms here have been converted to dormitories (W22,000), and when they're empty (which is more often than not) you'll effectively be getting a highish-end hotel room for peanuts. ❻

Gwanjang-dong

Though these interconnected hotels are among the best in the country, they're inconveniently located far to the east of town, in a nondescript area near Gwangnaru subway station on the purple line 5. From here a cab will cost

W2000, or there are free shuttle buses every twenty minutes. Both places listed below are on the Seoul map on pp.74–75.

Sheraton Grande Walkerhill Gwanjang-dong ⓣ02/455-5000, ⓦwww.sheratonwalkerhill.co.kr. With scented, plush-carpeted corridors and muted-tone rooms, it's not as showy as the *W* next door, but though the views are rarely as good it's immaculately designed nonetheless. There are some wonderful restaurants on the complex (you can also use those in the *W*), and with rack rates starting at W460,000, the hotel contains the most expensive rooms in the country – up to a colossal W15,000,000 per night. ⑨

W Seoul Walkerhill Gwanjang-dong ⓣ02/465-2222, ⓦwww.starwoodhotels.com/whotels. No doubt about it – the *W* is the most distinctive hotel in Korea. With artfully designed furniture in the rooms, neon gym rings in the elevators, sharp suited staff and a loungey beat pulsing through the lobby, every inch of it is achingly trendy – not to everyone's tastes. Particularly popular with Korean honeymooners, rooms range in style – and price; rack rates start around W570,000 – from "Wonderful" to "Extreme Wow", many coming with their own whirlpool and views over the river; there's also a gym, a juice bar and a great swimming pool. On-site restaurants are excellent, and the city's *nouveau riche* come to slurp fifteen-dollar cocktails in the *Woo Bar*. ⑨

The palace district

The area of central Seoul bounded by the five **grand palaces** is by far the most interesting in the city. During the Joseon dynasty, which ruled over the Korean peninsula from 1392 to 1910, each of the palaces at one time served as the country's seat of power, and no visit to Seoul would be complete without a visit to at least one or two. By far the most visited is **Gyeongbokgung**, the oldest of the group, though nearby **Changdeokgung** is the only one to have been added to UNESCO's World Heritage list. Literally a stone's throw away across a perimeter wall is **Changgyeonggung**, which probably has the most interesting history of the five, as well as the most natural setting, while further south are the smaller pair of **Gyeonghuigung**, home to some interesting Western-style buildings, and **Deoksugung**, the best palace to visit if you'd prefer to be alone. Note that the suffix *–gung* means palace, and once removed you're left with the two-syllable name of the complex.

While visits to only one or two of the palaces should suffice, there's much more to see in the area, from the trinkets and teashops on famed **Insadong-gil** to the more laid-back areas of **Samcheong-dong** and **Bukchon-dong**, the former studded with art galleries, the latter with traditional *hanok* buildings. Also in the area, just north of Gyeongbokgung, is **Cheongwadae**, the official residence of the Korean president.

One **day-trip** itinerary popular with tourists in Seoul is to start the day at Gyeongbokgung and take in the on-site museums before heading to Insadong-gil for a traditional Korean meal and a cup of tea; energy thus restored, you can then visit one or two nearby galleries and shop at the stalls, or the nearby palace of Changdeokgung, before taking a well-earned rest at Tapgol Park.

Gyeongbokgung

The palace of **Gyeongbokgung** (daily 9am–5pm; Nov–Feb to 4pm; W3000), with its glorious buildings hemmed in by the suitably majestic limestone crags of Bukhansan National Park to the north, is the single most popular tourist sight in the city; a large historical complex with excellent on-site **museums**, it can easily eat up the best part of a day. Construction was ordered by **King**

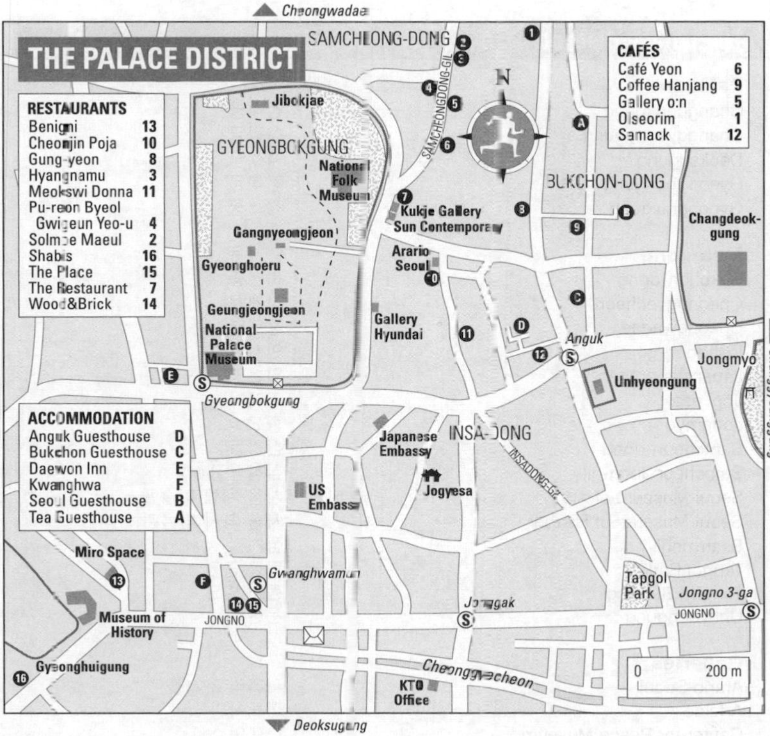

Taejo in 1394, and the "Palace of Shining Happiness" held the regal throne for over two hundred years. At its peak, the palace housed over four hundred buildings within its vaguely rectangular perimeter walls, but most were burnt down during the Japanese invasions in the 1590s. However, though few Koreans will admit to it, the invaders were not directly to blame – the arsonists were actually a group of local slaves, angered by their living and working conditions. The palace was only rebuilt following the coronation of child-king **Gojong** in 1863, but the Japanese were to invade again shortly afterwards, forcibly opening up Korea to foreign trade, and slowly ratcheting up their standing on the peninsula.

In 1895 **Empress Myeongsong**, one of Gojong's wives and an obstacle to the Japanese – who refer to her as "Queen Min" – was assassinated in the Gyeongbokgung grounds, a shady tale told in countless movies and soap operas, and a precursor to the full-scale Japanese annexation of Korea in 1910. During the occupation, which ended with World War II in 1945, the Japanese used Gyeongbokgung for police interrogation and torture, and made numerous changes in an apparent effort to destroy Korean pride. The front gate, Gwanghwamun, was moved to the east of the complex, destroying the north–south geometric principles followed during the palace's creation, while a Japanese command post was built in the sacred first courtyard in a shape identical to the Japanese written character for "sun". One interesting suggestion – and one certainly not beyond the scope of Japanese thinking at that time – is that Bukhansan mountain to the north resembled the character for "big" and City Hall to the south that of "root", thereby emblazoning

The palace district

Palaces	
Changdeokgung	창덕궁
Changgyeonggung	창경궁
Deoksugung	덕수궁
Gyeongbokgung	경복궁
Gyeonghuigung	경희궁
Insa-dong	인사동
Bukchon-dong	북촌동
Cheonggyecheon	청계천
Cheongwadae	청와대
Insadong-gil	인사동길
Japanese embassy	일본 대사관
Jogyesa	조계사
Jongmyo	종묘
Samcheon-dong	삼청동
Samcheondong-gil	삼청동길
Seoul Museum of Art	사울 시립 미술관
Seoul Museum of History	사울 역사 박물관
Ssamziegil	쌈지길
Tapgol Park	탑골 공원
Tong-in Building	통인 빌딩
Unhyeongung	운현궁
Galleries	
Arario Seoul	아라리오 사울
Artside	아트사이드
Center for Peace Museum	스페이스피스
doART	두아트 갤러리
Gallery Hyundai	갤러리 현대
Insa Art Centre	인사 아트센터
Insa Gallery	인사 갤러리
Kim Young Seob Photo Gallery	김영삽사진화랑
Kukje Gallery	국제 갤러리
Kyung-in Museum of Fine Art	경인미술관
Olseorim	올서림
Ssamzie-gil	쌈지길
Sun Art Center	선화랑
Sun Contemporary	선콘템포라리
Toto	토토

Seoul's most prominent points with the three characters that made up the name of the Empire of the Rising Sun.

Gyeongbokgung today, despite being restored with far fewer buildings than were once present, is quite absorbing, and the chance to stroll the dusty paths between its delicate tile-roofed buildings is one of the most enjoyable experiences Seoul can throw at you. Entering through the first courtyard – now minus the Japanese command post – you'll see **Geunjeongjeon**, the palace's former throne room, looming ahead. Despite being the largest wooden structure in the country, this two-level construction remains surprisingly graceful, the corners of its gently sloping roof home to lines of tiny guardian figurines. The central path leading up to the building was once

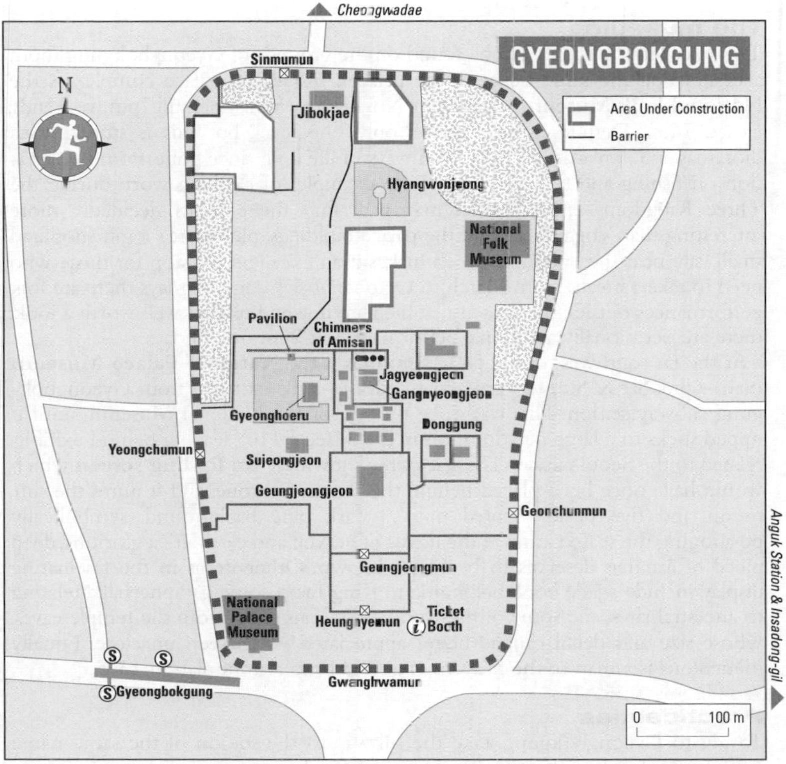

used only by the king, but the best views of its interior are actually from the sides – from here you'll see the golden dragons on the hall ceiling, as well as the throne itself, backed by its traditional folding screen.

After Geunjeongjeon you can take one of a number of routes around the complex. To the east of the throne room are the buildings that once housed **crown princes**, deliberately placed here to give these regal pups the day's first light, while behind is **Gangnyeongjeon**, the former living quarters of the king and queen, furnished with replica furniture. Also worth seeking out is **Jagyeongjeon**, a building backed by a beautiful stone wall, and chimneys decorated with animal figures. West of the throne room is **Gyeonghoeru**, a colossal pavilion looking out over a tranquil **lotus pond** that was a favourite with artists in regal times, and remains so today. The pond was used both for leisure and as a ready source of water for the fires that regularly broke out around the palace (an unfortunate by-product of heating buildings using burning wood or charcoal under the floor), while the pavilion itself was once a place for banquets and civil service examinations. North of the throne room, and right at the back of the complex, are a few buildings constructed in 1888 during the rule of King Gojong to house books and works of art. These structures were designed in the Chinese style that was the height of fashion at the time, and are markedly different from any other structures around the palace.

The museums

Two excellent museums can be found on the grounds of Gyeongbokgung (both accessible on the same ticket as the palace). Inside the palace complex is the **National Folk Museum** (9am–6pm, Nov–Feb to 5pm, open till 7pm weekends; closed Tues). Despite its size, there's only one level, but this is stuffed with dioramas and explanations of Korean ways of life long since gone, from information on fishing and farming practices to examples of clothing worn during the Three Kingdoms era. Children may well find the exhibits decidedly more interesting than slogging around the palace buildings, plus there's a gift shop and small café near the entrance, which makes it an excellent pit-stop for those who need to take a break. From March to October at 3pm on Saturdays there are folk performances outside the museum, which are free and usually well worth a look; there are occasionally additional performances at 2pm on Sundays.

At the far southwest of the palace grounds is the **National Palace Museum** (9am–6pm, Sat & Sun to 7pm; closed Mon) – take exit five from Gyeongbokgung subway station. This was once the site of the National Museum, until it upped sticks to a large new location in 2005 (see p.110), leaving behind exhibits related to the Seoul palaces. The star of the show here is a **folding screen** which would have once been placed behind the imperial throne, and features the sun, moon and five peaks painted onto a dark blue background, symbolically positioning the seated kings at the nexus of heaven and earth. It's a glorious, deep piece of art that deserves to be better known. Other items in the fascinating display include a jade book belonging to King Taejo, some paraphernalia relating to ancestral rites, and some of the wooden dragons taken from the temple eaves, whose size and detail can be better appreciated when seen up close. Equally meticulous is a map of the heavens engraved onto a stone slab in 1395.

Practicalities

To get to Gyeongbokgung, take the subway to the station of the same name (exit five), alternatively it's an easy walk from Insadong-gil. Try to time your

▲ Changing of the guards outside Gyeongbokgung

visit to coincide with the colourful **changing of the guard** ceremony, which takes place outside the main entrance every day except Tuesday on the hour from 11am to 3pm. There are free English-language **tours** of the grounds at 9.30am, 12pm, 1.30pm and 3pm, although the complex has information boards all over the place, and most visitors choose to go it alone. You can even visit the Gyeongbokgung's outer yard after closing; you can't go inside the palace itself, but its delicate tiled roofs can be quite captivating when bathed in the pinks or oranges of twilight, and Bukhansan's craggy peaks are thrown into silhouette behind the complex.

Cheongwadae

What the White House is to Washington, **Cheongwadae** is to Seoul. Sitting directly behind Gyeongbokgung and surrounded by mountains, this official presidential residence is named the "Blue House" on account of the colour of its roof tiles. In Joseon times, blue roofs were reserved for kings, but the office of the president is the nearest modern-day equivalent to regal rule. The road that borders the palace is open for public access, but don't venture too close to the entrance as it's understandably a high-security area. In 1968, a group of 31 North Korean soldiers were apprehended here during an attempt to assassinate then-President Park Chung-hee, but while you're unlikely to be accused of doing the same, those loitering or straying too close are likely to be questioned. Free **tours** (Tues–Fri 10am, 11am, 2pm & 3pm) of the grounds are available for those interested in taking a closer look; book online in advance at Ⓦenglish.president.go.kr.

Insa-dong

The undisputed hub of Korea's tourist scene, **INSA-DONG** is a city district whose tight lattice of streets is full to the brim with art galleries, shops, tearooms and traditional restaurants – you could quite happily spend most of the day here, and many return frequently throughout their stay in Seoul, especially to pick up souvenirs before their flight home. The appeal of the area lies in simply strolling around and taking it all in – most of the commerce here is pleasingly traditional in nature, particularly the food at the aforementioned restaurants. The galleries also display a fusion of old and contemporary styles very much in keeping with the atmosphere of the place. Should such delights bring your artistic muse out to play, there are numerous shops selling paints, brushes and handmade paper to sate your desires. Details of the most interesting **galleries** can be found in the box on p.95, and we have listed the area's best **restaurants** on pp.122–124, along with a selection of **tearooms** in the box on p.123.

Insadong-gil

Insa-dong's action is centred on **Insadong-gil**, the area's main street, which despite being cramped and people-packed is still open to traffic – be careful when walking here, as Korean taxis tend to be a law unto themselves. The one exception is Sunday, when the street is closed to vehicles; unless the weather's bad, you'll are likely to see music and dance performances or a traditional parade. At the northern end of the street – take exit six from Anguk station, walk up the main street for a few minutes and then turn left – there are a couple of **tourist information** booths, as well as the interesting **Ssamziegil** building, a spiralling complex of trendy trinket shops with a rooftop market. Tiny side streets branch off Insadong-gil as you head south along the road, most of which are lined with restaurants serving traditional Korean fare.

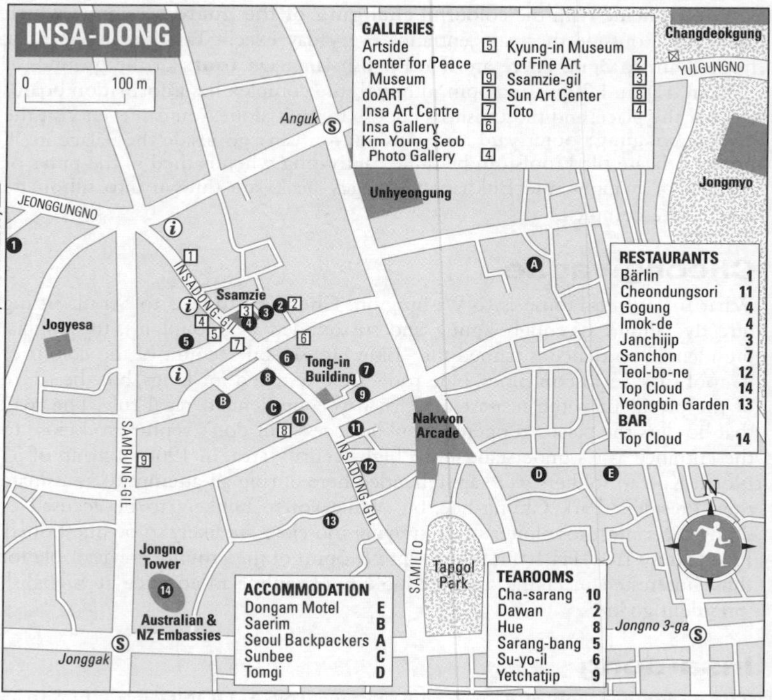

Continuing south, the street segues into the more westernized buildings of "regular" Seoul; look out for the *Starbucks* on the southern reaches of the road, which was the scene of traditionalist protests when it opened – it made a slight concession by having its name spelt in *hangeul*. In fact, the road has often been the scene of **anti-US protests** (see box, p.96). Insadong-gil finishes at small **Tapgol Park**, where a huge, stunning Joseon-era **stone pagoda** grandly titled official "National Treasure Number Two" sits resplendent inside. Sadly, though, its beauty is marred by the ugly glass box that has been placed around it for protection.

Around Insadong-gil

There are a number of mildly diverting sights within walking distance of Insadong-gil. Near the north end of the street is **Jogyesa**, the only major temple in the centre of Seoul. Created in 1910 and hemmed in by large buildings, it has neither history nor beauty to its credit, but for visitors with little time in the country it may represent the only chance to see a Korean temple of such size. The best times to visit are on Buddha's birthday or during the Lotus Lantern festival; see box on p.132 for more details.

Further east, and very close to Anguk subway station – take exit four – is the tiny palace of **Unhyeongung** (9am–7pm; closed Mon; W700). Having never been an official royal residence, it doesn't qualify as one of Seoul's "big five" palaces; accordingly, it's less showy than the others, but the relative lack of people makes it a pleasant place to visit – the bare wood and paper doors would

Insa-dong art galleries

There are hundreds of galleries on and around Insadong-gil; below are some of the most interesting. See Insa-dong map opposite.

Artside Ⓦwww.artside.org. With a sister gallery in Beijing, Artside is one of two galleries in Seoul (the other is Arario in Samcheong-dong) that regularly exhibits work from China's increasingly interesting contemporary art scene. Exhibitions change every month or so. Daily 10am–6.30pm; free unless there's a special exhibition.

Center for Peace Museum Ⓦwww.peacemuseum.or.kr. This unassuming but well-curated gallery west of Insa-dong has regular exhibitions of art and photography, all seeking to promote peace by highlighting the dangers of conflict. Monday to Saturday 10am–5pm.

doART Ⓦwww.doart.co.kr. This small but quirky two-level gallery regularly outdoes its more illustrious neighbours with exhibitions from young and emerging artists, and is a good place to keep your finger on the pulse of the Korean contemporary scene. Daily 10am–7pm; free.

Insa Art Centre This interesting building's seven floors of exhibitions could keep you busy for some time – the acres of wallspace display a wide range of modern styles. Those spending a while in Seoul can return for further helpings, as the place is stripped every week to make room for new works. Usually open 10am–7pm; closes early Tuesdat and opens late Wednesday to install new exhibitions; free unless there's a special exhibition.

Insa Gallery Ⓦwww.insagallery.net. This three-floored gallery's collection features some of the most interesting Korean artists of recent times. It's exploration of modern themes and styles is renowned in this competitive neighbourhood, and the twice-monthly changearounds keep things fresh. Daily 10am–6.30pm; free.

Kim Young Seob Photo Gallery Ⓦwww.gallerykim.com. A tiny photo gallery on the fourth level of a building that also features a café on the third floor, and a toy gallery-cum-shop on the second (see Toto below). The international collection of photographs continues to grow, and most notably includes a few from the highly influential Man Ray. Daily 10am–7pm; W3000.

Kyung-In Museum of Fine Art Exhibitions are rarely poor at this long-time local favourite, whose tradition-with-a-twist style reflects a desire to fuse the conventional with the contemporary. Its four rooms are pleasant and spacious, and are centred around a leafy traditional courtyard that's also home to a decent tearoom (see box, p.123). Daily 10am–6pm; free.

Ssamziegil Ⓦwww.ssamzie.com. A little too modern for some, this gallery hides away in the basement of the adventurous Ssamzie building (see p.93). On the same floor you'll find art for sale – sometimes from Asian artists of moderate or imminent fame – and *Gogung*, an excellent restaurant (see p.123). Daily 10am–6pm; free.

Sun Art Center Ⓦwww.sungallery.co.kr. Spoken about in hushed tones by curators at other Insa-dong galleries, this houses probably the most renowned collection in the area. The collection mainly consists of early twentieth-century works, and shows that modern art in Korea goes back way before the country's growth into an economic power – look for pieces by Kim Sou, who had a Rubens-like obsession with flesh, or the floral works of Kim Chong Hak. Daily 10am–6pm; free.

Toto Is it a gallery, a museum or a shop? Regardless, Toto is filled with planes, trains and automobiles, as well as action figures that wear their underpants on the outside. Some pieces are rare, but there are cheaper ones to take away as quirky souvenirs. Daily 10am–6pm; W1000.

The 2002 incidents

The 2002 World Cup fortified international ties that had been growing ever stronger since Seoul's hosting of the 1988 Olympics, but though the tournament was a resounding success the year will also be remembered for three incidents that gave rise to a palpable anti-Western sentiment. It started rather innocuously with the short-track **speed-skating** final of the Winter Olympics; Kim Dae-yung of South Korea crossed the line first but was harshly judged to have impeded Anton Ohno, an American of Japanese descent, coming into the final bend. Kim was disqualified and the gold went to the States. Incensed by this decision, the Korean public went ballistic to such an extent that within a couple of days a single titled "F***ing USA" went straight to the top of the music charts. The main subject of the song's vitriol, George W. Bush, put his foot in it shortly afterwards following his visit to Seoul, by grouping North Korea with Iran and Iraq in his infamous **axis of evil**. This did little to please South Koreans, many of whom harbour a strong desire for eventual reunification with their brothers in the North. A third event came just before the World Cup, when an American tank accidentally killed two Korean girls, just one reason for protests against American military presence that continue to this day. Although there's little chance of confrontation, Americans may sometimes receive a frosty reception in Korea, and Westerners tend to be deemed American until proven otherwise. Dutch travellers, on the other hand, can expect a free drink or three, thanks to Guus Hiddink, a manager from the Netherlands who led South Korea's minnows to an amazing fourth-place finish at the 2002 World Cup.

provide the perfect setting for a Japanese *anime*. Though he never lived here, King Gojong's marriage to the ill-fated Princess Myeongseong took place in Unhyeongung, and it was also the centre of Neo-Confucian thought during the Joseon period, which sought to base civil progress on merit rather than lineage (see p.231 for information on one of the main instigators).

West of Insadong-gil, and on the way to Gyeongbokgung, is the **Japanese embassy**. This may not sound like a tourist sight, but each Wednesday at noon an ever-decreasing number of elderly Korean women come to stage a **protest** – these are the "**comfort women**" who were forced into sexual slavery during the Japanese occupation of Korea, and are still awaiting compensation, or even an apology. "Say you're sorry!" and "You know you did wrong!" are the most popular chants, and it's not just the *ajummas* doing the shouting – though their numbers dwindle from year to year, they're being supplemented by younger protesters, whose demonstrations are likely to continue until Tokyo issues an official apology.

North of Anguk station

North of Anguk subway station, and between the palaces of Gyeongbokgung and Changdeokgung, lies Seoul's best-kept secret. **Samcheong-dong** and **Bukchan-dong** are two of the city's most characterful areas; despite being literally just across the road from Insa-dong and its teeming tourists, they feel a world apart - more traditional, but without the fuss.

Like Insa-dong, Samcheong-dong is crammed with quirky restaurants, cafés and galleries (see box opposite). Though most of the area remains charming and relaxed, one particular street has become rather popular; heading off from Gyeongbokgun's northeastern corner, and a five-minute walk from the palace's eastern exit, **Samcheongdong-gil** has an almost European air to it, its side streets snaking uphill in a manner reminiscent of Naples or Lisbon. A few of the cafés and galleries spill over into Bukchon-dong, an area characterized by the prevalence of traditional wooden **hanok buildings** – these once covered the whole country, but most were torn down during Korea's economic revolution and replaced with row upon row of fifteen-storey blocks. The city council spared this area the wrecking ball, and as a result there's some delightful walking to be done among its web of quiet lanes, where tiny restaurants, tearooms and comic book shops line the streets, and children play games on mini arcade machines, creating a pleasant air of indifference hard to find in the capital; a few of the buildings have even been converted into guesthouses (see box, p.85). The local authorities have produced an excellent booklet to the area; pick one up from one of Insa-dong's tourist booths (see map, p.94).

Changdeokgung

While Gyeongbokgung plays to the crowd, its smaller neighbour **Changdeokgung** (English-language tours 11.30am, 1.30pm & 3.30pm; palace closed Mon; W3000) is the choice of palace connoisseurs. Completed in 1412 and home to royalty as recently as 1910, this is the best-preserved palace in Seoul, and has been put on UNESCO's much-vaunted list of World Heritage sites. Entry here is regulated to a far greater degree than the other palaces, and for most of the week you'll have no option but to join a **tour**. These last around 80 minutes, during which time a *hanbok*-clad English-speaker guides groups through the complex, but though the information is interesting, you really can't beat the freedom of exploring the palace by yourself. To do this you will need to come on Thursday (April–Oct 9.15am–6.30pm), and you'll pay more for the privilege – W15,000. Note that snacks and drinks are not allowed in the palace – fill up before you go.

Art galleries north of Anguk station

As in Insa-dong, there are whole squads of galleries in the area. The following ones are particularly interesting, and are marked on the Palace District map, p.89.

Arario Seoul ⓦwww.ararioseoul.com. With a sister gallery in Beijing (as well as one in Cheonan; see p.328) Arario is often a great place to check out the latest offerings from the highly interesting art scene over the Yellow Sea. Tuesday to Sunday 11am–7pm; free.

Gallery Hyundai ⓦwww.galleryhyundai.com. This gallery is large, and possesses the most esteemed collection in the area; in existence since the 1960s, it's Korea's longest-running commercial gallery. The focus has long been on artists born before 1930, but times are changing and there's an ever-increasing emphasis on newer trends. Tuesday to Sunday 10am–6pm; free.

Kukje Gallery ⓦwww.kukjegallery.com. The Kukje is one of the most important players in the area, actively promoting Korean artists abroad, and hauling a wide, well-selected range of exhibits into its own space near the palace side of Samcheong-dong-gil. It's surrounded by excellent cafés and restaurants – including one adjoining the gallery (see p.124). Monday to Saturday 10am–6pm, Sunday till 5pm; free.

Olseorim Though it's a little hard to get to, and the art exhibited here is unlikely to be from high-profile artists, this gallery is well worth a visit. It doubles up as a café, and is adjoined to Korea's oldest dental practice (see p.128). Monday to Saturday 10am–6pm.

Sun Contemporary ⓦwww.sungallery.co.kr. The contemporary side of the excellent Sun Art Center in Insa-dong (see box, p.95), this gallery's collection is equally well put together, and occupies a few floors in a building near trendy Samcheongdong-gil. To get to other floors, you'll have to go through what looks like a fire escape from the entry room. Daily 9am–6pm; free.

▲ Lotus pond, Changdeokgung Palace

The suitably impressive **throne room** is without doubt the most regal-looking of any Seoul palace – light from outside is filtered through paper doors and windows, bathing in a dim glow the elaborate wooden beam structure, as well as the throne and its folding-screen backdrop. From here you'll be led past a number of buildings pertaining to the various kings that used the palace, some of which still have the original furniture inside. One building even contains vehicles used by **King Sunjong**, the Daimler and Cadillac looking more than a little incongruous in their palatial setting. Sunjong was the last ruler of the Joseon dynasty, and held the throne from 1907 until his country's annexation by the Japanese in 1910; his lineage still continues today, though claims are contested, and the "royals" have no regal rights, claims or titles. Further on you'll come to **Nakseondae**. Built during the reign of King Heonjong (ruled 1834–49), the building's Qing-style latticed doors and arched pavilion reveal Heonjong's taste for foreign cultures; without the paint and decoration typical of Korean palace buildings, the colours of the bare wood are ignited during sunset – look out for the circular sliding door inside, Star Trek in a Korean palace.

The **entrance** to Changdeokgung is a short walk from Anguk subway station – take exit three, walk straight up the main road, and it's on your left.

Biwon

Changdeokgung's highlight, however, is **Biwon**, the "Secret Garden". Approached on a suitably mysterious path, the garden is concealed by an arch of leaves. In the centre of the Biwon is a **lotus pond**, one of Seoul's most-photographed sights, and alive with colourful flowers in late June or early July. A small building overlooking the pond served as a library and study room, and the tiny gates blocking the entrance path were used as an interesting checking mechanism by the king – needing to crouch to pass through, he'd be reminded of his duty to be humble. This is the last stop on the tour, and most visitors take the opportunity to relax here awhile before exiting the complex.

Changgyeonggung and Jongmyo

Though not as heralded as its neighbouring palaces, **Changgyeonggung** provides one of Seoul's best-value days out – a W1000 ticket buys access not just to the palace, but also to the UNESCO-listed shrine of **Jongmyo**. These two sights are connected by footbridge, and can be seen in either order; while Changgyeonggung's entrance is harder to get to, starting here is recommended as it means that you'll wade into Jongmyo Park, one of Seoul's most chracterful areas, on exiting the shrine. The Changgyeonggung entrance is awkwardly located on the east side of the complex, and a confusing fifteen-minute walk from Hyehwa, the nearest subway station: it's usually better to take a bus from Anguk station – #150 and #171 are the most frequent (W900). It's also possible to walk here from Changdeokgung or Insadong-gil; allow 20–30 minutes. The

The murder of Crown Prince Sado

In 1762, a sinister event occurred in the grounds of Changgyeonggung, one whose story is, for some reason, omitted from the information boards that dot the palace grounds – a **royal murder**. A young prince named **Sado** was heir to the throne of **King Yeongjo**, but had been born mentally retarded, and had a rather unfortunate habit of killing people unnecessarily. Fearing dire consequences if the nation's power were placed into his son's hands, Yeongjo escorted Sado to Seonninmun, a gate on the eastern side of the palace, and ordered him to climb into a rice casket; his son obeyed, was locked in and starved to death. Sado's wife, Hyegyong, held the secret until after Yeongjo's death in 1776, at which point she spilled the beans in a book named *Hanjungnok* (published in English as *The Memoirs of Lady Hyegyong*). Sado's son **Jeongjo** became king on the death of Yeongjo, and built Hwaseong fortress in Suwon (see p.145) to house his father's remains. Jeongjo went on to become one of Korea's most respected rulers.

Jongmyo entrance is far easier to find: it's a short walk east down the main road from Jongno 3-ga subway station – exit eleven is best.

Changgyeonggung

Separated from Changdeokgung to the west by a perimeter wall, **Changgyeonggung** (daily except Tues 9am–5pm; free tours 11.30am & 4pm; W1000) tends to split visitors into two camps – those who marvel at its history and the relatively natural beauty of its interior, which is far greener than Seoul's other palaces, and those who feel that there's a little less to see.

King Sejong built Changgyeonggung in 1418 as a resting place for his father, the recently abdicated King Taejong. At its peak the palace had a far greater number of buildings than are visible today, but these were to suffer badly from fires and during the Japanese invasions. Almost the whole of the complex burned down in the Japanese attacks of 1592, and then again during a devastating inferno in 1830, two events that sandwiched the murder of a crown prince by his father (see box, p.99). When the Japanese returned in 1907, they turned much of the palace into Korea's first **amusement park**, and included a botanical garden, kindergarten and zoo, as well as a museum – the red brick exterior and pointed steel roof were very much in keeping with the Japanese style of the time, and pictures of this can still be seen around the palace entrance. The building and zoo themselves were tolerated by the Koreans for nearly a century before they were finally ripped down in 1983, whereas the **botanical garden** still remains today.

Considering its turbulent history, the palace is a markedly relaxed place to wander around. The buildings themselves are nowhere near as polished as those in the Gyeongbok or Changdeok palaces, which helps accentuate their validity; the history of each structure is chronicled on information boards. Be sure to look for **Myeongjeongjeon**, the oldest main hall of any of Seoul's palaces – it was built in 1616, and somehow escaped the fires that followed. From here, a number of paths wind their way to a pond at the north of the complex, many of which are highly beautiful, with some full of scent from herbs planted along the way. Near the pond are a couple of dedicated **herb gardens**, while also

▲ Locals playing Go outside Jongmyo Shrine

Korea's World Heritage sites

Jongmyo shrine was scribbled onto UNESCO's ever-growing list of **World Heritage** (@whc.unesco.org) in 1995, protected by the organization as a site of outstanding importance to the cultural heritage of humanity. The palace of **Changdeokgung** (see p.97) was also added in 1997, but these are just two of a small band of attractions around the country that have been protected in this way. The others are listed below:

Bulguksa and Seokguram Grotto Near Gyeongju, Bulguksa is one of the most popular temples in Korea; sumptuously painted, and dating from 774, its spectacular mountain setting also includes Seokguram, a grotto from which a beautifully carved Buddha stares out over the sea. See p.209 and p.210.

Dolmen sites The scattering of prehistoric dolmena long Korea's western flank are the most hard to reach World Heritage sites in the country. Two have been included in the Guide – Ganghwado, a bucolic Yellow Sea island west of Seoul (p.156), and those near Seonunsan National Park in Jeonbuk province (p.302).

Gyeongju Historic Areas As the former capital of the Silla dynasty – which ruled for nigh-on one thousand years from 69 BC – this wonderfully relaxed city remains chock-full of grassy regal tombs, traditional housing and ancient treasures, many of which have been placed under UNESCO protection. See p.206.

Haeinsa This temple, set into the mountains of western Gyeongnam, is the repository for the *Tripitaka Koreana*, the world's most complete collection of Buddhist texts; these were carved onto more than eighty thousand wooden blocks between 1237 and 1248, and can still be seen today. See p.225.

Hwaseong The fortress is located just south of Seoul in the city of Suwon, and was created by King Jeongjo in the late eighteenth century – excellent examples of the military architecture of the time, the walls still stand, and make for a great walk. See p.145.

Jeju volcanic island and lava tubes The most recent additions to the list, protected sights on Jeju Island include underground lava tubes (p.364), the glorious Sunrise Peak of Ilchulbong near Seongsan (p.362), and the extinct cone of Hallasan, the tallest mountain in the country (p.379).

visible are the white-painted lattices of the Japanese-built botanical garden. Those who still have energy after their palace sightseeing can head to the far southwest of the complex, where a footbridge crosses over to Jongmyo shrine.

Jongmyo

Along with the palace of Gyeongbokgung, the construction of **Jongmyo shrine** (9am–5pm; Nov–Feb to 4.30pm; closed Tues; W1000, or accessible on same ticket as Changgyeonggung) was on King Taejo's manifesto as he kicked off the Joseon dynasty in 1392. He decreed that dead kings and queens would be honoured here in true Confucian style, with a series of ancestral rites. These ceremonies were performed five times a year, once each season, with an extra one on the winter solstice, when the ruling king would pay his respects to those who died before him by bowing profusely, and explaining pertinent national issues to their **spirit tablets**. These wooden blocks, in which deceased royalty were believed to reside, are still stored in large wooden buildings that were said to be the biggest in Asia at the time of their construction. Jeongjeon was the first, but such was the length of the Joseon dynasty that another building – Yeongnyeongjeon – had to be added. Though the courtyards are open – take the opportunity to walk on the raised paths that were once reserved for kings – the buildings themselves remain locked for most of the year. The one exception being the first Sunday in May, which is the day of

Jongmyo Daeje (see box, p.132), a long, solemn ceremony (9am–3pm) followed by traditional court dances – an absolute must-see if you're in Seoul at the time.

On exiting the shrine from the main entrance, you'll find yourself in **Jongmyo Park**, one of the most atmospheric areas in Seoul – on warm days it's full of old men selling calligraphy, drinking *soju* and playing *baduk* (a Korean board game similar to Go). Find a spot to sit, close your eyes and listen to the wooden clack of a thousand game pieces.

West to Gyeonghuigung and Deoksugung

From Jongmyo, it's a westward trip to the palaces of **Gyeonghuigung** and **Deoksugung**, with more than one way to complete this journey. **Jongno**, one of Seoul's most important thoroughfares, runs directly from Jongmyo to Deoksugung, passing Tapgol Park, Insadong-gil and a statue of Korean hero Admiral Yi (see box, p.289 for more on him) along the way; it's 4km between shrine and palace – all heavily-trafficked – so it's a little too far to walk, but plenty of buses ply this road. A more pleasant alternative for those who don't mind giving their calves a work out is to make use of **Cheonggyecheon**, a creek that starts east of Jongmyo shrine, and runs parallel to Jongno for almost 6km. At its western end, a left turn will bring you to Deoksugung, and beyond this is Namdaemun market (see p.105). To get to Gyeonghuigung, take exit four from Seodaemun subway station and walk straight up the main road for a few hundred metres; the palace will be on your left.

Cheonggyecheon

Until recently, **Cheonggyecheon** was a mucky stream running under an elevated highway, but in 2003 the Mayor of Seoul decided to ditch the road and beautify the creek – this controversial project saw heads rolling on corruption charges, grumbles from local businesses and protests from environmentalists, but since completion in 2005 it has been looked upon as a resounding success. Both the stream and the walkways that flank it are below street level, and on descending you'll notice that Seoul's ceaseless cacophony has been diluted and largely replaced by the sound of rushing water. Heading west, you'll pass a series of interesting features including fountains, sculpture and stepping stones, before coming to an abrupt halt at a curious piece of modern art that some locals have described as an elongated red-and-blue dog turd.

Gyeonghuigung and the Museum of History

The most anonymous and least visited of Seoul's Five Grand Palaces (even locals who work in the area may struggle to point you towards it) is **Gyeonghuigung** (9am–6pm; closed Mon; free), which was built in 1616. Lonely and a little forlorn, it's a pretty place nonetheless, and may be the palace for you if crowds, souvenir shops and the necessity of avoiding camera sight-lines aren't to your liking. Unlike other palaces, you'll be able to enter the throne room – bare but for the throne, but worth a look – before scrambling up to the halls of the upper level, which are backed with grass and rock.

You might want to make your trip coincide with a visit to the **Museum of History** (Mon–Fri 9am–10pm, Sat & Sun 10am–7pm; closed Mon; W700), a large building sitting adjacent to the palace, and resembling for all intents and purposes a leisure centre. The permanent exhibition is on the third floor and focuses on Joseon-era Seoul. Here you find lacquered boxes with mother-of-pearl inlay, porcelain bowls and vases thrown in gentle shapes, and silk gowns with embroidered leaves and dragons; you may be surprised by how much you assumed to be quintessentially Japanese design actually started in Korea, or at least passed through here first on its way from China. There's a café on the first floor, and on exiting the museum keep an eye out for a strange piece of art across the road – a black metal statue of a man perpetually hammering, a mute reminder to folk from the nearby business district that life's not all about work.

Deoksugung and the Seoul Museum of Art

Its small size, central location and easy access – take exit two from City Hall subway station – ensure that **Deoksugung** (9am–8pm; closed Mon; W1000) is often very busy. This was the last palace of Seoul's Famous Five to be built, and it became the country's seat of power almost by default when the Japanese destroyed Gyeongbokgung (p.89) in 1592, and then again when King Gojong fled here after the assassination of his wife Myeongsong in 1895. Not quite as splendid as the other palaces, Deoksugung is overlooked by the tall grey towers of the City Hall business and embassy area, and includes a couple of Western-style buildings, dating back to when the "Hermit Kingdom" in the latter part of the Joseon dynasty was being forcibly opened up to trade. These neoclassical structures remain the most notable on the complex. At the end of a gorgeous rose garden is Seokjojeon, which was designed by an English architect and built by the Japanese in 1910; the first Western-style building in the country, it was actually used as the royal home for a short time. The second structure was completed in 1938, and was designed and built by the Japanese; inside you'll find the **National Museum for Contemporary Art** (W3000), which is well worth a visit. The steps of the museum are a favourite photo-spot for graduating students – usually in June you may find yourself surrounded by grinning young doctors, accountants or nurses, all dressed up to the nines.

There are English-language **tours** of the palace at 10.30am on weekdays and 1.40pm on weekends, and on every day but Monday traditional **changing of the guard** ceremonies take place outside the main entrance at 11am, 2pm and 3.30pm.

Come out of Deoksugung's main entrance and turn right, and you'll enter a quiet, shaded road that's feels a world removed from the bustle of the City Hall area; you may notice a near-total lack of couples on this road, as Seoulites have long held the superstition that those who walk here will soon break up. Along this road is the large, modern **Seoul Museum of Art** (10am–10pm; closed Mon; W700); it's well worth popping in for a look at what is almost always a fresh, high-quality exhibition of art from around the world. Continuing further up the road, you'll find a few restaurants and cafés, as well as **Chongdong Theatre**, which puts on regular *pansori* performances (see p.133). There's also an array of underground **shopping arcades** in and around City Hall station – one heads towards Myeong-dong, while another heads east for a number of kilometres under the main road of Euljiro.

North of the river

With the palace quarter forming just a tiny part of Seoul, it stands to reason that there's plenty more to see north of the Han, the river that bisects this huge city. The most interesting area is, in fact, that immediately south of the palaces, in a zone bound to the east and west by **Dongdaemun** and **Namdaemun**, two sprawling market complexes, and **Namsan**, a mountain sitting south of the palaces in the very centre of Seoul. The markets are two

North of the river

Markets	
Dongdaemun	동대문
Namdaemun	남대문
Myeong-dong	명동
Bank of Korea Museum	한국은행 박물관
Myeong-dong Cathedral	명동 성당
Namsan Park	남산 공원
Namsangol	남산골
N-Seoul Tower	N-서울 타워
World Cup Stadium	월드컵 경기장
Itaewon	이태원
Daehangno	대학로
Leeum Museum of Art	리움 미술관
Maronnier Park	마로니에 공원
National Museum of Korea	국립중앙박물관
War Memorial Museum	전쟁 기념관
Hongdae	홍대
Sinchon	신촌

of Seoul's must-sees, and most visitors try to visit at least one; whichever you choose, there's an amazing assortment of clothing, textiles, animals, insects, music, food, second-hand cameras and goodness knows what else. Namsan is not so much a must-see as a must-see-from; the mountain offers wonderful views of the city, especially in the evening, when the sun has set and Seoul is painted in swathes of garish neon.

Namdaemun and Dongdaemun

Between them, the colossal markets of **Dongdaemun** and **Namdaemun** could quite conceivably feed, and maybe even clothe, the world. Both are high up on most visitors' list of sights to tick off in Seoul, and deservedly so. Namdaemun literally means "big south door", and Dongdaemun "big east door", referring to the **Great Gates** that once marked the city perimeter; like the palace of Gyeongbokgung and Jongmyo shrine, these were built in the 1390s under the rule of **King Taejo**, as a means of glorifying and protecting his embryonic Joseon dynasty. Both the gates have since undergone extensive repairs, but although Dongdaemun still stands in imperial splendour today, surrounded by spiralling traffic day and night, an arson attack in February 2008 saw Namdaemun savaged by fire.

Dongdaemun market is the largest in the whole country, spread out, open-air and indoors, in various locations along the prettified Cheonggyecheon creek (see p.102). It would be impossible to list the whole range of things on sale here – you'll find yourself walking past anything from herbs to *hanbok* or paper lanterns to pet monkeys, usually on sale for reasonable prices. Though each section of the market has its own opening and closing time, the complex as a whole simply never closes, so at least part of it will be open whenever you decide to come. Night-time is when the market is at its most atmospheric, with clothes stores pumping out music into the street at ear-splitting volume, and the air filled with the smell of freshly made food sizzling at street-side stalls. Though some of the fare on offer is utterly unrecognizable to many foreign visitors, it pays to be adventurous – you may even find something you hadn't expected to like. The market is centred on the high-rise shopping malls south of the creek, in between Dongdaemun and Dongdaemun Stadium subway stations; with numerous floors bursting with cheap clothes, their customer base is usually young and female. Also in this area is the more rustic **Pungmul flea market**, a ramshackle collection of army surplus clothing, second-hand T-shirts and Chinese sex toys, all set in a decaying stadium. There's a **tourist information booth** (daily 9am–6pm) outside the stadium, facing the high-rise malls; they hand out maps of the area that are, in practice, of little use, but staff will be able to direct you to the right section of the market if you've a hankering for anything specific.

Smaller and more compact than Dongdaemun, you'll find essentially the same goods on offer at **Namdaemun market**, which stretches out between City Hall and Seoul station. It's best accessed through Hoehyeon subway station (exits five and six), while Dongdaemun market's spine road runs between Dongdaemun and Dongdaemun Stadium stations.

Myeong-dong

With a justifiable claim to being the most popular shopping area in the whole country, **Myeong-dong** is a dense lattice of streets that runs from the east–west thoroughfare of Euljiro to the northern slopes of Namsan peak. Though visitors to the area are primarily concerned with shopping or eating (see p.122 for a selection of restaurants), there are a couple of sights in the area that are worth a glance while you're here. Most central is the large **Myeong-dong Cathedral**; completed in 1898, it was Korea's first large Christian place of worship, and remains the symbol of the country's ever-growing Catholic community. It wouldn't win any prizes for design in Europe, but in Seoul the towering spire and red brick walls are appealingly incongruous. Nearby is the **Bank of Korea Museum** (10am–5pm; closed Mon; free), though the notes and coins on display are less interesting than the building itself, which was designed and built by the Japanese in the first years of their occupation. A little tricky to find, the museum is best accessed by walking south down the main road from exit seven of Euljiro 1-ga subway station.

East of central Myeong-dong is **Namsangol**, a small display village filled with traditional *hanok* buildings; though a much more interesting and entertaining folk village can be found just south of Seoul (see p.148), this is a more than acceptable solution for those with little time. Take exit three from Chungmuro subway station, and walk away from the main road.

Namsan Park

South of Myeong-dong station the roads rise up, eventually coming to a stop at the feet of **Namsan**, Seoul's resident mountain. There are spectacular **views** of the city from the 265m-high peak, and yet more from the characteristic **N-Seoul Tower**, which sits at the summit. Namsan once marked the natural boundary of a city that has long since swelled over the edges and across the river – some sections of the city wall can still be seen on the mountain, as can the remains of **fire beacons** that formed part of a national communication system during the Joseon period. These were used to relay warnings across the land – one flame lit meant that all was well, while up to five were lit to signify varying degrees of unrest; the message was repeated along chains of beacons that stretched across the

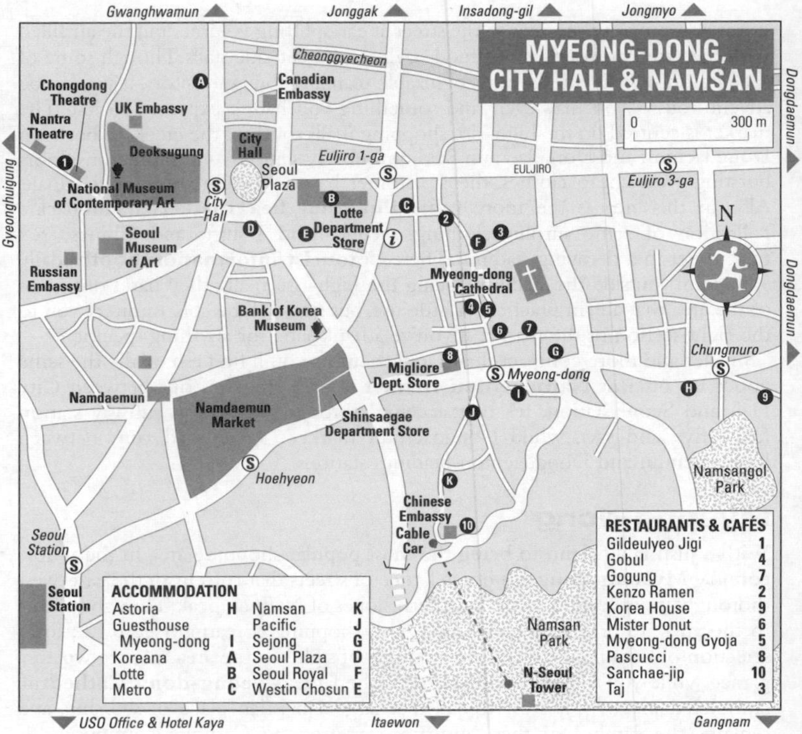

peninsula. Namsan's own are located just above the upper terminal of a **cable car** (daily 10am–11pm; W5000 one-way, W6500 return) that carries most visitors up to the summit. The base is an uphill slog south of Myeong-dong: leave the subway station through exit three, keep going up and you can't miss it. The mountain is also accessible on the yellow **buses** (W550) that ply local route #2 – the best place to catch these is outside exit four of Chungmuro station. It's also possible to **walk** up in under an hour from Seoul station.

The **N-Seoul Tower** (10am–11pm; W7000; Ⓦ www.nseoultower.com) sits proudly on Namsan's crown, newly renovated and recently renamed ("Seoul Tower" clearly wasn't trendy enough). Inside there's a viewing platform and an extortionately overpriced restaurant (meals for two W130,000). For many, the views from the tower's base are good enough, and coming here to see the **sunset** is recommended – the grey mass of daytime Seoul turns in no time into a pulsating neon spectacle. Unless you're up the tower itself, the best place to sit is at the rooftop restaurant near the cable car terminal, which faces north over Myeong-dong and the palaces – throw back a beer and some *pajeon*, and watch Seoul come to life.

Other sights north of the river

Though the palace district and the zone north of Namsan have Seoul's greatest concentration of sights, there are a number of interesting areas north of the Han. From west to east are the **World Cup Stadium**, surrounded by parkland and still home to the occasional big game, the **university areas** of **Hongdae**,

Sinchon and Edea are great for shopping during the day and drinking at night. **Itaewon** is Seoul's "foreigner capital" – a slightly seedy blend of soldiers and suits, but sprinkled with some great restaurants – while **Daehangno** is an arty part of town famed for its theatres.

World Cup Stadium and park

Purpose-built for the World Cup in 2002, this stadium had the honour of hosting the tournament's opening game – Senegal's shock victory over defending champions France – as well as South Korea's heartbreaking semi-final defeat to Germany. **Tours** of the ground are available and there's a small **museum** featuring boots and balls from the World Cup (both daily 9am–6pm; W1000), but the stadium has received fewer visitors since the country woke up to the fact that their 2002 success was something of a flash in the pan. Footie fans would do far better to visit on match day – the ground is now home to FC Seoul of the K-League, and the season runs from March to October, with most games taking place on Sundays. For others, the quiet riverside **park areas** surrounding the stadium are a pleasant place for a family outing, and there's even an excellent 24-hour **spa** inside the ground itself (W5000, or W8000 to stay the night); facilities include all manner of hot-tubs, steam rooms and massage benches, though – sadly – there are no views into the stadium. From here it's also possible to make use of a dedicated **cycle route** – one of the only such paths in the country – that runs for 21km from here to Olympic Park in the east of Seoul, via Yeouido (see p.116).

The university areas

Just west of the city centre lies Seoul's greatest concentration of **universities**, but this is no place to be bookish – as with most academic areas around the country, it's characterized less by what students do during the day than what they get up to at night, and streets are stuffed to the gills with **bars**, nightclubs, karaoke rooms and cheap restaurants. Though there are precious few tourist sights as such, it's possibly the best place in the land to get an understanding of what really makes Korea tick (see the box on p.108 for more on this).

Bound into just a few square kilometres are the universities of Hongik, Yonsei, Ehwa and Sogang. These are located at the peripheries of areas most commonly referred to as Hongdae, Sinchon and Edae, each with a distinctive atmosphere. Hongdae and Edae are colloquial terms for Hongik and Ehwa universities – the Korean tendency is to take the first syllable of the name

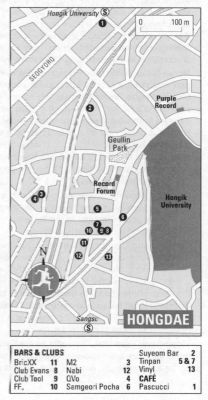

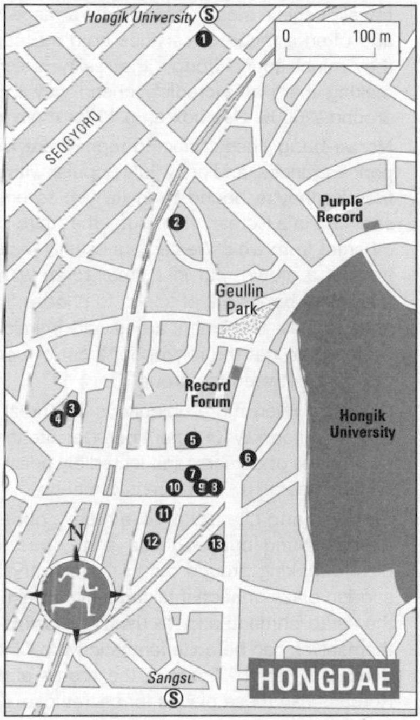

BARS & CLUBS					
BricXX	11	M2	3	Suyeom Bar	2
Club Evans	8	Nabi	12	Tinpan	5 & 7
Club Tool	9	QVo	4	Vinyl	13
FF.	10	Samgeori Pocha	6	**CAFÉ**	
				Pascucci	1

A banging good time

University areas are a good place to get a grip on the **"bang"** culture that pervades modern Korean life. The term is a suffix meaning "room", and is attached to all sorts of places where locals – and occasional foreigners – like to have fun. Below are a few of the most popular:

Da-bang These are a strange mix of café and hostess bar, where "coffee girls" occasionally serve more than just coffee; more often the customers merely pay for company and flattery. Though far less common in cities than they used to be, you'll still see plenty in provincial towns and villages, where women and customers alike tend to be much older; in cities, goods are usually relayed to thirsty customers by moped – if you see a young woman wearing a miniskirt and high-heels buzzing by on a 50cc engine, it's safe to assume that this is her line of work.

DVD-bang Imagine a small room with wipe-clean sofas, tissue paper on hand and a large television for movies – if it sounds a little sleazy, you'd be absolutely right. Though people do occasionally come to appreciate plot, cinematography or Oscar-winning performances, these places are more often used by couples looking for a cheap bit of privacy – going in by yourself, or with a person of the same sex, would draw some baffled looks. Figure on around W11,000 per movie.

Game-bang Filled with all manner of board-games, these rooms underwent a surge in popularity – a strange development, considering the country's love for digital forms of entertainment – but don't see many foreign guests.

Jjimjilbang Popular with families, teenagers and the occasional budget-minded traveller, these steam rooms have a range of hot and cold pools, and sauna rooms, and often a range of services from massage treatment to Internet booths. Though they might sound dodgy, the reality is somewhat tamer; most are open all night, making them an incredibly cheap way to get a night's sleep – prices tend to be around W6000. See box on p.41 for more information.

Norae-bang These "singing rooms" are all over the country, even outside national park entrances, and are wildly popular with people of all ages; if you have any Korean friends, they're bound to invite you to one before long, as *noraebang* are usually *sam-cha* in a Korean night out – the "third step" after meal and drinks. The system is different from what Westerners usually expect of a karaoke room – you don't sing in front of a crowd, but in a small room with your friends, where you'll find sofas, a television, books full of songs to choose from and a couple of maracas or tambourines to play. Foreigners are usually intimidated at first, but after a few drinks it can be tough to get the microphone out of people's hands. Figure on around W15,000 per hour between the group.

PC-bang Even more ubiquitous in Korea are places to get online, which cost an almost uniform W1000 per hour. Despite the prevalence of such places, they're often packed full of gamers, and incredibly noisy – you're likely to be the only one sending emails. See p.137 for more information.

Sarang-bang Literally a "love room", but essentially a motel, these can be found in teams around busy nightlife areas, bus terminals and train stations, but also in bizarre-looking groups out in the countryside – you may well see one appear in a sudden blaze of neon if taking a night train. Prices vary depending on the location of the establishment, and it's usually possible to pay by the hour. The building designs themselves can be quite fantastic: with Cinderella-style castle turrets on the outside, deep red "mood" lights in the rooms and heart-shaped beds to sleep on, many Koreans use these places for secret love.

Video-bang Essentially the same as the DVD-*bang*, but older, grubbier and half the price, these are slowly being phased out in the digital revolution, but are likely to hang on for a fair while yet. A movie here will cost around W7000.

and add the *–dae* from *daehakkyo*, which means university – and it's these names that you're most likely to hear.

Hongdae is one of the most beguiling areas in the whole country, teeming with young and trendy people at almost every hour. There's plenty to see during the day – many streets are lined with small shops selling stylish and used clothing, and there are quirky cafés on every corner – but it's at night that it really comes into its own. Packed with revellers every night of the week, it's without doubt Korea's most popular nightlife area; it starts getting busy from late afternoon, and slowly sucks in most of the city's clubbers and bar-crawlers (see p.128 for more information). Exit five from Hongik University subway station will put you in the thick of the daytime action, though most of the clubs and bars are nearer Sangsu station on line 6 – take exit one and walk uphill for a few minutes.

East of Hongdae – and just one subway station away on line 2 – is **Sinchon**; this area offers much the same delights as Hongdae, but is not as trendy or nearly as busy. Though a little confusing for the first-time visitor, the main area is situated north of Sinchon subway station – take exit two or three. **Edae**, two subway stops east (and sometimes written "Idae"), is the only major university in Seoul to cater exclusively to women. As a result, the area is packed not so much with bars and clubs, but with hundreds of shops selling clothes, shoes, make-up and fashion accessories.

Itaewon

One of Seoul's most famed quarters, **Itaewon** is something of an enigma. It has, for years, been popular with American soldiers, thanks to the major military base situated nearby. Expat businessmen and visiting foreigners have followed suit, and until English teachers started pouring into Korea by the planeload it was one of the only places in the country in which you could buy "Western" items such as leather jackets, deodorant, tampons or Hershey's Kisses. While it remains a great place to shop for cheap tailored suits and shoes, Itaewon's popularity also made it a byword for transactions of a more sexual nature – **hostess bars** sprung up all over the place, particularly south of the *Hamilton*, a hotel that marks the centre of the area, on the affectionately named "Hooker Hill". Times are changing, however. Most Western goods are available in cities across the country, and the gradual withdrawal of American troops has coincided with the opening of an ever more cosmopolitan array of restaurants

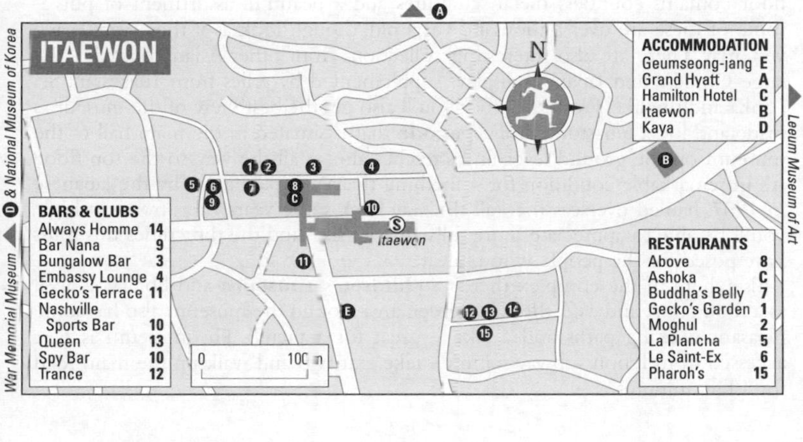

(see p.125), possibly the hippest in the city outside ultra-fashionable Apgujeong. The area is also heaving with clubbers on weekends, and from Hooker Hill also sprouts "Homo Hill", Seoul's only real gay area. For more details on Itaewon's bars and clubs, see p.130.

Sights in the area are set away from the centre of Itaewon. To the west is the **War Memorial Museum** (9.30am–5.30pm; closed Mon; W3000), a place of moderate interest that charts the history of warfare from ancient stones and arrows to more modern machines such as B-52 bombers and the Scud missile. Take exit twelve from Samgakji subway station. Those with less pugnacious tastes can head east of Itaewon to the excellent **Leeum Museum of Art** (10.30am–6pm; closed Mon; W10,000; Ⓦwww.leeum.org), which is not so much a museum as one of the most esteemed galleries in the country. It's split into several halls, each with a distinctive and original design; one, built in black concrete, was designed by acclaimed Dutch architect Rem Koolhaas, who has since busied himself on the fantastic CCTV headquarters in Beijing. The museum hosts the occasional special exhibition of world famous artists, both past and present – works from such luminaries as Mark Rothko and Damien Hirst have been displayed here. It's within walking distance from Itaewon, about fifteen minutes east of the subway station, but access is slightly faster from exit one of Hangangjin station.

National Museum of Korea

The **National Museum of Korea** (9am–6pm, Wed & Sat to 9pm, Sun to 7pm; closed Mon; W2000) used to be based in Gyeongbokgung, but was moved in 2005 to a huge building just north of the Han. This museum is a Seoul must-see for anyone interested in history, and houses over 11,000 artefacts in the museum's collection, including an incredible 94 official National Treasures; only a fraction of these will be on show at any one time. Among the many rooms on the ground level are exhibitions from the **Three Kingdoms** period, which showcase the incredible skill of the artisans during that time – gold, silver and bronze have been cast into ornate shapes, the highlight being a fifth-century crown and belt set that once belonged to a Silla king. Moving up a floor the focus shifts to paintings, calligraphy and wooden art, and there's usually a colossal **Buddhist scroll** or two, over ten metres high; some were hung behind the Buddha statue in temples' main halls, while others were used for such purposes as praying for rain. The museum owns quite a few, but due to the fragility of the material, they're put on a rota system and displays are changed regularly. The uppermost floor contains countless metal sculptures and a beautiful assortment of pots – some of these are over a thousand years old, though look as if they were made yesterday. There are also interesting collections from other Asian countries, the large Chinese and Japanese displays supplemented by relics from Turkestan, Sri Lanka and the like. From this floor you'll also get the best view of the museum's pride and joy, a ten-storey stone **pagoda** that is situated in the main hall of the museum on the ground level, and stretches almost all the way to the top floor. It's in remarkable condition for something that was taken apart by the Japanese in 1907, hauled overseas then all the way back some years later; from on high, you'll be able to appreciate more fully its true size, and the difficulties this must have posed for the people who built it.

Elsewhere in the complex there's a **children's museum** and library, as well as a food court and café; the wide, green area around the museum also has some pleasant walking paths and a lake – great for a picnic. The museum is best accessed from Ichon subway station – take exit two and walk up the main road for a few minutes.

Daehangno

With a buzzing yet artily alternative ambience, a near-total dearth of American soldiers or camera-toting tourists, and the cheapest guesthouses in Seoul (see box, p.82), studenty **Daehangno** has become very popular with backpackers in the know. Literally meaning "college street", it's actually the name of the road that heads north from Dongdaemun market, but most of the action takes place in a tightly packed area around Hyehwa subway station on line 4. The area has been a **student mecca** ever since the opening of Seoul National University in 1946; while this has since moved elsewhere, the presence of at least four more institutions keeps this place full of life. It's almost choked with bars, games rooms and cheap restaurants but has more recently attained national fame for its youthful **theatre scene**. Over thirty establishments big and small can be found dotting the side streets east of Hyehwa station – take exit one or two – but be warned that very few performances are in English. There are usually free shows in **Marronnier Park**, which lies a short walk along the road from Hyehwa station's exit two. Here performers make their first tentative steps on their hopeful road to stardom, seeking to drum up custom for later performances or showcase their talents, and you can often catch short bursts of magic, music, comedy or mime, all going on at the same time.

South of the river

Before Seoul outgrew its boundaries and spread over most of the northwest of the country, the city's southern perimeter ran through Namsan, north of the river. Accordingly, the capital's historical sights become sparser on the south side of the Han River; still, to appreciate just how life ticks along in this fine city you'd do well to spend some time here. Each district has its own particular flavour and breed of Seoulite – **Yeouido** has its mass of suits, **Gangnam** its fun-seekers, **Apgujeong** its flocks of ultra-fashionable. Heading east to the district of Jamsil, you can visit the grassy regal tomb mounds in **Samneung**

South of the river	
Yeouido	여의도
63 Building	63 빌딩
Gangnam	강남
Seorae Maeul	서래마을
Apgujeong	압구정
Dosan Park	도산 공원
Jamsil	잠실
COEX Mall	코엑스 몰
Lotte World	롯데 월드
Olympic Park	올림픽 공원
Olympic Stadium	올림픽 경기장
Samneung Park	삼능 공원
Seoul Grand Park	서울 그랜드 파크
National Museum of Contemporary Art	국립 현대 미술관
Seoul Land	서울 랜드

Park, go shopping at the gigantic **COEX mall**, or get your kicks at **Lotte World**, one of the largest theme parks in the country.

Yeouido

Though it's an island, you'd do well to banish any romantic visions before arriving in **YEOUIDO**. Meaning something akin to "useless land", it finally underwent development during Park Chung-hee's economic reforms in the 1970s, and is now one of South Korea's most important **business districts**, not to mention the home of its National Assembly and the 63 Building, formerly the tallest structure in the land. However, as Yeouido is manifestly a place to work, rather than live or go out, it has some of the quietest roads in the city. In fact, most of the northern fringe has been turned into a **riverside park**, which is a popular weekend picnicking place for Seoul families; here you can hire pedal-driven swan-boats, though **bike riding** is the most popular activity (mainly due to it being impracticable elsewhere in the city). There are hire stalls under Wonhyo bridge, the easternmost of three major roads that cross Yeouido to connect Seoul's north and south banks. Bikes are W3000 per hour, and double that for a tandem; kids' bikes are also available. A dedicated **cycle route** continues west to the World Cup Stadium (7km return; cross the river on Yanghwa bridge), or east all the way to Olympic Park. The latter is 35km return, though it's all same-level riding, and the pleasant views mean that this is one of the best ways to spend a sunny day in Seoul. It's also possible to take a **riverboat trip** from near Wonhyo bridge to Jamsil – there are round-trips (90min; W9900) every hour or so, and a few one-way trips each afternoon for the same price.

A short walk south of the bridge is the island's only real sight – the **63 Building**. A distinctive golden tower 249m in height, it was the tallest structure in Asia when completed in 1985, though had already lost the title by the time the Olympics rolled into town three years later, and is now even struggling to stay in the national top ten. The sixtieth-floor **observation deck** (daily 10am–11pm; W7000) provides predictably good views of Seoul, and is actually at the top of the building, the other three floors from the building's name being basement levels. Back near ground level are an **aquarium** (10am–10pm; W12,000) and an **Imax cinema** (10am–8pm; W8000), though both are somewhat dated and of questionable value.

Gangnam

Gangnam is one of those Seoul areas that is utterly devoid of traditional tourist sights, but an absorbing place to walk around. Streets around Gangnam subway station – especially to the northeast – are popular with young Koreans, and crammed full of cafés and cheap restaurants (see pp.125–126). One interesting place nearby, and one that doesn't feature on many tourist brochures, is **Seorae Maeul**, a peculiar "Frenchtown". Here live some of Seoul's more moneyed European expats, many drawn by the French school just up the way. The cosmopolitan nature is manifest in a tranquil air quite rare in Seoul, as well as a number of international restaurants (though, oddly, most of them are Italian, rather than French). While it's a little hard to track down, Seorae Maeul may appeal to those who need a breather from Seoul proper – take exit five from the Express Bus Terminal subway station, cross the main road and head right past the *Palace Hotel* until you see a footbridge; Seorae Maeul will be on your left.

Apgujeong

Seoulites refer to **Apgujeong** as "Korea's Beverly Hills", and the comparison is not far off the mark – if Louis Vuitton bags are your thing, look no further. Boutique clothing stores, chic restaurants and European-style outdoor cafés line streets frequented by a disproportionate number of Seoul's young and beautiful, but note that their good looks may not be entirely natural – this is also Korea's plastic surgery capital, and clinics are ubiquitous. Though there are no real sights as such, Apgujeong is one of the most interesting places in Korea to sit down with a skinny latte and people-watch.

The best cafés and restaurants (see p.126 for details) huddle in a pleasantly relaxed, leafy area outside the main entrance to **Dosan Park**. Heading further north, past the clothes shops and plastic surgeons, you'll eventually come out onto Apgujeongno, the area's main road, which features the most exclusive clothes shops and department stores in Korea (see p.135).

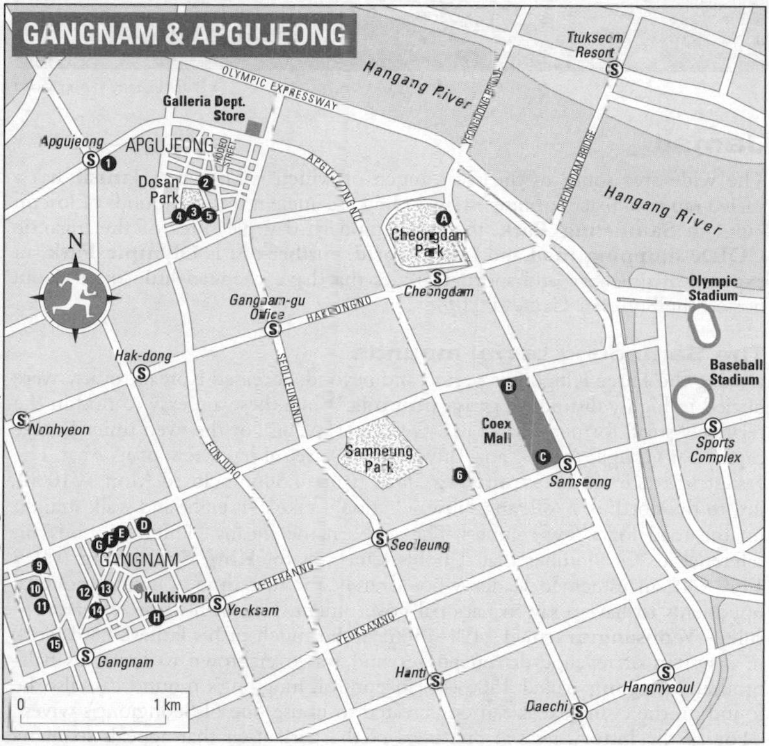

ACCOMMODATION		RESTAURANTS				CAFÉ	
COEX Intercontinental	B	Arte	7	La Trouvaille	8	Ceci Cela	5
Grand Intercontinental	C	Asian Live	C	Mashinneun Gogijip	9	Igloo	1
Jelly	H	Bombay	11	Oga-no Ju-bang	4	Jiin	5
Novotel Ambassador	F	Bongchu Jjim-dak	12	Pasha	15	Luxury Gongja	13
Richmond	D	Crystal Jade Palace	B	Pink Spoon	4	**BAR**	
Ritz-Carlton	G	Gorilla In The Kitchen	3	Slow Food	4	Blush	B
Riviera	A	Hakone	B	Sushiko	10	Marcie	6
Samjung	E	Hofbrauhaus	14	Tell Me About It...	2		

▲ Retail therapy in Apgujeong

Jamsil

The wide area south of the river, much of which is known as **Jamsil**, has a varied range of places of interest, including the ancient burial mounds of Joseon kings in **Samneung Park**, the more modern-day pleasures of the gigantic **COEX shopping mall** and **Lotte World**. Further east is **Olympic Park**, an expanse of greenery and sports facilities that have changed little since Seoul hosted the Summer Games in 1988.

The Samneung burial mounds

During the Three Kingdoms period and beyond, deceased Korean royalty were buried in highly distinctive **grass mounds**. While these are easy to find in the relatively small former Silla capital Gyeongju (p.206), or the even tinier Baekje capitals of Gongju (p.319) and Buyeo (p.323), Seoul has a few of its own. The easiest to reach are in **Samneung Park** (6am–4.30pm; closed Mon; W1000), just to the north of Seolleung subway station – take exit eight and walk straight up the road for a few minutes. The park's name means "Three Mounds" in reference to the number that it holds. One was for **King Seongjong** (ruled 1469–94), an esteemed leader who – rarely, for that time – invited political opponents to have a say in national government. Two of his sons went on to rule – **Yeonsangun** (ruled 1494–1506) undid much of his father's hard work in a system of revenge-driven purges, and was overthrown to leave his half-brother **Jungjong** (ruled 1506–44) in control. Jungjong's mound can also be found on the complex, as can one created to house one of Seongjong's wives.

For all the history, it's the prettiness of the park itself that appeals to many visitors, a green refuge from grey Seoul crisscrossed by gorgeous **wooded pathways**. The area is popular with employees from nearby offices, many of whom come here during their lunch break to munch a sandwich or go for a jog. Its early opening times mean that you'll be able to visit at daybreak, which can often be a rather atmospheric experience, dew sitting on the grass and the nearby buildings occluded by morning mist.

COEX Mall

This huge underground **shopping mall** is a popular place for tourists to spend a rainy day. The mass of shops, restaurants and wall-to-wall people can be quite bewildering, but there are a couple of tourist attractions on site; one of these is the **Kimchi Museum** (daily 10am–5pm, Sat & Sun from 1pm; W3000), the only facility in the land dedicated to this national dish (see the *Korean cuisine* colour insert), and worth a poke around. The **COEX Aquarium** (10am–8pm; W16,500) sees far more visitors and has been designed with flair – this must be the only aquarium in the world to use toilets as goldfish tanks, though mercifully there are normal facilities for public use. Sharks, manta rays and colourful shoals are on display, and most visitors come away impressed. Other activities within the mall include a pool hall, a board game café and a large multiscreen cinema. Also part of the complex are a couple of five-star hotels (see p.87), which house some of Seoul's best restaurants (pp.125–126).

Lotte World

This local version of Disneyland is incredibly popular – the complex receives over five million tourists per year, and it's hard to find a Korean child, or even an adult, who hasn't been here at some point. While it may not be quite what some are looking for on their visit to Korea, **Lotte World** (daily 9.30am–11pm; day-tickets W34,000 adults, W25,000 children; after 5pm W26,000 & W20,000; Ⓦ www.lotteworld.com) can be a lot of fun, particularly for those travelling with children. It comprises two theme parks: indoor Lotte World Adventure and outdoor Magic Island, the latter in the middle of a lake and accessed by monorail from the former. Also on the complex is a bowling alley (9am–midnight; W3000 plus shoe rental), an overpriced ice rink (10am–9pm; W12,000 plus skate rental), and a large swimming pool (noon–7pm, Sat & Sun to 8pm; W8000). The complex is an easy walk from Jamsil subway station; you'll see signs pointing the way from the ticket gates.

The 1988 Summer Olympics

Seoul's hosting of the **Olympic Games** in 1988 was a tremendous success, bringing pride not just to the city, but to the whole nation. In fact, it did much to make Korea the country that it is today, and has even been credited with bringing democracy to the nation. President **Park Chung-hee** had been first to toy with the idea of bidding for the games in the 1970s, seemingly wishing to win international approval for his authoritarian running of the country; he was assassinated in 1979, but the bid went ahead. However, large-scale protests against the government in the years running up to the games brought a hitherto unprecedented level of international scrutiny, and direct elections took place in 1987.

The games themselves were no less interesting and produced several moments which have become part of sporting folklore. The USA's **Greg Louganis** managed to win a second consecutive gold medal in the three-metre springboard dive after an incredible comeback; after bloodying the pool by walloping his head on the dive-board, he somehow followed with a perfect dive that was enough to propel him into first place. A lesser-known tale is that of Canadian sailor **Lawrence Lemieux**, who sacrificed a probable medal to race to the aid of two Singaporean competitors who had been thrown into the water in treacherous conditions. However, the Games' defining moment came in the final of the men's 100m, where **Ben Johnson**, also from Canada, sped to the line in a world record time of 9.79 seconds; once he'd finally slowed down enough for the drugs testing unit to catch up with him, he was revealed to have tested positive for steroid use, and the gold went instead to Carl Lewis of the USA.

Olympic Park

This large park (24hr; free) was built for the **1988 Summer Olympics**, which were held in Seoul (see box, p.115). It remains a popular picnicking place for Seoul families, and hosts a regular assortment of festivals – you're likely to see one if you turn up on a weekend. Near the eastern entrance to the park – take subway line 5 to Olympic Park – you'll see a number of facilities that remain from the games, including a couple of gymnasiums and the indoor swimming pool, though very few are actually open for public use – there's a general air of decay about the place but this is part of the appeal. The **tennis courts** are usually left unlocked, however, and though it can't be advised you could probably jump down and get a few games in before anybody notices. Interestingly, the order of play from the Olympics is still in place outside the ground, and through the peeling paint you can see the routes that Miroslav Macir and Steffi Graf took to their gold medals. On the way into the park, you'll pass by buildings and sculptures displaying the rather Stalinist themes that were in vogue in 1980s Seoul – some of this would look quite at home in Pyongyang, and those with interests in art and architecture may find the area quite absorbing. The park itself is crisscrossed by a great number of paths, but it's best to stick to the south where the main concentration of sights are. Past the Olympic velodrome – still a popular gambling venue for elderly Seoulites in summer months – is an interesting **sculpture park** and **SOMA** (10am–8pm; closed Mon; W3000), an excellent modern art gallery. Collections in the latter are interesting, but they're often outdone by the **Papertainer Museum** (daily 10am–6pm; W10,000) just down the way. The building's shell is made from old steel containers and paper tubes, while inside exhibits focus on such themes as marketing as art which sheds new light on the aims of corporate logos and the like. All of these places are best accessed from Mongcheontoseong subway station on line 8, as is the **Olympic Museum** (10am–5pm; closed Mon; W3000), which may appeal to sports buffs – there's a collection of Olympic torches from various games, as well as an exhibit showing just how terrifying Olympic mascots have been through the years (Atlanta's "Izzy" and Barcelona's "Cobi", the cubist Catalan sheepdog, being just two examples). Outside the museum, flags from the 159 countries that competed in the games stand in a semi-circle; though several countries have since merged, split or changed their flags, the authorities have decided to leave the originals as a symbol of what the world was like at the time of Seoul's biggest party – the Soviet and Yugoslav flags remain, but there's no South Africa, the country at that time having been banned from competing. The **Olympic Stadium** itself is actually a few subway stations to the west, and can usually still be entered during the day for a nose around.

Seoul Grand Park area

Seven subway stops south of the Han River on line 4 is **Seoul Grand Park** (daily 9.30am–9pm; W1500), one of the largest expanses of greenery in Seoul, and one of the best places in the capital to take children for a fun day out. The highlight is its **zoo**, home to animals from around the world, and the venue of daily animal shows (1.30pm & 3pm, also 11.30am & 4.30pm March–Oct). In 2005, six elephants escaped during one of these events, and were only caught hours later after trashing a restaurant and wading through a nearby resident's garden; needless to say, security has been tightened, and a repeat pachyderm performance is unlikely. To get to Seoul Grand Park, take exit two from the subway station of the same name. The entrance is just fifteen minutes' walk away, or you can take a tram train (W600) or a chairlift (W4500).

Other attractions in the park area are **Seoul Land** (same times; entry W12,000, day-pass for rides W28,000), a large amusement park with enough rollercoasters, spinning rides and spectacular performances to keep guests amused, and the **National Museum of Contemporary Art** (March–Oct Mon–Fri 10am–6pm, Sat & Sun to 9pm; Nov–Feb to 5pm, Sat & Sun to 8pm; closed Mon; W1000), an excellent collection from some of the biggest movers and shakers in the Korea modern art scene.

Bukhansan National Park

Few major cities can claim to have a national park right on their doorstep, but looming over central Seoul, and forming a natural northern boundary to the city, are the peaks of **BUKHANSAN NATIONAL PARK**, spears and spines of off-white granite that burst out of the undulating pine forests. Despite the park's relatively small size at just 80sq km, its proximity to one of earth's most populated cities makes it the **world's most visited** national park, drawing in upwards of five million visitors per year. Of course, most of these are lucky locals who can make their way from home to the park by subway, but

Culinary curiosities

While even "regular" Korean food may be utterly alien to most visitors, there are a few edibles that deserve special attention:

Baem soju Not strictly a food, but interesting nonetheless – this is regular *soju* with a snake (*baem*) marinating in the bottle, which is said to be extremely healthy, especially for the back muscles. Though many may feel that the bottles would make wonderful souvenirs, particularly with the larger serpents inside, be warned that international customs officials aren't too fond of you taking them.

Beonddegi In colder months, stalls selling this local delicacy – silkworm larvae – set up on pavements and riverbanks across the whole country. The smell of these mites boiled up in a broth is so disgusting that it may well breach international law. The treat is also served as bar snacks in many *hofs*, bursting in the mouth to release a grimy juice – perfect drinking game material.

Dak-pal So you've learnt the word for "chicken" in Korean (*dak*), spotted it on the menu and ordered a dish. Unfortunately, with this particular meal the suffix means "foot", and that's just what you get – dozens of sauced-up chicken feet on a plate, with not an ounce of meat in sight.

Gae-gogi This is dog meat, but let it be known that – contrary to the expectations of many a traveller – it rarely features on Korean menus: you're not going to get it on your plate unless you go to a dedicated restaurant. It's usually served in a soup: *yeongyangtang* and *bosintang* are its most common incarnations.

Pojangmacha Plastic chairs to sit on, tables littered with *soju* bottles, and a cackling *ajumma* serving you food that's still half-alive – these are the delights of the *pojang-macha*, ramshackle seafood dens that congregate on many a Korean street. They're usually distinguishable by their orange, tent-like covering; one good area to find them in Seoul is outside exits three to six of Jongno 3-ga subway station. Just watch out for the octopus tentacles – every year, people die of suffocation when their still-wriggling prey makes a last bid for freedom.

Sundae Don't let the romanization fool you – this is nothing whatsoever to do with ice cream. In Korea, it's actually a sausage made with intestinal lining, and stuffed with clear noodles – head to the nearest market to try some.

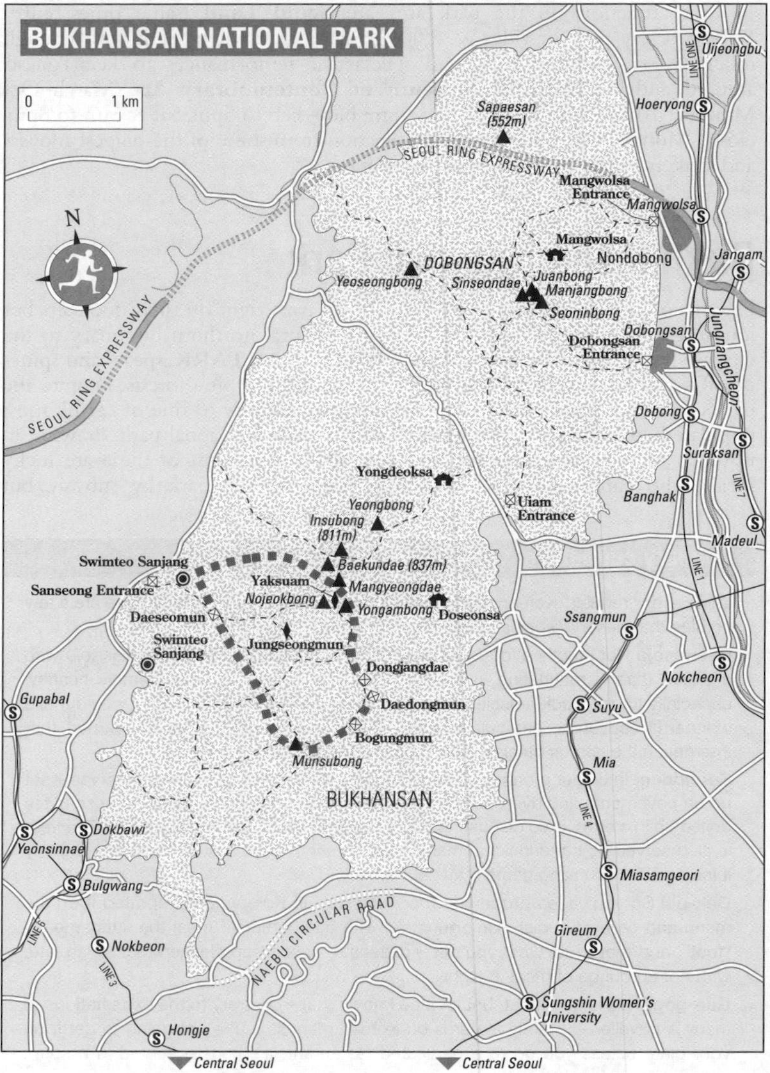

Bukhansan features on the schedules of many foreign visitors to the country. While an undeniably beautiful place, its popularity means that trails are often very busy indeed – especially so on warm weekends – and some can be as crowded as shopping mall aisles, hikers literally having to queue up to reach the peaks. Those looking for a more "natural" experience should consider heading to one of the other twenty-odd national parks around the country, though hiking is so popular in Korea that in peak season, some of these will be almost as full (see the *Hiking* colour section for more information).

With its position overlooking Seoul, the area has played a large role historically in protecting the city. In the second century a **fortress** was built during the capital's earliest days as the hub of the Baekje dynasty. Sizeable fortifications were constructed during the rule of King Sukjong (1661–1720), a leader notable for his peacemaking abilities in a time of national and international strife: not only did he pacify the warring factions that threatened to tear the peninsula apart, he negotiated with the Chinese Qing dynasty to define the borders between the two countries at the Yalu and Tumen rivers. These remain in place today, albeit under the control of Pyongyang, rather than Seoul, and it was while the two halves of Korea were jostling for control of the peninsula during the Korean War that much of Bukhansan's fortress was destroyed. Remnants of the wall can still be found, including much of the section that stretched down from the mountains to connect with Seoul's city wall – get off at Dongnimun station, one stop west of Gyeongbokgung on subway line 3, to reach the southern terminus of this linking section.

Hiking in Bukhansan

The national park can be split into the north and south areas. The southern section – **Bukhansan** proper – overlooks Seoul and is home to the fortress ruins, while 10km to the north is **Dobongsan**, a similar maze of stony peaks and hiking trails. Both offer good day-trip routes which are easy enough to be tackled by most visitors, but still enough of a challenge to provide a good work-out.

Southern Bukhansan

The southern half of Bukhansan is best accessed through **Sanseong**, an entry point on the western side of the park. To reach this, head first to Gupabal station on subway line 3, and walk from exit one to the small bus stop. From here, bus #704 (10min; W900) makes the run to the park entrance; get off when everyone else does. On the short walk to the clutch of restaurants that surround the entrance, you'll see the park's principal peaks soaring above; unless you're visiting on a weekend, the hustle and bustle of downtown Seoul will already feel a world away. There's some simple accommodation available at *Swimteo Sanjang* (❷), a small motel-restaurant a few minutes walk from the entrance.

It's around two hours from the entrance to **Baekundae** (837m), the highest peak in the park, though note that the masses tramping through Bukhansan have resulted in routes being closed off in rotation to allow them time to regenerate – bilingual signs will point the way. Around ten minutes into your walk you'll find yourself at **Daeseomun**, one of the main gates of the fortress wall. From here, it's a long slog up to Baekundae; once you've reached **Yaksuam**, a lofty hermitage, you're almost there (and will doubtless be grateful for the presence of spring-water drinking fountains). Continuing on, the route becomes more precipitous, necessitating the use of steel stairways and fences. Having finally scaled the peak itself, you'll be able to kick off your boots awhile and enjoy the wonderful, panoramic views. Hard to miss will be **Insubong**, an 811m-high peak faced with a sheer granite wall; though it's possible to scale, this is best left to professional climbers with the necessary equipment.

From Baekundae, the easiest route back to the park entrance is along the same route, though there are other options. One trail heads south, squeezing between some neighbouring peaks to Yongammun, another fortress gate. From here – depending on which paths are open – you can head downhill towards Jungseongmun (another gate) then follow the pretty stream to the park entrance, or take a half-hour detour along a ridge further south to Daedongmun gate. Those seeking a sterner challenge can head yet further southwest of

Daedongmun to **Munsubong** peak, then take the punishing up-and-down route back to the park entrance – from the entrance, the whole round-trip via Baekundae and Munsubong will be a full-day hike.

It's also possible to exit the park at different locations – from Baekundae, a two-hour route heads east to Uiam entrance via the temple of **Yongdeoksa**; while from Yongammun, a trail heads downhill to **Doseonsa**, the park's principal temple; and from Bogungmun – a gate just south of Daedongmun – a path drops down the **Jeongneung** valley to the entrance of the same name.

Northern Bukhansan

The scenery in the **Dobongsan** area is much the same as around Baekundae to the south – trees, sumptuous rock formations and wonderful views at every turn – though the hiking options are less numerous. Most choose to scale the main peak (740m) on a C-shaped route that curls uphill and down between **Mangwolsa** and **Dobongsan**, two subway stations on line 1. It's hard to say which direction is better, but most head from Dobongsan. From this station, cross the main road, then go left along the perimeter of a dense network of ramshackle snack bars, then right up the main road. Whichever way you go, it takes just over two hours up to the gathering of peaks at the top; like Baeundae to the south of the park, the upper reaches of the trail are patches of bare rock, and you'll be grateful for the steel ropes on which you can haul yourself up or down.

Eating

You're unlikely to go hungry in Seoul. Food is cheap by international standards and invariably of excellent quality, while the number of **restaurants** is nothing short of astonishing – there's almost literally one on every corner, and many more in between. Korean food has a well-deserved reputation as one of the spiciest around; those looking for something a little blander can make use of an ever-growing choice of global cuisine, or breakfast at one of the many **bakeries** strewn around the city (note, however, that Korean bread is rather sweet for many foreigners' tastes). Restaurants are usually open whenever you're likely to require food, and some are 24hr; if you do get stuck, you'll easily be able to track down one of Seoul's seemingly infinite number of **convenience stores** – large chains include 7-Eleven, Mini Stop and Buy the Way – which sell drinks and fast food. All have hot water for instant noodles and small tables outside for eating; partaking in this highly Korean activity will endear you to any passing locals. Those looking for something even more authentic should head to one of Seoul's many **markets**, those at Dongdaemun and Namdaemun being the most popular. Also note that the consumption of food has long been entwined with drink in Korea; many **bars**, including some of those listed from pp.129–131, serve meals every bit as good as you'd find in a restaurant.

Restaurants

Seoul's excellent choice of **restaurants** is growing more cosmopolitan with each passing year. They run the full gamut from super-polished establishments in five-star hotels to local **snack bars** where stomachs can be filled for just W1000; even in the cheapest places, you may be surprised by the quality of the food. With much of the national cuisine alien to most foreign guests, it may be easier to head for the **food courts** in department stores and shopping malls, where you can see plastic versions of the available dishes. Also popular are the

Seoul restaurants

Above	아버브
Arte	아르테
Ashoka	아쇼카
Asian Live	아시안 라이브
Bär in	베어린
Benigni	베니니
Bombay	봄베이
Bongchu Jjim-dak	봉추 찜닭
Buddha's Belly	부다스 벨리
Cheondungsori	천둥소리
Cheonjin Pocha	천진 포차
Crystal Jade Palace	크리스탈 제이드 팰러스
Gecko's Garden	게코스 가든
Gildeulyeo Jigi	길들여 지기
Gobul	고불
Gogung	고궁
Gorilla In The Kitchen	고릴라 인 더 키친
Gung-yeon	궁연
Hakone	하꼬네
Hofbrauhaus	호프브로이하우스
Hyangnamu	향나무 세그루
Imok-de	이목데
Janchijip	잔치집
Kenzo Ramen	켄조 라멘
Korea House	한국의집
La Plancha	라 플란차
La Trouvaille	라 트루바이
Le Saint-Ex	레 상텍스
Mashinneun Gogijip	맛있는 고기집
Meokswi Donna	먹쉬돈나
Mister Donut	미스터 도넛
Moghul	모글
Myeong-dong Gyoja	명동 교자
Oga-no Ju-bang	오가노 주방
Pasha	파샤
Pharoh's	파로스
Pink Spoon	핑크 스푼
The Place	더 플레이스
Pu-reun Byeol Gwigeun Yeo-u	푸른별귀큰여우
The Restaurant	더 레스토랑
Sanchae-jip	산채집
Sanchon	산촌
Shabis	샤비스
Slow Food	느리게걷기
Solmoe Maeul	솔뫼마을
Sushiko	스시꼬
Taj	타지
Tell Me About It...	텔미어바웃잇
Teol-bo-ne	털보네
Top Cloud	톱 클라우드
Wood&Brick	나무와벽돌
Yeongbin Garden	영빈 가든

snack chains such as *Gimbap Cheon-guk* and *Gimbap Nara*, who serve basic Korean staples such as *gimbap*, soups, *ramyeon* and pork cutlet at low, low prices (and often at incredible speed).

Reservations and tips are unheard of at all but the classiest places, and unlike elsewhere in the land, English-language menus are quite common; though note that romanization is woefully inconsistent. For example, *gimchi jjigae* can be rendered as *kimchi zzigae*, *gimchee chigae* and the like.

Many parts of Seoul have their own particular culinary flavour. Most popular with tourists are the streets around **Insadong-gil**, where restaurants almost exclusively serve traditional Korean food in an equally fitting atmosphere. Then there's cosmopolitan Itaewon, where local restaurants are outnumbered by those serving Indian, Japanese, Thai or Italian food, among others. Student areas such as Hongdae and Daehangno are filled with cheap eateries, while Gangnam is also popular with local youth, and trendy Apgujeong with the fashionistas.

Myeong-dong, City Hall and Namsan

All the places listed below are marked on the Myeong-dong, City Hall and Namsan map, p.106.

Gildeulyeo Jigi Jeong-dong ⓣ02/319-7083. The restaurant's name is a quote from the Korean translation of *The Little Prince*, and the decoration here is accordingly esoteric. Diners often fall in here on their way out of Chongdong Theatre (see p.133) underneath, to feast on spaghetti or grilled meat – salmon with herb pepper sauce is particularly recommended.

Gobul Myeong-dong. Cheap, filling food in a fresh-looking diner, where beads hang from the ceiling and the walls are decorated with plastic chilli peppers. W4500 will buy you chicken, octopus, beef or pork cutlet with rice and vegetables, all of which will be smothered in a spicy paste. Larger meals are also available.

Gogung Myeong-dong ⓣ02/776-3211. Once beyond the faux temple exterior, inside you can tuck into a variety of traditional Korean dishes. As in its other restaurant in Insa-dong (see opposite), *Jinju bibimbap* is the best dish, though there are lots more to choose from including *bulgogi* (W15,000) and huge seafood pancakes (*haemul pajeon*) for W13,000.

Kenzo Ramen Myeong-dong ⓣ02/757-7778. You can ruminate on the relative superiority of Japanese *ramen* to Korean *ramyeon* at this tiny noodle bar. Larger bowls, thicker noodles and less reliance on the hit of red pepper paste, a full stomach can be yours for just W5000. There's no English-language menu but pictures of the dishes should do the trick – *shoyu*, *shio* and *miso* are the most popular, washed down with an Asahi beer.

Korea House Toegyero ⓣ02/2266-9101. Delicious is not the word – this may well be the best food in Seoul. Sets go for W45,000 and up, and are made up of at least fifteen separate components, usually including broiled eel, ginseng in honey, grilled sliced beef and a royal hotpot. You'll dine in one of several traditional buildings which back onto Namsangol Folk Village, just south of Chungmuro subway station. Reservations recommended. Lunch noon–2pm; dinner 5.30–7pm & 7.20–8.50pm.

Mister Donut Myeong-dong. The only Korean branch of this chain caters to Japanese tourists who can't go without the sugary snacks for the duration of their stay; donut connoisseurs prefer it to the ubiquitous *Dunkin' Donuts*.

Myeong-dong Gyoja Myeong-dong ⓣ02/776-5348. Everything's W6000 at this wildly popular restaurant, which is often full to the brim with hungry visitors aching to try some of the famous meat dumplings. Noodle dishes are also available.

Sanchae-jip Namsan Cable Car ⓣ02/755-8775. The most pleasant of a small, slightly overpriced clutch near the Namsan Cable Car entrance. Pork cutlet, *bibimbap* and set meals are on the menu – some for cooking at your own table.

Taj Myeong-dong ⓣ02/776-0677. The best Indian restaurant in Seoul, according to English expats, and they should know; you'll be paying far more than you would for Korean food – curries start at W17,000 – but dishes are well made and absolutely delicious. Dinner sets are W35,000, though from noon–3pm on weekdays there are bargain lunch deals – just W10,000.

Insa-dong and around

Bärlin Susong-dong ⓣ02/722-5622. Those hankering for a bit of *bratwurst* or *sauerkraut* should hunt down this snazzy German eatery on the Somerset complex. Schnitzels can be made in Hunter, Gypsy or *Wiener* styles, and there's herring on the menu – extremely rare in Korea. See Insa-dong map, p.94.

Benigni Sinmunno 2-ga ⓣ02/3210-3351. An upper-class Italian restaurant on the ground floor of

Insa-dong tearooms

Insadong-gil and its surrounding alleyways are studded with **tearooms**, typically of a traditional or quirky style. You'll be paying W5000 or more for a cup, but most come away feeling that they've got value for money – these are high-quality products made with natural ingredients, and are likely to come with a small plate of traditional Korean sweets. Some of the teas available are listed in the box on p.47, but of particular interest are the *yak-cha* – these dark, bitter, medicinal teas taste just like a Chinese pharmacy smells, and are perfect for chasing away coughs or colds. All the places listed below are marked on the Insa-dong map, p.94.

Cha-sarang Swankier and more polished than others in the area, this multi-floor tearoom nevertheless manages to retain a warm, traditional style. Teas go from W5500, but there are some more unusual items on the menu.

Dawon Located in the grounds of the *Kyung-In Museum of Fine Art* (see box, p.95), in warm weather you can sit outside in the courtyard, while inside you'll find traditionally-styled rooms where guests are encouraged to add their musings to the graffiti-filled walls. Teas from W6000 are on the menu, alongside information about their purported health benefits

Hue Looking a little like a Korean temple roof that has fallen down and been compressed into four floors of tearoom, here you'll find interesting varieties such as medicinal herb and pomegranate, as well as a number of fruit juices and shakes. There's a great view from the fifth-floor terrace.

Sarang-bang On the second floor of an unassuming building west of Insadong-gil, this small tearoom is run by a Korean man and his Japanese wife, a friendly pair who are full of local information and money-saving tips.

Su-yo-il Built in a similar style to *Cha-sarang* across the road, though here the opportunity to see and be seen on the balconies overlooking Insadong-gil push prices a little higher. Also on offer are Earl Grey, Darjeeling and other teas that may be more familiar to Westerners.

Yetchatjip Though a little hard to find, this small upstairs tearoom is quite simply one of the most pleasurable places in Seoul. The comfy, soft-lit setting is agreeable enough, but add to this a team of amiable finches who happily chirp their way from wall to wall, occasionally stopping by to tilt a curious head at the guests. The tea's not bad, either.

the Miro Space complex near Gwanghwamun subway station. The menu concentrates on Tuscan specialities, and includes a range of pasta and risotto dishes (W14,000–16,000), as well as assorted meat steaks for around double the price – try the baked sea bass with fennel. See Palace District map, p.89.

Cheondungsori Insa-dong ☎02/732-3337. Possessing the typical rustic Insa-dong interior, this is a super-cheap place to fill up on excellent food. The roast fish set meal is a steal at W6000, as is the pork chop *ssambap* (W8000); both come with side dishes prepared with an attention to detail more typical of the Jeolla region in southwest Korea. Take Insa 8-gil, a side street off Insa-dong's main drag, and it's on your left. See Insa-dong map, p.94.

Gogung Gwanhun-dong ☎02/736-3211. Next to a gallery on the basement floor of the Ssamzie complex, the deco here is accordingly quirky, with walls festooned with threads and tie-dye. The food is traditionally Korean in nature – best is the *Jinju Bibimbap* (see p.296 and *Korean cuisine* colour insert) for W10,000. There are more options on the walk up Ssamzie's spiralling building. See Insa-dong map, p.94.

Imok-de Gwanhun-dong ☎02/739-3211. Like *Gogung*, this is located in the Ssamzie complex, but on the roof rather than in the basement. The *bibimbap* is delicious (W7000), and there are pretty views of the building's open-air interior. See Insa-dong map, p.94.

Janchijip Gwanhun-dong ☎02/732-0322. Tucked away behind Ssamzie, this rambling den is a real jack of Insa-dong trades – here you can munch traditional Korean food (such as the W7000 *pajeon* pancakes), sup traditional teas (W5000) or get drunk the traditional way with delicious, *insam*-infused *dongdongju*. Follow Insa 4-gil past Ssamzie, turn right, and it's on your left. See Insa-dong map, p.94.

The Place Sinmunno ⓣ02/722-1300. Next door to *Wood&Brick* (see below) though much cheaper, this increasingly attracts staff from the local banks and embassies. Pasta meals go from W8000, while the mini pizzas (W5000) are good for something light. Waffles and cakes are available for dessert, and there are plenty of coffee styles to choose from. See Palace District map, p.89.

Sanchon Insa-dong ⓣ02/735-0312. One of the most famous restaurants in the whole area, and an absolute must for vegetarians, the meals here are a slightly modern take on Buddhist temple food. The set meals (W20,000–35,000) are prepared with consummate attention, and the traditionally styled interior makes this one of the loveliest places to eat in Seoul. See Insa-dong map, p.94.

Shabis Sinmunno ⓣ02/722-0520. Though there's no English-language menu, most are here for the *shabu shabu* – thin rolls of meat boiled in a broth – which at W8000 per portion are under half the price of many similar places nearby. The interior has a faint Italian style to it, though on a warm day you're bound to be tempted by the leafy, multi-level courtyard outside. The restaurant is up some steps opposite the western end of Deoksugunggil, the road running from Deoksugung palace past Chongdong Theatre. See Palace District map, p.89.

Teol-bo-ne Gwanhun-dong. Immensely popular with Koreans and foreign tourists alike, this small stall on Insadong-gil often has dozens of people queuing up patiently to get their hands on some *hoddeok* – pronounced a bit like "hot dog". These are small, greasy pancakes with a syrupy filling made from cinnamon and brown sugar, and cost just W500 each. Delicious. See Insa-dong map, p.94.

Top Cloud Jongno Tower ⓣ02/2230-3000. Though the tower itself is only 24 storeys high, this restaurant contrives to be on the 33rd floor – it's hoisted high on what looks a frail barricade of steel. The views are tremendous, of course, and are almost equalled by the fusion food and grilled meats on offer. Lunch noon–2.30pm, dinner 6–10pm. See Insa-dong map, p.94.

Wood&Brick Sinmunno ⓣ02/735-1157. This long-standing embassy staff favourite dishes out scrumptious Italian food from W20,000 a dish, though many are here to take advantage of the excellent wine menu. Lunch sets go for W35,000 and up, and typically feature pasta or grilled meat, as well as a choice of dessert from the adjoining bakery. See Palace District map, p.89.

Yeongbin Garden Insa-dong ⓣ02/722-7237. Throw back some filling Korean food in a leafy outdoor courtyard at this gem of a restaurant, set back from Insadong-gil, and illuminated in the evenings by fairy lights. The beef *galbi* sets (W24,000) are enough to feed a small horse (or two people), with a similar pork option for just W11,000. Single diners can try one of the *jjigae* stews (W5000), which come with rice and a few side dishes. See Insa-dong map, p.94.

North of Anguk Station

All the places listed below are marked on the Palace District map, p.89.

Cheonjin Pocha Sogyeok-dong. Almost permanently packed, this small, steamy lair is so popular that you may have to take a number and wait outside while the Chinese chef doles out portion after portion of his famed Tianjin dumplings (*mandu*).

Gung-yeon Gahoe-dong ⓣ02/3673-1104. Few restaurants in Korea can claim to have a national treasure as a chef, but dishes here were created by Han Buk-ryo, who was President of the Institute of Korean Royal Cuisine, and made National Intangible Cultural Asset #38. Set menus here are immaculately designed, and cost W28,000–130,000; an English-language menu is available. In warmer months, you can eat in the garden area outside.

Hyangnamu Samcheong-dong ⓣ02/720-9524. An airy second-floor *galbi* joint overlooking Samcheongdong-gil, the most popular dish here is *moksal-sogeumgui* (W6000 per portion): this is pork from pigs bred on a special diet, which you get to fry yourself at the table and wrap in leaves before chowing down. There's also good tofu *jjigae* – a spicy broth – for just W5000.

Meokswi Donna Anguk-dong. In Korea, when places get popular, they get really popular – there's often a queue outside this plain-looking restaurant, all waiting to get their teeth around some *ddeokbokki*. This rice-cake smothered in a red-hot sauce is available all over the country, but *Meokswi* was the first place to experiment with ingredients such as seafood, cheese and *bulgogi*, and has built up a following. Dishes W3000 each.

Pu-reun Byeol Gwigeun Yeo-u Samcheong-dong ⓣ02/733-3325. Don't be daunted by the name, for this dim-but-funky little pasta refuge is one of the most pleasant eateries in trendy Samcheong-dong – it inhabits the upper floor of a corner building on the main drag. Primi are W16,000 or so, mains from W32,000.

The Restaurant Sogyeok-dong ⓣ02/735-8441. Connected to the excellent Kukje Gallery (see box, p.97), and within easy walking distance of Gyeongbokgung, here you can scoff pasta dishes, nibble baked goods or sip a skinny latte at slightly too-high prices.

Solmoe Maeul Samcheong-dong ⓣ02/720-0995. A sure-fire contender for the "Best Side Dishes in Seoul" award, should it ever come into being – you'll be in danger of filling up before the main course arrives. Traditional Korean sets (*jeongsik*) go from W18,000 per person, while *ssambap* meals are only marginally smaller and cost W8000. Try to nab one of the window tables if you don't fancy sitting Korean-style on the floor. It's on the second floor, overlooking Samcheongdong-gil.

Itaewon

All the places listed below are marked on the Itaewon map, p.109.

Above Itaewon-dong ⓣ02/749-0717. The mainly Korean customer base makes this stylish, dimly-lit restaurant a rather refreshing change in foreigner-heavy Itaewon. The menu is extremely varied, and contains dishes such as Spanish omelette, Belgian mussels and Polish cucumber salad, while there's a special night-menu to complement the excellent wine list.

Ashoka Itaewon-dong ⓣ02/792-0117. Capturing the feel of an English curry-house perfectly, this has long been a favourite with hungry expats, and sits on the third floor of the *Hamilton Hotel*. Tandoori meals are still the Rajasthani owner's pride and joy, but local competition for the curry dollar has seen renewed effort put into the dishes. There's also a daily buffet lunch.

Buddha's Belly Itaewon-dong ⓣ02/796-9330. While "Haewon style" once meant seedy and languid, this spick-and-span Thai restaurant is proof of the recent improvement to the area's restaurants. All of your favourite Siamese dishes from green curry and *pad thai* to chicken coconut soup are here, served in a wonderfully laid-back atmosphere – the comfy seating will tempt you to stay on for a glass of wine or two.

Gecko's Garden Itaewon-dong ⓣ02/790-0540. Not to be confused with *Gecko's Terrace*, an expat bar just down the way, this rambling restaurant is fenced off from Itaewon by a line of trees, and feels a world removed from smoky Seoul. The silver bistro tables impart a vaguely European air to the courtyard and the menu follows suit with pastas and risottos, while on weekends chefs will grill your choice of meat on an open barbeque.

Moghul Itaewon-dong ⓣ02/796-5501. Smaller and slightly cheaper than the *Ashoka*, a tree-fringed outdoor terrace simplifies the choice in the summer for those with curry cravings. Meals from W13,000.

La Plancha Itaewon-dong ⓣ02/790-0063. The decorations are a pretty Andalucian pink and there's meat, meat and more meat on the menu at this Spanish restaurant, located at the end of the restaurant-filled road that runs behind the *Hamilton Hotel*. Beefy *combos* are W14,000 per person, while the same amount will buy four plates of tapas.

Le Saint-Ex Itaewon-dong ⓣ02/795-2465. See the blackboard for the daily specials at this French bistro; these change a few times per week but generally include steaks and hearty salads. The desserts – teasingly set out near the exit – are hard to resist, and there's a good wine list. Lunch noon–3pm; dinner 6pm–midnight (last orders 9.30pm).

Pharoah's Itaewon-dong ⓣ02/798-5827. You'll find this pleasant Egyptian restaurant behind Itaewon fire station and surrounded by Seoul's most popular gay bars. As with the bars, it's empty for most of the week (and closed altogether on Mon), but can be full to the brim on Fri and Sat nights, when it stays open until 6am – this has to be one of the most interesting places in Seoul to people-watch. The food itself is excellent, with moussaka, houmous, felafel and all kinds of herby delights on the menu.

Gangnam

The places listed below are marked on the Gangnam and Apgujeong map, p.113.

Arte Banpo-dong ⓣ02/532-0990. Seoul's quirky little Frenchtown has – surprisingly – a fair share of Italian restaurants, of which this is the best. They're proud of their sautéed salmon with mushroom, though the steaks are succulent, and spaghetti dishes are good value at W17,000.

Asian Live COEX complex ⓣ02/3130-8620. Despite the rather tacky-sounding name, this is one of the city's top restaurants, sitting pretty on the second floor of the *COEX Intercontinental* (p.87) and an excellent place to clink glasses over a business deal. The kitchens are visible from many tables, meaning that you get to see the chefs whipping up what will invariably be excellent Indian, Chinese, Japanese or Korean food – figure on W70,000 or more per person.

Bombay Seocho-dong. Quite cheap for an Indian restaurant in Seoul, though portions are not as well made or authentic as you may find elsewhere. Still, the korma is good value at W10,000, and there's a tasty salmon curry on offer.

Bongchu Jjim-dak Yeoksam-dong ⓣ02/565-4593. Once inside, the smell of the food alone should be enough to make you stay, and the pleasant lighting makes the dining experience relaxed as well as tasty. *Jjim-dak* is steamed chicken, mixed with vegetables in a delicious stew. A W22,000 serving – one chicken – should be enough for two, though be sure to put on one of the bibs provided as there's bound to be some splashback.

Crystal Jade Palace COEX complex ⓣ02/3288-8101. As soon as you enter this restaurant located in the *Grand Intercontinental* (see p.87), you know you're in for something special. Part of a chain that includes branches in Bangkok, Jakarta, Shanghai and Ho Chi Minh, this top-notch Cantonese eatery is a strikingly beautiful place bathed in gentle light. The chefs are not adverse to harnessing elements of other Chinese cuisines – Peking duck is one of the most popular items on the menu, though there are far more adventurous things to choose from.

Hakone COEX complex ⓣ02/559-7623. This stylish restaurant is also in the *Grand Intercontinental*, and serves immaculately prepared Japanese cuisine. Courses laden with raw fish start at around W75,000, though some rice and noodle dishes are available for much less than that. Lunch 11.30am–3pm; dinner 6–10pm.

Hofbrauhaus Mani Building, ⓣ02/501-7770. Those looking to take an interesting break from Korean food could do worse than head to this approximation of a German *bierhalle*. Although Koreans are unlikely to get up and dance on the table, and the beef here actually comes from Austrian cows, it's all quite authentic – the owners particularly recommend their *Schweinshaxe* (roast pork knuckle), though some may find goulash, steaks or currywurst more appealing. There's also an on-site microbrewery pumping out beer made from German malt for W5400 a glass.

La Trouvaille Banpo-dong ⓣ02/534-0255. The best restaurant in the small French town near the express bus terminal, *La Trouvaille* has a pleasingly authentic European atmosphere. Friendly hosts dish out cuisine such as duck breast with gnocchi in a raspberry sauce – you'd have to look hard to find better-prepared food.

Mashinneun Gogijip Seocho-dong ⓣ02/593-3355. The "Delicious Meat House" is just as it claims to be, and the best place in Gangnam to savour the delights of cooking your own beef at the table. The meat is some of the best in Seoul, and pricey to match – W30,000 for 130g of sirloin – though those arriving before 5pm can take advantage of comparatively cheap lunch sets (W25,000 per person). For similar meals at lower prices head one road behind the restaurant, where there are a troupe of cheap *galbi* joints.

Pasha Seocho-dong ⓣ02/593-8484. Style and substance mix perfectly at this Turkish kebab house. The meals (from W15,000) are filling, with the familiar *doner* and *kofte* dishes supplemented by more unusual fish meals. *Pide* – a kind of Turkish pizza – is best washed down with some sour *ayran* yoghurt.

Sushiko Seocho-dong ⓣ02/3481-3071. Chefs chop up raw fish in front of an illuminated paper backdrop at this high-quality sushi den, which is within walking distance of a number of Gangnam's top hotels. Prices are extremely high – some courses are W100,000 per person – though weekday lunch menus are just W25,000 from 11.30am to 2.30pm.

Apgujeong

The places listed below are marked on the Gangnam and Apgujeong map, p.113.

Gorilla in the Kitchen Sinsa-dong ⓣ02/3442-1688. Glass and chrome interior, all-white furniture and surgical-white uniformed waitresses – this place has an air of arty European about it, but the calorie listings next to every single meal on the menu will serve as a reminder that you are, indeed, in waistline-conscious Apgujeong. The food here is innovative and delicious, with temptations including turkey steak with berry sauce, rice-covered tofu salad in sesame dressing, and peppered chicken breast on black rice; prices aren't extortionate, and lunch sets go as low as W27,000.

Oga-no Ju-bang Sinsa-dong. Though there's no English-language menu, sushi sets will feed two to three at this *izakaya*-style bar-cum-restaurant. This is one for the *sake* connoisseur – while the cheapest bottles are W15,000, some of Japan's finest are on sale here too.

Pink Spoon Sinsa-dong ⓣ02/514-0745. A small restaurant that offers valet parking – well this is Apgujeong, darling. Almost uniquely for a Thai restaurant, this below-street-level diner hasn't gone to town on the Siamese theme, concentrating instead on getting the food right. Spicy salads from W18,000, green and red curries for a little more, though the tastiest dish may well be the stir-fried chicken with roasted chilli and basil.

Slow Food Sinsa-dong. As the name suggests, you'll find a relaxed vibe at this restaurant, whose tables spill out onto the pavement outside as soon as the weather shows the slightest sign of warming up. It's an excellent place to sit with a crab and avocado sandwich and a skinny latte, watching beautiful people saunter by with their miniature poodles. The salads are tasty but poor value at W15,000; pasta dishes are more filling, and just a few thousand more.

Tell Me About It... Sinsa-dong ⓣ02/541-3885. This tapas bar has built up quite a following, with a funky atmosphere, menus that change with the season, and a pretty outdoor terrace for warmer months. Tapas dishes are W7000; there are also grill and pasta dishes, and that paradoxical Apgujeong staple – waffles for dessert.

Seoul's tearooms and cafés

Tearooms	
Cha-sarang	차사랑
Dawon	다원
Hue	휴
Sarang-bang	사랑방
Su-yo-il	수요일
Yetchatjip	옛찻집
Cafés	
Café Yeon	카페연
Ceci Cela	세시셀라
Coffee Hanjang	커피 한장
Gallery o:n	갤러리 온
Igloo	이글루
Jiin	카페지인
Luxury Gongja	락셔리 공짜
Olseorim	올서림
Pascucci	파스쿠치
Samack	사막

Cafés and teahouses

As well as a number of international **café** chains, a few local clones such as *Pascucci* and *The Coffee Bean and Tea Leaf* have popped up too; menus and prices are roughly equivalent to those in the West – a coffee will cost W2500–6000. See p.47 for more details on coffee in Korea. Seoul also has an admirable range of traditionally styled **tearooms**, most of which huddle around Insadong-gil; see the box on p.123 for details, and p.47 for listings of the most popular types of tea.

Café Yeon Samcheong-dong. Set around a tiny traditional courtyard hanging above trendy Samcheongdong-gil, this café puts forward a relaxed vibe that will doubtless appeal to backpackers. Vietnamese coffee, hydrangea tea and banana lassis are on the drinks list, and food is also available. See the Palace District map, p.89.

Ceci Cela Sinsa-dong. An Apgujeong institution, this is permanently full of young, fashionable females somehow keeping their waistlines intact while chowing down waffles, panini or slabs of cheesecake. Coffees and vitamin juices are also available, as are thick milkshakes. See the Gangnam and Apgujeong map, p.113.

Coffee Hanjang Bukchon-dong. Hard to find but worth tracking down; toys and music boxes stud the walls, while some tables are made out of butchered ping-pong tables. The coffee isn't bad, either. Take exit three from Anguk station, turn left and walk uphill for around ten minutes – the café will be on your left. See the Palace District map, p.89.

Gallery o:n Samcheong-dong. Set in a "floating" courtyard above Samcheongdong-gil, this airy café is quite representative of the area – traditional buildings with a sleek, modern vibe. Coffees and teas W7000. See the Palace District map, p.89.

Igloo Apgujeong. This café has achieved national fame for a rather strange reason – it's home to a clutch of famous dogs. Wandering freely around the premises, they've featured regularly on Korean television, and in the odd film. Female Apgujeongers waltz in for a drink with their own miniature poodles (stuffed into designer handbags, of course). Surreal. See the Gangnam and Apgujeong map, p.113.

Jiin Sinsa-dong. Double the price of most cafés, but one of Apgujeong's many places to be seen. A global choice of coffee can be imbibed in European-style surroundings, while shakes, chocolate drinks and waffles are also on the menu. See the Gangnam and Apgujeong map, p.113.

Luxury Gongjja Gangnam. Stylish, outlandish and nightmarish are three words that have been used to describe the decoration of this unusual café, which is highly popular with dating couples. There's Taiwanese-style "bubble tea" on the menu, as are thick milkshakes made with Haagen-Dazs ice cream. Head a few minutes up the main road from Gangnam station exit seven, then uphill on a road firing off diagonally before the CGV building; the café will be on your right. See the Gangnam and Apgujeong map, p.113.

Olseorim Gahoe-dong. A bizarre mixture of café, gallery and the oldest dental clinic in Seoul. Foreign visitors are so rare in this hard-to-reach place that the friendly owner will doubtless offer to escort you around the premises – the sight of people getting fillings in traditional wooden buildings is really quite something. Take exit two from Anguk station, and keep heading up; *Olseorim* is about 15min uphill, on the opposite side of the main road. See the Palace District map, p.89.

Pascucci There are branches of this *Starbucks*-like chain all around the city, though two are noteworthy places to people-spot – one on the main drag in Myeong-dong, and another peering over the subway exit in Hongdae. See the Hongdae map, p.107.

Samack Anguk-dong. The friendly, English-speaking owner is trying to create a "café for travellers", but though the rather out-of-the-way location means that she'll be lucky to get many foreign guests, this is a fabulously relaxed little den. The green tea latte is delicious, and you can snack out on fried rice or a *kimchi* omelette. See the Palace District map, p.89.

Nightlife and entertainment

Koreans love going out, whether it's with family, colleagues, social acquaintances or old study friends, making Seoul a truly 24-hour city – day and night, it simply hums with life. Those wanting to drink or dance can choose from myriad **bars** and **clubs**, with each area of Seoul having its own particular flavour. The city also has a thriving **theatre** scene that's surprisingly accessible to foreign visitors.

Bars and clubs

Clubs pumping out techno, trance and hip-hop to wiggling masses; loungey subterranean lairs filled with hookah smoke and philosophical conversation; noisy joints serving up feasts of live jazz and rock; neon-tinged cocktail bars in the bowels of five-star hotels. After a lengthy gestation, Seoul's nightlife scene is finally wide open, and the drinkers themselves are becoming ever more liberal. It wasn't so long ago that drinking in Seoul was pretty much a male-only affair, taking place in restaurants or at a "**hof**", the ubiquitous faux-Western bars that are still winning the battle for street-space, but are increasingly being looked over in favour of more genuinely Western ideas imported from overseas. That said, there are some more local elements that can be factored into a night out: Korean friends are likely to drag you before long into a **noraebang** singing room to belt out your favourite songs amid a cacophony of tambourines and castanets, while couples can end the night cuddled up at a DVD room (see box, p.108). Summer months see most of the city's convenience stores surround themselves with plastic tables and chairs; as strange as this sounds, it's a cheap and increasingly popular way to start a night out, and a great way to make a few new friends.

Most of the action is concentrated into just a few areas. Of these, **Hongdae** is by far the busiest. Its streets are infested with bars, clubs and restaurants, and full every day of the week from early evening on. Towards midnight the crowds are swelled further with Seoul's clubber population, who get on the last subway services of the day to Hongdae, party all night, then slink off home as dawn breaks. Almost as busy at the weekend is **Itaewon**, which has some of the best bars, clubs and restaurants in the capital. It has long been a popular watering hole for American soldiers from the nearby army base (though a mass military pull-

▲ The busy streets of Hongdae

out has long been mooted); this has resulted in a mass of "sexy bars" (expensive venues where the bar-girls wear bikinis, hot-pants and the like, and the customers pay for their company) and brothels, many lining the upward slope termed "Hooker Hill". The side street leading from this ("Homo Hill") has become the most popular **gay** area in the whole country, with some excellent bars catering to Seoul's ever-growing pink community. Also worth mentioning are **Sinchon**, one subway station from Hongdae and full of bars; studenty **Daehangno**, which is busy every evening (though most seem to flee the area for home or Hongdae as midnight approaches); as well as a few relaxing places to wine and dine in Samcheong-dong. South of the river, Gangnam has a couple of good bars (though is mainly an eating area), as does nearby Apgujeong.

Hongdae

All the places listed below are marked on the Hongdae map, p.107.

BricXX This candlelit underground lair is a popular place to take a date, with reasonably priced cocktails and excellent food – try the felafel. The seating areas are draped with curtains; try to get there in time to nab a seat in the ultra-chilled area lined with oriental silk pillows.

Club Evans Hongdae's most popular jazz venue by a mile, this is small enough to generate some decent acoustics, but large enough to create a good atmosphere. The acts are usually of more than acceptable quality, and the experience surprisingly refined for this nightclub-filled street.

Club Tool Some of the best electronica DJs in town descend on this extremely stylish dance club, though the size of the floor, coupled with the occasional frostiness of the door staff, means that it can feel rather empty at times: a place to go with a group rather than on your own.

FF Both Fs stand for "funky", though you're more likely to see some good ol' rock at this highly popular live music venue. A great many of the bands are foreign, bringing their pals and staying on for the DJ sets afterwards, so it's a great place to make new friends. Entry is around W11,000 while the bands are on, and free for the DJ sets.

M2 The area's top nightclub, and accordingly packed to the gills on weekends, *M2* manages to rope in the occasional top international DJ to spin out some house, but the music is good enough most of the time. Entry W10,000, Fri & Sat W15,000.

Nabi This pleasing underground bar has finally brought the word "bohemian" to Hongdae's nightlife. Marked only by a small sign on the outside, once you're through the door it may feel as if you've entered another world – candles

A real Korean night out

The "proper" Korean night out has long followed a similar format, one that entwines food, drink and entertainment. The venue for stage one (*il-cha*) is the **restaurant**, where a meal is chased down with copious shots of *soju*. This is followed by stage two (*i-cha*), a visit to a **bar** or **hof**; here priorities switch from food to drink, and beers are followed down with snacks (usually large dishes intended for groups). Those still able to walk then continue to stage three (*sam-cha*), the **entertainment** component of the night, which usually involves a trip to a *noraebang* room for a sing-along, and yet more drinks. Stages four, five and beyond certainly exist, but participants are unlikely to remember them clearly.

float on a small pond, arty folk sit on cushions passing the *hookah* around, and nobody feels as if they're in Seoul any more. Despite the secluded location, the secret is out, and it can get very crowded at weekends – if there's no floorspace, you'll just have to wait.

QVo Even though the music is usually hip-hop instead of house, *QVo* tends to mop up the overflow on the regular occasions that *M2* can't squeeze any more in. Add this to the dedicated hip-hop fans already bouncing away inside, and you're in for a good night. Entry W10,000, Fri & Sat W15,000.

Samgeori Pocha Though it's technically a restaurant, this is an integral part of Hongdae's nightlife – after a dance or a drink, Koreans love to eat (and drink a little more), so if you've made new friends you may well find yourself dragged along to this rustic-looking place, where raw fish and steaming broths are on the menu, and tables are littered with empty *soju* bottles.

Suyeom Bar In Korea if you want to save money on bar prices, you go to a convenience store for your beer. In Hongdae, you can go cheaper again, as a plastic cup of draught at this tiny road stall goes for W1000. There are only a few seats so you're bound to get talking to someone here – a perfect place to start a night out.

Tinpan A "meat market", yes, but Hongdae's best. It won't cost you a dime to get into either of the two *Tinpans* that face each other across nightclub road; once inside, drinks are cheap and the dance floors are heaving.

Vinyl Get takeaway cocktails from the window of this small bar, where you can get Pina Coladas and Sex on the Beach in what appear, at first glance, to be colostomy bags. Such ingenuity brings the price down – W4000 for a cocktail, or just W2000 for a slightly larger bag of beer.

Itaewon

All the places listed below are marked on the Itaewon map, p.109.

Bar Nana With its hanging fabrics, fake palm trees and relaxed vibe, this is the kind of bar you'd expect to find in Hongdae, and therefore a breath of fresh air in testosterone-filled Itaewon. Staff spin all kinds of music from ska to modern jazz, and there are regular live music nights.

Bungalow Bar Extremely popular, and fully deserving the hype. There are drinking options aplenty in this loungey, multilevel bar – sup sangria on the swing-seats, drink martinis in the sand pit, have a romatic glass of wine on a candle-lit table or kick back with a beer on the outdoor terrace.

Embassy Lounge This cocktail bar isn't quite as stylish as it pretends to be – the arty wall-projections and quirky seating derivative, rather than innovative – though it ropes in the weekend crowds with some excellent DJ sets. Cocktails from W8000.

Gecko's Terrace Unlike most Itaewon bars, *Gecko's* is busy every day of the week. A lively mix of Koreans and foreigners, it's popular with people who don't feel like dancing, or those filling up on cheap beer before a night on the tiles – draught Cass is just W2500, and pints of Guinness reasonable for Korea at W8000.

Nashville Sports Bar The name says it all – this is an American-style bar which shows Premier League football, Major League baseball or any other sport coverage in demand from Seoul's expat community. At quieter times, it's a pleasant place for a game of pool or darts, while during major sporting events you'll be lucky to find standing room.

Queen This bar is a "Homo Hill" institution, and quite possibly the most popular gay bar on the Korean peninsula (there being little competition in Pyongyang). The staff are inviting and the chairs highly comfortable, but on warm weekend evenings even these can't stop the crowd spilling out onto the street. Up the road, *Always Homme* shares much of the customer base, while close by is *Trance*, a thriving transgender bar.

Spy Bar Located on the basement level of a building that also houses the *Nashville Sports Bar*, weekends see this sometimes-house-sometimes-trance club heaving under the weight of a sexy, youthful crowd. American soldiers, expat teachers, scantily clad Korean girls and aspiring Eastern European models – a truer microcosm of Itaewon society would be hard to find. Fri & Sat entry W10,000.

Other areas

Blush COEX. A recent addition to the formidable array of swanky bars and restaurants in the *Grand Intercontinental*, this is one of Seoul's prime high-roller venues, though cheap enough to be a viable option for those that can walk the walk. Draught Cass goes for W9000, with cocktails around double that amount, and there's food on offer – try the chicken satay in peanut sauce. See the Gangnam and Apujeong map, p.113.

Comfort Zone Daehangno. The best bar in the area by a country mile. Here you'll be able to chill out over cocktails in the curtain-filled upstairs lounge (avoid the kiwi daiquiris though), pop downstairs for a beer and a game of darts, or have a quiet chat on the outdoor veranda. Brunch specials are on offer from 9.30am to 4pm – fried breakfast or french toast with maple syrup for W6000, with tea and coffee thrown in. Turn left out of exit four of Hyewha subway and walk along the road until you come to Burger King; it's down the alley to the left.

Dan Vie Daehangno. Tucked into a basement next door to *Comfort Zone*, this bar is a curious mix of decorative styles – some areas are cordoned off with dangling beads or shower curtains, others have space-station-style swivel chairs, and movies are projected onto the far wall. Though it rarely fills up, you'd still be lucky to nab the titchy upstairs room on a weekend evening.

Marcie Samseong-dong. Few bars in the country offer rooftop views of dead kings, but here you can slurp your beer while looking down on the green burial mounds of Samneung Park (see p.114), located a kilometre west of the COEX complex.

Top Cloud Jongno Tower. Slurp expensive cocktails – W15,000 and up – while enjoying a commanding view of Seoul's twinkling fairy lights: this 33-storey-high bar-restaurant (see p.124) sits perched nine levels above Jongno Tower on a pedestal of steel towers, and is an excellent place to impress dates or toast a business deal. See Insa-dong map, p.94.

Woo Bar Gwanjang-dong. Located in the entrance lobby of the futuristic *W Hotel*, this is almost a rite of passage for young Seoulites with a bit of cash to flash. Simply breathing ultra-trendiness, it won't appeal to everyone, but if egg-shaped chairs, UV-lit sofas or space-helmet-like DJ booths sound appealing, this is the place to head. Drinks are expensive, but the staff are way too cool to make any fuss about those who spend all night sipping a single beer. See Seoul map, pp.74–75.

Cinema, theatre and performance arts

Korean **cinema** has been the subject of growing worldwide attention and acclaim in recent times (see Contexts, p.436), but because almost no films are screened with English-language subtitles, it's probably best to hunt them down in your home country. Perhaps of more interest to visitors will be the wealth of **traditional performance** on offer, as well as a range of outlandish **musicals**.

Cinema

Wherever you find yourself in Seoul, you won't be too far from the nearest **cinema**. Foreign films are shown in their original language with Korean subtitles, though local films are Korean-only. Tickets cost W7000 or so, and some of the most popular places to go are Megabox in the COEX shopping mall, Lotte Cinema near Euljiro 1-ga subway station, and MMC in the Dongdaemun market area; the latter is open 24hr, while the others close around midnight. Two options for those looking for something more **arthouse** are the Korea Film Archive (Ⓦwww.koreafilm.org) near the Nambu bus terminal, which focuses on local and independent productions, and Mirospace (Ⓦwww.mirospace.co.kr), a small, hundred-seat cinema near the Seoul Museum of History. It's also possible to watch movies in a DVD- or video-*bang* – see box on p.108 for details.

Seoul festivals

As long as you're not in Seoul during the long, cold winter, you'll almost certainly be able to catch a **festival** of some kind. In addition to the traditional parades and street performances on Insadong-gil (usually every Thursday, Friday and Saturday), there are a whole host of events, of which a selection are detailed below.

April: Cherry Blossom Though the exact dates are determined by the weather, Seoulites get their picnicking equipment together as soon as the soft pink flowers are fluted through the cherry trees. Yeouido is the most popular place to go – bring a bottle of *soju* and make a bunch of friends.

April: International Women's Film Festival A week-long succession of films that "see the world through women's eyes" (even if they were created by men). See ⓦwffis.or.kr for details.

First Sun of May: Jongmyo Daeje Korean kings performed their ancestral rites at the Jongmyo shrine for hundreds of years prior to the end of the monarchy, and it's been carried forward to this day; the event is necessarily sober but very interesting, and is followed by traditional court dances.

May: Hi Seoul Festival Myriad events take place in this ten-day-long celebration of the coming of summer. From choreographed firework displays and tea ceremonies to men walking across the Han River by tightrope, there's simply no better time to be in Seoul. See ⓦhiseoulfest.org for details.

Late May: Buddha's Birthday With their courtyards strewn with colourful paper lanterns, temples are the place to be at this age-old event, which is also a national holiday. In the evening a huge lantern parade heads to Jogyesa temple along Jongno; get window-space early in one of the cafés overlooking the street.

Late May: Seoul International Cartoon & Animation Festival Koreans young and old are major cartoon addicts, but while most of the national fix is sated by Japanese fare, there's still a lot of local talent – *The Simpsons*, *Family Guy* and *Spongebob Squarepants* are among the shows inked and lined here. Screenings take place in several locations; see ⓦwww.sicaf.or.kr for details.

Early June: Korean Queer Culture Festival Not exactly an event trumpeted by the local tourist authorities – in fact, not so long ago the police were still trying to ban it – this is a great way to see Korea crawling out of its Confucian shell. A fortnight-long programme includes a film festival, art exhibitions and the obligatory street parade. See ⓦwww.kqcf.org for details.

June: Dano An age-old event centred around the shamanist rituals still practised by many Koreans, this takes place at locations across the city, but is best experienced in the Namsangol *hanok* village (see p.105). It's also your best chance to see *ssireum*, a Korean form of wrestling.

August: Seoul Fringe Festival This fortnight-long platform for all things alternative is highly popular with local students, and its semi-international nature means that certain events will appeal to visitors from overseas, with Hongdae usually the best place to be.

Late September and early October: Seoul Performing Arts Festival This increasingly acclaimed event has seen performances from as far afield as Latvia and Israel, though its main aim is to showcase Korean talent. It takes place in various locations around Seoul over a three-week period.

Early October: Seoul Drum Festival The crashes and bangs of all things percussive ring out at this annual event, which takes place in the Gwanghwamun area. See ⓦwww.drumfestival.org for details.

November: Kimchi Festival Get your hands and mouths around the many varieties of spicy fermented cabbage from all over the country – an event surprisingly popular with foreigners.

Theatre and performance arts

Stage buffs will have plenty to choose from in Seoul. Most popular with foreign travellers are traditional performances and musicals, though some will enjoy the relatively underground delights of the Daehangno theatres.

Chongdong Theatre Near City Hall Ⓦwww.chongdong.com. The 80min traditional shows of song and dance hosted by this theatre are extremely popular with foreign visitors. The theatre is located on a quiet road near the western wall of Deoksugung. Performances (daily except Mon; April–Sept 8pm; Oct–March 4pm; from W20,000) are in Korean, though English subtitles appear next to the stage. Also on offer are classes for the *janggu*, a Korean drum.

Dongsoong Art Center Daehangno Ⓦdsartcenter.co.kr. This Daehangno arts complex has long been putting on some of Seoul's best experimental drama, though as performances are in Korean only you'll need some language skills or an open mind. The on-site cinema shows some interesting films and documentaries from home and abroad.

Jump Cinecore Theater Ⓦwww.hijump.co.kr. Ever wondered what a family entirely made up of martial arts experts would be like? Live all the jumps and kicks in this musical, which takes place at the Cinecore Theater near Insa-dong. Performances Tues–Sat 4pm & 8pm, Sun 3pm & 6pm; W40,000.

Korea House Chungmuro Ⓦwww.koreahouse.or.kr. Highly polished traditional performances from some of the top artists in the country, combined with some of Seoul's best food (see p.122), make a visit to this collection of rustic buildings enjoyable. The wonderful shows include fan dances, *pansori* opera and the long-ribboned hats of the "farmers' dance". Take exit three from Chungmuro subway station and walk up the side street. Performances daily 7pm; W30,000.

Line 1 Hakchon Green Theatre, Daehangno Ⓦwww.hakchon.co.kr. The longest-running musical in Korea is an enjoyable parody of Seoul life and people, as viewed through the eyes of an ethnic-Korean born in China. People behind the scenes clearly have an eye for talent, as several performers have gone on to become movie stars. Performances with English subtitles Wed & Fri 7.30pm, Sun 4pm; W30,000.

Munye Theatre Daehangno. One of the most popular theatres with those studying performance arts in the area, this shrine to modern dance hosts regular shows, as well as a spring festival (see p.111).

Nanta Nanta Theatre, near City Hall Ⓦwww.nanta.co.kr. This madcap kitchen-based musical has gone down a storm, with song, circus tricks and all sorts of utensil drumming mixed with a nice line in audience participation. Performances Mon–Sat 4pm & 8pm, Sun 3pm & 6pm; W40,000.

Seoul Arts Centre Nambu bus terminal Ⓦwww.sac.or.kr. The home of Korea's national ballet and opera companies, as well as the symphony orchestra, there's always something interesting going on at this rambling complex: among other things, it contains an opera house, a concert hall and a couple of theatres. See website for details of upcoming events. See Seoul map, pp.74–75.

Sports and activities

Despite the seemingly never-ending rows of Seoul's apartment blocks and the near-permanent foulness of its air, there are a number of ways to keep in shape in the city, or merely watch other people getting paid to do so. An hour or two of **taekwondo** practice features on the travel schedules of many a backpacker, while others choose to sample Korea's unique take on **football** and **baseball**. In warmer months it's possible to have a dip in one of several outdoor **swimming pools** or rent a bike; the Han-side banks of Yeouido are the best places (though, Japanese visitors actually come here to save money) for both. Korean golf courses are among the most expensive in the world and usually require membership, but there are plenty of small **driving ranges** dotted around Seoul – look for the buildings topped with green nets. You'll be able to find **pool tables** in many of Itaewon's foreigner bars, usually free to use. More common are pool halls that cater to **four-ball**, a pocketless version of the game so popular in Korea that live matches are regularly broadcast on television.

Taekwondo

The home of Korea's national sport is **Kukkiwon** (Mon–Fri 9am–5pm; free), a hall near Gangnam station; here there are occasional performances and tournaments, though it's empty at other times. Perhaps of more interest to travellers is the chance to have a go yourself – there are **training sessions** at Gyeonghuigung palace (daily except Mon; W15,000 per session). The 10.30am sessions are for basic moves, 1.30pm for self-defence and 3.30pm for "breaking techniques" (pine boards, not people). Reservations can be made through a tourist information office, who can also organize longer programs: figure on around W50,000 per day.

Football

Those wanting to watch some **K-League** action can catch FC Seoul at the World Cup Stadium (tickets from W6000; Ⓦwww.fcseoul.com), with games taking places on weekends from March to October. Seongnam and Suwon, the two most dominant Korean teams of recent times, also play near Seoul; the atmosphere at all grounds is fun but a little empty, unless you're lucky enough to be around for a major international game (Ⓦwww.fifa.com).

Those who prefer to play rather than watch football can try their luck with the highly competitive **foreigners' football league** (Ⓦssflkorea.com); this has been in operation for a number of years, and most of the competing teams are based in Seoul, though as the standard is quite high you'll have to be a decent player to get a regular game (unless you're playing for Daejeon De La Cuba).

Rugby

Though it may be a minority sport in Korea, rugby players can keep in shape by training with **Seoul Survivors RFC** (Ⓦwww.survivorsrfc.com), an expat squad who practice most Sundays on Yeouido. They've little competition in Korea, but make occasional international tours, including an annual pilgrimage to a 10s tournament in the Philippines. There's also **Seoul Sisters** (Ⓦwww.ssrfc.com), a women's team which has confounded the men by surviving for more than a couple of years; they also play in international tournaments, and a few exhibition games around Korea.

Baseball

Seoul has two main professional teams: **LG Twins** and the **Doosan Bears**, who both play in Jamsil Baseball Stadium – take subway line 2 to Sports Complex station, exit five or six. Games take place most days from April to October, and tickets can cost as little as W3000. Avid players can get some practise at a number of **batting nets** dotted around the city, particularly in student areas; these cost just W1000 for a minute's worth of balls.

Shopping

Shopaholics will find themselves quite at home in Seoul: the city has everything from trendy to traditional and markets to malls. High on the itinerary of many tourists are the colossal markets of **Dongdaemun** and **Namdaemun** (see pp.104–105 for more details).

Clothing

There are **department stores** all over the city. Beware, though; as soon as you dare to even look at something, a grinning girl in uniform will race up to you, and stay by you until you try something on or leave. The bustling streets of **Myeong-dong** host stores from the biggest nationwide chains – Migliore, Shinsaegae, Lotte and Galleria – among many others. Note that the preponderance of Japanese tourists ensures that Japanese-influenced styles are most prevalent. **Apgujeong** has the country's grandest department stores, notably the twin *Galleria* malls (one of these is covered with soft light cells, and glows like a spaceship at night), while further up the road is a parade of brand-name flagship stores – such as Gucci, Prada and Louis Vuitton; there is also a clutch of boutique stores around nearby Dosan Park. **Itaewon** has long been popular with foreign businessmen, so most shopkeepers can speak a little English; an increasing number actually hail from abroad. Here you can get all sorts of things, including leather shoes and jackets, tailored suits and fake watches. Outside Itaewon, foreign travellers should note that sizes tend to be on the small side, particularly around the hips for females.

Arts, crafts and antiques

The best place to head for anything vaguely arty is **Insadong-gil** and its side streets. As well as numerous galleries (see box on p.95 for some of the most interesting), there are **craft** shops selling paints, brushes, calligraphy ink and hand-made paper. There are also countless trinket shops, many of which set up stalls in the spiralling indoor walkway of the fantastic Ssamzie complex near the top of the road; this also has a rooftop market on weekends, selling all manner of quirky arts and crafts. Further down the road is the **Tong-in Building**, which has whole floors full of **antique** cases, cupboards, medicinal racks and the like, many in a distinctively oriental style; at least one of the proprietors will be able to speak English, and the store can arrange shipping.

Books and music

Most of Seoul's larger **bookstores** have dedicated English-language sections stocked with novels, history books and language study guides for those studying Korean or teaching English. Two of the most useful are near Insa-dong: Kyobo

▲ Dongdaemun market

Books in the Kyobo Building outside exit four of Gwanghwamun subway station, and the equally large Bandi & Luni store in the basement of nearby Jongno Tower (Jonggak subway, exit three). Itaewon has a couple of smaller, more intimate shops selling second-hand books – Abby's Book Nook and What the Book.

The Korean **music** scene may be flooded with K-pop and local hip-hop, but there are a few shops dotted around Seoul that dare to venture underground. These include Purple Record and Record Forum, two stores on the main road outside the entrance of Hongik University; the former has a selection of post-rock unequalled in Korea, while the latter has a mix of everything from blues to bossa nova. There are also a couple of options in Daehangno, including SKC Plaza, a large music shop though mostly full of K-pop, or Gomapss, a tiny store on the Hongik university entrance road. Even smaller is Harvest Music, opposite *Gogung* restaurant in Myeong-dong, which has a few gems amid its second-hand vinyl collection. A couple of the bookshops listed above also have surprisingly well-stocked music sections. Those who prefer making music of their own should head straight to the upper floors of the large Nakwon arcade in Insa-dong; here more than a hundred shops sell **musical instruments**, with customers and shop owners alike testing the products.

Cameras and electronic equipment

Technophiles have two main choices – one is Yongsan Electronics Mart, a multi-level giant rising up alongside the train and subway station of the same name, and the other Techno Mart, near Gangbyeon subway station on line 2. At both, many staff speak a little English (particularly Yongsan, thanks to its proximity to Itaewon). Prices are generally about twenty percent less than elsewhere in the land; this can rise to fifty percent for imported goods.

Listings

Airlines Aeroflot ⓣ02/551-0321; Air Canada ⓣ02/3788-0100; Air China ⓣ02/774-6886; Air France ⓣ02/3483-1033; All Nippon Airways ⓣ02/752-5500; American Airlines ⓣ02/319-3401; Asiana Airlines ⓣ02/1588-8000; Cathay Pacific ⓣ02/311-2800; China Eastern Airlines ⓣ02/518-0330; China Hainan Airlines ⓣ02/779-0600; Delta Airlines ⓣ02/754-1921; Japan Airlines ⓣ02/757-1711; KLM ⓣ02/2011-5500; Korean Air ⓣ02/1588-2001; Lufthansa Airlines ⓣ02/3420-0400; Malaysian Airlines ⓣ02/777-7761; Northwest Airlines ⓣ02/732-1700; Philippine Airlines ⓣ02/774-3581; Qantas ⓣ02/777-6871; Singapore Airlines ⓣ02/755-1226; Thai Airways ⓣ02/3707-0114; Turkish Airlines ⓣ02/777-7055; United Airlines ⓣ02/757-1691; Uzbekistan Airways ⓣ02/754-1041; Vietnam Airlines ⓣ02/757-8920.

Airport information The information line for both Incheon Airport (ⓦwww.airport.or.kr) and Gimpo Airport (ⓦwww.airport.co.kr) is ⓣ02/1577-2600.

Banks and exchange Banks will exchange foreign currency or travellers' cheques, while some have a "Global ATM" that can be used with cards from around the world. Those with debit cards may find it easier to head to one of the main convenience stores such as 7-Eleven or Mini Stop.

Car rental Prices run from around W60,000 per day. The main companies are Hertz ⓣ02/797-8000 and Avis ⓣ02/1544-1600; both have desks at Incheon International Airport.

Credit cards For lost credit cards call the relevant toll-free 24hr number: American Express ⓣ02/1588 8300; Mastercard ⓣ0031/113886; Visa ⓣ0120/133173.

Embassies Australia ⓣ02/2003-0100; Canada ⓣ02/3455-6000; China ⓣ02/738-1173; Ireland ⓣ02/774-6455; New Zealand ⓣ02/736-0341; Russia ⓣ02/752-0630; South Africa ⓣ02/792-4855; UK ⓣ02/3210-5500; US ⓣ02/397-4114.

Emergencies Call the tourist information line on ⓣ1330; staff here have teamed up with the emergency services to provide the fastest possible foreign-language advice. Staff at the top hotels will also be willing to provide assistance, even to non-guests. Alternatively, emergency numbers are ⓣ112 for the police and ⓣ119 for ambulance and the fire brigade.

Hospitals and clinics To find an English-speaking doctor, or a clinic suited to your needs, call the Seoul Help Center's medical line on ⓣ010/4769-8212.

Immigration There are immigration offices at both Incheon and Gimpo airports, as well as one in City Hall. Call ⓣ02/2650-6212, or go to ⓦwww.immigration.go.kr.

Information for foreigners The Seoul Help Center for Foreigners can provide all sorts of assistance, from visa enquiries to job-hunting. Their office is on the second floor of City Hall, or call ⓣ02/797-8212.

Internet access Found all over Seoul and costing W1000 per hour, with a one-hour minimum fee. There are free terminals in the main KTO tourist information centre south of Jonggak subway station (see p.75 for directions). Top-range hotels usually have LAN connections, charging up to W20,000 per day.

Left luggage Most subway, train and bus stations have storage lockers costing W1000 per day, though these are too small to accommodate suitcases or large backpacks. Some hotels offer left luggage facilities, and a couple of guesthouses are willing to put your bags somewhere safe while you travel around the country.

Lost property The national lost property hotline is ⓣ02/2299-1282, but since staff are unlikely to speak English it may be best to go through the tourist information line on ⓣ1330. There are also lost property offices in City Hall and Chungmuro subway stations, as well as the main train stations.

Post offices There's a post office in every neighbourhood of the city, all of which can handle international mail – just ask for the nearest *ucheguk* (usually Mon–Fri 9am–5pm). The main office in along Jongno Road is open to 8pm on weekdays; 6pm on weekends (ⓣ02/3703-9011).

Taxis All taxis are metered and fares start at W1900, increasing in W100 increments for each additional 144m.

Ticket agencies The big bookstores (see p.135) have ticket booths, or go online at ⓦwww.ticketlink.co.kr.

Tours From Gwanghwamun, tour buses (W10,000) head around the city's main sights every 30min on two loops – one downtown (9am–7pm) and another around the palaces (9am–4pm); there's also a night course (W5000) at 8pm, and guided walking tours are available. For further information see ⓦwww.visitseoul.net.

Travel details

Trains

The trains between the major cities listed below are the fastest, most direct services; on some lines there exist slower, cheaper trains.

Cheongnyangni station to: Andong (11 daily; 4hr–5hr 30min); Chuncheon (hourly; 2hr); Gangneung (10 daily; 6hr 45min); Wonju (9 daily; 1hr 45min–2hr).

Seoul station to: Busan (regularly; 2hr 40min); Cheonan (regularly; 40min); Daegu (regularly; 1hr 35min); Daejeon (regularly; 50min); Suwon (regularly; 30min).

Yongsan station to: Cheonan (regularly; 35min); Daejeon (regularly; 50min); Gwangju (regulary; 2hr 50min); Iksan (regularly; 1hr 45min); Jeonju (direct 3hr 30min, for faster trains change in Iksan); Mokpo (regularly; 3hr 10min); Suwon (regularly; 30min).

Buses

Dong-Seoul Terminal Express section to: Busan (10 daily; 4hr 30min); Cheongju (every 30min; 1hr 40min); Daegu (every 30min; 3hr 30min); Daejeon (every 25min; 1hr 50min); Gangneung (35min; 3hr 20min); Gwangju (every 30min; 3hr 50min); Jeonju (every 45min; 2hr 50min); Jinju (5 daily; 3hr 50min); Samcheok (9 daily; 3hr 40min).

Intercity section to: Andong (34 daily; 2hr 50min); Buan (5 daily; 4hr); Cheonan (49 daily; 1hr 20min); Cheongju (25 daily; 1hr 40min); Chuncheon (every 15min; 1hr 30min); Gangneung (20 daily; 3hr 10min); Gongju (12 daily; 2hr 10min); Guinsa (20 daily; 3hr 30min); Gyeongju (18 daily; 4hr); Haeundae (14 daily; 5hr); Incheon (34 daily; 1hr 10min); Jeongdongjin (3 daily; 3hr 30min); Sokcho (every 20min; 3hr 30min); Songnisan (12 daily; 3hr 30min); Suanbo (13 daily; 2hr 30min);

Taean (4 daily; 4hr); Taebaek (26 daily; 4hr 30min); Wonju (70 daily; 1hr 40min).

Express Terminal Gyeongbu section to: Busan (every 20min; 4hr 30min); Cheonan (every 10min; 1hr 10min); Cheongju (every 10min; 1hr 40min); Daegu (every 20min; 3hr 30min); Daejeon (every 5min; 1hr 50min); Gongju (every 30min; 2hr 20min); Gyeongju (every 30min; 4hr 15min); Pohang (every 20min; 5hr); Tongyeong (11 daily; 5hr). Honam section to: Buan (hourly; 3hr 10min); Chungju (every 30min; 2hr 10min); Daecheon (hourly; 2hr 10min); Gangneung (every 20min; 3hr 10min); Gwangju (every 5min; 3hr 55min); Jeonju (every 10min; 2hr 50min); Jinan (2 daily; 3hr 30min); Jindo (4 daily; 6hr 10min); Mokpo (every 25min; 4hr 20min); Samcheok (every 45min; 3hr 50min); Sokcho (every 30min; 4hr 10min); Suncheon (every 35min; 5hr); Wando (4 daily; 6hr); Wonju (every 15min; 1hr 30min); Yeosu (every 50min; 5hr 40min).

Nambu Terminal to: Anmyeondo (12 daily; 3hr); Buyeo (19 daily; 2hr 10min); Cheonan (every 20min; 1hr); Cheongju (every 30min; 1hr 40min); Daecheon (6 daily; 2hr 10min); Gongju (every 25min; 1hr 30min); Jeonju (18 daily; 2hr 50min); Jinju (29 daily; 4hr); Mallipo (5 daily; 3hr); Muju (5 daily; 3hr 20min); Songnisan (3 daily; 3hr 30min); Taean (22 daily; 2hr 20min); Tongyeong (13 daily; 4hr 30min).

Sinchon Terminal to: Ganghwa-eup (every 10min; 1hr 10min); Oepo (hourly, 2hr); Onsuri (hourly; 2hr).

Flights

Gimpo to: Busan (every 30min; 1hr); Gwangju (7 daily; 50min); Jeju City (every 15min; 1hr 5min); Jinju (3 daily; 55min); Mokpo (1 daily; 55min); Pohang (4 daily; 50min); Ulsan (hourly; 55min); Yeosu (8 daily; 55min).

2

Gyeonggi and Gangwon

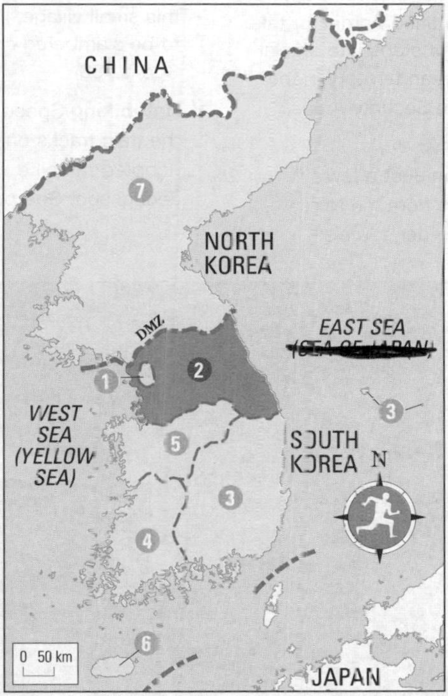

CHAPTER 2

Highlights

- **Suwon** Scramble up a UNESCO-listed fortress wall, visit a nearby folk village, or join what may be the world's only toilet tour. See p.143
- **West Sea islands** Clean air, homely villages and a thriving fishing industry are what make a visit to the islands worthwhile; all this and only a day-trip from Seoul. See p.155
- **The DMZ** Walk through a tunnel under the world's most heavily fortified border, or take a couple of steps into official North Korean territory in the eerie Joint Security Area. See p.159
- **Cheorwon** Just a few kilometres from the North Korean border, there's tension in the air and some interesting sights related to the neighbours across the way. See p.169
- **Seoraksan National Park** With its tall pines and naked rock, Koreans are in near-unanimous agreement that this is the most beautiful national park in the country. See p.178
- **Jeongdongjin** An American warship and a North Korean submarine lie side by side near this small village, just begging to be clambered around. See p.188
- **Rail-biking** Speed 7km down the train tracks on a specially adapted rail-bike, north of Jeongseon. See p.194

▲ Rail-biking near Jeongseon

2

Gyeonggi and Gangwon

Gyeonggi and **Gangwon**, South Korea's northernmost provinces, couldn't be much further apart in character, despite both being bounded to the north by the **Demilitarized Zone**, often described as one of the most dangerous places on Earth. In the small north-western corner of the country, Gyeonggi (officially known as Gyeonggi-do) is a busy rabble of eleven million people much cut up by roads and buzzing with industry. It encircles the two cities of Seoul and Incheon; though these are administratively separate, the combined urban mass of 24 million people – around half of South Korea's population – makes little Gyeonggi one of the world's most densely populated areas.

Seoul functions as the province's beating heart by providing work to the masses, though most of Gyeonggi's surrounding cities are commuter-filled non-entities, whose sights are few and far between. However, **Incheon** to the west of the capital and **Suwon** to the south merit a visit; the former was the first city in the country to be opened up to international trade, and remains Korea's most important link with the outside world thanks to its international airport and ferry terminals. The airport squats on an island just west of Incheon in the West Sea, which also contains myriad nearby **islands** of a more tranquil nature. Heading inland, the Gyeonggi countryside is home to one of the most interesting sights in the country: **Panmunjeom** is a village sandwiched in the demilitarized zone between North and South Korea, where it's even possible to step across the border in the renowned Joint Security Area.

By comparison, Gyeonggi's rugged next-door-neighbour Gangwon (or Gangwon-do) has managed to remain the country's most natural mainland province. A lofty range of mountains score its eastern flank, mopping up national and provincial parks along the way; these include **Seoraksan**, a limestone-heavy mass of beautiful rocky crags and spires, and **Odaesan**, a similar but much less touristed national park just down the coast. Elsewhere around the province it's possible to **raft** down white-water rivers, go skiing, laze on a selection of unspoilt **beaches**, or fire down a rural valley on a specially built rail-bike (see p.194). Even Gangwon's cities are relaxed; **Gangneung** is home to a wonderful Confucian shrine; salty **Sokcho** on the east coast has enough on its periphery to keep you occupied for a few days; and **Chuncheon**, the region's capital, is unhurried enough to allow for some pleasant bike-riding.

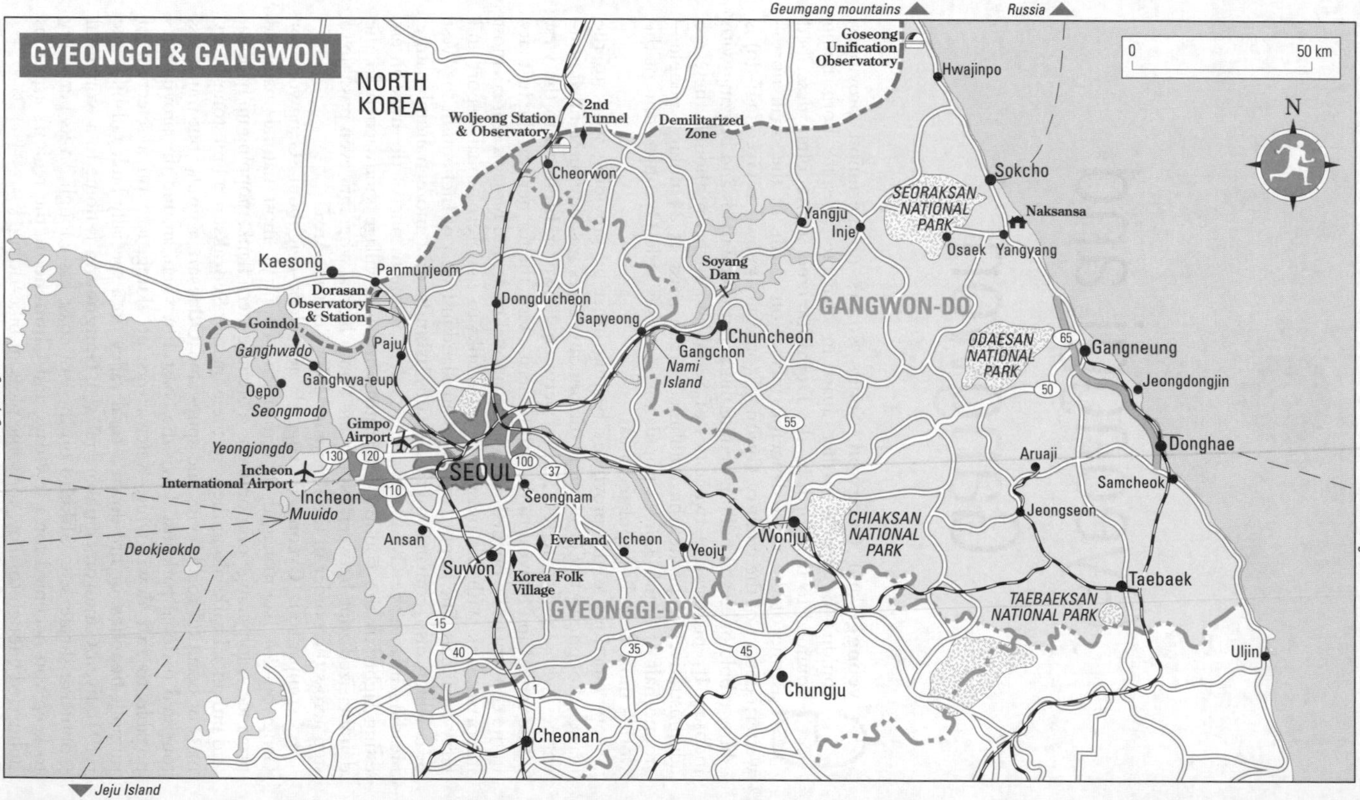
GYEONGGI & GANGWON
NORTH KOREA
Geumgang mountains
Russia
Goseong Unification Observatory
Hwajinpo
0
50 km
N
Woljeong Station & Observatory
2nd Tunnel
Demilitarized Zone
Cheorwon
Sokcho
SEORAKSAN NATIONAL PARK
Naksansa
Yangju
Inje
Osaek
Yangyang
Kaesong
Panmunjeom
Dorasan Observatory & Station
Dongducheon
Soyang Dam
GANGWON-DO
Goindol
Gapyeong
Chuncheon
Ganghwado
Paju
Gangchon
Nami Island
ODAESAN NATIONAL PARK
65
Gangneung
Ganghwa-eup
Oepo
Seongmodo
Jeongdongjin
50
55
Gimpo Airport
Yeongjongdo
130
120
Donghae
Incheon International Airport
SEOUL
100
37
Aruaji
Samcheok
Baengnyeongdo
110
Incheon
Muuido
Seongnam
Jeongseon
Ulleungdo
Deokjeokdo
Ansan
Everland
Icheon
Yeoju
Wonju
CHIAKSAN NATIONAL PARK
China
Suwon
Korea Folk Village
Taebaek
GYEONGGI-DO
TAEBAEKSAN NATIONAL PARK
15
40
35
45
Uljin
Chungju
1
Cheonan
Jeju Island

Gyeonggi-do

Despite the presence of one of the world's biggest cities at its centre, **GYEONGGI-DO** is a somewhat anonymous province. The long steel and concrete tentacles of Seoul stretch across the region, smothering the appeal of what must once have been a corner of commendable natural beauty. Because of this, travellers tend to bypass the area entirely on their way around the country, which is a shame because the bulky cities of **Suwon** and **Incheon** have some intriguing sights, and with both connected to Seoul by subway they make enjoyable day-trips from the capital. Suwon's main draw is the UNESCO-listed fortress, while Incheon is an important transport hub and sports the country's most thriving Chinatown.

A residue of traditional Korean life can be found off the mainland in the West Sea. Better known internationally as the Yellow Sea, it's home to a legion of **islands** from whose shores fishermen roll in and out with the tide as they have for generations. Some of the more notable isles are **Yeongjongdo**, surprisingly pretty despite being the site of Korea's main international airport; **Deokjeokdo**, a laid-back and refreshingly unspoilt retreat from Seoul; and **Ganghwado**, an island within spitting distance of the North Korean border (not that you're allowed even to see North Korea from its army-controlled shores, let alone spit at it). Those who want to go catch a glimpse of the neighbours should head to **Panmunjeon**, a village inside the **Demilitarized Zone** that separates North and South Korea. With security so tight, access is understandably subject to the conditions of the time, but most should be lucky enough to take a step across the world's most fortified border to what is technically **North Korean territory**. Alternatively you can make do with a view of the empty "Propaganda Village" on the opposite side of the DMZ, or a scramble through tunnels built by the North in readiness for an assault on Seoul.

Suwon and around

All but swallowed up by Seoul, **SUWON** is a city with something of an identity crisis. Despite a million-strong population, and an impressive history of its own – best embodied by the **UNESCO-listed fortress** at its centre – it has had to resort to unconventional methods to distance itself culturally from the capital, the best example being the dozens of individually commissioned public toilets that pepper the city. The city, in fact, came close to usurping Seoul as Korea's seat of power following the construction of its fortress in the final years of the eighteenth century, but though the move was doomed to failure, Suwon grew in importance in a way that remains visible to this day – from the higher parts of the fortress wall, it's evident that this once-little settlement burst through its stone confines, eventually creating the noisy hotchpotch of buildings that now forms one of Korea's largest cities.

An hour away from central Seoul, Suwon is certainly within easy **day-trip** territory of the capital, though those who choose to stay will benefit from cheaper accommodation, and get the chance to explore an interesting nightlife scene. East of the centre lie a number of interesting sights, though these can usually be reached just as easily from Seoul.

Arrival, information and orientation

Though **buses** run from Seoul to points all over Suwon, the most popular way for visitors to arrive is by rail, with the main station just about within walking distance of the fortress. It's about an hour from central Seoul on the capital's **subway** line 1, though bear in mind that this splits south of the river, with many trains heading to Incheon on the west coast: be sure to board a train bound for Suwon, or Cheonan, a city another hour down the line. Suwon is also a major stop on the overland **train** line heading in or out of Seoul (though not, notably, for the KTX high-speed trains), meaning that those heading into Suwon from further south will not have to transit via the capital. Those heading from Seoul can cut the subway time in half by using this line, though after factoring in interchange and waiting times, most choose to stay on the subway, a move that also avoids the need to buy another ticket. Those who have a Seoul **transport card**, such as T-Money or Upass, can also use it for buses or subway trains in Suwon.

A useful **information office** (daily 7am–10pm; ⓣ031/228-4672) can be found just outside Suwon station – take a left from the train exit, and look for a squat, traditional-style building; tours of the city start here at 10am and 2pm every day except Monday, lasting two or three hours and costing W8000. Buses to all places of interest can be picked up from the main road outside.

Accommodation

Despite the fact that accommodation in Suwon is markedly cheaper than similar places up the road in Seoul, most travellers visit on **day-trips** from the capital. There are troops of motels in the area bounded by the fortress wall, but you'd do well to disregard all images that staying inside a UNESCO-listed sight may bring to mind, as it's one of the seediest parts of the city. True budget-seekers can make use of the *Grand Sauna*, an excellent *jjimjilbang* just off Rodeo Street, where for just W7000 you can clean off the city grime and put your head down in a dorm room for a night's rest.

Arrows Park Janganmun. Just inside the fortress gate, this motel's clean rooms make it a blessing in the surprisingly seamy area bounded by the fortress walls. The *Ruby* opposite has slightly inferior rooms at marginally lower prices. ❷

Hotel Castle Uman-dong ⓣ031/211-666, ⓦwww.hcastle.co.kr. Suwon's best hotel, though in an uninteresting corner of the city, attracts well-heeled visitors – primarily Europeans here on business – though rooms are of questionable value

Suwon

Suwon	수원
Everland	에버랜드
Hwaseong Fortress	화성
Korean Folk Village	한국 민속촌
Accommodation	
Arrows Park	아로즈 파크
Gwangmyeong Yeoinsuk	광경 여인숙
Hotel Castle	호텔캐슬
Hotel Central	호텔 센트럴
Motel Gremmy	모텔 그레미
Restaurants	
Bonsuwon Galbi	본수원 갈비
Hwaseong Byeolgwan	화성 별관
Sukbong Toast	숙봉 토스트
Yeonpo Galbi	연포 갈비

for those who have to foot their own bill. A nightclub, a sauna and some quality restaurants can be found on the premises. ⑦

Hotel Central Gyo-dong ⓣ031/246-0011, ⓕ031/246-0018. In an excellent location for the fortress, as the name suggests, and not too run down for a Korean tourist hotel. Rooms are reasonably good value and have cable TV; a mini-buffet breakfast is also thrown in for free, but staff are unlikely to speak English, and the bar-filled street outside can get noisy at night. ⑤

Gwangmyeong Yeoinsuk Maesanno. Just across the main road from the train station, rooms here are perfect for those on a tight budget. You wouldn't normally expect beds or private bathrooms at this price level, but they're here, unfortunately accompanied by a curious smell ①

Motel Gremmy Maesanno 2-ga ⓣ031/254-7557. Most Korean motels are a little "love-oriented", but at least this one is honest about it – racy pictures in the corridors, laid-on contraception and "special interest" videos to choose from in the lobby. It's obviously not for everyone, but rooms are large and clean with the more expensive ones housing cavernous bathrooms. ③

Hwaseong fortress

Central Suwon has but one notable sight – **Hwaseong fortress** (free), one of Korea's few entries on the UNESCO list of world heritage, and the most accessible outside Seoul. Completed in 1796, the complex was built on the orders of **King Jeongjo**, one of the Joseon dynasty's most famous rulers, in order to house the remains of his father, Prince Sado. Sado never became king, and met an early end in Seoul's Changgyeonggung Palace at the hands of his own father, King Yeongjo (see box, p.99); it may have been the gravity of the situation that spurred Jeongjo's attempts to move the capital away from Seoul.

Towering almost ten metres high for the bulk of its course, the **fortress wall** rises and falls in a 5.7km-long stretch, most of which is walkable, the various peaks and troughs marked by sentry posts and ornate entrance gates. From the higher vantage points you'll be able to soak up **superb views** of the city, but while there's also plenty to see from the wall itself, the interior is disappointing: other fortresses around the country – most notably those at Gongju, Buyeo and Cheongju – have green, tranquil grounds with little inside save for trees, squirrels, pagodas and meandering paths, but Hwaseong's has had concrete poured into it, and is now a cityscape filled with restaurants, honking traffic and ropey motels. Even on the wall itself, it's hard to escape the noise, which is often punctuated by screaming aircraft from the nearby military base. Another complaint from visitors is that the wall looks too new, the result of copious restoration work, but as this slowly starts to "bed in", it will once again don thin veils of moss and ivy, achieving a look more proximate to the original appearance.

Most visitors start their wall walk at **Paldalmun** – a gate at the lower end of the fortress, exuding a well-preserved magnificence now diluted by its position in the middle of a traffic-filled roundabout – before taking the steep, uphill path to Seonammun, the western gate. Just after this you'll find a platform where W1000 will buy you three gongs of a giant, twelve-ton bell – one for your parents, one for a healthy, harmonious family, and one for whatever you desire. The path then winds its way down past lookout towers, munitions points and other military installations – their respective functions explained on English-language information boards – before crossing a stream, and rising again on the other side. Notable structures here include a brick fire beacon, which was once part of a network that relayed warnings around the country.

In the centre of the area bounded by the fortress walls is **Hwaseong Haenggung**, once a government office, then a palace, and now a fine place to amble around; its pink walls are punctuated by the green lattice frames of windows and doors, which overlook dirt courtyards from where you can admire the fortress wall that looms above. There's a martial arts display (Tues–Sun 11am), and traditional dance and music performances take place at 2pm on Saturdays and Sundays from April to November.

Several **buses** ply the route to Paldalmun from the train station, including #11, #13, #36 and #39, while the #300 heads there from the bus terminal.

Around the city

Away from the fortress, central Suwon carries precious little sightseeing potential, though one interesting modern facet is what may be the world's greatest concentration of high-quality **public toilets** – armed with the relevant pamphlet from the tourist office, it's even possible to fashion some kind of toilet tour. The idea came about from a former mayor of the city who

▲ Hwaseong fortress

went on to become the head of the World Toilet Organization (the other WTO). Seeking to improve his homeland's facilities for the World Cup in 2002, and doubtlessly spurred on by the organization's finding that the average human being spends three years of their life on the toilet, he chose to design dozens of individual facilities. Features may include skylights, mountain views or piped classical music, though such refinement is sadly sullied, as it is all over Korea, by the baskets of used toilet paper discarded throne-side. The World Cup also prompted the city to build one of the best and most distinctive **stadiums** in the country, a move rewarded by an incredible twenty goals in just four games, which included two of the tournament's best – Brazil's 5–2 win over an equally attack-minded Costa Rica, and the hugely entertaining three-all draw between Senegal and Uruguay. The "Big Bird", as the stadium is nicknamed, is now home to the **Suwon Bluewings**, multiple champions of country and continent and, therefore, one of the best teams to watch if you want to experience Korean football – see Ⓦwww.fcbluewings.com for more information.

Eating and drinking

Suwon is famous for a local variety of *galbi*, whereby the regular meat dish is given a salty seasoning. There's an excellent **food court** just above the main concourse of the train station, which serves hundreds of big dishes at surprisingly reasonable prices: there's no English-language menu, but plastic versions of the dishes on offer will help you make your choice; the cashier will then give you a numbered ticket and tell you which counter to collect from. You will more than likely find something appealing on **Rodeo Street**, where the city's youth flocks to in the evening to take advantage of the copious cheap restaurants on offer. Food segues into **drink** as the evening goes on – *Team* and *S* are two popular Western-style bars for local cowboys and cowgirls, with a more local flavour found at *Ddaengjumak*, a *makkeolli* den just after the main Rodeo drag. Hip-hop-heavy *NB* is the most popular club, a taxi-ride away in Ingae-dong.

Bonsuwon Galbi Uman-dong. Around the back of *Hotel Central*, and therefore a little out of the way for those not staying there, is what may well be the best *galbi* restaurant in the city. The succulent meat doesn't come cheap, but is worth it for the chance to try Suwon's local take on Korea's most pyromanial eating experience.

Hwaseong Byeolgwan Paldallo 2-ga. Not far from the entrance to Haenggung, this presentable restaurant – though devoid of English-language menus – serves extremely cheap *bibimbap* and pork cutlet, as well as more expensive meat specials. The *galbitang jeongsik* – beef stew with an array of side dishes – is great value at W7000. Look for the sign saying "Korean Royal Palace Cuisine".

Sukbong Toast Paldalmun Rotary. Fill yourself with grease at this tiny booth before – or, more sensibly, after – climbing the fortress wall. The Korean version of toast makes a good breakfast for those who don't feel like rice or red pepper paste; it is made from squares of lightly fried bread, ham, egg and other ingredients, detailed on an English menu of sorts ("nude toast" is merely the plainest variety).

Yeonpo Galbi Buksu-dong. In a quiet area just inside the fortress wall lies the best restaurant in the area. The *galbi* meat is rather expensive, but cheaper noodle dishes are available, and those who arrive before 3pm can get a huge *jeongsik* (set meal) for W15,000, which includes several small fish and vegetable dishes.

Around Suwon

Making up for the dearth of sights in Suwon itself, is an interesting and varied range of possibilities in a corridor stretching east of the city. Twenty kilometres away, the **Korean Folk Village** is a vaguely authentic portrayal of traditional Korean life; though too sugary for some, it redeems itself with some high-quality dance, music and gymnastic performances. Twenty-five kilometres further east is **Everland**, a huge amusement park that, to Koreans, needs no introduction, and whose outdoor summer beach is proving popular with the country's surgically enhanced.

Korean Folk Village

This re-creation of a traditional **Korean Folk Village** (March–Oct 9am–6.30pm; Nov–Feb 9am–5pm; W11,000) has become one of the most popular tourist draws in the area, its thatch-roofed houses and dirt paths evoking the sights, sounds and some of the more pleasant smells of a bygone time, when farming was the mainstay of the country. Its proximity to Seoul makes this village by far the most-visited of the many such facilities dotted around the country, which tends to diminish the authenticity of the experience. Nevertheless, the riverbank setting and its old-fashioned buildings are impressive, though the emphasis is squarely on performance –shows of seesaw-jumping (a traditional village game that remains popular in modern-day Korea), tightrope-walking and horse-riding take place regularly throughout the day. The fun usually kicks off at 11am, lasting for an hour or two, before starting again at 3pm. The traditional wedding ceremony provides a glimpse into Confucian society, with painstaking attention to detail including gifts of live chickens wrapped up in cloth like Egyptian mummies. Don't miss the **farmers' dance**, in which costumed performers prance around in highly distinctive ribbon-topped hats amid a cacophony of drums and crashes – quintessential Korea.

Free **shuttle buses** to the folk village leave from outside Suwon's tourist information office every half-hour from 10.30am to 2.30pm (30min; free with entry ticket), though the last one back to Suwon departs the village frustratingly early – usually 5pm. Regular city buses are available for those who want to stay a little longer.

Everland

The frequency with which Korea utilizes Western-sounding product names that are impossible to pronounce in the national tongue is rather curious. **Everland** (usually 9.30am–10pm; W27000, discounts after 5pm; Ⓦwww.eng.everland.com), which the Korean alphabet forces locals to pronounce as "Eborendu", is a colossal theme park that ranks as one of the most popular domestic tourist attractions in the country – male or female, young or old, it's hard to find a *hangukin* who hasn't taken this modern-day rite of passage. Most are here for the fairground rides, and the park has all that a rollercoaster connoisseur could possibly wish for. Other attractions include a **zoo**, which features a safari zone that can be toured by bus, jeep or even at night, a speedway track, a golf course, and the surprisingly good **Hoam Museum**, which contains a few excellent examples of Buddhist art, and some interesting French sculpture in an outdoor garden.

The most popular part of the park is **Caribbean Bay** (usually 9.30am–5pm, closes 7pm Sat & Sun; W30,000, discounts after 2.30pm), with an indoor zone that's open year-round containing several pools, a sauna and a short river that you can float down on a tube, as well as massage machines and relaxation capsules. The **outdoor section** (same times June–Aug; W40,000–60,000 depending on date, slight discounts after 5pm) with its man-made beach is what really draws the summer crowds. It's no longer just the beach that's artificial – despite a fairly innocent beginning, when it was marketed squarely at family groups, this has become one of the most popular places for Korea's silicon crowd to show off their new curves. Off the beach, facilities include a water

▲ Farmers' dance at the Korean Folk Village

bobsleigh, which drops you the height of a ten-floor building in just ten seconds, and an artificial surfing facility.

Most locals usually drive to Everland, creating long queues on busy days, whereas foreign visitors tend to take the **bus**. These leave on the half-hour from outside the train station in Suwon, and take around an hour. Several routes head here from Seoul; one of the most frequent and useful runs from the Dong-Seoul bus terminal via Jamsil subway station (50min; W2 200), and a second from just north of Gangnam subway station exit six, via Yangjae (40min; W1,600).

Incheon and the Yellow Sea islands

INCHEON is an important port and Korea's third most populous city. It's also home to the country's main international airport, though few foreign travellers see anything of the city itself, with the overwhelming majority of people preferring to race straight to Seoul on a limousine bus. However, in view of its colourful recent history, it's worth at least a day-trip from the capital. This was where Korea's "Hermit Kingdom" finally crawled out of self-imposed isolation in the late nineteenth century and opened itself up to international trade, an event that was spurred on by the Japanese following similar events in their own country (the "Meiji Restoration"). The city was also the landing site for **Douglas MacArthur** and his troops in a manoeuvre that turned the tide of the Korean War (see box, p.154). However, despite its obvious importance to Korea past and present, there's a palpable absence of civic pride, possibly due to the fact that Incheon is inextricably connected to the huge Seoul metropolis – the buildings simply don't stop on their long march from the capital. This may be about to change, however, as it has been chosen as the host of the **2014 Asian Games**, and is busily setting about smartening itself up in preparation for the event.

Incheon's various sights can easily be visited on a day-trip from Seoul, which is an hour away by subway train. The most interesting part is **Jung-gu**, the

Incheon

Incheon	인천
Chinatown	차이나타운
Jayu Park	자유공원
Wolmido	월미도
Ferry terminals	
International ferry terminal 1	1 국제 여객 터미날
International ferry terminal 2	2 국제 여객 터미날
Yeonan ferry terminal	연안 여객 터미날
Accommodation	
Athene Motel	아테네 모텔
Buseongjang Yeogwan	부성장 여관
Paradise Hotel	파라다이스 호텔
Wolmido Motel	월미도 모텔
Restaurants	
Cana Well-Being Buffet	가나 웰빙부페
Cheonggwan	청관
Hyangmanseong	향만성
To-chon	토촌
Yejeon	예전

country's only official Chinatown, a small but appealing area where you can rub shoulders with the Russian sailors and Filipino merchants who – after the Chinese – make up most of Incheon's sizeable foreign contingent. It sits below **Jayu Park**, where a statue of MacArthur gazes out over the sea. Along the coast is the island of **Wolmido**, home to umpteen seafood restaurants and an amusement park popular with Incheon's young and young-at-heart. Incheon is the starting point for **international ferries** to a number of Chinese cities, as well as a number of Korean islands; see box on p.152 for more information.

Arrival, orientation and information

Importantly, there's no need to transit in Incheon to get to and from the **international airport**, which is actually on an island west of the city proper and connected to the mainland by bridge: there are dedicated airport bus connections from Seoul and all over the country. To get to Incheon from the airport, you can go via one of several limousine bus routes, or city bus #306 to Incheon subway station. A second important point is that despite the city's size, there's **no train station**: to get to Incheon from other parts of Korea by train you'll first need to head to Seoul. Gwangmyeong station to the south of the capital is the most convenient transfer point if coming from the south. Entering or departing Incheon by **bus** avoids the need to change in Seoul; the terminal is handily situated next to the "Terminal" subway station, a stop on Incheon's subway line, which intersects with Seoul's line 1 at Bupyeong. Those who have a Seoul **transport card**, such as T-Money or Upass, will be able to use it on Incheon's buses and subway trains. International **ferries** dock at one of two terminals; see p.196 for details.

The city itself spreads far and wide in an unruly sprawl of buildings and industry, with its western fringe dissolving into the sea in a mess of cranes, ships and containers. Incheon's main sights lie in Jung-gu, a western district of the city best accessed via Incheon or Dong-Incheon **subway** stations, the last two on Seoul's

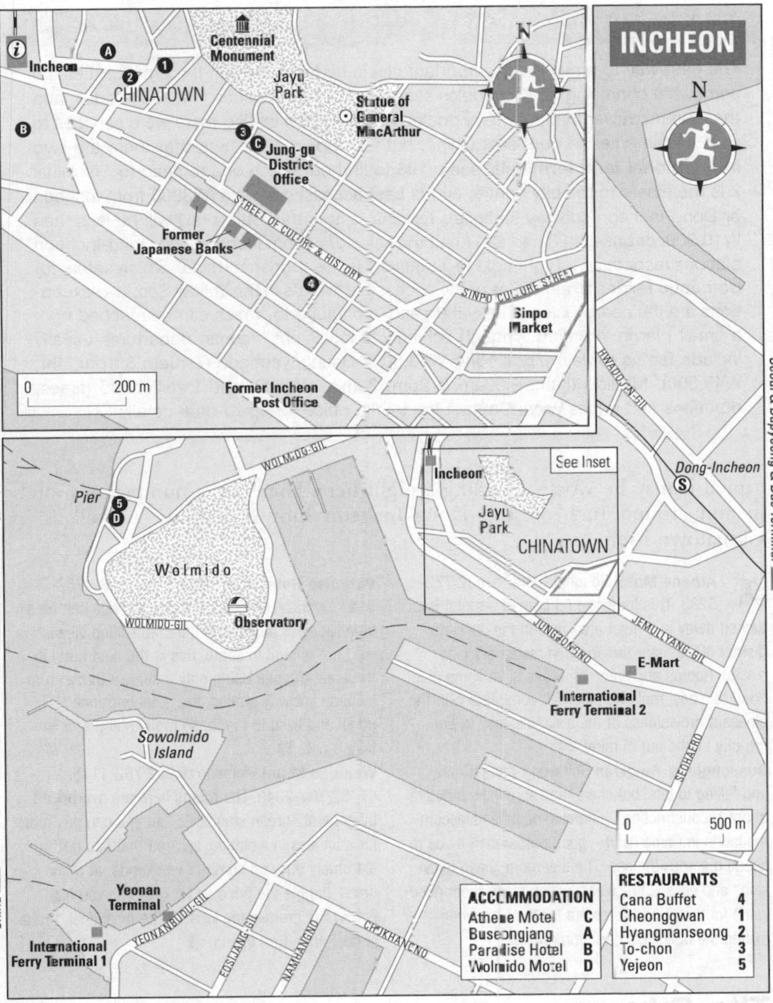

line 1. From Seoul, be sure to board a train bound for Incheon, as line 1 splits south of the capital and heads to Suwon and Cheonan. Outside Incheon subway station is a helpful **tourist information** office (daily 9am–6pm; ⓣ032/773-2225), which usually has an English-speaker; further offices can be found in the international ferry terminals. From here, there are six daily **tour buses** to the island of Yeongjongdo (see p.155), costing W6000 and taking almost three hours to complete the trip, while a special "historical experience" tour of Incheon leaves at 10am on Saturdays – call the tourist office to make a reservation.

Accommodation

Like Suwon, Incheon's proximity to Seoul means that most people choose to visit on a day-trip, but with accommodation prices a little lower than in the

Incheon ferry connections

The best way to arrive in this important city is by **ferry**, though the practicalities are somewhat confusing: the schedules seem to change almost as fast as the tides, and there are no fewer than four ferry docks. At the time of writing there were services to at least ten cities in northeast China, but it's important to note that there are **two international ferry terminals**: see p.196 to find out which one to head for. Terminal 2 is the closer to the city centre, and is best accessed by taxi (W3000 from Incheon or Dong-Incheon subway stations). Terminal 1 is further out; a taxi will be less than W10,000, or buses #28 and #24 head the same way from Incheon and Dong-Incheon stations respectively. Right next to Terminal 1 is the Yeonan terminal, which caters for **domestic ferries** to almost all of the accessible islands in the Yellow Sea; two exceptions are the nearby isles of Jakyakdo and Yeongjongdo, which can be reached from a small pier in Wolmido. Though achingly inconsistent, Yeonan departures usually include ferries to Jeju (7pm; 13hr; W53,500), Baengnyeongdo (7.10am & 1pm; 4hr; W49,500), Muuido (8am, 9.30am & 2pm; 30min; W9500) and Deokjeokdo (times, durations and prices vary). Contact the tourist office for up-to-date details.

capital it may be worth spending a night here. There are a number of motels in and around Incheon and Dong-Incheon subway stations, as well as in Chinatown itself.

Athene Motel Songhak-dong ⓣ032/772-5233. This hard-to-find gem of a motel is tucked away in a quiet area behind the Jung-gu district office, near the *To-chon* restaurant (see p.155). Rooms and common areas have some nice floral touches, real and pictorial; combined with the pleasant drowsiness of the area, it's easy to put big-city bustle out of mind. ❷

Buseongjang Yeogwan Bukseong-dong. Crusty and falling to bits, but cheap and somehow redolent of pre-reconstruction Chinatown or, indeed, accommodation in China itself – good preparation if you're heading across the sea. The tiny rooms have televisions and en-suite facilities, which make them good value for the price. Watch out for the step when exiting the building's dark corridor. ❶

Paradise Hotel Hang-dong 1-ga ⓣ032/762-5181, ⓕ032/763-5281. Though service can be a little ropey at times, and the crane-filled views may not appeal to some, this is the best hotel in the area. Despite being only a stone's throw from Incheon subway station, the hotel entrance is uphill and hard to reach, so many still prefer to take a cab. ❼

Wolmido Motel Wolmido ⓣ032/762-1115, ⓕ032/761-2349. The rooms here are overpriced by general Korean standards, but you can pay more for a lot less in Wolmido, an area that can get extremely busy on summer weekends; at other times, haggle the price as far down as you can. Follow the promenade west of the ferry dock to the anchor, then turn inland. ❹

The City

To get to **Jung-gu**, Incheon's most absorbing district, you should head to Incheon subway station, which sits at the end of a line that runs all the way from Seoul. On exiting the gate, you'll immediately be confronted by the city's gentrified Chinatown, sitting across the main road and demarcated by the requisite oriental gate. Not so long ago, this area was dowdy and run-down, and lent an unintentional air of authenticity by displaying cracked roads, rubble and grime; it has since been given a makeover, and is now a pleasant and surprisingly quiet area to walk around with a belly full of Chinese food. Uphill roads heading northeast from Chinatown lead to **Jayu Park**, also within easy walking distance of the subway station, and home to a statue of **General Douglas MacArthur**, staring proudly out over the seas that he conquered during the Korean War (see box, p.154). Also in the park is the Korean-American Centennial Monument, made up of eight black triangular shards

Korean cuisine

For many people visiting Korea, food forms one of the biggest highlights. The country's distinctive cuisine gets surprisingly little coverage internationally, which can make each mealtime feel like a voyage of discovery. Those with little experience of spicy food should be warned that there's very little respite from it – most meals come with lashings of red-pepper paste (*gochujang*), and some take spiciness to eye-watering extremes. Korean food was uniformly mild until the seventeenth century, when chillies arrived on the ships of Western traders. Nowadays, it's almost impossible for a Korean to eat without a *gochujang* "hit". Though there's plenty of choice for visitors, there are three popular Korean dishes to try.

Gimchi ▲

Red chillies ▼

Gimchi

No country on earth is as closely entwined with its national dish as Korea is with its beloved **gimchi**: a spicy mix of fermented vegetables, which is served as a complimentary **side dish** at pretty much every restaurant in the land. Many traditionally minded families still ferment their own *gimchi* in distinctive earthenware jars, but home-made or not it's an important part of breakfast, lunch and dinner in most Korean homes. Because of the known redolence of the dish, many even have a dedicated *gimchi* fridge, quartered off to separate the four main types. The two most common varieties are **baechu gimchi**, made with cabbage, and **ggakdugi gimchi**, which are cubes of radish in a red-pepper sauce, but there are others made with cucumber or other vegetables.

Salt, garlic and a hearty dollop of **red-pepper paste** are almost mandatory in a good *gimchi*, though additional ingredients vary from home to home and restaurant to restaurant. Many of the best recipes are shrouded in secrecy and handed down from generation to generation, but some of the most popular components include onion, brine, ginger and fish paste. Needless to say, the effect on the breath can be unsavoury to say the least.

Fermented *gimchi* was once used as a means of maintaining vegetable intake through Korea's long, bitter winters, but even today the health benefits are proclaimed proudly by Koreans. Foreigners often have a tough time adjusting, but love it or loathe it, there are few better ways to endear yourself to the locals than by chowing down on a bowlful of *gimchi*.

Galbi

Galbi is a carnivore's dream come true. Here, you get to play chef with a plate of raw meat commonly placed on a grill over **charcoal**, and a pair of scissors to cut it all up. As excess fat drips off the meat onto the briquettes it releases the occasional tongue of flame, which lends a genuine air of excitement to the meal.

In dedicated *galbi* restaurants the dish is usually eaten sitting on the floor, but many cheaper places have outdoor tables, and on warmer weekends Koreans even drag their own mini barbeque set to a park or riverbank for an *al fresco* picnic. In all cases, it's traditionally washed down with a bottle or three of *soju* – Korea's answer to vodka.

Most restaurants serve **beef** (*so-galbi*), but some places offer pork too (*dwaeji-galbi*, or *samgyeopsal* for fattier belly roll), and always with a range of free **side dishes**, known as *banchan*. Ranging from three to well over twenty, these include the obligatory *gimchi*, as well as bowls of pulses, tofu, leek, potato and tiny fish, all lovingly prepared and replenished at no extra cost. A boiling bowl of egg broth and a tray of leaves are also usually thrown in for the group to share – *galbi* is not a meal to eat on your own – and each person is given a bowl of chopped-up greens and a pot of sesame oil.

In Confucian Korea, it's common for the "lowest" adult member of the party – usually the youngest female – to cook and dish out the meat. To eat it, first place a leaf or two from the tray onto your left hand, then with your chopsticks add a piece of meat, a smudge of soybean paste and a few morsels from the *banchan*; roll the leaf around to make a ball, and you're ready to go.

▲ Traditional beef galbi

▼ Eating al fresco in Seoul

▼ Traditional meal with side dishes

Bibimbap meal in Jeonju ▲

Seafood is a popular ingredient in Korean dishes ▼

Bibimbap

Literally meaning "mixed rice", **bibimbap** consists of a bowl of rice topped with seasoned vegetables, red-pepper paste, minced beef and a fried egg. It was originally a religious dish derived from the five principal colours of Korean Buddhism – **red** for the paste, **yellow** for the egg yolk, **white** for the rice, **blue** for the meat and **green** for the vegetables – and is one of the easiest dishes to find in Korea. Some restaurants serve it in a heated stone bowl (*dolsot bibimbap*), those in the countryside may make it using only vegetables sourced from the surrounding mountains (*sanchae bibimbap*), while certain establishments in Jeonju have elevated the dish to an art form, serving it with umpteen side dishes.

Culinary curiosities

▸▸ **bulgogi deop-bap** Thanks to its lack of red-pepper paste, this dish – strips of marinaded beef over rice – is a favourite with newbies to Korea.

▸▸ **gimbap** You're rarely far from your nearest roll of *gimbap* in Korea – cylinders of seaweed-coated rice with a variety of delicious fillings: cheap and filling snack solutions for a hike or a long bus-ride.

▸▸ **haemul ajeon** These sumptuous, seafood-filled, savoury pancakes are the default Korean choice for an after-hike meal, particularly if washed down with a pot of *dongdongju* (creamy rice wine).

▸▸ **nakji bokkeum** Seeing the tentacles chopped off a baby octopus that's stir-frying to death on a tray of salad isn't everybody's idea of fun, but there's no easier (or more delicious) way to ingratiate yourself with new Korean friends.

▸▸ **twigim** Indisputably unhealthy, these are deep-fried stall-snacks given one more quick dunk in scalding oil before they're sliced and served, preferably smothered in spicy *ddeokbokki* sauce.

that stretch up towards each other but never quite touch – feel free to make your own comparisons with the relationship between the two countries. Views from certain parts of the park expose Incheon's port, a colourful maze of cranes and container ships that provide a vivid reminder of the city's trade links with its neighbours across the seas.

The cultural district

South of Jayu Park lies a quiet but cosmopolitan part of town, where the streets are lined with Russian shops and sailor bars plastered with Cyrillic writing, as well as restaurants run by – and catering for – the city's Filipino community. From Chinatown, it's possible to take a pleasant, relatively traffic-free walk through Incheon's past on the way to Dong-Incheon station – pick up the *History through Modern Architecture* pamphlet from the tourist office, which will guide you directly to a road studded with distinctive **Japanese colonial buildings**. Surprisingly Western in appearance, three of these were originally banks, though one has now been turned into a small **museum** (9am–5pm, closed Mon; free) and is worth popping into for a look at life in colonial times. The staff will be more than happy to play you an English-language DVD detailing the opening up of the country to international trade in the late eighteenth century. On the street outside are some fascinating pictures taken here on what was then a quiet, dusty road almost entirely devoid of traffic, peopled with white-robed gents in horsehair hats – images of a Korea long gone. However, one block to the north on a parallel road, the city has tried to evoke this bygone era on the slightly bizarre **Street of Culture and History**; the new wooden fronts added to the buildings are the only discernable things that constitute such a grand title, though they look decidedly pretty. The businesses that received a facelift were tiny shops such as confectioners, laundries and electrical stores, but with the city likely to pour more money into the area, you can expect these to be replaced by galleries and arty cafés when their rent triples.

Wolmido

Along the coast to the south of Incheon subway station is **WOLMIDO**, once a just-offshore island but now largely absorbed by the city. Families arrive by the busload to eat at raw fish restaurants, let off small fireworks and have fun at an **amusement park** where three thirty-metre-long ships scud up, down and around, much to the delight of those on board. From the seafront promenade you may be able to see planes humming in and out of the airport on Yeongjongdo, an island across the water (see p.155); sea mist and pollution regularly conspire to erase views of the aircraft, though you'll be able to get closer to the action on regular **ferries** to the island which leave from the promenade's pier (every 20–30min; 20min; W2000). There are also hourly ferries to neighbouring **Jakyakdo** (10.40am–5.40pm; 20min; W5000), a pretty speck of land whose trails and rural charm make it worth a brief visit.

Eating and drinking

Rarely for a Korean city, and perhaps uniquely for a Korean port, Incheon isn't renowned for its food, though with such excellent fare on offer this may come as a surprise to many visitors. One major variation from other cities is, of course, the presence of a large and thriving **Chinatown** – in culinary terms, this is the most authentically Chinese place in the country. It's also worth noting that the Korean take on Chinese cuisine is usually far from authentic. Away from

General MacArthur and the Incheon landings

"We drew up a list of every natural and geographic handicap... Incheon had 'em all."

Commander Arlie G. Capps

On the morning of September 15, 1950, the most daring move of the **Korean War** was made, an event that was to alter the course of the conflict entirely, and now seen as one of the greatest military manoeuvres in history. At this point the Allied forces had been pushed by the North Korean People's Army into a small corner of the peninsula around Busan, but **General Douglas MacArthur** was convinced that a single decisive movement behind enemy lines could be enough to turn the tide.

MacArthur wanted to attempt an amphibious landing on the Incheon coast, but his plan was greeted with scepticism by many of his colleagues – both the South Korean and American armies were severely under-equipped (the latter only just recovering from the tolls of World War II), Incheon was heavily fortified, and its natural island-peppered defences and fast tides made it an even more dangerous choice.

The People's Army had simply not anticipated an attack on this scale in this area, reasoning that if one were to happen, it would take place at a more sensible location further down the coast. However, the plan went ahead and the Allied forces performed **successful landings** at three Incheon beaches, during which time North Korean forces were shelled heavily to quell any counterattacks. The city was taken with relative ease. MacArthur had correctly deduced that a poor movement of supplies was his enemy's Achilles heel – landing behind enemy lines gave Allied forces a chance to cut the supply line to KPA forces further south, and Seoul was duly retaken on 25 September.

Despite the Incheon victory and its consequences, MacArthur is not viewed by Koreans – or, indeed, the world in general – in an entirely positive light, feelings exacerbated by the continued American military presence in the country. While many in Korea venerate the General as a hero, repeated demonstrations have called for the **tearing down** of his statue in Jayu Park, denouncing him as a "war criminal who massacred civilians during the Korean War", and whose statue "greatly injures the dignity of the Korean people". Documents obtained after his eventual dismissal from the Army suggest that he would even have been willing to bring nuclear weapons into play – on December 24, 1950, he requested the shipment of 38 atomic bombs to Korea, intending to string them "across the neck of Manchuria". Douglas MacArthur remains a controversial character, even in death.

Chinatown, there are teams of **restaurants** serving fresh fish on the promenade in Wolmido, and Sinpo Market has an extremely popular chicken restaurant, *Dakgangjeong* – just look for the queue.

Cana Well-being Buffet Jungang 3-ga. Not far from International Ferry Terminal 2, and perfect for those who've just arrived from China, anyone who requires a full belly should head straight here. There's no menu, but W5000 will pay for an all-out assault on the delicious buffet selection, which contains enough variety to provide a decent primer on Korean cuisine. The mushrooms, *bulgogi* and buckwheat noodles are particularly worth a second – then a third – trip to the buffet bar.

Cheonggwan Bukseong-dong 3-ga. Downhill from the western Jayu Park entrance you'll find Chinatown's best restaurant, which serves genuine Chinese food in pleasant, upper-floor surroundings. Try the sautéed shredded beef with green pepper, or spicy *mapo* tofu, and finish off your meal with fried, honey-dipped rice balls. Though prices are generally high, cheap rice and noodle dishes are available, most notably the *beokkeumbap* – fried rice with black bean sauce and vegetables, topped with an egg and served with spicy seafood soup.

Hyangmanseong Bukseong-dong 2-ga. Various Chinese dishes are on offer at this small but impressively authentic Chinatown institution, which has been operating for over forty years. There's usually a special "delectable course sampler" on offer for W8000, with the main dishes coming in at much higher prices; they're proudest of their braised prawns in chilli sauce.

To-chon Songhak-dong. A wonderful, rustic lair, whose ground floor is surrounded on three sides by interconnected fish tanks. Fishy set meals go for W23,000 or more, though cheaper dishes are available, such as delicious mountain *bibimbap* for W7000.

Yejeon Bukseong-dong 1-ga. Though it may seem that the culinary options on Wolmido run to fish, fish and more fish, this restaurant dishes out pizza, steak and pork cutlet to those desperately seeking something that hasn't been trawled from the sea. The lunch specials are good value, and the cocktails go down nicely in the evening.

West Sea Islands

Gyeonggi's perforated western coast topples into the West Sea in an expanse of mud flats – the **tidal range** here is said to be the second biggest in the world after the Bay of Fundy in eastern Canada, though this is challenged by Britain's Bristol Channel. Whoever the silver medallist, the retreat of the tides is fantastic news for hunters of clams and other sea fare; it does, however, mean that beaches are in short supply. Fear not, Korean land rises again across the waves in the form of dozens of **islands**, almost all of which have remained pleasantly green and unspoilt; some also have excellent **beaches**. Life here is predominantly fishing-based and dawdles by at a snail's pace – a world away from Seoul and its environs, despite a few being close enough to be visited on a day-trip. Quite a number of these have next to no traffic, making them ideal places for a ride if you can find a bike to bring along.

Yeongjongdo receives thousands of foreign guests each day, a fact entirely attributable to the international airport that was constructed here in 2001, though only a small number of people stay longer than it takes them to find a bus or train out. Further up the Gyeonggi coast is **Ganghwado**, a slightly over-busy dot of land, though its UNESCO-listed dolmen betray an ancient history. Both these islands are connected to the mainland by bus, but there are others that can take hours to reach by ferry; two of these are **Deokjeokdo** and **Baengnyeongdo**, both beautiful and sufficiently far away from "regular" Korea to provide perfect escapes for those in need of a break. Swarms of less-visited islands are also there for the taking, if you're in an adventurous mood.

Yeongjongdo

On the face of it, things don't look good – **YEONGJONGDO** is a small island, and has had one of the world's busiest airports slapped down in the centre – but the reality is somewhat more appealing. Here once lay two islands – Yeongjongdo to the east and Yongyudo to the west – but following a mammoth **land reclamation project**, the two were connected and Incheon International Airport was built, with the first flights taking off in 2001. The island's western coast is dotted with pleasant **beaches**, and "Airport New Town" – a collection of hotels, restaurants and apartments – has been built just a few kilometres east of the airport.

For information about leaving the airport, see the box on p.34. To get to Yeongjongdo for sightseeing, there are a few options. A few daily **tour buses** head from Incheon to the island's main sights, while some Seoul tour companies also make the trip. From Incheon it's also possible to take a ferry from Wolmido – see p.153 for more details. Most people prefer to get to the airport and make their own way around Yeongjongdo – take bus #202 to the west of the island for the beaches, and buses #203 or #223 to the Airport New Town. **Motels** aplenty can be found in both areas; a few of the more interesting accommodation options are listed below.

▲ Take a boat trip to one of the West Sea islands

Accommodation

Best Western Incheon Airport Unseo-dong ⓣ032/743-1000, ⓦwww.bestwestern.com. Right next to the airport, and a popular choice for business travellers in need of a rest after their flight. Rooms are well equipped and large by Korean standards, and though a few visitors feel stung by restaurant prices, there's plenty of culinary choice nearby. ❻

Guesthouse Korea Airport New Town ⓣ032/747-1872, ⓦwww.guesthousekorea.co.kr. An excellent guesthouse – modern, spotlessly clean, not too expensive (dorm beds W20,000; private rooms are also available) and the perfect choice for budget travellers arriving late at night, or those whose flight schedule necessitates an early-morning dash from Seoul. There's free Internet access and cooking facilities, and the staff will collect you from the airport. ❷

Hyatt Regency Incheon Unseo-dong ⓣ062/745-1234, ⓦincheon.regency.hyatt.com. Just a couple of minutes away from the airport is the island's most upmarket hotel. The facilities and attention to detail are as you'd expect from the chain – the rooms are kitted out with large, flat-screen TVs and goose-down duvets, and guests can take a swim in the large indoor pool. ❼

Ganghwado

Unlike most Yellow Sea islands, **GANGHWADO** is close enough to the mainland to be connected by road – buses run regularly from Sinchon bus terminal in Seoul via Gimpo, taking around ninety minutes to arrive in **Ganghwa-eup**, the ugly main settlement; from here local buses dash to destinations across the island, though the place is so small that journey times are rarely more than half-an-hour long. While this accessibility means that Ganghwa

The Yellow Sea

The West Sea is far better known abroad as the "**Yellow Sea**", a reference to the vast quantity of silt deposited into it by the Yellow River, which flows from the Chinese desert. But be warned that few Koreans will take kindly to this term, even though it's the accepted international name; there's nowhere near the intensity of debate that the East Sea/Sea of Japan on the other side of the country has inspired (see box on p.185 for more information), but those who want to stay on the better side of their Korean friends should refer to the body of water off the Gyeonggi coast as the "**West Sea**".

lacks the beauty of some of its more distant cousins, there's plenty to see. One look at a map should make clear the strategic importance of the island, which not only sits at the mouth of Seoul's main river, the Han, but whose northern flank is within a frisbee throw of the **North Korean border**. Would-be adventurers should note that this area is chock-full of military installations, and closed to the public – see p.416 for information on the best places to catch a glimpse of the neighbours' homeland.

Before the latest conflict, this unfortunate isle saw **battles** with Mongol, Manchu, French, American and Japanese forces, among others (see p.426). However, Ganghwado's foremost sights date from further back than even the earliest of these fisticuffs – a clutch of **dolmen** scattered around the northern part of the island, dating from the first century BC and now on UNESCO's World Heritage list. Misty remnants from bygone millennia, these dolmen are overground burial chambers consisting of flat capstones supported by three or more vertical megaliths. The Korean peninsula contains over 30,000 of these ancient tombs – almost half of the world's total – and Ganghwado has one of the highest concentrations in the country. Most can only be reached by car or bike, though one is situated near a main road and accessible by bus. From Ganghwa-eup, take one of the buses bound for Changhu-ri, which depart every hour or so, and make sure that the driver knows where you want to go – ask to be dropped off at the *Goindol* (24hr; free), a granite tomb which sits unobtrusively in a field as it has for centuries: a stone skeleton long divested of its original earth covering, with a large five-by-seven-metre capstone. The surrounding countryside is extremely beautiful, and you can combine a visit to the dolmen with a delightful walk. One of the best places to head to is the village of **Hajeom**, not far to the west, where the roofs of some houses have been traditionally decorated with distinctive patterns. From the hills above Hajeom it's possible to view the North Korean bank of the Hangang, though sadly the propaganda that the North once boomed across the border from giant speakers can no longer be heard. Visual propaganda still remains, however, in the form of giant slogans best seen from the small mountain of **Bongcheonsan**, a forty-minute walk north of Hajeom – the message visible across the border translates as "Yankees go home", a request that would doubtless be more effective were it not written in Korean.

To the south of the island is **Jeondeungsa**, a pretty temple dating from the fourth century – when Buddhism was just taking root on the peninsula – making it one of the oldest temples in the country. It was also the venue for the creation of the famed *Tripitaka Koreana*, eighty-thousand-plus blocks of carved Buddhist doctrine which now reside in Haeinsa temple near Daegu (see p.225). To reach the temple, take one of the half-hourly buses bound for Onsu-ri. About five kilometres west of Onsu is **Manisan**, the main peak of the island, which affords wonderful views of the surrounding islands.

Studding Ganghwado's east coast are three **fortresses** – Gwangseongbo, Deokjinjin and Chojijin – which are best seen by making use of the bicycle lanes that run alongside the main road; otherwise, buses run every hour or so. Gwangseongbo (daily 9am–6pm; W1000) is the northernmost and most interesting of the three, and dates from the mid-seventeenth century; its strategic importance will be obvious to all visitors, as it peers out over the channel that separates Ganghwado from the mainland.

The small settlement of **Oepo** (pronounced "Way-paw") on the island's western coast is by far the most appealing place to stay; small and delightfully old-fashioned, it's a little like stepping into the Korea of the 1970s, before the country's "economic miracle" mopped up old traditions by the bucketload. There are no particular sights, so wandering around to soak up the atmosphere is the order of the day. There's an appealing little fish market near the dock, and restaurants all around it; you can even stay above one at the impossible-to-miss *Santa Lucia* (ⓣ032/933 2141; ❷), the only building to take advantage of the village's views of **Seongmodo**, another island just across the water. Half-hourly ferries run to the island, with the journey taking around ten minutes; though be warned Oepo must be the seagull capital of Korea, with local flocks having an endearing habit of swirling around the ferry for its entire journey. Seongmodo itself is achingly beautiful, with precious few settlements; the main sight here is Bomunsa, a small temple surrounded by trees to which buses run at ten-minutes past the hour from a small stop just uphill from the ferries. There are restaurants near the dock if you need to wait awhile, and even *minbak* accommodation, with some more places near the temple.

Deokjeokdo and further afield

Possibly the prettiest and most tranquil of the Yellow Sea isles, **DEOKJEOKDO** feels a world away from Seoul, though it's quite possible to visit from the capital on a day-trip. There's little in the way of sightseeing, and not much to do, but that's just the point – the island has a couple of stunning beaches and some gorgeous mountain trails, and makes a refreshing break from the hustle and bustle of the mainland. Around the ferry berth are a few shops, restaurants and *minbak*, while a bus meets the ferries and makes its way round to **Seopori Beach** on the other, quieter side of the island – also home to a few *minbak*. Most who stay here for a day or two spend their time chatting to locals, lazing or throwing back beers on the beach, going fishing or taking the easy climb up to the island's main peak. Some adventurous souls make their way to **Soyado**, an island facing the ferry berth, and only a few minutes away if you can flag down a fishing boat. There's even less to do than on Deokjeokdo, though there are a couple of places to stay if you look hard enough, and you can rest assured you'll be one of very few foreigners to have over-nighted on the island.

Four hours' ferry-ride from Incheon is **BAENGNYEONGDO**, almost tickling the North Korean coastline and one of the most popular points of access for those fleeing North Korea to seek a better life in the South; you're unlikely to see any defectees, much less be mistaken for one, but steer well clear of military installations. The island is so named because of its apparent resemblance to an ibis taking flight, and although the reality is somewhat different you'll find yourself gawping at Baengnyeongdo's spectacular **rock formations**, best seen from one of the tour boats that regularly depart the port. Some of the most popular are off Dumujin, to the west of the island, while at Sagot Beach the stone cliffs plunge diagonally into the sea.

The tranquil nature of these islands is sometimes diluted by swarms of summer visitors – it's best to visit on weekdays, or outside the warmest months. **Ferries** run to Deokjeokdo from Incheon's Yeonan pier, but schedules are erratic to say the least; there are usually two fast services a day at times determined by the tides, the day of the month and goodness knows what other random factors, and a slower ferry leaving Incheon at 7.45am. Ferries to Baengnyeongdo leave from the same pier three times daily; for all sailings, contact the tourist information office in Incheon (☎032/773-2225) for up-to-date information.

The Demilitarized Zone

As the tour bus crawls out of Seoul and heads slowly north through the traffic, the seemingly endless urban jungle slowly diminishes in size before disappearing altogether. You're now well on the way to a place where the mists of the Cold War sill linger on, and one that could well have been ground zero for the Third World War – the **DEMILITARIZED ZONE**. More commonly referred to as "the DMZ", this no-man's-land is a four-kilometre-wide buffer zone that came into being at the end of the Korean War in 1953. It sketches an unbroken spiky line across the peninsula from coast to coast, separating the two Koreas and their diametrically opposed ideologies. Although it sounds forbidding, it's actually possible to enter this zone, and take a few tentative steps into North Korean territory – thousands of civilians do so every month, though only as part of a **tightly controlled tour**. It's even home to two small communities; see the box on p.162. Elsewhere are a few platforms from which the curious can stare across the border, and a **tunnel** built by the North, which you can enter.

Details given here are for the area surrounding Panmunjeom, but there are a number of other ways to get a handle on the North. Free tours from the town of Cheorwon take in observatory visits and a tunnel walk under the DMZ (p.171), and there's another observatory on the east coast, just north of Sokcho (p.176). Thanks to the Hyundai Corporation's lease of some North Korean land, it's also possible to take a tour through the DMZ to the wonderful Geumgang mountains just across the border (p.413), or go for broke and become one of those rare souls who can say they've been on a tour to Pyongyang (p.399).

Some history

For the first year of the **Korean War** (1950–53), the tide of control yo-yoed back and forth across the peninsula (see p.428 for more details). Then in June 1951, General Ridgeway of the United Nations Command got word that the Korean People's Army (KPA) would "not be averse to" armistice talks. These talks took place in the city of Kaesong, now a major North Korean city (see p.411), but were soon shifted south to **Panmunjeom**, a tiny farming village that suddenly found itself the subject of international attention.

Cease-fire talks went ahead for two long years and often degenerated into venomous verbal battles littered with expletives. One of the most contentious issues was the repatriation of prisoners of war, and a breakthrough came in April 1953, when terms were agreed; exchanges took place on a bridge over the River Sachon, now referred to as the **Bridge of No Return**. "Operation Little Switch" came first, seeing the transfer of sick and injured prisoners (notably, 6000 returned to the North, while only a tenth of that number walked the other way); "Operation Big Switch" took place shortly afterwards, when the soldiers on both sides were asked to make a final choice over their preferred destination. Though no **peace treaty** was ever signed, representatives of the KPA, the United Nations Command (UNC) and the Chinese Peoples' Liberation Army put their names to an **armistice** on July 27, 1953; South Korean delegates refused to do so. The room where the signing took place was built specially for the occasion, and cobbled together at lightning speed by KPA personnel; it now forms part of most tours to North Korea (p.413).

An uneasy truce has prevailed since the end of the war – the longest military deadlock in history – and the DMZ is now something of a natural haven filled with flora and fauna that's been left to regenerate and breed in relative isolation. However, there have been regular spats along the way. In the early 1960s a small number of disaffected American soldiers **defected** to the North, after somehow managing to make it across the DMZ alive (see box, p.437), while in 1968 the crew of the captured USS *Pueblo* (p.408) walked south over the Bridge of No Return after protracted negotiations. The most serious confrontation took place in 1976, when two American soldiers were killed in the **Axe Murder Incident** (see box, p.164), and in 1984, a young tour leader from the Soviet Union fled North Korea across the border, triggering a short gun battle that left three soldiers dead.

Panmunjeom and the Joint Security Area

There's nowhere in the world quite like the **Joint Security Area** ("the JSA"), a settlement squatting in the middle of Earth's most heavily fortified frontier, and the only place in DMZ territory where visitors are permitted. Visits here will create a curious dichotomy of feelings: on one hand, you'll be in what was once memorably described by Bill Clinton as "the scariest place on Earth", but as well as soldiers, barbed wire and brutalist buildings you'll see trees, hear birdsong and smell fresh air. The village of **Panmunjeom** itself is actually in North Korean territory, and has dwindled to almost nothing since it became the venue for armistice talks in 1951. But such is the force of the name that you'll see it on promotional material for most **tours** that run to the area; these are, in fact, the only way to get in.

The JSA tour

"The visit to the Joint Security Area at Panmunjeom will entail entry into a hostile area, and possible injury or death as a direct result of enemy action": disclaimer from form issued to visitors by United Nations Command.

Situated just over an hour from Seoul is **Camp Bonifas**, an American army base just outside the DMZ. Here you'll meet your guides, usually young recruits from the infantry whose sense of humour makes it easy to escape the seriousness of the situation, and be given a briefing session reminding you of the various dos and don'ts. Back on the bus look out for the white-marked stones pushed into the wire fence – these are detection devices that will fall out should anyone try to climb over. On both sides of the road you'll see hilltop points from where UNC forces keep a constant lookout across the border for any military build-up that would precede a large-scale attack.

Once inside the **JSA** itself, keep your fingers crossed that you'll be allowed to enter one of the three meeting rooms at the very centre of the complex, which offer some serious travel kudos – the chance to step into North Korea. The official Line of Control runs through the very centre of these cabins, the corners of which are guarded by South Korean soldiers, who are sometimes joined by their Northern counterparts, the enemy soldiers almost eyeball-to-eyeball. Note the microphones on the table inside the room – anything you say can be picked up by North Korean personnel. The rooms are closed to visitors when meetings are scheduled, which is just as well since some of them have descended into farce. One such charade occurred when members of one side – it's not clear which – brought a bigger flag than usual to a meeting. The others followed suit with an even larger banner, and the childish process continued until the flags were simply too large to take into the room; at this point, both sides agreed on a standard flag size.

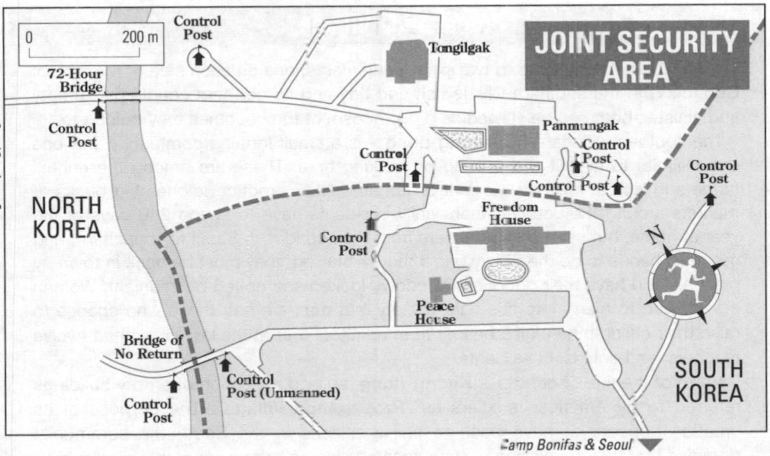

From an outdoor **lookout point** near the cabins you can soak up views of the North, including the huge flag and shell-like buildings of "**Propaganda Village**" (see box, p.162). You may also be able to make out the jamming towers it uses to keep out unwanted imperialist signals – check the reception on your phone. Closer to the lookout point, and actually within JSA territory, is the **Bridge of No Return**, the venue for POW exchange at the end of the Korean War (and also for James Bond in *Die Another Day* – though for obvious reasons it was filmed elsewhere).

On arriving back at Camp Bonifas you'll usually have time to pop into a gift shop, stocked with "I did the DMZ" T-shirts and a nice line in North Korean blueberry wine. Also in the area is a golf course once named by *Sports Illustrated* as the most dangerous on Earth, but there's only one hole (a par-three) and you won't be allowed to use it.

Practicalities

Almost all **tours** to the DMZ start and finish in Seoul, and there are a great number of outfits competing for your money, though as schedules and prices vary, it pays to shop around. Check that the tour actually heads to the JSA (off limits to South Korean nationals). Most people go with the USO (Ⓦ www.uso.org/korea; US$44), the recreational arm of the American military, whose schedule includes the JSA, Dorasan observatory and the Third Tunnel of Aggression; tours should be booked at least four days in advance, and start at 7.30am from outside their office – take exit ten from Samgakji subway station and walk up the main road. Other operators include Young Il Tours (Ⓦ www.iloveseoultour.com), which follows up a visit to the Third Tunnel of Aggression with a trip to the rifle range (W105,000), and Panmunjom Travel Center (Ⓦ www.panmunjomtour.com), which offers a tour led by a North Korean defector (W70,000).

For all these tours you'll need to bring your **passport** along. Note that these excursions come with a number of **restrictions**, most imposed by the United Nations Command. Citizens of certain countries are not allowed into DMZ territory, including those from most nations in the Middle East, some in Africa, and communist territories such as Vietnam, Hong Kong and mainland China. A dress code also applies (no flip-flops, ripped jeans, "clothing deemed faddish"

Daeseong-dong and "Propaganda Village"

The DMZ is actually home to two small settlements, one on each side of the Line of Control. With the southern village rich and tidy and its northern counterpart empty and sinister, both can be viewed as a microcosm of the countries they belong to.

The southern village – **Daeseong-dong** – is a small farming community, but one out-of-limits to all but those living or working here. These are among the richest farmers in Korea: they pay no rent or tax, and DMZ produce fetches big bucks at markets around the country. Technically, residents have to spend 240 days of the year at home, but most commute here from their condos in Seoul to "punch in", and get hired hands to do the dirty work; if they're staying, they must be back in town by nightfall, and have their doors and windows locked and bolted by midnight. Women are allowed to marry into this tight society, but men are not; those who choose to raise their children here also benefit from a school that at the last count had twelve teachers, and only eight students.

North of the line of control is **Kijong-dong**, an odd collection of empty buildings referred to by American soldiers as "**Propaganda Village**". The purpose of its creation appears to have been to show citizens in the South the communist paradise that they're missing – a few dozen "villagers" arrive every morning by bus, spend the day taking part in wholesome activities and letting their children play games, then leave again in the evening. With the aid of binoculars, you'll be able to see that none of the buildings actually has any windows; lights turned on in the evening also seem to suggest that they're devoid of floors. Above the village flies a huge **North Korean flag**, one so large that it required a fifty-man detail to hoist, until the recent installation of a motor. It sits atop a 160m-high pole, the eventual victor in a bizarre game played out over a number of years by the two Koreas, each hell-bent on having the loftier flag.

or "shorts that expose the buttocks"), but most things are OK. Also be warned that schedules can change in an instant, and that in certain areas **photography** is not allowed – you'll be told when to put your camera away. Lastly, remember that you'll be entering an extremely dangerous area – this is no place for fooling around or wandering off by yourself.

The Third Tunnel of Aggression

A short drive south of Panmunjeom is the **Third Tunnel of Aggression**, a sight that often forms part of day-tours to the DMZ. In 1974, a South Korean army patrol unit discovered a tunnel that had been burrowed under the DMZ in apparent preparation for a military attack from the North; tip-offs from North Korean defectors and some strategic drilling soon led to the discovery of another two, and a fourth was found in 1990. North Korea has denied responsibility, claiming them to be coal mines (though strangely devoid of coal), but to be on the safe side the border area is now monitored from coast to coast by soldiers equipped with drills and sensors. The third tunnel is the closest to Seoul, a city that would have been just a day's march away if the North's plan had succeeded. Regularly included in DMZ tour packages, it also gets the most visitors, though many emerge from the depths under-whelmed – it is, after all, a tunnel, even if you get to walk under **DMZ territory** up to the line of control that marks the actual border. On busy days it can become uncomfortably crowded – not a place for the claustrophobic. Before entering the tunnel, which runs up to 70m below the ground, visitors are usually ushered into a small theatre to be shown an explanatory movie. This is a ghastly but mercifully brief pro-unification shocker that gives no account at all of how the separation actually occurred, preferring instead to show the ground literally splitting to force a young girl from her family. Some locals may find its shallow sentiment moving, but feel free to ask questions about how the economic and ideological differences between the countries would be reconciled on reunification.

The observatories and Dorasan train station

South of the Third Tunnel, and also part of many tour schedules, are the **observatories** of Dorasan and Odusan, from which for W500 visitors are able to stare at the North through binoculars – a cheap price to satisfy a bit of curiosity. From Dorasan, which is right next to Panmunjeom, you can try to judge for yourself what does and doesn't happen in "Propaganda Village" across the way. Unlike most other sights in the area, it's possible to access **Odusan** (daily 9am–5pm; W1500) on public transport – head to Geumchon from Seoul by bus #158-2 or #912, then take a local bus (hourly; W900) or a taxi (W8000–10,000) to the observatory. **Dorasan** has to be visited on a tour, which usually combines a visit to the nearby **train station**. This is the last stop on the Gyeongui line that once connected Seoul to China, via Pyongyang, though as one sign says, "it's not the last station from the South, but the first station toward the North". Despite the total lack of any services heading Pyongyang-way, a gleaming, modern station has been built. The investment was rewarded in May 2007, when the first train in decades rumbled up the track to Kaesong in North Korea, another going in the opposite direction on the east coast line; regular freight services got going in December of the same year. The station itself is full of images from the peace process, and there's a wall map showing which parts of the world Seoul will be connected to should the line ever see regular service, as well as a much-photographed sign pointing the way to Pyongyang.

Gangwon-do

For Koreans, **GANGWON-DO** (its official name) exerts a magnetic pull. Enclosed by Gyeonggi to the west, Gyeongsang to the south, North Korea and the East Sea, it's a lush green land blessed with beaches, lakes and muscular peaks, whose rugged topography ensures that it remains the least-populated part of the country: despite being Korea's second largest province, it has a smaller population than many of its cities. Not that Gangwon is an undiscovered paradise – those in the know will direct you here, rather than to the more obvious tourist draw of Jeju Island. In summer, tour buses galore make a beeline for the region, especially the east coast beaches and the national parks, while skiers work their way around several resorts in the winter. Visitor numbers are still on the rise, thanks in part to a number of films and soap operas set in the province's more spectacular areas, which have roped in telly-addicts from all over Asia (see box, p.170).

The Axe Murder Incident

Relations between the two Koreas took a sharp nose-dive in 1976, when two American soldiers were killed by a pack of **axe-wielding North Koreans**. The cause of the trouble was a **poplar tree** which stood next to the Bridge of No Return: a UNC outpost stood next to the bridge, but its direct line of sight to the next Allied checkpoint was blocked by the leaves of the tree, so on the 18th of August a five-man American detail was dispatched to perform some trimming. Although the mission had apparently been agreed in advance with the North, sixteen soldiers from the KPA turned up and demanded that the trimming stop. Met with refusal, they launched a swift attack on the UNC troops using the axes the team had been using to prune the tree. The attack lasted less than a minute, but claimed the life of First Lieutenant Mark Barrett, as well as Captain Bonifas (who was apparently killed instantly with a single Karate chop to the neck). North Korea denied responsibility for the incident, claiming that the initial attack had come from the Americans.

Three days later, the US launched **Operation Paul Bunyan**, a show of force that must go down as the largest tree-trimming exercise in history. A convoy of two dozen UNC vehicles streamed towards the plant, carrying more than eight hundred men, some trained in taekwondo, and all armed to the teeth. These were backed up by attack helicopters, fighter planes and B-52 bombers, while an aircraft carrier had also been stationed just off the Korean shore. This carefully managed operation drew no response from the KPA, and the tree was successfully cut down.

Chuncheon is Gangwon's capital and major city, but though it's an agreeable enough place most aren't visiting the province to sate urban pleasures. There are four **national parks** in the province, each differing in topography and popularity, and whose acknowledged champion, **Seoraksan**, contains some of the highest peaks in the land.

Beaches are even easier to come by – unlike Korea's indented, island-peppered southern and western coasts, Gangwon's eastern shore sketches a fairly straight line from the North Korean border to the Gyeongsang provinces, so you're never far away from a perfect sunrise. Neither are you likely to be far from a rushing blue river, a mountainside village, or lofty trees and peaks that recede into the distance – regular Korea can feel a world away.

Despite the natural attractions, Gangwon hasn't always been a paragon of serenity. Its historical boundaries actually extend far into North Korea, but since the end of the Korean War the province has been divided by the twin perimeters of the **Demilitarized Zone**. During the war, the mountainous terrain that for so long preserved Gangwon's tranquillity became a curse, with ferocious battles fought for strategically important peaks. Even today, the tension is palpable – much of the region's coast is fenced off to protect against attacks from the North, and even some of the most popular beaches are fringed with barbed wire and military installations – from the end of the Korean War until the signing of the armistice in 1953, all land above the 38th Parallel (which hits the coast at a point roughly halfway between Sokcho and Gangneung) came under **North Korean control**, and was eventually exchanged for an area almost equal in size north of Seoul. Tunnels under the DMZ were found in the 1970s, and a spy-filled North Korean submarine crashed on the Gangwon coast in 1996 (see box, p.189); the latter can still be seen, next to an old American warship, near the small village of **Jeongdongjin**. Not that you should feel in danger – bus-loads of tourists head to peek over the border from the observatory in Goseong, and there's a quieter collection of sights related to the northern neighbours in the area around **Cheorwon**, a dusty frontier town only a matter of kilometres from the border.

Chuncheon and around

Despite its status as Gangwon's capital city, **CHUNCHEON** remains small and relaxed; in fact, it's the country's smallest provincial capital. Mountain-fringed and surrounded by artificial **lakes**, the fresh air is a welcome change to those who've been cooped up in a larger city, particularly on the small island of **Jungdo**. All this may be about to change, however – the city's proximity to Seoul, combined with Korea's heavy investment in public transport and the gradual shift of business from the capital, means that in national terms, Chuncheon's stock is going up. A new expressway should be finished by 2009, bringing it within an hour's drive of the capital; the KTX line will follow by 2013, so it's hard to see how Chuncheon can avoid becoming a commuter town. Although there's not an awful lot to see in the city itself, the surrounding countryside is beautiful and makes a pleasant stop on the way from Seoul to the eastern coast, especially if you plan to skip across the lakes by **ferry** along the way.

Arrival, information and transport

Until the **KTX line** is completed, to get to Chuncheon from Seoul you'll have to jump on a regular train from Cheongnyangni in the east of the capital. The station formerly known as "Chuncheon" is defunct and Nam-Chuncheon, right at the end of the line, is the city's terminal, located a short taxi ride south of the city centre. Buses stop about a kilometre away at the **intercity bus terminal**; there's also a tiny express terminal nearby, but it only serves Daegu and Gwangju. There's a small **information booth** inside the intercity terminal, which is fine for maps, but for quality information about Chuncheon and Gangwon province head downhill, past the E-Mart, and across the main road to the larger and more useful **Gangwon information centre** (daily 9am–6pm; ⓣ033/244-0088). Though there are **buses** into the city centre, the wait proves too much for some so it's much easier to take a taxi; this also goes for journeys around town, which should cost no more than a few thousand won. If you wish to head on to the east coast by **ferry**, you'll need to get to Soyang Dam, half an hour away on hourly local buses from the intercity bus terminal – see p.169 for more details.

Accommodation

There's a line of reasonable, fairly new motels across the main road from the Gangwon tourist centre; older places are dotted around the city's shopping district. As is often the way in provincial Korea there's little real quality at the top end of the scale.

Chuncheon Bears Tourist Hotel Samcheon-dong ⓣ033/256-2525, ⓦwww.hotelbears.com. West of the centre and near the Jungdo ferries, Chuncheon's main tourist hotel has only been open since 1991, but is already in need of a serious revamp. There's a slightly Chinese feel to the place (and a restaurant in similar style), but some rooms have tranquil views of the lake. ❺

Grand Motel Okcheon-dong ⓣ033/243-5021 or 2. The motel of choice for foreign backpackers can feel like a youth hostel at times, with helpful staff able to advise on the area. They even offer a free pick-up from the tourist office or bus station, but you won't be allowed to leave without signing the guestbook. The rooms are fine, and it's near Chuncheon's main shopping area. ❸

Jjimjilbang Twigye-dong. Chuncheon's best *jjimjilbang* is a short distance from the bus terminal and is perfect for lone or budget travellers – a tiny fee will buy you a night's sleep, even if it's on the floor in a communal room. ❶

Motel I ... Twigye-dong ⓣ033/242-2154. One of a row of motels opposite the Gangwon information centre, this is within walking distance of the bus terminal (or even the train station, at a push), and offers funky rooms in a variety of styles. Some have Internet access for a higher fee, but all have fantastic showers. ❸

New Seoul Yeoinsuk Namchuncheon-yeok-ap ⓣ033/254-8874. Some rooms in this *yeoinsuk* are surprisingly big for the price. Though many of them have private facilities, it's prudent to check that the showers and hot water work before handing over your cash. Head straight down from the train station, and it's just before the river on the left-hand side. ❶

The City

Chuncheon is more of an "activity" destination than a collection of sights – here you can race a bike around small islands, go hiking on nearby hills or watch puppeteers and mime artists perform at two of the country's most interesting **festivals**. The main draw for Koreans, however, is the chance to sample *dak-galbi*, a famed local dish (see box, p.168). Many choose to get around by bicycle – a **cycleway** runs along the lake, and there are a number of short tracks on the island. The best place to rent a bike (bikes W3000 per hr or W15,000 a day) is on the west of town next to the **Ethiopian Veterans' Memorial Hall**, a building that was being constructed at the time of writing. Dedicated to Ethopian fighters that lost their lives in the Korean War, its distinctive golden domes gleam in the sun, making it look somewhat like a half-submerged Russian church. From here, it's a relatively simple ride across the bridge and out to the ferry dock.

Ferries run every half-hour to the island of **Jungdo**, returning immediately (9am–6pm; W4300 return, bikes W1000 extra). In addition to the cycle tracks – some of which provide fantastic views of Chuncheon's surrounding mountains – you can also try your hand at rowing and water skiing, though such mirth tends to restrict itself to weekends and holidays; at other times the island can be near-empty. There's a passable restaurant just inland from the ferry dock, as well as some cabin-style pension accommodation (❹) for those who want to stay on the island; in warmer months it's also possible to camp.

Back on the mainland and heading the other way from the Ethiopian Veterans' Hall, a dedicated cycle route heads north along the waterfront, reaching another

Chuncheon and around

Chuncheon	춘천
Gangchon	강촌
Inje	인제
Jungdo	중도
Nami Island	남이섬
Sangjungdo	상중도
Soyang Lake	소양호
Wido	위도
Accommodation	
Chuncheon Bears Tourist Hotel	춘천 베어스 관광 호텔
Grand Motel	그랜드 모텔
Jjimjilbang	찜질방
Motel If...	모텔 이프
New Seoul Yeoinsuk	뉴서울 여인숙
Restaurants	
Daewon Dak-galbi	대원 닭갈비
Pihwa-ne Ddeokbokki	피화네 떡복이
Spoon	스푼
Umai	우마이
Umi Dak-galbi	우미 닭갈비

memorial after a few kilometres, this one in honour of the locals who died in the Korean War. This is best done in the evening, when – as long as the weather agrees – you'll get views of the sun setting behind the mountains to the west.

Two more small but pleasant islands lie further up the river – **Sangjungdo** and **Wido**. Next to the latter, which is connected to the city's northern flank by a bridge, is Chuncheon's colourful Puppet Theatre; each August, performers from Korea and abroad take part in a delightful **puppet festival** (ⓦwww.cocobau.com). Other popular annual events include a **mime festival** (ⓦwww.mimefestival.com), which takes place in May at venues across town, and a city **marathon** in October; ask at tourist offices in Chuncheon or in Seoul for up-to-date information.

Eating and drinking

Galbi's the word in Chuncheon; **dak-galbi**, to be precise (see box, p.168), and the shopping area in the city centre has a whole street of restaurants – Dakgalbi-golmok – on which to sample this speciality. Another local favourite is *makguksu* – cold buckwheat noodles with soup and hot pepper paste, and a bargain feed at about W3000 per bowl.

Restaurants

Daewon Dak-galbi On-ui-dong. One of a number of similar places opposite the bus terminal, at the time of research this was serving the biggest portions of *makguksu* in the shortest time. It's straight across the footbridge from the terminal – look for the red sign.

Pihwa-ne Ddeokbokki Dak-galbi St. Flash-fried snacks from W200 each, together with the free *kimchi*, soup and pickled radish on offer, mean that it's possible to fill your belly here for next to nothing – just point at what you want, sit, then chow down. Look for a small booth opposite *Umi Dak-galbi*.

Spoon Hyoja 3-dong. A fresh face in the university area, *Spoon* is without doubt the most stylish restaurant in the city, with mood music, latticed wood frames, and tatami mats to sit on. *Galbijjim* is the recommended dish, but simple meals such as *naeng-myeon* noodles and *galbitang* are also available, at reasonable prices.

Umai Hyoja 3-dong. A stylish Japanese restaurant in the university area, where you can sink *sake* while your *okonomiyaki* (something like a fried pizza topping) gets cooked in front of you by skilled chefs. There is, of course, a wide choice of raw sea-fare available, though it may pay to take a local friend along as the menu is in Korean only.

Umi Dak-galbi Dak-galbi St. The most popular of a whole squadron of similar restaurants on the same street, this place is usually jam-packed; it may be hard to see what differentiates it from the rest, but bear in mind that when it comes to food, the Koreans are rarely wrong. It costs W8500 for a portion of the good stuff, and unlike many competitors they're willing to cater for single diners.

Cafés and bars

There's only really one place to head for a good night out, and that's the area around **Gangwon University**. Chuncheon's take on the student party zone is a tad more stylish than most provincial cities, with a whole host of well-designed bars, restaurants and karaoke rooms opening up. Local expats make a beeline for the *Hard Rock Bar* on the main drag, though the customer base remains predominantly Korean. The American army once threw down the dollars in hostess bars near the old train station; the military pulled out of nearby Camp Page in 2004, but the good-time girls are still there, wondering where their customers went. As far as **cafés** go, *Ethiopia Espresso* deserves a mention. The coffee comes from Ethiopia, as you might expect, and the friendly owner (who speaks English and Russian) will help out with translating duties if you want to rent a bike from the rack opposite.

Dak-galbi

You may have sampled regular *galbi*, whereby you cook (or to be more precise, set fire to) meat at your own table. **Dak-galbi** is a little different – it's made with chicken meat, rather than beef or pork, and is grilled in a wide pan so there's no visible flame action for regular *galbi* arsonists to enjoy. You'll find this dish pretty much anywhere in Korea, but for some reason Chuncheon gets the glory. Imagine throwing a **raw chicken kebab** into a hot metal tray to boil up with a load of veg – you get to do this at your table for around W8000 per portion. You usually need at least two people for a meal, and once you're nearly finished it's common, or perhaps obligatory, to throw some **rice or noodles** into the pan for a stomach-expanding second course.

Gangchon

Chuncheon's surrounding area is alluringly green and undulating, and well worth delving into. One of the most accessible places is the small town of **GANGCHON**, a pretty and seemingly tranquil place just west of Chuncheon. Although it has a national reputation as a student "MT" centre par excellence – Membership Training is a somewhat non-studious exercise that usually involves lots of drinking, singing and buzzing about on quad bikes – such revelry tends to confine itself to student holidays, and at other times it's a far more relaxing place to stay than Chuncheon for those who want a taste of inland Gangwon. The major sight here is **Gugok-pokpo** (daily 8am–7pm; W1600), a tumbling waterfall surrounded by hills and trails that make for a rewarding few hours of exploration. It's 5km away from Gangchon down a highly picturesque valley studded with tiny houses, but the rural charm of this area is likely to be heavily diluted by the new high-speed KTX train line being built through it. The journey from Gangchon to the falls is best made by bike on a cycle path that heads into the valley from town; roadside stalls in the village offer **cycle and scooter rental**, with bikes going for W2000 per hour or W10,000 per day, scooters for about six times that price, and quads for a little more again. From the train station, head through town and take the first right after the stream. Bus #50 heads there along the parallel road that runs down the stream's opposite bank.

Gangchon is one stop before Chuncheon on the train line from Seoul's Cheongnyangni station, and there are also regular buses from Chuncheon. The village has enough motels and restaurants to cater for the students during their holidays, and an excess for the rest of the year; one comfy **place to stay** is the *Good-Time Motel* (Ⓣ033/261-4720; ④) on the main road, which has large, clean rooms with big televisions. Cheaper and more rural *minbak* accommodation can be found in the valley linking the town with Gugok-pokpo; along this same road is a **youth hostel** (Ⓣ033/262-1201 to 3; dorm beds W16,000) and *Lorellai*, a pleasant cabin-style **tearoom** and restaurant.

Nami Island

Further downstream from Gangchon is tiny **Nami Island**, which has achieved international fame for being the scene of the main characters' first date and kiss on the hugely successful *Winter Sonata* soap opera (see box, p.170). The programme was most successful in Japan, and the island is often packed with Nipponese tourists, mostly middle-aged and female, some of whom bizarrely choose to sport **wigs** in an attempt to impersonate the male lead. Soap hysteria aside, you're likely to enjoy the island, which has plenty of paths lined with gingko and chestnut trees, maples and white birches that will make for a beautiful walk;

you might even encounter the occasional ostrich. Unless you're on a tour bus – ask at tourist offices in Chuncheon, Seoul or Tokyo for information – the easiest way to get here is by taxi from Gapyeong (see map, p.142), a small city connected to Chuncheon by intercity bus, and also a stop on the train line.

Soyang Lake to Inje

For those heading from Chuncheon to Sokcho or vice versa, it's possible to cover much of the route to Sokcho by ferry on **Soyang Lake**, an artificial lake which affords fantastic views. **Bus** #11 and #12 (40min; W1000) run from outside Chuncheon's intercity bus terminal to the huge Soyang dam; the ferry dock is then a short walk along the road. From here those heading east – or on a day-trip from Chuncheon – can take a detour to the temple of **Cheongpyeongsa**. The temple's appeal lies not in superb architecture or historical importance (though it's over a thousand years old, it was razed to the ground and rebuilt several times), but in the watery approach – ferries are the easiest way of getting here – and even then, it's a half-hour walk from the ferry dock. Unfortunately, the secret is out, and the temple is now fronted by restaurants, snack stalls and *minbak* of a small tourist village.

Ferries run on the hour from Soyang Dam dock to a small port on the other side of the lake where local buses will be waiting to take you ten minutes up the road to **Yanggu** town (30min; W5000), from where buses head on to Sokcho, though whether you're heading east or west you may have to change in **INJE**, a popular centre for adventure sports. Many choose to stay in Inje because of the abundance of accommodation and **activities** in the area, which include bungee jumping, rock climbing, mountain biking, four-wheel driving, paragliding and the "Flying Fox", a high-speed steel-cable ride. If all this fails to engage the hairs on the back of the neck, note that you can partake in a spot of rafting from April to October, though the activity is not in the white-water league. All can be arranged through the tourist information centre (Ⓣ033/460 2170) downhill from the bus station; it rarely has English-speaking staff, so to arrange in advance it's best to get a Korean friend to call ahead.

The North Korean border area

A few sights relating to **North Korea** are clustered north of the town of **Cheorwon**, which sits almost too close for comfort to the border. Gangwon province extends across the border, passing the sumptuous Geumgang mountain range just across the border and stretching to Wonsan, a major North Korean port; however, people on opposite sides of the Demilitarized Zone that separates the two countries have next to no chance of meeting one another. The Geumgang mountains across the border can be visited on costly tours that run from Seoul (see p.413), but unless you fancy taking an even more expensive trip to Pyongyang you'll have to make do with staring across the border from certain vantage points on the southern side – one of these, the Goseong Unification Observatory, is north of Sokcho on the east coast (see p.176), and there are a couple near Panmunjeom to the west (p.163).

Cheorwon

Though those interested in getting a feel of North Korea from the South usually make a beeline to Panmunjeom and its surrounding sights, similar and

Winter Sonata

Though too cheesy for many Western palates, **Korean drama** has recently enjoyed enormous popularity across Asia, with snow-filled **Winter Sonata** the biggest success to date. The story runs as follows: a boisterous girl named **Yujin** meets withdrawn **Junsang** on a bus. Despite being total opposites they fall in love and Yujin lends her gloves to her new man, who promises to give them back on New Year's Eve. He doesn't turn up, and Yujin hears that he died in a car accident on the way. Fast forward ten years to Yujin's engagement ceremony, when she thinks that she sees Junsang – now choosing to wear pink lipstick for some reason – through the crowd. She later finds out that it isn't Junsang but **Min-hyung**, a successful American architect. Yujin ends up working at the same company, and one further car-crash later it transpires that unbeknown to Yujing not only is the man Junsang after all, but that he's Yujin's half-brother. As the pair part ways, Yujin hands him the blueprints for a beautiful house she'd designed as a farewell present. Of course, they're not related after all, and when Yujin returns to Korea from France three years later she finds out that Junsang is in fact the half-brother of her erstwhile fiancé. She then happens across the house that she once handed Junsang in blueprint form, finds him inside – now blind, just to heighten the tragedy – and they fall in love once more.

Although he may look like an effeminate Asian Harry Potter, Junsang got hearts racing all over Asia; **Bae Yong-jun**, the actor who played him, is now an international superstar whose face is plastered across all kinds of merchandise – just look at the socks on sale in Seoul's Myeong-dong district. Nowhere was he more successful than in Japan, where he is now revered as *Yon-sama*, a title roughly equivalent to an English knighthood – *Winter Sonata*'s popularity across the sea was one major reason behind a 32 percent growth in Korea's foreign tourist numbers from 2003 to 2004. Junsang also helped the stereotypically strong-but-sensitive Korean male replace the martial arts hero as Asia's role model, and Korean men now enjoy considerable demand from females across the continent.

much less touristed delights are on offer north of **CHEORWON**, a frontier town facing one of the world's largest and least-understood armies. From here the **DMZ** is close enough to walk to, but you wouldn't get very far: as the closest urban base in the country to the border, there's a great military presence, and checkpoints are all over the place. It's not unusual to hear explosions either – training usually takes place once a week, more often if the North has been making similar noises. Be sure to look out for the large lumps of concrete suspended over the roads – their purpose is to block the path of North Korean military vehicles, should they ever arrive. Note that there are landmines and barbed wire around the border area, but you won't be allowed to venture anywhere dangerous.

Dusty, ramshackle Cheorwon somehow manages to maintain a frontier atmosphere despite the total lack of anything crossing the border. It's also quite spread out for its population, with its major districts separated by mountains and rice fields. Old Cheorwon has the most character, while across the river Dongsong is a newer and slightly tidier part of town. Very few foreigners make it here, and as it's not exactly heaving with domestic tourists either, it can be hard to get around – you may have to rely on hitching rides with locals. A **tourist office** from where tours leave (see opposite) forms part of a small clutch of buildings surrounding **Goseokjeong**, a rocky crag that pokes up through an extremely pretty section of the river that flows through Cheorwon. Buses head to this countryside location from all across the city; if you have time to kill before or after a tour, be sure to head down to the riverbank – take the steps downhill from the small restaurant complex – where it's often possible to **hire a boat** for small trips (W9000 per group).

North Korea-related sights

Though you can't step over the border, those wishing to get a sniff of North Korea can make use of a **free tour** laid on by the local authorities. Unfortunately it's only available to **those with their own car** – a guide comes with you in the vehicle – but it may be possible to join a ride with others taking the trip. However, be warned that although Koreans are generally extremely hospitable to foreigners – and even more so in a remote place such as this – the area is so quiet that it's quite common for nobody to turn up all day. Travellers either in possession of a car or willing to give hitching a bash should head to the **tourist information office**, near Goseokjeong, which is within the large building visible from the bus stop. Tours run from here four times a day (9.30am, 10.30am, 1pm & 2.30pm).

The tour is quite a thrill, and much cheaper than those operating from Seoul; guides will direct your route through beautiful countryside around the barbed wire, landmines and checkpoints to any of the official sights – there aren't many to choose from. The most popular stop is the **Second Tunnel of Aggression**, an excavated burrow discovered in 1975, and made by North Korea in apparent preparation for an attack on the South. Only wide enough for foot soldiers, it's tall enough to walk through without crouching – wear decent footwear as the tunnel floor is rather wet. An armed guard will escort you deep under the DMZ itself to within a few hundred yards of official North Korean territory. This is not a place for clowning around – the bullets in the guard's gun are real – and as the kilometre-plus tunnel goes up to 150m below the surface, neither is it a place for those who are claustrophobic. After seeing what the DMZ looks like underground, most tourists are eager to peer over the border into the North itself, which you can do from **Cheoluisamgak Observatory**, a short drive west of the tunnel, through pair of binoculars (W500). Just outside the observatory is the disused **Woljeong-ri train station**, the last stop on the line that heads into the North. This is one of three main lines that headed across what is now the border prior to the division of the peninsula, and the carcass of one of the trains that used to ply the line is still on the tracks. The sign above the track reads "the train wants to go", but the rusty and crumbling vehicle is in no state to make requests; it'll be a long time before anything makes it down the line to Gagok, the first station on the other side of the DMZ. While this line remains idle, the other two lines connecting North and South Korea have actually seen some recent activity – amid much fanfare, trains finally rolled over the border in a special ceremony in May 2007 (see p.163).

On your way back to Cheorwon you'll be able to spot plenty of bombed out buildings and landmine signs – the guide may allow you to stop your vehicle and get out to take a couple of pictures, but you won't be allowed anywhere near the buildings themselves.

Practicalities

There are **buses** to Cheorwon from Seoul and several cities across Gangwon province, but it pays to make sure where you're going – buses head to both Dongsong, the city's newer half to the west, and Old Cheorwon ("Gu-Cheorwon") to the east, though there's a large, field-filled gap between these two halves. **Dongsong** makes the most comfortable place to stay; the *Tanto Motel* (Ⓣ033/455-4200; ❸) near the bus terminal is the best choice in the area, and has some funky rooms. Nearby is *Maengbal*, an interesting North

Korea-styled *galbi* restaurant. There are few decent places to stay around **Old Cheorwon**. Try *Royal Park* (☎033/452-8222; ❷), a short walk from the bus station; rooms are acceptable, and to while away night-time hours you can hire videos from a nearby shop. *Rainbow* is a stylish Japanese-style restaurant visible from the bus-side of the station, standing out in contrast to its drab surroundings to serve up nachos, *teriyaki* and more. For more rustic dishes head down the road to *Ddong-gae*, literally "shit-dog" (the colloquial name of the breed usually eaten by Koreans); you may be grateful that the menu is in Korean only. It's also possible to stay in the countryside between these two districts near Goseokjeong. Most places in this extremely quiet area have closed down in recent years but one that has remained open is *Sun Leisure-tel* (☎033/455-1350 or 1; ❸), which has small linoleum-floored rooms, and can organize rafting on nearby rivers. There are a lot of restaurants in the area, the best of which is *Hyeonmuam*, which serves huge *dwoenjang-jjigae* sets for W5000. For those with their own transport, there are lots of houses for rent in the surrounding countryside.

Sokcho and around

Heading north along Korea's eastern coast, the appealingly ugly coastal city of **SOKCHO** is the country's last major settlement before the barbed wire of the DMZ. Despite its size, it still leans heavily on the fishing industry; all around you'll see racks of squid, hung out to dry in the sun like laundry. Brackish, decaying and a little over-large, it's a tough city to love, though repeated attempts have been made at sprucing it up a bit, particularly in the area around Expo Park, by adding walking trails and a small amusement park. Despite its faults, Sokcho receives more visitors than any other city in Gangwon-do, though most of them are on their way to the wonderful crags of **Seoraksan National Park**, which lies within visible range to the west. It's also possible to venture north to the DMZ for a look at North Korea, or south to Naksan Beach and its resident temple. Sokcho's own sights are few and far between with only one a unique experience – the winch-ferry journey to tiny **Abai Island**. Both north and south of the city, the coast is littered with small packs of motels and restaurants, but though accessible by bus, their scattered positions means that they're better visited with private transport.

Arrival and information

Sokcho curls around Cheongcho Lake in a C-shape, one loosely tied together in a very literal sense by the twin steel cables along which tiny ferry-platforms winch their way to Abai Island. To the north of the city are the **intercity bus terminal** and **passenger ferry terminal**; from the latter there are twice-weekly connections to Zarubino in Russia, regularly full of Korean tour groups on the long haul to Paekdusan (a mountain straddling the North Korea–China border; see p.415), though the intricacies of Russian visa applications mean that it's a route rarely used by westerners. Local buses aplenty trundle through the city centre from the intercity bus terminal, passing Expo Park and eventually reaching the **express bus terminal** in the south. Buses #7 and #7-1, from either bus terminal, continue on to Seoraksan National Park. Others head further down the coast to the local **airport** at Yangyang, but though there are flights from Seoul, journeys by express bus are far cheaper and take little longer when waiting times and transport to and from the airports are factored in.

Tourist offices are located outside both bus terminals, but at the time of writing these were among the least helpful in the country. There's another south of town, at the T-junction where the coastal road splits to head to Seoraksan; all can give you maps, but for assistance it may be better to call tourist enquiries on ⓣ033/1330.

Accommodation

Most places to stay in Sokcho were built in the 1970s during the first big burst of domestic tourism, and today they're looking rather drab. Motels can be found around both bus terminals and pretty much anywhere along the lakefront in between, with the newest places around Expo Park. More numerous, and much cheaper, are those around the bus terminals, and for real budget-seekers there are a few grimy *yeoinsuk* by the water opposite the City Hall.

Chuncheon Hoet-jip Cheonho-dong ⓣ033/ 633-8333. There's only one available space in this family home on Abai Island, but it's massive – three rooms, cooking facilities and a private bathroom. Head straight up from the winch-ferry and turn left after the restaurants. ❷

Deokwon Motel Joyang-dong ⓣ033/635-3477. Tucked away behind the express bus terminal, this motel has some large, good-value rooms – try to score the large ones at the end of the corridor, if you can put up with the "romantic" circular beds. ❷

Donggyeong Motel Dongmyeong-dong ⓣ033/631-5444 or 5. Right next to the express bus terminal, this busy, family-run motel is where the tourist office usually points backpackers. Though the lobby may look ramshackle, rooms are perfectly acceptable. ❷

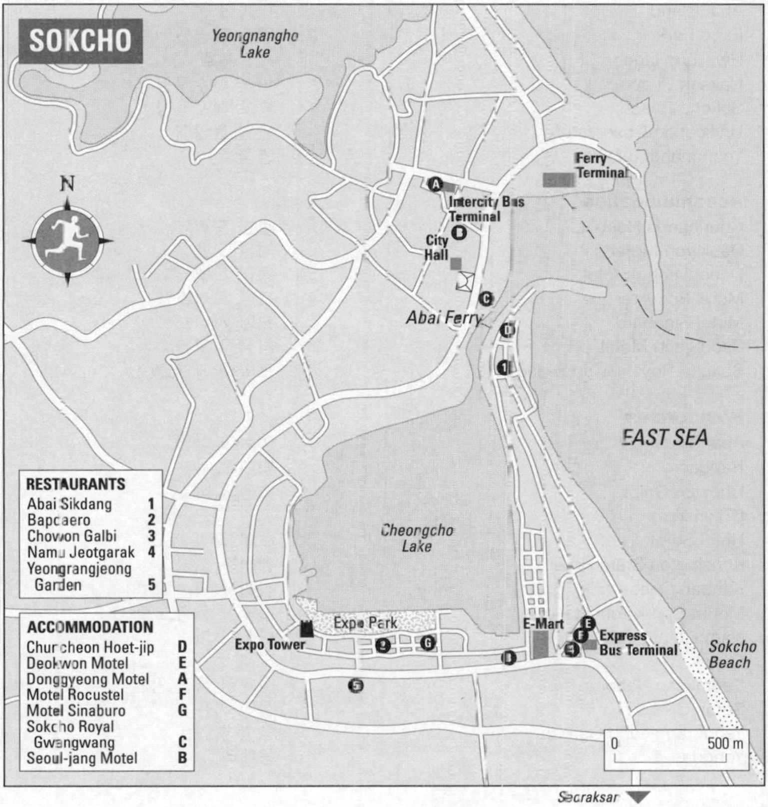

Motel Rocustel Joyang-dong ⓣ033/633-4959. You can't miss this pink jalopy of a building behind the express bus terminal. It's too brash for some, but has nice rooms with a bit of thought put into their design. Prices are a little high in peak season. ❹

Seoul-jang Motel Dongmyeong-dong ⓣ033/633-3477. Off-season it's just about possible to haggle this place down to get a room with a bed and private facilities for the same price as the sleep-on-the-floor box-rooms of the local *yeoinsuk* lodgings. Rooms here are comfy enough and the owners are very friendly indeed – the lady of the house will want your name in her guestbook. ❷

Motel Sinaburo Joyang-dong ⓣ033/636-5959, ⓕ033/638-6400. The best of a small patch of new motels near Expo Park allows you to choose your room from a menu in the lobby. Note that not all of them face the lake – maybe a good thing, as there's a small funfair outside. ❹

Sokcho Royal Gwangwang Hotel Facing Abai Island ⓣ033/631-8700. Despite the soulless lobby and the downright ugliness of the surrounding area, this hotel provides the comfiest possible stay in central Sokcho, which admittedly isn't saying much. Rooms are stylishly decorated and have wooden floors, with views of the city's port from the hotel's top levels. Ask about discounts off-season, when it can become quite a bargain. ❻

The City

There's little to see in Sokcho itself, and most of the attractions popular with visitors lie outside the city. One exception is tiny **Abai Island**, the most

Sokcho and around

Sokcho	속초
Abai Island	아바이 섬
Expo Park	엑스포 공원
Hwajinpo lagoon	화진포호
Naksan Beach	낙산 해수욕장
Sokcho Beach	속초 해수욕장
Unification Observatory	통일 전망대
Yeongnangho Lake	영랑호
Accommodation	
Chuncheon Hoet-jip	춘천 횟집
Deokwon Motel	덕원 모텔
Donggyeong Motel	동경 모텔
Motel Rocustel	모텔 로커스텔
Motel Sinaburo	모텔 시나브로
Seoul-jang Motel	서울장 모텔
Sokcho Royal Gwangwang Hotel	로얄 관광 호텔
Restaurants	
Abai Sikdang	아바이 식당
Bapdaero	밥대로
Chowon Galbi	초원 갈비
Green Yard	그린 야드
Hotel Sorak Park	호텔 설악 파크
Kensington Stars Hotel	켄싱턴 호텔
Kimbap Cheon-guk	김밥 천국
Mount Sorak Tourist Hotel	설악산 관광 호텔
Namu Jeotgarak	나무 젓가락
Osaek	오색
Seoraksan National Park	설악산 국립 공원
Sorak Garden	설악 가든
Yeongrangjeong Garden	역랑정 가든
Yongdae-ri	용대리

brackish part of this salty city, and connected to it by road and winch-ferry. Seemingly transported here from a bygone era, Abai's warren of tight lanes is well worth a wander, and it's is also famed for the peculiar dish *sundae* (see below). The island is connected on its southern side to the express bus terminal road by an unnecessarily large bridge, and to the City Hall area by an incredibly cute ferry service. Little more than a platform attached to steel cables, it runs day and night along a winch line, the two operators using what look like giant tuning forks to haul the ferry across. It's quite a spectacle, and may well be the cheapest thrill you can get in Korea – just W200 per person. Near central Sokcho is **Expo Park**, a family area where bikes and mini quads are available to rent; there's also a small amusement park and a viewing tower, the latter looking something like a space-age *hareubang*.

A twenty-minute walk north of the intercity bus terminal will bring you to **Yeongnangho**, a tranquil lake set away from Sokcho's brine and bustle. From its eastern shore, you can see Ulsanbawi – Seoraksan's distinctive spiny rock ridge – reflected in the water. It's a great area for a **bike ride** – the nearest rental outlets are in the city centre (see p.175). To get here by bus, take number #1 or #1-1 from Sokcho's main road.

South of the city centre, and within walking distance of the express bus terminal, is **Sokcho beach**; this small stretch of sand can get extremely busy in the summer months, at which time you'll be able to rent out rubber rings or take a banana boat ride.

Eating and drinking

Like the accommodation, **restaurants** in Sokcho have a general air of decay about them; nonetheless, there are some decent places to eat. *Sundae* is the local speciality, but it has nothing to do with ice cream, rather it's a kind of sausage whereby various odds and ends are stuffed into intestinal lining; like haggis, most people find the dish somehow tastes better than the sum of its parts. Though *sundae* is available all over Korea – mainly in markets – the squid variety (*ojing-eo sundae*) is an Abai speciality, and the island is the best and most

▲ Squid drying, Sokcho

atmospheric place in Sokcho to eat all varieties of the dish. Sokcho lacks a decent **drinking** area, and even weekend nights can be awfully quiet. However, *Tara Burn*, a short taxi ride to the north, can often become jam-packed with foreigners from all over Gangwon. One of the most distinctive bars in Korea, almost every square inch is filled with detail, and the beer's reasonably priced.

Abai Sikdang Cheonho-dong. If you really fancy getting into the local groove and chowing down on stuffed intestine, this restaurant on Abai Island is the best place to try it. *Abai Sundae* – a local take on the dish – is a little expensive at W10,000, but is big enough to feed two or three.

Bapdaero Joyang-dong. All you can eat for W5000 – if that doesn't tempt you, you're not hungry enough. Despite the low price and the canteen atmosphere, the food is actually pretty good – just the treat for hungry hikers. Near the motels in Expo Park.

Chowon Galbi Joyang-dong. Grilled pork ribs go for W8000 at this popular second-floor *galbi* joint, as well as rib-eye steak or amazingly cheap *naeng-myeon* noodles. Head straight on from E-Mart, and look for the pig sticking its thumbs up.

Kimbap Cheon-guk This chain restaurant offers a long list of cheap, filling Korean specialities such as *gimbap*, *ramyeon* and *rabokki*, which are served up within minutes of your order. There are several branches on the main road.

Namu Jeotgarak Joyang-dong. An acceptable choice in the culinary waste-ground surrounding the express bus terminal, with chicken cutlet from W4000, or *ojing-eo sundae* at W5000. Come out of the terminal and turn right down the main road.

Yeongrangjeong Garden Joyang-dong. Food in this mushroom-like building near Expo Park is expensive, but locals swear it's the best in town. The English-language menu has a list of succulent beef to barbeque from W26,000 per person, or there are cheaper noodle dishes.

Listings

Bike rental Bikes can be rented in Expo Park from underneath the large *hareubang*-like tower for W2000 per hour, or W8000 per day.

Car hire Several companies have offices outside the express bus terminal, including *Avis* and *Juseong*. Rates start at around W35,000 per day.

Hiking equipment There are numerous stores on the main road of the city centre, including *Treksta* and *North Face*, both conveniently located opposite City Hall.

Post Office The main branch (Mon–Fri 9am–6pm) is located near the intercity bus terminal, just a short walk from City Hall.

Supermarkets There's an E-Mart a short walk from the express bus terminal – come out of the main exit and head right down the main road, then right again at the next main junction.

North of Sokcho

Travelling north of Sokcho by road, tensions emanating from the area's proximity to North Korea become more and more apparent. Huge chunks of concrete sit suspended at the roadsides, ready to be dropped to block the path of any North Korean military vehicles that might one day come thundering along. The coast, as it is along most of Gangwon's shore, is fenced off with barbed wire, growing in ferocity until it hits the ordnance-strewn no-man's-land of the DMZ. The **unification observatory** at Goseong – an hour north of Sokcho by bus – draws a fair number of Koreans eager to get a glimpse of their neighbours over the border. Unfortunately most are on chartered tour buses from other Korean cities, and the area is otherwise hard to get to without your **own transport** – few foreigners make it this far. Tourist offices in Seoul (see p.75) or Sokcho (p.172) may be able to help you join a tour bus with a little advance notice, but public transport is limited to the buses that run up the coast from Sokcho (#1 and #1-1; 1hr); these stop a kilometre or so at the ticket office, from where the observatory is still well out of walking range. From here, hitching is the only option – you could do worse than asking for a ride with one of the many **tour buses** that head on up to the observatory, as all have to stop at the ticket office. From the observatory you'll be able to make out the **Geumgang range** in North Korea, which is similar to Seoraksan to the south but bigger and more visually arresting. Although they lie across the border, you may spot one of the few tour buses that **cross the DMZ** and head to the mountains (see p.413). Near the observatory are shops selling North Korean booze, including beer, mulberry wine, and some acrid-tasting hooch made from mushrooms (though not, it must be said, of the hallucinogenic variety). On the other side of the car park, a few train carriages that used to serve the now-defunct line across the border have been converted into a cheap restaurant – one car even allows you to eat while sitting on old train seats.

Hwajinpo lagoon

With the scenery so similar to the South, there's only so much time you can spend looking at North Korea. Therefore it's good to take a day out of observatory visiting to make a trip to **Hwajinpo**, a lagoon once used as a holiday escape by the Korean great and good – summer villas belonging to three prominent Korean politicians can be visited on the same ticket (daily 9am–5pm; W2000). **Kim Il-sung** (North Korea's creator, "Great Leader" and still the country's president despite his death in 1994) had a base here before the area was given to the South after the Korean War; this building was destroyed, but a replica has been built in its place, and now contains a mildly interesting collection of photographs; two particular displays are titled "Ceaseless provocations and atrocities by North Korea" and "Nothing has changed at all" – hardly in the spirit of reconciliation. **Syngman Rhee** and **Lee Ki-boong** had villas here too; Rhee was President of South Korea from 1948 to 1960, when protests forced him to flee to Hawaii, at which point his deputy, Lee, killed himself, shortly after shooting his parents. It's possible to walk between all three villas, but none are particularly interesting, and all could have been restored with far greater care; the beauty of the lagoon, however, makes a visit worthwhile, as does its sandy beach – white sands cordoned off by barbed wire and traps for North Korean frogmen (don't go swimming too far). There's also an aquarium in the area (same times; W1000).

It's just about possible to tour these sights from Sokcho with **public transport** – take the #1 or #1-1 bus and get off at Chodo stop; the lagoon is then a short walk down a side road. There are also plenty of *minbak* (❷) around the bus stop if you feel like staying the night.

South of Sokcho

Twelve kilometres south of Sokcho, and accessible on buses #9 and #9-1, is **Naksan Beach**, by far the longest along this stretch of coast. Almost unbearably popular in the summer, it's accordingly surrounded by hundreds of motels and seafood restaurants. Just north of the beach is **Naksansa** (free), a temple situated on the shore; despite the highly photogenic beauty of temple and sea, this combination is almost unique on the Korean peninsula. Naksansa is undergoing restoration work after being savaged by fire in 2005 – you can still see the charred tree trunks and stumps. A walk to the elegant white Goddess of Mercy statue at the top of the complex affords great views of the sea to the east and Seoraksan National Park to the west, with the gleaming teeth of Ulsanbawi particularly evident from here. The temple is breezy and open, with plenty of nooks and crannies to explore, particularly around the rocky shore area.

Accommodation prices in the area go up and down with the temperature, but motels get newer and cheaper as you move away from the beach and main access road. The only distinctive place is *Hotel Naksan Beach* (❼) near the temple entrance, but with its old, stuffy rooms and the faintly Soviet-era atmosphere of the lobby it represents poor value for money – you're better off at a decent motel on Naksan Beach. Their seawater **sauna**, however, is nicer than it sounds and can be used by non-guests for W6000.

Seoraksan National Park

Koreans gush about **SEORAKSAN NATIONAL PARK**, and with good reason. The nation's northernmost park, it contains some of the tallest peaks in the country, with mist-fringed bluffs of exposed crag that could have come straight from a Chinese painting. The name gains ambiguity in translation, but roughly translates as "Snow-cragged Mountains"; these bony peaks are pretty enough on a cloudy day, but in good weather they're set alight by the sun, bathed in spectacular hues during its rising and setting.

The park stretches around 40km from east to west and about the same size north to south, with the wide area crisscrossed with myriad **hiking trails**: the routes mentioned here are by no means exhaustive. Also bear in mind that some are closed off from time to time in rotation in order to protect the land: in peak season there can be literally queues of hikers stomping along the more popular routes, and this pressure takes its toll. The park offers several two-day hikes heading around Daecheonbong, its highest peak, but the focal point is undoubtedly **Ulsanbawi**, a beautiful spine of jagged rock to the north which resembles a stegosaur spine, a crocodile jaw, or a thousand other things depending on your angle, the time of day, and the weather. The time of year is important, too; Seoraksan is one of the highest parks in the country and as a result is usually the first to display the reds, yellows and oranges of autumn.

Seoraksan can be roughly split into three main areas. **Outer Seorak** is where most of the action takes place as it's the most accessible part of the park from Sokcho. **South Seorak** looms above the small spa town of Osaek, while to the west are the less crowded peaks of **Inner Seorak**.

Outer Seorak

It's extremely easy to get from Sokcho to **Seorak-dong**, the main Outer Seorak (*Oe-Seorak*) entrance – buses #7 and #7-1 (W950) leave frequently from the city's main road. The transition from the beaches and seafood restaurants of the coast to the peaks and pine lodges of the mountains can be surprisingly swift, sometimes taking as little as twenty minutes, though bear in mind that on warm weekends and holidays the access road can be blanketed by one huge traffic jam, and **delays** of over an hour are not uncommon before you're finally released outside the *Kensington Hotel*.

Just beyond the Seorak-dong entrance is the entry terminal of a **cable car** (W5000 one-way, W8000 return), which whisks people up to the top of a nearby peak for some great views. From the base of the cable car lead three easy and rewarding two-hour round-trip hikes; everything is signposted in Korean and English, though it's prudent to nab a map from the park entrance (W1000). The most popular trail heads to **Heundeulbawi** (literally "the rocking rock"). On the way you'll pass Sinheungsa, a modest temple-with-a-view founded in the seventh century but rebuilt several times over; this is home to a large bronze Buddha and some wonderfully detailed "Heavenly Kings", four painted guardians that watch over the temple. The trail then continues up to Gyejoam, a **cave hermitage** chiselled from the rock – this has for centuries been a place of meditation, but given the popularity of the trail you'll have to arrive very early to get any sense of serenity – from where it's a short distance to Heundeulbawi, a sixteen-ton boulder, which, despite its size, can be (and is, frequently) rocked to and fro by groups of people. Many visitors choose to stop here for a picnic, and there's also a small snack bar – it's hard to resist the sweet-smelling waffles on sale, though tea made from local fruits is a healthier option for those wishing to head beyond the rock, where the path becomes much steeper. An hour up this trail, which consists of metal stairways, vertigo-inducing bridge passes and over eight hundred steps, is the summit of **Ulsanbawi**, a highly distinctive 873m-high granite crag thrusting out of the surrounding pine trees. Legend has it that the large rock formation was once a living being that came from Ulsan, a city in southeast Korea. It heard one day that a new mountain range was being put together – the Geumgang mountains in present-day North Korea – which were to be the most beautiful on the whole peninsula. Finding on arrival that there was no more room for gargantuan masses of rock, Ulsanbawi headed back home, but fell asleep in the Seorak mountains and never woke up.

From the cable-car base, a second popular hike heads southeast through a tight ravine, taking in a few **waterfalls** on the way – Yukdam, Biryeong and Towangseong. **Yukdam** is less a waterfall than a collection of tumbling cascades; hence its name, which means "Six Pools". The **Biryeong** fall further on is far taller, toppling almost forty metres down a cliff face. Almost an hour into the ravine, most hikers turn back here, but though it looks like the end of the line the last waterfall, **Towangseong**, is a further twenty-minute hike away.

A third walk – arguably the most pleasant in the whole park – heads west from Sinheungsa to the lofty cave of **Geumganggul**. Just over half an hour's walk from the cable car, this grotto sits almost halfway up one of the many spires of rock that line the valley; it was created as a place of meditation, though the height of the cave and the commanding views it provides make it hard to truly relax. From here, many head back the way they came, but among the day-trippers you'll see people setting out for an assault on the park's highest peak, **Daecheongbong** (1708m), an otherworldly confusion of rock, and the third-highest peak in the country. From the cave it's a tough all-day hike, but it's possible to cut out some of the upward climb by taking a well-signed route from the top of the cable car. Either way, you'll probably need to spend the night at one of several **shelters** – see p.181 for details.

Osaek and South Seorak

Sitting pretty at the southern border of the national park, **Osaek** is a small village famed for the **hot spring waters** that course beneath its rolling hills. Osaek actually means "five colours", though this was a reference to the flowers fed by the nutritious springs, rather than the waters themselves. The subterranean bounty can be imbibed at several points in the village – the taste something close to an infusion made from flat lemonade and copper – or bathed in at the communal washrooms of numerous *yeogwan*, many of whose facilities are open to non-guests.

To get to Osaek, take one of the half-hourly buses from Sokcho's intercity bus terminal (W3500). From the village, it's possible to make an attempt on Daechongbong, the park's highest peak, which is just within day-hike territory – four hours up, three down.

Inner Seorak

If you want a quiet hike, this is the place for you. Further away from Sokcho than the Outer Seorak range, there is less to see at **Inner Seorak** (*Nae-seorak*),

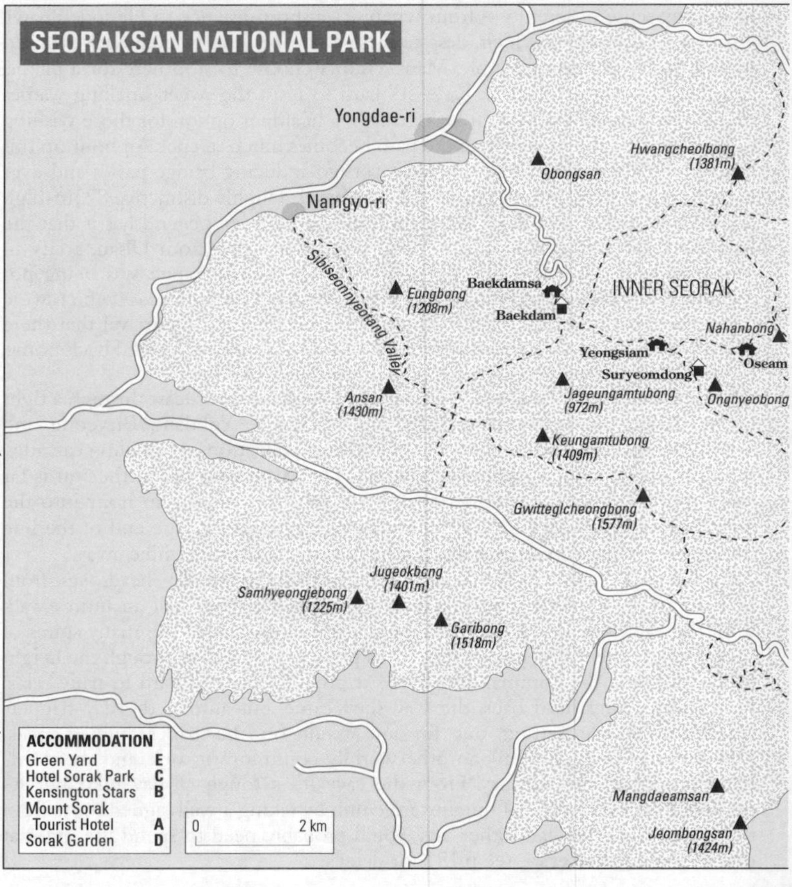

and it receives a fraction of the visitors. The area is still accessible from Sokcho, although there are only a few buses a day; these head from the intercity bus terminal to within hiking distance of Baekdamsa, a temple in the northwestern side of the park, on the way passing Yongdae-ri, a small village that has *minbak* and restaurants for those who want to stay as close as possible to the mountains. Inje, a town just 15km west of the park, is another alternative base (see p.169).

Ninety-minutes' walk from Yongdae-ri, a route also plied by the occasional bus, is **Baekdamsa**, a temple with a curious history. It started life much further west in the seventh century, but a series of unexplained fires led to several changes of location, until the monks finally settled in Seoraksan surrounded by water – Baekdamsa actually means "The Temple of a Hundred Pools". From here, there are a number of hiking options – one day-long trail heads to Seorak-dong at the east of the park, while others converge on Daecheongbong; one of the most pleasant is a ridge route that runs from Daeseungnyeong, a peak lying around four hours' hike south of Baekdamsa. Daeseungnyeong can also be reached via the **Sibiseonnyeotang valley**, one of the prettiest routes in Inner Seorak, which heads southeast from Namgyo-ri, a village west of Yongdae-ri,

and also connected to Sokcho by bus. Getting to Daecheongbong on either of these routes will certainly necessitate an overnight stay at a park shelter.

Accommodation

The bulk of Seoraksan's **accommodation** is situated a downhill walk from the Seorak-dong entrance on the east of the park; there are a few classy hotels near the park gates, and a clutch of much cheaper motels around twenty-minutes' walk back down the access road. It's also possible to stay at **Osaek**, the spa village at the southern end of the park; most of the *yeogwan* here pump **hot spring water** into the bedrooms, and some have communal hot spring baths that can be used by non-guests (W5000–10,000); room prices vary from W35,000 in the winter to over W65,000 in summer and autumn. The top choice is *Green Yard* (Ⓣ033/672-8500; ⑤), a hotel with good-value rooms and a couple of restaurants. Simpler *minbak* accommodation (from W20,000 per room) is on offer at **Yongdae-ri**, a village on the park's northwest boundary. If your hiking schedule necessitates an overnight stay in the mountains, you'll need to hunt down one of several basic **shelters**. These make for an atmospheric stay, and cost from W5000 to W7000 per night (an extra W1000 for blankets). While you're unlikely to be kicked out on a wet evening, to guarantee a place you'll have to book ahead on Korea's national park website (Ⓦwww.knps.or.kr) or reserve through the Seoraksan park office (Ⓣ033/636-7700). Unfortunately, you'll have to select the specific shelter in advance, which is a pain for those whose hike takes them longer than expected; most popular are the Yangpok and Jungcheong shelters, which generally allow for the most

▲ Seoraksan National Park

leeway. Sleeping at the peaks themselves is not allowed, though some intrepid hikers do so in their sleeping bags, waking sodden with dew in the midst of empty trails and wonderful views – just make sure you're well hidden. Rudimentary **camping facilities** are also available from W500 per tent at Seorak-dong and Jangsudae. Book ahead in summer or on weekends in the autumn, when the leaves are turning and the trails are at their busiest. All places listed below are in Seorak-dong; note that prices from June to October tend to be far higher than at other times of year, especially on weekends.

Kensington Stars Hotel ⓣ033/635-4001, ⓦwww.kensington.co.kr. A favourite of visiting dignitaries, the *Kensington* has a genuinely English feel to it, with London buses parked up outside, suits of armour in the faux library, and mahogany everywhere. Built in 1971, it's managed to keep itself on form, with excellent rooms; hefty discounts can be enjoyed off-season, plus slightly smaller ones for giving breakfast a miss. ❼

Mount Sorak Tourist Hotel ⓣ033/636-7101–5. Very simple rooms for the price, but you can chop the rack rate in half off-season. It's actually inside Seoraksan itself, and guests can enter the park for free, as the hotel's entrance road circumnavigates the park gates. ❻

Sorak Garden ⓣ033/636-7156. This motel lies, as the name suggests, in a leafy setting just off the main road in Seorak-dong's main motel area. Rooms are simple, lino-floored and have televisions; there's also a cheap restaurant in the lobby. ❸

Hotel Sorak Park ⓣ033/636-7711, ⓦwww.hotelsorakpark.co.kr. Views of Seoraksan's peaks are particularly good from the balconies of this scrupulously clean hotel; from some rooms, you'll be able to see the sea at the same time. There are a few excellent restaurants, and free shuttle buses to Yangyang airport. ❼

Down the coast

Gangwon's coast runs in an admirably straight line from the North Korean border to Gyeongbuk provice, a route hugged almost the whole way by coastal roads. Beach-fringed **Gangneung** is the first city of note south of Sokcho, and makes a good base for the pleasant national park of **Odaesan**, a short way inland, and is home to a couple of interesting temples. South of Gangneung is the small village of **Jeongdongjin**, much favoured with couples and home to two rather bizarre attractions.

Heading further down the coast, the two neighbouring cities of Donghae and Samcheok are both surrounded by beaches and navigable caves. **Donghae** has been stretched like bubblegum to an improbable size by the rewards of industry, and its unwieldy bulk means that it's frustrating to get around; **Samcheok** has better beaches, bigger caves and a far more compact layout, making for a more enjoyable visit.

Gangneung

In terms of size and numbers, **GANGNEUNG** is a big player in Gangwon terms – it's the biggest city on the northeastern coast and, like its provincial buddies Sokcho and Donghae, is spread thinly over a large area. The city's relaxed atmosphere makes it a popular place to hole up for a few days and explore the surrounding area, especially for hikers heading on to **Odaesan National Park**. That said Gangneung has a couple of sights of its own, including excellent **beaches**. If you can, try to time your visit around the fifth day of the fifth lunar moon – usually in May – when the riverside **Dano festival** is held. Events take place all over the country on this auspicious date, but the biggest is in Gangneung, a five-day event which has commemorated the "Double Fifth" with dancing and shamanist rituals for over four hundred years.

The festival also marks your best opportunity to see *ssireum*, a Korean version often compared to sumo, but actually far more similar to Mongolian wrestling.

Gangneung's main sight is **Ojukheon** (daily 9am–6pm; W2000), a network of floral paths and traditional buildings, and the birthplace of **Lee Yulgok**, also known as Yi-Yi, a member of the *yanbang* – Korea's Confucian elite – and one of its most famous scholars (see box, p.186). The complex is quite large, and much of it is paved, but there's a pleasant green picnic area surrounded by tall pines, as well as a patch of rare black bamboo to stroll through. Ojukheon is especially popular in the autumn, when its trees burst into a riot of flame. Rice fields surround the complex so it can be a little hard to know when to get off the bus – be sure to tell the driver where you want to go; take number #202 from outside the train station or bus terminals, though as the route braches off halfway be sure to board one bound for **Gyeongpo beach**. This long stretch of white sand is one of the most popular beaches in the province, and there's all kinds of water-based fun to be had in the summer, when it can be absolutely heaving with people from all across the province. Well-informed locals prefer **Anmok beach**, a more relaxed stretch of sand further south, which rarely fills up. In between the beach and Ojukheon you may care to disembark the bus at **Gyeongpoho**, a lake overlooked by an ornate pavilion, or the slightly bizarre **Chamsori Edison Gramophone Museum**, which claims to be the largest gramophone museum in the world (those doubting the existence of any others should note that there's another in Jeongdongjin, just down the road).

Practicalities

Although Gangneung is part of Korea's **rail** network, the service running along the coastal line is so sparse it's usually more convenient to arrive by **bus**. The city's express and intercity terminals are joined at the hip in the west of the city, with two helpful **tourist information** centres outside (Ⓣ033/640 5129); another info booth can be found outside the train station. Most of the city's main sights lie on one **bus route** – pick up #202 from outside the train station or bus terminals, and make sure that the final destination is **Gyeongpo beach**, as some head elsewhere. Gangneung's main shopping and restaurant area lies near where the train line crosses **Jungangno**, a main road twenty-minutes' walk from the train station.

Half-a-dozen new **motels** have sprung up in the area behind the bus terminal and provide the city's most comfortable accommodation, if not the best located. *Equus* (Ⓣ033/643-0114; ④) is the pick of the bunch, with wood-lined rooms, mood lighting and heavenly showers (most of which you can see into from the bedrooms). It's the sand-coloured building with a clock on top. If you're looking to stay around the train station, look for the # *Motel* (Ⓣ033/645-9692 or 3; ④) – the neon hash sign is just about visible from the train station exit.

Down the coast	
Gangneung	강릉
Jeongdongjin	정동진
Odaesan National Park	오대산 국립 공원
Samcheok	삼척
Taebaeksan National Park	태백산 국립 공원
Wonju	원주
Yongpyeong Ski Resort	용평 스키 리조트

Victims of nautical nomenclature

The victim mentality drilled into Korean students during their history lessons is such that any perceived slant against the nation, no matter how slight, can turn into a serious issue that has the whole country boiling with rage. Anger is further magnified should the insult come from Korea's one-time colonial masters, the Japanese – witness the case of the waters east of the Korean mainland, generally known across the world as the **"Sea of Japan"**. Koreans insist that this name is a symbol of Japan's imperial past, and youth hostel wall-maps around the world have had the name crossed out by *gimchi*-chomping Korean travellers and replaced with **"East Sea"**. Korean diplomats raised enough of a stink to take the issue to the United Nations, which tentatively sided with the Japanese, but left the topic open for further discussion. Although both terms have been used for centuries, neither is strictly correct – Korea controls a large portion of the waters yet the sea lies plainly to Japan's west – so while this storm in a teacup continues to rage on, feel free to send your own suggestions of compromise to the UN: "Sea of Peaceful Diplomatic Negotiations", perhaps?

Eight funky styles of room can be selected from a menu behind the counter – try room C, which is like Kubrick's *2001* with flowers. For a cheaper sleep with no frills whatsoever, the grimy *Samil Yeoinsuk* (❶) is literally the first building on the left as you leave the train station; there are teams of similar places to the right of the station exit, though an abundance of pink lighting suggests that any prices quoted may be for more than just the room.

Restaurants are ubiquitous and well priced. *Dorstop*, near the train station, has some extremely cheap meat to fry, with prices starting at W2500 per person; look for the Chinese lanterns under a yellow pig-nose logo. Those arriving in the city or about to depart for pastures new can make use of the food court on the upper floor of the bus terminal; the restaurants here may look a little crusty, but there's nothing wrong with the food. Should you fancy a drink, there are several friendly **bars** in and around the main shopping area, of which *Warehouse*, on Gotgamjeon-gil, is the busiest and best, and usually closes when the last person decides to leave.

Odaesan National Park

A short ride to the west of Gangneung is **ODAESAN NATIONAL PARK**, markedly smooth and gentle compared with its jagged Gangwonese neighbours. Full of colour in the autumn, and with magnificent views from the stony peaks, it's relatively empty for a Korean national park as hikers tend to be sucked into the Seoraksan range a short way to the north.

Odaesan has two main entrance points – one in the pretty Sogeumgang area to the north of the park, and a south gate reached via the small town of Jinbu. Between the two are two temples and innumerable shrines, some of which are quite remote and receive next to no visitors – just the treat for adventurous hikers.

Sogeumgang ("Little Geumgang") is named after the spectacular range just over the border in North Korea. A maze of tumbling waterfalls, bare peaks and thickly forested slopes, Odaesan is more than a little similar to its renowned northern cousin, but substantially easier to get to. The south of the park contains two sumptuous **temples** – Woljeongsa and Sangwonsa. **Woljeongsa** dates from 645, and contains an impressive octagonal nine-storey pagoda from the early Goryeo dynasty, adorned with wind chimes and

Star of the five-thousand-won note

Lee Yulgok (1536–84), more commonly known by his pen name **Yi-Yi**, is one of the most prominent Confucian scholars in Korea's history, and once lived in the **Ojukheon** complex in Gangneung. A member of the country's *yangban* elite, he was apparently able to write with Chinese characters at the age of 3, and was composing poetry by the time he was 7 years old, much of it on pavilions surrounding the glassy lake at Gyeongpoho just down the road. At 19 he was taken to the hills to be educated in Buddhist doctrine, but abandoned this study to excel in **political circles**, rising through the ranks to hold several important posts, including Minister of Personnel and War. At one point, he advised the King to prepare an army of 100,000 to repel a potential **Japanese invasion** – the advice was ignored, and a huge attack came in 1592, just after Yi-Yi's death. His face is on one side of the **W5000 note**, while on the other is the famed "Insects and Plants", painting from his mother, **Sin Saimdang** (1504–51), who was a well-known poet and artist.

striking a perfect balance with the thick fir trees surrounding the complex. It faces an ornate, and rare, kneeling Buddha. The complex as a whole addresses function rather than beauty, though in the main hall are two elaborate Buddhist paintings – most interesting is the one on the left-hand side, which features some hellish scenes of torture. Ten kilometres away through the pine trees is **Sangwonsa**, a complex containing what is believed to be Korea's oldest bronze bell, which dates from 725. Sangwonsa's appeal is its magical setting, facing a mountain ridge swathed with a largely deciduous wall of trees; in a country where pine-green reigns supreme, the blaze of colour that these create in the autumn is rather welcome. There's also a little **tearoom** by the temple in which to rest.

A **hiking** trail leads from Sangwonsa to **Birobong**, the highest peak in the park at 1563m. Although the ascent can be made in under two hours, it's steep and not an easy walk. Those who get to the top can continue along a ridge trail to Sangwangbong, or even attempt a U-shaped day-hike to Dongdaesan via Durobong – this walk is particularly tough on the legs. A waterfall-strewn day-hike heads up through Sogeumgang via Noinbong to Odaesan's spine road; unfortunately, this twisty thoroughfare sees no public transport, limiting onward movement from the park to hitchhiking or a lengthy walk.

Practicalities

City bus #303 heads to Sogeumgang from outside Gangneung's bus terminal. To get to the temples in the south of the park you'll have to change in Jinbu, to which regular **buses** run from Gangneung, as well as a few from Dong-Seoul. However, onward connections to the park are infrequent – there's one every hour or so, though some only go as far as Woljeongsa. Don't worry about the misleading signs on the way – you'll know when to get off. There's a pleasantly low-key **minbak** area downhill from the southern park entrance, with rooms in traditional houses going from W30,000. Further down again is the rather more comfortable *Odaesan Hotel* (Ⓣ033/330-5000, Ⓕ033/330-5123; ❼). Inside the park itself, there's a tiny **shelter** between Woljeongsa and Sangwonsa, with the few rooms going for W30,000. There's also a **campsite** nearby; it costs up to W6000 per tent in July and August, but though it's free for the rest of the year the shower facilities will be unavailable. Sogeumgang also has a *minbak* area, as well as a campsite. **Hiking maps** can be bought for W1000 at the park entrances.

Yongpyeong ski resort

In Pyeongchang county, just west of Gangneung, is **YONGPYEONG** (ⓦwww.yongpyong.co.kr), Korea's largest ski resort, also known as Dragon Valley. Facilities here are so good that Pyeongchang came within a whisker of being selected as the host of the 2010 **Winter Olympics**, but was usurped by Vancouver in the final ballot, and suffered defeat again to the Russian resort Sochi for the 2014 games.

▲ Sangwonsa temple, Odaesan National Park

The resort has all kinds of activities from snowboarding to sledding available in the winter and a mammoth **31 slopes** to choose from, accessed on fifteen ski lifts and gondolas. Prices depend on what time of day you'd like to ski – it's even possible (and cheapest) to do it at night under strong lights, but most go for the W68,000 lift-and-gondola pass, which will see you through morning and afternoon. Equipment is available to hire; skis and clothing for the same times would cost a combined W51,000, though this too can rise or fall depending on your exact schedule. The *Dragon Valley Hotel* (call the resort on Ⓣ033/335 5757; ❼) is the deluxe accommodation option on site, but there are many *yeogwan* and a **youth hostel** in the area too.

To get to Yongpyeong from Gangneung, take a **bus** from the intercity terminal to Hoenggye – there's one every ten or twenty minutes. From Hoenggye there are free shuttle buses during the ski season; at other times you can take a local bus. There are direct bus services to the resort from Gangneung and the capital's Dong-Seoul terminal. If you're looking for smaller, less-crowded ski resorts, go to Phoenix Park and Hyundae Sungwoo further down the Yeongdong highway, in the direction of Wonju.

Jeongdongjin

For those bored with temples, war museums and national parks, the area around **JEONGDONGJIN** has some more unusual attractions which should float your boat, if you'll pardon the pun. Near this small, windswept coastal village lie two retired nautical vessels – an **American warship** from the Korean War, and an equally authentic **North Korean submarine**. From Gangneung, trains make the short trip down the coast, much of which is cordoned off with barbed wire, before stopping at what is apparently the world's closest train station to the sea. A short stretch of sand separates the track from the water, and it's here that Korean couples flock to hold hands and watch the sunrise – the area was featured in *Sandglass*, a romantic Korean drama (truly a truism, since all Korean dramas are romantic). There's not too much to see in the town itself, but the **Sun Cruise Hotel** is as much a tourist attraction as a place to stay. Designed to look like a boat, you really can't miss it – just look for the ship hanging precariously from a cliff. Although its souvenir shop is only on the ninth floor, the combined height of hotel and cliff means that you're a whopping 165m above sea level, and as you walk out of the shop onto the **viewing platform**, it's tempting to let your mind soar and imagine that you're up on the deck of the world's largest ship. One floor up is a revolving bar, where cocktails start at a reasonable W7000. Squatting a hundred yards from the hotel is another land-lubbing ship, this one a **museum** containing old gramophones, phonographs, TVs and radios, as well as a floor dedicated to the inventions of one Thomas Edison. On the way back to the station, look out for the **giant egg-timer** – the sand inside takes exactly twelve months to fall through, and couples gather to watch it being turned over each New Year.

Tongil Park

Jeongdongjin's resident warship and sub are permanently moored next to each other at **Tongil Park** (March–Oct 9am–6pm; Nov–Feb till 5pm; W2000), four kilometres north of the village on the coast, and joined to Gangneung and Jeongdongjin by bus #11 (every 15min; W900). The ship saw action, having served in the Korean War, but the **submarine** has an even more interesting tale to tell, having made a dramatic final voyage – see box opposite. It's hard to imagine that this small metal tube could hold a crew of thirty, as even with

Espionage in the East Sea

Those who deem the Cold War long-finished should cast their minds back to September 1996. On the fourteenth, a submarine containing 26 **North Korean spies** arrived at Amin, on South Korea's Gangwon coast. Three disembarked, and made it back to the submarine after completing their surveillance mission on the Air Force base near Gangneung, but the waves were particularly strong that day and the sub came a cropper on the rocks. Eleven non-military crew members were killed by the soldiers, lest they leaked classified information to the South, and important documents were incinerated inside the vessel – the ceiling of the cabin in question is still charred with burnt North Korean spy material. The remaining fifteen soldiers attempted to return to the North overland, with their Southern counterparts understandably keen to stop them; the mission continued for 49 days, during which seventeen South Korean soldiers and civilians lost their lives. Thirteen of the spies were killed, one was captured, and the whereabouts of the last remains a mystery.

nobody else on board it's tough enough to navigate without bumping your head; with just one dark, cramped corridor, you're unlikely to be inside for long. By compari-son, the US-made **warship** is 120m long, and it can take an hour or so to hunt down every nook and cranny; in the bridge you can play with the chunky steering equipment, twiddle some knobs, check the dials, and shoot imaginary torpedoes at your enemies. Though the ship is on dry land, nearby military installations and the waves crashing below can make it easy to let your imagination go wild, and if your karma is in credit there'll be fighter jets from the local Air Force base roaring overhead.

Practicalities

Jeongdongjin is best accessed by **train**, though Gangwon's coastal line operates a frustratingly infrequent service so it pays to find out times in advance. Otherwise, it's accessible by **local bus** from Gangneung – #109 runs from the bus terminal, and #111, #112 and #113 from various stops around the city, passing by Tongil Park on the way.

The whole town trades on the romance dollar, with amorous couples arriving to hold hands and watch the sunset year-round, so there are plenty of **rooms** and **restaurants** to choose from. The *Sun Cruise Hotel* (ⓣ033/610-7000; ❻) can be surprisingly cheap off-season; mercifully the nautical theme isn't carried through into its plain rooms, but the whole place could do with a refurb, and the staff are somewhat inattentive. Just down the hill is the *Hyang-gi* (ⓣ033/642-7512 or 3; ❺), which tries to be stylish and sits in a prime location at the very end of the beach, but the immediate patch is cordoned off with barbed wire, and rooms are a little stuffy and of questionable value. Cheap **motels** (❸) can be found near the train station, with a newer and slightly more expensive flock under the *Sun Cruise*; if you choose the latter, make sure you're out of the ship-hotel's sonic range – the piped seagull, wave and foghorn noises that emanate from the "deck" would try the patience of a saint. Even cheaper are the *minbak* that sit on the quiet road between the two motel clusters (❷).

Restaurants are plentiful, though one which deserves a special mention is *Sseon Hansik*, a European-style white cottage on the main road near the train station; try *sundubu*, a local speciality made from tofu in a spicy sauce – W20,000 for two people. Close by is *Café Sun*, serving coffees from around the world with great sea views, or cocktails when the sun has gone down.

Samcheok and around

Although **Donghae** is the largest city in the area after Gangneung, it's a little too cumbersome to be of much interest to travellers, other than those heading to the stunning East Sea island of Ulleungdo (see p.231), to which daily ferries run from March to October from a port next to Mukho train station. However, the beaches and caves of Donghae are well and truly trumped by more impressive versions around the smaller and more manageable town of **SAMCHEOK**, just to the south, which makes for a far more comfortable base. Samcheok is best approached by bus, as the train station is some distance from the centre and in any case carries a sparse service. The city's two bus terminals – express and intercity – lie almost side by side on the southern flank of a quadrilateral of roads that form the city centre; these are home to plenty of chain restaurants and high-street clothing stores, while much of the interior is taken up by an appealingly grimy market. A **tourist information booth** is located just outside the express terminal, the helpful staff able to advise on accommodation, as well as the ever-changing details of local transport.

With Samcheok's main tourist draw – the colossal Hwanseon Cave – some way to the west, there's little to see in the city itself, though the **port area** to the east is worth a stroll. Here, it's common to see acres of squid hung out like laundry to dry in the sun, and there are more fish restaurants than you can count. Unfortunately, few buses head here from Samcheok centre, so taxis are usually the best way to go. A few kilometres north is **Samcheok Beach**, which attracts a young crowd in the summer; like many other beaches in the province, much of it is cordoned off with **barbed wire**. This makes it a rather interesting place to sunbathe; the wire is in place to prevent amphibious North Korean landings such as the one that occurred up the coast in Jeongdongjin in 1996 (see box, p.189); also keep an eye out at night for the large spotlights used to keep an eye on the seas. Further south there are several more beaches, as well as Haesindang, a coastal park of **phallic sculpture**. Unfortunately, this once-beautiful coast is steadily being eroded, not so much by crashing seas as by the development of coastal highways.

Accommodation

With the exception of *Hotel Palace*, all accommodation options listed here are in central Samcheok, and within easy walking distance of its **bus terminals**. For a more old-time coastal Gangwon atmosphere, adventurous travellers could do worse than head to the cheap guesthouses sprinkled around the **port area** east of town, an area whose restaurants and shops are almost entirely dedicated to fish, and home to something of an end-of-the-world atmosphere. Samcheok beach is also a pleasant place to stay, though bear in mind that prices at its various motels rise in summer months.

Hanil Motel Namyang-dong ⓣ033/574 8277 or 8. Right next to the bus terminal, this motel has reasonably large rooms, though the mattresses are a little hospital-like. The rosy silk wallpaper in the halls mercifully stops before the rooms. ❷

Jjimjilbang Jeongsang-dong. For those willing to sleep on the floor of a darkened communal room, this is a budget option right next door to the *Moon Motel*; your W6000 entry fee pays for use of the pools and steam rooms, as well as the hire of a fetching set of matching T-shirt and shorts.

Moon Motel Jeongsang-dong ⓣ033/572 4436. The *Moon* lies in a quiet part of town between the bus terminal and the river, and has clean, comfy rooms that are remarkably stylish for a Korean motel. ❹

Hotel Palace Jeongha-dong ⓣ033/575 7000. Way out of town on the coast, Samcheok's luxury option has several large restaurants and banquet halls; the cavernous rooms are linoleum-floored, making it feel a little like a well-tended Korean apartment. You can cut the rate in half off-season, or even more if you don't require a sea view. ❼

Samil Yeoinsuk Namyang-dong ⓣ033/5732038. Take the small alley opposite the bus terminal's information booth to get to the *Samil*, which has *ondol*-heated rooms, as well as some with a bed for a few dollars more. All rooms have a TV and private bathroom, although you may have to ask for hot water, and even with heating the whole place may be a little too cold for comfort in the winter. ❶

Hwanseondonggul

Though Korea contains a fair number of navigable caves, **Hwanseondonggul** (daily: March–Oct 8am–5.30pm; Nov–Feb 8.30am–4.30pm; W4000) is the one

▲ Hwanseondonggul

that can most justly be described as "cavernous" – hiding away under a sumptuous range of hills west of Samcheok, the local tourist board claims that it's the **largest cave in Asia**. Superlatives aside, it's certainly a whopper – the system is over 6km in length, featuring umpteen rooms and some subterranean water features. Hwanson's largest chamber measures 100m by 30m, its dimensions, shading and vaguely creepy atmosphere bringing to mind a Gothic cathedral. Only 1.6km is open to the public, most of which is traversed by platforms and staircases; be sure to bring suitable shoes and an extra layer of clothing, as it's damp and not very warm down there. Also bear in mind that the cave entrance is a rather steep half-hour trek from the ticket office, next to which are some examples of the area's traditional wooden mountain housing. Bus #60 heads to the cave from Samcheok bus terminal (7 daily; 50min), though only five of these will allow you enough time to tour the cave, the latest of which is the 2.20pm service; the last bus back is at 7.30pm.

South of Samcheok

The Gangwon coast continues on down from Samcheok, squeezing numerous **beaches** into a fairly short stretch along the way, although continued development of the coastal roads and the resulting increase in traffic means that in addition to the one in Samcheok only two are actually worth visiting – **Maengbang** and **Yonghwa**. The former is one of the largest in the area and its calm waters make it good for swimming. Surrounded by pine trees, it's usually quite peaceful as it's a twenty-minute walk from the nearest bus stop and *minbak* village. The beach at Yonghwa is smaller – only 200m in length – and much closer to the road, but equally attractive.

A little further on from Yonghwa beach is the rather curious **Haesindang Park** (daily 9am–6pm; W3000); take the hourly bus #24 from Samcheok's bus terminal, though bear in mind that some maps and bus drivers refer to this area as Sinnam. Inside the park, paths are lined with **penis sculptures** of metal, stone and wood – one is lined with nails, several are carved into people-like shapes, and one metal ithyphallus is mounted on cannon wheels. There is method to the madness – one local folk tale tells of a young bride-to-be who died by the shore in a violent storm, after which her angry spirit chased the fish from the seas; the only way around this, apparently, was to placate the newly dead's soul with carved wooden phalluses. The main building's **folk exhibition** can be safely ignored, and is interesting only for a small display showing how local squid are lured to their deaths, and an almost comically bad simulation of a boat ride. It gets better in the **sculpture zone**, which has replicas of ancient pornographic statuary from Asia and beyond – don't leave until you've checked out the Greek god's horny pose. Various trails make for a pleasant walk around the park – though one often made brisk by the seaside winds – with views of the sea crashing on to the crags below. You can go all the way down to the shore, which is pebbly and certainly not safe for swimming. A few *minbak* and some stalls selling grilled fish from as little as W1000 can be found around the park's southern end.

Taebaek to Wonju

Heading west from the coast towards Gyeonggi-do and Seoul, you'll pass through some magnificent Gangwonese scenery, its swathe of rolling hills rising up to a couple of relatively untouristed **national parks**. The more easterly of the two, **Taebaeksan**, can be accessed from the relaxed city of Taebaek, while **Chiaksan** National Park lies east of Wonju, near the confluence of the Gangwon, Gyeonggi and Chungbuk borders.

Taebaek

The small, sedate city of **TAEBAEK** is one of the most typical of the Gangwonese interior. Surrounded by mountains and with little large-scale commerce to speak of, its elevation means the air is clean and fresh, and the climate is usually a little colder here than on the coast. It's mainly used as a transit point for the thoroughly enjoyable maze of hiking trails that is Taebaeksan National Park – see the account below for details.

The train station, bus terminal and information booth (daily 9am–5pm; ⓣ033/550 2081) are all corralled around the same roundabout at the top of town, together with a range of cheap **places to stay**. You can't miss the *Aegis Motel* (ⓣ033/553 9980; ④), with its white frame towering over the train station; rooms here are large and clean, though as the train line has some early morning services, it may not be ideal for light sleepers. Further down the road is the *Garden-jang Yeogwan* (②), which has basic but adequate rooms, or roll out a futon on a heated floor at the *Bohye Yeoinsuk* (①). For decent **food** you'll have to make your way into the city centre – walk down from the train station and turn right at the main road – where the two best places are *Chueok-ui Yeontanbul*, which serves *samgyeopsal* with a great range of side dishes, and *Simigi-peunmeul*, a traditionally-styled drink-'n'-snack place on the second floor of a building opposite Hwangji pond.

Taebaeksan National Park

Within half-an-hour of Taebaek's bus terminal is the main entrance to **Taebaeksan National Park**, which is said to be especially beautiful in winter months, and makes a much prettier place to stay than the city centre. The entrance is already 870m above sea level, and from here a pair of easy two-hour routes run to the twin peaks of Munsubong (1517m) and Cheonjedan (1561m), two of the highest in Korea. These are of particular importance to **shamanists**, as Taebaeksan is viewed as Korea's "motherly mountain" – ancient Korean kings were said to perform rituals here, and at the summits it's still common to see offerings left behind by hikers in honour of **Dangun**, the legendary founder of Korea (see Contexts, p.420). Cheonjedan plays host to a shamanist ceremony every year on October 3 – "National Foundation Day" in Korea, and a public holiday – as does the Dangun hall near the entrance. A rather less spiritual **coal museum** sprawls out just below the park entrance; the Taebaeksan area was once the heart of Korea's coal industry, and this museum charts its gradual decline. The top floor shows some interesting pictures of coal village life, and there are a couple of surprise simulations in store too.

Near the park entrance is a two-storey parade of buildings, with **restaurants** on the ground floor and **minbak** accommodation above. Nearby motels offer greater comfort, including *U-kin*, whose attached restaurant allows you to eat in little private huts. Further downhill is a bunch of newer, homelier *minbak*, all charging around W25,000 per room.

The Jeongseon route

At **Jeungsan**, 35km west of Taebaek, a spur splits from the main train line and barrels up north through an extremely picturesque valley, whose undulating hills and unspoilt scenery carry echoes of Shikoku in Japan. A single carriage train plies this route, heading through Jeongseon to Aruaji, though its modern swivel-chairs are somewhat incongruous with the surrounding bucolic scenery and the small, unassuming towns on route. Situated near the end of the line, **Jeongseon** is the only stop en route that could possibly be termed "touristy" – most of the valley's accommodation and restaurants can be found here, and there's a market on every date ending with a 2 or a 7, along with coinciding assorted cultural performances from April to November. For the most enjoyable attraction on the route, you'll have to head to **Aruaji** at the end of the line: shuttle buses meet the trains and head further up the track to a now-disused station, from where you can cycle the 7km back down the train line to Aruaji on a specially crafted **rail-bike** (W18,000 per pair). Its popularity means that it can be booked solid at weekends, though on slacker days curious foreigners may be given a free hundred-metre dash – don't forget to brake. Also at the station is an odd burger-bar-cum-café in the shape of two fish.

Wonju

From Taebaek, trains barrel up and across a gorgeous succession of valleys and crests, and make a full 360-degree turn inside a mountain before arriving at **WONJU**. Sadly, Wonju is a sure-fire contender for the worst city in Korea, with a level of poverty rarely seen in urban South Korea, some downright seediness around the train and bus terminals and a large military presence from local army camps. When soldiers are coming or going, the PC rooms near the bus station can be full of young soldiers blowing up digitized armies while wearing real-life military fatigues – a surreal sight. Wonju is only really useful as a jumping-off point for the surrounding hills, particularly the **Chiaksan National Park** to the east. Also within striking distance are several **ski resorts** – Oak Valley to the west, Hyundai Sungwoo to the east on the way to Gangneung, and Phoenix Park further along again. See Ⓦenglish.tour2korea.com for more info.

The **train** station and intercity **bus** terminal are both in the city centre, within a short cab ride or a twenty-minute walk of each other, while arrivals from Seoul, Gangneung or Gwangju may be set down at the more pleasant express bus terminal, a building which also houses the city's **tourist information** office. The area around it has some good restaurants, though the sleek **motels** are pricier (and even more blatantly love-based) than elsewhere in Korea. One of these is the *Kingdom Motel* (Ⓣ033/748-6691; ❹), a green building across from the terminal; the rooms are good for a motel but poor value at this price. There are a couple of decent options near the train station; turn left on the main road outside and you'll soon come across the *Rinbiato Hotel* (Ⓣ033/743-6677; ❷), which has clean rooms with powerful showers, and a free choice of DVDs to watch. The *Pau Motel* opposite offers much the same at similar prices. **Bus** #41 takes you to the main entrance of Chiaksan National Park; you can pick it up from stops near the train station and intercity bus terminal, but they're a little hard to find so ask around.

Chiaksan National Park

Visible from parts of Wonju are the principal ridges of **CHIAKSAN NATIONAL PARK**, the dozen or so 1000-metre-plus peaks rifling across the sky like a torn page, but despite its proximity to Seoul, and Wonju just to the west, the park is rarely overrun with visitors. This is partly due to the infrequency of public transport heading to the park – though several buses connect various park entrances to Wonju, only the #41 appears regularly, heading to the main entrance at the north of the park every half-hour or so; unless you find one of the others, you may have a tough job getting back without resorting to hitchhiking, a mission simplified by the fact that almost all cars heading from the park will be heading towards Wonju.

Near the main entrance is **Guryeongsa**, a small but well-formed temple complex dating from the dawn of Unified Silla rule in the mid-seventh century. From here a three-hour hiking route heads on via a small waterfall to **Birobong** (1288m), the park's highest peak, and continues along a ridge to Namdaebong, a slightly less lofty peak four hours or so to the south. From Birobong it's also possible to drop down past the lonely Ipseoksa temple to the Hwanggol entrance on the west of the park, though onward transport to Wonju is patchy at best.

Outside the Guryeongsa entrance is one of the most pleasingly rural *minbak* villages of any Korean national park, entirely devoid of the neon signs, trinket shops and pumping grandmother techno that often sully park entrances; staying here is highly recommended if you're looking for a peaceful – if rustic – getaway. From the bus stop, go downhill and over the bridge crossing the stream – *minbak* dot the small valley for a few hundred metres; just choose the one you like the look of, as they're all very spartan and cost around W25,000 per room. All should be able to cook you something, but for the local speciality, *gamja pajeon*, a kind of savoury pancake eaten with soy sauce, you'll probably have to head up to the restaurants near the bus stop. At the bottom of the mountain is the excellent *Motel NYX* (Ⓣ033/732-4338; ④), a quirky place with great rooms.

Travel details

Trains

Chuncheon to: Gangchon (hourly; 16min); Seoul (hourly; 2hr).
Gangneung to: Jeongdongjin (16 daily; 14min); Seoul (10 daily; 6hr 45min); Taebaek (10 daily; 2hr 33min).
Jeongdongjin to: Gangneung (16 daily; 14min).
Suwon to: Seoul (regularly; 29min).
Taebaek to: Gangneung (10 daily; 2hr 33min); Seoul (10 daily; 4hr 40min).
Wonju to: Andong (9 daily; 2hr 43min); Seoul (9 daily; 1hr 45min–2hr).

Buses

Cheorwon to: Chuncheon (12 daily; 2hr 30min); Daejeon (2 daily; 3hr 30min); Seoul (regularly; 2hr).
Chuncheon to: Andong (1 daily; 2hr); Busan (14 daily; 6hr); Cheorwon (12 daily; 2hr 30min); Daegu (5 daily; 3hr 30min); Daejeon (7 daily; 2hr 50min); Gangneung (regularly; 3hr); Incheon (regularly; 2hr 30min); Jeonju (2 daily; 4hr 15min); Samcheok (10 daily; 4hr); Seoul (regularly; 1hr 30min); Sokcho (frequently; 2hr 30min); Suwon (regularly; 2hr 20min); Taebaek (1 daily; 5hr); Wonju (regularly; 1hr 30min).
Gangneung to: Busan (10 daily; 7hr); Cheonan (8 daily; 4hr); Cheongju (5 daily; 4hr); Chuncheong (regularly; 3hr); Chungju (regularly; 2hr 50min); Daegu (regularly; 5hr); Gwangju (6 daily; 5hr); Incheon (hourly; 4hr); Samcheok (regularly; 1hr); Seoul (regularly; 3hr 20min); Sokcho (regularly; 1hr 10min); Suwon (12 daily; 3hr 30min); Taebaek (regularly; 2hr 30min); Wonju (regularly; 2hr).
Incheon to: Andong (regularly; 4hr 10min); Busan (11 daily; 4hr 30min); Cheongju (regularly; 2hr); Chuncheon (regularly; 3hr); Daegu (hourly; 4hr 30min); Daejeon (regularly; 2hr 45min); Gangneung (hourly; 4hr); Gwangju (every 30min; 4hr); Jeonju (hourly; 3hr 10min); Mokpo (15 daily; 4hr 30min); Seoul (regularly; 1hr 10min); Sokcho (10 daily; 4hr 10min); Taebaek (3 daily; 4hr 25min); Wonju (regularly; 2hr); Yeosu (3 daily; 5hr 40min).
Samcheok to: Busan (10 daily; 5hr); Chuncheon (10 daily; 4hr); Daegu (regularly; 5hr); Gangneung (regularly; 1hr); Gyeongju (regularly; 5hr); Seoul (8 daily; 4hr 30min); Sokcho (9 daily; 3hr); Taebaek (regularly; 1hr 10min).

Sokcho to: Busan (10 daily; 7hr); Chuncheon (regularly; 2hr 30min); Daegu (10 daily; 4hr 30min); Gangneung (regularly; 1hr 10min); Gwangju (4 daily; 6hr); Samcheok (9 daily; 3hr); Seoul (regularly; 3hr 30min); Wonju (8 daily; 3hr 30min).
Suwon to: Busan (7 daily; 5hr); Daegu (14 daily; 3hr 30min); Daejeon (8 daily; 1hr 30min); Gwangju (regularly; 3hr 30min); Jeonju (12 daily; 2hr 40min); Mokpo (7 daily; 4hr 30min); Sokcho (8 daily; 4hr 30min).
Taebaek to: Andong (5 daily; 3hr); Busan (5 daily; 4hr 30min); Daegu (7 daily; 4hr 30min); Gangneung (regularly; 2hr 30min); Samcheok (regularly; 1hr 10min); Seoul (regularly; 3hr 30min).
Wonju to: Cheongju (regularly; 1hr 40min); Chuncheon (regularly; 1hr 10min); Chungju (regularly; 1hr 20min); Daegu (15 daily; 2hr 30min); Gangneung (regularly; 1hr 40min); Guinsa (6 daily; 2hr); Seoul (regularly; 1hr 30min); Sokcho (8 daily; 4hr).

Ferries

Of the many services to China, the route to Tianjin's port at Tanggu will put you closest to Beijing. Note that the Tues sailings arrive at a far more amenable hour than Thurs departures.
Incheon International Terminal 1 to: Dalian (5pm Tue, Thurs, Sat; 17hr); Dandong (5.30pm Mon, Wed, Fri; 16hr); Qinhuangdao (7pm Mon, 1pm Fri; 23hr); Shidao (6pm Mon, Wed, Fri; 14hr); Yantai (8pm Tue, Thurs, Sat; 14hr); Yingkou (8pm Tue, noon Sat; 24hr).
Incheon International Terminal 2 to: Lianyungang (7pm Tue, 3pm Sat; 24hr); Qingdao (5pm Tue, Thurs, Sat; 15hr); Tianjin (1pm Tue, 7pm Fri; 24hr); Weihai (7pm Mon, Wed, Sat; 14hr).
Wolmido Terminal to: Jagyakdo (hourly; 20min); Yeongjongdo (every 20min; 20min).
Yeonan Terminal to: Baengnyeongdo (3 daily; 4–8hr); Deokjeokdo (five daily; 2hr 30min–5hr); Jagyakdo (hourly; 30min); Jeju City (7pm Mon, Wed, Fri; 13hr).Ro doluptatum augait, quismolor

3

Gyeongsang

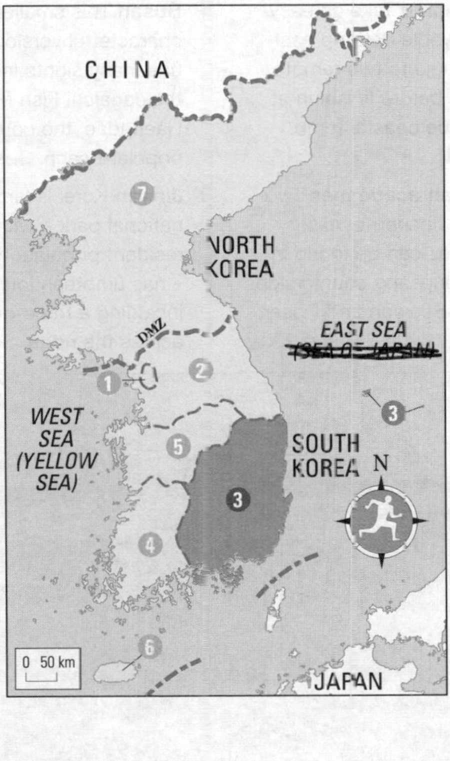

CHAPTER 3

Highlights

* **Gyeongju** Once the Silla kingdom's capital and now Korea's most laid-back city, Gyeongju has enough sights to fill at least a week. See p.201
* **Bulguksa** Combine a trip to the country's busiest temple with a visit to Seokguram, a holy grotto set in the mountains above. See p.209
* **The Underwater Tomb of King Munmu** Take an easy but enjoyable day-trip east of Gyeongju to two remote temples, before finishing at this unique coastal tomb. See p.216
* **Confucian academies** Two stunning Joseon-dynasty academies can be found in the Gyeongsang countryside – Oksan Seowon and Dosan Seowon. See p.217 & p.230
* **Folk villages** Savour a taste of Korean life long forgotten at Yangdong, a village near Gyeongju, and Hahoe, an equally gorgeous version near Andong. See p.217 & p.229
* **Ulleungdo** This island's isolation out in the East Sea makes it the perfect place to see traditional life first-hand, or kick back and relax for a few days. See p.231
* **Busan** This smaller, more characterful version of Seoul has many sights including the Jagalchi Fish Market and Haeundae, the country's most popular beach. See p.238
* **Jirisan** Korea's largest national park – with its own resident population of bears – has umpteen lofty trails, including a three-day hike across the ridge. See p.258

▲ Haeundae beach, Busan

3

Gyeongsang

The surprisingly low number of travellers who choose to escape Seoul usually make a beeline to the **Gyeongsang provinces** at the southeast of the country, and with good reason – a land of mountains and majesty, folklore and heroes, this area is home to some of the most wonderful sights that Korea has to offer. Gorgeous **Gyeongju** was capital of the Silla kingdom that ruled for nearly a thousand years (see box below), and there is more to see than in Korea's modern-day capital, all crammed into a fraction of

The Silla dynasty

In 69 BC a young Herod was learning how to talk, Julius Caesar was busying himself in Gaul and Spartacus was leading slave revolts against Rome. Legend has it that at this time, a strange light shone down from the East Asian sky onto a **horse** of pure white. The beast was sheltering an egg, from which hatched **Hyeokgeose**, who went on to be appointed king by local chiefs at the tender age of 13. He inaugurated the **Silla dynasty** (sometimes spelt "Shilla", and pronounced that way), which was to go through no fewer than 56 monarchs before collapsing in 935, leaving behind a rich legacy still visible today in the form of jewellery, pottery and temples. Many of the regal burial mounds can still be seen in and around **Gyeongju**, the Silla seat of power.

Initially no more than a powerful city-state, successive leaders gradually expanded the Silla boundaries, consuming the smaller **Gaya kingdom** to the south and becoming a fully-fledged member of the **Three Kingdoms** that jostled for power on the Korean peninsula – Goguryeo in the north, Baekje to the west, and Silla in the east. Silla's **art and craft** flourished, Buddhism was adopted as the state religion, and as early as the sixth century a detailed social system was put into use – the *golpuljedo*, or "bone-rank system" – with lineage and status dictating what clothes people wore, who they could marry and where they could live, and placing strict limits on what they could achieve.

Perversely, given their geographical positions on the "wrong" sides of the peninsula, Baekje were allied to the Japanese and Silla to the Chinese Tang dynasty, and it was Chinese help that enabled Silla's **King Muyeol** to subjugate Baekje in 660 (see box, p.317). Muyeol died the year after, but his son, **King Munmu**, inherited the throne and promptly went one better, defeating Goguryeo in 668 to bring about a first-ever unified rule of the Korean peninsula. The resulting increase in power drove the state forward, though abuse of this new wealth was inevitable; pressure from the people, and an increase in the power of the nobility, gradually started to undermine the power of the kings from the late eighth century. Gyeongju was sacked in 927, and eight years later **King Gyeongsun** – by that time little more than a figurehead – finally handed over the reigns of power to **King Taejo**, bringing almost a millennium of Silla rule to a close, and kicking off the Goryeo dynasty.

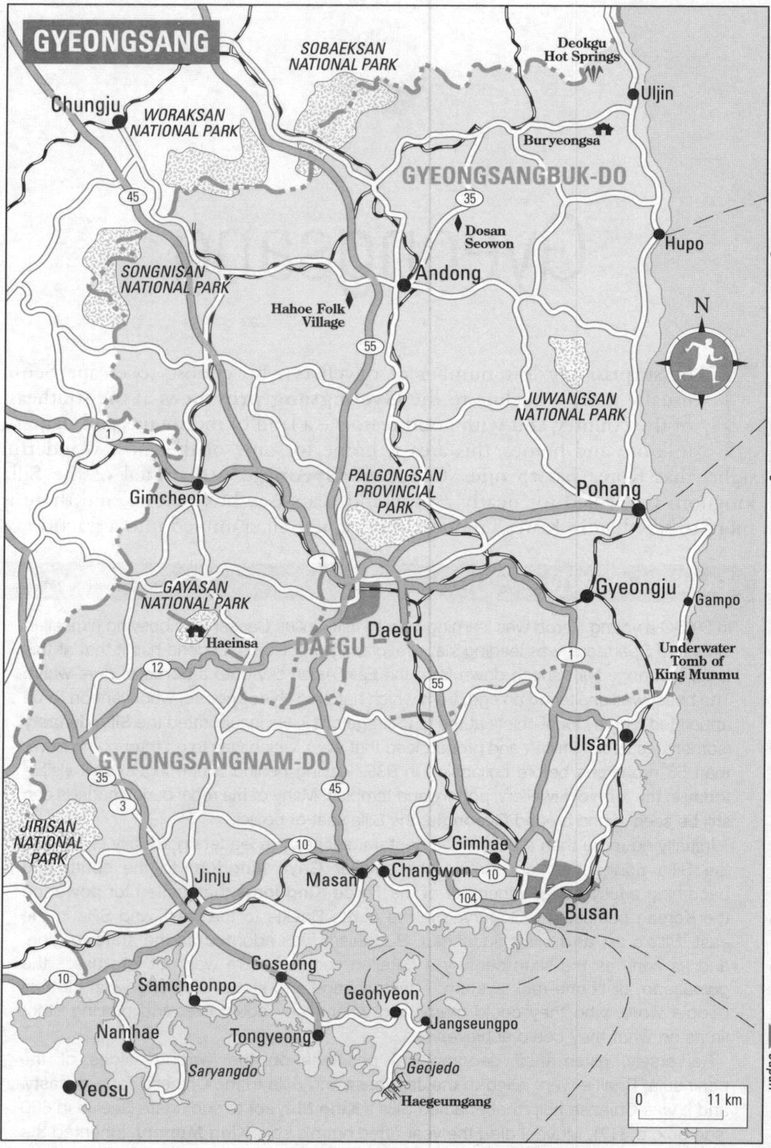

Seoul's area. A dynastic seat of power from 57 BC to the tenth century, but now pleasantly carefree, Gyeongju has preserved its long history well, and evidence of imperial times can be found all over town. The main sights here are the **regal tombs**, small hillocks that held the city's kings, queens and nobles; **Bulguksa**, one of the country's most revered temples; and **Namsan**, a holy mountain criss crossed with paths, and studded with relics of Silla times.

Evidence of later dynasties can be seen in the **Joseon-era** folk villages and **Confucian** academies around Gyeongju and **Andong**, a similarly relaxed city, while **Busan**, the major urban base in the region and the second biggest in the country, had a pivotal defensive role to play in both the Japanese invasions of the late sixteenth century and the **Korean War** in the 1950s.

Though the Korean capital was transferred to Seoul following the collapse of the Silla dynasty, Gyeongsang has continued to exert influence on the running of the country. Since independence and the end of Japanese occupation, the majority of Korea's leaders have been Gyeongsang-born, with the resulting distribution of wealth and power making the area the country's most populated, and industrial, outside Greater Seoul. Despite this, Gyeongsang is well known for its beautiful countryside; **national parks** line the provincial borders, and the southern coast is surrounded by hundreds of stunning **islands**. Its richly traditional hinterland provides the biggest contrast to the rest of the country – here you may be lucky enough to see ancestral rites being performed, or beasts ploughing the fields, and villages of thatch-roofed houses.

Gyeongsangbuk-do

Covering one-fifth of the country, the largely rural province of **GYEONGSANGBUK-DO** ("North Gyeongsang") is South Korea's largest, and one of the most popular with visitors. Here, age-old tradition lingers on to a degree unmatched anywhere else in Korea, with sights strewn around the area providing a chronological view into more than two thousand years of history. Wonderful **Gyeongju** was once capital of the **Silla empire**, which reigned over the southeast of Korea from 57 BC to 668 AD, and then the whole peninsula until 935 AD, and is now a repository to the resulting treasures. Traces of the **Joseon dynasty**, which ruled the peninsula from 1392 until its annexation by the Japanese in 1910, are also evident in a number of Confucian academies and traditional villages; both of which can be found around **Andong**, a small, peaceful city that's becoming ever more popular with foreigners. The years immediately preceding Korea's mass industrialization in the 1980s can be savoured on the scenic island of **Ulleungdo**, where fishing and farming traditions exist unadulterated by factory smoke or sky-high apartment blocks. Stepping forward in time once more the saccharine delights of present-day Korea can be savoured in **Daegu**, the largest city in the region, and a fun place to hole up for a couple of days.

Gyeongju

A green jewel in Korea's tourist crown, **GYEONGJU** is a city that deserves a little more fame. Here you can walk among kings from a dynasty long expired and view the treasures accumulated during a millennium of imperial rule, while strolling around a city infinitely more traditional in nature than any other in the country. If this sounds a little similar to Kyoto, you'd be half-right – like the

Japanese city, it's a **former capital** with some achingly beautiful quarters, but while many visitors to Kyoto feel cheated after seeing that its bulk is traffic-filled and busy, Gyeongju as a whole impresses guests with its lack of bustle. Strangely, much of Gyeongju's present beauty is all down to a bit of good, old-fashioned dictatorship: in the 1970s and 1980s, authoritarian President **Park Chung-hee** managed to ensure that Korea's most traditional city stayed that way at a time when rapid economic progress was turning the country upside-down. He introduced height restrictions on structures built anywhere near historical remains – in other words, pretty much all of the centre – and passed a bill requiring almost everything static to have a traditional Korean-style roof. While it's a little strange to see petrol stations and post boxes under such ornamental coverings, it's a welcome change.

Chief among Gyeongju's sights are the dead kings' tombs, rounded grassy hills that you'll see all over town; it's even possible to enter one for a peek at the ornate way in which royalty were once buried. To the east of the centre there's **Anapji Pond**, a delightful place for an evening stroll under the stars, and a museum filled with assorted trinkets and fascinating gold paraphernalia from Silla times. Further east is **Bulguksa**, one of Korea's most famous temples; splendidly decorated, it's on the UNESCO World Heritage list, as is **Seokguram**, a grotto hovering above it on a mountain ridge. A less-visited mountain area is **Namsan** to the south of the centre, a wonderful park filled with trails and carved Buddha images, where a bicycle or some hiking boots are enough to keep the energetic occupied for a full day.

Some history

The most interesting period of Gyeongju's lengthy history was during its near-millennium as capital of the **Silla kingdom** (see box, p.199).

After so long as Korea's glamourpuss, the degree to which Gyeongju faded into the background is quite surprising – having relinquished its mantle of

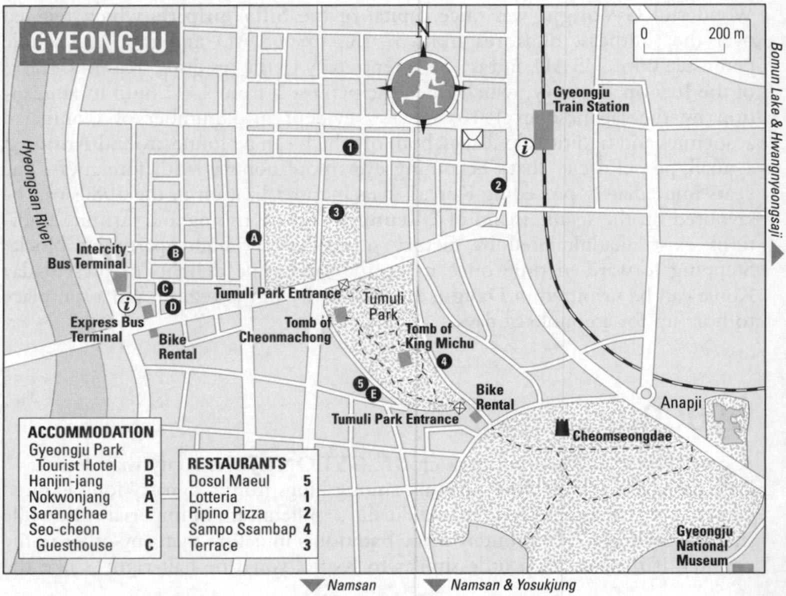

power, the city lived on for a while as a regional capital, but then fell into a **steep decline**. The Mongols rampaged through the city in the fourteenth century, the Japanese invasions a couple of hundred years later stripped away another few layers of beauty, and from a peak of over a million, Gyeongju's population fell to next to nothing.

Ironically, centuries after carrying countless spoils of war across the sea after their successful invasion, it was the Japanese who reopened Gyeongju's treasure-chest of history, during their occupation of the country in the early twentieth century. In went the diggers, and out came hundreds of thousands of relics, so that, even today, much visible evidence of the dynasty still remains around the city. Not all of this is above ground – excavations continue, and new discoveries are made every year.

Arrival, information and city tours

The small **train** station is on the east of the city centre, but because the line that runs through Gyeongju has few services, most choose to arrive by **bus**. Both terminals – express and inter-city – sit side by side on the west of the city centre. Outside the train and bus stations are excellent **information booths** (daily 9am–6pm; ⓣ054/772-9289), usually staffed by friendly English-speakers eager to dole out pamphlets.

Although the real joy of the city lies in putting together and following your own schedule, those with limited time may want to join a **city tour**. Two daily services are available, starting at 8.30am and 10am, and lasting about eight hours; these leave from outside the tourist information kiosk next to the express bus terminal, and cost W12,000 per person.

Orientation and city transport

Central Gyeongju is small enough to **walk** around, while the number of landmarks dotted around town – and the fact that you can actually see them, without any apartment blocks getting in the way – makes navigation easy in relation to other Korean cities. A great number of tombs are situated in the city centre, though Gyeongju's most interesting sights are a bus-ride away. Buses are regular and fares are cheap. **Taxis** between central locations shouldn't cost any more than two or three thousand won, though one excellent way of getting around – almost uniquely, for a Korean city – is by **bicycle**. Rental outlets can be found all over town, including outside the main entrance to Tumuli Park and opposite the bus terminal information booth. You'll need to hand over some form of identification for security (those unwilling to part with their

Gyeongju festivals

Throughout the year the city puts on many shows and events to please its guests. In warmer months, regular performances of traditional song and dance take place on **Bomun Lake** (see p.209) and around **Anapji Pond** (see p.208) at 8pm on Saturdays from April to October, but the biggest event by far is the **Silla Cultural Festival**, a three-day fest which takes place every October and is one of the best and most colourful in the land. On the menu are wrestling, archery, much singing and dancing, and a parade in which a mock Silla king and queen are carried down the streets. Other events include the **Cherry Blossom Marathon**, held each year on the first Saturday of April, and a **Traditional Drink and Rice-cake Festival** in late March, while on December 31 the New Year's crowd heads to King Munmu's seaside tomb (see p.216) to ring in the change of digits and enjoy the first sunrise of the year.

passports may be able to use a library card or something similar), and a bike will be yours for around W7000 per day – see box, p.211 for details on touring Namsan by bike.

Accommodation

For a city that trades so heavily on the tourist dollar, central Gyeongju's range of **accommodation** is a little poor. Its five-stars stand proud in a swanky collective around Bomun Lake, a short way east of the centre; all have the conveniences you'd expect at such places, including LAN connections in the rooms, for which you'll pay an extortionate price of around W20,000 per day for connection. Rack rates can fall by up to fifty percent at quieter times of the year, but rooms are on the small side and lack character. Cheaper motels can be found together with some lower-end hotels near the bus terminals, though prices tend to be higher here than elsewhere in Korea. One thing unique to Gyeongju is a selection of backpacker-oriented **guesthouses**, which generally allow free use of their Internet and cooking facilities, and provide common rooms in which to hang out with fellow travellers. Those on an even tighter budget should head left down the main road from the train station to the *yeoinsuk* area – these are guesthouses from days before Korea took off as an economic power, and possess nothing more than a few blankets, a television and some toilet paper for use in a grubby shared toilet. They generally charge around W10,000 per night; if you're quoted anything higher than W20,000, it won't be just for the room.

City centre

All the places listed below are marked on the Gyeongju map, p.202.

Gyeongju Park Tourist Hotel Sincheon 4-dong T 053/759-7002, W www.gjpark.com. Not a bad place to stay – cheaper than most official tourist hotels, and largely devoid of the regular scruffy floors – it has the faint air of a European hotel, and prices often drop as low as W50,000. The lobby contains a café and a small restaurant, and though the size of the rooms is little different from those of the surrounding motels, all come with large televisions, and some provide free Internet access. 5

Hanjin-jang Yeogwan Noseo-dong T 054/771-4097, W www.hanjinkorea.wo.to. "Charmingly grubby" is probably a fair description of this place, which is popular with foreign guests. It's a great place to meet people, especially when evenings are warm enough to allow for a spot of drinking on the roof terrace. The owner, Master Kwon, is a curious sort but tries his best to inform and entertain – ask for a calligraphy lesson, or to see his "scorpion show". 2

Nokwonjang Yeogwan Chukhyeop-ap T 054/741-6277. In a quiet, relaxed area immediately to the west of the Noseo-ri tombs – look for the green building. Rooms are basic but perfectly acceptable, though the strange window constructions mess up what should really be a fine view of the tombs. 2

Sarangchae Hwangnam-dong T 054/773-4868, W www.kjstay.com. Quite possibly the best backpacker guesthouse in the country, the *Sarangchae* throws friendly, informative management, free use of Internet and cooking facilities and some friendly dogs into a gorgeously traditional courtyard setting. Rooms are cheap at W20,000 but those on a budget are welcome to share a room with fellow backpackers for just W12,500. Book ahead though as there are only a few rooms and it's popular with Korean families. 1

Seo-cheon Guesthouse Noseo-dong T 054/772-1631. This homely guesthouse is popular with foreign backpackers; rooms cost just W20,000, or W15,000 if you're willing to share shower facilities. The friendly owner has been guiding tourists around his city for years, and is a font of local information.

Bomun Lake

All the places listed below are marked on the Around Gyeongju map, p.215.

Commodore Hotel Gyeongju Chosun Sinpyeong-dong T 054/745-7701, F 054/740-8349. Rooms here are as tastefully designed as the lobby, and come with a choice of hill or lake view – the latter is preferable but marginally more expensive. There are a few good restaurants on site, as well as a lovely spa. 7

Gyeongju Hilton Sinpyeong-dong ⓣ054/745-7788, ⓦwww.hilton.com. Possessing a slightly more international ambience than its neighbours, facilities at the *Hilton* include a swimming pool, gym, squash court and jogging track. Fans of Spanish surrealism will be pleased by the Miró in the lobby. ❽

Hotel Concorde Sinpyeong-dong ⓣ054/745-7000, ⓕ054/745-7010. Largely shunned by the convention crowd, this may be the place for those who want a more relaxed stay. The hotel doesn't try as hard as its neighbours. Rooms are good value for money, and all come with balconies facing the lake. ❻

Gyeongju and around

Gyeongju	경주
Anapji Pond	안압지
Bomun Lake	보문호
Bulguksa	불국사
Cheomseongdae	첨성대
Confucian School	향교
Girimsa	기림사
Golgulsa	골굴사
Gyeongju National Museum	경주 국립 박물관
Nodong-ni	노동리
Noseo-ri	노서리
Oksan Seowon	옥산 서원
Seokguram	석굴암
Tumuli Park	대릉원
Underwater Tomb of King Munmu	문무대왕수중능
Wolseong Park	월성 공원
Yangdong Folk Village	양동 민속 마을
Accommodation	
Commodore Hotel Gyeongju Chosun	코모도 호텔 경주 조선
Gyeongju Hilton	경주 힐튼 호텔
Gyeongju Park Tourist Hotel	경주 파크 관광 호텔
Hanjin-jang	한진장
Hotel Concorde	호텔 콩코드
Hotel Hyundai	호텔 현대
Kolon Hotel	코오롱 호텔
Nokwonjang	녹원장
Sarangchae	사랑채
Seo-cheon Guesthouse	서천 게스트하우스
Restaurants	
Baeri Samjeon-seokbul	배리 삼전석불
Borisa	보리사
Dosol Maeul	도솔 마을
Lotteria	롯데리아
Namsan Park	남산 공원
O-neung	오릉
Pipino Pizza	피피노 피자
Poseokjeong	포석정
Samneung	삼릉
Sampo Ssambap	삼포 쌈밥
Terrace	테러스
Tomb of King Jima	지마왕릉
Tongiljeon	통일전
Yosukjung	요수중

Hotel Hyundai Sinpyeong-dong ⓣ054/748-2233, ⓦwww.hyundaihotel.com. This hotel probably offers the best lake views in the area, though rooms with a hill view are a little cheaper. Rooms are pleasing, with some nice touches and relatively large bathrooms, and service is of a high quality; there are also Italian, Chinese, Korean and Japanese restaurants to choose from, as well as a coffee shop that serves delectable pecan pie. ⑧

Bulguksa

Kolon Hotel Ma-dong ⓣ054/746-9001, ⓦwww.kolonhotel.co.kr. See Around Gyeongju map, p.215. Despite the unfortunate name, this is a quality place to stay, out of town and just down the road from Bulguksa, in a tree-surrounded setting that includes a nine-hole golf course. Rooms are a little dated, but views over the course and trees are lovely. Rooms are cheaper at weekends. ⑥

Tumuli Park

Gyeongju is often described by the Korean tourist board as an open-air museum, thanks to its large number of grassy regal, burial mounds. The tombs in question are known as **Tumuli**, which are prolific across the city and quite impossible to miss. Right in the centre of town, the walled-off **Tumuli Park** (daily 9am–10pm; W1500) contains over two dozen tombs. It's hard to imagine that this was until quite recently a functioning – though quiet – part of town, but in the 1970s the buildings were removed and the area beautified, creating a path- and tree-filled park that's wonderful for a stroll. Entrances are located at the east and north of the complex, but its most famous hump sits to the far west. Here lies **Cheonmachong**, the only tomb in Korea that you can actually enter. Its former inhabitant is not known for sure, but is believed to be a sixth- or seventh-century king whose many horse-related implements gave rise to the name – Cheonmachong means "Heavenly Horse Tomb". Excavated in 1973, it yielded over 12,000 artefacts, which was the largest single haul in the country, and although many went to Gyeongju Museum, a few decorate the inner walls of the tomb. There's also a full-scale mock-up of

▲ Burial mounds, Gyeongju

What's green and lumpy?

Every culture has its own solutions for what to do with the deceased. Tibetan corpses are often left on a mountainside for vultures to carry away, certain Filipino societies place the departed in a coffin, and pack it into a cliff, while the Yanomami of the Amazon rainforest choose to cremate their dead then eat the ashes with banana paste. Koreans have long preferred burial – a slightly more prosaic journey to the afterlife, for sure – and those who have travelled around the country a while will doubtless have seen the little green bumps that dot hills and mountains in the country's rural areas. Larger versions used to be a matter of course for Korean royalty.

Literally hundreds of **tombs** from the **Silla dynasty** can be found all over Gyeongju and its surrounding area. However, the identities of few of the tombs' occupants are known for sure – there were only 56 Silla kings, so the others seem likely to have been created for lesser royals, military leaders and prominent members of society. Equally mysterious are the **interiors**, as the super-simple green parabolas give almost no hints as to their construction; however, a look inside **Cheonmacheong** in Tumuli Park should provide a few hints. Layers of gravel and stone make up the base of the tomb, with a wooden chamber placed in the centre to house the deceased – unlike a Pharaoh, he or she would not have supervised the construction, but as in Egypt they would have been buried with some of their favourite belongings. The chamber was then covered with large, rounded stones (these would eventually crush the chamber, after sufficient putrefaction of the wood), which in turn was covered with clay and dirt, and sown with grass.

Given the riches inside, surprisingly few of the tombs were plundered for their treasures – while such an endeavour would be long and rather conspicuous, that didn't stop thievery elsewhere in the country. Over the past century, many tombs have been carefully excavated, yielding thousands of artefacts, many of which are now on display in Gyeongju's National Museum.

how the inhabitant was buried. Elsewhere in the complex is the large **tomb of King Michu**, who reigned from 262 to 284 and fought many battles to protect his empire from the neighbouring Baekje dynasty. According to legend, he even dispatched a ghost army from beyond the grave when his successor was losing one particular bout of fisticuffs; these phantoms disappeared during the resulting celebrations, leaving behind only the bamboo leaves that had infested the cavities of the enemy dead. For this reason, the tomb is often referred to as the "Tomb of the Bamboo Chief". One other tomb of note is the double-humped **Hwangnam Daechong**, which was almost certainly the resting place of a king and queen.

Noseo-ri and Nodong-ri

Across the main road, the tumuli continue, though less abundantly, into the city's main shopping district. Split by a road into two sections known as **Noseo-ri** and **Nodong-ri**, these areas are not walled off, and are free to enter at any time of the day or night. Here lie some colossal mounds, as big as those you'll find in Tumuli Park – one, known as Bonghwangdae, is 22m high, with a 250m circumference. Although you're not allowed to climb onto any of the tombs, a faint path heading up this largest hump indicates that some find the temptation too great to ignore, and you'll usually find a couple of people seated here after the sun has gone down. Opposite, in Noseo-ri, is a monument dedicated to **Prince Gustav Adolf VI** of Sweden, who participated in the excavations here in 1926 before inheriting his country's throne.

Wolseong Park area

A short walk southeast of Tumuli Park will bring you to the pretty patch of greenery called **Wolseong Park** (24hr; free), in and around which are some of the city's most popular sights. The paths that run through the park are pedestrianized, but you can also take a short horse-and-carriage ride around the area – you'll see them lined up opposite the main entrance to Tumuli Park. There are plenty of tombs around, though most Koreans make an eastward beeline to have their picture taken next to **Cheomseongdae** (daily 9am–6pm; W500), an astronomical observation tower dating from the seventh century. Looking a little like a rook from a giant chessboard, its simplicity conceals a surprising depth of design: the twelve stones that make up the base represent either the months of the year or the signs of the Chinese zodiac, while the 27 circular layers were a nod to Queen Seondeok, ruler during the tower's construction and the 27th ruler of the Silla dynasty. Added to the two square levels on top and the aforementioned base, this equals thirty, which is the number of days in a lunar month, while the total number of blocks equals the number of days in a year. Even more amazingly, the various gaps and points on the structure are said to correspond to the movements of certain celestial bodies.

South of Cheomseongdae and making up much of the park is **Banwolseong**, which was once a fortress; today only a few stones remain, though you're able to walk the tree-lined path that heads around the earthen wall. Down the northern fringe and across the road is **Anapji** (8am–10pm; W1000), a pleasure garden constructed in 674 by the fantastically named **King Munmu** (see p.216). Numerous battles in the preceding decade had led to a first-ever unification of the Korean peninsula, after which Munmu built what was – and still remains – a tranquil, tree-filled area around a **lotus pond** whose shape roughly mirrored that of his kingdom. In an interesting twist of fate, this was where the empire also came to an end, being the scene of King Gyeongsun's handover of power to King Taejo, founder of the Goryeo dynasty. In the following centuries, the area fell into disrepair until 1975, when it received its first modern makeover. When the pond was dredged it revealed a few relics from Silla times at the bottom. That few then grew to hundreds, then thousands – much of the bounty, including a whole barge, now sits in the National Museum just down the road. Relics were found in even greater numbers at **Hwangnyeongsaji**, a temple ruin a short walk to the north across the railroad tracks. The original was built here in the sixth century, then destroyed and rebuilt several times over before rampaging Mongol hordes finished it off for good in the thirteenth century. Apparently, at one point it contained a 70m-high wooden pagoda; support stones from this structure are still visible, and hint at its former size. **Bunhwangsa**, a short walk further north again, is an active temple; though small, it's worth a look around at what was once a large nine-storey stone pagoda (only three levels remain).

Gyeongju National Museum

Back on the perimeter of Wolseong Park, **Gyeongju National Museum** (9am–9pm; Nov–March until to 6pm; closed Mon; W1000) is a repository of riches from the surrounding area, and with the exception of the one in Seoul's own National Museum (p.110), it's quite possibly the best in the country. The rooms run in chronological order from locally sourced stone tools and ancient pottery to modern times, via the Bronze Age. But it's the **Silla** bling that most are here to see. Royalty of the time evidently had a partiality for gold, silver and bronze, and one can only marvel at the considerable skill that went into the making of their assorted trinkets. Earrings, pendants and other paraphernalia were cast into spectacular shapes, and often adorned with tiny golden discs or leaves. You'll also find pottery, golden antlers and some uncomfortable-looking spiked bronze shoes, but the undisputed star of the show, and accordingly hidden away in its own private room, is a glorious golden sixth-century crown, intricately sculpted and boasting an array of dangling bean-shaped jades. Outside lies the **Emille Bell**, a veritable beast dating from 771. Known to Koreans as the Bell of King Seongdeok – in whose memory it was created – this is the largest existing bell in the country, and one of the biggest in the world; though estimates of its weight vary for some reason, even the smallest – nineteen tons – makes it a whopper by any standard. Legend surrounding the bell says that when it was first cast it failed to ring, only doing so once its constituent metal was melted back down and mixed with the body of a young girl. Her death-cry "Emille" (which rhymes with "simile") was a word for mother in the Silla dialect, and can apparently still be heard in the ring of the bell.

Bomun Lake

A few kilometres east of Wolseong Park, and on the bus route towards Bulguksa temple, you'll come to **Bomun Lake**. Surrounded by five-star hotels, it has become a venue of choice for the well heeled; largely devoid of the historical sights found elsewhere in the city, it's still a good place to head for a bit of easy fun. Swan-shaped pedaloes – the doyens of Korea's artificial waterways – can be hired (30min; W5000), as can bikes for the cycle-trails around the lake, while those seeking entertainment of a more highbrow nature can head to the **Sonjae Museum of Contemporary Art** (10am–6pm; W3000) on the grounds of the *Hilton*. There are also regular cultural and musical performances at the Bomun Outdoor Performance Theater just down from the *Commodore Hotel*; these usually take place at 8.30pm from July to October on every day except Wednesday, and at weekends only during May and June. A number of **golf courses** can be found in the area around the lake, ranging in size from nine to thirty-six holes.

Bulguksa and around

Sitting comfortably under the tree-lined wings of the surrounding mountains, **Bulguksa** (daily 7am–6pm; W4000) was built in 528 during the reign of King Beop-heung, under whose leadership Buddhism was adopted as the Silla state religion. It was almost destroyed by the Japanese invasions in 1593 and, though it's hard to believe now, was left to rot until the 1970s, when dictatorial president Park Chung-hee ordered its reconstruction. It has subsequently been added to the UNESCO World Heritage list. As one of the most visited temples in the country, it can be thronged with people, many of whom combine their visit with a picnic on and around the path leading from the bus stop to the ticket office. Once through the gates, you'll walk a pretty path past a pond and over a bridge, before being confronted by the temple. Here **two staircases** lead to the upper level; these are officially "four bridges" rather than two flights of steps, leading followers from the worldly realm to that of the Buddha. Both are listed as national treasures, so you're not actually allowed to ascend them. Having entered the main courtyard from the side, you'll be confronted by yet more treasures, this time two three-level **stone pagodas** from the Unified Silla period: one plain and one ornately decorated, representing Yin and Yang.

From the courtyard, it's best to stroll aimlessly and appreciate the views. The whole complex has been elaborately **painted**, but the artistry is particularly impressive in Daeungjeon, the main hall behind the pagodas, whose

▲ Bulguksa temple

eaves are painted both inside and out with striking patterns. At the top of the complex, another hall – Gwaneumjeon – looks down over Bulguksa's pleasing array of roof tiles; the steep staircase down causes problems for Korean girls in high heels, but there are other ways back. Making your way across the rear of the complex you'll come to Nahanjeon, a hall surrounded by bamboo and a cloak of maple leaves. Behind this building lie small towers of stacked stones, to which you're welcome – even expected – to add your own. Those needing a rest at this point can head to the **tearoom** underneath the nearby trinket shop.

Seokguram Grotto

After the temple, a visit to the Buddhist grotto of **Seokguram** (same times; W4000) may feel a little anti-climactic. However, the views from its lofty position alone justify the trip up, especially at sunrise. The East Sea is visible on a good day, and it is said that the statue was built to provide spiritual protection to the country from the Japanese across these waters. Until fairly recently, access was only possible via a 3km mountain path from Bulguksa, but while it's still possible to do this today, if only to appreciate how hard it must have been for the grotto's builders to transport the necessary blocks of granite to such a height, most choose to take the bus instead.

Once past the ticket booth, a winding but easy ten-minute walk through the trees leads to the grotto itself; inside its keyhole-shaped chamber sits an image of the Sakyamuni Buddha, surrounded by art of a similarly high calibre. However, the chamber has been sealed off in order to protect it from the elements and visitors. Unfortunately, this could and should have been done better – a pane of glass separates you from the art and its beauty, and many tourists also have gripes about the ugly little protective hut that now stands in the way of the grotto. As a result, it's almost impossible to appreciate the elegance and attention to detail that many experts consider to be the finest example of Buddhist art in the country.

Practicalities

Buses #10 and #11 ply the Bulguksa route regularly from around Gyeongju city centre; on the way you'll pass the **Folk Art Village**, a countryside parade of shops selling tea sets, cups and other fired paraphernalia, and a great place to go souvenir shopping. Next to the bus stop is a useful **tourist information** booth, usually staffed with an English speaker. Bulguksa itself is an uphill walk from its bus stop, and the trail continues up to Seokguram along a 3km path that runs to the right of the temple's ticket booth; you can judge for yourself how far it is by looking up at the horizon from the Bulguksa bus stop – that's the Seokguram ticket booth on top. However, most people take the **bus** – those going up leave Bulguksa at forty minutes past the hour, with the last at 5.20pm, and come back on the hour, the last at 6.20pm.

For food, there are dozens of **restaurants** across from the Bulguksa bus stop, many of which have menus in English. There are also a few **places to stay** in the area, including one top-end hotel (the *Kolon*; see p.206), but these motels and guesthouses are generally the preserve of youth and family groups. Still, the quietness of the place at night is quite appealing.

Namsan Park

Central Gyeongju's rag-tag assortment of buildings fades to the south, turning from urban to rural. Mercifully, development of this area is unlikely as the city is hemmed in on its southern flank by **Namsan Park**, a small mountain area absolutely packed with trails and sights. New discoveries of ancient relics are made here regularly, but even if you don't find yourself unearthing a piece of Silla jewellery, this is another of the city's must-sees. Roads run along the park's perimeter, giving access to a wealth of sights on both sides, while the interior is strewn with carved Buddhas and offers some fantastic hikes. Namsan is best tackled either by **bicycle** around its pleasantly traffic-free perimeter (see box below), or with a pair of hiking boots through its interior.

From Gyeongju, buses #500 to #503 run down the western side of the park, while #10 and #11 can be used for some of the sights on the eastern side.

Touring Namsan by bike

For those with the inclination, and as long as the weather agrees, a **bike-tour** around Namsan is one of the most enjoyable ways to spend a day in Gyeongju. To reach the mountain, come out of Tumuli Park and turn right at the main road; the tombs of Wolseong Park should be on your left and a few tourist shops and restaurants to your right. Turn left at the T-junction and head over the bridge. When you reach the end of the road turn left to get to Namsan's eastern flank, or right for the west. For the **west side**, turn left after the golden Buddha and you'll be at the northeast corner of **O-neung**; the entrance is down the main road on the south side. After seeing the sights on the western flank, those who don't feel like returning on the main road can make use of the labyrinthine farm tracks that spread out between the road and the parallel river further back. On Namsan's **east side** a patchwork of fields provides more opportunities to get away from the main roads than on the west, and you can use your own initiative to hug Namsan's skirt of trees.

There are numerous places to **hire bikes** (W7000 per day) in Gyeongju, but the most convenient place is the outlet in the car park outside the main entrance to Tumuli Park.

The western flank

The first sight that you'll come to on the western flank is **O-neung** (9am–6pm; Nov–Feb until 5pm; W500), which means "five tombs". The grassy area just inside the perimeter wall is popular with picnicking families in the summer, but if you make your way through the pines along one of the park's lovely paths you'll soon come to the tomb of Hyeokgeose (ruled 57 BC to 4 AD), the **first king** of the Silla dynasty and accordingly quite an important chap. Little else is known about him, but a history this long deserves to be acknowledged with a little perspective: Hyeokgeose was born in 69 BC, the same year as Cleopatra – Hyeokgeose's hump has been around for a seriously long time. Nearby mounds contain three of his immediate successors – Namhae, Yuri and Pasa were the second, third and fifth Silla monarchs respectively – as well as Hyeokgeose's wife, **Alyeong**, who was apparently born as a dragon in a nearby well, and therefore suitably auspicious. The well can still be seen, just follow the signs. Hyeokgeose himself trumped his future wife's spectacular birth by hatching from an egg laid by a phantom horse; his birthplace is outside the park, just down the road at Najeong, but the site is badly neglected in comparison.

Heading south and across the main road you'll soon come across **Poseokjeong** (same times; W500), an uninteresting site, but one that's hugely popular with Korean tourists. Here once lay a villa in which Silla kings held regular banquets, but with the buildings long gone, you may wonder what all the fuss is about. The draw is actually a six-metre-long water canal set within a loose perimeter of rocks – don't step inside – which was once used for royal **drinking games**: one member of the party would reel off a line of poetry, choose another guest to supply a suitable second line, and float a cup of wine down the water course. If the drink reached the challenger before he could think of a line, he had to drain the cup. Just across the way, and signposted from the Poseokjeong car park, is the **Tomb of King Jima**, who was the sixth Silla king, but now finds himself isolated among the trees. The neighbouring village of **Poseok** remains charming, and is worth a nose around. It's also home to some good, cheap **restaurants**, though the best eatery is across the main road at *Chogadeungji*, a tiny thatch-roofed bungalow where you can get a filling *jeong-sik* for just W6000 – perfect food for hungry cyclists.

Further down either the road or the footpath from from Posekjeong you'll find a couple of tiny temples housing a standing Buddha trio known as **Baeri Samjeon-seokbul** (24hr; free), which are said to date back to the early seventh century. This area is a pretty place, and the starting point for a number of paths into Namsan's interior. Just south of the Buddhas is a good place to stop for food; *Jungnim Nongjang* is a tiny farm-cum-restaurant where you can slurp *kalguksu* noodles under a flower-covered canopy. Continuing south is **Samneung** (24hr; free), a small, pretty complex that contains three tombs. Here lies Adalla, the eighth Silla king, who ruled from 154 to 184 AD, next to Sindeok and Gyeongmyeong, the 53rd and 54th leaders, who ruled for just a few years each in the early tenth century as the empire struggled to its close.

The eastern flank and the interior

There's a little less to see on Namsan's eastern side, though those travelling by bike will be able to get off the main road and head through some farm villages; here, it will be quite hard to imagine that you're within a few kilometres of Tumuli Park and its swarm of tourists. There are lots of little roads, but as long as you keep between the main road and the park it doesn't really matter where you head – small houses, trees, fields and drying laundry greet you at every turn. There are also a number of carved Buddhas, placed on Namsan's eastern side so that they may face the rising sun, though you'll need to trek a short way into the park to see them – the tourist office will have detailed **maps** of the area, and some guesthouses create their own.

One of the first Buddhas you'll reach on your way from Gyeongju is also the most accessible – follow signs for Woljeongsa temple – but the one uphill behind **Borisa**, the largest functioning temple on Namsan, is more interesting, dating from the eighth century and backed by richly detailed stonework. A path from here leads all the way to a viewing platform on the top of the mountain, after which you'll have a choice of heading west to Poseokjeon, south to the ruin-surrounded peak of Geumosan, or east to **Tongiljeon**. This "Palace of Reunification" (daily 9am–6pm; Nov–Feb until 5pm; W300) was constructed on the orders of Park Chung-hee in 1977, though with little apparent ambition – there's not much to see, but its secluded park-like location means that you may well find yourself alone. After climbing several large outdoor staircases, there's a sudden hush as you enter the topmost courtyard, the cream-coloured walls of which are lined with paintings depicting legends from Silla times. Those who've not yet had their fill of regal mounds can take one of two paths that push a short way into Namsan's pines just north of the palace; both lead to the tombs of Heongang and Jeonggang, two ninth-century kings who, in this isolated position, would doubtless appreciate the company. Beyond Tongiljeon you'll find a pond sporting a gorgeous pavilion; this area is dotted with rural temples that are historically unimportant, but pretty nonetheless.

Eating and drinking

The best food can be found in the **five-star hotels** that surround Bomun Lake. However, there's plenty of choice in the centre. Gyeongju is not known for its food, but one interesting variation from other cities is the simply incredible number of small bakeries selling *gyeongju-bbang*. These are small, sweet cakes, which are eagerly snapped up by Japanese tourists seeking their *omiyage* (near-compulsory edible travel souvenirs). While most restaurants serve Korean fare, those who just can't live without burgers, pizza or pasta will also be kept happy – a few of the more interesting places are listed below. Despite the high number of foreigners that visit the city, few restaurants have English-language menus.

Dosol Maeul Hwangnam-dong. Near the *Sarangchae* guesthouse and very similar in appearance, here you can eat *pajeon* pancakes and quaff *dongdongju* – a milky Korean wine – by the bucketload in traditional rooms set around an equally rustic courtyard. A great place to chill out with fellow backpackers.

Lotteria Hwango-dong. Respite from Korean cuisine is available here in a sesame-seeded sandwich. Though regular beef- or cheeseburgers are yours for the taking, those who want to impart at least a little local flavour to their meal can choose the *bulgogi* or *galbi* burgers instead.

Pipino Pizza Hwango-dong, ⓣ054/773-0987. While there are Western pizza chains in Gyeongju, *Pipino* offers a slightly more Korean experience for W10,000 and up. Toppings include vegetarian, sweet potato, *bulgogi* or "super special". Those able to speak Korean, or find someone willing to translate, can call for free delivery – perfect on a rainy day.

Sampo Ssambap Hwangnam-dong. Filled with assorted Korean bric-a-brac, this is the most atmospheric of a line of restaurants near the main entrance to Tumuli Park, all of which serve the same dish, *ssambap* – a delicious meal whereby a seemingly infinite range of mostly vegetable side dishes is placed on your table, and a fantastic way to fill your stomach for around W8000. Unlike most such restaurants, this one is willing to feed single travellers.

Terrace You can see the green resting places of kings through the bamboo from this tasteful restaurant, located on the northern side of the

Nodong-ni tomb area. Steak, pasta dishes and Thai chicken salad are among the choices on the menu, and are all available at reasonable prices.

Yosukjung Gyo-dong. A fabulous place for fabulous food at high prices, set around a traditional courtyard in a quiet area facing Namsan Park. There's no English menu, but good traditional food is guaranteed – set meals here go from W30,000 to W100,000 per head, though there's a two-person minimum.

Listings

Banks There are a number of banks with money exchange facilities around town, including the Korea First Bank opposite the train station, as well as ATMs at 24hr convenience stores such as Family Mart or 7-Eleven.

Car rental The city's five-star hotels and tourist information booths will have the most up-to-date info about hiring a car; alternatively, book through Avis at Ⓦ www.avis.com.

Cinemas Myeongbo, Daewang, Silla and Primus cinemas can be found on the main downtown thoroughfare; ticket prices average around W7000.

Farm stay An interesting farm stay programme is on offer near Oksan Seowon, to the north of Gyeongju (p.217). There you may find yourself helping to plant rice, or roasting chestnuts around an open fire. Ask at one of Gyeongju's tourist information centres for details, or call Ⓣ 054/762-6148.

Internet Some motels and all of the main backpacker guesthouses offer Internet for free, or there are cafés available all over town which charge W1000 per hour – just look for the letters "PC", or ask for a "*pishi-bang*".

Martial arts Seonmudo courses are available at Golgulsa, a secluded temple to the east of Gyeongju – check below for details, or log onto Ⓦ www.golgulsa.com.

Post The main post office is just opposite the train station (Mon–Fri 9am–5pm; Ⓣ 054/740-0114).

Around Gyeongju

An almost overwhelming number of sights litter the countryside around Gyeongju – those listed here make up just a fraction of the possibilities, so be sure to scour local maps and pamphlets for things that might be of particular interest to you. **Transport** to sights is not always regular – you may need to spend some time waiting for buses, if possible, try to get the latest timetable from one of Gyeongju's tourist offices. While hitchhiking is never totally safe and can't be wholeheartedly recommended, you'll rarely get a better chance than on the run east to the **Underwater Tomb of King Munmu**, where the road is lightly trafficked and everyone is heading to or from Gyeongju. To the north of Gyongju are **Oksan Seowon**, one of the country's best examples of a Joseon-era Confucian academy, and **Yangdong Folk Village**, a collection of traditional housing. To the west of the city and within cycling range are yet more regal tombs.

East of Gyeongju to the Underwater Tomb of King Munmu

On the way to see King Munmu and his watery grave, and easily combined as part of a day-trip, you'll pass a rural spur road leading to two out-of-the-way temples that inhabit a wonderfully unspoilt valley east of Gyeongju. **Golgulsa** is the nearer of the two, and famed as a centre of *seonmudo*, a Zen-based martial art. From the bus stop near the village of Andong-ni (#150, the same bus that heads to Munmu), it's just under a kilometre to the temple turn-off on the left. It's all uphill from here, with the track heading past a teahouse before rising into the small complex, from where it becomes even steeper. Backing the complex is a sixth-century Buddha, carved into a cliff navigable on some short but

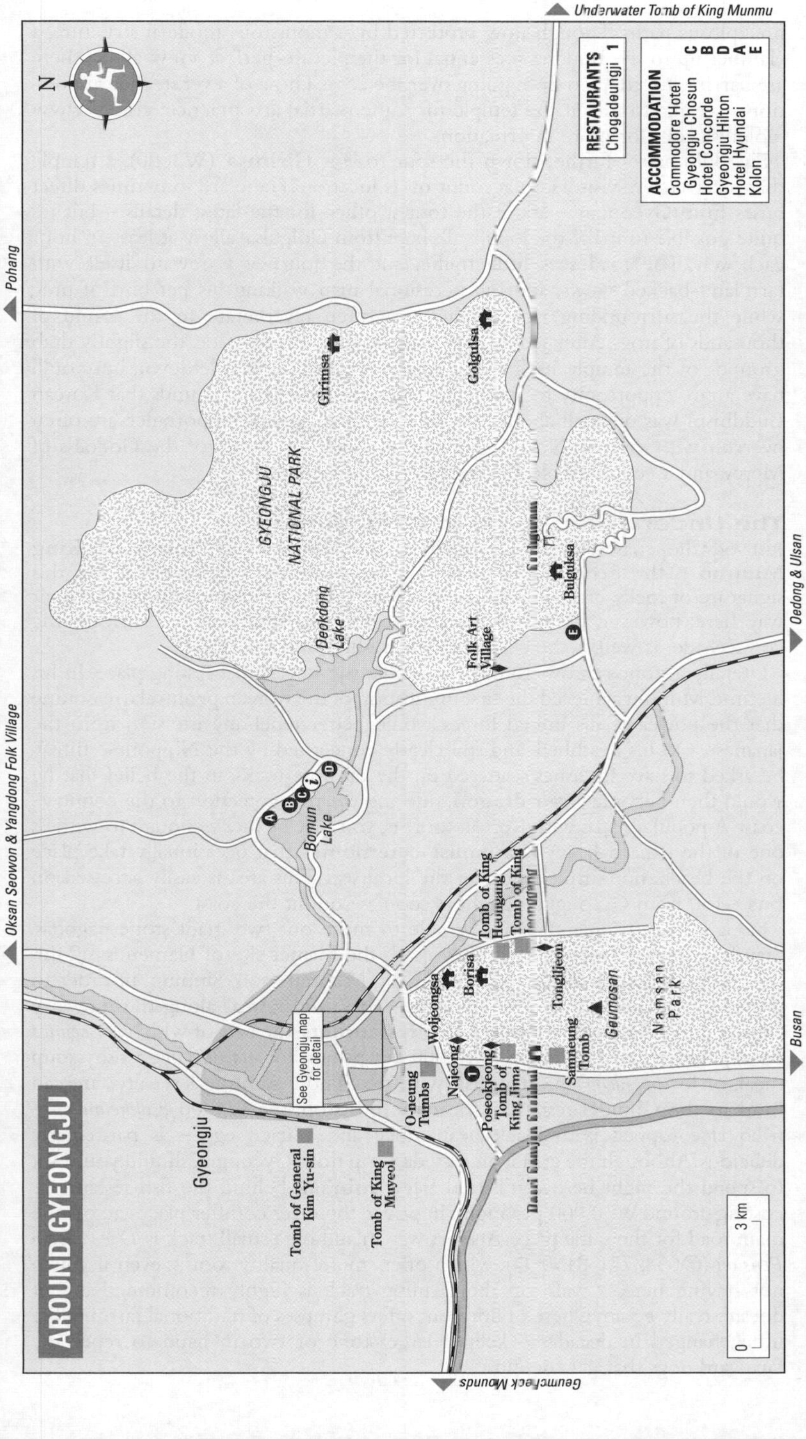
AROUND GYEONGJU
Underwater Tomb of King Munmu
Pohang
Oksan Seowon & Yangdong Folk Village
Oedong & Ulsan
Busan
Geumcheok Mounds
N
RESTAURANTS
Chogadeungji 1
ACCOMMODATION
Commodore Hotel C
Gyeongju Chosun B
Hotel Concorde D
Gyeongju Hilton A
Hotel Hyundai
Kolon E
GYEONGJU NATIONAL PARK
Girimsa
Golgulsa
Deokdong Lake
Bulguksa
Folk Art Village
Bomun Lake
See Gyeongju map for detail
Gyeongju
Tomb of General Kim Yu-sin
Tomb of King Muyeol
O-neung Tumbs
Najeong
Poseokjeong
Tomb of King Jima
Woljeongsa
Borisa
Tomb of King Heongang
Tomb of King Jeonggang
Tongiljeon
Samneung Tomb
Geumosan
Namsan Park
0
3 km

precipitous paths. Though now protected by a monstrous modern structure, a clamber up to the Buddha is essential for the picture-perfect **view** alone; there are barriers to stop you from going over the edge. Those of a yet steelier disposition may like to stay at the temple for some martial arts practice; visit Ⓦwww.golgulsa.com for more information.

Five kilometres further down the spur road is **Girimsa** (W3000), a temple that receives few visitors on account of its location. There are sometimes direct buses from Gyeongju – ask at the tourist office for the latest details – but it's quite possible to make the long walk here from Golgulsa: allow at least an hour each way. The road sees little traffic, but the journey is reward itself with farmland-backed views, and the occasional man walking his pet bird of prey, while the surrounding rice paddies can often reverberate to the sound of thousands of frogs. After soaking up such majestic countryside, the slightly drab grounds of the temple itself may come as something of a letdown, but you'll have a rare opportunity to appreciate the sights, smells and sounds that Korean Buddhism was once all about – temples of such age and importance are often overrun with visitors. Notable here are a couple of statues of the Goddess of Mercy, and a centuries-old Bodhi tree.

The Underwater Tomb of King Munmu

Just off the coast east of Gyeongju is the **Underwater Tomb of King Munmu** (24hr; free). The name would be fitting for a good novel, but this signature of rocky crags may come as an anticlimax to visitors who make their way here; however, it's worth the trip to see the beauty of the surrounding countryside, as well as the chance to eat freshly caught seafood.

Literally a stone's throw from the coast lies the king's final resting place. In his lifetime, Munmu achieved the first unification of the Korean peninsula, reasoning that the power of his united forces would better repel any invasion from the Japanese. On his deathbed, and still clearly concerned by the Nipponese threat, he asked to have his ashes scattered on the offshore rocks, in the belief that he would then become a **sea dragon**, offering eternal protection to the country's coast. A popular place with Korean tourists, you may be lucky enough to witness one of the banana-heavy **shamanist ceremonies** that occasionally take place on the beach, honouring spirits of the local seas. This area is easily accessed on **bus** #150 from Gyeongju – alight as soon as you hit the coast.

Just a kilometre inland you'll be able to make out two giant stone pagodas. Standing thirteen metres high, they mark the former site of Gameunsa (24hr; free), a temple built on the orders of King Munmu's son, Sinmun, in order to provide his father – now a sea-dragon – an inland retreat along the now-dry canal. Lining the beach are several **fish restaurants**, the best of which is *Saemteo Hoetjip*; dishes start at around W10,000 per person for *maeun-tang*, a fishy soup meal, or for *hoe-deopbap* – raw fish with rice. Those wanting less salty fare can head to the Chinese restaurant near the bus stop; the W4000 *beokkeumbap* – fried rice topped with black bean sauce and a fried egg – is particularly delicious. Although the area is an easy day-trip from Gyeongju, should you want to spend the night here you'll find a few **minbak** behind the fish restaurants costing around W30,000 per night; however, there are comfier places across the main road for the same price. A short way inland on a small track is *Daewangam Pension* (Ⓣ054/771-8190; ③), which offers motel-quality rooms; even if you're not staying here, a walk up the farming track is highly recommended – it doesn't really go anywhere of note, but offers glimpses of traditional farming life little changed in decades – keep a large stone or two in hand to repel any farmyard dogs that get too close.

North of Gyeongju

After the Silla-era delights in and around Gyeongju, you can leap forward in time to the **Joseon dynasty** by making a trip 30km north of town to **Oksan Seowon**, a Confucian school and shrine established in 1572 under the rule of King Seonjo. During this period Confucianism was the primary system of belief, particularly for the *yangban* aristocracy. However, most such places were closed in the 1870s at a time of social upheaval, and many were destroyed, making Oksan one of the oldest in the country, and quite possibly the most enjoyable to visit (though tiny Dosan Seowon near Andong gives it a run for its money, see p.230). It was dedicated to **Yi Eon-jeok** (1491–1533), a Confucian poet, **scholar** and all-round theological handyman who, while not as revered as his contemporaries Yi-Yi (see p.186) or Toegye (p.231), certainly exerted an influence on neo-Confucian thought. Now restored, following years of neglect and the occasional fire, the complex still manages to put forward a gentle atmosphere in keeping with its original function as a place of study and reflection, helped along by the stream bubbling away below, as well as the gorgeousness of the surrounding countryside and the surprisingly low number of visitors. It's also home to a copy of the **Samguk Sagi**, the only concise records of the Three Kingdoms period (albeit one that seems to be biased towards the Silla dynasty). To get to Oksan Seowon take **bus** #203 from Gyeongju; they leave very sporadically – check the return schedule at the academy as soon as you arrive. For those with a bit more time, there's a **motel** and a few *minbak* around the academy, as well as some places to eat.

Just a short walk beyond Oksan Seowon is Yi Eon-jeok's former abode at **Dongnakdang**. Some of his descendants still live in the cramped compound, which appears be hiding under the skirt of a large tree, and is every bit as tranquil as the academy itself. Further ahead again are **Jonghyesa**, a temple famed for its curiously shaped pagoda and **Dodeokam**, a tiny hermitage with a view balanced high up on the rocks. All are just about within walking distance of each other, though considering the rather poor bus connections from Gyeongju, it may be best to stay the night near Oksan Seowon.

Yangdong Folk Village

Korea has a number of "**folk villages**" dotted about, a product of Park Chung-hee's desire to keep alive rural traditions at a time when large-scale economic growth was smothering the nation in concrete. Usually they consist of a rural group of houses and associate buildings, and are fun places to amble around dusty paths, absorbing the sights and smells. Some openly exist for show alone, while others are living, breathing communities whose denizens work the local fields, rewarded for their enforced deprivation of urban amenities with governmental subsidy. **Yangdong Folk Village**, tucked into a countryside fold near the village of Angang-ni, is one of the best in the country, and home to some real history. Dating from the 1400s, this was once a thriving community of **yangban**, the aristocracy that ruled the country during the Joseon dynasty. Yi Eon-jeok, the great Confucian scholar to whom Oksan Seowon was dedicated, was born here in 1491; his life and the academy's history is relayed on information boards. As you walk around try to suspend belief for a short while, and imagine yourself back in nineteenth-century Korea (though it probably smells much more pleasant now). Some buildings are permanently open to the public, and you may even be lucky enough to be invited into a private house for a nose around. Several **buses** (presently #200, #208, #212 and #217, but these have been known to change) run from Gyeongju to a stop 2km from the village – a blessing in disguise, as it necessitates a short walk through the Gyeongsang countryside.

West of Gyeongju

The sights west of Gyeongju are quite scattered, making exploration a little tricky. For those not yet weary of dead Silla kings, a few **tomb complexes** lie a couple of kilometres beyond the River Hyeongsan, which runs along the western side of the city. The closest two are accessible **by bike** – there's a rental place opposite the tourist information booth near the bus terminals, just head over the bridge, and follow the signs. The **tomb of King Muyeol** – who defeated the rival Baekje kingdom in 660 – lies just to the south of the bridge, though as the road is both a little too narrow and a little too busy for comfortable walking or cycling, it's advisable to head through the fields. Turn left down the bumpy riverside track immediately after the bridge, then down the first decent road that falls off to the right, and under the railway bridge. Navigating the labyrinthine trails of the farming village across the road is difficult (but thoroughly enjoyable), so head a short way down the main road, and the tombs will be on your right.

Several kilometres further down this main road is the beguiling **Geumcheok** collection of tomb-mounds. Legend has it that Hyeokgeose, the first Silla king, once owned a golden stick (*geum-cheok*) that could restore the dead to life. However, the village got so overcrowded with Silla-dynasty undead that the townsfolk decided to bury the rod in a mound – forty decoy mounds were also raised in the area, and to this day nobody knows which one houses the stick.

A right-turn after the Hyeongsan bridge near Gyeongju will take you in the direction of the tomb of **General Kim Yu-sin**. Records in the *Samguk Sagi* (see box, p.317) state that in between his birth in 595 and his death in 673, he led the battles that defeated the Baekje and Goguryeo kingdoms, paving the way for Silla rule over the whole peninsula. The road leading here is quieter than those heading elsewhere from the bridge, but unfortunately for walkers and cyclists there are no real side-routes to make use of.

Daegu

DAEGU surfed the crest of various waves – notably medicine, textiles, machinery and computers – sucking in people from the surrounding area and beyond, quickly becoming Korea's **fourth largest city** by population. Such business savvy has had an interesting effect, as central Daegu can now be looked upon as one large shopping mall, the department stores supplemented by a lattice of streets devoted to particular products. Herbal Medicine Street is the best known, as the city has for centuries been a centre of **herbal medicine**, but you may also wish to head to Steamed Rib-Meat Street or Rice Cake Street if you're hungry, Shoe Street or Sock Street if your feet need clothing, or **Washing Machine Appliance Street** if, well, your washing machine needs maintenance.

For all this commerce, it has to be said that Daegu as a city is not particularly attractive. However, in a country obsessed with appearance, it's hard to talk to a Korean about Daegu without being told how beautiful its women are; the city is based in a geological bowl, which makes for very hot summers, very cold winters and very delicious apples – this fruit that pops out of the surrounding countryside is said to keep the skin pimple-free, as well as providing the blanching effect that all Korean girls crave.

There are few notable sights in central Daegu, but it's a pleasant place to go shopping, or catch up on your **partying** if you've been trawling the Gyeongsang countryside. This is aided by the fact that it has quite possibly the largest expat community outside Seoul, many of whom are soldiers from one of four American military bases around town; the additional English teachers and South Asian migrants lend Daegu an increasingly cosmopolitan air. Outside the city boundaries there are some excellent places to visit: **Palgongsan** is a wonderful park to the north of town, while **Haeinsa** is one of Korea's best-known temples, and just a bus-ride to the west.

Arrival and information

Daegu sprawls far and wide across the geological basin it calls home, which can make orientation more than a little tricky. Arriving by **bus** is particularly confusing, as there are **several terminals** across the city, though only a few of these are likely to be used by tourists. The Bukbu terminal and Seodaegu express terminal are frustratingly far (9km) to the northwest of the centre, as is the Seobu terminal to the southwest. The Dongbu terminal is marginally more central, but best is the Dongdaegu express (*gosok*) terminal, which connects with trains and the subway system – to get here from other Korean cities you should head to their own *gosok* terminal. It's far better to arrive by **train** – Daegu station stares straight down at the main downtown area. For high-speed KTX services you'll have to head to Dongdaegu station, one stop to the east. The

The Daegu subway fire

On February 18, 2003, a calamitous event took place under Daegu's downtown streets, one that was to have a heavy impact on the Korean psyche, and a terrible comedown after the spectacular success of the previous year's World Cup. The simple facts of the matter – around two hundred killed in a **subway fire** – do not even begin to tell the story, with failings before, during and after the event bringing about a national sense of shame, and a level of introspection previously unseen in a country accustomed to looking abroad for excuses.

A few months before the fire, a man named **Kim Dae-han** had suffered a stroke which left him partially paralysed. Ostracized by his family and friends, and losing his sanity, he decided to take his frustrations out on society. During a Tuesday morning rush-hour, he wandered into a subway train armed with gasoline-filled containers, which caught fire as the train pulled into Jungangno station. The fire spread rapidly through the carriages, owing to the lack of any fire-extinguishing apparatus on board; both the seats and the flooring also produced toxic smoke as they burned. Kim managed to escape, along with many passengers from his train, but the poor safety procedures on the line meant that the train driver arriving in the opposite direction was not informed of the problem, and pulled in to a plume of thick, toxic smoke. At this point the fire detection system kicked in and shut off power on the line, leaving both trains stranded. The driver of the second train told passengers to remain seated while he attempted to contact the station manager, and when finally put through was told to leave the train immediately. He duly scurried upstairs, but in his haste had removed the train's key, shutting off power to the doors, and effectively sealing the remaining passengers inside – death on a large scale was inevitable. The total count has never been fully established, as some bodies were burnt beyond all recognition.

The families of the victims, and the country as a whole, needed someone to blame. The arsonist, Kim Dae-han, was sentenced to life in prison, avoiding the death penalty on the grounds of mental instability; he died in jail soon afterwards. The incident raised some serious questions, primarily about **safety** being compromised by a thirst for profit, and the treatment of the **disabled** in Korean society – a baptism of fire for incoming president Roh Moo-hyun. Safety on Daegu's subway has since been significantly improved, and facilities for the disabled have started to appear. At least some good may be coming out of one of Korea's biggest modern-day disasters.

city's **international airport** is a short bus or taxi ride east from Dongdaegu train station. However, there are only a handful of connections to other Asian cities, and Daegu's location in the centre of a small country means that you're unlikely to be using it for a domestic flight.

Both train stations have **tourist information** booths, with English-speakers most likely at Dongdaegu (daily 9am–7pm; ⓣ053/939-0080). The stations are also connected to the city's two-line **subway system**, which is cheap and efficient.

Daegu and around

Daegu	대구
Apsan Park	압산 공원
Daegu Hyanggyo (Confucian school)	대구 향교
Dalseong Park	달성 공원
Gyesan Cathedral	계산 성당
Haeinsa	해인사
Herbal Medicine Market	한약 시장
Jae-il Church	재일 교회
Palgongsan Provincial Park	팔공산 도립 공원
Seomun Market	서문 시장
Yangnyeongsi Exhibition Hall	약령시 박물관
Yasigolmok	야시골목
Accommodation	
Anpyongjang	안평장
Canel Motel	카넬 모텔
Hotel Ariana	호텔 아리아나
Hotel Inter-Burgo	호텔 인터불고
Jjimjilbang	찜질방
Motel Milano	모텔 밀라노
Restaurants	
Ariana Brau	아리아나 브로이
Geumgok Samgyetang	금곡 삼계탕
Little Italya	리틀 이탈야
Mimi	미미

As with all Korean cities, Daegu's **local bus** network is comprehensive, though likely to bewilder foreign tourists. Those staying in the city for more than a couple of days may wish to make use of the Daegyong **travel card**, which gives slight discounts and avoids the need to rummage in your pockets for change – just beep your card over the sensor at the front of the bus, or on the subway entrance gate. Cards cost W2000 and can be bought at subway stations, or from kiosks next to some bus stops; W10,000 is the minimum top-up. Short-term visitors can hop on a **city tour**, which leaves daily at 10am from Dongdaegu station and can be reserved by phone. Routes vary, but usually last around seven hours.

Accommodation

For a city of its size, Daegu has a real dearth of decent **accommodation**. The tourist information booths outside the train stations will be able to help you find a suitable room – **motels** aplenty can be found near both terminals, and there are some cheaper *yeogwan* within staggering distance of the nightlife area around Jungangno subway station.

Hotel Ariana Dusan O-geori ⓣ053/765-7776, ⓦwww.ariana.co.kr. With clean, fresh and relatively spacious rooms, this hotel in Deurangil is the best choice in the city at this price level, but it's still overpriced unless you can land a discount; the "Deluxe" rooms are far bigger than the "Standard", and cost just a little more. Beer lovers should note that there's a microbrewery on site in the German restaurant. 6

Anpyongjang Yeogwan Jungangno area ⓣ053/424-0355. Cheap, cheerful and convenient for the downtown area, this *yeogwan* has decent enough en-suite rooms, though they occasionally rock to the sounds of a nearby *noraebang* singing room. Head to Jungangno subway station, and take the road opposite Brannigan's. 2

Canel Motel Namseongno ⓣ053/252-4466. Located near the western end of the Herbal Medicine Street, and, therefore, within walking distance of the downtown area, this motel will suffice for those on a tight budget. 4

Hotel Inter-Burgo Manchon-dong ⓣ053/602-7114, ⓦhotel.inter-burgo.com. Though it may look like a leisure centre from outside, this is billed as Daegu's top hotel. It's overpriced and in an uninteresting part of town, though mercifully a short taxi-ride from either the airport or the train station. Book at the tourist office outside Dongdaegu station for big discounts. 8

Jjimjilbang For those on a real budget, or just in need of a good scrub, there is a decent *jjimjilbang* (W6000) right outside Daegu Station. There are similar options in downtown and near Dongdaegu catering to a younger crowd, the noise from whom can sometimes make it hard to sleep. 1

Motel Milano Dongdaegu Yeok-ap. A good choice near Dongdaegu train station, rising above its competitors by laying on free Internet in many rooms. All the regular Korean motel conveniences are present and correct, from the free can of coffee in the fridge to the shampoo in the bathroom. 2

The City

Though the best sights are outside the city, Daegu's biggest draw is the variety of **shopping streets** that cover its centre. **Yasigolmok** is a web of largely pedestrianized roads representing the city's modern heart – a collection of clothes shops, bars, cheap restaurants, to the west is the **Herbal Medicine Market**, which first got going in the 1650s. These markets used to be found all over the country but only a few remain, and today almost half of the country's buying and selling of medicinal herbage is undertaken on these streets: here you'll find everything from fruits to roots, bark to bugs and lizard tails to deer antlers. Practitioners here are able to whip up combinations of weird and wonderful ingredients for a range of ailments, but though the attraction for most foreign visitors is purely visual, it must be said that the area isn't as picturesque as its contents make it sound. On this street is the **Yangnyeongsi Exhibition Hall**

▲ Shoppers in Daegu

(9am–5pm; Sun from 10am; free), a mildly diverting display of medicinal ingredients and how they're used, though very little information is in English. Alongside this is the **Jae-il Church**, Daegu's first Christian place of worship, while the Gothic-style **Gyesan Cathedral** is just around the corner.

The medicinal street finishes with a flourish at its western end, marked with a traditional gate. Across the main road you'll find a whole array of shopping streets, each with a particular theme – the goods on Towel Street and Sewing Machine Street are unlikely to be of interest to most foreigners, but Motorcycle Street pulls in expats from far and wide. Just south of the gate is **Seomun Market**, one of the best-known marketplaces in the country. Like the herbal marketplace, it has been trading since the seventeenth century, but although there's little sign of this longevity it's a great place to hunt cheap clothing or sniff around for food. Near here is **Daegu Hyanggyo**, a former Confucian academy that's usually pretty quiet, and a good place to walk around.

Forming a western boundary to the specialist shopping street area is **Dalseong Park**, which was created on the site of what was apparently the oldest fortress in Korea; just around the corner from the entrance is a small **folk museum** (daily 9am–5pm; closed Mon; free). Daegu has many other parks – the **National Debt Repayment Movement Park** near the city centre, is worth mentioning for the splendid name alone – but the only other one of note is **Apsan Park**, a large green stretch to the south of the city; here you'll find plenty of temples and pavilions, a small exhibition on the Korean War, and a cable car that rises to a ridge and provides wonderful views of Daegu's sprawl.

Eating and drinking

There's a good, cheap **restaurant** around every corner in Daegu, and the rising number of foreigners living here means that the choice is becoming ever more cosmopolitan. Indian restaurants are increasingly popular in the suburbs and it won't be long before decent ones start penetrating the city centre. **Coffee** and morning snacks are far easier to hunt down in the Jungangno downtown area – the *Tous Les Jours* bakery near the Kyobo Building is a good choice for both, and you can surf the net for free – as are Western joints such as *TGI Friday's* and *Brannigan's*. Another place crammed with restaurants is the Deurangil district, located a few kilometres south of downtown.

The downtown area also has some great places to **drink**, most notably the *Thunderbird Lounge*, a chic, foreign-owned bar that revels in relative isolation a short walk from the main drag, and a great place to make new friends over a chilled Jagermeister, or a microbrewed Alleykat pale ale. Beer central *Commune's*, which often plays music that's surprisingly underground for a Korean bar, also has live music at least once a week, and a quiz night every second Saturday. In the same area is Rodeo Street, which contains all of the city's most popular **clubs** – try *Frog*, *Bubble* or *Monkey* – and lures local expats by the dozen at weekends to dance until dawn.

Ariana Brau Dusan O-geori. Fill up on Bratwurst and Sauerkraut at this German restaurant under the *Hotel Ariana*, and try a range of beers from the on-site microbrewery. Prices are a little high, so it's best to show up on Sat for the W17,000 buffet.

Geumgok Samgyetang Gongpyeong-dong. *Samgyetang* is a soup containing a small chicken stuffed with rice and ginseng roots, which some foreign inductees find a little bland, and others delicious. This restaurant has a surprisingly un-Korean feel for such a dish, which is usually served in more traditional surroundings; still it's the best place in the city to give it a try.

Little Italya Gongpyeong-dong. Unlike most Italian restaurants in the city, chefs here prepare the dishes with real, fresh herbs – a difference not lost on hungry Daegu expats. Pizzas go for W10,000 and upwards, with pasta dishes a little cheaper, and there's some drinkable wine on the menu.

Jjim-galbi Street One of many cuisine-centred streets in the city, this is the best place to tuck into *jjim-galbi*, steamed rib meat that goes down particularly well with a few shots of *soju*.

Mimi Gongpyeong-dong. The best of a small Japanese-style collection tucked into a corner just off the main nightlife drag; here you can throw back *sake* and chicken *teriyaki* amid a feast of paper lanterns and Japanese sketches.

Listings

Books Kyobo Bookstore, in the Kyobo Building near Jungangno subway station, has plenty of English teaching materials and books. Youngpoong Bookstore, under the Samsung Financial Plaza just down the road, has much of the same.

Cinemas The most convenient is the *Academy Cinema* in the downtown area, which charges W7000 per mainstream film or Korean melodrama.

Hospitals Kyungpook University Hospital, 50 Samdeok 2-ga (ⓣ053/422-1141), or Kwak's Hospital, 18 Su-dong (ⓣ053/252-2401). Eastern remedies are available at Daegu Oriental Medicine Hospital,165 Sang-dong (ⓣ053/749-1010).

Immigration Alien Registration office, 1012 Geomsa-dong (ⓣ053 980-3505), best accessed via Dongchon subway station.

Internet Web cafés can be found all over the city – look for the letters "PC" on an upper floor – and cost W1000 per hour, with a one-hour minimum fee.

Post The main post office is west of Jungangno subway station (Mon–Fri 9am–8pm, Sat 9am–6pm, closed Sun). There is also a post office in every *dong* district (Mon–Fri 9am–6pm); all have the facility to handle international mail.

Sport The city's football club is Daegu FC, who play at the World Cup Stadium, way to the east of the city centre near Daegongwon subway station; this will also be the venue for the 2011 World Athletics Championships. An adjacent stadium is home to the Samsung Lions (ⓦwww.samsunglions.com), Daegu's baseball team, who are regularly among the challengers for the national title.

Palgongsan Provincial Park

Just twenty kilometres north of Daegu, the land rises and folds, creating a peak-lined ridge and a series of valleys now studded with temples, hermitages and the odd carved Buddha, an area known as **PALGONGSAN PROVINCIAL PARK** – an ideal setting for a day of relaxed hiking. Dating way back to 493, **Donghwasa** is the park's most famous temple, though a little over-hyped by the local authorities. Visitors are most likely to be impressed by a seated Buddha that is thought to date from the eighth century, and the gloriously intricate interior of the main hall. More modern is the mammoth **Tongil Buddha**, which stands next to next to some similarly outsized stone pagodas and lanterns. These uninspired creations were placed here in the hope that the two Koreas will one day become one – *Tongil* means "reunification" – but though the religion-lite powers-that-be in Pyongyang are unlikely to approve of the Buddha, they're sure to be impressed by a liberal use of concrete rarely seen outside Communist societies.

Gatbawi, another carved Buddha, occupies a lofty and far more natural setting, providing a view that's not quite top-of-the-world, but at least high enough to present Daegu in all its apartment block-filled glory. Situated up near the peak of Gwanbong (850m), it's around an hour's walk from the tourist village at the bottom of the trail. Many people make the journey on the first or fifteenth of the month to make a wish, as it is claimed that the Buddha will hear one from every visitor on these occasions. **Hikers** wanting to head from here to Donghwasa can do so without too much difficulty; a few hours should be enough to bring you to Yeombulbong (1121m), from which you can drop down the trail back to Donghwasa, stopping at Yeombulam, a hermitage on route. Those with tired legs could even take the cable car to or from an observation point near the hermitage – this runs from the tourist village beneath Donghwasa, and costs W3500 one way or W5500 return.

Palgongsan is fairly easy to get to by **bus**; from Dongdaegu station, #105 heads to Donghwasa and #104 to Gatbawi, each taking just under an hour to arrive. There's a small **information booth** near Donghwasa that can provide maps of the park; these should also be available at similar offices in Daegu.

Haeinsa

A bus-ride away from Daegu, the secluded temple of **Haeinsa** is part of Korea's holy trinity of "Jewel Temples" – the other two are Tongdosa and Songgwangsa (see p.284), which represent the Buddha and Buddhist community respectively, while Haeinsa symbolizes the religion's teachings, or *dharma*. These doctrines have been carved onto more than eighty thousand wooden blocks, known as the **Tripitaka Koreana** (see box below), and remain visible through the vertical wooden rungs of the buildings that house them. Still in use today, Haeinsa's various buildings are pleasant enough; its location, however, is nothing short of spectacular: the path leading up to the main entrance is worth the trip alone, being lined on both sides with colossal trees, while the complex backs onto **Gayasan National Park**. Fame and beauty conspire to make the complex uncomfortably crowded at times, but few venture off the beaten track to enjoy the surrounding area. This is a shame, as a few hermitages can be found on the opposite side of the stream, and innumerable paths snake their way through the trees to peaks, farmland and secluded villages.

Practicalities

The temple sits just across the border in Gyeongsangnam-do; however, the easiest access is via Daegu. Regular direct buses head from the Seobu terminal, taking just over an hour to arrive; from the bus stop, it's a short but unnecessarily convoluted walk to the temple. There are, however, plenty of **places to stay** in the winding streets that surround the small terminal. The best rooms are on high at the *Haein Tourist Hotel* (Ⓣ055/933-2000, Ⓕ055/931-1108; ⑤); though it possesses the stained carpeting and slight chemical odour typical of official Korean tourist accommodation. The views, however, can be stunning, particularly on misty mornings. More interesting is the *Sanjangbyeoljang Yeogwan* (Ⓣ055/932-7245; ②), whose rooms may be spartan but the building is in traditional style in keeping with its natural surroundings. Those in a persuasive mood could even try to wangle a berth at **Haeinsa** itself – you'll have to be up early, but dawn at the temple is simply magical.

The Tripitaka Koreana

One of the most famous sights in the land, the eighty-thousand-plus wooden blocks of Buddhist doctrine known as the **Tripitaka Korea** were first carved out in the eleventh century, over a 76-year period, in an attempt to curry the favour of the Buddha in a time of perpetual war. Though the originals were destroyed by rampaging Mongol hordes in the thirteenth century, the present set were carved shortly after that, and once again every possible measure was taken to please the Buddha. The best wood in the area was tracked down then soaked for three years in seawater before being cut to shape and boiled. The slabs then spent another three years being sheltered from sun and rain but exposed to wind, until they were finally ready for carving. Incredibly, not a single mistake has yet been found in over **fifty million** Chinese characters, a fact that led other countries to base their own Tripitaka on the Korean version. A superb feat of craft patience and devotion, the outer spines of these blocks are still visible today at Haeinsa temple, and the set has been added to UNESCO's World Heritage List.

Andong and north Gyeongbuk

Surrounded by picturesque countryside and magical sights, **ANDONG** is deservedly one of the most popular draws in the region for foreign travellers. Whatever the Korean tourist booklets say about its history, don't go expecting a mini-Gyeongju – such a comparison is unfair and misguided, as there's little in the city itself. However, the wonderful sights on Andong's periphery mean that it has enough to be respected on its own terms. The centre is small, pleasant and unhurried, with the main sights located well out of town – **Dosan Seowon** to the north is a stunning Confucian academy dating from Joseon times, while to the west is **Hahoe Folk Village**, a rustic approximation of traditional Korean life. A similar village can be found nearer the centre, next to a rather absorbing folklore museum.

Arrival, information and orientation

Andong's **train** and **bus** stations are a few minutes' walk from each other, both on the same road to the south of the city centre. Outside the train station is an excellent **tourist information office**; staff here are helpful and informative, especially with regard to finding a place to stay, and there's usually an English-speaker on hand. Central Andong is extremely compact, so you won't need to travel far to find somewhere to stay and eat. For the main sights both in Andong and its surrounding countryside, you're likely to need to use taxis or buses.

Accommodation

Andong's **accommodation** simply hasn't caught up with its increasing popularity as a tourist destination, and the city centre's only official tourist hotel – the *Andong Park* (④) – could credibly claim to be the worst in the country. All this means that those seeking **luxury** are advised to stay in Gyeongju and visit Andong on a tour or day-trip. Less picky souls should be able to find an acceptable place within walking distance of the train or bus stations; the tourist information office outside the former is an invaluable source of information, and will even ring ahead to book a room if required.

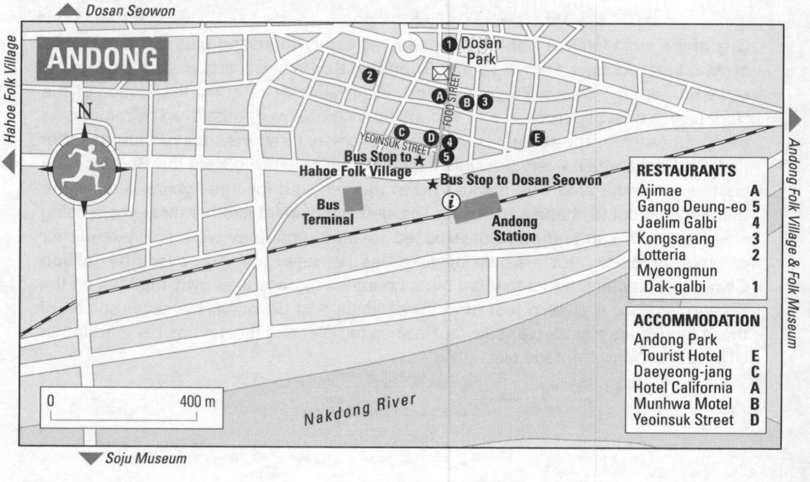

Andong and around

Andong	안동
Dosan Seowon	도산 서원
Folk Museum	민속 박물관
Hahoe Folk Village	하회 마을
Juwangsan National Park	주왕산 국립 공원
Soju Museum	소주 박물관
Accommodation	
Andong Park Tourist Hotel	안동 파크 관광 호텔
Daeyeong-jang	대영장
Hotel California	호텔 켈리포니아
Munhwa Motel	문화 모텔
Restaurants	
Ajimae	아지매
Gango Deung-eo	강오 등어
Jaelim Galbi	재림 갈비
Kongsarang	콩사랑
Lotteria	롯데리아
Myeongmun Dak-galbi	명문 닭갈비
Rosebud	로즈버드

Hotel California Samsan-dong ⓣ054/854-0622. Under friendly ownership and everything the *Andong Park* fails to be, this is the best place to stay in town – surprisingly stylish for a motel, posters of Klimt and similar art can be found in the corridors, while rooms are just as flash, and come with great showers. It may be worth paying extra for the more expensive deluxe rooms, which are simply huge. ❸

Daeyeong-jang Yeogwan Samsan-dong. Rooms at this *yeogwan* on Yeoinsuk St (see below) have toilets and showers, comfy beds and windows, as well as a television and drinking water in the fridge – just the same as most motels, but cheaper at around W25,000. ❷

Munhwa Motel Dongbu-dong ⓣ054/857-7001. With powerful showers, and mood lighting, this isn't a bad choice if the *California* is full. When demand is low, you'll be able to haggle the price down to near-*yeogwan* levels. ❸

Yeoinsuk Street Samsan-dong. Though extremely cheap at around W12,000 per person, all you'll get is a tiny linoleum room with a couple of blankets, and a television if you're lucky. This said true budget travellers should not require anything more, and there are few more authentically Korean places to stay. ❶

The City

For all the amazing sights around the city, there's not too much to see in Andong itself. The centre of the city, though relaxed, is for eating, drinking and sleeping in between excursions to the surrounding countryside, with a few attractions within a short taxi- or bus-ride. Just outside the main body of the city, and accessible on bus #3 – get off immediately after the river – is a small **folk village** (24hr; free). With its buildings mere models, rather than functioning abodes, this is basically a heavily-diluted version of the terrific folk village at Hahoe to the west of the city (see p.229), but it's worth a quick nose around, especially if the bus schedules from Andong to Hahoe or Dosan Seowon have left you in the city centre with an hour or two to spare. Those with more time can stop at one of the restaurants at the top of the complex, a rustic bunch primarily occupied with the making and selling of *pajeon* – a fried Korean pancake made with a number of possible ingredients. Prefix *pajeon* with *haemul* for seafood (tentacles and things), *goju* for chilli pepper, *baechu* for cabbage or *buchu* for leek; all will cost around W5000, and are best washed down with *dongdongju*, a milky rice wine. After seeing the village, it's possible to cross the river on a zigzagging pedestrian bridge then catch the bus back to Andong from the other side of the road. Don't leave without seeing the **Folk Museum** (daily 9am–6pm; W1000) near the entrance to the complex, which is chock-full of interesting information about local culture and practices – including why Korean women give birth facing the south or east – and altogether more explanatory and less obsessed with cold, hard facts than most Korean museums. The museum also has dioramas portraying village games – some of which still go on in the countryside on occasion – and some fascinating collections of clothing and headwear; on a good day, you may even walk out with a free scroll of calligraphy from an on-site artist. Another museum detailing a markedly more current aspect of Korean culture can be found a couple of kilometres to the south of town. **Soju**, of which Andong is home to a particularly strong variety, is the grog that oils the wheels of the whole country, and the town has a whole **museum** (Mon–Sat 9am–5.30pm; free) dedicated to the stuff. Unfortunately, it isn't too interesting, but you're welcome to buy a bottle of the local variety which, at about 45 percent alcohol by volume, is nearly twice as strong as any other. It's best to take a taxi from the bus or train stations (W2500); stand on the opposite side of the main road.

Eating

A dedicated **food street** starts just opposite the train station – look for the gate with the mask – though the best restaurants are to be found away from this road. The tourist booth outside the train station is an excellent source of information – one member of staff has even drawn up a cursory **restaurant map** for visiting foreigners. Those seeking to sate their caffeine cravings have a choice of **cafés** – *Rosebud* to the north of the centre is popular with the city's youth, with its assortment of garden chairs giving it an outdoorsy feel, while nearby is *Tous Les Jours*, a bakery good for a non-spicy breakfast.

Ajimae Samsan-dong. Stylish and amicable, this restaurant under the *Hotel California* has a menu featuring those Andong rarities: pictures and English translations. The assorted beef set – W30,000 and big enough to feed three people – is the star of the show, but cheaper dishes are also available.

Gango Deung-eo Sikdang Unheung-dong. Across the main road from the train station, here you can dine on salted mackerel, an Andong speciality. Ask for the *jeong-sik* – a belly-filling set course featuring this dish plus an array of side dishes, and yours for just W7000.

Jaelim Galbi Unheung-dong. Though Andong has a dedicated Galbi Street, this is the best joint in town, and very popular with foreign tourists. Unlike most such restaurants, they're just about willing to cater for single diners – put on your biggest smile. Pork *galbi* is W7000 per portion, with marinated *bulgogi* a little more. The best meat, *hanu galbi*, costs a whacking W17,000 per portion, but is absolutely delicious.

Kongsarang Unheung-dong. A small restaurant with a stone-clad exterior, this is a good place to try simple Korean dishes such as *bibimbap* (mixed vegetables on rice) or *sundubu jjigae*, which is a spicy tofu broth, served with rice and vegetable side dishes. Those with calories to burn after the meal can head across the road to an indoor driving range.

Lotteria This burger joint originated in Japan; even so there are still some interestingly Korean items on the menu, such as *galbi* or *bulgogi* burgers. More regular buns, fries and shakes are also available.

Myeongmun Dak-galbi Facing Ungbu Park. Just to the north of the city centre, this is the most popular place in town for *dak-galbi*, a delicious meal in which chicken meat and assorted vegetables are thrown into a hot pan to cook at the centre of your table.

Around Andong

The **countryside** around Andong is full of beauty and interesting sights, but given the general dearth of public transport, most tourists settle with the two main sights – the folk village at **Hahoe**, a bus-ride west of the city, and **Dosan**

Seowon, a Confucian academy to the north. There are buses to both from Andong, though services are not too frequent – it's just about possible to see both in a day, if you time it right. Alternatively, some intrepid travellers choose to stay the night at the folk village. Some way east of Andong is **Juwangsan National Park**, one of the least-visited in the country.

Hahoe Folk Village

Korea has made many efforts to keep alive its pastoral traditions in the face of rapid economic growth, with one particularly interesting example being the number of preserved **folk villages** sprinkled around the country. While some, such as the one near central Andong, exist purely for show others are functioning communities where life dawdles on at an intentionally slow pace, the residents surviving on a curious mix of home-grown vegetables, government subsidy and tourist-generated income. **Hahoe Folk Village** (24hr; entry W2000) is one of the best and most popular in the country, a charming mesh of over a hundred **traditional countryside houses** nestling in the gentle embrace of an idle river. This charming mix of mud walls, thatched roofs and dusty trails is no mere tourist construct, but a village with a history stretching back centuries, and you'll be able to eat up at least a couple of hours exploring the paths, inspecting the buildings and relaxing by the river. The village's past is told on information boards that you'll find outside the most important structures – seek out the Yangjin residence, for example, the oldest in the village, and built in a blend of Goryeo- and Joseon-era styles. The village can sometimes get a little busy with visitors, but it's easy to escape and find some space of your own – try the riverside at the far end of the village, past the church.

On site are several trinket shops, and more than a few restaurants; all are pleasantly rustic in nature, and the prices reasonable. Rather temptingly, there are also a number of *minbak* at which you can **stay the night**, costing about W30,000 for a spartan room, and heated in colder months with the underfloor *ondol* system. The tourist information office in Andong will be happy to book

▲ Farm land surrounding Andong

you into one of these, and it's well worth staying to experience the sights, sounds and smells of the village at night, when the vast majority of its visitors have gone home. **Bus** #46 runs to the village from Andong, taking around forty minutes to arrive, but there are only eight services per day – a shame, given that another excellent sight is two kilometres back down the road, and a frustratingly long distance to walk: the **Hahoe Mask Museum** (9am–6pm; W1000) is home to an absorbing collection of facewear from around the world.

Dosan Seowon

Dosan Seowon is a Confucian academy, surrounded by some of the most gorgeous countryside that the area can offer. To get here take **bus** #67 from Andong – there are only a few per day, so check the return schedules at Andong's tourist information office. Not long after getting on you'll find yourself winding your way past rice paddies and some pleasantly unspoilt countryside, before ducking down to the academy's entrance (9am–6pm; Nov–Feb until 5pm; W1500). From here it's a short walk to the complex itself; the wide **valley** to your right is simply stunning, the sound of rushing water from the stream occasionally augmented by the splutter of a faraway tractor.

The academy was established in 1574, in honour of Yi Hwang, a well-respected Confucian scholar also known as **Toegye** (see box opposite). It no longer functions as a place of study, but a refurbishment in the 1970s gave back the tranquility of its original *raison d'être*: this was a highly important study place during the Joseon era, and the only one outside Seoul, for those who wished to pass the notoriously hard tests necessary for governmental officials. Opposite the main entrance, you may notice a little man-made hill topped by a **traditional-style shelter**; the stele underneath once marked an important spot for the aforementioned government exams, with the original location somewhere towards the bottom of the lake that you pass on the bus-ride in. As you enter the complex, beyond the flower gardens and up the steps are two libraries whose nameplates are said to have been carved by Toegye himself; the buildings were built on stilts to keep humidity to a minimum. Further on are buildings that were once used as living quarters, the main lecture hall, as well as a shrine to Toegye, though this last one is usually closed-off. Passing back down under a cloak of maple – which flames roaring red in late autumn – you'll find an **exhibition hall** detailing the great man's life and times, as well as an astrolabe for measuring the movements of celestial bodies.

Beyond the academy you'll find numerous other Toegye-related sights, all backed by **Cheongnyangsan**, a mountainous park. These scholarly sights are of more interest to Koreans than foreigners, but Onhye, Toegye's birth village, is a pretty place, and descendants of the don can still be found in one of his old abodes. A couple of daily buses on the #67 route continue past Dosan Seowon to Onhye and the park, but it's rather hard to do as a day-trip without your own transport. A number of *minbak* are located near the park entrance if you'd like to stay the night. Such accommodation is also available in Dosan Seoburi, a small village just before the academy on the bus route from Andong.

Juwangsan National Park

Just over 50km east of Andong, is the small, unheralded **JUWANGSAN NATIONAL PARK**. While many such places in Korea can be full to the brim with hikers, *pajeon*-eaters and *dongdongju*-quaffers, Juwangsan's relative inaccessibility keeps it largely free of bustle. Yet here you'll find almost everything you could ask of a Korean national park – the deep green of a thousand pine trees, crags and spires of bare limestone, small waterfalls and scenic temples, all connected by good, sign-posted trails.

Toegye, neo-Confucianist

Poet, scholar, all-round good guy and bearded star of the thousand-won note, **Toegye** (1501–70) is one of Korea's most revered historical characters. Born Yi Hwang, but better known by his pen name (pronounced Twegg-yeah), he exerted a major influence on the politics and social structure of his time. The country was then ruled by the **Joseon dynasty**, one of the most staunchly **Confucian** societies the world has ever known – each person was born with a pre-defined limit as to what they could aspire to in life, forever restricted by their genetics. The aristocracy oversaw a caste-like system that dictated what clothes people could wear, who they could marry, and what position they could hold, among other things.

Toegye was lucky enough to be born into privileged society. He excelled in his studies from a young age, and eventually passed the notoriously difficult governmental examinations necessary for advancement to the higher official posts. Once there, he refused to rest on his laurels and live the easy life – he hunted down those he thought to be corrupt, and as a reward for his integrity was **exiled**, several times, from the capital. However, his intelligence made him a force to be reckoned with, and he set about introducing **neo-Confucian thought**, much of it borrowed from the Song dynasty in China; he advocated, for example, advancement based on achievement rather than heredity. After his death, the Confucian academy **Dosan Seowon** was built in his honour; it retains the contemplative spirit of the time, and of Toegye himself.

The bulk of Juwangsan's sights lie in the small valley that runs up from the park's main bus stop – pick up a map from the information booth near here before you set off. Just beyond the park entrance you'll find **Daejeonsa**, residing in a setting that should be the envy of many a Korean temple. Impossible to miss from here is **Giambong**, a crag of rock worn like a mohican hairdo, standing tall and proud as if to protect the temple. From the temple a streamside path heads up through the valley, and past a number of interesting rocky features before coming to three waterfalls; from here you can turn left or right and head back to the park entrance on the mountain ridges that enclose the valley.

Access to the park is from the small town of Cheongsong, a short way to the west. This town has direct **bus** connections with Andong, Daegu and Busan, as well as the Dongseoul terminal in the capital. Near the park entrance you'll find a small tourist village, which has a decent number of small restaurants, and simple accommodation on offer.

Ulleungdo

With island groups dotted all around Korea's southern and western coasts, you may feel it prudent to forgo the three-hour ferry-ride to a small turret of land between Korea and Japan, and head instead to a closer isle. However, this would be a mistake – **ULLEUNGDO**, covered in a rich, green cloak of trees and fringed with juniper, is simply stunning and refreshingly unspoilt. Its volcanic origin and the flora splashed around on account of its nutritious soils mark it out as a mini Jeju (see p.349). But while increasingly popular with Korean travellers, Ulleungdo's isolation has kept it largely free from the ravages of mass tourism. With no Family Marts or five-star hotels, and just one bumpy main road tracing a vague parallel to the coast, the only time that the island's pulse seems to quicken is in the half-hour window surrounding ferry arrivals, when *ajummas* race around trying to draw tourists back to their *minbak* accommodation. One of the main reasons for Ulleung's popularity with armies of middle-aged Korean tourists is its proximity to **Dokdo**, an even smaller speck of land claimed by both Korea and Japan, and recently the focus of nationalistic demonstrations (see box opposite).

Few islands in Korea can provide as spectacular an arrival as Ulleungdo's main settlement, **Dodong-ni**, whose port makes a sudden appearance in a sumptuous pirate-like cove hidden and encircled by precipitous mountains, and squeezed in on both sides by the valley walls. Ulleungdo's second main settlement, **Jeodong-ni**, lies just up the coast, slightly smaller, but relatively open and rather different in character. These two villages, both an untidy but undeniably appealing mishmash of *minbak* and fish restaurants, give guests a taste of what the rest of the island is like. **Naribunji** is a farming area of tremendous beauty to the north of the island, whose flatness will come as a great surprise to those who've travelled the bumpy coastal road to get there. On the way, picturesque fishing settlements dot the coast, while there's some good **hiking** to be enjoyed around the rugged, volcanic peaks that rise up in the centre of the island, almost totally unspoilt by modern life.

Arriving by ferry

Due to the absence of an airport on the island, there's only one way to arrive – by **ferry**. At the time of writing, all services were using the port at the main settlement of Dodong-ni, but plans have long been afoot to make a larger terminal elsewhere on the island. Ferry schedules were also in a constant state of flux – most get here from **Pohang**, a large but uninteresting city near Gyeongju on the mainland's eastern coast. Services leave each morning at 10am, costing W55,000 one-way and taking three hours to complete the journey, before making the return trip at 4pm. The terminal at Pohang is a short taxi journey

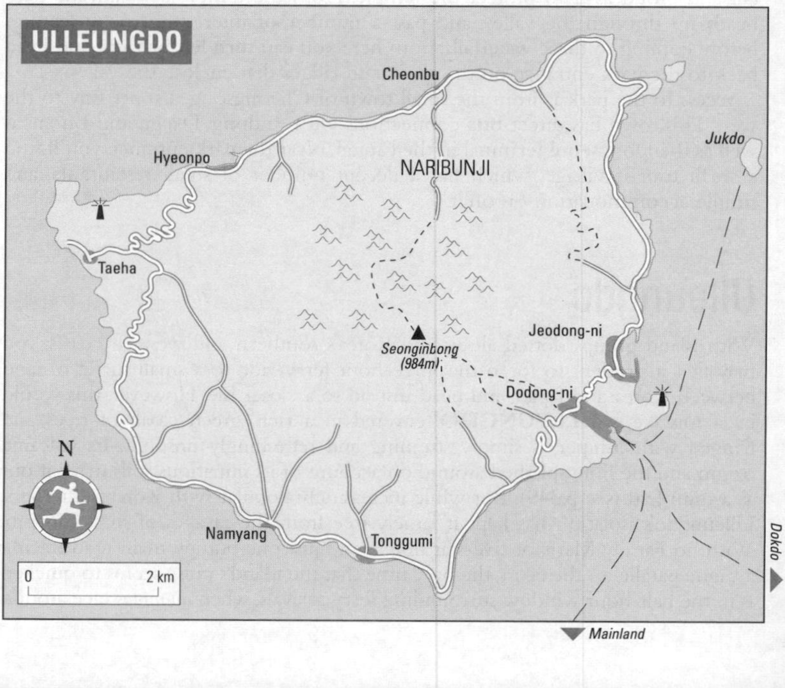

Dokdo

Ninety kilometres east of Ulleungdo lies a remote, straggly bunch of rocks, a small archipelago that seems to be good for little bar fishing, fighting and assertions of national identity. **Dokdo** to the Koreans, **Takeshima** to the Japanese, it is claimed by both nations, and like the East Sea/Sea of Japan dispute (see box, p.185), the issue is unlikely to be resolved any time soon. The problem centres not on the land itself, but about the territorial claim, one that includes a substantial amount of water, and contains an equally substantial amount of **fish**. This means that Dokdo and its surrounding waters are of importance to the economies of both countries. Then there's political rivalry resulting from Korea's Japanese occupation, which lasted from 1910 until the end of the Second World War – Koreans tend to take even the slightest whiff of Nipponese neo-imperialism quite seriously.

In the decades following the war, a number of **armed confrontations** took place in and around the islands, but after things eventually died down Korea took the upper hand, and built a wharf, a lighthouse and a helicopter-landing pad, around which are stationed a couple of permanent residents. In 2004, Korea issued a set of stamps featuring the islands; Japan took this as a claim of ownership, and a couple of years later sent two ships to Dokdo on an unauthorized survey mission. After protracted talks, Japan agreed to suspend the survey, but shortly afterwards Korea sent in ships to do exactly the same thing.

Today, **right-wing elements** in Korea use Dokdo in promotional materials, and the islands have become the focal point of a new nationalist wave. A few of the biggest mobile telecom operators in the country recently built communications towers on the island – totally for show, given the puny local population – and flag-waving ferry-loads of Korean tourists regularly make the journey across from Pohang. It's quite possible for foreign travellers to do likewise, but few choose to do so – without the bombastic fervour, it's not quite the same.

from the train station or either bus terminal. Fortunately, the ferry bay is one of the quieter, more pleasant areas in a generally ugly city, and those unlikely to arrive in time to get the ferry can make use of one of several **motels** around the terminal, including *Joy-tel* and *N.Beach* (both ④), both of which face a pleasant beach. There's also a 24-hour sauna in the *Pos Town* tower, where a night's sleep can be yours for just W6000. It's possible, with an early start, to wake up in Gyeongju and make it to Pohang in time to catch the ferry.

There's also an Ulleungdo service from the Mukho terminal near **Dongdae** in Gangwon province, but it's imperative to call the Korean tourist information line (Ⓣ1330) for the latest information, as you're unlikely to find an English-speaker at any of the relevant ports; tourist offices in Gyeongju will also be able to help.

Information and transport

On Ulleungdo there's a small **tourist information** office just uphill from the ferry terminal – where the water stops, look to your left. Though you'll be lucky to find an English speaker here, staff will be able to hunt down accommodation across the island, and arm you with the requisite maps and pamphlets. One very important thing to consider is **money** – those who have been travelling around Korea with their foreign bank card will run out of luck on Ulleungdo, though a few banks here will be able to exchange foreign cash. **Getting around** the island is also harder than you might expect – the coastal road runs in a "U" rather than a circle, ending in the northeast of the island, and just seven daily **buses** bump their way around, making it impossible to use them for more than a couple of sights per day. Making the short trip from Dodong-ni to Jeodong-ni is far easier – **taxis** cost a standard W2400 per person. You can use these to get to locations around the island, but including travel and waiting time, the total price is going to be expensive – getting on for W100,000 per day. The island is guaranteed to put a few miles of wear and tear on your walking boots, as even in Dodong-ni the few sights are a sweaty clamber away.

Accommodation

Korea's developers must have a fear of long ferry-rides – Ulleungdo is almost entirely devoid of modern **accommodation** facilities, bar one tourist hotel and a few overpriced motels in the main settlements, Dodong-ni and Jeodong-ni; there are also a few condominiums around the island, though these almost exclusively cater to well-off Koreans. The most comfortable place to stay is just out of Dodong-ni at the *Ulleung Dae-a Resort* (Ⓣ054/791-8800; ❻), which has stylishly decorated rooms and good sea views, but little going on around it.

The popularity of little Ulleungdo is such that almost every building in Dodong-ni seems to have **minbak** rooms, while such dwellings can also be found in Jeodong-ni and other settlements. You won't need to go hunting for offers, as elderly women will scream them at you on your walk up from the ferry. A fair price for a room sleeping two is usually around W30,000; don't be afraid to see a couple, or to play the *ajummas* off against each other – haggling is expected, maybe even mandatory. Heading around the island, there are a few tiny settlements where it's possible to stay, but the best by far is **Naribunji** in the north: there's a campsite here, as well as a few *minbak*; the best of the latter is the *Neulporeun-sanjang* (Ⓣ054/791-8181), which has rooms for around W30,000 per night, and doubles as a restaurant.

Dodong-ni

Seonginbong Motel Ⓣ054/791-2677. Just up from the ferries on the right-hand side of the road, this is the best motel in the village, though the quality and accessibility mean that it's often packed with tour groups, and the price is accordingly a little high. ❹

Skyhill Pension Ⓣ054/791-1040. A good option, in relative isolation at the top of the village but still within walking distance of dozens of restaurants, this clean pension has cooking facilities in a communal area, and videos for free hire in reception. ❹

Ulleung Hotel Ⓣ054/791-6611. This is the one official tourist hotel in the village, but not too overpriced, especially when the off-peak discounts kick in, and some of the more expensive rooms are colossal. Walking up from the ferries, keep on the right-hand side, and you'll eventually see the hotel up some stairs to your right. There's a good restaurant on the ground floor, and another – the *Eddiang* – underneath. ❺

Jeodong-ni

Bideulgi Motel Ⓣ054/791-7090. Located a block uphill from the main road that skirts the seafront, this motel has acceptable rooms; try to stay on the top floor for the best views. ❷

Motel Jaeil Ⓣ054/791-2637. Set back from the seafront, next to a small park visible from the waterfront, this is the best of Jeondong-ni's motley selection of accommodation. Rooms are surprisingly large and well appointed, and some have pretty sea or mountain views; there's also an attached sauna, in which you can scrub off the day's whatever for a few thousand won. ❷

Dodong-ni

Though still just a village in population terms, **DODONG-NI** is the largest settlement on Ulleungdo and its main port, and as a result houses most of the island's overnight guests. However, despite the large number of visitors, it has remained surprisingly true to its old ways. The atmospheric village sits in a tight valley up from the ferry terminal, its few roads all heading uphill past a looping parade of *minbak*, small shops and raw fish restaurants. There are few sights as such, but many visitors find themselves heading to a **lighthouse** to the east of town, which can be reached on a number of routes; the most scenic is the half-hour walk around the jagged coast from the ferry terminal. You can walk a short way on the opposite side of the terminal, but all you'll find here – if you're lucky – are a couple of fish snack shacks.

If you head uphill from the ferries and stick to the left, you'll eventually come across a sign pointing to the **Dokdo Museum** (9am–6pm; free), which together with the adjacent historical museum form part of a small park. The former is the most interesting, as it details the Korean claim on Dokdo, a tiny scrawl of rock east of Ulleungdo (see box, p.233 for more information). Also in the park is a "healthy water" spring (the metallic taste presumably proof of some kind of goodness), while those who still have some energy after the climb can bounce off any remaining calories on the see-saw at the very top. The walk up is quite a slog, and most who make the climb are heading to the base of a **cable car** (W7000 return), ready to be whisked up a nearby peak to take in some wonderful views: on clear days, you may be able to see Dokdo across the seas.

Those who follow one of Dodong-ni's upward trails from the ferry terminal will, after what may seem like a never-ending climb, eventually come to the island's main "coastal" road. Turn left, then immediately right again, and you'll find **Daewonsa**, a tiny temple that marks the beginning of most hikes into the interior (see box on p.236 for more details).

Jeodong-ni

A short taxi-ride – or a half-hour walk – away from Dodong-ni is another small settlement called **JEODONG-NI**. Open-plan and spread out along a harbour,

Ulleungdo

Ulleungdo	울릉도
Cheonbu	천부
Daewonsa	대원사
Dodong-ni	도동리
Dokdo Museum	독도 박물관
Ferry terminal	여객 터미널
Hyeonpo	현포
Jeodong-ni	저동리
Jukdo	죽도
Namyang	남양
Naribunji	나리분지
Taeha	태하
Tonggumi	통구미
Accommodation	
Bideulgi Motel	비둘기 모텔
Seonginbong Motel	성인봉 모텔
Skyhill Pension	스카이힐 펜션
Ulleung Hotel	울릉 호텔
Restaurants	
99 Sikdang	99 식당
Eddiang	에띠앙
Hyangu-chon	향우촌

Hiking

Wherever you are on the island, you're likely to see the sea on one side, and a group of verdant peaks hovering over you on the other. These unspoilt, richly forested slopes offer some wonderful **hiking** opportunities, and fortunately the walk up to the main summit, **Seonginbong** (984m), and back can be done in one day-trip. There are several paths into and around the interior, but the main access point is just north of Dodong-ni, near Daewonsa, a small temple. A spur-road just before the temple leads uphill to the right, marking the start of a clammy 4.1km walk to the top. From here, you can either turn back, or make your way further north to the opposite trailhead at Naribunji, 4.5km from the summit. Trails are well signposted, though as there's almost nothing on route, be sure to bring water and some snacks.

rather than wedged into a valley, it's something like a flattened version of its neighbour; while Dodong hasn't exactly been ravaged by tourism, here you'll see far fewer visitors, fewer *minbak*, and therefore an atmosphere more in keeping with the general nature of the island. It's the kind of place where you can idle away a fair few hours doing nothing at all. The **harbour** is a great place for a walk, full of fishing boats dangling dozens of high-wattage bulbs, used to lure squid to their doom. To its right-hand side is a ramshackle group of corrugated metal cabins dangling precariously from the hillside; from here there's a good view of the harbour, and the tall finger of stone that protrudes through its outer wall, called "**Candlestick Rock**", the village's defining landmark. You can take a stroll up to the rock, on the way to the harbour passing two **large concrete penguins** whose decidedly phallic appendages are used to load material onto waiting boats – if you can see one in action, it's likely to be the funniest moment of your stay.

Around the island

For those wishing to escape the main villages and see the rest of Ulleungdo there are two ways of doing so: ferry, bus and taxi. Using the former it's possible to take one of the round-island **ferry tours** (W18,000) which run nine times a day in the summer, and twice a day at other times, and take two hours to sail around the island. Another service heads to **Jukdo** (W10,000), a smaller island north-east of Ulleungdo, and a perfect place for a walk and a picnic.

Others could travel by taxi – just about affordable for a group of three or more – or make use of the frustratingly infrequent **buses** that rattle along Ulleungdo's only main road. These leave from outside the tourist information booth in Dodong-ni, and travel around the island clockwise to Cheonbu, a port fifty minutes away on the northern coast, before heading back again an hour later – Ulleungdo's tourist office will be able to provide you with a Korean-only schedule. With so few buses, and around two hours in between each service, it's hard to put together a full day-trip. A few small settlements are dotted on the coast along the way, and it's possible to stay at some – **Tonggumi** is a small but delightful village, and a popular place to fish or dive. Prices, including wet-suit hire, are usually around W100,000 per person. **Namyang** is a similarly laid-back fishing village a little further on, with amazing views across the ocean from the slopes above. Continuing on the bus, the road rises uphill, passes through a tunnel, and then dives down into **Taeha**, a port on the far northwestern cape of the island. Within hiking distance of this village are Seongha Shrine, some interesting rock formations, and a remote lighthouse. Rising up again, the road finally descends to Ulleungdo's northern coast, and the twin harbour towns of **Hyeonpo** and **Cheonbu**. Like all of the places mentioned here, they're small and bursting with character, and their secluded location on an already remote island means that few foreigners have ever made it this far.

To the north of the island lies a geographic anomaly – **Naribunji**. It is the only flat space on Ulleungdo, a dreamy patchwork of fields entirely encircled by mountains. To get there, you'll have to get off the coastal road bus at Cheonbu, where a 4WD will be waiting to take passengers over the hill to Naribunji (W1000). This is short but pleasantly bumpy journey: one traveller reported having to help the vehicle back onto the road with sticks and stones after it ploughed into the roadside vegetation and lost traction.

Naribunji is a fantastic place to spend a day or two walking through fields, taking in the surrounding forest, or doing absolutely nothing – those who have spent a few months teaching at a *hagwon* on the mainland will know just how necessary this can be. It's also a good start or finish point for a **hiking trip** up and over the mountain; you may notice cable-car wires heading up into the hills, but unfortunately, this service is for the use of local military only.

Eating

There are plenty of **restaurants** in both Dodong-ni and Jeodong-ni, mostly centred around fare culled from the sea, though less fishy things are available – the island's most famous edible product is, in fact, **pumpkin taffy**. Visitors used to Korea's open-all-hours culture may be in for a surprise, as even in Dodong-ni everywhere may be shut by 9pm. The most interesting places to eat in both main villages are the **raw fish outlets** – in good weather, a few cling limpet-like to the cliffs near Dodong-ni's ferry terminal, and there's an upper-floor parade above the one in Jeodong-ni. Selections at both depend on the season, the weather and the fortunes of local fishermen, but W10,000 per person should be enough for a belly full of fish; your food will be killed and sliced up in front of you, and some of the hardier creatures will still be wriggling on the plate. There are more regular restaurants around, too, and those who have made it this far should know a few Korean dishes by now – a good thing, as English-language menus are nonexistent. Alternatively, there's an Italian restaurant in Dodong-ni or a bakery next to the bus stop in Jeodong-ni.

99 Sikdang This friendly restaurant has whipped up quite an army of fans, following appearances on Korean TV. Prices have stayed low, and there's an English menu of sorts, including spicy fish soup, steamed rice with mussels, and the house special – spicy grilled squid known as *ojingeo bulgogi*. All meals come with seasonal side dishes.

Eddiang Under the *Ulleung Hotel*, this homely place offers spaghetti, steak and pizza, making it the perfect respite from the ubiquitous fish restaurants. Prices are also reasonable.

Hyangu-chon Way up near the *Skyhill* at the top of Dodong-ni, this is a great place to tuck into filling *sanchae bibimbap* – mountain vegetables on rice – though most are here to barbeque beef or pork and throw it back with a few shots of soju. *Yak-so jumulleok* is a popular dish; this is beef from cows raised on medicinal herbs and plants.

Gyeongsangnam-do

Korea's most southeastern province, **GYEONGSANGNAM-DO**, also known as Gyeongnam, is as closely connected to the sea as its northern neighbour,

Gyeongbuk, is to the land. The southern coast splinters off into an assortment of cliffs, peninsulas and **islands**, many of the latter preserved as the **Hallyeo Haesang National Park**. Here you can head by ferry to minute specks of land where life goes on as it has for decades, free of the smoke, noise and neon often hard to escape on the mainland. This greenery is not just confined to the province's saltier fringes – **Jirisan**, to the west, is the largest national park in the country. It's a real favourite among hikers, and not just for its size, or its beauty – a chain of **shelters** runs across the park's central spine, making multi-day hikes a possibility. These may well be Gyeongnam's most atmospheric places to stay; the park also has a small **bear population**. Despite these earthy features, Gyeongnam is no natural paradise. Nearly eight million people live in the area, making it the most densely populated part of the country outside Greater Seoul. Many of the cities are drab, ugly places – Ulsan is home to a million, while the knot of Masan, Changwon and Jinhae beats even that when combined, yet there's little to see in any of them. It's something of a relief, then, that **Busan**, the second biggest city in the land, is a fantastic place, with good beaches, excellent nightlife, and a friendly, earthy nature.

Busan

Those who've visited Barcelona, Osaka, Marseille or Melbourne will know what to expect of **BUSAN**. A serious victim of second-city syndrome, a strange mix of inferiority and superiority complexes, Busan has emerged from the provincial shadows full of pep and character. By turns brackish, glamorous, clumsy and charismatic, it prides itself on simply being different from Seoul, and many travellers end up preferring it to the capital. Like the cities listed above, the locals alone make it worth a visit: more characterful than those from the capital, Busanites talk almost as fast as their city moves, spouting provincial slang in a distinctive staccato that many foreigners initially mistake for Japanese.

Busan is not just Korea's second-biggest city, but the fifth-largest container **port** in the world – its salty fringes tumble away into a colourful, confetti-like jumble of corrugated containers. This connection to the sea is evident at two of Busan's most visited areas – **Haeundae**, a beach area sprinkled with five-star hotels, and **Jagalchi Fish Market**, quite possibly the smelliest place on earth. Those with calories to burn will have temples and mountains to amble around, or you can shop till you drop at a variety of places from grimy markets to designer shopping malls. In the evenings, the setting sun throws the ships into cool silhouette on a sea of gold, and Busan's youth come out to paint the town red. While the nightlife here is second only to that in Seoul, for sheer verve there's no contest – Busan is the champion.

Some history

Even before it became the whirring economic dynamo that it is today, Busan played a pivotal role in the country's history. Though it was once part of the short-lived **Gaya kingdom** swallowed whole by the Silla dynasty (see box p.199), it was at that time little more than a collection of fishing villages. In the fifteenth century it benefited from its proximity to Japan, when a trade treaty opened it up as a port to international trade – up until that point, most goods had been leaving the area as loot on pirate ships. This competitive advantage promptly swung around and hit Busan squarely in the face when the city was attacked by the Japanese in 1592; under the astute leadership of **Admiral Yi Sun-shin** (see box, p.289) damage was limited, but still devastating.

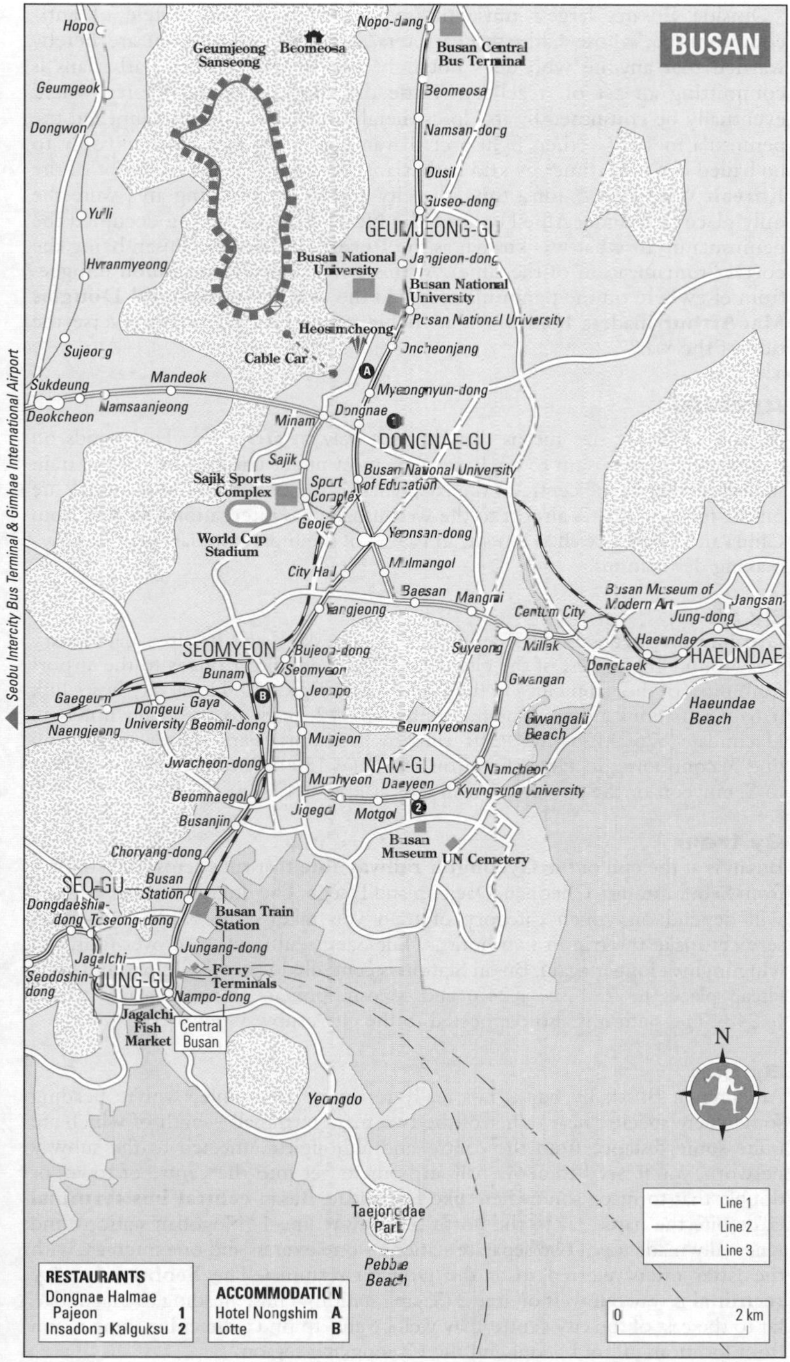
BUSAN
Seobu Intercity Bus Terminal & Gimhae International Airport
Hopo
Geumgeok
Dongwon
Yulli
Hwanmyeong
Sujeong
Sukdeung
Deokcheon
Mandeok
Namsaanjeong
Geumjeong Sanseong
Beomeosa
Nopo-dong
Busan Central Bus Terminal
Beomeosa
Namsan-dong
Dusil
Guseo-dong
GEUMJEONG-GU
Busan National University
Jangjeon-dong
Busan National University
Pusan National University
Heosimcheong
Cable Car
Oncheonjang
Myeongnyun-dong
Dongnae
Minam
DONGNAE-GU
Sajik
Sajik Sports Complex
Sport Complex
Busan National University of Education
World Cup Stadium
Geoje
Yeonsan-dong
Mulmangol
City Hall
Baesan
Mangmi
Yangjeong
Busan Museum of Modern Art
Jangsan
Centum City
Jung-dong
Haeundae
HAEUNDAE
Suyeong
Millak
Dongbaek
SEOMYEON
Bujeon-dong
Seomyeon
Bunam
Jeonpo
Gwangan
Gaegeum
Dongeui University
Gaya
Naengjeong
Beomil-dong
Haeundae Beach
Gwangalli Beach
Geumnyeonsan
Munjeon
Jwacheon-dong
NAM-GU
Munhyeon
Daeyeon
Namcheon
Kyungsung University
Beomnaegol
Jigegol
Motgol
Busanjin
Busan Museum
UN Cemetery
Choryang-dong
SEO-GU
Busan Station
Dongdaeshin-dong
Toseong-dong
Busan Train Station
Jungang-dong
Jagalchi
Seodoshin-dong
JUNG-GU
Ferry Terminals
Nampo-dong
Jagalchi Fish Market
Central Busan
N
Yeongdo
Taejongdae Park
Pebble Beach
Line 1
Line 2
Line 3
RESTAURANTS
Dongnae Halmae Pajeon 1
Insadong Kalguksu 2
ACCOMMODATION
Hotel Nongshim A
Lotte B
0
2 km
Geojedo
Japan

Outside Busan's largest museum (see p.245) is a stone "stele of anti-compromise", whose Chinese characters read "All countrymen are hereby warned that anyone who does not fight against the western barbarians is committing an act of treachery." Little did they know that Korea would eventually be consumed by its closest neighbour – the Japanese annexed the peninsula in 1910 – then fight a civil war against its own brothers, only to be bailed out both times by said barbarians. Busan was at the forefront of the **Korean War**; indeed, for a time, the city and its surrounding area were the only places left under Allied control, the North Koreans having occupied the peninsula up to what was known as the **Pusan Perimeter** (Pusan being the correct romanization of the time). At this point, up to four million refugees from elsewhere on the peninsula crowded the city, before **General Douglas MacArthur** made a bold move at Incheon (see box, p.154) to reverse the tide of the war.

Arrival

Busan's unwieldy size means that the best way to arrive largely depends on exactly where you want to go. In general, most prefer **train** to **bus** as the train station is right in the centre of the city, whereas the two main bus terminals are on the fringes. Busan's airport to the west usually has international **flights** from China and Japan, as well as Russia, and a few of the more popular Asian holiday-making destinations.

By air

Gimhae airport is Busan's connection to the skies, and lies in a flat estuary area around 15km west of the city centre. There are direct **buses** to the airport from most of the main cities in the Gyeongsang region, and local city buses link it to destinations around Busan. Shuttle bus #2 heads to the main hotels in Haeundae (W6000), while #307 runs to the Sports Park subway station on line 3, continuing to Deokcheon on line 2 (W1500). A **taxi** from the airport to Seomyeon or the city centre will cost at least W15,000.

By train

Busan is at the end of the **Gyeongbu railway line** that runs across the country from Seoul through Cheonan, Daejeon and Daegu. The duration of the journey will depend on which category of train you take – the KTX high-speed services make the trip in two hours, while Saemaeul trains take over four, and Mugunghwa longer again. Busan Station is centrally located, and surrounded by cheap places to stay (see p.243) and a cosmopolitan range of places to eat (p.248). The station is also connected to the city's subway network.

By bus

Arriving in Busan by bus is not really recommended, unless you're heading somewhere specific near either of the two main terminals – both of which are quite some distance from the centre, and although connected to the subway network, you'll need to allow half an hour to get into the centre of town, or double that to reach somewhere like Haeundae. Busan **central bus terminal** is, despite the name, far to the north on subway line 1 (Nogodan station), and is actually made up of two separate stations – one express and one intercity, with the latter often referred to as the Dongbu terminal. The **Seobu intercity terminal** is way out west on line 2 (Sasang station). Those heading to Haeundae, far to the east of the city centre, may well be able to find a direct bus connection from locations around Seoul and the Gyeongsang region.

By ferry

No doubt about it – the most spectacular way to arrive into Busan is by sea. The city has two **ferry** terminals; one is for international services, the other for domestic, and both are near Jungang-dong subway station in the centre of town,

Busan	
Busan	부산
Beomeosa	범어사
Busan Museum	부산 박물관
Busan Museum of Modern Art	부산 시립 현대 미술관
Busan Tower	부산 타워
Geumjeong Sanseong	금정산성
Haeundae	해운대
Heosimcheong	허심청
Jagalchi Fish Market	자갈치 시장
Seomyeon	서면
UN Cemetery	유엔 기념공원
Yeongdo	영도
Yongdusan Park	용두산 공원
Transport	
Busan Station	부산역
Domestic Ferry Terminal	부산 여객 터미날
International Ferry Terminal	부산 국제 여객 터미날
Accommodation	
Blue Backpackers Hostel	블루 백팩커스 호스텔
Grand Blue Beachtel	그랜드 블루 비치텔
Gwangjang Tourist Hotel	광장 관광 호텔
Hotel Busan Arirang	호텔 부산 아리랑
Hotel Commodore	호텔 코모도
Hotel Nongshim	호텔 농심
Hwankum Hotel	환금 호텔
Lotte Hotel	롯데 호텔
Paradise Hotel	파라다이스 호텔
Phoenix Hotel	피닉스 호텔
Saehan Hotel	새한 호텔
Seacloud Hotel	씨클라우드 호텔
Westin Chosun	웨스틴 조선
Restaurants	
Dongnae Halmae Pajeon	동래 할매 파전
Donjangsa	돈장사
Harbour Town	하버 타운
Insadong Kalguksu	인사동 칼국수
I-rae	이래
Minami	미나미
Omutopia	오므토피아
Pocheonidong Eol-eum Makkeolli-wa Saengtak	포천이동얼음 막걸리와 생탁
Pojangmacha	포장마차
Shobu Izakaya	쇼부 이자까야
Sutbul Galbi	숯불 갈비
Wonhyangjae	원향재
Yugane	유가네

just minutes from each other by foot. At the time of writing, there were connections from Fukuoka, Shimonoseki and Osaka in Japan, with the first especially popular with *hagwon* teachers heading to that city's Korean embassy on visa runs. There are also domestic connections to Jeju Island (see p.353), and Geojedo, a pretty island a short way to the west (p.251).

Orientation and information

With buildings sprawling across the whole horizon, filling the gaps between the city's mountains and swamping some of the smaller hills entirely, Busan can be quite confusing for the first-time visitor. The de facto centre of the city, known as **Jung-gu**, is the area heading south from the train station down to Jagalchi Fish Market; on the way, you'll pass the ferry terminals, Busan Tower and Nampo-dong's maze of shops, cinemas, markets and restaurants. A short way north of the train station is trendy **Seomyeon**, a brand-name shopper's paradise, but also home to some of the earthiest restaurants, and excellent nightlife. A way east of here you'll find **Haeundae**, a fascinating beach area that's home to rich Koreans and five-star hotels, but still manages to retain much of its fishing village character.

For a city of such size, and with so many foreign visitors, Busan has a surprisingly poor network of **tourist information offices**. The most useful one is in the train station (Ⓣ051/441-6565): you're unlikely to find any English-speakers at the offices in Haeundae and Seomyeon. Five-star hotels can come in very handy, but if you need some English-language information in a hurry, it's best to call Ⓣ1330 (though add an area code if using a mobile phone – Busan's is 051). There's also a special Foreigners' Service Centre in Choryang 1-dong (Ⓣ051/441-3121).

Accommodation

Unlike most Korean cities, Busan has plenty of choice at the **top end** of the accommodation range. The five-stars are almost all located in **Haeundae**, a beach district far to the east of the centre, but here you'll also be able to find *minbak* and *yeoinsuk*, simple guesthouses that are dirt-cheap for most of the year,

Busan festivals

Busan plays host to an incredible number of **festivals**, though many of them are quite incredibly bad – those dedicated to anchovy-rubbing or egg-rolling might sound comical, but they're really not worth the effort. However, there are a number of good ones – the most popular is PIFF, the **Pusan International Film Festival** (Ⓦwww.piff.org), which takes place over a week or so each October. One of the biggest such events in Asia, it draws the cream of the continent's talent, and has recently expanded its scope to please non-mainstreamers too – you wouldn't have seen a Tajikistani black-and-white back in 2002, but now, you never know. Most of the action takes place around Nampo-dong and Haeundae, with the latter a great place to star-spot – you might find yourself pitching ideas to a director over *soju*. Also interesting are the **Busan Biennale** (Ⓦwww.busanbiennale.org), a festival of contemporary art that takes place on even-numbered years, though in seemingly random months, and the **International Rock Festival** (Ⓦrockfestival.co.kr), which takes place in early August on Dadaepo Beach. The **Polar Bear Swim Contest** sees participants splash through the cold Haeundae waters each January, and is followed by the **Straw-Heap Burning Festival**, an event that does what it says in the title, ostensibly to ward off evil. Worth mentioning for the name alone is the **Mass-Media Cutting-Edge Marine Fireworks Festival**, an event that sees things go bang over Gwangalli Beach each November.

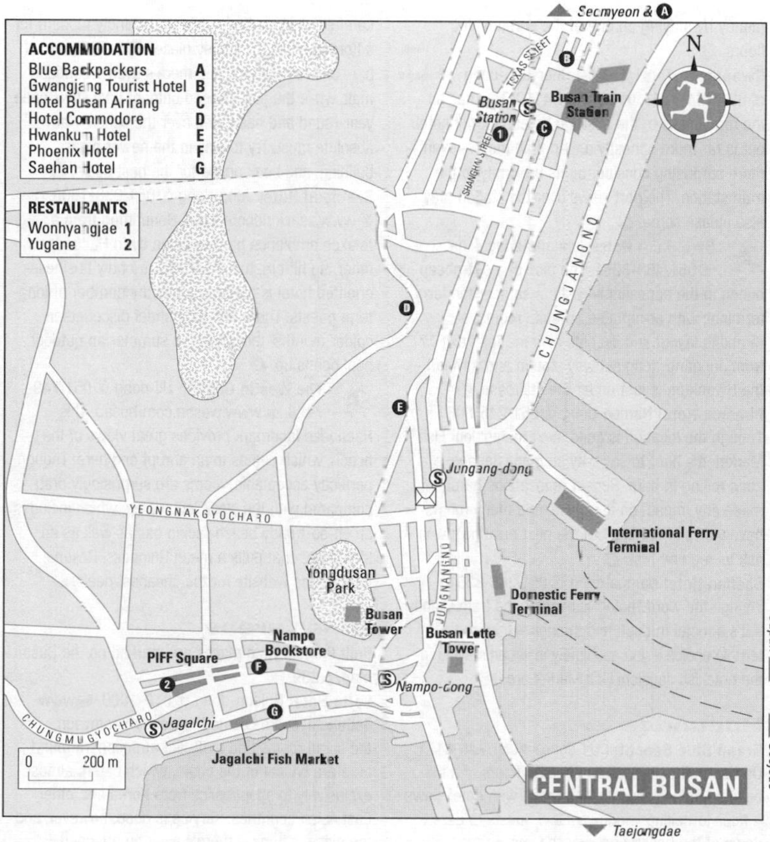

but raise their prices for the summer season. There are cheap motels all over the city; if you want to go out at night you're best basing yourself in Seomyeon or around the university drinking areas (see p.249), whereas sightseers should head for the cheap areas around the **train station** or **ferry terminal**. Those who really want to save cash can get a nights sleep for less than W10,000 in a *jjimjil-bang* (see box, p.41); two of the most convenient are *Vesta*, east of the main hotel district in Haeundae, and *Nokju* in central Seomyeon.

Central Busan

Blue Backpackers Hostel Beomcheon 2-dong ⓣ051/634-3962. Essentially a regular Korean apartment kitted out with bunkbeds and facilities for backpackers, the friendliness of the hosts makes this a popular place despite the circuitous arrival – cross the footbridge from exit three at Beomnaegol subway station, turn left then across the bridge, and it's in apartment block 106 on the right, apartment number 1802. Dorm beds ❶.

Hotel Busan Arirang Choryang-dong ⓣ051/463-5001, ⓕ051/463-2800. Just as close to the train station as the *Gwangjang*, and equally good value. Some rooms here have computers and free Internet access. ❹

Hotel Commodore Yeongju-dong ⓣ051/466-9101. Visible from the port, this distinctive fusion of skyscraper and temple is highly popular with Japanese tourists and a short taxi-ride from the main train station. The sliding windows are a nice feature, even more so given the views – Busan's crane-filled port on one side, and what passes for a Korean version of Naples on the other. Discounts are available outside peak-season, and you'll save money by staying on one of the unrenovated floors. ❻

Gwangjang Tourist Hotel Choryang-dong ⓣ051/464-3141, ⓕ051/464-4150. This has all the drawbacks of the average Korean tourist hotel, but is far more honestly priced than most – even more surprising considering its proximity to the train station. The port views over the station may also please some. ❹

Hwankum Hotel Jungang-dong 4-ga ⓣ051/463-3851. The pick of a dirt-cheap bunch in the appealingly rustic area near the ferry terminal, with acceptable en-suite rooms, a rambling layout and likeable owners. Take exit 17 from Jungang-dong subway station and turn left – the Hwankum is just under the staircase. ❶

Phoenix Hotel Nampo-dong ⓣ051/245-8061. Though the location is good, next to Jagalchi Fish Market, it's hard to say why so many Japanese keep rolling in here. Recent renovations hardly made any impact on the place, and many rooms have views of nothing but the next building's wall – ask to see one first. ❹

Saehan Hotel Nampo-dong ⓣ051/246-6251. Though the word "hotel" is bending the truth slightly – it's a motel through and through – this isn't a terrible choice if you absolutely insist on staying in the brackish Jagalchi Fish Market area. ❷

Haeundae

Grand Blue Beachtel Uil-dong ⓣ051/746-8171. On the tenth, eleventh and twelfth floors of a tall building, this is essentially a motel with hotel views – floor-to-ceiling windows allow guests to gaze down at the beach and over the sea. Reasonably good value, unless you stay on a weekend, and some interesting bars and restaurants are just an elevator ride away. ❺

Paradise Hotel Jung-dong ⓣ051/749-2111, ⓦwww.paradisehotel.co.kr. With widescreen televisions in the rooms, stylish lighting in the corridors and W6,000,000 suites, the *Paradise* has been carefully designed in a style refreshingly modern for a Korean hotel. It's a busy place with all manner of bars and restaurants, and there's even a boutique mall, while the pine-fringed outdoor pool stays open year-round and has views over the beach – an absolute must. Try to stay in the newer main building, and book online for the best deals. ❽

Seacloud Hotel Jung-dong ⓣ051/933-1000, ⓦwww.seacloudhotel.com. Benefitting from a relaxed ambience hard to come by in Haeundae's other big hitters, this smart-but-friendly business-oriented hotel is home to a healthy number of long-term guests. There are substantial discounts in colder months, though in the summer an outdoor pool opens up. ❽

The Westin Chosun Uil-dong ⓣ051/749-7428, ⓦwww.westin.com/busan. This Haeundae landmark provides great views of the beach, which comes to an abrupt end here. Though perfectly acceptable, rooms are surprisingly drab compared with the sleek lobby area, which includes an oh-so-trendy beach-facing bar, as well as an Irish "pub" that pulls a mean Guinness. Reserve through the website for the cheapest deals. ❽

Other areas

Both the following places are marked on the Busan map, p.239.

Lotte Hotel Bujeon-dong ⓣ810-1000, ⓦwww.lottehotel.co.kr. Located in trendy Seomyeon, the small rooms and mall-like atmosphere found here are typical of the chain, which caters almost exclusively to shopaholics from Korea and other East Asian countries; service is good, however, and the place is huge – there's even an attached shopping mall. ❽

Hotel Nongshim Oncheon-dong ⓣ051/550-2100, ⓕ051/550-2105. Rooms are modest for the price, though you're paying for the hotel's proximity to Heosimcheong, the mammoth hot springs complex next door (p.248). Hefty discounts are usually available from the rack price. ❽

Downtown

The city's **downtown** spreads south from the train station to Jagalchi Fish Market. This area, often referred to as Jung-gu, is dripping with character but rather run-down, though it's likely to undergo substantial transformation in the near future, having been earmarked for renovation by the city council. The powers that be are officially aiming for a Sydney-style harbour area, but even the most rosy-spectacled official would privately admit that this is an impossible dream. One interesting development here is the **Busan Lotte Tower**, which could be the start of a mushrooming series of super-tall skyscrapers – scheduled for completion in 2009, but almost certain to be delayed, it's expected to rise to 510m in height, surely high enough to put it into the world's top ten for a few months at least. Traffic around here can be intense, though travellers can escape this – or inclement weather – by making use of an **underground walkway** that follows the subway line all the way from Jungang-dong station to Nampo-dong, one stop down the line, a route studded all the way with cheap shopping stalls and snack bars.

Heading across the main road from Busan train station, you'll come to **Shanghai Street**, a pedestrianized "Chinatown" road filled with restaurants, and marked with the oriental gates mandatory for such areas. This joins onto **Texas Street**, which has yet more places to eat – predominantly Russian and South-East Asian – but it's not all about the food. This area rivals Haeundae for the title of most cosmopolitan part of the city, though has an entirely different air to it: whereas Haeundae draws in beach bums and the convention crowd, here you may find yourself rubbing shoulders with Russian sailors, American soldiers, Filipino restaurateurs and lost tourists, and it is a great place to people-watch.

Yongdusan Park

Until the completion of the *Lotte*, you'll have to make do with **Busan Tower** (9am–10pm; W5000), a comparatively puny structure, though one still affording **excellent views** of Busan's boat-filled surroundings. This long-standing city landmark is now crying out for renovation; this will hopefully be forthcoming, as Seoul recently gave its own tower a makeover, and Busan's city government is notoriously competitive towards the capital. The tower is the crowning glory of **Yongdusan Park**, a popular area for elderly walkers. The top of the park is already high enough for good views – take an early morning walk to the top, buy some instant *ramyeon* from the convenience store and watch the sun break through the mist. There's also an **aquarium** (same hours) near the base of the tower, and accessible on the same ticket, but this is hardly worth a visit, especially as all the fish you could ever want to see are just down the road at Jagalchi Fish Market.

Nampo-dong and Jagalchi Fish Market

To the south of the park is **Nampo-dong**, one of the city's main shopping and dining areas. Less modern than other parts of Busan, but catching up fast, the tiny alleys and markets make aimless wandering quite pleasant. The foremost sight in the area, and one of the most atmospheric places in the whole country, is **Jagalchi Fish Market**. A Busan institution, it's primarily for locals but many foreign visitors to Busan pop by for a look around. The market itself is a mix of outdoor and covered stalls, as well as two large buildings that house some interesting restaurants – see p.248 for details.

East of the centre

In **Nam-gu**, a district between Busan Station and Haeundae, lie a couple of sights commemorating Busan's interesting past. A short walk south of Daeyeon subway station is **Busan Museum** (daily 9am–6pm; W500), which charts the local area's history and its remains from the Neolithic era to the present day; interesting exhibits include a **gilt-bronze crown** once worn by a Silla king, and a **standing Bodhisattva** of similar age and material. More recent history is generally presented in diorama form, with one of the more interesting displays showing Busan Station in the 1920s; the building has, of course, changed somewhat. Unfortunately, the more modern part of the exhibit leaves a rather bad taste in the mouth, stemming from the sad inevitability of the museum's choice to focus on the Japanese occupation rather than the Korean War. In the museum, there's just a single wall commemorating the tens of thousands of foreign troops who died here when Korean fought Korean; a pattern repeated all over the country – in classrooms as well as museums – but here it's at its most galling considering that many of the fallen are lying just outside in the **UN Cemetery**. Here you'll find over two thousand dead soldiers from Britain, Turkey, Canada, Australia, the Netherlands, France, the USA, New Zealand, South Africa and Norway; many more, of course, were never found, and those from Belgium, Ethiopia, Colombia, Thailand, Greece, India and the Philippines, as well as the vast majority of Americans, were repatriated. The photographic exhibition on site provides a small, mute tribute, but mercifully the grounds are welcoming and pretty.

Haeundae

On the eastern side of Busan, and about 25 minutes away by subway, **HAEUNDAE** is without a doubt the most popular **beach** in Korea. But whether it's the best or not is open to question – in the summer it draws in families, teens and bronzed beach bums by the bucketload, though at only two kilometres in length, space here is tighter than a Brazilian's Speedos, while the sand gradually becomes a composite of cigarette butts, firework ash and other debris. Like it or not, it's an interesting place – Haeundae is not just the name of the beach, but also its surrounding area, one that attracts all sorts throughout the year: the **Busan Film Festival**, one of the biggest in Asia, rolls into town each October with a cast of directors, actors, wannabes and hangers-on; the super-fit come to splash and dash out a **triathlon** course each October; hungry Koreans come to chow down **raw fish** and throw back a few bottles of *soju* from the comfort of a plastic chair; affluent expats, trendy locals and the international convention crowd populate the many luxury apartments and **five-star hotels**, while youngsters come from all over the country to spend a starry night on the beach. If you catch it at the right time, Haeundae can be quite magical.

The **beach** itself is good for swimming; tubes and boats are also available to rent, and the purchase of puny, multi-round fireworks is near compulsory. There are also a couple of sights by the shore: situated on the beach is **Busan Aquarium** Mon–Fri 10am–7pm, Sat & Sun 9am–9pm; W15,000; Ⓦwww.busanaquarium.com), where three million litres of water suspend up to 30,000 fish. Penguins and crocodiles are also on the complex, plus a touch pool for the kids. There's an underwater tunnel for those who want to see fish from below, or you can pay an extra W5000 to ride a glass-bottomed boat and see them from above instead. At the end of the beach, past a clutch of raw fish stalls and behind the *Westin Chosun*, there's **Dongbaek Park**, a pleasant place for a stroll, skate or bike-ride, while one subway station away from Haeundae is the **Busan Museum of Modern Art**, an interesting gallery that keeps its exhibitions fresh; get off at the station of the same name – take exit number five and walk for a hundred metres or so.

Yeongdo

Facing Jagalchi Fish Market in downtown Busan is **Yeongdo**; although it's technically an island, its double-bridge connection to Nampo-dong makes it feel more like a peninsula. There's not much to see here, but a walk around **Taejongdae**, a pretty park at the far end of the island, is worthwhile. A number of bus routes head from Busan's main centres to the entrance, including #88 from Seomyeon, via the train station and ferry terminals, and #30 from Nampo-dong. From here, regular train-shaped shuttle buses run to **Pebble Beach**, a rocky outcrop at the very end of the island, but as roads are otherwise

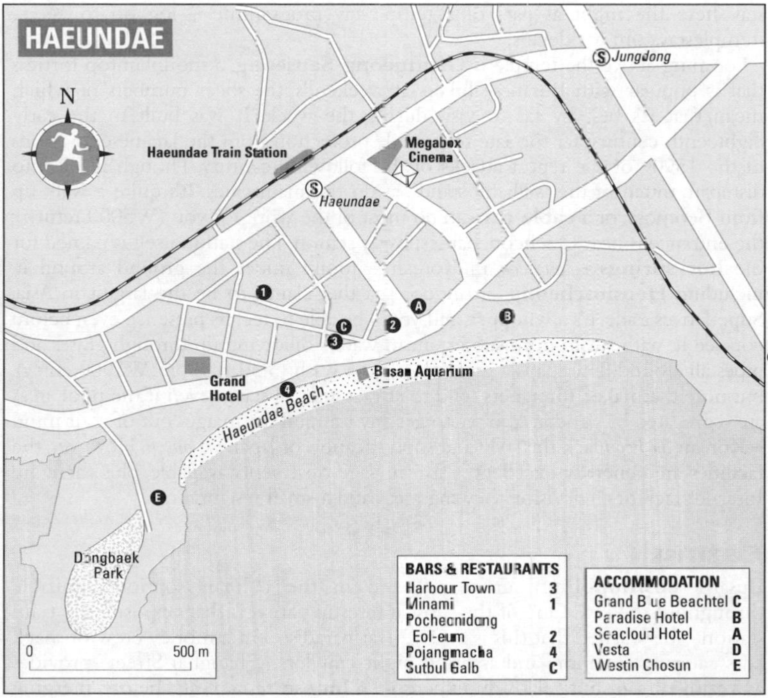

empty it makes a pleasant walk, particularly at sunset, when the sun sets over the mainland peninsula west of Yeongdo, casting the ships into silhouette on a golden sea.

Northern Busan

A half-hour subway ride to the north of central Busan, you'll find one of the best sights in the city. The temple of **Beomeosa** dates from 678 and occupies a spectacular setting high above town, and is a popular choice for foreigners looking to **templestay**. Despite the age of the complex, most of its buildings were built much later, the result of the occasional fire or destruction during the Japanese invasion. The first main gate, Iljumun, dates from 1781 and continues to carry its age well, the eaves radiating rich colour from its four pillars. Ascending past a patch of bamboo, you'll pass through four bearded guardians to the main concourse, and Daeungjeon, the main hall and scene of fervent morning prayer. In the courtyard there's a three-storey stone pagoda dating from the ninth century. However, the main appeal of the place lies not in its buildings, but in its **mountainous setting** – the forested slopes are impressive enough, and there's a surprising preponderance of deciduous trees for a Korean mountain area, providing obvious spectral benefits in the autumn. On the complex itself, smaller trees and shrubs lend their own spindly nuances to an enchanting scene. The temple is a 3km uphill walk from a subway station of the same name, though you can chalk most of this off by making use of the **buses** just uphill from the station, which leave every fifteen minutes. Many choose to stay here the night as part of a templestay programme – log on to ⓦeng.templestay.com for details.

Looming above the temple is **Geumjeong Sanseong**, a mountaintop fortress that is popular with Busanese hikers at weekends, the sheer numbers of which mean that it's best by far to visit during the week. It was built in the early eighteenth century, far too late to provide protection from the Japanese invasions of the 1590s, or the repeat attacks of the following century. Though it fell into disrepair, much of the wall still stands, as do the main gates. It's quite a walk up from Beomosa, or a **cable car** can do most of the work for you (W5000 return); the entrance is near Oncheonchang subway station. The station itself is named for the **hot springs** – *oncheon* in Korean – found under the ground around it, including **Heosimcheong**, an indoor spa that claims to be the largest in Asia. Superlatives aside, it's a whopper, and you'll be able to feel its presence even before you see it, with steam from subterranean waters billowing up through grates and pipes all around. The spa is a great place for a wash (5.30am–9pm; W7900 entry), but note that naked foreigners tend to attract a lot of stares, even if the pool areas are segregated by gender. Also try to get any tranquil spa images out of your mind – Korean *oncheon* lack the style and sophistication of Japanese *onsen*. However, the facilities are generally excellent, with massage treatments available, plus there are Internet facilities, television viewing areas and a small restaurant.

Eating

Busan's **cosmopolitan** air is reflected in the culinary options available throughout the city. One of the most interesting areas is that opposite the train station – be warned that this is no five-star paradise, but a motley crew of snack bars catering to sailors and assorted night-crawlers. "Shanghai Street" provides a wealth of safe but relatively expensive **Chinese** restaurants, before merging effortlessly into "Texas Street", home to a lower-key choice of outlets; despite the American name, the most appealing food here lies in the cheap, cheerful Filipino snack-halls. You'll notice a fair few **Russian** restaurants, but those hankering for a bit of *borshch* will be disappointed to find that these concentrate squarely on alcohol, primarily catering to drunken sailors of an evening. The area running from the station to Jagalchi Fish Market is uninspired, though any of the Korean staples are easy to track down, while the student areas (see "Nightlife", opposite) are predictably cheap, as are the tiny, *galbi*-filled side streets around Seomyeon. Those looking for something a little classier should head to one of the five-star hotels around Haeundae beach.

Central Busan

Jagalchi Market Nampo-dong. One of Busan's foremost attractions most of the dishes here will be utterly confusing to the average Westerner. Easiest on both brain and palate are the fried slabs of tuna (*chamchi*) served at the outdoor stalls (W5000 for four). The truly brave should make their way to one of the two large buildings for some raw seafood action. The smaller, older market is more atmospheric, its ground floor swimming with seawater, and wooden yellow booths surrounded by tanks and baskets. The upstairs floor is more like a restaurant, though the fare is the same – W10,000 to W15,000 should be enough for a bellyful of fish.

Wonhyangjae Shanghai Street. This Chinese restaurant is one of several good options on this interesting road near Busan Station. Meals are fairly pricey by Korean standards – figure on at least W15,000 per head – though simple rice and noodle dishes are delicious and cheap.

Yugane Nampo-dong 5-ga. If you don't fancy raw fish, you could do worse than heading to this large, fresh hall, full to the brim of an evening with the young, hungry and budget-conscious. Staff will do the necessary chopping and mixing on your table – meat and fried rice are yours for around W4000, or chicken *galbi* for W5500, and unlike most places that serve the latter, single diners are welcome. There are branches around the city, including one in Seomyeon.

Haeundae

Harbour Town Uil-dong. A perfect fallback for those who can't stand Korean food, or at least need a short holiday from it, this large complex houses a *Starbucks*, an *Outback Steakhouse* and a *TGI Friday's*, as well as *Ganga*, a worthy Indian restaurant.

Minami Jungil-dong. Set back a couple of streets from the beach behind the *Grand Hotel* is this approximation of a Japanese *izakaya*, where you can throw back fish, beer and *sake* till morning. The place really comes to life during the film festival, when it often becomes a mingling place for the movie crowd.

Pocheonidong Eol-eum Makkeolli-wa Saengtak Jungil-dong. The colossal name hides a high-class *makkeolli* joint, but though most head to this bar-cum-restaurant opposite the *Seacloud Hotel* for the hooch, the purchase of expensive, but well-prepared, side dishes is pretty much obligatory.

Pojangmacha Beachside. A quintessential Korean dining experience – raw fish and assorted seafood served up by an equally salty *ajumma*. Look for the tarpaulin-covered stands sheltering tanks of fish, and prepare your stomach – some of your prey may still be moving.

Sutbul Galbi Uil-dong. On the fifth floor of a building that also houses the *Grand Blue Beachtel*, and with similar views of sea and beach, this *galbi* restaurant is open around the clock. Portions are W6000 per diner, with a two-person minimum.

Seomyeon

I-rae Bucheon-dong. Highly popular, though the Korean-only menu is almost entirely centred around *juk-bal*, which translates as "cow foot" (look out for the stylized hoof on the outside) with a medium-sized portion big enough to feed two. This restaurant can become rather boisterous of an evening – there can be few better places to get a handle on the distinctive Busanese dialect.

Omutopia Bucheon-dong. *Omurice* is a Japanese attempt at culinary fusion now popular in Korea, whereby something like a portion of rice is wrapped in something resembling an omelette, then usually covered in tomato ketchup. Here, mercifully, you'll be able to try other sauces and side-servings, starting at around W5000 per meal.

Other areas

Dongnae Halmae Pajeon Bokchun-dong. See Busan map, p.239. Way off the beaten tourist track is this fascinating restaurant – despite the modern interior, it has nearly a century of history behind it, and the food is accordingly excellent. People come for the eponymous *pajeon*, a local version of the Korean pancake, and quite possibly the best example of the dish in the country. The restaurant is near the *Dongnae Gucheon* district office, within a W2000 taxi-ride of Dongnae subway station.

Donjangsa Jangjeon-dong. A popular sit-on-the-floor meat house on a side street in front of the Busan National University entrance. Students are no doubt happy with the cheap *samgyeopsal* – pork belly slices that you cook at the table – just W3900 per portion.

Insadong Kalguksu Daeyeon 1-dong. See Busan map, p.239. Near the museum entrance – on the right-hand side of the road heading back to Daeyeon subway station – and well worth hunting down, this friendly, family-run restaurant often has some amazingly cheap deals; though no information is in English, the pictures on the wall come in useful. Usually good value are the *shabu-shabu* sets – a boiling bowl of delicious meat broth, supplemented by excellent side dishes.

Naebang Oncheon-dong. Next door to the *Nongshim Hotel* is one of the city's finest restaurants. Though the interior isn't as pretty as the building's traditional outer styling might suggest, food here is prepared with an attention to detail hard to come by in the Gyeongsang provinces, and more similar to that found in Jeolla-do – sets start at around W80,000 per person, with the fried sea bream and broiled beef especially tasty.

Shobu Izakaya Jangjeon-dong. Ideal for group grazing, this Japanese-style restaurant-cum-bar draws in students from the nearby Busan National University with moderately priced sashimi sets. The picture menus aid foreign diners who can also take advantage of cheap noodle dishes, and there's outdoor seating in warmer months.

Nightlife

Busan has an excellent and varied **night scene**, spread in uneven clumps across various parts of the city – a single evening can see you sipping *soju* over raw fish at sunset, rubbing shoulders with Russian sailors near the train station, throwing back beer with new student friends in one of the university areas, then dancing all night at a hip-hop club. Each of the main nightlife zones has a character of its own, but given the distances between them it pays to plan your night in advance. Some clubs have a cover charge, which is unlikely to be more than W10,000, and very few will close before 4am.

Busan National University

The area around the **university** is obviously popular with local **students**. And although its star is on the wane, it has long been drawing in expats with an interesting collection of **cheap bars**, many of which are hemmed into a tight area north of the subway station on and around Jeonwon 1-gil. At the time of writing, *Basement* was the best of these, with super-friendly staff and fantastic theme nights on Hallowe'en, St. Patrick's Day and the like. Nearby *Monk* has some great live music nights, and between the two relaxed *Crossroads* is often the setting for impromptu jams. In the same area, *Soul Trane* and *Moe's* complete a popular line-up.

Seomyeon

A shopping area by day, Seomyeon can also get quite hectic of an evening, and caters to more of a **dance crowd**, with weekend entry fees of around W10,000 – *Foxy Club* and *Hollywood Star* get jam-packed at weekends with expats, and nearby *New York New York* sometimes transforms from regular beer bar to crowded dance floor.

Kyungsung University

East of Seomyeon is this **up-and-coming** nightlife zone, arguably the most vibrant in the city at the time of writing. Here you'll find *Vinyl Underground*, a bar that hosts occasional movie nights, live music and other events, *Bar Code*, a laid-back and pleasantly pretentious haunt of local artsy folk, and *Birra*, so named as it has anything up to a hundred varieties of bottled beer from around the globe. Many nights start, bizarrely, on the patio outside the *Family Mart*, which has even been the scene of a couple of live music sets – a fantastic place to meet people (if the weather agrees) before putting together a battle plan. From here, a short taxi-ride to the coast will bring you to **Gwangalli Beach**, facing a bridge that becomes a kaleidoscope of colour of an evening, and home to some cool waterfront bars and clubs; these include *Garbage*, a small but trendy bar with plans to move to a bigger place in the pipeline, and *Beach Bikini*, a huge, glass-fronted bar-with-a-view that could be up there with the trendiest in town if they knew how to pick a decent DJ.

Haeundae

Further east again is **Haeundae**, also a beach area and a markedly more expensive place to party than most, though the summer crowds barely seem to notice. Here you can wine and dine at posh hotel bars, including the *Panorama Lounge* and *Kim's* – a trendy wine bar and mock Irish pub, respectively – in the *Westin Chosun*, or sip free cocktails while throwing your money around at the *Paradise Hotel Casino*. Bar *110* is a stylish place on the ninth floor of the building that houses the *Grand Blue Beachtel*, while two floors further down is *Money Money*, a transgender bar. Others seeking tradition, instead of snazz or glam, go for a spot of al fresco *soju*-drinking at the *pojang macha* – raw fish stands – that line the beach.

Around Busan Station

The area opposite Busan's main train station – known as **Texas Street** – is a highly male-oriented haunt of soldiers, sailors and suits flocking to the numerous **hostess bars**, and a sure contender for the seediest district in Korea.

It's still pretty safe, though, and can make for an interesting night out (even for females, though play it safe and don't go unaccompanied).

Listings

Books *Nampo Bookstore*, across the main road from the Jagalchi fish market, has a good selection of books covering Korean language and culture, as well as the usual Rowlings and Grishams.
Cinemas Four large multiscreens stand almost eyeball-to-eyeball on PIFF Square in Nampo-dong. When PIFF rolls into town in October there are also showings at the big cinemas in Haeundae.
Embassies and consulates China, 1418 Ui-dong ⓣ051/743-7984; Japan, 1147-11 Choryang-dong ⓣ051/465-5101; Russia, 10F Korea Exchange Bank BD, 89-1 Jungang-dong 4-ga ⓣ051/441-1104.
Hospitals Pusan National University Hospital, 10 1-ga, Ami-dong (ⓣ051/254-0171), is most likely to offer English-language help or try the more central Maryknoll Hospital, 4-ga Daecheong-dong (ⓣ051/465-8801).
Internet PC cafés can be found all over Busan with prices an almost uniform W1000 per hour, with a W1000 minimum fee, and W100 increments added on every six minutes thereafter. There are also coin-operated computers in the train station and ferry terminals.
Post The largest post office is just south of Jungang-dong subway station on the main road (Mon–Fri 9am–8pm, Sat 9am–6pm), but there are smaller branches in every city suburb.
Sport Despite being the country's second-largest city, Busan's sporting teams usually fail to make waves in their national leagues. Busan I'Park is the city's football team, and play in red-and-white-quartered shirts at the Asiad Stadium. The Lotte Giants are one of the best-known baseball teams in Korea, and you can catch them at the Sajik Baseball Stadium.

The South Sea coast and islands

Gyeongnam's south coast is surrounded by squadrons of islands. One of these, **Geojedo**, is the second largest in the country; despite a heavy amount of industrialization, it retains some worthwhile sights, particulary rocky **Haegeumgang**, a coastal formation best viewed by boat. Dozens of other islands have been protected under the salty banner of **Hallyeo Haesang**, one of only three national marine parks in the country; these are best accessed from **Tongyeong**, a coastal city whose square harbour must rank as one of Korea's most scenic.

Geojedo

Just an hour by ferry from Busan, but also connected to the mainland by road, is **GEOJEDO**; measuring forty kilometres by twenty-five, this is Korea's second-largest island, and a craggy paradox of stone and steel. Here can be found large swathes of forest and some of the most impressive **coastal scenery** in the land, but while the island is famed for its natural vistas, parts of it have been shattered by industry – around a third of the world's container ships are built here in the two mammoth **shipyards** that now define the island, and provide much of its employment.The island's main centre of population is **Gohyeon**, tucked in to the north and sheltered from the South Sea. Other sights include **Haegeumgang**, where a simply gorgeous rock formation – quite possibly the most beautiful on the whole Korean coast – rises from the sea just offshore, and **Oedo**, a tiny island covered with flowers, and incredibly popular with Korean tourists.

Gohyeon

During the Korean War, Geojedo was also the base of one of the allied forces' main **prisoner of war camps**, which kept Chinese and North Korean captives

Leaving Busan by ferry

Even though there's plenty to see inside it, **leaving Busan** can be one of the most rewarding experiences of your stay – it's as easy as getting on a **ferry**. Domestic departures invariably head west, so try to get a seat on the right-hand side of the vessel; this will ensure you have sweeping views of the sloping rows of tightly crammed buildings that prompt some to compare Busan to Naples.

While ferries to Japan quickly find themselves in open sea, domestic **routes** take you past Jagalchi fish market, and a whole armada of ships, cranes, buoys and bays, all backed by an undulating mess of grimy buildings. The city soon fades away, waves pounding instead against cliffs that fall into the sea in ice-creamy diagonal bands of yellow and purple – evidence that Busan once rode high above the waters, before being toppled down to sea level by the drift of plates. Lighthouses poke up from the crags like lonely crayons, backed all the way to your destination by a hurried scrawl of mountain scenery.

almost as far as possible from the wavering line of control. The largest of several such bases was in **Gohyeon**, now the island's biggest town and main travel hub. Visitors to the island can visit the freshly spruced-up **Prisoner of War Camp Museum** (daily 9am–6pm; W3000), which recreates part of the original camp. Despite being diorama-heavy, the open-air display is surprisingly diverting for a Korean historical exhibition, right from the introductory escalator-based greeting from Mao, MacArthur, Kim and their cardboard comrades. Simulated gunfire, explosions and revolutionary music crackle around the squat buildings and dirt tracks, much of which is cordoned off by barbed wire, but the effect is spoilt somewhat – in Korean fashion – by the new flyover swooping above the complex. There's little information in English, but some of the exhibits speak for themselves – keep an eye out for the interesting video footage of what life was like in the camp. This exhibition is just about within walking distance of Gohyeon bus terminal, which is uphill and poorly signed – a taxi won't cost more than a couple of thousand won.

Haegeumgang and Oedo

The Geumgang Mountains in North Korea are rightly revered as the most beautiful on the peninsula, a Chinese painting come to life where tree-fringed scoops of sculpted rock rise through the mist. Similar sights – far smaller, but infinitely more accessible – are on offer at **Haegeumgang** off the south coast of Geojedo – *hae* means sea – where the precipitous crags lift their skinny fists like antennas through the waters, rather than the North Korean hinterland. Topped with a sprinkling of camellia and highly photogenic, it's possible to get a look at Haegeumgang from dry land – a network of trails web out from a nearby village, heading to a viewing point that's perfect for a picnic, but becomes yet more majestic under the light of the moon. However, as the peaks lie a few hundred metres offshore, they're most commonly viewed by boat on the way to **OEDO** (pronounced "way-dough"), an island possessing a different kind of beauty. The brainchild of a couple of botanists from Seoul, it has been almost entirely covered with flowers, and is now one of the most popular sights in the country for Korean tourists, pulling in a couple of million each year.

The South Sea and Islands:

Geojedo	거제도	Tongyeong	통영

Though the flowers are beautiful, it's one of those experiences that appeals to Koreans far more than it does to foreign visitors, and the island's tight paths can get uncomfortably crowded – don't dare to go against the current.

Practicalities

Thanks to the mammoth bridge to Tongyeong, Geojedo is easily accessible by **bus** from many mainland destinations – Gohyeon has by far the best connections, and its bus terminal is surrounded by motels and restaurants. The best way to arrive, however, is by **ferry** from Busan – regular ferries depart the city's domestic Yeonan terminal for several Geoje destinations; most head to Gohyeon or **Jangseungpo**, a small fishing village on the east of the island. One-way rides cost around W17,000, and take just over or under an hour, depending on which Geoje port you use. Wherever you land, regular **local buses** speed between the island's major centres. Ten **ferries** a day do the three-hour circuit to Oedo from Jangsuengpo, costing W17,000 on weekdays and W19,000 on weekends, when it can be hard to get a ticket. You'll get ninety minutes on the island – more than enough – and a pass saying which ferry you have to return on. Ferries also depart from Haegeumgang, and sometimes from Tongyeong.

There are **places to stay** all over Geojedo, but for convenience, most make do with Jangseungpo or Gohyeon. Near the former, *Hotel Art* (ⓣ055/682-0075; ❺) is the best and most prominent place to stay, with some rooms overlooking the harbour – it's part of a large, Guggenheim-esque complex visible from the harbour, which contains a modern art gallery (free) on the sixth floor. Cheaper rooms can be found at the *Sky* and *Sun Park* motels (both ❸), painted in mint and peach tones respectively, and both visible from the main road. Gohyeon is busier and less appealing; an easy walk from the bus terminal lies the crusty *Geoje Tourist Hotel* (ⓣ055/632-7002; ❹), whose standards of cleanliness and service couldn't get much worse, plus the usual cheap motels. Culinary choices are similarly insipid, but near the bus terminal there's *Gimbap-gwa Spaghetti*, a cheap respite from all things fishy. Haegeumgang is a wonderful area to stay, with the village containing several *minbak* and a *yeogwan* (both ❷).

Tongyeong and the South Sea islands

Straddling the neck of the Geosong peninsula, affable **TONGYEONG** occupies a special place in Korean hearts as the base from which **Admiral Yi Sung-Shin** orchestrated some of his greatest victories against the invading Japanese (see p.289). The town is now a pleasantly laid-back place concentrating as much on its present as its past, with enough diversions to keep visitors occupied for a day, after which you may care to head off to the emerald confetti of islands that surround it (see p.254 for more details).

Tongyeong's four-sided **harbour** – known as Ganguan – forms the focal point of the city. The **promenade** lining its western flank can be a relaxing place to drink on warm evenings, the Bossa Nova piped through the PA system augmented by the gentle lapping of moored fishing boats. The north bank forms the base of a small hill, with a maze of houses, tiny lanes and drainage channels snaking their way to the top. Back at the harbour you'll be able to see, and taste, the city's pride and joy – **Chungmu Gimbap**. Despite every town in Korea having an official famous food, Tongyeong may be unique in that its own local dish – small rice rolls with radish *kimchi* and chillied squid – actually tastes markedly different here than it does elsewhere in the country. The western side of the harbour is almost entirely occupied by tiny restaurants, each serving this local speciality on old newspaper – most outlets have pictures of female proprietors present and past on their nameboards; as a general rule of thumb, the older the *ajumma*, the more rustic the restaurant, and the better the food.

A steep five-minute walk from the harbour brings you to **Sebyeonggwan**, a huge single-floor house built in 1605 as the headquarters of the Admiralty, and one of the oldest wooden structures in the country. Its lack of walls, windows or doors makes it almost unrecognizable as a house, but in the summer the giant roof, balanced on top of fifty carved wooden columns, provides welcome shade for *gimbap*-munching tourists. Just down the road lies the **Folklore & History Museum** (9am–5pm; closed Mon; free), which concentrates on Tongyeong's military triumphs but also features interesting examples of local craft and costume. East of the harbour, Nammangsan hill is the home of an excellent international **modern sculpture park** (24hr; free) and a statue of Lee Sung-Shin. The bearded Admiral Yi stands with his back to the art, fixing a patriotic gaze at the island-peppered scene of his victories.

Practicalities

Although there's no train station, Tongyeong is something of a local transport hub, with regular **ferries** heading to the surrounding islands in all seasons. Most popular are the forty-minute trip to the twin peaks of Saryangdo and the half-hour hop to Jeseungdang (both 8 daily), and there's a twice-daily summer service to the tourist mecca of Jeju Island (see p.349). Tongyeong's **bus** station, inconveniently hidden in the northern suburbs, offers regular services to most cities in Korea, including half-hourly connections to Busan and Daegu. The station has a **tourist office**, though your chances of finding an English-speaking member of staff are slim. Tongyeong is the proud host of a genuinely international summer **music festival**, for which performers gather in a feast of modern and classical tunes. For those who prefer muscles to music, Korea's number one triathlon sees competitors splash, dash and cycle through the city each June.

Accommodation can be found around the bus station, but by far the most pleasant place to stay is the harbour. Standing out like a sore thumb is the *Napoli Motel* (Ⓣ055/646-0202; ❹), one of the tallest buildings around, and a little overpriced, but pleasant enough. A clockwise right-angle around the harbour is the *Geumjeong-jang Motel* (❷), which though cheaper, and with similar views, may be a little seedy for some. More motels, *yeogwan* and cheap-as-chips *yeoinsuk* line the busier sides of the harbour, together with an acceptable *jjimjilbang*.

Islands of the South Sea

An almost innumerable number of islands radiate out into the South Sea like emerald stepping-stones. Much of this area is protected as the **HALLYEO HAESANG NATIONAL PARK** and, as in other island groups around the country, offers a look into the heart of traditional Korean life. Here ports and villages have changed little for generations, places inextricably connected to their surrounding waters where the busy urban realities of modern Korea are little more than memory.

Mainland Tongyeong is the area's main transport hub, and from here you can hop to dozens of islands by ferry. **Mireukdo** is immediately opposite the ferry terminal, but is built up and a little too industrial, and in any case connected to Tongyeong by bridge. Just 20km to the west of Tongyeong, the twin-peaked island of **Saryangdo** is far more serene, and popular with young travellers in the summer on account of some good beaches; at these times, many choose to camp under the stars, but there are *minbak* available. **Hansando** is even closer to Tongyeong, and was once home to Admiral Yi's main naval base; nowadays it's best known for

Jeseungdang, a large shrine. Just off its northeastern flank is the relaxed island of **Bijindo**, whose long, east-facing beach is a wonderful place to watch the sunrise over a smattering of small islets. Further afield, **Yeohwado** is home to a remote temple, as well as the *yeongmori* – needles of rock protruding from the eastern cape. These are just a few possibilities in the area – allow yourself a few days, armed with a map of the area, and forget about the mainland for a while. Many of the islands have simple *minbak* accommodation, but as banking facilities are next to nonexistent it's essential to bring the necessary funds along from the mainland.

Jinju

A small city typical of Korea's southern coast, but slightly more redolent of those found across the border in laid-back Jeolla-do, **JINJU** is worth dropping into on account of its superb **fortress** alone – this was the scene of one of the most famous suicides in Korean history when a girl jumped to her death into the river below during the Japanese invasions of the 1590s, dragging an enemy general with her. Here you can walk for hours along pretty paths, gaze over the river from traditional pavilions and pop into the odd temple. The beauty of of Jinju is that all you need is within easy walking distance – the fortress is close to the intercity bus terminal, and surrounded by places to stay and eat. Unlike most towns in the region, the city is famed for its food, and a clutch of excellent **eel restaurants** can be found outside the fortress entrance. Jinju even has its own take on *bibimbap* – a popular dish across the nation, but one prepared here with consummate attention – or track down one of the few restaurants still serving ostrich meat. The city also makes a good base for those keen to tackle the nearby national park of **Jirisan** (see p.258), one of the most popular in the country.

Arrival, information and orientation

With the **train** line seeing few daily services, and the domestic **airport** 20km away and similarly quiet, most of Jinju's visitors arrive by **bus**. The express terminal is to the south of town, past the train station, but the intercity terminal is well located in the thick of things, just north of the Nam River and within walking distance of the fortress. There's a small **tourist information** booth outside the main fortress entrance, where staff can usually do little more than hand out maps, or perhaps shed some light on the bullfights that the city

Jinju	
Jinju	진주
Jinjuseong	진주성
Accommodation	
Dongbang Tourist Hotel	동방 관광 호텔
Lotte Motel	롯대 모텔
Songjuk-jang	송죽장
Restaurants	
Eel restaurants	장어 식당
Gwallamgaek	관람객
Ilsin Galbi	일신 갈비
Zio Ricco	지오 리꼬

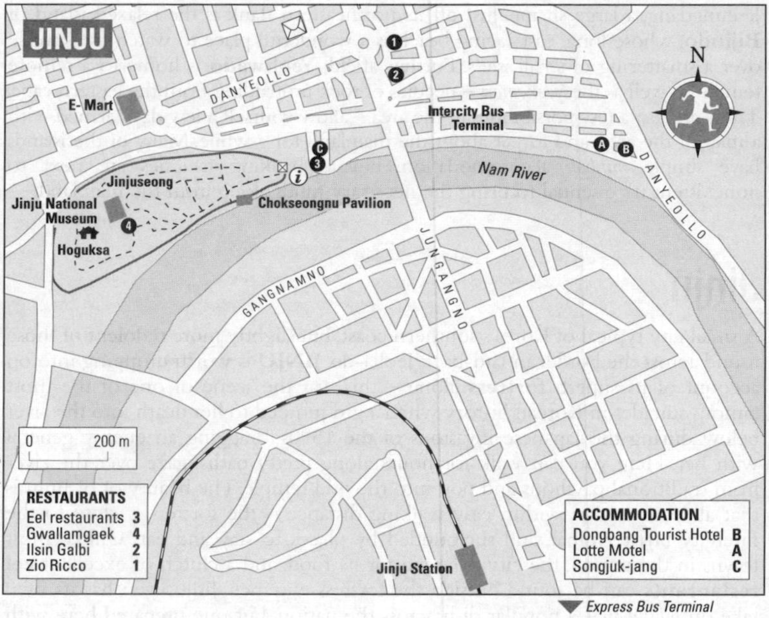

occasionally hosts. There's also an annual **festival** commemorating local heroine Nongae (see box, p.258) with a whole weekend's worth of events taking place by the fortress at the end of May.

Accommodation

While there are **places to stay** all over the city, there's little point in basing yourself anywhere other than the strip running from the bus station to the fortress, which is dotted with cheap motels and *yeogwan*. There are also a few crusty *yeoinsuk* lying around, which are extremely cheap at just W10,000 per room, but the room is all you'll get, with nothing inside but a couple of blankets, a television, and some toilet roll for use in the communal washrooms – not quite the *Ritz*, but a quintessentially Korean experience nonetheless.

Dongbang Tourist Hotel Okbong-dong ⓣ055/743-0131, ⓕ055/742-6786. Better than the average Korean tourist hotel, though this really isn't saying much, and rooms are heavily overpriced. The river-facing location, however, is a plus. ❻

Lotte Motel Okbong-dong ⓣ055/741-4888. Right next to the *Dongbang*, but much cheaper. Rooms here are smallish but spotless, and come with fetching his 'n' hers nightgowns; some also have pleasing river views. ❸

Songjuk-jang Jeongmun-ap. A cheap, interesting place run by a gaggle of *ajummas*-to-be, opposite the main entrance of the fort and down a side street. Rooms have their own toilet, which means that they're fine for the price. ❷

The City

The focal point of the city and its best sight by far is the walled-off riverside fortress of **Jinjuseong**, which can easily eat up half a day of your time. Constructed in 1379 to protect the city from Japanese invasions, it did its job in 1572 during the first attacks of what was to be a prolonged war (see box, p.258).

Just in from the entrance you'll find **Chokseongnu**, a beautiful pavilion facing the river; if you're lucky, you may find it full of old men in white, chatting and playing *baduk*. From here a network of pretty, tree-lined trails spider-web across the complex, with something to see at every turn. One of the most impressive sights is little **Hoguksa**, a temple at the opposite end – small and unheralded, but highly atmospheric. The compact central square is surrounded by an immaculately balanced amphitheatre of palms, bamboo and other foliage, especially pleasing when augmented by the drones and wooden clacks of morning prayer. There's also a large **museum** on site (Tues–Fri 9am–6pm, Sat & Sun until 7pm; W1000), which has been built in an unnecessarily modern style, at odds with its surroundings. However, it is good on history, with an inevitable focus on the 1592 Japanese invasions, several battles from which are depicted in folding screen form.

Near the fortress you'll find several restaurants specializing in **eel** (see p.258 for details) as well as Insadong-gil, a street lined with **antique shops**. The Nam River is dammed a short distance upstream, with Jinyangho, the resulting **lake**, now a popular place with Korean couples here you'll also find an amusement park, and a small zoo. The river itself comes alive during an annual **lantern festival**, which takes place at the beginning of October; this usually coincides with one of Korea's only **bullfighting** events, though you may be cheered to hear that the bulls fight each other, and don't die in front of a baying crowd.

Eating

The **food** is good, even by Korean standards. **Jeollanese** influence has clearly crept across the provincial border – meals are often served with a copious array of **side dishes**, and there's even a local take on that Jeonju favourite, the *bibimbap*. Surprisingly few Jinjuites will be able to point you to a restaurant serving this delectable dish, though one can be found fairly close to the fortress entrance. Even harder to find are the few restaurants still serving **ostrich** meat,

▲ Chokseongnu pavilion

The Japanese attacks on Jinju

Jinju's fortress received its first serious test in October of 1592, during the first attacks of what was to be a prolonged Japanese invasion. Like Admiral Yi along the coast in Yeosu (see box, p.289), **General Kim Si-min** held fort despite being heavily outnumbered, with records claiming that 30,000 Japanese soldiers were seen off by just 3800 local troops. The following June, the Japanese returned in greater numbers, with up to 100,000 soldiers eager to obliterate the shame of their previous defeat, and it is estimated that 70,000 Koreans were killed during a week-long siege. Every tragedy needs a hero – or, in this case, a heroine – and this time a local girl named **Nongae**, one of several girls selected to "entertain" the Japanese top-dogs after their victory, stepped into the breach. After using her charms to lure Japanese general Keyamura to what should have been a suspiciously lofty position on the riverside cliff, she jumped to her death, bringing the general down with her. A **festival** commemorating Nongae's patriotic valour takes place in the fortress each May, while General Kim's memory lives on in statue form at the centre of the fortress.

a Jinju speciality, but on the decline – one of these, *Tajobaelli*, is a short taxi-ride from the fortress area.

Eel restaurants Outside the main gate to the fortress lies a parade of restaurants, all devoted to the same dish – eel. There's precious little to choose between them in terms of price or quality, and all now have English-language menus; the *Yujeong* has made the most effort in terms of decoration, but *Gangnaru* may overshadow it on the taste front. At all places, river eel costs around W15,000, with sea eel a couple of thousand won cheaper.

Gwallamgaek Sikdang Jinjuseong. Actually located inside the fort itself, and, therefore, a perfect place to fall back and fill up if you're spending a while here. Noodle dishes are cheap at W3000, but the *bibimbap* is better value at W5000.

Ilsin Galbi Dongseong-dong. Though most come for the *galbi*, it would be a shame to turn down the fantastic local speciality, which is one of the most delicious dishes available for miles around – Jinju *bibimbap*. Extremely similar to the Jeonju style, but half the price at just W5000, meticulous care goes into the meal and its accompanying side dishes. *Doenjang jjigae*, a *miso*-style stew, is also a bargain at just W3000. The restaurant is on a small alley near the bus station and a little hard to find – it's just in front of the *Dongbo Motel*, which is somewhat easier to track down.

Zio Ricco This Italian restaurant is a *kimchi*-free refuge for Jinju's small expat community, with its proximity to the bus station and fortress also making it a good choice for tourists. Pasta forms the bulk of the menu, and is inevitably served with the sweet pickles that Koreans must assume to be a regular side dish in Italy.

Jirisan National Park

Korea's largest national park, **JIRISAN**, pulls in hikers from all over the country, attracted by the dozen peaks measuring over 1000m in height, which includes Cheonwangbong, the South Korean mainland's highest. It has also found fame for its **resident bear population**; a park camera spotted an Asiatic Black Bear wandering around in 2002, almost two decades after the last confirmed Korean sighting. The bear group was located and placed under protection, and the species continue to breed successfully. Although you're extremely unlikely to see them, it lends the park's various twists and turns an extra dash of excitement – nowhere else in Korea will you be fretting over the sound of a broken twig. Jirisan is one of the only national parks in the country with an organized system of overnight **shelters** – there are few more atmospheric places to fall asleep in this corner of Korea. This makes **multi-day**

hikes an exciting possibility; one popular route heads across the main spine of the park from east to west, and takes three days to walk. There are large peaks all the way along this central ridge, from which numerous picturesque valleys drop down to the fields and foothills below. It's impossible to detail all of the possible hikes and sights in the park, better instead to arm yourself with the park map (available at park entrances and nearby tourist offices for W1000) and find your own lofty piece of paradise.

The park actually sprawls across three provinces, with its most popular access point – the temple of **Hwa-eomsa** – on the west of the park, across the provincial border in Jeonnam (see p.284). The eastern side of Jirisan, in Gyeongnam province, lacks such a focal point – there are dozens of entrances, but though none are particularly popular or easy to get to, this usually makes for a quieter visit than you'd get at other national parks. One of the most popular trails is up from **Ssanggyesa**, a beautifully located temple at the south of the park. There's little of historical worth here, bar a stone tablet apparently dating from 887, but the surroundings are delightful, particularly in the early mornings when the sun has not yet risen beyond Jirisan's muscular peaks; it may also be Korea's loudest temple in terms of birdlife. **Daewonsa** is another pretty temple, this one on the park's eastern fringe, which also has trails leading up to the peaks.

Hiking Jirisan National Park

A few of Jirisan's hundreds of routes are particularly popular. The biggest is the **26km-long trail** heading along the east–west main spine of the park. The hike connects **Nogodan**, a 1507m-high peak in the west, best accessed from Hwa-eomsa, and **Cheonwangbong** (1915m) in the east, the highest peak on the South Korean mainland and the second highest in the country. This trail takes most people three days to walk, with a couple of overnight stays at the shelters sprinkled along the way; there are eight of these on the spine, costing from W5000 to W7000 per person, and all are marked on the map. The westernmost shelter, at Nogodan, is very often full due to its proximity to a bus stop: to guarantee a place at any of the shelters you're asked to reserve a berth in advance through Korea's national park website (Ⓦ english.knps.or.kr). This can prove frustrating, as it's hard to tell where you will run out of daylight or energy on your hike, but reserving beds at Samdobong and Seseok should give you enough leeway whether you're heading east or west.

Numerous valleys head up to the park's main spine, and most make for excellent day-hikes. One of the most popular runs from **Jungsan-ni**, a village connected to Jinju by bus, up to the principal peak of Cheonwangbong and back again, though many choose to continue north and emerge out of the park at Chuseong, down a valley lined with small waterfalls. Others start at the temples of Daewonsa and Ssanggyesa, which are a little far away from the spine for a day-trip, so you'd have to overnight at a shelter.

Practicalities

Because there are dozens of places to start an assault on the Jirisan peaks – including Hwa-eomsa in Jeollanam-do (see p.284) – none enjoy particularly good bus connections. The temple at **Ssanggyesa** is usually the easiest to get to; direct buses head here from Jinju, though these pass through Hadong, a small town nearer the park that you may be able to get to directly from other cities. The village of **Jungsan-ni** also has bus connections to Jinju, but the park entrance is a frustratingly long uphill walk from the bus stop.

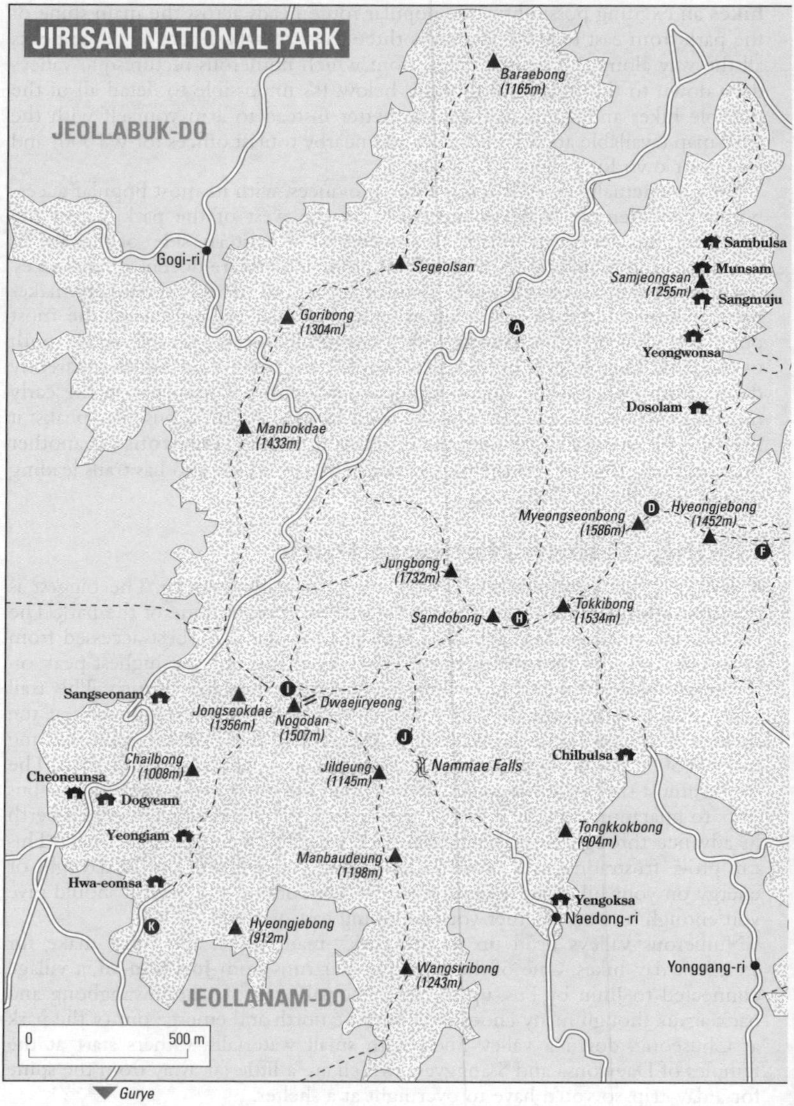

In addition to the shelters detailed earlier, there are **places to stay** and **eat** outside both of these main park entrances, as well as a smattering of campsites. The best place to eat is near the Jungsan bus stop at *Geomoksan-jang*, where a friendly man with his own unique English dialect serves some pretty good *pajeon* pancakes – just the treat after a long hike. A twenty-minute uphill walk brings you to the park entrance, where there's a clutch of *minbak* (❷), though the remoteness of the place makes for a rather lonely stay. The Ssanggyesa entrance

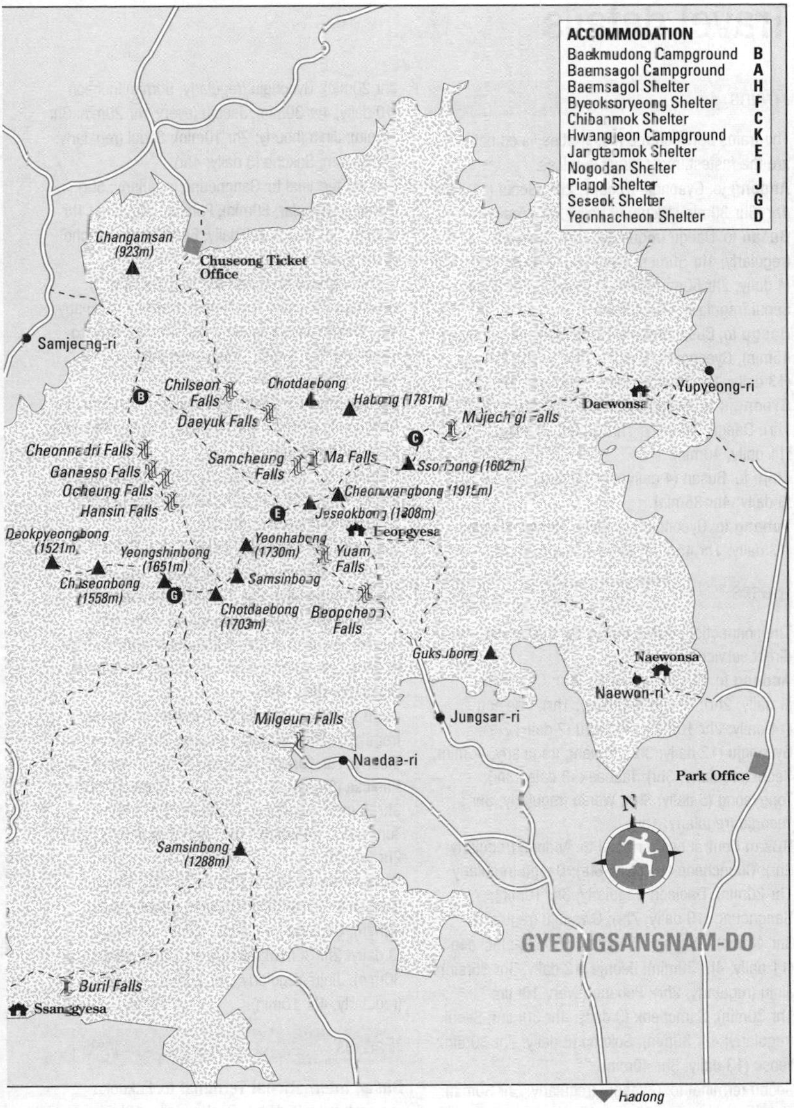

is a better option – just as bucolic but more open-plan, with *minbak* and restaurants spread over a wide area. The rustic *Joh-eun Sesang* (1) on the access path to the temple is a family home that caters for both needs; rooms are basic but come with private bathrooms, and the owners have been known to whip up free bowls of *ramyeon* in the evening if foreign guests look hungry. Those on a multi-day hike may be able to buy basic provisions in some park shelters, but while water is easier to find, it's advisable to bring your own food.

Travel details

Trains

The trains between the major cities listed below are the fastest, most direct services.

Andong to: Gyeongju (6 daily; 2hr); Seoul (11 daily; 4hr–5hr 30min); Wonju (9 daily; 2hr 45min).

Busan to: Daegu (regularly; 1hr); Daejeon (regularly; 1hr 50min); Gyeongju (2 daily; 1hr); Jinju (4 daily; 2hr 50min); Mokpo (3 daily; 7hr 30min); Seoul (regularly; 2hr 40min).

Daegu to: Busan (regular; 1hr); Daejeon (regularly; 45min); Gyeongju (16 daily; 1hr 25min); Pohang (13 daily; 1hr 45min); Seoul (regularly; 1hr 35min).

Gyeongju to: Andong (6 daily; 2hr); Busan (2 daily; 1hr); Daegu (16 daily; 1hr 25min); Pohang (11 daily; 40min).

Jinju to: Busan (4 daily; 2hr 50min); Mokpo (3 daily; 4hr 35min).

Pohang to: Gyeongju (11 daily; 40min); Daegu (13 daily; 1hr 45min); Seoul (2 daily; 5hr).

Buses

The connections listed below are the fastest, most direct services available.

Andong to: Busan (regularly; 3hr); Chuncheon (1 daily; 2hr); Daegu (regularly; 1hr); Daejeon (14 daily; 2hr 10min); Gwangju (2 daily; 3hr); Gyeongju (12 daily; 3hr); Pohang (regularly; 40min); Seoul (regularly; 3hr); Taebaek (3 daily; 3hr); Tongyeong (5 daily; 3hr); Wonju (regularly; 3hr); Yeongju (regularly; 1hr).

Busan Central bus terminal to: Andong (regularly; 3hr); Chuncheon (14 daily; 6hr); Daegu (regularly; 1hr 20min); Daejeon (regularly; 3hr 10min); Gangneung (10 daily; 7hr); Gwangju (regularly; 3hr 40min); Gyeongju (regularly; 50min); Incheon (11 daily; 4hr 30min); Jeonju (12 daily; 3hr 35min); Jinju (regularly; 2hr); Pohang (every 10min; 1hr 30min); Samcheok (3 daily; 4hr 30min); Seoul (regularly; 4hr 30min); Sokcho (8 daily; 7hr 30min); Yeosu (13 daily; 3hr 40min).

Seobu terminal to: Gwangju (regularly; 3hr 30min); Jinju (regularly; 1hr 30min); Mokpo (7 daily; 5hr 40min); Ssanggyesa (3 daily; 2hr); Tongyeong (regularly; 2hr); Wando (5 daily; 6hr 40min).

Daegu Express terminal to: Andong (9 daily; 1hr 20min); Busan (every 50min; 1hr 40min); Daejeon (regularly; 2hr 20min); Gwangju (every 40min; 3hr 20min); Gyeongju (regularly; 50min) Incheon (10 daily; 4hr 30min); Jeonju (every 1hr 20min; 3hr 30min); Jinju (hourly; 2hr 10min); Seoul (regularly; 3hr 50min); Sokcho (3 daily; 4hr).

Dongbu terminal to: Gangneung (regularly; 5hr); Gyeongju (regular; 50min); Pohang (regularly; 1hr 20min); Samcheok (11 daily; 6hr 30min); Sokcho (8 daily; 7hr).

Seobu terminal to: Busan (8 daily; 1hr 50min); Gyeongju (19 daily; 1hr 10min); Haeinsa (regularly; 1hr 30min); Jinju (regularly; 1hr 40min); Pohang (regularly; 1hr 30min); Tongyeong (regularly; 2hr 40min); Yeosu (7 daily; 4hr).

Bukbu terminal to: Andong (regularly; 1hr 30min); Gangneung (9 daily; 4hr); Guinsa (1 daily; 4hr); Muju (3 daily; 3hr 30min).

Geojedo to: Busan (regularly; 3hr 20min); Jinju (every 30min; 2hr 50min); Seoul (6 daily; 6hr); Tongyeong (regularly; 40min).

Gyeongju to: Andong (12 daily; 3hr); Busan (regularly; 50min); Daegu (regularly; 50min); Daejeon (regularly; 2hr 40min); Gangneung (16 daily; 5hr 30min); Gwangju (2 daily; 3hr 30min); Incheon (every 50min; 5hr 30min); Jinju (6 daily; 2hr 30min); Seoul (regular; 4hr 15min); Sokcho (2 daily; 8hr).

Jinju to: Busan (regularly; 1hr 30min); Daegu (regularly; 2hr); Daejeon (hourly; 2hr); Daewonsa (hourly; 1hr 10min); Gwangju (2 daily; 2hr 40min); Haeinsa (3 daily; 2hr 20min); Seoul (every 30min; 3hr 35min); Suncheon (15 daily; 1hr 30min); Tongyeong (regularly; 1hr 30min); Yeosu (3 daily; 2hr 20min).

Tongyeong to: Busan (regularly; 2hr); Daegu (regularly; 2hr 40min); Daejeon (regularly; 2hr 40min); Geojedo (regularly; 40min); Gwangju (3 daily; 2hr 30min); Haegeumgang (2 daily; 1hr 30min); Jinju (regularly; 1hr 30min); Seoul (regularly; 4hr 10min).

Ferries

Busan International Terminal to: Fukuoka (several daily; 3–15hr); Osaka (daily; 18hr); Shimonoseki (daily; 14hr).

Busan Domestic Terminal to: Gohyeon (5 daily; 1hr); Jangseungpo (7 daily; 45min); Jeju Island (7pm daily except Sun; 11hr).

Pohang to: Ulleungdo (10am daily; 3hr).

4

Jeolla

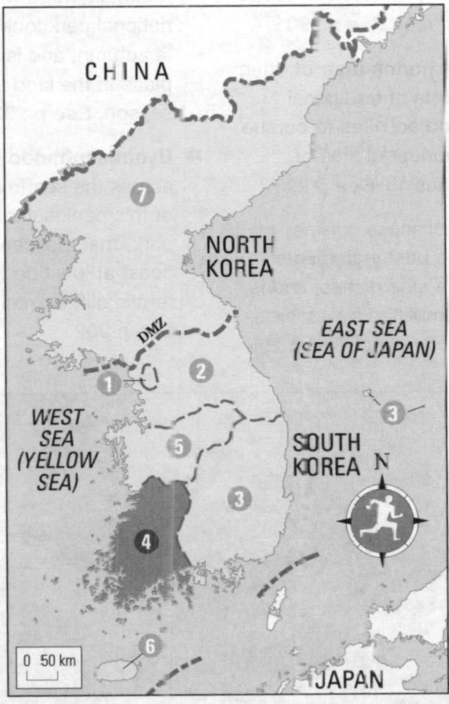
CHINA
NORTH KOREA
DMZ
EAST SEA (SEA OF JAPAN)
WEST SEA (YELLOW SEA)
SOUTH KOREA
N
JAPAN
0 50 km
1
2
3
3
4
5
6
7

CHAPTER 4

Highlights

* **Mokpo** This characterful seaside city is the best jumping-off point for excursions to the emerald isles of the West Sea. See p.274
* **Hyangiram** A tiny hermitage hanging onto cliffs south of Yeosu, and the best place in the country in which to see in the New Year. See p.290
* **Jeonju's hanok district** There are all sorts of traditional sights and activites to pursue in this wonderful area of *hanok* housing. See p.293
* **Food** Jeollanese cuisine offers the best ingredients and more side dishes, and is best exemplified by Jeonju's take on *bibimbap*. See p.296
* **Tapsa** This cute temple, nestling in between the "horse-ear" peaks of Maisan Provincial Park, is surrounded by gravity-defying towers of hand-stacked rock. See p.297
* **Naejangsan** The circular mountain ridge within this national park looks stunning in autumn, and is the best place in the land to enjoy the season. See p.299
* **Byeonsanbando** Look out across the sea from the peaks of this peninsular national park, then descend to the coast at low tide to see some terrific cliff formations. See p.302

▲ Jeonju's hanok district

4

Jeolla

If you're after top-notch food, craggy coastlines, swathes of undulating green fields, and islands on which no foreigner has ever set foot, go no further. Jeju Island has its rock formations and palm trees, and Gangwon-do pulls in nature-lovers by the truckload, but it's the **Jeolla provinces** where you'll find the essence of Korea at its most potent – a somewhat ironic contention since the Jeollanese have long played the role of the renegade. Here, the national inferiority complex that many foreigners diagnose in the Korean psyche is compounded by a regional one: this is the most set-about part of a much set-about country. Although the differences between Jeolla and the rest of the country are being diluted daily, they're still strong enough to help make it the most distinctive and absorbing part of the mainland.

A look at any map of the country will tell you what makes Jeolla special. The Korean coast dissolves into thousands of **islands**, the majority of which lie sprinkled like confetti in Jeollanese waters. Some such as Hongdo and Geomundo are popular holiday resorts, while others lie in wave-smashed obscurity, their inhabitants hauling their living from the sea and preserving a lifestyle little changed in decades. The few foreign visitors who make it this far find that the best way to enjoy the area is to pick a ferry at random, and simply go with the flow. Many of the islands lie under the protective umbrella of **Dadohae Haesang**, a marine national park. In addition to this, there are no fewer than five national parks on the mainland: Wolchulsan and Jirisan lie in South Jeolla province (**Jeollanam-do**), while Byeonsanbando, Naejangsan and Deogyusan are in the north (**Jeollabuk-do**).

Jeolla isn't all about natural delights. Pleasures of an urban bent can be found in **Gwangju** and **Jeonju**, the two regional capitals. Jeonju is the smaller of the two but one of the most likeable cities in the country, with its **hanok district** of traditional buildings a particular highlight. Both capitals are young, trendy cities with a reputation for art and political activism, and also the best places to sample the **Jeollanese cuisine** that's the envy of the nation – pride of place on the regional menu goes to *Jeonju bibimbap*, a local take on one of Korea's favourite dishes (see box, p.296). Jeolla's culinary reputation arises from its status as one of Korea's main food-producing areas, with shimmering emerald rice paddies vying for space in and around the national parks. The Jeollanese themselves are also pretty special – they're fiercely proud of their homeland, with a devotion borne from decades of social and economic repression. Speaking a dialect sometimes incomprehensible to regular Koreans, they revel in their status as outsiders, and make a credible claim to be the friendliest people in the country.

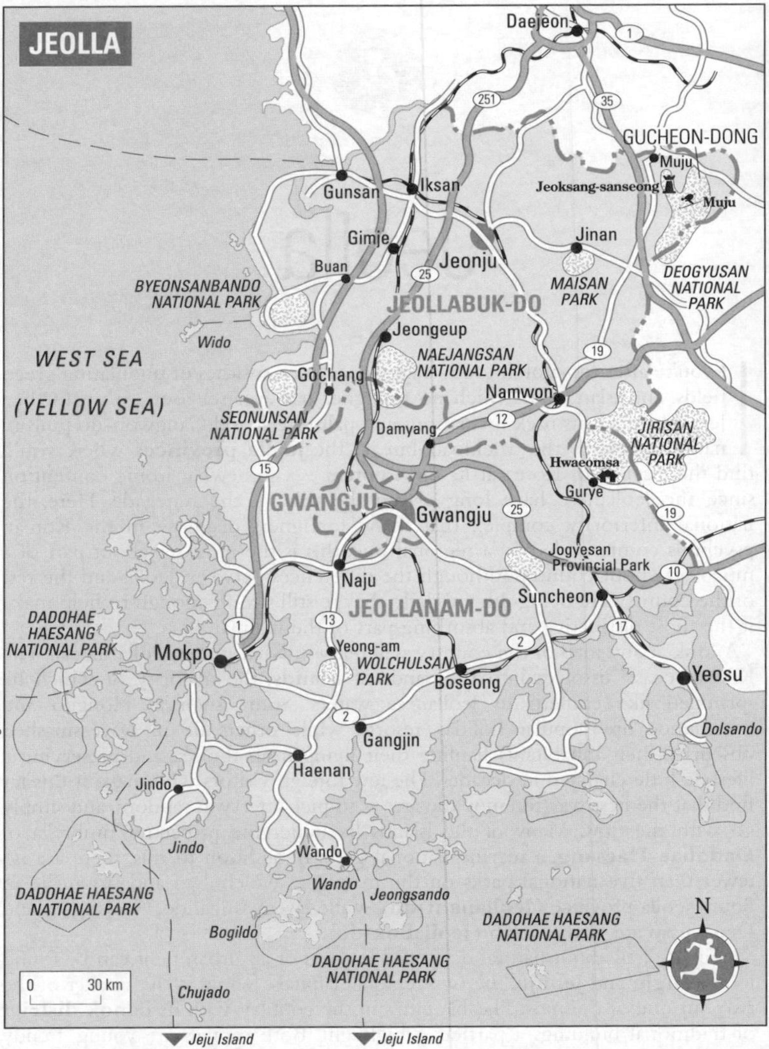

Some history

Jeolla's gripe with the rest of the country is largely political in nature. Despite its status as the **birthplace** of the Joseon dynasty that ruled Korea from 1392 until its annexation by the Japanese in 1910, most of the country's leaders since independence in 1945 have hailed from the southeastern Gyeongsang provinces. Seeking to undermine their Jeollanese opposition, the central government deliberately withheld funding for the region, leaving its cities in relative decay while the country as a whole reaped the benefits of the "economic miracle". Political discord reached its nadir in 1980, when the city of Gwangju was the unfortunate location of an event which left hundreds of civilians dead (see box, p.270). National democratic reform was gradually fostered in the following years, culminating in the election of Jeolla native and eventual Nobel Peace Prize laureate **Kim Dae-jung**. Kim attempted to claw his home province's living standards up to scratch with a series of big-money projects, notably in the form of highway connections to the rest of the country once so conspicuous by their absence. Despite these advances, with the exception of Gwangju and Jeonju, Jeolla's towns and cities are still among the poorest places in Korea.

Jeollanam-do

With its mountainous mainland melting into a gathering of islands too numerous to count, **JEOLLANAM-DO**, or Jeonnam for short, is something akin to the country of Greece transported to oriental climes. However, comparisons are not purely cartographic in nature; the region is littered with ports, and the surrounding waters are bursting with seafood. Low-rise buildings snake up from the shores to the hills, and some towns are seemingly populated entirely with salty old pensioners. The region's capital and largest city, **Gwangju**, is worth a look around, as is the coastal city of **Mokpo**, which after years of being denied public money is now spending it with abandon. It's here that you'll best sense the differences between Jeolla and the rest of the country. A constellation of little-visited islands swarm around the coastal route between Mokpo and **Yeosu**, near the border with Gyeongsang, while further inland the province's interior is green and lush, particularly around **Wolchulsan** and **Jirisan** national parks, and **Boseong**, home to the mainland's biggest tea plantations. All in all, Jeonnam is quite possibly the most fascinating quarter of the country.

Gwangju and around

GWANGJU is the gleaming, busy face of "new Jeolla", and the region's most populous city by far. Once a centre of political activism, and arguably remaining so today, it's hard for Koreans to hear the name without thinking of the brutal **massacre** that took place here in 1980, an event that devastated the city but highlighted the faults of the then-government, thereby ushering in a more democratic era. A **cemetery** for those who perished in the struggle is located on the city outskirts. There's little else of note to see in Gwangju itself, except perhaps the shop-and-dine area in its centre, which is largely pedestrianized, and one of the busiest and best such zones in the country. This is the obvious place to see at first hand why Gwangjuites are deemed to be among the most fashionable folk on the peninsula, as well as the best place in which to sample the Jeollanese cuisine. Also located in this area is "**Art Street**", a warren of studios and the figurehead of Gwangju's dynamic **art scene**. Although most funding is now thrown at contemporary projects, the city's rich artistic legacy stems in part from the work of **Uijae**, one of the country's most famed twentieth-century painters and a worthy poet to boot. A museum dedicated to the great man sits on his former patch – a building and tea plantation on the slopes of **Mudeungsan Park**, which forms a natural eastern border to the city.

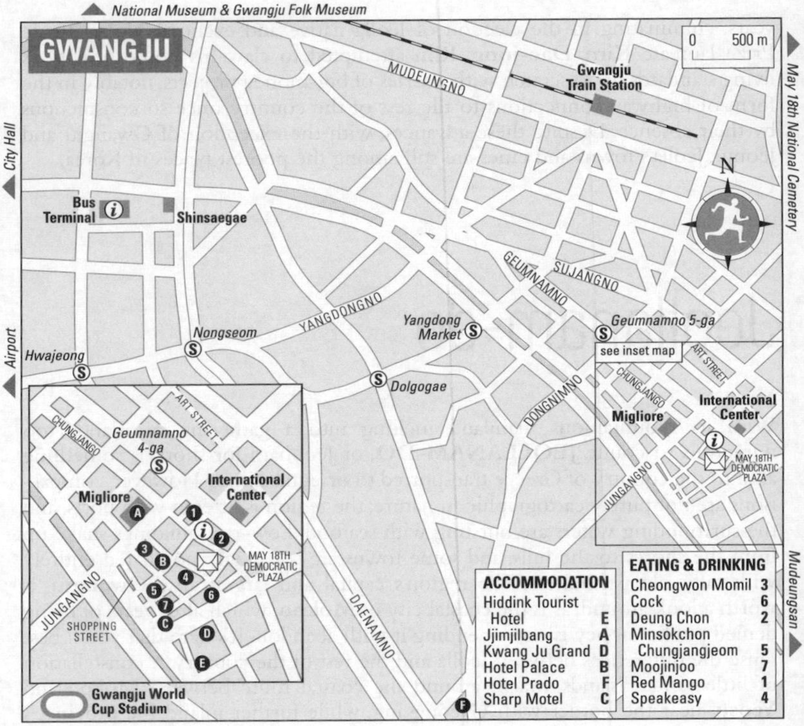

Arrival, information and orientation

Despite the substantial funds thrown at it by the city government, Gwangju's public transport network is poor for a Korean city. A brand-new **subway** line fires through the centre from east to west, but for some reason doesn't actually connect with the **train** station or **bus** terminal (both of which are fairly central); this is particularly odd considering that the latter, a mall-style structure that serves both express and intercity buses, is also new. Getting away from this terminal to other points in the city is tough – the area is full of traffic, and the bus stops on the busy main road outside are blocked by cars and taxis waiting for passengers. Those who wish to take a **local bus** often have to run out into the traffic – that's if they manage to see their bus coming. Add to that a confusing series of bus numbers and you have a recipe for chaos. Alighting from the **train** station is far simpler, making it a more convenient way to arrive in Gwangju. The **airport** is located just over 6km west of the centre, and is served by a couple of short-haul international services; it will eventually be a stop on the subway line. In the meantime, you can catch one of the city buses to the centre, or a taxi should cost less than W10,000.

Gwangju is far too unwieldy to be covered on foot so you'll have to rely on the subway (W900 per ride), buses (W1000) or taxis to get around. The majority of the sights are on the city's perimeter, and all are easily accessible on public transport. Most tourists base themselves around **Geumnamno**, the major road and travel artery in the downtown area, near the democratic plaza in Gwangju's main shopping district. The city's beating heart, the area is busy with shoppers by day, and drinkers by night. On the same road is a **tourist information centre** (daily 9am–6pm; ⓣ062/226-1050), which sits almost directly opposite the surprisingly homely **Gwangju International Center**, an excellent source of local information, with a selection of second-hand English language books and films. The centre also puts on Korean language classes for resident foreigners.

Accommodation

Gwangju's **accommodation** is relatively poor by Korean standards, and hasn't kept pace with the city's other advances. There are a couple of decent options at the higher end of the price range, and motels can be found in groups around the train and bus stations, as well as the city centre. The area around the bus station isn't a pleasant place to stay, as not only is it a convoluted walk from the station to the motels, but the establishments are even more brazenly "love"-based than elsewhere in the country – those around Geumnamno are far more pleasant.

Hiddink Tourist Hotel Bullo-dong ⓣ062/227-8500, ⓦwww.hotel-continental.co.kr. Named after national hero Guus Hiddink, South Korea's manager in the 2002 World Cup, this is where the team stayed before their surprise quarter-final win over Spain. It's acceptable but not amazing, and prices have been inflated because of its famous guests – check out the name plaques on the room doors. ❺

Jjimjilbang Chungjang-dong. On the top floors of the downtown Migliore department store, this large jjimjilbang is one of the flashiest (and most popular) around, and perfect to fall into after a night out nearby. ❶

Kwang Ju Grand Hotel Bullo-dong ⓣ062/224-6111, ⓕ062/224-8933. Though the rooms are large, they're dating fast, and the whole hotel is in dire need of a refit. Facilities include a sauna, nightclub and restaurant, but room prices are poor value, even with the free trip back to the 1970s thrown in. ❺

Hotel Palace Hwanggeum-dong ⓣ062/222-2525, ⓕ062/236-2511. Smallish yet immaculate rooms in the very centre of the city and much better value

Gwangju

Gwangju	광주
Art Street	예술의거리
Geumnamno	금남로
Gwangju Folk Museum	민속 박물관
May 18th National Cemetery	국립 5.18 묘지
Mudeungsan	무등산 도립 공원
National Museum	국립 박물관
Uijae Art Museum	의재 미술관
Accommodation	
Hiddink Tourist Hotel	히딩크 호텔
Hotel Palace	팔레스 호텔
Hotel Prado	호텔 프라도
Jjimjilbang	찜질방
Kwang Ju Grand Hotel	그랜드 호텔
Sharp Motel	샤프 모텔
Restaurants	
Cheongwon Momil	청원 모밀
Cock	코크
Deung Chon	등촌
Minsokchon Chungjangjeom	민속촌 충장점
Moojinjoo	무진주
Paris Baguette	파리 바게뜨
Red Mango	레드 망고

The Gwangju massacre

"At 10.30 in the morning about a thousand Special Forces troops were brought in. They repeated the same actions as the day before, beating, stabbing and mutilating unarmed civilians, including children, young girls and aged grandmothers... Several sources tell of soldiers stabbing or cutting off the breasts of naked girls; one murdered student was found disembowelled, another with an X carved in his back... And so it continues, horror piled upon horror."

Simon Winchester, *Korea*

Away from the bustle of Gwangju, in what may at first appear to be a field of contorted tea trees, lie those who took part in a 1980 **uprising** against the government, an event which resulted in a brutal **massacre** of civilians. The number that died is still not known for sure, and was exaggerated by both parties involved at the time; the official line is just over two hundred though some estimates put the death toll at over two thousand. Comparisons with the **Tiananmen** massacre in China are inevitable, an event better known to the Western world despite what some historians argue may have been a similar death toll. While Beijing keeps a tight lid on its nasty secret, Koreans flock to Gwangju each May to pay tribute to those that died.

In an intricate web of corruption, apparent communist plots and a presidential assassination, trouble had been brewing for some time before **General Chun Doo-hwan** staged a **military coup d'état** in December 1979. Chun had been part of a team given the responsibility of investigating the assassination of President Kim Jae-kyu, but used the event as a springboard towards his own leadership of the country. On May 17, 1980, he declared martial law in order to quash **student protests** against his rule. Similar revolts had seen the back of a few previous Korean leaders (notably Syngman Rhee, the country's first president); fearing the same fate, Chun authorized a ruthless show of force that left many dead. Reprisal demonstrations started up across the city; the MBC television station was burnt down, with protestors aggrieved at being portrayed as communist hooligans by the state-run operator. Hundreds of thousands of civilians grouped together, mimicking the tactics of previous protests on Jeju Island by attacking and seizing weapons from police stations. With transport connections to the city blocked, the government were able to retreat and pool their resources for the inevitable crackdown. This came on May 27, when troops attacked by land and air, retaking the city in less than two hours. After having the protest leaders executed, General Chun resigned from the Army in August, stepping shortly afterwards into presidential office. His leadership, though further tainted by continued erosions of civil rights, oversaw an economic boom; an export-hungry world remained relatively quiet on the matter.

Also sentenced to death, though eventually spared, was **Kim Dae-jung**. An opposition leader and fierce critic of the goings-on, he was charged with inciting the revolt, and spent much of the decade under house arrest. Chun, after seeing out his term in 1987, passed the country's leadership to his partner-in-crime during the massacre, Roh Tae-woo. Demonstrations soon whipped up once more, though in an unexpectedly conciliatory response, Roh chose to release many political prisoners, including Kim Dae-jung. The murky world of Korean politics gradually became more and more transparent, culminating in charges of corruption and treason being levelled at Chun and Roh. Both were pardoned in 1997 by Kim Dae-jung, about to be elected president himself, in what was generally regarded as a gesture intended to draw a line under the troubles.

than the more expensive hotels in the area. There's a funky café on the ground floor, as well as free Internet and sauna facilities, but it's slightly hard to find in the middle of a bank of clubs and restaurants. ④

Hotel Prado Baek-un-dong ⓣ062/654-9999, ⓦwww.pradohotel.co.kr. Set in a fairly quiet quarter of the city, the *Prado* is the hotel of choice for those with cash to splash, though it's still very affordable (rooms W121,000). It has good restaurants, excellent service and super-clean rooms; online discounts are available. 6

Sharp Motel Bullo-dong ⓣ062/228-2929. Clean if slightly musty rooms, and half the price of the official tourist hotels in the area. There are free videos to rent, a surprisingly large proportion of which are not sexual in nature. 2

The City

The city's sprawling **downtown area**, covering a largely pedestrianized grid of tight streets from Geumnamno 4-ga subway station to the Democratic Plaza, is an unrelenting mix of cafés and restaurants, shops and shoppers, sound and vision. Most of the action takes place south of Geumnamno, the area's main thoroughfare, though the most interesting road lies a short walk to the north. Affectionately known as **Art Street**, it's a funky collection of shops and studios, selling art materials and works by local artists. There are similar streets in other Korean cities, but by comparison this one is larger, much more accessible and draws enough visitors to form an active part of city life. Traditional art styles remain dominant but they're complemented – and sometimes sent up – by a more contemporary set. A few arty cafés and restaurants can be found in or just off the road, though as this area is also Gwangju's centre of after-school education, the discussions you'll hear are more likely to be about pop than Picasso. The less artistically inclined can take a walk north of Geumnamno to **Shopping Street**, a parade of well-designed clothes shops that mainly caters to females, many of which are one-off boutiques – a rarity for a Korean shopping area.

Gwangju's **museum district** lies on the northern fringe of the city, around the Honam Expressway. The **National Museum** (Mon–Fri 9am–6pm, Sat & Sun to 7pm; closed Mon; W1000) is set in a typically oversized, quasi-traditional building, a grubby place despite its relative youth. The most interesting rooms here are those devoted to **Yuan-dynasty ceramics** scavenged from a Chinese trading boat, sunk off the Jeolla coast in the fourteenth century on its way to Japan, which lain undiscovered until 1975. Yuan dynasty artisans were renowned across East Asia for their celadon pottery, and many of the pieces on display can be traced to **Jingdezhen**, China's most famous centre of ceramic production. Despite the underwater centuries endured by the ware, most pieces are in pretty good condition, a testament to the procedures of the time. Another section is devoted to items scavenged from a Korean wreck found nearby in 1983, though these pieces lack the gentle balance of their Middle Kingdom counterparts. Through a tunnel under the expressway is the less interesting **Gwangju Folk Museum** (same hours; W1000), a diorama-centric look at Jeollanese costumes and customs from as far back as the Three Kingdoms period. You can reach the museums on city buses #16, #19 and #26.

The city outskirts

One of Gwangju's most important sights, the **May 18th National Cemetery** (daily 8am–5pm; free), is located in rolling countryside around forty minutes north of the city centre by bus, and is the resting place of those killed in the **1980 massacre** (see box opposite) the thousands of participants who survived also have the right to be buried here. Though Gwangju has many sights related to this event, some even forming part of a rather macabre tour detailed in the official tourist literature, this is the least morbid and most factual. An overlarge oval of walkways and sculpture, the visitor centre is more of a testament to concrete than to the lives of the demonstrators, though it's worth a visit for the

▲ May 18th National Cemetery, Gwangju

photograph exhibition hall – there are some astonishing pictures on display, and the tension of the time is painfully palpable. Be warned that many are rather graphic, though the worst have mercifully been cordoned off into a section of their own. The cemetery itself is a badly signed five-minute walk away. It's possible to get to the site by city bus – at the time of writing it was best to take #518, though check for the latest information before setting out.

While the massacre may well have been Gwangju's lowest ebb, the works of Ho Baeknyon, better known by his pen name of **Uijae** (1891–1977), probably represented the city's high-water mark in terms of artistic endeavour. His old house and tea plantation, as well as a museum dedicated to his work, stand on the slopes of **Mudeungsan**, a park bordering Gwangju on its eastern side, crisscrossed by a pleasant network of walking trails along which city-dwellers stretch their legs at weekends. A stream flows down from the hills to the park entrance, making it easy to locate the **Uijae Art Museum** which it passes on the way (10am–5pm; closed Mon; W1000). Uijae was an important painter-poet-calligrapher, and in uniting those fine arts was one of the main catalysts behind Gwangju's dynamic art scene. This museum is largely filled with contemporary Asian art, but the top floor is devoted to the great man's work; the most interesting piece is a ten-picture **folding screen**, whose images are said to represent the world's rainbow of personal characteristics: are you bamboo-, blossom- or orchid-like in temperament? The museum was started by Uijae's grandson, and nearby is the artist's old **tea plantation**, now tended by Buddhist monks, and stretching up to **Jeungsimsa** temple.

Eating and drinking

The Jeollanese pride themselves on their **food**, and as with other cities in the region, Gwangju cuisine is excellent – dishes are large and rarely will you be far from a restaurant serving a mouth-watering array of edibles. To an even greater degree than elsewhere in Korea, the best advice is to follow your nose and try your luck. The area around the bus terminal can be largely avoided, though if you're hungry on arrival you could try one of the fast-food bars in the complex itself. All of the establishments listed below are in the city's **downtown** area, which surrounds the democratic plaza.

Cheongwon Momil Bullo-dong. Opposite the Migliore department store, this little restaurant has been serving cheap noodles since 1960, making it almost Jurassic in Korean terms. The buckwheat noodles (*momil*) are similar to Japanese *soba*, and the proprietors recommend *bibim momil*, a bargain at W3500.

Cock Hwanggeum-dong. This restaurant stands out for more than just the name – it's known by locals as one of the cheapest places to get a filling meal, including chicken fillet, and *dak galbi* (like a chicken kebab cooked in a wide pan at your table) for just W5000 per portion. The free side dishes are also worthy of a mention, as they usually venture beyond the *kimchi* and pickled radish served just about everywhere else.

Deung Chon Chungjang-ro 1-ga. In a side street behind the downtown tourist centre, this is by far the most popular restaurant with Gwangju's expat population, in no small part thanks to the presence of English-speaking staff. *Shabu-shabu* is the dish of choice (W10,000 per person), though noodles and fried rice are available too.

Minsokchon Chungjangjeom Honam-dong. Twinned with *Moojinjoo* across the road, this meat restaurant serves up delicious but slightly expensive *galbi* in a pleasant atmosphere.

Moojinjoo Bullo-dong. Set on several stylish levels, this adventurous restaurant is the most aesthetically pleasing in the city. Unfortunately the menu is full of strange dishes and in Korean only, so take a local with you to get the most out of it; recommended dishes are *modeum bosam*, pork slices with a variety of succulent vegetable side dishes, or *yeongyang dolsotbap*, an energy-giving rice dish.

Red Mango Chungjang-ro. This chain serving low-fat iced yoghurt rode the crest of the healthy living wave that swept across the country in recent times. Its star is fading a little now but with a variety of toppings to choose from you're still in for a tasty snack.

Cafés and bars

The city's **downtown** area can be a sea of people even on weekday evenings, and has a few interesting clubs that keep going through the night. *Speakeasy*, the city's main expat bar, is an excellent place to meet people and hosts regular live music; other establishments tend to be rather transient in nature. By night the action centres on bars and clubs, but by day downtown is also Gwangju's capital of **café culture**, and you'll be spoilt for choice. The café above the *Paris Baguette* bakery on Chungjangno is usually heaving with university students filling themselves with confectionery half the price of the *Starbucks* down the road.

Listings

Books The large bookshop in the bus terminal has a wide selection of English-language books and magazines, as well as an array of English-teaching materials.

Cinema The Migliore and Lotte department stores each have cinemas with several screens.

Convention centre The modern Kimdaejung Convention Center (Ⓦwww.kdjcenter.or.kr) near City Hall plays host to regular exhibitions and conferences.

Hospital Chonnam University hospital can be found between the KT building and the river (Ⓣ062/220-6902).

Post Office There's a post office in every district of the city (*-dong*), usually open Mon–Fri 9am–5pm. The most convenient for travellers will be the one in the bus terminal and the one just west of the May 18th Democratic Plaza.

Magazines The excellent monthly *Gwangju News* is one of the best expat magazines in the country, and although it's aimed at residents, visitors are sure to find it useful. Copies are available at the Gwangju International Center.

Shopping Gwangju is awash with department stores, including Lotte and Migliore in the city's downtown area, and Shinsaegae near the bus terminal. The funky shops of Clothes Street can also be found near Migliore.

Spectator sports Gwangju Sangmu is the only military football team in Korea's top division, and plays at the World Cup Stadium to the south of the city. Players are sourced from men taking their two-year compulsory military service.

Mokpo

The Korean peninsula has thousands of **islands** on its fringes, but a glance at the map will show that the seas around the coastal city of **MOKPO** have by far the most concentrated number. Though many of these are merely bluffs of barnacled rock poking out above the West Sea (also known as the Yellow Sea), dozens are accessible by **ferry** from Mokpo; beautiful in an ugly kind of way, this curious city gives the impression that it would happily be an island if it could.

Korea's southwestern train line ends quite visibly in Mokpo city centre. The highway from the centre of the country does likewise with less fuss, but was not completed until fairly recently. For much of the 1970s and 1980s, public funding also ran out before it hit southern Jeolla – poor transport connections to the rest of the country are just one example of the way this area was neglected by the central government. For much of this time, the main opposition party was based in Mokpo, and funding was deliberately cut in an attempt to marginalize the city, which was once among the most populous and powerful in the land. Though the balance is now being addressed with a series of large projects, much of the city is still run-down, and Mokpo is probably the **poorest** urban centre in the country. Some Koreans say that taxi drivers are a good indicator of the wealth of the cities, and here cabbies have a habit of beeping at pedestrians in the hope that they want a lift, occasionally swinging around for a second go. Things are changing, however, especially in the new district of Hadang, which was built on land reclaimed from the sea, but it'll be a while before Mokpo's saline charms are eroded.

Arrival, information and orientation

Mokpo, it has to be said, is not the easiest Korean city in which to get your bearings. The most logical way to arrive is by **train**, as the main station is right next to a busy shopping area in the centre of the city; **buses** terminate some way to the north, just a few thousand won by taxi to the centre, to which several city bus routes also head (15min; W900). The most useful of these is #1, which passes

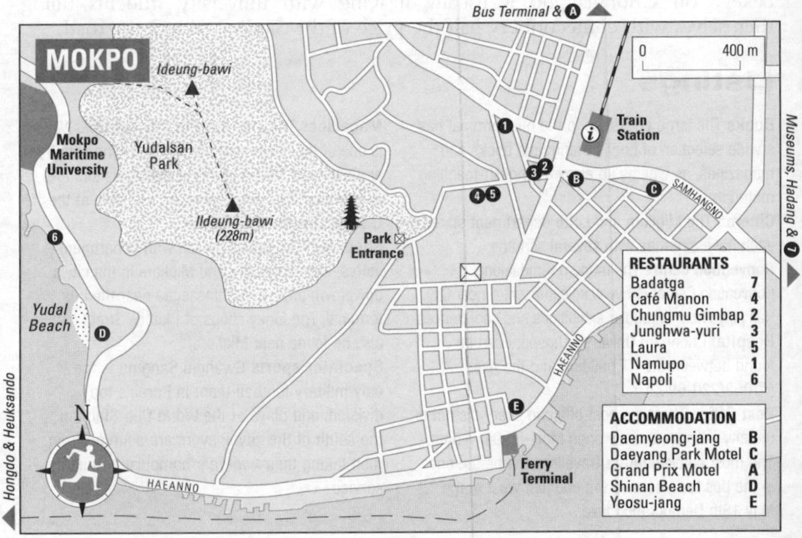

Mokpo

Mokpo	목포
Hadang	하당
Maritime Museum	문화예술회관
Natural History Museum	자연사 박물관
Pottery Museum	남공기념관
Yudalsan	유달산
Accommodation	
Daemyeong-jang	대명장
Daeyang Park Motel	대양 파크 모텔
Grand Prix Motel	그랑 프리 모텔
Shinan Beach Hotel	신한 비치 호텔
Yeosu-jang	여수장
Restaurants	
Badatga	바닷가
Café Manon	카페 마농
Chungmu Gimbap	충무 김밥
Junghwa-yori	중화요리
Laura	라우라
Namupo	나무포
Napoli	나폴리Mincipit aut alisisit

both the bus and the train station on its way to the **ferry terminal** on the city's southern shore. There were once half-a-dozen terminals, though by the time you read this all departures for the islands should leave from this new one, a large, lavishly funded structure standing incongruously in an area of apparent decay, and as such one of the most telling symbols of modern Mokpo.

Although things should improve as the city grows, **tourist information** has never been one of Mokpo's strong points. The booth in the train station offers twice-daily **tours** (10.10am & 1pm) of the city's main sights, and has maps to hand out. However, the best place to go fact hunting is the small info-hut outside the Natural History museum. The sparsely populated museum district lies a few kilometres east of the centre; further east again is Hadang, a modern new zone created on reclaimed land.

Accommodation

Despite the city's newfound wealth, there are few options at the **top end** of the accommodation range. Numerous places are springing up in Hadang, east of the centre, which may become the best place to stay in the city. Further down the price scale, there are dozens of fairly decent **motels** around the bus terminal, and an older collection of *yeogwan* by the train station. Fans of *jjimjilbangs* will find a brand-new one five-minutes' walk north of the bus terminal, on the same main road.

Daemyeong-jang Yeogwan Opposite train station ⓣ061/244-2576. This *yeogwan* is usually the cheapest around the train station, often offering discounts for single travellers. The rooms are fine (and cockroach-free, unlike some neighbouring *yeogwan*), and have a television, a/c and private bathroom. ❶

Daeyang Park Motel Chukbok-dong ⓣ061/243-4540. One of the better options in this area, the stairwells and corridors are lit up with ultraviolet lights, stars and planets. After this NASA-friendly introduction the rooms are disappointingly plain – though clean, with big televisions and free toiletries. ❸

Grand Prix Motel Next to the bus terminal, this motel offers a clean, cheap sleep, and has free Internet access in most rooms. ❷

Shinan Beach Hotel Seongsan-dong ⓣ061/243-3399, ⓕ061/243-0030. Cut off from the city centre by the mountains and with views of the sea, this was for decades Mokpo's no.1 tourist hotel. Nowadays its stylings feel a little Soviet, especially the chunky metal world map (and the service) behind the reception desk, and continued neglect will surely kill it off before long. ❼

Yeosu-jang 2–74 Hang-dong ⓣ061/244-0103. A cramped little lair within the briny ferry terminal area, the pale yellow paint gives this *yeogwan* a slightly Neapolitan air. Your bed will be a mattress on an *ondol* floor, but rooms have private facilities. ❶

The City

Mokpo is a city of dubious charms that the short-term visitor may be unable to appreciate. Its main draw lies outside the city with the mind-boggling number of **islands** accessible by ferry (see p.278). Many of these are visible from the peaks of **Yudalsan** (daily 8am–6pm; W700), a small hill-park within walking distance of the city centre and train station. It's a popular place, with troupes of hikers stomping their way up a maze of trails, past manicured gardens and a sculpture park, towards **Ildeung-bawi**, the park's main peak. After the slog to the top – a twenty-minute climb of 228m – you'll be rewarded with a **spectacular view**: a sea filled to the horizon with a swarm of emerald islands, some large enough to be inhabited, others just specks of rock. Similar views can be had from Yudalsan's second-highest peak, **Ideung-bawi**, just along the ridge past a large, precariously balanced boulder. Between the peaks, a trail runs west to a small **beach**. The waters around here are not suitable for swimming, but there are hour-long **ferry cruises** to nearby islands which run regularly from outside the nearby *Shinan Beach Hotel*. These tours offer delightful views of the islands that surround Mokpo, but bear in mind that the regular ferry routes from the city's main terminal are cheaper, longer, and offer a greater opportunity to observe island life.

The museum district

A handful of museums lie to the east of the centre, accessible on bus #111, but better approached by taxi. The most popular of this modern collective is the

▲ View from Yudalsan in Mokpo

Maritime Museum (Mon–Fri 9am–6pm, Sat & Sun to 7pm; closed Mon; W600), whose prime exhibits are the remains of a ship sunk near Wando in the eleventh century – the oldest such find in the country. Preserved from looting by its sunken location, celadon bowls and other relics scavenged from the vessel are on display, alongside a mock-up of how the ship may have once looked. Across the road is the large, breezy and modern **Pottery Museum** (same times; free), which although newly built, contains almost nothing of interest. Along the road, and marginally more interesting, is the **Natural History Museum** (same hours; W3000), home to an artily arranged butterfly exhibit, as well as a collection of dinosaur skeletons that is sure to perk up any sleepy youngster. Accessible on the same ticket, the building next door contains sights of a more highbrow nature, including calligraphy and paintings from **Sochi**, a famed nineteenth-century artist from the local area. Sochi was a protégé of Chusa, one of the country's most revered calligraphers (see p.376). More works from this talented duo and their contemporaries are on display here, as is a collection of modern works by Oh Sung-oo, a Korean impressionist who painted modern takes of oriental clichés.

Eating and drinking

In Mokpo, it's unlikely you'll walk five minutes without strolling past a dozen **restaurants** serving cheap, delicious food. The main downtown area west of the train station is packed with all kinds of places to eat, from cheap-as-chips snack bars to swanky *galbi* dens. One particularly good "eat street" – nameless, for all extents and purposes – runs straight through this quarter from the train station to Yudalsan, passing *Daemyeong-jang Yeogwan* (p.275), *Laura* (see below) and *Café Manon* (p.278) along the way.

Restaurants

Unless otherwise mentioned, the establishments listed below are in and around Mokpo's main shopping quarter, which lies between Yudalsan and the train station.

Badatga Yuhae-dong. Sitting in monopolistic comfort in the Maritime Museum, this is the only place to eat in the area and prices are, accordingly, a little high. Pizza and lobster are among the items on a Western-orientated menu, while *bibimbap* or the W10,000 cutlets won't break the bank.

Chungmu Gimbap Downtown. This small chain serves up cheap but passable versions of the dish it's named after – spicy octopus with *kimchi* and laver-rolled rice, a speciality of Tongyeong in Gyeongsang province – plus the regular chain dishes.

Junghwa-yori Downtown. Not a remarkable restaurant, but somewhere to wean yourself onto Chinese dishes if you're about to board the ferry to the Middle Kingdom. As with every Chinese restaurant in the country, *jajjang-myeon* is the favoured dish – stir-fried noodles in a black bean sauce.

Laura Cheuk-hu-dong. Just down the road from *Café Manon* (see p.278), this well-designed restaurant serves up Korean versions of Western dishes at reasonable prices, including delicious smoked chicken.

Namupo Downtown. Head here for the juiciest *galbi* in town, and right in the city centre to boot. There's a variety of meat styles to nuke and scoff down on the illustrated, English-language menu, though the dish of choice is the aromatic *Namupo Galbi*.

Napoli Jukgyu-dong. Steaks and seafood fried rice are among the dishes on offer at this two-storey restaurant, located on the waterfront near Yuda Beach, on the western side of Yudalsan. Sadly, the pretty sea views aren't always matched by the dishes.

Cafés and bars

Hadang, a newly built area south of the bus terminal, is the best place to head for a night out. On one particularly alcohol-fuelled street, *Wa Bar* and the *New York Bar* fight it out for the expat dollar, with the latter putting on a dance party every last Friday of the month. Between them is *Plastic*, surprisingly stylish for a Korean bar, though it remains to be seen how long it will last. For a caffeine fix or a green tea latte, head to *Café Manon* on the access road to Yudalsan, a friendly escape from Korea for those who need it, and filled with turntables, gramophones and the like.

West Sea islands

Looking west from Mokpo's Yudalsan peaks, you'll find a sea filled to the horizon with an assortment of **islands** – there are up to three thousand off Jeolla, and though many of these are merely bumps of rock that yo-yo in and out of the surf with the tide, hundreds are large enough to support fishing communities. The quantity is so vast, indeed, that it's easier to trail-blaze here than in some less-developed Asian countries – many of the islands' inhabitants have never seen a foreigner, and it's hard to find a more quintessentially Korean experience.

Much of the area is under the protective umbrella of **Dadohae Haesang National Park**, which stretches offshore from Mokpo to Yeosu. The two most popular islands in the park are **Hongdo**, which rises steeply from the West Sea, and neighbouring **Heuksando**, a miniature archipelago of more than a hundred islets of rock. Both lie some way to Mokpo's west, but those interested in seeing Korea's rural underbelly will have plenty of less touristy places to choose from. Further down the coast are **Jindo**, which owes its popularity to the local tide's annual parting of the sea, and **Wando**, connected to the mainland by road, but surrounded by an island constellation of its own.

Around Mokpo

The key to enjoying the islands around Mokpo is to kick back like the locals and do your own thing – just pick up a map, select an island at random, and make your way there; if you stop somewhere nice along the way, stay there instead. The **islanders** are among the friendliest people in Korea – some travellers have found themselves stuck on an island with no restaurants or accommodation, only to be taken in by a local family. These islands are not cut out for tourism and possess very few facilities, particularly in terms of banking so be sure to take along enough **money** for your stay. It's also a good idea to bring a **bike** or some **hiking boots**, as the natural surroundings mean that you're bound to be spending a lot of time outdoors.

One of the most pleasing ferry circuits connects come of Mokpo's closest island neighbours – a round-trip will take around two hours, and there are several ferries per day. The only island that sees any tourists whatsoever is **Oedaldo**, which has a decent range of accommodation and restaurants. Only a few kilometres from the mainland, though hidden by other islands, little **Dallido** (population: 104) offers some of the best walking opportunities. Beyond these lie a pack of much **larger islands**, accessible on several ferry

West Sea islands	
Heuksando	흑산도
Hongdo	홍도
Jindo	진도
Wando	완도

routes from Mokpo (Korean-only maps are available at the ferry terminal). Most of these will have beaches and hills to climb. However, public transport on the islands is poor or nonexistent so bring a bike from Mokpo if you can.

Hongdo and Heuksando

Lying on their own, well clear of the emerald constellations that surround Mokpo, and more than 100km west of the mainland, are this oddly matched pair of islands. Furthest-flung is **Hongdo**, whose slightly peculiar rock colouration gave rise to its name, which means "Red Island". Those who make it this far are less likely to be interested in its pigment than its spectacular shape. Spanning around six kilometres from north to south the island rises sheer from the waters of the West Sea to almost 380m above sea level, with valleys slicing through the deep expanses of dense forest as though pared by a gigantic knife. It may seem like a hikers' paradise, but much of the island has been placed under protection, which means that most views of the rock formations will have to be from a boat. **Tours** (2hr 30min; W15,000) run from the tiny village where the ferry docks, one of only two on an island whose population barely exceeds five hundred; most trips go around the rocky spires of **Goyerido**, a beautiful formation just north of Hongdo.

In contrast to Hondgo's chunk of steep terrain, **Heuksando** is a jagged collection of isles that's fully open for hiking. There are some great trails, with the most westerly ones highly recommended at sunset, when Hongdo is thrown into silhouette on the West Sea; most people head to the 227m-high peak of Sangnabong. Ferries usually dock at Yeri, Heuksando's main village, from where **boat tours** (2hr 30min; W15,000) of the dramatic coast are available, though some choose to hire a taxi (W60,000 for around 3hr) to see the island's interior.

Practicalities

Both islands are accessed by **ferry** from the terminal in Mokpo, almost always on the same services; these head first to Heuksando (1hr 45min; W28,000), then Hongdo (2hr 15min; W32,000). There are at least three per day throughout the year, though extra services are laid on in the height of summer when thousands of tourists descend on the islands. At these times, ferries can be packed to the gills: it's advisable to book tickets in advance through a tourist information office (even those in Seoul will be able to help). Both islands have collections of *yeogwan* (❸), and if you're coming during the summer holidays, you are advised to book your accommodation prior to arrival through the tourist offices in Mokpo or Gwangju.

Jindo

As the coast curls southeast from Mokpo, the bewildering array of islands shows no sign of letting up. **JINDO**, one of the most popular, is connected to the Korean mainland by road, but every year in early March the tides retreat to create a 3km-long land-bridge to a speck of land off the island's eastern shore, a phenomenon that Koreans often compare to Moses' parting of the Red Sea – this concept holds considerable appeal in an increasingly Christian country, and "**Moses' Miracle**" persuades Koreans to don wellies and dash across in their tens of thousands. For the best dates to see this ask at any tourist board in the area, or call the national information line on ⓣ1330.

Jindo is also famed for the Jindo-gae, a white breed of **dog** with a distinctive curved tail; unique to the island, this species has been officially classified as National Natural Treasure #53. The mutts can be seen in their pens at a research centre –

fifteen-minutes' walk from the bus terminal – which occasionally hosts short and unappealing dog shows, as well as a canine beauty pageant each autumn. Jindo is accessible from Mokpo by both **bus** and **ferry**, with free shuttle buses from the terminal to the relevant stretch of coast during the annual parting of the seas.

Wando and around

Dangling off Korea's southwestern tip is a motley bunch of more than a hundred islands. The hub of this group and the most popular is **WANDO**, owing to its connections to the mainland by bus and Jeju Island by sea. Not that there's nothing to detain you here – a journey away from **Wando-eup**, the main town, will give you a glimpse of Jeolla's pleasing rural underbelly. **Gugyedeung** is a pleasant rocky beach in the small village of Jeongdo-ri on the island's southern coast, while north of Wando-eup is **Cheonghaejin**, a stone park looking over a pleasant island which, despite its unassuming pastoral mix of farms and mud walls, was once important enough to send trade ships to China. Both of these sights can be reached on regular buses from Wando-eup's bus terminal.

In Wando-eup itself, most of the action is centred around the bus station, but the area around the main ferry terminal makes a quieter and more pleasant place **to stay**; *Naju Yeoinsuk* is visible as you exit and has the cheapest rooms around (❶), while *Hilltop Motel* (❷) just behind it is for those who prefer to sleep on a bed rather than *ondol* flooring. Overlooking the sea between the two terminals is the pale yellow building of the *Dubai Motel* (Ⓣ061/553-0688; ❷), whose rooms are excellent value. For **food**, there's a fish market right next to the ferry terminal, and plenty of restaurants serving both raw and cooked fare. Those looking for something other than seafood should head a short way along the coast to *Jjajjaru*, a Chinese restaurant offering huge two-person courses that could feed three or four.

Heading further afield, you'll be spoilt for choice, with even the tiniest inhabited islands served by ferry from Wando-eup. **Maps** of the islands are available from the ferry terminal, where almost all services depart, with a few leaving from *Je-il Mudu* pier, a short walk to the north. At the time of writing, **Jeongsando** was the island most visited by local tourists, mainly due to the fact that it was the scene of *Spring Waltz*, a popular drama series. Nomenclature alone should tell you that spring is the busiest time of year – and quite beautiful, with the island's fields bursting with flowers – though it remains a sleepy place for much of the year. More beautiful is pine-clad **Bogildo**, a well-kept secret accessible via a ferry terminal on the west of Wando island – free hourly shuttle-buses make the pretty twenty-minute journey here from the bus terminal in Wando-eup. In the centre of tadpole-shaped Bogildo is a lake, whose craggy tail stretches east, taking in a couple of popular beaches on the way.

Mokpo to Yeosu

The large coastal cities of Mokpo and Yeosu are connected by road, though in the summer it's possible to travel between them by ferry – a beautiful journey that jets passengers past whole teams of islands. Travelling on the overland route, you'll pass by the bald crags of **Wolchulsan National Park**, just outside Mokpo, the tea plantation at **Boseong** and two gorgeous temples further east in the city of **Suncheon**. From here, Yeosu lies around 30km down a narrow peninsula to the south, while heading north you'll reach the fringes of **Jirisan**, Korea's largest national park, and home to the popular temple **Hwa-eomsa**.

Hiking in Korea

If you're wondering what keeps Koreans in such great shape, here's your answer – hiking. The activity is so popular that it thoroughly eclipses taekwondo, the national sport, and most of Korea's parks are busy year-round with a steady trail of locals enjoying a day out.

Ulleungdo ▲

Seoraksan National Park ▼

Where to go

There are no fewer than **seventeen national parks** on the mainland - their names all end with the suffix "-san", which means mountain or mountains. The national parks are supplemented by an even greater number of lesser parks, mountains and hills. Wherever you are in the country, you're always within walking distance of a hiking trail. For a list of Korea's most popular hikes see the box overleaf. Alternatively, you can escape the hustle and bustle of the mainland entirely and head to one of the 4000 or so islands surrounding the coast. **Jeju Island** is the largest - and deservedly most popular - while gorgeous little **Ulleungdo** (see p.231) sits alone in the East Sea, but literally hundreds more can be accessed by ferry from the main hubs of Mokpo, Incheon and Tongyeong. Many are tiny specks of land where fishing is the only way of life, and time passes at a snail's pace; tantalizingly, some have never played host to a foreign visitor.

What to do

Hiking in Korea is extremely **user-friendly**. English-language **maps** are available at all park offices, trails are well marked with dual-language signs, and each national park has a cluster of accommodation and restaurants outside its main entrance. Some are mini-towns bursting with neon signs and karaoke rooms, which dilutes the experience somewhat, but a hike is not complete unless it's finished off with a good meal: *pajeon* is the most popular post-hike dish, a kind of savoury pancake made with mountain vegetables, while a creamy rice wine named *dongdongju* is the drink of choice. Deceptively mild in taste, it can pack a punch, especially the next morning.

What to see

It must be said that none of Korea's parks is huge, and there's very little fauna to see; since all parks are likely to be teeming with budding hikers, you're unlikely to get lost, either. However, they're usually awash with natural spectacles such as gorgeous peaks and **waterfalls**, and sprinkled with functioning **temples** and hermitages – some spectacular feasts of intricate architecture and colourful paintwork, others remote hideaways where the monks can contemplate existence in near solitude. The beauty of hiking in Korea is not knowing what you will see on the way; the occasional holy grotto, **fortress** wall or hillside-carved Buddha make it easy to weave a spot of sightseeing into a good walk.

When to visit

Despite the wealth of choice available, many of Korea's trails contrive to be packed to the gills, especially during **holidays** and warm **weekends**, when the parks are full with locals enjoying a day out. Many families bring along sizeable picnics to enjoy on their way to the peaks, and lone travellers may be invited to join in – Koreans hate to see people on their own. Special mention must be made of the fascinating **ajumma** brigade: Korean grandmothers are little short of indestructible, and these elderly women rock up to mountain ranges in huge, bubble-permed packs of up to fifty. Wearing fishing jackets identical but for the choice of red or blue, they laugh, shout and sing all the way up, then all the way down again, and put many a Westerner to shame with their strength and energy. You know when you've been *ajumma*-ed.

▲ Beopjusa Temple, Songnisan National Park

▼ Seek out one of Korea's forested trails

Wolchulsan National Park ▲

Hallasan's Peak, Jeju Island ▼

Popular hikes

▸▸ **Day-trips from the city** With so much of the country covered by mountains, it's possible to see any Korean city from the vantage point of its surrounding peaks. Even Seoul has a national park. **Bukhansan** (see p.117) is the world's most visited, though occasionally offers surprising serenity.

▸▸ **Multi-day hikes** Only a couple of parks have shelters in which you can stay the night. **Jirisan** (see p.258) is the largest in the country, and features a three-day, 26km-long spine route, and a small bear population. **Seoraksan** (see p.178) is not quite as expansive, but is considered the most beautiful in the country, with great clumps of rock peeking out from the pines like giant skulls; waking up on its misty peaks provides a top-of-the-world feeling.

▸▸ **Scaling peaks** South Korea's highest peak is on Jeju Island. The 1950m-high extinct volcanic cone of **Hallasan** (see p.379) dominates the island, but is surprisingly easy to climb, as long as Jeju's fickle weather agrees. The highest mountain on the whole peninsula is **Paekdusan** (2744m) on the Chinese–North Korean border (see p.415); its sumptuously blue crater lake, ringed by jagged peaks, is a font of myth and legend.

▸▸ **Getting away from it all** Hiking is so popular in Korea that some trails resemble supermarket queues, but there are a few splendid ways to get away from it all. **Woraksan** (see p.339) is one of the least visited national parks in the country, its spine road home to just a few quaint villages, while **Chiaksan** has a wonderfully rustic range of *minbak* homestays. The small park of **Wolchulsan** sees few visitors dash across the vertigo-inducing bridge that connects two of its peaks, and though popular on account of its enormous golden Buddha, **Songnisan** (see p.335) has a tiny, secluded guesthouse; when the sun goes down, you'll be alone with nature, a trickling stream and a bowl of creamy *dongdongju*.

Mokpo to Yeosu	
Boseong	보성
Hwa-eomsa	화엄사
Jogyesan Provincial Park	조계산 국립 공원
Suncheon	순천
Wolchulsan National Park	월출산 국립 공원

Wolchulsan National Park

A short bus-ride east of Mokpo is **WOLCHULSAN NATIONAL PARK**, the smallest of Korea's national parks and also one of its least visited – the lack of historic temples and difficulty of access are a blessing in disguise. Set within the achingly gorgeous Jeollanese countryside, Wolchulsan's jumble of mazy rock rises to over 800m above sea level, casting jagged shadows over the surrounding rice paddies. Just five buses a day make the fifteen-minute trip to the main entrance at Cheonhwangsaji from the small town of **Yeong-am**; alternatively, it's an affordable taxi ride, or an easy walk. Yeong-am itself is well connected to Mokpo and Yeosu by bus. From here a short but steep hiking trail heads up to **Cheonhwangbong** (809m), the park's main peak along the way, you'll have to traverse the "Cloud Bridge", a steel structure slung between two peaks – not for vertigo sufferers. Views from here, or the peak itself, are magnificent, and with an early enough start it's possible to make the tough hike to **Dogapsa**, an uninteresting temple on the other side of the park, while heeding the "no shamanism" warning signs along the way. There's no public transport to or from the temple, but a forty-minute walk south – all downhill – will bring you to **Gurim**, a small village on the main road between Mokpo and Yeong-am. A couple of kilometres south of Gurim is the **Yeongam Pottery Centre** (daily 9am–6pm; free). Due to the properties of the local soil, this whole area was Korea's main ceramics hub throughout the Three Kingdoms period, and local artisans enjoyed trade with similarly minded folk in China and Japan. Sadly, the centre is as dull as the clay itself, though the on-site shop is good for souvenirs; you may get a chance to throw your own pot for a small fee, and there's a decidedly brutalist sculpture outside the main entrance which would look at home in Pyongyang (were it not for the South Korean flag). The downhill walk from Gurim to the centre is much more interesting – the town remains an important base for pottery production, and accordingly many of its houses have eschewed modern-day metals for beautiful, **traditional tiled roofs**. There are few concessions to modern life here, and a wander round will give you a peek into Jeolla's rural belly.

Boseong

The town of **BOSEONG** is famed for the **tea plantations** that surround it, and visitors flock to them during warmer months to take pictures of the thousands of tea trees that line the slopes. They may not be as busy or as verdant as those in Sri Lanka or Laos, for example, but they're still a magnificent sight, particularly when sepia-tinged on early summer evenings. Pluckers comb the well-manicured rows at all times of year, though spring is the main harvest season, and if you're lucky you may be able to see the day's take being processed in the on-site factory. **Green tea** (*nok-cha*) rode the crest of the "healthy living" wave that swept the country shortly after the turn of the century, and here you can imbibe the leaf in more ways than you could ever have imagined. A couple of on-site restaurants serve up

▲ Boseong tea fields

green tea chicken cutlet, green tea *bibimbap* and green tea with seafood on rice, as well as a variety of dishes featuring pork from pigs raised on a green tea diet. There's also a café serving *nok-cha* ice cream and snacks, and if you've never tried a *nok-cha* latte, you'll never get a better opportunity.

Daehan-dawon (summer 5am–8pm; winter 8am–6pm; W1600) is the main plantation, and to get here on public transport you'll first need to head to

Boseong itself. From there, head coastward on one of the half-hourly buses to Yulpo, and get off at the tea plantation – let the driver know where you're going. Further up the same road are a few less-visited plantations that can be entered for free, one of which stretches down to a rather cute village by the water's edge.

Suncheon

SUNCHEON is a surprisingly large place – indeed, first-time visitors discovering this may have given rise to the city's official slogan, "Aha! Suncheon". However, there's little to see in the city itself, its main use being a handy base for nearby **Jogyesan Provincial Park** (see below). Suncheon's two **bus terminals**, as well as its **train station** are all located on the same main drag, a large road that runs right the way through the centre of the city; all are a little too far from each other to be walked between, but taxi rides cost no more than W4000. A visit to both sides of Jogyesan will probably necessitate a stay in Suncheon (unless you're staying in the park itself). The best place to motel-hunt is the district of Yeonhyang-dong, which also has some good places to drink. Price-wise there's not much between the motels, and it's near impossible to haggle them down; *Dodgers Motel* (ⓣ061/722-2115; ❷) is usually the cheapest, and has rooms that are more than acceptable for the price. There are several decent *galbi* **restaurants** and **bars** in the area, including *Baekso*, which serves an impressive array of side dishes with your *galbi* or *samgyeopsal*, and *Julianna*, by far the most popular **bar** with Suncheon's expat community (a fact evident in the number of motorbikes parked outside on weekend evenings).

Jogyesan Provincial Park

The small but pretty, **JOGYESAN PROVINCIAL PARK** is flanked by two splendid temples, **Seonamsa** and **Songgwangsa**, both of which are accessible by bus from Suncheon (see above). As long as you get up early enough, it's possible to see both temples in a single day, taking either the hiking trail that runs between them, or one of the buses that heads the long way around the park.

Seonamsa, on the park's eastern side, is the closer temple of the two to Suncheon, but the journey will still take almost an hour. On the way in from the ticket booth you'll pass by Seungseongyo, an old rock bridge; its semicircular lower arch makes a full disc when reflected in the river below: slide down to the water to get the best view. There has been a temple here since 861 – the dawn of the Unified Silla period – but having fallen victim to fire several times, the present buildings are considerably more modern. The temple is apparently too poor to afford a full-scale refurbishment, but provides a pleasant visit as a result, despite the fact that a couple of the once-meditative ponds have been carelessly lined with concrete. Its entrance gate is aging gracefully, though the dragon heads are a more recent addition – the original smaller, stealthier-looking ones can be found in the small museum inside. Notably, the temple eschews the usual four heavenly guardians at the entrance, relying instead on the surrounding mountains for protection, which look especially imposing on a rainy day. The main hall in the central courtyard is also unconventional, with its blocked central entrance symbolically allowing only Buddhist knowledge through, and not even accessible to high-ranking monks – this is said to represent the egalitarian principles of the temple. The hall was apparently built without nails, and at the back contains a long coffin-like box which holds a large picture of the Buddha that was once unfurled during times of drought, to bring rain to the crops. A smaller version of this picture hangs over the box.

Around the complex are a number of small paths, one leading to a pair of majestic stone turtles; the one on the right-hand side is crowned by an almost Moorish clutch of twisting dragons. Another path fires west across the park to Songgwangsa, a four-hour walk, more if you scale Janggunbong (885m), the main peak, on the way.

To the west of the park is **Songgwangsa**, viewed by Koreans as one of the most important temples in the country, and this is one of the "Three Jewels" of Korean Buddhism (see p.225). Large, well maintained and often full of devotees, it may disappoint those who've already appreciated the earthier delights of Seonamsa. The temple is accessed on a peculiar bridge-cum-pavilion, beyond which can be found the four guardians that were conspicuously absent at Seonamsa. Within the complex is Seungbojeon, a hall filled with 1250 individually sculpted figurines, the painstaking attention to detail echoed in the paintwork of the main hall; colourful and highly intricate patterns spread like a rash down the pillars, surrounding a trio of Buddha statues representing the past, present and future. Unfortunately, the Hall of National Teachers is closed to the public – perhaps to protect its gold-fringed ceiling.

Practicalities

The simplest way to get to the park is on one of the **tour buses** that leave from outside Suncheon's train station every day at 9.50am. As well as Seonamsa temple, tours take in a film set on which historical dramas are regularly shot, and the interesting **Nagan folk village**, which is set within authentic Jeoson fortress walls, and is a pleasingly rural place to stay. On weekends, another tour bus leaves at 9.40am, though it goes to Songgwangsa temple, rather than Seonamsa. To get to the park on public transport, take bus #1 from central Suncheon to Seonamsa, or #111 to Songgwangsa. Both buses take an hour or so from Suncheon, and if moving between the two you'll save a lot of time by transferring at Seopyeong-maeul, a small village near Seonamsa, where the bus routes split. Also note that there are occasional buses to Songgwangsa from Gwangju.

There are low-key **accommodation** and **restaurant** facilities at both entrances to the park; *minbak* offer the most authentic Korean experience, but for a little more comfort try *Saejogyesan-jang* (Ⓣ061/751-9200; ❷) outside the Seonamsa entrance. The restaurants outside Songgwangsa are in traditionally styled buildings; *Suncheon Sikdang* deserves a mention, if only for the charming way in which its name has been spelled out in Korean. As in many Korean rural areas, *sanchae bibimbap* is a favoured dish, and is made with local ingredients.

Hwa-eomsa

Although it's not on the main Mokpo to Yeosu route, the temple of **HWA-EOMSA**, locked in the muscular embrace of **Jirisan National Park**, is a highly worthy detour. The park itself spans the tri-state junction of Jeonbuk, Jeonnam and Gyeongnam and is one of Korea's best in terms of hiking; it's covered in more detail in the Gyeongsang chapter (see p.258). The temple (sunrise–sunset; W3800) is a kilometre-plus uphill walk from the bus stop just outside the park entrance – an early morning visit is recommended, as you'll avoid any school groups and, hopefully, be able to see the sun rise over the peaks. At the entrance to Hwa-eomsa, the **temple guardians** are worth a look – the three regular bulgy-eyed fellows are joined by a serene buck-toothed figure strumming an instrument with huge fingers. Inside the complex are two **pagodas**; the western one is the more interesting, carved in Silla times with Buddhist figures that remain visible to this day. Nearby is a **stone lantern** that is – if you believe the Korean tourist authorities – the largest such sculpture in the world, an oversized beast emblazoned with cloud and lotus motifs, stretching over six metres from the ground. Subtler in its approach is the neighbouring stone pagoda, its main block balanced on the heads of four smug-looking lions. You'll see that some of the buildings around the complex are painted while some remain bare; attempts were made at repainting the whole lot, but these were quashed by a lack of funds and the deteriorating quality of the wood. **Gakgwangjeon** is a particularly appealing hall. Looking all the better for its lack of renovation, its largely bare wooden structure forms a delicious contrast with the huge pictures that hang inside – a rhapsody in red. If you're looking for some solitude, head behind the heart of the complex to **Gu-am**. This hermitage is not as old or pretty as the buildings in the main complex, but filled as it is with vegetable plots, birdsong and mossy paths, and almost no signs of modern life, it's quite enchanting.

From the Hwa-eomsa bus stop it's possible to hike up to **Nogodan peak** (1507m), a walk of around three hours, though many save time and energy by taking a connecting bus most of the way up. Times are infrequent but there's one roughly every hour from 7am to 6pm – check at the small **information centre** near the bus stop for the latest details. If you choose to take the bus, the remaining distance to the top is an easy walk of an hour or so – make sure you leave enough time if catching the last bus down. From the summit you'll see Cheonwangbong in the distance, at 1915m it is the highest peak on the Korean mainland. For hardcore hikers there's a **three-day trek** that takes you from Nogodan all the way across the national park, finishing at Daewonsa in the east – the information office at the Hwa-eomsa bus stop can supply you with a map.

Practicalities

Direct **buses** run to the park entrance below Hwa-eomsa from the major Jeollanese cities of Jeonju, Gwangju and Yeosu, as well as from Busan in Gyeongsang province. From other cities, you'll have to change at the small town of Gurye, from where there are regular bus connections to the temple. Around the bus stop are plenty of places to stay and eat; one of the most distinctive restaurants is *Iyagi*, an attractive place just across the road from the *Chirisan Swiss* hotel, which has steak, spaghetti and *gingko* fried rice on the menu at reasonable prices.

Accommodation

Campsite Located near the temple entrance and open year-round, tents cost W3000–5000, depending on their size.

Chirisan Swiss Tourist Hotel ⓣ061/783-0700, ⓕ061/782-1571. The only deluxe accommodation on offer in the area. However, the rooms are a little on the "cosy" side, and the mattresses could be softer. Make sure to ask about discounts off-season. ❺

Little Prince Pension ⓣ061/783-4700, ⓕ061/782-0741. The best of a string of similar places in this area, this vaguely log-cabin-like pension has big rooms, including some duplexes. The terrace at the back sometimes hosts *soju*-filled night-time feasts over the fire. ❹

Minbak Village There are plenty of *minbak* around the bus stop, but the nicer ones are close to the *Chirisan Swiss* a couple of hundred metres down the road. ❷

Nogodan Sanjang Up in the park itself near Nogodan peak (see above for transport details), this is one of most accessible mountain shelters in the country, and despite a 140-person capacity is often full – book online at ⓦwww.knps.or.kr. If you haven't brought along your own bedding, you can rent some for a small fee. ❶

Worldeung Park Hotel ⓣ061/782-0082. Not a beautiful place by any means, and woefully overpriced at high season, but this hotel has a certain 1970s charm that is somewhat in keeping with the area – wooden furniture in the bedrooms, and plastic fittings from the age of invention in the bathrooms. Choose from bed or *ondol* rooms. ❹

Yeosu and around

YEOSU is by far the most appealing city on Jeonnam's south coast. Sadly, it sees few tourists now that ferry services to Jeju Island have been discontinued, despite there being more than enough here to eat up a whole day of sightseeing. Beautifully set in a ring of emerald islands, the wonderful views over the South Sea would in any case justify a trip down the narrow peninsula. Though parts of the coast remain rugged and pristine, the area around Yeosu has been heavily industrialized, especially the gigantic factory district to the city's north, and consequently many of Yeosu's foreign visitors are here on business. However, in 2012 Yeosu plays host to an international **Expo**, an event set to take place in the area between the mainland and the islet of Odongdo that could put Yeosu firmly back on the tourist map.

Despite the city's sprawling size, many of the most interesting sights are just about within walking distance of each other in and around the city centre. These include **Odongdo**, a bamboo-and-pine island popular with families, and a replica of Admiral Yi's famed **turtle ship**. Beyond the city limits are the black-sand beach of **Manseongni**, and **Hyangiram**, a magical hermitage at the end of the Yeosu peninsula.

Arrival, information and orientation

Buses and **trains** arriving into Yeosu squeeze down the narrow isthmus, which opens out as it hits the city. The new **airport** lies around 20km to the north – take a bus from the city's main bus terminal – and has flights to and from Seoul and Jeju Island. Whether you are arriving by train or bus, the stations are located frustratingly far from the action. A number of **bus routes** head into the centre from both, but you'll barely pay any more money in a taxi. The **ferry terminal**, on the other hand, is in an area bristling with shops and motels. This is Yeosu's heart, with plenty of raw fish restaurants and markets, and many of the city's best sights within walking distance. From around the ferry terminal you'll see the triangular red masts of Dolsan Bridge, which connects the city to the island of Dolsando. For a city of Yeosu's size, good **travel information** is hard to come by, with the only decent point being a small booth near the entrance to Odongdo, a small, gentrified island connected to Yeosu by causeway.

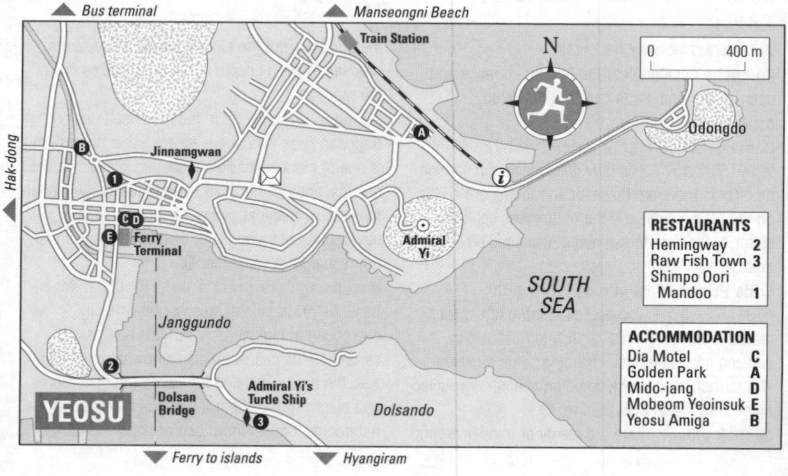

Yeosu

Yeosu	여수
Admiral Yi's Turtle Ship	거북선
Hyangiram	향일암
Jinnamgwan	진남관
Manseongni	만성리 해수욕장
Odongdo	오동도
Accommodation	
Dia Motel	디아 모텔
Golden Park Hotel	골든 파크 호텔
Mido-jang	미도장
Mobeom Yeoinsuk	모범 여인숙
Yeosu Amiga Hotel	여수 아미가 호텔
Restaurants	
Hemingway	헤밍웨이
Shimpo Oori Mandoo	심포우리만두

Accommodation

You'll find **motels** near all of Yeosu's main travel junctions, but due to the out-of-the-way location of the bus terminal and the seedy environs of the train station it's best to head to the **ferry area**, which is within walking distance of many sights and the city's main shopping district. There are some also extremely cheap *yeoinsuk* immediately opposite the exit to the building. However, those aiming even lower on the price scale – or just in need of a good wash after spending time on the Jeonnam coast – should head to a *jjimjilbang* on the shore near Admiral Yi's turtle ship, on the way to Hyangiram, which offers excellent sea views from some of its pool rooms.

Dia Motel Gyo-dong ⓣ 061/663-3347. Near the ferry terminal, this motel is just down the road from the *Mido-jang*, but the rooms are slightly plusher, and the prices accordingly higher. ❸

Golden Park Hotel Sujeon-dong ⓣ 061/665-400. Poky *ondol* rooms make this more of a motel than a hotel, though it's a good option on the entrance road to Odongdo, and is also within walking distance of the train station. ❸

Mido-jang Gyo-dong. This downtown motel, within a few minutes' walk of the ferry terminal, has perfectly acceptable rooms with private facilities. The owners offer slight discounts to foreigners. ❶

Mobeom Yeoinsuk Ferry terminal area ⓣ 061/663-4897. Just one of a whole clutch of *yeoinsuk* in a pleasantly brackish area opposite the ferry terminal, this is a friendly, family-run place with dirt-cheap rooms. ❶

Yeosu Amiga Hotel Chungmu-dong ⓣ 061/663-2011. Yeosu's best hotel has cosy rooms with great showers, and is just a short walk from the main shopping area. A popular choice with Korean honeymooners (though less so since the ferries to Jeju stopped), it has a decent on-site restaurant and café, and offers airport pick-up. Ask about discounts off-season – usually around thirty percent. ❺

The City

For many visitors the real joys of Yeosu can be found wandering around a fish market or pouring over one of the many restaurants' menus. However, the city centre is home to a cache of interesting, unassuming sights. In the very centre of town, and just ten-minutes' walk northeast of the ferry terminal, is **Jinnamgwan**, a pavilion once used as a guesthouse by the Korean navy. The site had previously been a command post of national hero **Admiral Yi** (see box, p.289), but a guesthouse was built here in 1599, a year after his death, and replaced by the current

▲ Admiral Yi's turtle ship, Yeosu

structure in 1718. At 54m in length and 14m high it's the country's largest single-storey wooden structure. In front of the guesthouse is a stone man – initially one of a group of seven – that was used as a decoy in the 1592–98 Japanese invasions (see box opposite). The guesthouse sits on a rise, and the scene of the battles must once have made a spectacular view; just below the pavilion is a small museum (9am–6pm; closed Mon; free) detailing the area's maritime fisticuffs.

A statue of Admiral Yi stands to the east of the city centre, on a hill overlooking the small island of **Odongdo** (daily 9am–6pm; W1600). Essentially a botanical garden, it's crisscrossed by a deliciously scented network of pine- and bamboo-lined path, and has become a popular picnicking destination for local families. A 700m-long causeway connects it to the mainland, and if you don't feel like walking you can hop on the bus – resembling a train – for a small fee. The island's paths snake up to a lighthouse, the view from which gives a far clearer rendition of Yeosu's surroundings than can be had from Jinnamgwan in the city centre. In the summer, kids love to cool off in the fountain by the docks on the northern shore – the water show comes on every twenty minutes or so. A number of **boat tours** operate from Odongdo – operators are unlikely to speak English, so these are best arranged through the tourist information centre outside the main entrance; routes include cruises across the harbour to Dolsan Bridge, and a longer haul to Hyangiram (p.290) and back.

Across Dolsan Bridge is a replica of **Admiral Yi's turtle ship** (daily 8am–6pm; W1200), a small, rounded vessel with a wooden dragon head at the front that spearheaded the battles against the Japanese in the sixteenth century – the boats were so-called because they were tough to attack from the top, due to its iron roof covered with spiked metal. Inside the replica is a modern-day regiment of mannequins showing what once went on at sea, though the outside of the ship is decidedly more interesting.

Eating and drinking

For a city that prides itself on the food it culls from the sea, Yeosu's **restaurants** are surprisingly poor by Jeolla standards. If you're feeling brave, and

Admiral Yi, conqueror of the seas

"...it seems, in truth, no exaggeration to assert that from first to last he never made a mistake, for his work was so complete under each variety of circumstances as to defy criticism."

Admiral George Alexander Ballard, *The Influence of the Sea on the Political History of Japan*

Were he not born during the Joseon dynasty, a period in which a nervous Korea largely shielded itself from the outside world, it is likely that **Admiral Yi Sun-shin** (1545–98) would today be ranked alongside Napoleon and Horatio Nelson as one of the greatest generals of all time. A Korean national hero, you'll see his face on the W100 coin, and **statues** of the great man dot the country's shores. The two most pertinent are at Yeosu, where he was headquartered, and Tongyeong (then known as Chungmu; see p.253), the site of his most famous victory.

Yi Sun-shin was both a beneficiary and a victim of circumstance. A year after his first major posting as Naval Commander of Jeolla in 1591, there began a six-year wave of **Japanese invasions**. Although the Nipponese were setting their sights on an eventual assault on China, Korea had the misfortune to be in the way and loyal to the Chinese emperor, and 150,000 troops laid siege to the country. Admiral Yi achieved a string of well-orchestrated victories, spearheaded by his famed **turtle ships**, vessels topped with iron spikes that were adept at navigating the island-dotted waters with ease.

Despite his triumphs, the Admiral fell victim to a Japanese spy and the workings of the Korean political system. A double agent persuaded a high-ranking Korean General that the Japanese would attack in a suspiciously treacherous area; seeing through the plan, Admiral Yi refused the General's orders, and as a result was stripped of his duties and sent to Seoul for torture. His successor, Won Gyeun, was far less successful, and within months had been killed by the Japanese after managing to lose the whole Korean fleet, bar twelve warships. Yi was hastily **reinstated**, and after hunting down the remaining ships managed to repel a Japanese armada ten times more numerous. Peppering the enemy's vessels with cannonballs and flaming arrows, Yi waited for the tide to change and rammed the tightly packed enemy ships into one another. Heroic to the last, Yi was killed by a stray bullet as the Japanese retreated from what was to be the final battle of the war.

have a decent command of Korean seafood menus, you will find that the shopping area north of the ferry terminal has a wealth of choice, as does **Raw Fish Town** – a parade of restaurants near Admiral Yi's turtle ship. Prices at the latter aren't cheap, and establishments cater for groups rather than solo travellers – large spreads are the order of the day (figure on paying W30,000 or more for a meal). Alternatively there's *Hemingway*, near Dolsan Bridge, which serves passable steak and pork cutlet dishes with splendid views back over the city. The shopping area has a lot of grimy Korean fast-food dens but *Shinpo Oori Mandoo* stands out from the crowd, and has an English-language picture menu to boot. The downtown area is quiet even on weekend evenings – for a **night out** you're much better off heading to the new area west of the centre called **Hak-dong**, though it's over half an hour away by bus, and expensive to reach by taxi. Here, the expat-friendly drinking den *Elle Lui* continues to get good reviews.

Around Yeosu

Around 4km north up the coast from Yeosu's train station, you'll find *minbak* and raw fish restaurants aplenty at **Manseongni**, which is revered as the only **black sand** beach on the Korean mainland – in truth, this volcanic material is actually rather grey in appearance. Mid-April is said to be the time of year when the beach "opens its eyes", and people flock to bury themselves in the allegedly nutritious sand, an experience somewhat akin to being a cigarette butt for the day.

South of the city centre, the mainland soon melts into a host of **islands**, many of which can be accessed from Yeosu's ferry terminal. As with Jeolla's other island archipelagos, these are best explored with no set plan in mind. **Dongsando** is the most visited as it's connected to the mainland by road, and is most famed for **Hyangiram**, a hermitage dangling over the crashing seas. Further south are **Geumodo**, a rural island fringed by rugged cliffs and rock faces, and **Geomundo**, far from Yeosu – and briefly occupied by Britain during the 1880s, during an ill-planned stab at colonizing Korea's southern coast – but now an increasingly popular holiday destination. From Geomundo you can take a tour boat around the assorted spires of rock that make up **Baekdo**, a protected archipelago containing a number of impressive formations.

Hyangiram

Clinging to the cliffs at the southeastern end of Dolsando is the magical hermitage of **Hyangiram** (daily pre-dawn–8pm; W2000), an eastward-facing favourite of sunrise seekers, and a popular place to ring in the New Year. Behind Hyangiram is a collection of angular boulders which – according to local monks – resembles an oriental folding screen, and are soaked with camellia blossom in the spring. To get to Hyangiram, take a local bus from Yeosu's city centre – #111 also runs directly from the train station and Odongdo. Although the trip can take around an hour, on a bumpy, winding course, the journey costs just W1000. Outside the hermitage is a small town of motels and restaurants – *Hwangtobang* (Ⓣ061/644-4353; ❷), near the entrance, offers both of these as well as a café, though other motels have better sea views.

Jeollabuk-do

Green and gorgeous, **JEOLLABUK-DO** (Jeonbuk) is home to four excellent **national parks**, and it's to these that most of the province's visitors head. Jeonju aside, you're unlikely to be coming here for the cities: Iksan is rather dull and best used as a transport hub, Gunsan on the coast is just as devoid of sights and near a major army base, and Namwon relies on a romantic myth to get visitors into town. All the more surprising, then, that the regional capital **Jeonju** is one of the most likeable cities in the country.

The best of Jeonbuk's wonderful array of parks lie in the southwest of the province and includes **Naejangsan**, **Seonunsan** and **Byeonsanbando**. To the east of the province, **Deogyusan** is popular with skiers, while the arresting "horse-ear" mountains of **Maisan Provincial Park** accentuate the appeal of Tapsa, a glorious temple that sits in between its distinctive twin peaks. Part of Jirisan National Park lies in Jeonbuk, and is covered in the Gyeongbuk chapter (see p.258).

Jeonju

JEONJU marked the beginning of one of the longest lines of kings that the world has ever seen. It was here in the fourteenth century that the first kings of the **Joseon kingdom** were born, and the dynasty went on to rule over Korea for over five centuries. Overlooked as the dynastic capital in favour of Seoul, Jeonju is not over-endowed with historical riches, but is well worth a visit. Gingko-lined streets help to create an ambience notably relaxed for a Korean city, while its splendid **hanok village** of traditional housing contains more than enough for a full day of sightseeing. Jeonju also has one of the greatest concentrations of cinemas in the country, and those who visit in the spring may be able to take advantage of JIFF (Ⓦ eng.jiff.or.kr), by far the most eclectic major **film festival** in the country; this usually runs for nine days between late April and early May.

The city also remains the most important in the country for papermaking – both hand-made and industrial. However, it's **food** that Koreans most readily associate with Jeonju. Many of the differences are too subtle to be noticed by foreigners – and in the cheapest places nonexistent – but you're likely to find a greater and more lovingly prepared number of *banchan* (side dishes) around your meal, and a slightly greater emphasis on herbal seasoning than the somewhat less cultivated tastebud-tinglers of salt and red pepper paste. Of particular interest is Jeonju's take on the tasty Korean staple, **bibimbap**; see box, p.296 for details.

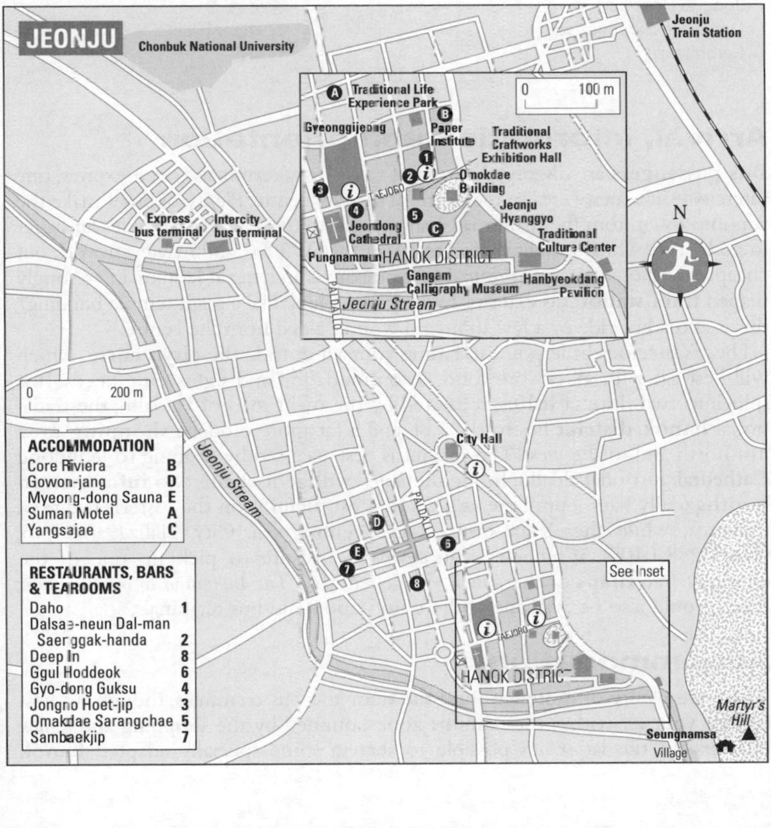

Jeonju

Jeonju	전주
Gyeonggijeon	경기전
Hanbyeokdang	한벽당
Hanok District	한옥 마을
Jeondong Cathedral	전동 성당
Jeonju Hyanggyo	전주 향교
Jinnamgwan	진남관
Korean Traditional Life Experience Park	한옥생활체험관
Pungnammun	풍남문
Accommodation	
Core Riviera	코아 리베라 호텔
Gowon-jang	고원장
Myeong-dong Sauna	명동 사우나
Suman Motel	수만 모텔
Yangsajae	양사재
Restaurants and tearooms	
Daho	다호 찻집
Dalsae-neun Dal-man Saenggak-handa	달새는 달만 생각한다
Ggul Hoddeok	꿀 호떡
Gyo-dong Guksu	교동국수
Jongno Hoet-jip	종로 횟집
Omokdae Sarangchae	오목대 사랑채
Sambaekjip	삼백집

Arrival, information and orientation

Bus passengers are disgorged at one of two crusty terminals – one express, one intercity – in a messy area to the north of the city centre. Plenty of buses make the run into town from the main road a short walk to the east. However, it's far easier to go by taxi, which is unlikely to cost more than W3000, and may even work out cheaper for those in a small group. More pleasant is arriving at Jeonju's interestingly shaped **train station** (its exterior looking something like a giant temple building); this is also a bus ride or a few thousand won in a taxi from the centre.

There's precious little point in basing yourself outside the **city centre**, which will best cater for all of your food, accommodation and sightseeing needs. It is split into two distinct halves, separated by the main road of Paldallo; the traditional **hanok district** lies to the east, and a far more modern **shopping area** just north and to the west. The former is best accessed by heading to Jeondong Cathedral, just off Paldallo. Inside the *hanok* village itself are two **information booths** (daily 9am–6pm); the larger and most useful is on the eastern fringe of the area, while there's an even bigger centre near City Hall (9am–9pm; ⓣ063/288-0105). Whichever you head to, be sure to pick up one of the excellent free **maps** of the *hanok* village, entitled *The Invitation to our Tradition*; these should also be available at the train station and bus terminals.

Accommodation

There are plenty of motels around the train and bus terminals, though it's best to base yourself within the comfort zone bounded by the shopping and *hanok* quarters. In the latter, it's possible to stay in some specially adapted **hanok** buildings – as these are traditional dwellings don't expect large rooms or too much comfort. The experience is unique, nonetheless, especially in winter when your feet are toasted by the *ondol* floors.

Core Riviera Hanok Village ⓣ063/232-7000. Not to be confused with its lesser brother the *Core Hotel* near City Hall, this modern hotel stands defiantly over the *hanok* district. All rooms are carpeted and homely, but make sure you get one with a westward view over the traditional area below. ⑥

Gowon-jang Jungang-dong ⓣ063/286-3211. One of a string of motels opposite the CGV cinema in the town centre, and usually the easiest to haggle down in price. Rooms are decent enough, and most have private facilities and cable TV. ②

Korean Traditional Life Experience Park Hanok Village ⓣ063/280-7000, ⓦwww.jjhanok.com. As the name suggests, this establishment sees guests staying in traditional *hanok* rooms. The place is highly popular with Korean tourists, so try to book at least a week in advance. It's also possible for non-guests to see the performances that take place each Sat at 8pm in the delightful courtyard. ④

Myeong-dong Sauna Jungang-dong. Despite being older than other *jjimjilbang* in the area, this one is extremely central, and you'd struggle to find a cheaper sleep in the city. ①

Suman Motel Gyeongwon-dong 2-ga ⓣ063/231-7770. Though a little soulless with its yellow linoleum rooms, this motel is as close as you'll get to Gyeonggijeon – a beautiful shrine in the *hanok* village – and is also within an easy walk of the shopping quarter. ②

Yangsajae Hanok Village ⓣ063/282-4959, ⓦwww.jeonjutour.co.kr. One of the hanok district's traditional dwellings, this is smaller and less polished than others, and provides a more authentic experience. Its setting in the more rustic southern half of the district also helps, and although the rooms are tiny they're pleasant and *ondol*-heated. ④

The City

Jeonju's main attraction is undoubtedly its splendid **hanok district**, a city-centre thatch of largely traditional housing in which visitors can get to grips with the various facets of Korean customs. Highlights include a cathedral, an ancient shrine and a former Confucian academy, as well as museums for calligraphy, paper and wine; almost all sights are free, and there's enough to keep you busy for a full day. Nearby is Jeonju's main shopping quarter, a noisy mishmash of clothes shops and cheap restaurants; here you'll find **Cinema Street**, which becomes the centre of attention when the city's international film festival (JIFF; see p.291) rolls into town. Outside these areas, Jeonju's other sights are spread far and wide, and few are worth the effort of getting to, though many will enjoy the excellent walk from the *hanok* district to **Martyr's Hill**.

The hanok village

The best way to enjoy Jeonju's **hanok village** is simply to turn up and have a wander around – whether it be a museum, a traditional restaurant or a photogenic house, there's something to see around every corner. Note that there are no opening times or entry fees to the area and it remains a functioning part of the city. Only a few sections have been tarted up for tourism, so don't go expecting anything too grand.

Most visitors start their journey by making their way to a sight just outside the village, just across the main road that marks its western boundary. Here lies **Pungnammun** (24hr; free), an ornate city gate whose present structure dates from 1768, but was originally built here in the late fourteenth century as part of Jeonju's city wall. Now surrounded by a circle of rather ugly modern buildings, it holds a gruesome secret – this is where the heads of martyred Christians were displayed after purges in 1801 (see p.295). Inside the village is **Jeondong Cathedral**, which almost looks authentically European with its brown brick walls and soaring spire. It was one of the first cathedrals to be built in Korea, and remains an active place of worship. The cathedral lies on the southern side of **Taejoro**, a road that bisects the *hanok* area. Lightly trafficked and studded with small lights that glow at night, this is the best place to get your bearings, and has two information offices that can provide you with maps of the area.

Almost directly opposite the cathedral is **Gyeonggijeon** (daily 9am–6pm; free), a park-like shrine area full of ornate buildings and beautiful trees – quite a sight in the autumn. It was built in 1410 to preserve a portrait of **King Taejo**, first leader of the famed Joseon dynasty and native to Jeonju, who had died two years previously after arguably the most productive reign in Korea's long regal history (see p.72). The portrait itself shows Taejo resplendent in an embroidered robe, against a pale yellow background, and sits proudly in a hall to the rear of the complex. It's surrounded by other members of his family, who were only officially made royals after Taejo's death, a move that gave posthumous legality to his bringing down of the Goryeo dynasty (see p.424).

Near the southeastern corner of the *hanok* area is **Jeonju Hyanggyo** (opening hours vary; free), a former Confucian academy. Present here since 1603, and still housing a few of the original buildings, it sees surprisingly few visitors – a very good thing, as you'll appreciate more its contemplative *raison d'être*. Most notable are a number of large gingko trees, a couple of which – rather incredibly – actually predate the complex; with a majesty all of their own, these alone make a trip to this *hyanggyo* worthwhile.

Museums and activities

In addition to a number of interesting **museums**, the hanok village contains a few places in which to get hands-on experience of Korean culture. Near the eastern end of Taejoro, the road bisecting the area, you'll find the **Traditional Craftworks Exhibition Hall** (10am–7pm, Nov–Feb to 6pm; closed Mon; free), a traditionally-styled wooden structure which holds crafts created by Jeonju artisans – a great place to hunt for souvenirs. If you're lucky you may get to see one of the shows of traditional song and dance that are occasionally held just outside the complex – there's a list of performance times on the Hanok Village map. North of Taejoro you'll find the **Traditional Wine Museum** (9am–7pm, Sept–May to 6pm; closed Mon; free); it is rather hit and miss as the exhibits aren't terribly interesting, but the beauty of the *hanok* building – and the fact that free tipples are occasionally handed out – make it worth a quick peek. Of more interest is the **Korean Paper Institute** (same times; free), where beautiful examples of products made with *hanji* – hand-made paper – are on display, many available to buy; if you ask nicely, you may even be able to try your hand at making a kite or lantern.

South of Taejoro, and overlooking the stream that marks the *hanok* area's southern boundary, is the **Gangam Calligraphy Museum** (10am–5pm; free); stored inside are wonderful examples of writing from some of Korea's best-known calligraphers. Artistic beauty of a different kind can be found a five-minute walk east along the streamside road, at the **Traditional Culture Center**, which puts on *pansori* shows (see box opposite) every Wednesday at 7.30pm (W5000). The mournful singing and sparse drum-raps are complemented well by the old-fashioned beauty of the building, and the performers are usually of extremely high calibre – the shows are not over-long, making this an absolute must-see. Other nights of the week see similar performances, though of slightly lower quality. Also of interest are the various programmes run by the centre – there's a free tea ceremony course every third Thursday of the month from 10.30am to noon, and irregular cheap lessons (W5000–10,000) in cooking, fan-making, traditional music and the like; consult a tourist office for details.

Elsewhere in the city

Although there's more to Jeonju than its *hanok* district, most other city sights are spread far and wide, and it's debatable whether or not they're worth the trek. One exception is a fantastic walk south of the *hanok* area that can easily take up half a day and which manages to peer into the ancient heart of the city. The logical place to start is **Hanbyeokdang** (free), a pavilion dangling off a rock face across the road from the *hanok* district's southeast corner. A place for poets and contemplation, one can only speculate on how beautiful the view must have been when this was built in 1404, before the main road arrived. From here continue south along the river, where before long, you'll be rewarded with a **picturesque village**, whose paths snake between walls of rock, and up the hill to the pine forest behind. Despite the noise from the road the atmosphere is something special, especially considering its proximity to the city centre. The Andalucian ambience and cute, hand-painted name signs on many buildings disguise the fact that this little hamlet may have been the true **birthplace** of Joseon-era Korea – local rumours suggest that this was the source of the dynasty's first royals. Nowadays it's home to **Seungamsa**, a simple, deserted but intricately painted temple. It's possible to access **Martyr's Hill** behind the village via a path starting a little further down the river. The martyrs in question include Yi Hang-geom, killed in 1801 along with six of his family for his religious beliefs, his head displayed on Pungnamun in the city centre to show the populace what happened to Catholics. A thirty-minute slog will take you to his tomb, from where you can follow a number of paths back to the city, many of which are studded with yet more delightfully secluded temples and hermitages.

Eating and drinking

Jeonju has a national reputation as a city of culinary excellence and visitors should not leave without trying the city's wonderful **bibimbap** (see box, p.296 for details). There exist a number of excellent traditional restaurants in the *hanok* village, together with some rustic tearooms (see box, p.47 for the most popular kinds of tea). The eateries around the bus and train stations are surprisingly poor.

There are countless places to **drink** or dance the night away in the **student zones** around the universities, but the one outside Chonbuk National University is generally regarded as the best. Two of the most popular **clubs** here are *Music Bank* and *Jukebox*, unpretentious places with reasonably decent sound

Pansori

Usually marketed to foreigners as "Korean opera", **pansori** performances are a modern-day derivative of the country's shamanist past. Songs and incantations chanted to fend off evil spirits or ensure a good harvest slowly mutated over the years into ritualized presentations. As might be expected, the themes also evolved, with tales of love and despair replacing requests to spirits unseen.

A good *pansori* may go on for hours, but each segment will be performed by a cast of just two – a female singer (the *sorikkun*) and a male percussionist (*gosu*). The *sorikkun* holds aloft a paper fan, which she folds, unfolds and waves about to emphasize lyrics or a change of scene. While the *gosu* drums out his minimalist finger taps on the *janggo*, he gives his singer words – or, more commonly, grunts – of encouragement known as *chuimsae*, to which the audience are expected to add their own. The most common are "*chalhanda!*" and "*olshi-gu!*", which are roughly equivalent to "you're doing good!" and "hm!", a grunt acknowledging appreciation, usually delivered with a refined nod. Just follow the Korean lead, and enjoy the show.

systems. *Deep In* is a bar very popular with foreign residents and visitors alike, but due to its location just south of the shopping quarter – a ghost town at night – it's a little hit and miss, and can be empty during the week.

Restaurants and tearooms

Daho Hanok Village. One of the most picturesque tearooms in the area, where you sit down on tatami-matted rooms around a central courtyard. The teas are excellent, with the ginger variety particularly tasty here.

Dalsae-neun Dal-man Saenggak-handa Hanok Village. The extravagant name (meaning "Moon-birds think only of the Moon") is bigger than the tearoom itself – there are just four tables here for the taking. But the menu has been translated into English of a sort, and the teas are top-notch.

Ggul Hoddeok Pungnam-dong. The name of this little booth is as much of a mouthful as the gloopy sugar-and-rice pancakes on sale for just W500 each – *hoddeok* (pronounced a little like "hot dog") are extremely popular winter snacks, and on a cold evening are hard to beat.

Gyo-dong Guksu Hanok Village. There are just two items on the menu at this tiny eatery – you can have your noodles in a spicy sauce for W3000, or a marginally blander soup for W2500. Cheap but delicious, and a great place to fall into after a day in the *hanok* district.

Jongno Hoet-jip Hanok Village. Not the most atmospheric restaurant serving up genuine Jeonju *bibimbap*, but the location next to Gyeonggijeon is pretty impressive, as is the dish itself. For W10,000 you get the meal and a mouth-watering array of side dishes – the mushrooms, in particular, are nothing short of heavenly.

Omokdae Sarangchae Hanok Village. Yet more traditional food is on offer at this smartly designed restaurant, which sits just south of the Traditional Craftworks Exhibition Hall; a visit is particularly recommended in the evening, when the interior is bathed in a dull glow. Jeonju *bibimbap* is available for W9000.

Sambaekjip Jungang-dong. On the fringe of the shopping quarter, and for decades an extremely popular place with lunching Koreans, this restaurant is famed for its *kongnamul gukbap* – a rice-and-veg dish cooked in a hot stone pot. Try the *moju*, a hot, spicy drink.

Listings

Bike hire The tourist office at the eastern end of Taejoro in the *hanok* village offers free bike rental, though you'll probably have to get there early to nab one, and there are talks of charging for use in the future.

Emergencies To get in touch with the police or to call an ambulance, your best option by far is to ring the tourist number on ⓣ1330; there are English-speaking operators available 24hr.

Jeonju bibimbap

Though the whole of Jeolla province is renowned for its food, **Jeonju** can credibly claim to be the country's **culinary capital**, and its most famous dish is, without doubt, Jeonju *bibimbap*. Regular *bibimbap* – a mixture of vegetables served on a bed of rice, with a fried egg and meat on top – is available across the country (see the *Korean cuisine* colour insert), but in Jeonju they've picked up the formula and run with it. Recipes vary from place to place, but the ingredients are always well chosen and may include anything from pine kernels to bluebell roots or fern bracken in addition to the usual leaves and bean sprouts. Plus your meal will invariably be surrounded by a selection of up to twenty free side dishes, made with just as much care, and an even greater variety of ingredients. Beware of restaurants that claim to serve authentic Jeonju *bibimbap* – many places, particularly around the train station and bus terminals, will simply give you a regular version of the dish (though genuinely made in Jeonju, and thereby circumnavigating Korea's already weak product description laws). One way to sort Jeonju wheat from Jeonju chaff is the price – for the real deal, you shouldn't be paying less than W8000, but even at double this price it's likely to be money well spent.

Football Jeonbuk Football Club, winners of the Asian Champions League in 2006 and usually there or thereabouts as far as the K-League is concerned, plays at the Jeonju World Cup Stadium, far to the north of town. A quick fact of little importance – they once had a Brazilian player named Raphael Botti.

Internet There are *PC-bangs* all over the city, each charging a standard W1000 per hour to surf the web.

East of Jeonju

With few urban areas to speak of, it's bucolic countryside all the way east of Jeonju. Easily accessible on a day-trip from the provincial capital are the wonderful twin peaks of **Maisan Provincial Park**. Between these lies **Tapsa**, one of Korea's most distinctive temples, surrounded by otherworldly spires of stacked rock that, though built without bonding agents and attacked by regular typhoons and snowstorms, continue to stand tall. Pushing on further east you'll soon hit the slopes of **Deogyusan National Park**, home to the popular ski resort **Muju**.

Maisan Provincial Park

Korea's pine-clad mountain ranges have a habit of looking rather similar to each other. One exception is tiny **MAISAN PROVINCIAL PARK**, or "horse-ear Mountains", so-named after two of its peaks. It's easy to reach Maisan by bus on a day-trip from Jeonju, via the small town of **Jinan**. The park is within walking distance of Jinan's decaying bus terminal, but most opt for taking a taxi along the lake to the main entrance north of the park – the fifteen-minute trip should cost around W4000, though many taxi drivers will try to get you to go to the more distant Tapsa entrance for around three times that price. At the northern entrance are restaurants and a couple of places to stay, and from here steep flights of energy-sapping stairs take you between the horses' ears and over the scalp, where you'll probably need a rest. Unfortunately it's not possible to climb the peaks, which were closed for regeneration at the time of writing; the path up the western ear is due to reopen in 2014. Despite the threat of heavy fines and the fact that hikers stand out like a sore thumb, people still flout the rule.

If you continue between the peaks, you'll soon come to Unsusa, a dainty temple surrounded by flowers in warmer months, while further down the mountain is the highly popular temple of **Tapsa**, Maisan's real gem, which sits in a surreal clasp of stacked rock. Mildly Gaudíesque in appearance, the near-hundred-strong towers were the work of one monk, Yi Kap-myong (1860–1957), who apparently used no adhesive in their construction, even though some are over ten metres in height.

Muju and Deogyusan National Park

Locked into the northeast of Jeonbuk province is **Deogyusan National Park**, whose lofty yet gentle terrain rises up south of **Muju ski resort**, then spills down in an undulating series of valleys. Both park and resort can be reached on regular buses via Muju town itself along a typically relaxed slice of rural

East of Jeonju	
Deogyusan National Park	덕유산 국립 공원
Maisan Provincial Park	마이산 도립 공원
Muju	무주

▲ Stone towers outside Tapsa temple

Jeolla – the 19km drive in from the west is astonishingly beautiful. Buses continue past the resort on to Gucheon-dong, the main entrance to Deogyusan; there are also free hourly shuttle buses linking this entrance with the ski resort.

Muju ski resort

Despite being one of the warmest and most southerly ski resorts in Korea, **MUJU** (Ⓦwww.mujuresort.com) is one of the peninsula's most popular, and attracts hordes of skiers throughout the winter, a season artificially elongated with the aid of some hefty snow machines. Less bulky ski equipment is available for hire, and whether you're a ski veteran or an absolute beginner, you'll have more than twenty slopes from which to choose from. It's also possible to sled or go cross-country skiing, or take part in non-snow related activities from golf and paintball to bungee-jumping and bike-rides. There's plenty of fun to be had in **warmer months** too, which is a great time of year to go, when accommodation prices plunge.

It'll cost a pretty penny to stay next to the slopes. The cushy *Hotel Tirol* (Ⓣ063/320-7617, Ⓕ063/320-7609; ❼), situated right next to the ski runs and resembling an Austrian cabin, is absurdly expensive during the peak winter season, and far from cheap at other times. Things are much cheaper down the hill in the area's main **motel** district; few of the establishments are worthy of special mention, and it will always pay to shop around, but the best are on and around Baebang-gil, near the main road at the bottom. The longest-serving of these is the grandly titled *Uri-duri Neorang-narang Condo Pension Muju* (Ⓣ063/322-3425 or 6; ❹), a rambling light-brick complex with large rooms, and a steal off-season (though they can get a little grubby during these times). Below the *Hotel Tirol* is **Carnival Street**, a collection of over-expensive restaurants and cafés, whose wintry, quasi-Austrian atmosphere can make a refreshing change if you've been in Korea for a while. Otherwise there's *Mujunori*, near the top end of the village on the way to the resort, which deserves a shout for its adventurous decor and succulent *galbi*.

The rest of the park

A popular hike – one that almost every visitor to Deogyusan follows – links Muju ski resort with the main park entrance at Gucheon-dong. Though it's not an especially taxing walk, much of the upward slog can be chalked off by **cable car** from the ski resort, which whisks passengers up the 1520m peak of Seolcheon-bong. From here it's a 6.2km hike back down to the ski area, or a longer, more beautiful one to the park's main entrance at Gucheon-dong. This latter trail is riddled with rocks, small waterfalls and pools.

In another section of the park is the fortress **Jeoksang-sanseong**, located near the bus route from Muju town to the resort and park, though sadly not directly on any public transport routes. Unless you hitch, you'll have to walk from the nearest bus stop, which is in the village of Bukchang-ri – let your driver know where you want to get off – from where the fortress is an hour's signposted walk away.

Motels and **restaurants** line the stream in Gucheon-dong, a village-like area below the park entrance, and much smaller and quieter than the similar district below Muju ski resort. The most pleasant places to stay are on the western side of the water, with the best-priced place *Shilla Motel* (Ⓣ063/322-0663; ❸), whose friendly owners give occasional discounts to foreigners. Across the creek are two neighbouring restaurants which, bizarrely, both go under the name *Jeonju Sikdang*: the one at the end of the row is marginally less amicable, but is the only establishment along here that has views of the park, rather than the road. *Minbak* line the main road all the way from the Muju resort turnoff and, unless you're camping, represent the cheapest accommodation any time of year – especially important during ski-season, when the hotels and motels still manage to stay full despite some hardcore price-hikes. There's also a **campsite** near the park entrance (from W3000 per tent).

West of Jeonju

If you're looking for **national parks** you'll be spoilt for choice in the western half of Jeonbuk province – there are three to choose from, and each offer plenty of outdoor activities. **Naejangsan** lies closest to Jeonju, and is famed for its riot of colour in the autumn. **Seonunsan**, near the Jeonnam border, is Korea's main magnet for rock-climbing, while on the coast is **Byeonsanbando**, a rural peninsula park that's also the scene of a controversial land reclamation project. **Iksan** and **Gunsan**, the major cities of the region, have too few attractions to merit a visit, though the former is an important junction on the KTX line linking Seoul with Mokpo and Gwangju, and the latter has occasional ferry services to Qingdao in China.

Naejangsan National Park

NAEJANGSAN NATIONAL PARK is one of Korea's most popular parks, with its ring of peaks flaring up like a gas ring in the autumn, pulling in visitors from across the country. Maple trees are the stars of the show in this annual incandescence, with squads of elm, ash and hornbeam also adding their hues to the mix. There are plenty of trails and peaks across the park, keeping hikers happy throughout the year, though most visitors head to the amphitheatre-shaped mountain circle in the northeast, where the nearby village has plenty of accommodation and places to eat. This area's topography allows for two **hiking routes**: a short temple loop around the interior, or a far more punishing circuit around the almost circular ridge.

West of Jeonju

Byeonsanbando National Park	변산반도 국립 공원
Naejangsan National Park	내장산 국립공원
Seonunsan National Park	선운산 국립 공원

The **temple route** takes in three sights, and should take less than two hours. A pleasant, maple-lined path takes you from the entrance to **Naejangsa**, an unremarkable but pretty temple whose complex is dotted with informative English-language signs. Heading further up the valley you'll come to isolated **Wonjeogam**, a tiny hermitage home to a couple of monks and an abnormally large golden statue, before the trail swings back along the mountain face towards **Baengnyeonam**, another hermitage that marks the final sight on this route. Built in 632, the structure has been destroyed and rebuilt several times since then, and enjoys the most arresting setting of the three – bamboo stalks in a grove behind the main building point up towards the sheer rock crags of Naejangsan's main ridge, while in the other direction is the awesome view of a distant pavilion nestling beneath the peaks.

There are some eight main peaks on the **ridge route**, and it's possible to scale them all on a calf-burning 13.8km day hike, but most visitors content themselves with a shorter trip up and down – wherever you are on this circular route, you won't be far from a path heading back towards Naejangsa in the centre, and it's even possible to take a **cable car** up to a restaurant (usually pumping with loud *ajumma* music) within a short hike of the southern ridge.

Practicalities

Jeongeup is the main access point to the park – buses run from its bus terminal to the park's main entrance, and there are also a few direct buses from Gwangju that pass through the town. Whichever way you come, if you've reached Jeongeup's bus terminal and the next bus to the park isn't due for a while, head outside to the main road, from which **local buses** are far more frequent. Alighting at Naejangsan's main bus stop, entry to the park can be a little confusing; buses usually drop off outside the Family Mart, and from here you should turn left and follow the road. It's a fair walk to the entrance, but cheap shuttle buses run through the day, and it's also possible to pedal the route on a hired bike. Ask at the park's **information office** (daily 9am–5pm), which is around five minutes' walk up the road from the Family Mart, and usually staffed with an English speaker. Almost directly opposite is the *Swegobil Motel* (ⓣ063/538-8122; ④), which continues to get good reviews, though prices are a little high. Connected to this is *Gwangju-daegwal Sikdang*, a restaurant that serves delicious mountain fare, and has the advantage of being next to the information office if you need help with the menu. If you're looking for something much more rustic, on the other side of the Family Mart is a small, friendly village of family homes, many of which lease out *minbak* rooms from W25,000 or so.

Seonunsan National Park

SEONUNSAN NATIONAL PARK has more than a few aces hidden up its leafy sleeves. It offers some of the country's best **rock-climbing** opportunities and a few enjoyable hikes; these are not as well signed as others in Korea, though some may find this somewhat liberating. A streamside path, lined with stalls selling delicious mountain berry juice in the summer and autumn, heads straight from the main entrance to **Seonunsa**, a dusty collection of buildings, stupas and the like that appear to have been thrown together with little apparent care. It's quite possibly the least satisfying temple complex in the province, and the small hermitages strewn around the park are of more interest.

Once past the temple, you'll have a diverse range of trails to choose from. **Hikers** should head for the hills; the peaks are puny by Korean standards, rarely

▲ Totem poles on protest site, near Buan

reaching above 400 metres, but this makes for some easy day-hikes, and you may be rewarded with occasional views of the West Sea. For more hardcore thrills, continue further on the temple path, across the river; hidden a ten-minute hike behind a small restaurant is a spectacular **rock-climbing** course. This is a tough route and should not be attempted alone or without equipment – see Ⓦwww.koreaontherocks.com for climb details, and to contact the few Koreans (and expats) au fait with holds, conglomerates and juggy overhangs. Back towards the entrance, an underused side path heads along the temple wall and up a gorgeous valley, lined with rows of tea trees, and a few rustic dwellings. You'll soon come across a small and highly beautiful farming village, where one house offers *minbak* accommodation (❶); as long as you don't mind sharing a bathroom and sleeping on the floor, it's the best place to stay for miles around. A motley collection of poor **hotels** lies outside the park entrance, including the over-expensive *Sun Un San* (Ⓣ063/561-3377; ❺) and the dilapidated *Dongbaek* (Ⓣ063/562-1560 or 1; ❸) – it's far better to stay elsewhere. There's also a small **tourist information** booth near the park bus stop.

Seonunsan is a day-trip from Jeonju or Gwangju, though access to the park is usually via **Gochang**, the closest town and connected to it by regular buses. On the way back to Gochang, some bus drivers may be willing to drop you off within walking distance of a dolmen site (*Gochang Goindol*). This collection of ancient rocks is one of few Korean sites saved for posterity by **UNESCO World Heritage**, but it may be one of the least-visited places on their list, and is only worth the effort of getting to if you've time, patience and a love of the countryside.

Byeonsanbando National Park

In addition to the usual mix of peaks and temples found in Korea's parks, **BYEONSANBANDO NATIONAL PARK** throws in some unexpected treats including wonderful sea views and a monkey school. Best accessed by bus

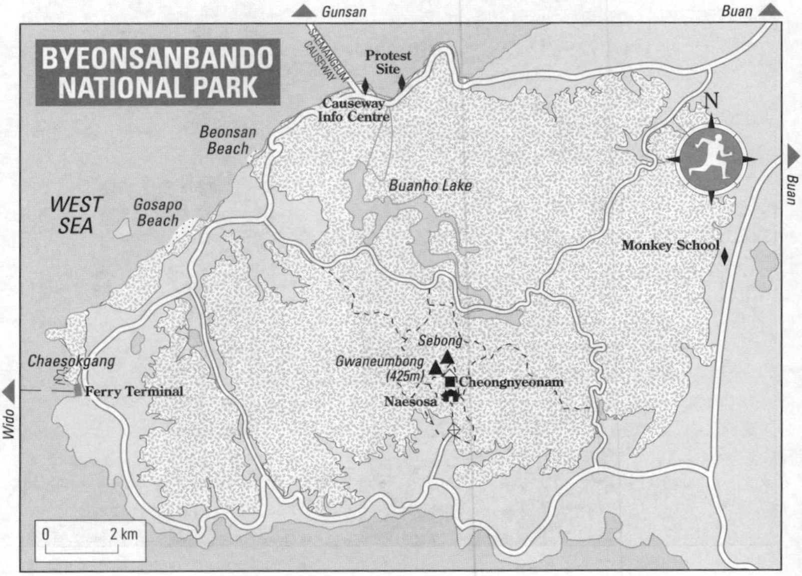

When I was a boy, all this was waves...

On the north Byeonsanbando National Park lies a bizarre sight. Sketching a long line between sea and sky is a **traffic-bearing causeway** of 33 kilometres in length, which stretches all the way north to Gunsan. Prior to construction more than 40,000 hectares east of this concrete snake were part of the West Sea, but are now slowly being converted into rice fields, a change large enough to be clearly visible on maps of the country.

Understandably, this mammoth project ruffled feathers in Korea's largely toothless **environmental lobby**, which was concerned about what the loss of the area's mud flats would do to the local fish and bird populations, and why a country with a shrinking population needed so many new rice fields; Korea has long been forced to subsidize rice to prevent cheaper imports from destroying an important national industry. One interesting protest, dubbed "Three Steps, One Bow", saw demonstrators making a two-month, 300km pilgrimage to Seoul, taking three steps at a time before prostrating themselves on the ground. The protest failed to meet its goals, and the date of completion has been set for 2011; the road to Gunsan should be open by 2008, though the main **protest site** near Buan – an area of large wooden poles, carved with anguished faces, rising from the sand of the former shore – may well have been drowned by then.

On the southern end of the causeway is the project's **information centre**; there's almost no information in English, but the staff will be willing to play you an unintentionally hilarious English-language DVD, in which a cute cartoon hostess communicates the benefits of the dam: "The blue ocean and the endless embankment!" she screams in introduction, before a token foreigner dreamily declares that it must be the most beautiful place he's ever seen. Though Kim Jong-il may have produced less balanced pieces of film, few could better the parody.

(30min) via the town of **Buan**, the park is spread around a small, rural **peninsula** on the west coast from which it takes its name (*bando* literally means "half-island"). However, this is being hauled towards the mainland on its northern side with the aid of a 33km causeway, a development which will yield thousands of hectares of new farmland, but has caused one hell of a stink with Korean environmental groups (see box above). Heading west by bus from the end of the dam, you'll pass a couple of pleasant beaches, before arriving at the unusual rock formations of **Chaesokgang** (daily 9am–6pm; W1600). You have to time it right to get the most out of the place – for much of the day it's just a bunch of pretty cliffs, but the surrender of the tide reveals page-like leaves of rock piled up like rusty banknotes, and teeming with crabs and other oceanic fauna. Chaesokgang is serviced by four buses an hour from Buan, though its entrance is badly signed – from the bus stop (the last stop on the route), head back along the road for 100m or so, then turn left through an area of motels and fish restaurants. Near the port south of the cliffs is a ferry terminal, which has services to, and occasionally beyond, the island of **Wido**, though this too has provided cause for environmental concern, and was at one point slated for the storage of nuclear waste.

The charming southern side of the peninsula offers more trails and temples. The temple complex of **Naesosa** is more notable for its rural, mountain-backed setting than any of its buildings, and is the most accessible place from which to start a hike. Persimmon trees surround the entrance (from where it's a short walk to the temple, and its adjacent *minbak* village), these shed their leaves at the slightest sniff of autumn, leaving behind naked baubles of bright orange fruit. The temple's main building's exterior is almost entirely devoid of paint, while inside four dragons ascend to heaven, two headless, one gnawing a fish. From here, **hiking** routes head up to Gwaneumbong (425m), one via Cheongnyeonam, a small hermitage with great sea views. It's possible to continue down the north face of the mountains to an artificial lake, though public transport here is nonexistent. From the main entrance outside Naesosa, hourly **buses** head to and from Chaesokgang and Buan, the latter a convoluted route passing little-visited temples and innumerable small villages, one of which is home to a bizarre **Monkey School**. This is popular with Koreans but probably not to the average foreigner's tastes, as the daily shows feature dressed-up simians balancing on balls and riding around on little bikes. If you really want to see this, ask your driver to let you off at "Monkey Hakkyo".

Travel details

Trains

Gwangju to: Daejeon (regularly; 1hr 45min); Iksan (regularly; 55min); Seoul (regularly; 2hr 50min).
Iksan to: Gwangju (regularly; 55min); Jeonju (hourly; 20min); Mokpo (regularly; 1hr 25min); Seoul (regularly; 1hr 45min).
Jeonju to: Daejeon (hourly; 1hr 20min); Iksan (hourly; 20min); Seoul (11 daily; 3hr 30min); Suncheon (hourly; 1hr 30min); Yeosu (hourly; 2hr).
Mokpo to: Busan (3 daily; 7hr 25min); Iksan (regularly; 1hr 25min); Jinju (3 daily; 4hr 35min); Seoul (regularly; 3hr 10min).
Suncheon to: Jeonju (hourly; 1hr 30min); Yeosu (hourly; 35min).
Yeosu to: Jeonju (hourly; 2hr); Seoul (11 daily; 5hr 10min); Suncheon (hourly; 35min).

Buses

Gwangju to: Busan (every 30min; 3hr 40min); Chuncheon (4 daily; 5hr); Daegu (every 40min; 3hr 40min); Daejeon (every 20min; 2hr 50min); Gurye (every 30min; 1hr 30min); Gyeongju (2 daily; 3hr 30min); Incheon (hourly; 3hr 40min); Jeonju (every 30min; 1hr 40min); Jindo (every 40min; 2hr 50min); Jinju (3 daily; 2hr); Mokpo (every 30min; 1hr 30min); Naejangsan (5 daily; 1hr 30min); Seonunsan (8 daily; 1hr 40min); Seoul (every 5min; 3hr 55min); Sokcho (4 daily; 6hr); Wando (every 40min; 2hr 40min); Yeosu (regularly; 2hr).
Jeonju to: Buan (regularly; 1hr 20min); Busan (11 daily; 3hr 35min); Daegu (hourly; 3hr 30min); Daejeon (every 20min; 1hr 20min); Gurye (regularly; 2hr); Gwangju (every 30min; 1hr 40min); Jinan (regularly; 50min); Jinju (regularly; 3hr 30min); Mokpo (regularly; 3hr); Muju (regularly; 2hr 30min); Seoul (every 10min; 2hr 50min); Suncheon (11 daily; 2hr 20min); Yeosu (11 daily; 4hr).
Jindo to: Busan (2 daily; 6hr 30min); Gwangju (regularly; 2hr 30min); Mokpo (regularly; 1hr 10min); Seoul (4 daily; 5hr).
Mokpo to: Busan (9 daily; 5hr); Gwangju (regularly; 1hr 30min); Jeonju (regularly; 3hr); Jindo (regularly; 1hr 10min); Seoul (regularly; 5hr 20min); Wando (7 daily; 2hr); Yeosu (every 40min; 3hr 30min).
Muju to: Daejeon (regularly; 1hr 30min); Gwangju (regularly; 3hr 40min); Jeonju (regularly; 2hr); Seoul (5 daily; 2hr 40min).
Suncheon to: Busan (regularly; 3hr); Gwangju (every 20min; 1hr 30min); Gurye (regularly; 1hr); Jeonju (11 daily; 2hr 20min); Jinju (regularly; 1hr 30min); Mokpo (regularly; 2hr 50min); Seoul (6 daily; 5hr); Yeosu (every 5min; 50min).
Wando to: Gwangju (regularly; 2hr 40min); Mokpo (every 50min; 2hr); Seoul (4 daily; 6hr).
Yeosu to: Busan (hourly; 3hr 40min); Gwangju (regularly; 2hr); Jeonju (11 daily; 4hr); Mokpo (every 40min; 3hr 30min); Seoul (regularly; 5hr 40min).

Ferries

Mokpo to: Heuksando (3 daily; 1hr 30min); Hongdo (3 daily; 2hr 30min); Jeju City (2–3 daily; 3hr 10min–4hr 30min).

5

Chungcheong

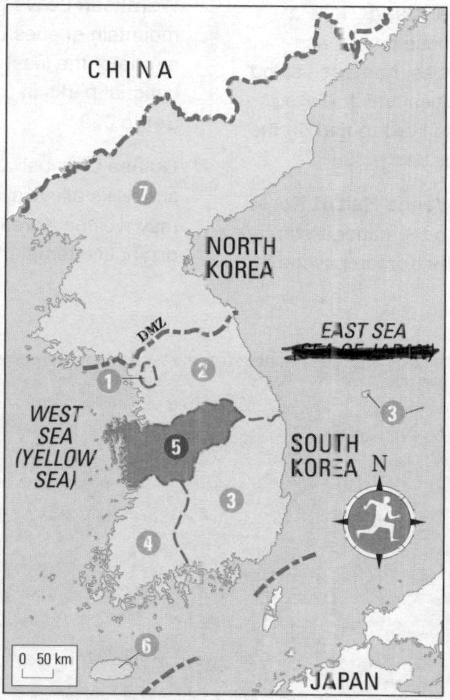

CHAPTER 5

Highlights

* **Gongju and Buyeo** Head to the former capitals of the Baekje dynasty to feast your eyes on their regal riches. See p.317 & p.321

* **Boryeong mud festival** Get dirty on the beach at the most enjoyable festival on the Korean calendar. See p.324

* **West Sea islands** Take a ferry to these tiny, beach-pocked isles, home to fishing communities and a relaxed way of life hard to find on the mainland. See p.326

* **Independence Hall of Korea** Delve into the nationalistic side of the Korean psyche at this huge testament to the country's survival of Japanese occupation. See p.329

* **Beopjusa Temple** Gaze in awe at the world's tallest bronze Buddha, before taking a hike in the surrounding national park. See p.335

* **Woraksan** Leave the mountain queues behind at one of the least-visited national parks in the country. See p.339

* **Guinsa** Clamber around the snakelike alleyways of what may well be Korea's most distinctive temple. See p.343

▲ Baekje jewellery, Gongju National Museum

5

Chungcheong

Of South Korea's principal regions, **Chungcheong** is the least visited by foreign travellers, most choosing to rifle through it on buses and trains to Gyeongju or Busan in the southeast, or over it on planes to Jeju-do. But to do so is to bypass the heart of the country, a thrillingly rural mishmash of rice paddies, ginseng fields, national parks and unhurried islands.

Today split into two provinces, Chungcheong was named in the fourteenth century by fusing the names of Chungju and Cheongju, two of its major cities, which now form part of **Chungcheongbuk-do** province (meaning "North Chungcheong"). **Chungcheongnam-do** ("South Chungcheong") is home to Cheonan, and surrounds the municipality of **Daejeon**. If these tongue-twisters sound confusing, then know that north and south Chungcheong lie manifestly to the east and west, respectively. Daejeon, the region's biggest city, has become an important administrative hub and may succeed Seoul as the country's centre of government if certain politicians get their way, while the other urban centres of **Chungju**, **Cheongju** and **Cheonan** are pleasant enough places, though admittedly with few sights to share between them.

Those who take the time to enjoy Chungcheong's **hinterlands** will testify that this is where the appeal of the region lies. The area has some good **beaches** – the strip of white sand in Daecheon is one of the busiest in the country, with the summer revelry hitting its zenith each July at an immensely popular mud festival. There are also scores of rolling green mountains, many of which have been cordoned off into **national parks** – Songnisan has a 33m-tall golden Buddha at its foot, and Sobaeksan is bordered by Guinsa, possibly Korea's most distinctive temple complex. Chungcheong is also one of the biggest ginseng producing regions in the world (see box, p.309), with the black plastic nets of the *insam* fields standing in stark contrast to the emerald of the rice paddies. Off the west coast are a number of accessible **islands** – tiny squads of rock stretch far beyond the horizon into the West Sea, and sustain fishing communities that provide a glimpse into pre-karaoke Korean life. If you're craving some history, you won't be disappointed with **Gongju** and **Buyeo**, the former capitals of the **Baekje kingdom** (18 BC 660 AD; see box, p.317). Both are home to fortresses, regal tombs and museums filled with gleaming jewellery of the period, which went on to have a profound influence on Japanese craft.

One less obvious Chungcheong attraction is the local populace – the Chungcheongese are noted throughout Korea for their **relaxed nature**. Here you'll get less pressure at the markets, or perhaps even notice a delay of a second or two when the traffic lights change before being deafened by a cacophony of car horns. An often regaled tale tells of a Chungcheongese town

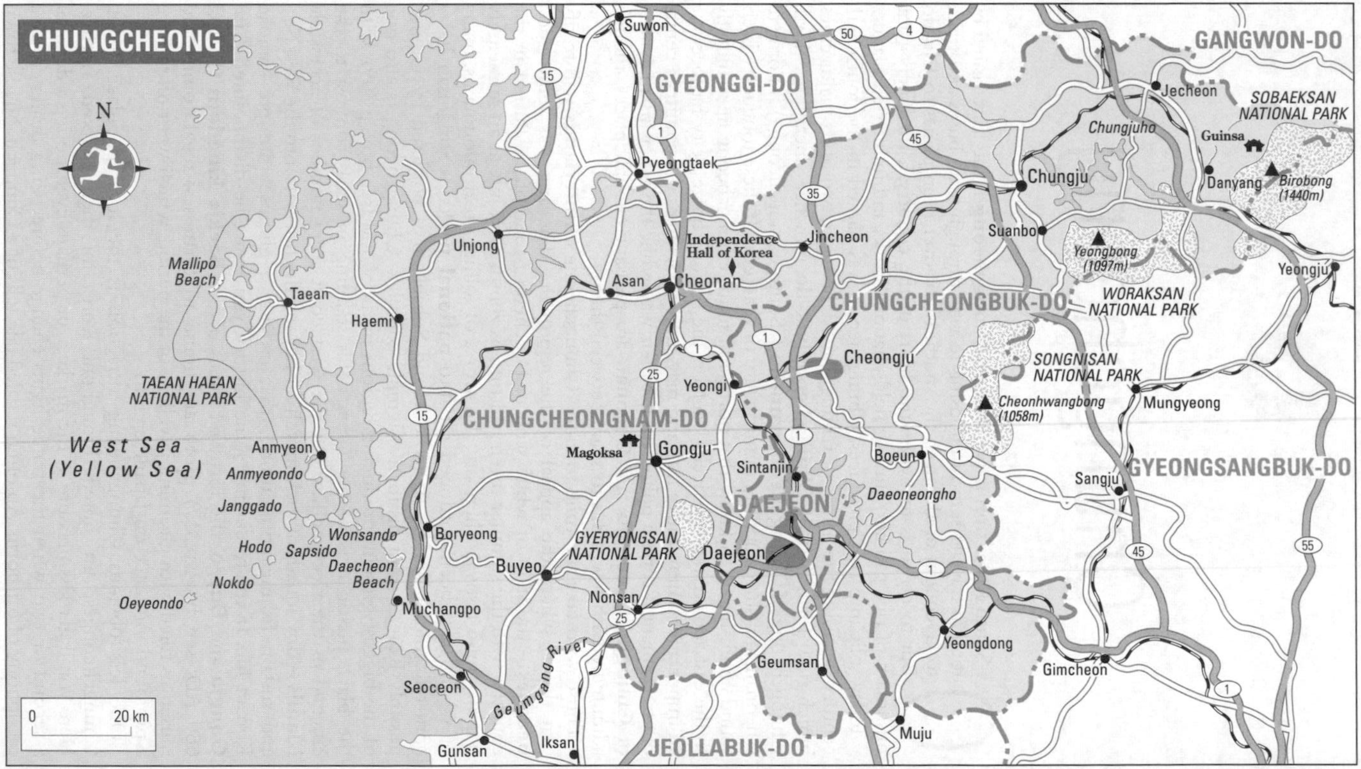
CHUNGCHEONG
N
GANGWON-DO
GYEONGGI-DO
CHUNGCHEONGBUK-DO
CHUNGCHEONGNAM-DO
GYEONGSANGBUK-DO
JEOLLABUK-DO
DAEJEON
SOBAEKSAN NATIONAL PARK
WORAKSAN NATIONAL PARK
SONGNISAN NATIONAL PARK
GYERYONGSAN NATIONAL PARK
TAEAN HAEAN NATIONAL PARK
Suwon
Pyeongtaek
Jecheon
Chungjuho
Guinsa
Danyang
Birobong (1440m)
Chungju
Suanbo
Yeongbong (1097m)
Yeongju
Jincheon
Independence Hall of Korea
Cheonan
Asan
Unjong
Mallipo Beach
Taean
Haemi
Cheongju
Yeongi
Cheonhwangbong (1058m)
Mungyeong
West Sea (Yellow Sea)
Anmyeon
Anmyeondo
Janggado
Wonsando
Hodo
Sapsido
Daecheon Beach
Nokdo
Oeyeondo
Boryeong
Magoksa
Gongju
Sintanjin
Boeun
Daeoneongho
Sangju
Buyeo
Daejeon
Nonsan
Muchangpo
Geumgang River
Seoceon
Gunsan
Iksan
Geumsan
Yeongdong
Gimcheon
Muju
0
20 km
15
1
50
4
45
35
25
55

that was destroyed by a falling boulder because locals were unable to elucidate their warnings in a speedy enough manner. The Chungcheongese do indeed speak at a slower pace than other Koreans (particularly the staccato *patois* of Gyeongsang province), though this is only really noticeable in the countryside, where some *cheon-nom* (a term that vaguely translates as "country bumpkins") speak in a drawl that can even have non-native students of the language rolling their eyes and looking at their watches in frustration. The Chungcheongese themselves seem quite happy with their relaxed reputation; this feeds into the region's main cities, which are noticeably laid-back by Korean standards.

Chungcheongnam-do

Representing the western half of the Chungcheong region, **CHUNGCHEONGNAM-DO**, or Chungnam for short, has something for everyone. Glittering regal relics from the old **Baekje capitals** of Gongju and Buyeo are laid out in splendid museums, while on the west coast some of Korea's best **beaches** cater to the more contemporary pleasures of sand and sunbathing. Although not technically part of Chungnam province, **Daejeon** is the biggest city in the area, and despite white-collar leanings and a lack of sights it packs a punch with great nightlife. South of the city is one of the world's most important **ginseng**-producing areas, while near Cheonan is the **Independence Hall of Korea**, a huge museum complex detailing the Japanese occupation.

The cure-all root

For centuries, perhaps even millennia, the **ginseng** root has been used in Asia for its medicinal qualities, particularly its ability to retain or restore the body's **Yin–Yang** balance; for a time, it was valued more highly by weight than gold. Even today, Korean ginseng is much sought after on the global market, due to the country's ideal climatic conditions; known locally as **insam**, much of it is grown in the Chungcheong provinces under slanted nets of black plastic. The roots take anything up to six years to mature, and suck up so much nutrition from the soil that, once harvested, no more ginseng can be planted in the same field for over a decade.

The **health benefits** of ginseng have been much debated in recent years, and most of the evidence in favour of the root is anecdotal rather than scientific. There are, nonetheless, hordes of admirers, and ginseng's stock rose further when it rode the crest of the "healthy living" wave that swept across Korea just after the turn of the millennium. Today it's possible to get your fix in pills, capsules, jellies, chewing gum or boiled sweets, as well as the more traditional tea or by eating the root raw. As the purported benefits depend on the dosage and type of ginseng used (red or white), it's best to consult a practitioner of oriental medicines, but one safe – and delicious – dish is **samgyetang**, a soup made with a ginseng-stuffed chicken. Or for a slightly quirky drink, try mixing a sachet of ginseng granules and a spoon of brown sugar into hot milk – your very own **ginseng latte**.

Daejeon and around

Every country has a city like **DAEJEON** – somewhere pleasant to go about daily life, but with little to offer the casual visitor. This major city in the Chungcheong region is a rising star in the worlds of science and administration, and has started to suck away people and investment from Seoul and its satellites. In due course, it may even become the "new" Seoul – parliamentary big-shots are exploring the idea of transferring Korea's capital to the Daejeon area.

There are a number of mildly diverting attractions dotted in and around the city should you find yourself with time on your hands here. Most vaunted are **Expo Park**, built for an exposition in 1993 and still a source of local pride, and **Yuseong**, the therapeutic hot-spring resort situated on the western flank of the city. Further west is **Gyeryongsan**, a small but pretty national park flanked by two decent temples, and filled to the brim with steep but simple day-hikes. South of Daejeon is the small town of **Geumsan**, around which most of Korea's ginseng is grown; it's not an especially interesting place, though it comes to life on **market days**, which are held on days of the month ending with a two or a seven. Ginseng is on sale, of course, and so are other "health" products – roots and fungi, scorpions and dried scaly things.

Arrival, information and transport

Daejeon has excellent **bus** connections to every major city in the country, though arrivals are often hampered by the city's incessant traffic. Rather

Daejeon

Daejeon	대전
Bomunsan	보문산
Dunsan-dong	둔산동
Eunhaeng-dong	은행동
Expo Park	엑스포 과학 공원
Gyejoksan	계족산
Gyeryongsan National Park	계룡산 국립 공원
Hanbat Arboretum	한밭 교육박물관
Kumdori Land	꿈돌이 랜드
Namseon Park	남선 공원
Uam Historical Site	우암 사적 공원
Yuseong	유성
Accommodation	
Best Western Legend	베스트 웨스턴
Carib Theme Motel	카리브 테마 모텔
Hote Riviera	호텔 리베라
Jjimjilbang	찜질방
Motel Bobos	모텔 보보스
Yousung Hotel	유성 호텔
Restaurants	
Galbi Street	갈비 골목
Pungnyeon Samgyetang	풍년 삼계탕

confusingly, there are three main bus terminals: buses from most Chungcheong destinations arrive at the Seobu terminal to the south of the city, while the other two – the express (*gosok*) terminal and the intercity Dongbu terminal – sit across the road from each other to the northeast. The city also has two **train** stations: Daejeon station is right in the centre and sits on the Seoul–Busan line, while Seodaejeon station is a W3000 taxi-ride away to the west of the city and is on a line that splits off north of Daejeon for Gwangju and Mokpo. Daejeon station has an excellent **tourist information office** on the departures level upstairs (daily 9am–5pm; ⓣ042/221-1905), which can help out with accommodation or bus routes; there's a slightly less useful one outside the express bus terminal.

The size of the city and the amount of traffic makes getting around frustrating. The **city bus** network is comprehensive but complicated, with hundreds of routes – two of the most useful are the #841, which connects Daejeon station to all three bus terminals, and the #102, which runs from the express terminal via Yuseong to Gyeryongsan (see p.315). After years of delays, a new **subway** line bisects the city; tickets come in the form of cute blue plastic tokens, and it costs a uniform W900 to get from the Daejeon station to City Hall and Yuseong, among other destinations.

Accommodation

Finding a **place to stay** in Daejeon shouldn't be too much trouble, though don't go expecting much in the centre – Daejeon's higher-end lodgings are all way out west in **Yuseong**, the default base for the city's many business visitors and dotted with some fantastic hotels. Many of these squat over **hot springs**, the mineral-heavy waters coursing up into bathrooms and communal steam rooms; non-guests can usually use the latter for a fee (W6000–25,000). The city centre's main **motel** areas are notoriously sleazy, particularly the one surrounding the bus terminals. Pickings are even slimmer by the train station, but if you come out of the main exit and turn right onto the side street before the main road, you'll come across a warren of near-identical **yeoinsuk** – bare rooms with squat toilets and communal showers set around courtyards, but dirt-cheap at W10,000.

Best Western Legend Yuseong ⓣ042/822-4000, ⓦwww.legendhotel.co.kr. The cheapest and friendliest of Yuseong's top hotels, the stylish *Legend* gives five-star service at four-star prices. The rooms are decked out in relaxing tones, and there's an on-site restaurant and spa. ❼

Carib Theme Motel Yuseong ⓣ042/823-8800. Just around from the *Legend*, this is one of the best cheap sleeps in Yuseong. Ask to see a few rooms – some have Internet access, some are carpeted, and some even trump the upmarket hotels with steam saunas. ❸

Jjimjilbang Jungangno. For a real only-in-Korea experience, head to Dongbang Mart, a department store by the creek a few minutes walk away from the train station. Here on the upper floors, you can freshen up and grab a super-cheap night's sleep for W6000. ❶

Motel Bobos Express Bus Terminal area. The zone around the main bus terminals is awash with sleazy motels, and this is just as love-oriented as its competitors, but rooms here are the cushiest in the area.

Hotel Riviera Yuseong ⓣ042/823-2111, ⓦwww.hotelriviera.co.kr. The plushest hotel in the area features Japanese and Chinese restaurants, as well as a stylish lounge bar, and is large enough to seem quiet most of the time. The rooms have been pleasantly decorated and have Internet connections, though not all have bathtubs. ❼

Yousung Yuseong ⓣ042/820-0100, ⓦwww.yousunghotel.com. Plush-carpet corridors lead the way to rooms that are slightly disappointing for the price, though service is excellent and the staff are full of helpful information about the area. Even if you're not staying here, the retro-chic café on the ground floor makes a good coffee-and-cake stop. ❼

The City

On the northern fringe of the city, just past the Gapcheon River (officially a stream, but fairly wide), you'll find Daejeon's official draw, **Expo Park** (9am–6pm; closed Mon; W3000), along with a clutch of surrounding sights. The park was built for Expo '93, a "World's Fair" that took place in the city. Its buildings were designed almost a decade in advance of the festival itself, meaning that they already looked dated by the time the party rolled into town, and do so to an even greater degree today. While it won't appeal to everyone, this unintentional creation of an urban dystopia has its own unique appeal, particularly when allied to the fact that the park is almost totally empty other than on national holidays. Behind the park is **Kumdori Land** (daily 9am–7pm; W20,000), an amusement park named after the little yellow alien mascot of the Expo.

The banks of the Gapcheon come alive in the summer with picnickers, and the park-like area immediately south of the river, across the pedestrianized Expo Bridge, is a popular weekend hang-out venue for Daejeonite families. You can rent bikes for W3000 per hour from a booth just south of the bridge. Also here is **Hanbat Arboretum** (daily 9am–6pm; summer evenings until 9pm; free), a peaceful area containing some interesting tree life, and an excellent **modern art gallery** (10am–5pm; closed Mon; W2000). Further on is the **National Government Complex**, four large, sinister cuboids that would look quite at home in Pyongyang. While there's nothing to see inside, these are the most visible examples of Korea's recent attempts to shift its capital from Seoul to the Daejeon area, a move delayed – perhaps indefinitely, and after considerable expense – following the discovery that it violated the national constitution. On the western flank of the complex is Dunsan Prehistoric Site, an almost laughable collection of straw huts that ostensibly provide a glimpse into Daejeon's ancient past. The site is set within **Dunsan-dong**, the city's dedicated "new" centre, and home to some great bars and restaurants (see pp.314–315).

Eunhaeng-dong

Daejeon's de facto city centre – known as **Eunhaeng-dong** – stretches west from the train station, a typical Korean **downtown area** with clothes shops, restaurants and cafés, pumping music into streets crammed with the young and trendy. Milano 21 and Galleria are two popular department stores along Jungangno, the main road that starts opposite the train station, while under this thoroughfare runs an underground shopping arcade. There's also a typically grimy **market** south of Jungangno (head away from the train station then turn left when you hit the creek), a fascinating area where you'll likely come across intestines bubbling away in witch-like vats, hard-to-pin-down smells and possibly enough *hanbok* to clothe the whole country.

Daejeon's other sights are scattered around the city. Budding hikers should make their way to **Bomunsan**, a 458m-high mountain that marks the city's southern fringe. It's a simple, invigorating climb that provides fantastic views of Daejeon to the north, and rolling mountainous countryside to the south. Avoid the abysmal zoo adjacent to the mountain, unless you want to see lonely seals, miserable penguins and what must be the world's saddest eagles. Also worth a climb is **Gyejoksan**, a similarly sized peak rising cone-like from a plateau to the northeast, and particularly popular when the weather looks like creating a good sunset. Both peaks take a couple of hours to get up and down, and signs point the way to secluded temples and hermitages. Gyejoksan also has a couple of sections of fortress wall from the Baekje era. Several **bus** routes head to Bomunsan from all across Daejeon, with the most useful being the #724 from Daejeon station and the #113 from City Hall. Gyejoksan is also on a number of routes, including the #720 and #102; on all routes you're unlikely to be kept waiting for any more than fifteen

▲ Traditional house in village outside Gapsa, Gyeryongsan National Park

minutes. Back in the main body of the city, and near City Hall, is the much smaller peak **Namseon Park**, a spiders' web of quiet, pine-lined paths that offers pleasant walking opportunities at any time of the year. On the grounds is a rooftop astro-turf football pitch with pleasing views of Daejeon and its surrounding mountains; arrive at the right time and you may be able to weasel your way into a game. Just east of the express bus terminal is **Uam Historical Site**, a little collection of traditional buildings nestled between a quiet part of town and some forested mountain slopes that somehow best suits a rainy day.

Eating and drinking

Daejeon's culinary scene is unremarkable but you should still eat well in the city. There are a tremendous number of **restaurants** spread out over the city centre, within walking distance of Daejeon station; locals are particularly fond of Galbi Street, a whole row of establishments south of Jungangno devoted to the dish. The restaurants near the express bus terminal are more tightly packed, and a good place to hunt down a healthy local favourite called *samgyetang*, a ginseng-infused chicken soup. Ten minutes' walk southwest of the terminals along Dongseoro, *Pungnyeon Samgyetang* is the oldest and most famed establishment, though several places serve the same dish closer to the buses – figure on W8000 or more per head.

Daejeon's **nightlife** is excellent. The city centre has a number of bars that are wildly popular with local expats, the most popular formula being a few beers, a game of pool and a chat with the friendly staff at *J-Rock*, before heading to nearby *Watermelon Sugar* to overdose on cheap cocktails. Both are within walking distance of Jungangno subway station – take exit four. The student area in Kung-dong, over the river Gapcheon on the way to Yuseong, has been on the wane since the closure of the legendary *Zoo Bar*, and interest has shifted to the ever-growing "new downtown" area of Dunsan-dong, near City Hall, many

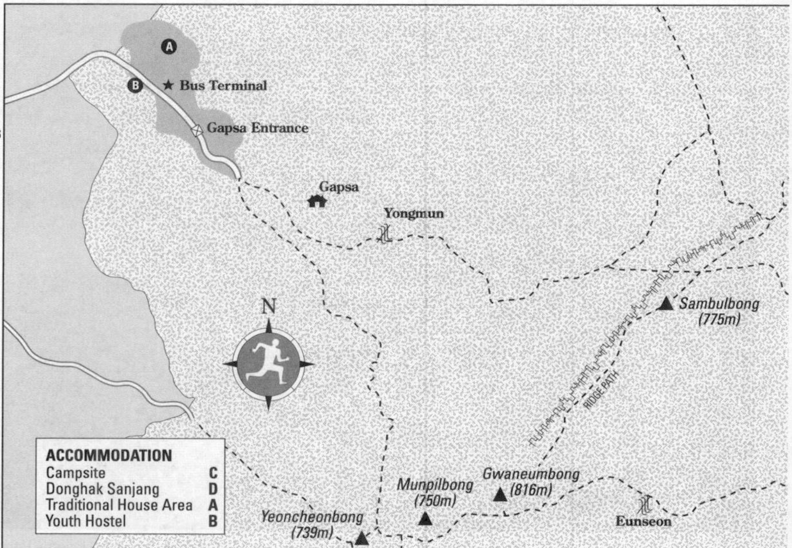

of whose bars wouldn't look out of place in Seoul's trendier areas. Here you can puff on a hookah (W10,000) in *Ethnic*, a faintly Arabic subterranean lair centred around a small pond, or dance the night away at *Booby Booby*, a hip-hop club that attracts a predominantly young crowd.

Gyeryongsan National Park

Despite its comparatively puny size relative to its Korean brethren, **GYERYONGSAN NATIONAL PARK** is a true delight, with herons flitting along the trickling streams, wild boar rifling through the woods and bizarre long net stinkhorn mushrooms – like regular mushrooms, but with a yellow honeycombed veil – found on the forest floors. It is said to have the most *gi* (life-force) of any national park in Korea, one of several factors that haul in 1.4 million people per year, making it the most visited national park in the Chungcheong region. The main reasons for this are accessibility and manage-ability – it lies equidistant from Gongju to the west and Daejeon to the east, and easy day-hikes run up and over the central peaks, connecting Gapsa and Donghaksa, two sumptuous temples that flank the park, both of which date back over a thousand years. The smaller of the two, **Donghaksa** in the east is best accessed from Daejeon and is said to look at its most beautiful in the spring. It has served as a college for Buddhist nuns since 724, and its various buildings exude an air of restraint (though some have been renovated rather too modernly). More open-plan than its eastern neighbour, **Gapsa** is closer to Gongju and better suits the fiery colours of autumn, thanks to its surrounding cloak of maple trees. Although the temples are pretty, most people are here for the **hike** between them – two main routes scale the ridge and both should have you up and down within four hours, including rests; given the terrain, it's slightly easier to hike east to west if you have a choice. Heading in this direction, most people choose to take the path that runs up the east side of Donghaksa, which takes in a couple of ornate

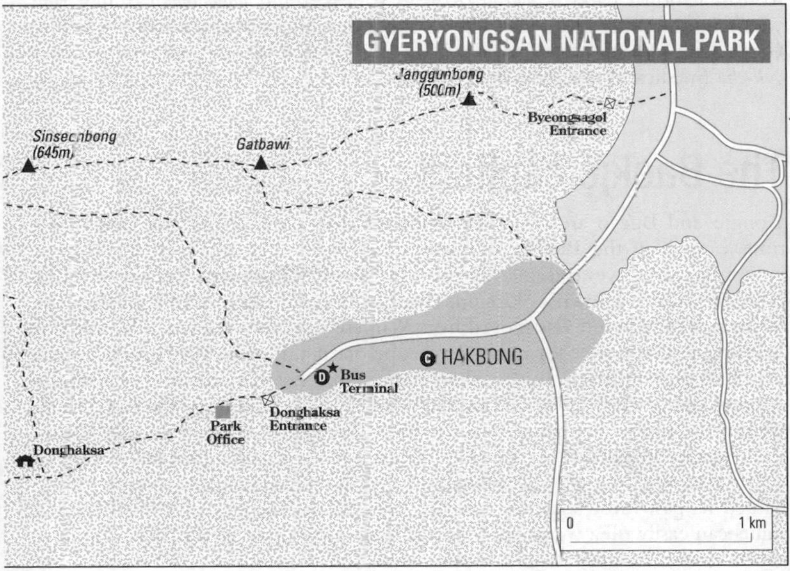

stone pagodas on its way to Gapsa. Others take a faster but more challenging route south of the temple, which heads up the 816m-high peak of Gwaneumbong; these two routes are connected by a beautiful **ridge path** that affords some excellent views. Whichever way you go, routes are well signposted in Korean and English, though the tracks can get uncomfortably busy at weekends; a less crowded (and much tougher) day-hike runs from Byeongsagol ticket booth – on the road north of the main eastern entrance to the park – to Gwaneumbong, taking in at least seven peaks before finally dropping down to Gapsa.

Practicalities

From Daejeon, **buses** #102, #103 and #120 run via Yuseong to the Donghaksa entrance every fifteen minutes or so. There are also half-a-dozen buses per day to the Gapsa entrance at the west of the park, though it's easier to get there on the half-hourly buses from Gongju. The bulk of Gyeryongsan's **rooms and restaurants** are located around the bus terminal below Donghaksa, but not all are of high quality; the Gapsa end is prettier and more relaxed. *Donghak Sanjang* (ⓣ042/825-4301; ❸) has average rooms but is right above the Donghaksa bus terminal and consequently one of the first to sell out. Nearby is a **campsite** (from W3000 per tent). Below Gapsa are some very rural *minbak* (❶), while on the other side of the car park is an achingly sweet village of **traditional houses** with simple rooms for rent – at night the cramped, yellow-lit alleyways create a scene that is redolent of a bygone era, and make for a truly atmospheric stay. Rooms go from W20,000, but hunt around to find the best and try to haggle the price down. There's also a **youth hostel** in the Gapsa area (ⓣ041/856-4666 or 7; dorm beds W12,000 for members, W15,000 non-members), which is just as soulless as others around the country. You won't go hungry at either end of the park; indeed, the local *ajummas* will go out of their way to lure you into their establishments. The best **restaurants** are on a leafy streamside path running parallel to the main Donghaksa access road, where – as at other Korean national parks – *pajeon* (Korean pancake) and *dongdongju* (milky rice wine) are the order of the day. There's also an excellent **teahouse** just below Gapsa temple, with a variety of teas on sale for W4000 – in winter the bitter *yak-cha* (medicinal teas) are hard to beat.

The Baekje capitals

Gongju and Bueyo are two small settlements in Chungnam that were, for a time, capitals of the **Baekje dynasty** which controlled much of the Korean peninsula's southwestern area during the **Three Kingdoms** period (see box opposite). Once known as Ungjin, **Gongju** became the second capital of the realm in 475, when it was moved from Wiryeseong (now known as Seoul), but held the seat of power for only 63 years before it was passed to **Buyeo**, a day's march to the southwest. Buyeo (then named Sabi) lasted a little longer until the dynasty was choked off in 660 by the powerful Silla empire to the east, which went on to unify the peninsula. Today, these three cities form an uneven historical triangle, weighed down on one side by Gyeongju's incomparable wealth of riches. Although the old Silla capital is the most interesting place to visit, having hauled its past most faithfully into the present, the Baekje pair's less heralded sights can easily fill a weekend. Many of these echo those of the Sillan capital – green grassy mounds where royalty were buried, imposing fortresses, lofty

The Baekje dynasty

The **Baekje dynasty** was one of Korea's famed **Three Kingdoms** – Goguryeo and Silla being the other two – and controlled much of southwestern Korea for almost seven hundred years. The *Samguk Sagi*, Korea's only real historical account of the peninsula in these times, claims that Baekje was a product of sibling rivalry – it was founded in 18 BC by Onjo, whose father had kick-started the Goguryeo dynasty less than twenty years beforehand, in present-day North Korea; seeing the reins of power passed on to his elder brother Yuri, Onjo promptly moved south and set up his own kingdom.

Strangely, given its position facing China on the western side of the Korean peninsula, Baekje was more closely allied with the kingdom of Wa in Japan – at least one Baekje king was born across the East Sea – and it became a conduit for art, religion and customs from the Asian mainland. This fact is perhaps best embodied by the Baekje artefacts displayed in the museums in Gongju (p.319) and Buyeo (p.323), which contain lacquer boxes, pottery and folding screens not dissimilar to the craftwork that Japan is now famed for.

Though the exact location of the first Baekje capital is unclear, it's certain that Gongju and Buyeo were its last two seats of power. Gongju, then known as Ungjin, was **capital** from 475 to 538; during this period the aforementioned Three Kingdoms were jostling for power, and while Baekje leaders formed an uneasy alliance with their Silla counterparts the large fortress of Gongsanseong (see p.319) was built to protect the city from Goguryeo attacks. The capital was transferred to **Sabi** – present-day Buyeo – which also received a fortress-shaped upgrade (see p.322). However, it was here that the Baekje kingdom finally ground to a halt in 660, succumbing to the Silla forces that, following their crushing of Goguryeo shortly afterwards, went on to rule the whole peninsula.

Though local rebellions briefly brought Baekje back to power in the years leading up to the disintegration of Unified Silla, it was finally stamped out by the nascent Goryeo dynasty in 935. Despite the many centuries that have elapsed since, much evidence of Baekje times can still be seen today in the form of the regal burial mounds found in Gongju and Buyeo.

pavilions and ornate **regal jewellery**. Unabashedly excessive, yet at the same time achieving an ornate simplicity, Baekje jewellery attained an international reputation and went on to exert an influence on the Japanese craft of jewellery making; some well-preserved examples in both cities can be found at their **museums**, which are two of Korea's best.

Gongju

Presided over by the large fortress of Gongsanseong, the small, sleepy city of **GONGJU** is one of the best places to see relics from the Baekje dynasty that it ruled as capital in the fifth and sixth centuries. **King Muryeong**, its most famous inhabitant, lay here undisturbed for over 1400 years, after which his tomb yielded thousands of pieces of jewellery that provided a hitherto unattainable insight into the splendid craft of the Baekje people. Largely devoid of the bustle, clutter and chain stores found in most Korean cities, and with a number of wonderful sights to choose from, Gongju is worthy of a day's exploration.

Arrival, information and city transport

Gongju is divided by the Geumgang River, with its dilapidated **intercity bus terminal** standing defiantly on the north bank. There are direct buses here from cities and towns across the Chungcheong provinces, as well as Seoul and a few cities in Gyeonggi-do; to get here from elsewhere you may need to

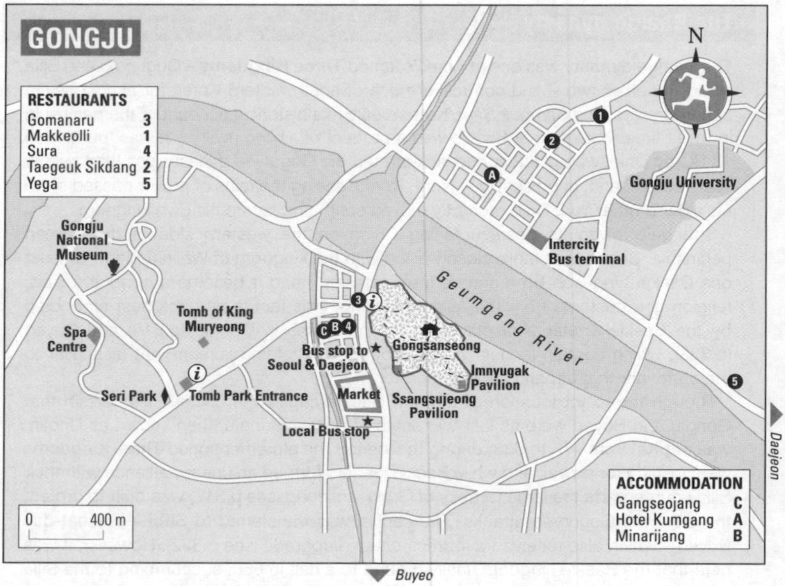

change in Daejeon. There's also a small terminal near the fortress for services to Gongju's periphery.

There are local buses, though Gongju's small size means that it's often cheaper for small groups to get around by **taxi**; it's also quite possible to walk between the centre and the main sights with a little effort. From the intercity bus terminal, a W2000 ride will get you to Gongsanseong, or it's a fifteen-minute walk via the bridge – though it may look impassable, only one lane is for traffic, the other for bicycles and pedestrians.

The main **tourist information** centre (☎041/856-7700; daily 9am–6pm; winter to 5pm) is located under Gongsanseong, and usually has helpful, English-speaking staff. Free **tours** of the city's main sights (entrance fees not included) start here every Sunday at 10am, though it's wise to book ahead. A

Gongju

Gongju	공주
Gongju National Museum	공주 국립 박물관
Gongsanseong	공산성
Magoksa	마곡사
Tomb of King Muryeong	무령왕릉
Accommodation and restaurants	
Gangseojang	강서장
Gomanaru	고마나루
Hotel Kumgang	호텔 금강
Minarijang	미나리장
Sura	수라
Yega	예가

smaller and less helpful information centre can be found at the entrance to King Muryeong's tomb.

Gongsanseong

For centuries, Gongju's focal point has been the hilltop fortress of **Gongsanseong** (daily 9am–6pm; winter until 5pm; W2000), whose 2.6km-long **perimeter wall** was built from local mud in Baekje times, before receiving a stone upgrade in the seventeenth century. It's possible to walk the entire circumference of the wall, an up-and-down course that occasionally affords splendid views of Gongju and its surrounding area. The grounds inside are worth a look too, inhabited by stripy squirrels and riddled with paths leading to a number of carefully painted **pavilions**. Of these, Ssangsujeong has the most interesting history – where this now stands, a Joseon dynasty king named Injo (ruled 1623–49) once hid under a couple of trees during a peasant-led rebellion against his rule; when this was quashed, the trees were made government officials, though sadly are no longer around to lend their leafy views to civil proceedings. Airy green Imnyugak has been painted with meticulous care and is the most beautiful pavilion; press on further west down a small path for great views of eastern Gongju. Down by the river there's a small temple, a refuge to monks who fought the Japanese in 1592, and on summer weekends visitors have the opportunity to dress up as a Baekje warrior and shoot off a few arrows. An hourly Baekje **changing of the guard** takes place at 2pm (April–June, Sept & early Oct).

Around the city

Heading west over the creek from Gongsanseong, you'll eventually come to the **Tomb of King Muryeong** (daily 9am–6pm; W1500), one of many regal burial groups dotted around the country from the Three Kingdoms period, but the only Baekje mound whose occupant is known for sure. Muryeong, who ruled for the first quarter of the sixth century, was credited with strengthening his kingdom by improving relations with those in China and Japan; some accounts suggest that the design of Japanese jewellery was influenced by gifts that he sent across. His gentle green burial mound was discovered by accident in 1971 during a civic construction project – after one-and-a-half millennia, Muryeong's tomb was the only one that hadn't been looted. All have now been sealed off for preservation – the fact that you can't peek inside is disappointing, but the sound of summer cicadas whirring in the trees, and the views of the rolling tomb mounds themselves, make for a pleasant stroll. A small exhibition hall contains replicas of Muryeong's tomb and the artefacts found within. Opposite the entrance is a small patch of land dedicated to female golfer **Seri Park**, Gongju's most famous daughter, who owns a boat-restaurant that you may spot incongruously "moored" on the side of the from Daejeon.

To see the actual riches scavenged from Muryeong's tomb head west to **Gongju National Museum** (9am–6pm, until 7pm weekends and holidays; closed Mon; W1000), set in a quiet wooded area by the turn of the river. Much of the museum is devoted to jewellery, and an impressive collection of Baekje bling reveals the dynasty's penchant for gold, silver and bronze. Artefacts such as elaborate golden earrings show an impressive attention to detail, but manage to be dignified and restrained with their use of shape and texture. The highlight of the exhibition is the king's flame-like **golden headwear**, once worn like rabbit ears on the royal scalp, and now one of the most important symbols not just of Gongju, but of the Baekje dynasty itself. Elsewhere in the museum are exhibits of wood and clay, showing the dynasty's history of trade with Japan and China.

Near the museum, you can relax at a small **hot spring** spa resort; the W5000 entrance fee allows you entry to the pools and sauna facilities, and is a small price to pay to emerge clean and refreshed.

Practicalities

Gongju's **accommodation** is centred around two areas; north of the river to the west of the bus terminal is a bunch of new establishments, while a group of older cheapies lie south of the river across the road from Gongsanseong – a quainter and more atmospheric area, and slightly closer to the sights. North of the river, the 𝟘 *Hotel Kumgang* (ⓣ041/852-1071 to 3, ⓕ041/852-1074; ❸) has friendly staff, spacious bathrooms, free Internet access in most rooms and a moderately priced restaurant on the second floor. The best option south of the river is the red-brick *Gangseojang* by the creek (ⓣ041/853-8323; ❷), which has decent enough rooms; ask for the one with a computer terminal and free Internet access. Nearby, and also acceptable, is the similarly priced *Minarijang*.

Two excellent **restaurants** can be found near Gongsanseong. Immediately across from the tourist information booth is *Gomanaru*, whose leafy interior is a good place to fill up with *ssambap-jeonsik*, a tableful of mostly vegetable dishes that are usually eaten rolled up in leaves; at just W5000 per person, this should keep you going for the best part of the day. A short walk south is *Sura*, a *galbi* den that may not look special from inside or out, but doles out *galbi* with a commendable array of side dishes. For something a bit more fancy, head east of the bus terminal to *Yega*, a bustling two-floored restaurant overlooking the river road. Its menu is written in English and almost entirely rib-based, and there are some delicious raspberry wines to sup during your meal; staff may also offer you delicious iced plum tea to wash down your food. The area around Gongju University has some interesting places to **drink**, with *Makkeolli* a focal point; open until late and busiest during term-time, the full version of its name translates as something like "W10,000 can make you happy", and the deceptively smooth rice wine proves this point night after night. Nearby is *Taegeuk Sikdang*, an almost hilariously right-wing restaurant-cum-*soju* bar adorned with slogans such as "Let's unite with North Korea, so that we can attack Japan with missiles" and "Dokdo belongs to us, earthquakes to Japan" (see box, p.233 for information on the latter dispute). Sparrows, pigskin and *dakddongjip* are on the menu, the latter literally translating as "chicken excrement house" and basically a platter of bird tails – if you can't smell the nationalist sentiment three blocks away, look out for the Korean flags.

Magoksa

A beautiful 45-minute bus ride through the countryside west of Gongju is **Magoksa** (daily 8am–6pm; W3000). The exact year of this temple's creation remains as mysterious as its remote, forested environs but it's believed to date from the mid-seventh century. It is now a principal temple of the Jogye order, the largest sect in Korean Buddhism. Although the most important buildings huddle together in a tight pack, rustic farmyard dwellings and auxillary hermitages extend into nearby fields and forest, and can easily fill up a half-day of pleasant meandering if you're not temple-tired. The hushed vibe of the complex provides the main attraction, though a few of its buildings are worthy of attention. Yeongsanjeon is a hall of a thousand individually crafted figurines, and has a nameplate said to have been written by King Sejo, a Joseon-dynasty ruler perhaps best famed for putting his brother to the sword. At the top of the complex, Daeungbojeon is a high point in more than one sense; the three golden statues in this main hall are backed by a large yet highly detailed Buddhist painting, and look down on a sea of fish-scaled black roof tiles.

Magoksa can be reached on **buses** #7 and #18 from the small bus terminal near the fortress in Gongju. If staying in such natural surroundings is an appealing prospect, note that on the way from the bus stop to the temple you'll find a number of **motels** and **restaurants**, the best of which are the *Magok Motel* (ⓣ041/841-0047; ③), a pretty swanky place considering the unabashedly rural location, and *Gareung-binga* just down the hill, a restaurant-cum-teahouse that serenades diners with traditional piped music.

Buyeo

Smaller and sleepier than Gongju, **BUYEO** still has enough sights to make it equally worthy of a visit. The Baekje seat of power was transferred here from Gongju in 538, and saw six kings come and go before the abrupt termination of the dynasty in 660, when General Gyebaek led his five thousand men into one last battle against a Silla–Chinese coalition ten times that size. Knowing that his resistance would prove futile, the general killed his wife and children before heading into combat, preferring to see them dead than condemn them to slavery. Legend has it that thousands of the town's women threw themselves off a riverside cliff when the battle had been lost, drowning both themselves and the Baekje dynasty. Today, this cliff and the large, verdant **fortress** surrounding it are the town's biggest draw, along with an excellent **museum** stuffed with treasures from a time when little Buyeo was one of the most important places in the land.

Arrival, information and orientation

Buses arrive at the station in the centre of town; from here most major sights – as well as the majority of motels and restaurants – are within walking distance, though it's easy to hunt down a cab if necessary. Buyeo's main street runs between two roundabouts – Boganso Rotary to the north, and Guncheon Rotary a kilometre to the south. By the latter is a statue of General Gyebaek, while east of the northern roundabout is a **tourist information office** (daily 9am–6pm; ⓣ041/830-2523), next to the fortress entrance, where's there's usually an English-speaker on hand. **Bus tours** (8hr) of the town set off from here every Sunday morning from July to November, taking in all the main sights; though the ride is free, entry fees will set you back W9000 or so. It's advisable to book ahead if possible.

Buyeo	
Buyeo	부여
Busosan	부소산
Buyeo National Museum	부여 국립 박물관
Gungnamji	궁남지
Jeongnimsaji	정림사지
Accommodation and restaurants	
Dingle Dangle	딩글당글
Minsokgwan	민속관
Motel VIP	모텔 VIP
Sky Motel	스카이 모텔
Youth hostel	유스 호스텔

Busosan

Buyeo's centre is dominated by its large fortress. **Busosan** (March–Oct 7am–7pm; Nov–Feb 8am–5pm; W2000) lacks the perimeter wall of Gongju's Gongsanseong, but with its position perched high over the river Baengman, plus a greater variety of trees and a thoroughly enjoyable network of trails, many visitors find this one even more beautiful. It also has history on its side,

▲ Bronze incense burner on display at Buyeo National Museum

as this is where the great Baekje dynasty came to an end after almost seven centuries of rule.

On entry to the fortress, you'll happen upon one of the many **pavilions** that dot the grounds, though the scattered nature of the trails mean that it's neither easy nor advisable to see them all. Yeonggillu is nearest the entrance and has a particularly pleasant and natural setting; it's also where kings brought local nobility for regular sunrise meetings, presided over by a pair of snakelike wooden dragons that remain today. Paths wind up to Sajaru, the highest point in the fortress and originally built as a moon-viewing platform. The path continues on to the cliff top of **Nakhwa-am**; from here, it is said, three thousand wives and daughters jumped to their deaths after General Gyebaek's defeat by the Silla–Chinese coalition, choosing suicide over probable rape and servitude. This tragic act gave Nakhwa-am its name – **Falling Flowers Rock** – and has been the subject of countless television epics. Down by the river is **Goransa**, a small temple backed by a spring that once provided water to the Baekje kings on account of its purported health benefits – servants had to prove that they'd climbed all the way here by serving the water with a distinctive leaf that only grew on a nearby plant. The spring water is said to make you three years younger for every glass you drink. The best way to finish a trip to the fortress is to take a **ferry ride** from a launch downhill from the spring. These sail a short way down the river to a **sculpture park** and some of the town's best restaurants; in summer there's a ferry every half-hour or so (W3000 one-way), but the service can be annoyingly infrequent in winter months.

Around the city

Heading south of Busosan's main entrance, you might want to swing by **Jeongnimsaji**, a small but pretty temple site (daily: March–Oct 7am–7pm; Nov–Feb 8am–5pm; W1000), inside of which is a five-storey stone pagoda – one of only three survivors from Baekje times – and a seated stone Buddha dating back to the Goryeo-era. Of more interest is **Buyeo National Museum** (9am–6pm, Sat & Sun until 7pm; closed Mon; W1000), a large but slightly out-of-the-way place due east of the city centre statue of General Gyebaek. As with other "national" museums in Korea, it focuses exclusively on artefacts found in its local area; here there's an understandable focus on riches from Baekje times. Some rooms examine Buyeo's gradual shift from the stone to the Bronze Age with a selection of pots and chopping implements, but inside a room devoted to Baekje treasures is the museum's pride and joy – a **bronze incense burner** that now serves as a symbol of the town. Elaborate animal figurines cover the outer shell of this two-foot-high egg-shaped sculpture, which sits on a base of twisted dragons; it's considered one of the most beautiful Baekje articles ever discovered, showing off the dynasty's love of form, detail and restrained opulence.

A short walk south of General Gyebaek's statue is **Gungnamji**, a beautiful lotus pond with a pavilion at its centre, and surrounded by a circle of willow trees; outside this weepy perimeter lie acres of lotus paddies, making this peaceful idyll feel as if it's in the middle of the countryside. To the east of town is a cluster of seven **Baekje tombs**; their history is relayed in a small information centre, though none of the former occupants are known for sure. A taxi from central Buyeo should cost not much more than W3000.

Practicalities

As long as you're not too fussy, **accommodation** is easy to find in Buyeo. The best rooms are at *Motel VIP* (Ⓣ041/832-3700; ③), near Boganso Rotary. The place is spotless, with mood lighting in the rooms and piped music in the corridors. Another good choice, and slightly cheaper, is the *Sky Motel* (☎041/835-3331; ❷), whose rooms are clean, airy and agreeably furnished; some have Internet access, though you'll pay more for these. Look for the building with the stone-clad exterior. The town's **youth hostel** (☎041/835-3101; HI members W11,000, non-members W16,000) is near the river and within walking distance of central Buyeo; though cheap for single travellers, bear in mind that Korean youth hostels are the almost exclusive preserve of Korean youth groups, so you're infinitely more likely to hear flute recitals than the Red Hot Chili Peppers. Try to avoid the immediate vicinity around the bus terminal, which contains some rather insalubrious places to stay.

Some of the town's best **restaurants** can be found on the road that leads past the youth hostel to the ferry dock. One of these is *Minsokgwan*, just past the hostel – the name is in Chinese characters so it's a little hard to spot, look for a sign with a pair of stone turtles straining their necks towards it. It's a traditionally styled place, with a courtyard full of old-Korea paraphernalia, and the tables and chairs inside fashioned from tree trunk segments. The *naeng-myeon* noodles – served in a cold but spicy soup – are good for cooling off in the summer, or try the home-made *kimchi*-tofu mix. If you're looking for somewhere closer to the bus terminal, your safest bet is *Dingle Dangle*, at the southern end of the main road; this fresh and colourful restaurant serves "fusion" food such as chicken cutlet and *omurice* (rice wrapped in an omelette), and has garden chairs to swing on and board games to play, as well as the best (or only) espresso in Buyeo.

Coastal Chungnam

Within easy reach of Seoul, Chungnam's coast is a popular place for those seeking to escape the capital for a bit of summer fun. Inevitably, the main attractions are the **beaches**, with the white stretches of Mallipo and Daecheon the most visited; the latter is the scene of an annual **mud festival**, one of the wildest and busiest events on the peninsula. It's a short ferry trip from the mainland's bustle to the more traditional lifestyle enjoyed on the offshore **islands**, a sleepy crew strung out beyond the horizon and almost entirely dependent on the fishing trade.

Daecheon beach

Long, wide and handsome, **DAECHEON BEACH** is by far the most popular on Korea's western coast, hauling in a predominantly young crowd. In the summer this 3km-long stretch of white sand becomes a sea of people, having fun in the water by day, then drinking and letting off fireworks until the early hours. The revelry reaches its crescendo each July with the **Boryeong mud festival**, a week-long event that seems to rope in (and sully) almost every expat in the country. Mud, mud and more mud – wrestle or slide around in it, throw

Coastal Chungnam

Cheonan	천안
Daecheon	대천
Independence Hall of Korea	독립기념관
Taean Haean National Park	태안해안 국립 공원

it at your friends or smear it all over yourself, then take lots and lots of pictures – this is one of the most enjoyable festivals on the calendar (see Ⓦwww.mudfestival.or.kr for more details). Those arriving outside festival season can still sample the brown stuff at the **Mud Skincare Center**, the most distinctive building on the beachfront, where guests can treat themselves to all-over mud massages from W25,000. There's also a sauna on the premises, and all manner of mud-based cosmetics on sale. During July or August watery fun of all kinds is available to rent – banana boats, jet-skis and large rubber tubes – as well as **minibikes** that you can ride up and down the prom.

Getting to Daecheon beach can be a little tricky. It's just 15km from the town of **Boryeong**, and the two places have been known to trade names on occasion – hence "Boryeong" Mud Festival. **Buses** to Daecheon will drop you at a bus terminal that goes by the name of Daecheon or Boryeong, from where you'll have to catch another bus to the beach (*Daecheon-bichi*). These usually go on to **Daecheon Harbour** (*Daecheon-hang*), from where ferries can be caught to the islands of the West Sea. Alternatively, it's a W4000 taxi ride from terminal to beach. Nine kilometres south of the beach is **Muchangpo**, a settlement that becomes popular for a few days every month when the tides retreat to reveal a path linking the beach with a small nearby island, an event inevitably termed "**Moses' Miracle**"; the sight of a line of people seemingly walking across water is quite something. For up-to-date advice on the tides phone the tourist information line on Ⓣ041/1330.

Practicalities

There's an **information booth** near the mud centre where staff can reserve accommodation both in Daecheon and – helpfully – on the offshore islands, but you'd be lucky to find an English-speaker here; a map and some controlled mime should be enough to land you a booking. **Motels** and *yeogwan* are everywhere, and even at the peak of summer you can usually find a bed without too much difficulty; prices can go through the roof on summer weekends and holidays, though with time and patience you should find a room for W30,000 or less. Generally speaking, things get cheaper the further you get from the twin axes of the beach and the mud centre access road; travellers often save money by cramming as many people as possible into a room, or staying out all night on the beach with a few drinks. There are a few clean, consistently good options near the access road – the *Sanho Beach Hotel* (Ⓣ041/931-1020; ❹) and *Motel If* (Ⓣ041/931-5353; ❹) have reasonable rooms, while those under the distinctive oriental roof of the *Moktobang Motel* (Ⓣ041/931-7172; ❹) are wood-panelled and quite pleasing. There's a small **campground** with shower facilities behind the mud centre, which costs W5000 per tent in July and August, but is free to use at other times.

Daecheon's culinary scene is simple – fish, fish and more fish. The seafront is lined with **seafood restaurants** and the competition is fierce, with most places displaying their still-alive goods in outdoor tanks – among the myriad options are eel, blue crabs, razor clams and sea cucumbers. Note that seafood in Korea is generally far costlier than other fare, and that no restaurants here have English-language menus – just let the restaurateur know how much you plan to spend (figure on no less than W10,000 per person). A way to get around the problems of price or language is to order the *hoe-dop-bap*, chunks of raw fish with spicy sauce served on a bed of rice and leaves. A more rustic patch of eateries can be found near **Daecheon harbour**; these are quite atmospheric, especially in the evenings when the ramshackle buildings, bare hanging bulbs and coursing sea water may make you feel as though you've been shunted back in time a couple of decades. Those who desire something other than fish will find their choices slim, and may have to rely on **snack stalls** or instant noodles from one of the convenience stores; the latter are also the source of most of the alcohol consumed in Daecheon, though there are plenty of **bars** lining the seafront.

West Sea islands

From Daecheon harbour, a string of tiny islands stretches beyond the horizon into what Koreans term the **West Sea**, a body of water known internationally as the Yellow Sea (see box, p.156). From their distant shores, the mainland is either a lazy murmur on the horizon or altogether out of sight, making this a perfect place to kick back and take it easy. **Beaches** and **seafood** restaurants are the main draw for most visitors, but it's also a joy to sample the unhurried island lifestyle that remains unaffected by the changes that swept through the mainland on its course to First World status; these islands therefore, provide the truest remnants of pre-industrial Korean life. Fishing boats judder into the docks where the sailors gut and prepare their haul with startling efficiency; it's sometimes possible to buy fish directly from them. Restaurants on the islands are usually rickety, family-run affairs serving simple Korean staples.

All islands have *minbak* **accommodation** in or around family homes, though don't expect anything too fancy – the rooms will be small and bare, and you'll probably have to sleep on a blanket on the floor. Prices start at W20,000 per night, and increase in summer months. Remember to bring enough money for your stay as most of the isles lack **banking facilities**, but most have mini-markets (sometimes hard to find as they tend to double as family homes). **Ferries** connect the islands in two main circuits, though with so few sailings, you won't be able to see more than one or two islands in a day.

Circuit one

This circuit fires 53km out to sea, terminating at the weather-beaten island group Oeyeondo, before heading back to the mainland on the same route; as the ferries are for foot passengers only, the islands they visit are **quieter** than those on loop two.

The first stop is **Hodo**, which attracts visitors for its beaches without the fuss of those on the mainland; the island's best beach is a curl of white sand just a short walk from the ferry dock and is great for swimming. Around the terminal are plenty of *minbak* rooms – pretty much every dwelling in the village will accept visitors, though there are only around sixty on the whole island. Try to track down Mr Choi at *Gwangcheon Minbak*, who's the proud owner of the only land vehicle on Hodo (a beat up 4WD) and can be persuaded to give free night-time rides through the forest, or a splash across the mudflats if the tide is out – tremendous fun. Next stop is **Nokdo**, the smallest island of the three and home to some superb hill trails. Unlike the other islands, the hillside town and its accommodation options are a fair walk from the ferry dock – everyone will be going the same way so you should be able to hitch a lift without too much bother. The ferries make their final stop at **Oeyeondo**, a weather-beaten family of thickly forested specks of land. This has the busiest port on the loop, with walking trails heading up to the island's twin peaks, as well as a tiny beach that's good for sunsets.

There are two **sailings** per day from Daecheon leaving at 8.10am and 3pm; ferries take 40 minutes to get to Hodo, 20 minutes more to Nokdo and a further 30 minutes to Oeyeondo, from where return sailings depart at 10am and 4.40pm.

Circuit two

This is a proper loop, with ferries heading both ways around a circle that starts and ends in Daecheon. These boats can accommodate vehicles, meaning that the islands here are busier than on the aforementioned circuit; however, the salty and remote appeal remains. All have *minbak* accommodation from around W20,000 (more in summer months).

Heading clockwise, the first port of call is **Sapsido**, the most popular island in the whole area (and pronounced sap-shi-do). Its shores are dotted with craggy rock formations, some with a hair-like covering of juniper or pine, while the island's interior is crisscrossed with networks of dirt tracks – it's possible to walk from one end of the island to the other in under an hour. Depending on the tides, ferries will call at one of two ports – there are *minbak* aplenty around each, and both have decent beaches within walking distance, but make sure that you know which one to go to when you're leaving the island. Next stop is **Janggodo**, whose name derives from its contours, which are said to be similar to the Korea *janggo* drum (though it's actually shaped more like a banana). Home to some Algarve-like rock formations, it's popular with families and, thanks to some particularly good beaches, the trendier elements of the Korean beach set. Local buses wait at the northern terminal (there are two) to take passengers to the *minbak* area (it's a little far to walk). It's then a short hop across a strait usually filled with fishing nets to little **Godaedo**, an island renowned for its seafood, proof of which is a pungent aroma that can often be smelt from the ferry. The next stop is **Anmyeondo**, the largest island in the group, and the only one connected to the mainland by road. Depending on the ferry and the tides, you may also stop at **Wonsando** and **Hyojado** on your way back to Daecheon.

At least three **sailings** per day head around this loop; those leaving Daecheon at 7.30am and 12.50pm head clockwise, arriving first at Sapsido, while the 4pm sailing heads in the opposite direction, stopping first at Anmyeondo.

Taean Haean National Park

Despite its status as a national park, **Taean Haean** is actually more developed than the islands of the West Sea, and a visit here is of questionable value. Although it ropes over a hundred islands into its perimeter, most are uninhabited crags of rock, and only **Anmyeondo** – connected to the mainland by road – is of any size. The small town of **Taean** is the principal gateway to the park; from here hourly buses run to the excellent **beach** at Mallipo. The most popular in the area, it gets crowded on summer weekends with Seoulite refugees escaping city life, and allows camping in summer months. **White sand beaches** fill in the tiny coves that dot Anmyeondo's western coast, many of which are only accessible by footpath from a small road that skirts the shore between Anmyeon, the island's main settlement and transport hub, and Yeongmok, a port village at the southern cape that receives ferries from Daecheon and other West Sea islands. Connecting the two are **buses** which meet the ferries and run approximately once an hour; Anmyeon has bus connections to several mainland cities. It's tempting – and advisable – to savour the wonderful countryside on the way by getting off the bus for a stroll.

Cheonan and around

After years in the shadows, **Cheonan** is a city on the up: now connected to Seoul by the steel veins of tube and high-speed train, it's awash with money from those deserting the capital, and improving at a rate of knots. The population has boomed in recent years, both with disaffected office workers from Seoul, and migrants from Asia who have been brought over to work on one of the many construction projects. The new **KTX line** has enabled commuters to work in Seoul while living in a cheaper, more manageable city, and Cheonan has even been connected to the capital's **subway** system. One of the longest metropolitan lines in the world, it's a fair couple of hours to central Seoul, and another to Soyosan at the northern end of the line.

However, despite the flashy new department stores and housing complexes, there's not much here to detain the traveller – visitors mainly use Cheonan as a jumping-off point for the largest museum in the country, the fascinating **Independence Hall of Korea** (see opposite). One exception is the excellent **Arario Gallery** (daily 11am–7pm; W5000) right next to the bus terminal, which is linked to the contemporary gallery in Seoul (see p.97), and makes a good pit stop en route to the independence hall. Outside the main entrance sits one of Damien Hirst's body-with-bits-exposed sculptures, alongside a tall tower of car axles that pokes fun at the city's ever-declining reputation as a mere transit hub; inside are two exhibition floors, both small but almost always brimming with high-quality modern art. The gallery's bosses have excellent connections to China (there's another Arario in Beijing's 798 gallery-cum-warehouse complex), which means that it's often possible to catch glimpses of the burgeoning art scene across the West Sea. There's also a great café beneath the gallery itself.

Practicalities

Cheonan's **train** and **bus** stations are fairly close to each other in the city centre; outside the former is a small **tourist information** booth (daily 9am–5pm; ⓣ041/550-2445). Note that high-speed KTX services terminate at a dedicated station some way to the west, next to Onyang, a hot spring resort. Good **accommodation** is a little thin on the ground, but the *Hotel Metro* (ⓣ041/622-8211 to 4, ⓦwww.hotelmetro.co.kr; ❻), visible to the left of the train station exit, is a reliable option, and also offers an airport shuttle service. The carpeted rooms are decent with vault-like doors, though bathroom goings-on can be sometimes too visible through the frosted glass that separates them from the bedrooms. The best area for **budget-seekers** is to the left of the bus station exit; just up the road from *TGI Friday's*, the *Western Hotel* (ⓣ041/551-0606, ⓕ041/551-0070; ❸) is excellent value and offers free Internet access, soft drinks, snacks and international calls. On the same road is *Yewonjang Motel* (ⓣ041/556-4311 or 2; ❷), without the frills but slightly cheaper. Nearby, the *Hotel California* (ⓣ041/566-3311 or 2; ❷) also deserves a mention; rooms are furnished with black tiles and dark wood, and you'll find a free can of beer waiting in the fridge. There's also an extremely decent *jjimjilbang* near the crossroads by the exit of the bus station.

For **eating and drinking** (especially drinking), head to the lattice of bar-and restaurant-filled streets immediately opposite the bus station exit. Here, *Z-Pasta* is an excellent refuge for those who want a menu free of red pepper paste. It's a stylish place under the same ownership as the Arario Gallery, which attracts a suitably arty crowd, and has pasta dishes from W7000. There's also a bar, a café and a Japanese restaurant underneath. Korean tourists love to sample regional specialities – sometimes making trips solely for this purpose – and for them no visit to Cheonan is complete without buying a box of *hodu-gwaja*, small **nut cakes** that the city is famous for. These near-compulsory souvenirs are rather tasty, and sell by the dozen in *Apgujang Kimbap*, just outside the train station, which also has simple Korean mains on offer at low prices. As far as **nightlife** goes, the bus station area is full of bars with little to choose between them, but the hottest club is *St. 101*, home to a popular weekly hip-hop night (W5000 entry).

Independence Hall of Korea

Set in a wooded area east of Cheonan, Korea's largest museum, the **Independence Hall of Korea** (9.30am–5pm, Nov–Feb until 4pm; closed Mon; W2000; Ⓦwww.independence.or.kr), is a concrete testament to the country's continued

▲ Independence Hall of Korea

struggle for independence during its most troubled time from 1910 to 1945, when it suffered the indignity of being **occupied by Japan**. Though this was a relatively short period, the effects were devastating (see box below), and despite the Korean government's initial appeal for locals not to be "filled with bitterness or resentment", the popularity of the place and the size of its seven large exhibition halls – each of which would probably function quite well as individual museums – show that the wounds are still sore. Scarcely an opportunity is missed to insert a derogatory adjective against the Japanese people and policies of the time, it's this combination of vitriol and history that makes the place an absorbing visit.

Each of the halls highlights different aspects of the occupation, with the most important displays labelled in English. However, many locals head straight for those detailing **Japanese brutality** during the colonial period – "Torture done by Japan", a life-size display featuring some unfortunate mannequins, is one of the most popular exhibits, but there are also numerous photographs on show. Should you tire of the unrelenting indignation, the "Hall of National Heritage" is filled with less bombastic displays detailing traditional Korean life.

A number of city **buses** run to the museum from the bus and train stations in central Cheonan (all have three-digit numbers beginning with 4); the journey takes around half an hour. Ask for *Dongnip Ginyeom-gwan*, if you can get your tongue around it, and the driver will drop you off outside.

Japanese occupation

If you've done any sightseeing in Korea, you'll no doubt have come across information boards telling you when, or how often, certain buildings were burnt down or destroyed by the Japanese. The two countries have been at loggerheads for centuries, but the 1910–45 **occupation period** caused most of the tension that can still be felt today. In this age of empire, Asian territory from Beijing to Borneo suffered systematic rape and torture at the hands of Japanese forces, but only Korea experienced a full-scale assault on its **national identity**. Koreans were forced to use Japanese names and money, books written in *Hangeul* text were burnt and the Japanese language was taught in schools. These measures were merely the tip of the iceberg, and Japan's famed attention to detail meant that even the tall trees were chopped down: straight and strong, they were said to symbolize the Korean psyche, and they were replaced with willows which drifted with the wind in a manner more befitting the programme, the apparent hope being that Korean minds would achieve the same flexibility. The most contentious issue remains the use of over 100,000 **comfort women**, who were forced into slave-like prostitution to sate the sexual needs of Japanese soldiers.

The **atomic bombs** that brought about the end of the World War II also finished off the occupation of Korea, which slid rapidly into civil war. This post-occupation preoccupation kept both factions too busy to demand compensation or apologies from Japan – they were, in fact, never to arrive. While some countries have bent over backwards to highlight wartime misdeeds, Japan has been notoriously stubborn in this regard – its prime ministers have regularly paid respects at **Yasukuni**, a shrine to those who died serving the empire, but notably also to at least a dozen Class A war criminals, and school textbooks have increasingly glossed over the atrocities. This has led to repeated and continuing protests; surviving comfort women, still devoid of compensation, hold **demonstrations** every Wednesday at noon outside the Japanese Embassy in Seoul (see p.96). Korea, for its part, has failed to debate successfully the role of **local collaborators** during the resistance, or to acknowledge fully in its own schoolbooks or museums the foreign influence that ended both the Japanese occupation and the Korean War. Until the nations of the Far East stand up to their own histories, it's hard to see how the region will truly move forward.

Chungcheongbuk-do

As Korea's only landlocked province, **CHUNGCHEONGBUK-DO** could be said to represent the heart of the country. It is a predominantly rural patchwork of fields and peaks, with three national parks within its borders. **Songnisan** is deservedly the most popular, and has a number of good day-hikes emanating from Beopjusa, a highly picturesque temple near the park's main entrance. **Woraksan** and **Sobaeksan** are less visited but are just as appealing to hikers; both surround the lakeside resort town of **Danyang**, which makes a comfortable base for exploration of the province's eastern flank where caves, fortresses and the sprawling temple of **Guinsa** are on the menu.

Cheongju and around

CHEONGJU, along with Chungju, gave part of its name to the greater region of Chungcheong in 1356. Despite this evidence of age-old importance – and the fact that it's home to **Jikji**, the first book ever produced with movable metal type (see box, p.334) – there's little history on show for you to see. Cheongju is best reserved as a convenient base for visiting the surrounding area, or to take in the urban pleasures of **shopping** and **drinking**: the city has a sizeable and switched-on **student population**; students pour out of the universities and into nearby neighbourhoods crammed full of bars and cheap restaurants.

Arrival, information and orientation

Though there's a small international **airport** 9km north of Cheongju (best accessed on bus #747 from the centre; W850), the overwhelming majority of travellers are likely to arrive by train or bus. However, with the **train station** frustratingly located outside the city to the west, its best to choose the latter option; the express and intercity **bus terminals** are close to central Cheongju, and stare each other down across a road just west of the city centre. Between the stations is a helpful **tourist office** (daily 8.30am–7pm, winter until 6pm; ⓣ043/223-8430), with English-speaking staff who can advise on both Cheongju and Chungnam province as a whole.

Cheongju itself divides neatly into **three main sections**: the bus stations and most accommodation options to the west; the shopping and restaurant district to the east; and Jungmun, a pulsating nightlife district outside Chungbuk University, playing the slightly inebriated piggy in the middle.

Cheongju and around	
Cheongju	청주
Early Printing Museum	고인쇄 박물관
Gongwondang	공원당
Jjol-jjol Hoddeok	쫄쫄호떡
Jungmun	중문
Sangdangsanseong	산당산성
Songnisan National Park	속리산 국립 공원
Tourist Hotel Newvera	관광 호텔 누베라

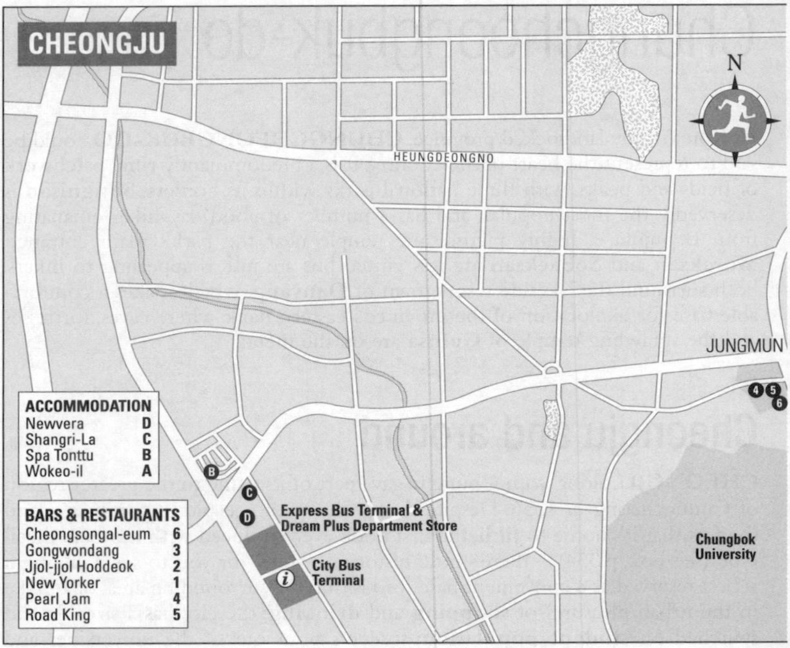

Accommodation

An assortment of motels and **mid-range hotels** lie near the bus stations, on the north side of the Dream Plus department store. A slightly cheaper but much seedier **motel district** lies in between the shopping area and the nearby stream; there are also some scruffy digs in and around the Jungmun area.

Shangri-La Gagyeong-dong ⓣ043/231-8632, ⓕ043/231-8636. This turreted motel is the best of a new, clean bunch in a surprisingly quiet area near the bus terminals. The decor is more European than Himalayan, and there are a few styles of room to choose from. ❸

Spa Tonttu Bokdae-dong. Big, clean and new, you'd do well to find a better *jjimjilbang*. Green tea bathing pools, sauna facilities and the use of exercise bikes and treadmills are all yours for W6000, which includes a night's stay (albeit on a mat in a darkened room, surrounded by snoring locals). ❶

Tourist Hotel Newvera Gagyeong-dong ⓣ043/235-8181 to 4, ⓦwww.newvera.co.kr. Comfy and within walking distance of the bus terminals, this hotel is the default recommendation of the local tourist office. Staff are amiable, and the cosy rooms are decked out in slightly different styles; suites are comparatively poor value. ❺

Wokeo-il Motel Seomun-dong ⓣ043/254-5231. Probably the best in a slightly run-down area between the river and the shopping centre. Inside, it's a decent enough place with acceptable rooms. ❸

The City

Most of the area's attractions lie outside Cheongju; with few actual sights in the city itself, you should be able to cover most places in a few hours, perhaps spending the evening soaking up the atmosphere in the bars of the Jungmun student area. The most appealing attraction is the **Early Printing Museum** (9am–5pm; W1000), near the centre of the city, and easily accessible by city bus

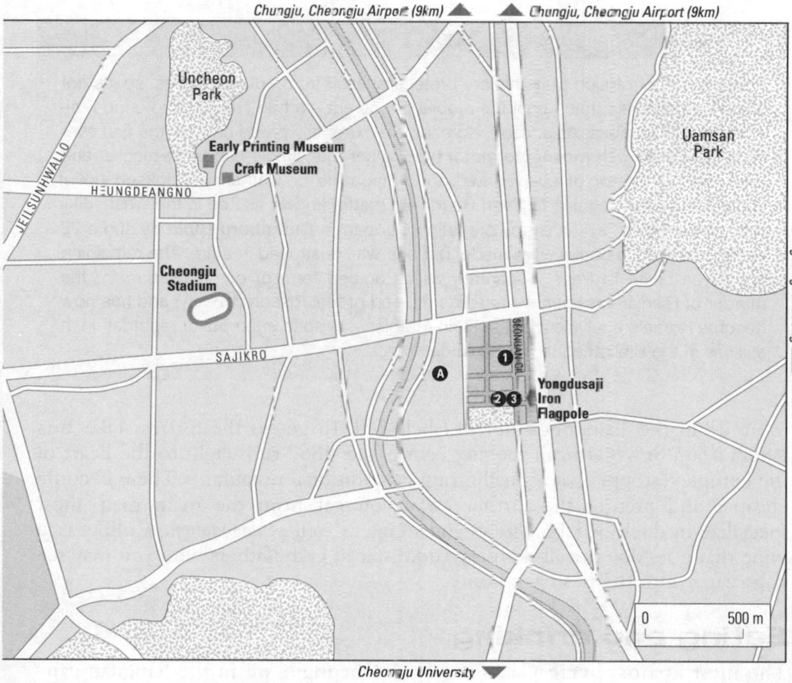

#831 (15min; W850) from the bus terminals. Looking somewhat like a mushroom spaceship from the outside, it's dedicated to **Jikji**, the great-great-granddaddy of all printed work, though the book itself was confiscated by the French some time ago (see box, p.334). On site, there are exhibition halls detailing the creation of Jikji, as well as some showcasing the history of print throughout the world. Just across the road is a somewhat dull **Craft Museum** (same hours; free), with its two upper floors mostly filled with tea sets, though the ground floor shop is a good place to hunt for souvenirs.

Another of Cheongju's official attractions (and officially Korean National Treasure #41) is a metal stick that pokes somewhat incongruously out of the shopping district to the east of the city – the **Yongdusaji Iron Flagpole** has been here since 962, and was once used to display banners on religious occasions; now seemingly content to proffer an iron finger at the area's teeming commerce, it serves as a favoured meeting point for the hip young things who populate the area's innumerable shops, cafés and restaurants, though unless you're in the area it hardly merits a visit.

Set high above the city to the east is **Sangdangsanseong** (free), the city's fortress. Surrounded by an outer wall, much of which is still standing, the fortress was built in the Baekje era, a perilous time when the Korean peninsula was being pulled apart from within by the famed Three Kingdoms of the time, and attacked from without by Japanese forces. Having undergone extensive facelifts during the Unified Silla and Joseon periods, it's now possible to walk along part of the outer wall, which affords great views of the hills and fields that surround Cheongju. The fortress **interior** is equally worthy of a stroll, with stepped rice paddies, and farming residences in various states of disrepair and habitation. Check out the wooden statues outside number 96, and "conference

Jikji

Korea has spent much of its history protecting itself from outside forces, so it's not much of a surprise that – until the mobile phone era – it had little time to enrich the world with inventions. As a result, Koreans are extremely proud of **Jikji**, the first ever book produced with **moveable metal type** rather than single-use page-blocks, and is a direct ancestor of every newspaper, magazine or Catherine Cookson novel you've ever read. A guide to *Seon* Buddhism (better known as Zen in the West), Jikji was produced in 1377, thereby predating Germany's **Gutenberg Bible** by some 78 years; initially two books were made, but one was destroyed in a fire. The remaining copy was taken to Paris, apparently as an agreed form of compensation for the murder of French missionaries towards the end of the Joseon dynasty, and has now become Korea's equivalent of the Elgin Marbles – despite attempts at repatriation, it still lies in the Bibliothèque Nationale de France.

room 1" in the abandoned hut just below it. To get to the fortress take **bus** #862, #863 or #864 from the city centre; the #862 runs right to the heart of the complex, stopping at a small group of traditional restaurants. These become cheaper and prettier the further away you get from the main road; most specialize in duck or rabbit stews and soups, as well as *dongdongju*, a milky rice wine that goes down well with the ruddy-faced grandfathers who you may see staggering onto the bus back home.

Eating and drinking

The most **atmospheric** places to eat in Cheongju are in the Sangdangsan-seong fortress just out of town, though the city's three main districts are all packed with places to fill your belly. The area around the bus stations has a collection of cheap **restaurants**, including some decent *galbi* joints for meat-loving pyromaniacs. There's also a wealth of choice in the food court of the blue Dream Plus department store – here cheap Korean dishes vie with Japanese and Italian fare, plus there's a good noodle bar covered almost head-to-toe with Post-It note messages from previous diners. The student districts outside Chungbuk and Cheongju universities are awash with cheap **snack bars**, but for something a little more upmarket you should head for the eateries lining the pedestrianized streets of the main shopping district. *Jjol-jjol Hoddeok* is a simple restaurant as hard to find as it is to pronounce, but is often the endpoint of long queues waiting their turn for a W500 *hoddeok* or four. These syrupy rice pancakes are popular Korean snacks but can usually only be found in the wintertime, so this small restaurant gets lots of sweet-toothed custom year-round. A pancake throw away is *Gongwondang*, a popular Japanese-style place with lots of chicken cutlets on offer, or try the buckwheat noodles (*momil guksu*, otherwise known as *soba* in Japanese). Also in the shopping district is *New Yorker*, the slick multi-floor capital of Cheongju's **café society**, and a great place to people-watch over a green tea latte. Although it looks for all the world like a *Starbucks*, it's not part of a chain, and also has free Internet access.

The city's liveliest nightlife area is student-heavy **Jungmun**, a tangle of bars and snack stalls around Chungbuk University, and not to be confused with the quieter, less interesting area of the same name around Cheongju University. The city's motley expat crew usually gather outside the Hi-Mart of a summer evening, before heading to *Road King* or *Pearl Jam*, two bars that rock to live music most weekends. For something more Korean try *Cheongsongal-eum*, a nearby *makkeolli* den packed almost every evening with red-faced students gamely holding down the cheap snacks.

Songnisan National Park

The muscular **SONGNISAN NATIONAL PARK** is justly one of the most popular parks in Korea, partially due to its position dead centre of the country, but also thanks to its temple and the visually arresting **33m-high bronze Buddha**, the tallest such figure in the world. Songnisan's myriad trails are a joy to hike, the paths winding uphill alongside gentle streams to heady thousand-metre-high peaks, but though the park's name translates as "mountains far from the ordinary world", the area between the bus terminal and the main park entrance couldn't be more typical of a Korean tourist hotspot, with more souvenir shops, restaurants and karaoke rooms than you'd expect to find in the midst of such tranquil environs. Once inside, a short, shaded path leads to the park's main draw – the glorious temple **Beopjusa**. Entirely surrounded by pine and peaks, its name means – somewhat tautologically – "the temple where Buddhist teachings reside", and it is indeed still an active place of worship and religious study. Standing with his back to the west (the direction of his death), the huge bronze Buddha statue faces an unconventional five-storey building that, despite a rather squat appearance fostered by the shallow lattice windows, is also the tallest such structure in Korea. Nearby are two elaborately decorated **stone lanterns**; two lions hold up the torch segment on one (though the flames have long been extinguished), while the other is adorned with four carved devas and a statue of a bodhisattva. This deity incarnate once held an incense burner until he was consumed by fire, presumably reaching nirvana during his show of determination.

Plenty of **hiking** opportunities lie beyond Beopjusa. The main target is the 1054m-high summit of Munjangdae, an easy three hours away from Beopjusa; locals often make a wish after their third visit to this peak. A short walk from here is the peak of **Birobong** (1008m). Geographically speaking, this can credibly claim to be the centre of the country, as rain falling here – depending on what face it lands on – will end up flowing down the Nakdong River to Busan in the south, running through Gongju on its way to the west coast, or

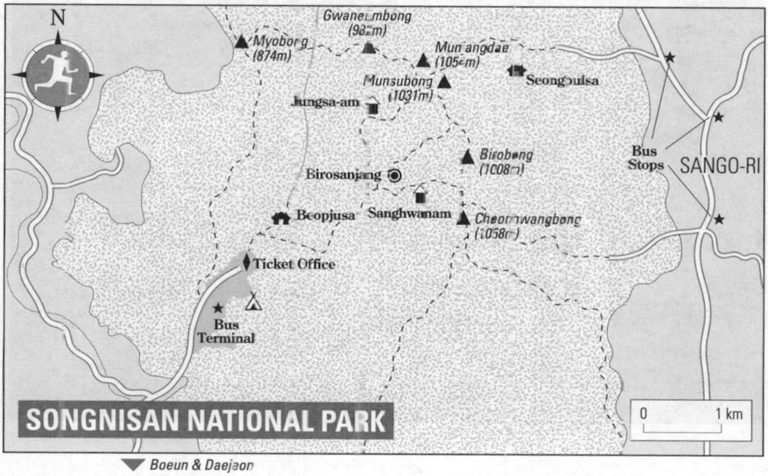

pouring north into the Han River and exiting the mainland through Seoul. An easy ninety-minute ridge trail connects Munjangdae to **Cheonhwangbong**, the park's highest peak at 1058m; a further two-hour walk west will bring you back down to the main park entrance, or you can continue east towards Sango-ri in Gyongsang province.

▲ Bronze Buddha, Beopjusa temple

Practicalities

There are direct **bus** connections to Songnisan every twenty minutes or so from Cheongju, as well as regular services from Daejeon and even the Dong-Seoul terminal in the capital. Buses stop just under a kilometre away from the park entrance itself, and their arrival is often delayed on summer weekends by the solid traffic running into the park. The best **accommodation** in the area is at *Lake Hills* (Ⓣ043/542-5281 to 2, Ⓦwww.lakehills.co.kr; ❻), a hotel snuggled up next to the park entrance. Prices at this heavyweight champ of the Songnisan circuit pack a bit of a punch (W148,000) but the rooms are just about worth the rate. Further down the price scale before you reach the ubiquitous *minbak* rooms – cheap, simple and often part of family homes, these go for around W30,000 per night – is *Youn Song* (Ⓣ043/542-1500, Ⓦwww.songnisanhotel.com; ❹), a cavernous hotel whose rooms are fair value for money. There's a fascinating budget option inside the park itself – the *Birosanjang* (Ⓣ043/543-4782; ❷) is essentially a *yeoinsuk* with a motel price tag, though the location is worth the extra cash – it hangs over a trickling stream, around which chipmunks, frogs and colourful moths pop by for regular visits. Despite the remote location, food is available, and occasionally the *dongdongju* flows well into the night. Remember to sign one of the guestbooks, which date back over thirty years (notable for the chance to see the word "groovy" used with no sense of irony).

Songnisan's **restaurants** are excellent; corn jelly (*dotorimuk*) is the official local speciality but the *pajeon* (a kind of Korean pancake) here are possibly the best in the country, and are usually slung back with a pot of *dongdongju*. One good place to fill up on these comestibles and more is the family-run *Chanumul*, an orangey building south of the main road.

Chungju and around

Chungju is a moderately sized city in the north of Chungbuk province, but while there's little to see here, there's plenty to see in the surrounding area, for which the city makes an agreeable base. Close by is **Suanbo**, a relaxed hot spring resort popular with Korean families, as well as a ski resort. A short push further on will bring you to **Woraksan**, one of the country's quietest national parks. **Danyang**, another resort town, lies on the other side of the park, and is best approached by **ferry** from Chungju. The lake itself is man-made, but is surrounded by soaring mountains and numerous valleys; there are also some interesting rock formations by the water's edge on the approach to Danyang. Ferries run from the Chungjuho ferry terminal (*seonchak-jang*) just past the dam to the east of Chungju city centre, and accessible on bus #301. Schedules are irregular, depending on the season, the water height and whether the captain sleeps in or not, so it's best to contact the tourist office for information before you set off. Around Danyang, there are several **cave systems** that have been opened up for tourist exploration, as well as **Guinsa**, surely the most distinctive temple in the land.

Chungju and around	
Chungju	충주
Suanbo	수안보
Woraksan National Park	월악산 국립 공원

Chungju

Most travellers use **CHUNGJU** as a place from which to get elsewhere, particularly the stunning ferry route east of Danyang. One exception is **Jungangtap**, a seven-storey stone pagoda dating from the late eighth century and, at over fourteen metres high, the tallest structure to survive from those times. The site is pleasant and has been developed into a tourist attraction, with examples of traditional housing and a small museum. Bus #400 runs here from Chungju's bus terminals. A more transient Chungju attraction rolls into town once a year – the **martial arts festival**, which takes place in early October, is a slap-fest that draws pugilists from around the world to perform and practise their own local brands of martial fisticuffs.

Chungju's bus and train stations are within walking distance of each another. The gleaming new **bus station** has onward connecting services to Suanbo and Woraksan, and contains a helpful **tourist information** centre (daily 9.30am–6pm; ⓣ043/850-7329); staff here can book accommodation, and offer discounts at the tourist hotels. The **train station** faces a motel area that, despite feeling slightly seedy, is a good option for those arriving on a late train. Two decent motels on the road heading straight ahead from the train station exit are the *Hollywood Hotel* (ⓣ043/855-6836; ❸), a clean pad with free Internet access and dressing gowns, or the slightly more expensive *Hotel M★tel* (ⓣ043/852-1250; ❸), a funky place with large, comfy rooms and a choice of free DVDs to watch, though prospective guests at both will be provided with free contraceptives on the bedside tables. Those seeking something a little classier should head to the *Friendly Hotel* (ⓣ043/848-9900, ⓕ043/842-9403; ❺), where the staff live up to the name. Rooms here are a little scruffy but some have great views of the adjacent reservoir. Filling your stomach in Chungju shouldn't be a problem; one easy option for those arriving or departing is the **food court** in the bus station, which has a number of cheap, clean restaurants – *Yong-u-dong* has an English-language picture menu, and a greasy though tasty range of chicken cutlets.

Suanbo

A short bus ride east of Chungju is the hot spring resort **SUANBO**, a quiet village that's small and untrafficked enough to be navigated easily on foot. As with many tourist spots built on Korea's sudden economic growth a few decades back, it feels a little like a dog that's had its day, but remains a relaxing place nonetheless. The village's slumber is punctuated by regular festivals and special events, including the national **arm wrestling championships** in late July, but many use Suanbo as a base for tours of the local area, which includes a ski resort, golf courses and the peaks of Woraksan National Park. Hotels and motels squat over the **springs** themselves, pumping healthy hot water to communal spa facilities, or directly to guest bathrooms. If you're only here on a day trip, head to the **spa complex** (6am–8pm; W5000) to the north of town; it may look a little like a nuclear waste facility from the outside, but the interior is more presentable and a great place to wind down if you've been travelling hard. One place to work up a sweat is **Sajo Village**, just a couple of kilometres from Suanbo and one of the most petite **ski resorts** in the country. A lack of crowds and fuss, as well as the chance to night-ski, have made it popular with those in the know; free shuttle buses run here regularly to and from Suanbo during the ski season.

Bus #246 heads from Chungju to Suanbo's bus station, where a fairly useful **tourist information** booth situated nearby can provide you with maps and advise on accommodation. Suanbo has a decent range of **accommodation** with all of the top hotels – and some cheaper ones – having spa facilities. The *Chosun Tourist Hotel* (ⓣ043/848-8833, ⓦsuanbo.co.kr; ❻) at the far edge of town is a decent enough place, and more presentable than the cheaper but slightly Soviet-styled *Sangnok Hotel* near the information booth – off-season discounts can bring the price down to the same level. Cheaper alternatives include *Sinhung-jang* (ⓣ043/846-3711; ❸) near the info booth, which has a spa in the basement but only traditional *ondol* rooms (guests sleep on blankets, not beds), and the *Hotel Gloria* (ⓣ043/856-7008; ❸), whose bathrooms are pumped with spa water. A short cab ride out of town is the sprawling *Suanbo Park Hotel* (ⓣ043/846-2331 to 6, ⓦwww.suanbopark.co.kr; ❼), which is usually full of affluent Korean families drawn to its spa featuring a couple of outdoor pools – highly recommended if you have the money. Suanbo is famed for several **culinary specialities**, of which pheasant, duck and rabbit are the most interesting; these usually come in group-based meals served in the form of large stews accompanied by side dishes (around W40,000 for four people). For solo diners, there's *Jeonju Sikdang*, a restaurant near the spa complex which serves pheasant dumplings as well as stews. More regular Korean fare is available at restaurants all over the town, including the local favourite, *sundubu*, a spicy tofu stew.

Woraksan National Park

Korea has a great range of national parks to choose from, but such is the popularity of hiking that many can be uncomfortably crowded on summer weekends. However, if you prefer peaks to people, **WORAKSAN NATIONAL PARK** could be the one for you. Despite the easy access provided by the spine road running through its centre, this area still has a remote feel and the hiking routes here rarely get crowded. The three small settlements – Songgye, Deokju and Mireuk – located en route from north to south manage to retain a rural air, utterly devoid of the packs of restaurants and *noraebang* that often infest the entrance to Korean parks. It's also one of the only places in the country where the endangered **goral antelope** can be found; six were released into the park and at the last count have managed to triple their numbers, though they're notoriously shy and chances of seeing one are extremely slim.

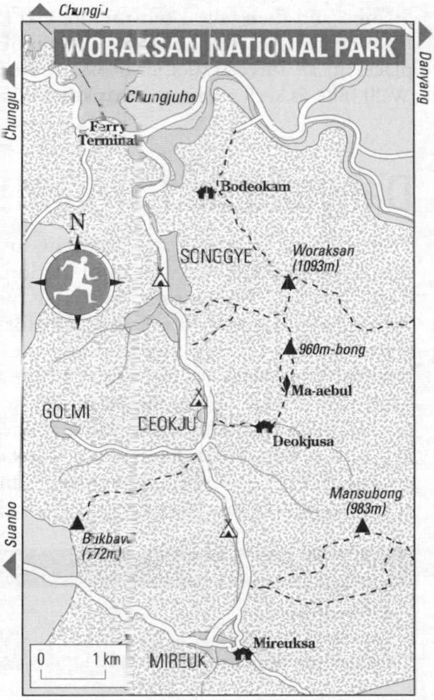

Mireuk is the most common access point for visitors to the park, as it's marked by a stone Buddha and the Mireuksa temple ruins; the latter were, at the time of writing, undergoing extensive restoration, and the end result promises to be an interesting approximation of the temple that once stood on the same spot. Many visitors content themselves with a short walk to a small waterfall, but a trickier three-hour-loop hike also starts here, running to the nearby peak of Mansubong (983m) and back. Hikers prefer the harder four- to five-hour hike that starts from Doekju, which follows the route up Mansubong then back down to Songgye; allow a little more time if you want to branch off and scale Woraksan, the park's highest peak at 1093m. The views from the top are superb – keep an eye out for the waters of Chungjuho to the north – but you'll see plenty on your way up. Just fifteen minutes from the Deokju trailhead you'll come to **Deokjusa**, a small but highly colourful temple, then **Ma-aebul**, an engraved stone Buddha that likely dates from the early Goryeo period. Ma-aebul was designed to face the aforementioned standing Buddha in Mireuk, and investigations have shown that somehow, despite the trees and peaks in the way and the total absence of measuring equipment, the designers got it almost spot-on. A less-visited three-hour route runs southwest from Deokju to Bukbawi (772m), and down to the Suanbo road; this trail is closed off periodically by the park authorities to preserve the natural environment, but makes for a stimulating hike if you find it open.

Practicalities

Buses **from Chungju** approach Woraksan from both north and south. The #222 heads in via lake Chungjuho to stop at the far north of the park and is arguably the more beautiful route, whereas the #246 (via Suanbo) heads along the park's spine road to stop at all three settlements; both journeys take around 45 minutes. Annoyingly, the routes don't quite connect in the middle, and the times are irregular – get the latest timetables from the information office in Chungju or Suanbo. If there are no buses for a while, it may be easier to get to Suanbo and then take a ten-minute taxi ride. *Minbak* dot this route all the way from Suanbo, so you should have few problems finding a simple room; there are places in all three settlements on the main road, with prices starting at about W20,000, as well as three **campsites** that each charge W5000 per tent.

Danyang and around

From the river dam near Chungju, an artificial lake spreads east, spilling into valleys along the way until settling into river-like normality near the sleepy town of **Danyang**. Traversable by ferry, this route is a serious rival to Soyang in Gangwon-do (see p.169) for the title of Korea's prettiest inland waterway. With its mountain air and laid-back nature, Danyang makes a good base for the highly scenic surrounding area. Three national parks sit almost back-to-back in an expanse of green, pine-covered ripples – Woraksan (see p.339) and Chiaksan (p.194) are best accessed from other provinces, but you can visit pretty **Sobaeksan** from Danyang. The parks form natural tri-state boundaries to the Chungcheong, Gangwon and Gyeongsang regions – accordingly, the area has played host to a number of battles over the centuries,

Danyang and around	
Danyang	단양
Guinsa	구인사
Sobaeksan National Park	소백산 국립 공원

and some fortress ruins from these heady times can still be seen. The highlight of the area, however, is **Guinsa**, one of the most distinctive temples in the whole of the land.

Danyang

Home to a rarified and almost resort-like air, **DANYANG** is – despite its puny size – the major settlement in the predominantly rural eastern arm of Chungcheonbuk-do province. The artificial lake that curls river-like along its shore swallowed what was once the town centre; as a result, its replacement has a slightly fresher and less pastoral feel than one might expect for the town's size and location, and is squeezed between the shore and **Daesongsan**, a pretty hill of walking trails. The surrounding sights are scattered and hard to reach by bus so this area is best visited with your **own transport**. The region's roads are quiet by Korean standards, and motels and restaurants are dotted all

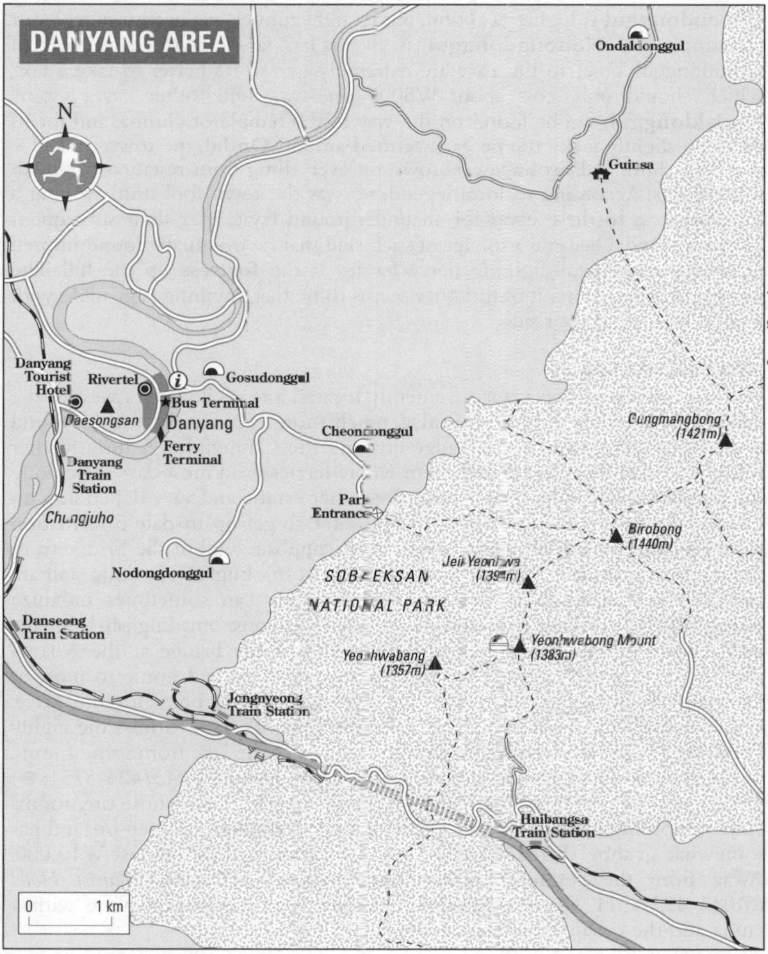

over the place, which makes for some pleasant touring on two wheels or four. If you arrive by ferry from Chungju be sure to look out for the oddly shaped rocks and crags found around the lake area: those travelling by bus or car may catch glimpses of these when the roads dive down to the waterside on their approach to Danyang.

Danyang's biggest draw is the abundance of cave systems that lie to the north and east of town. Within walking distance of the centre is **Gosudonggul** (9am–5pm; W4000); dating back millennia, this 1.7km-long grotto was discovered less than forty years ago. Underground, its honey-yellow stalagmites and stalactites ripple through the dim, damp tunnel, and are visible from metal walkways and staircases. Note, however, the cave is a popular stopover with families out for a weekend drive through the countryside, and can become uncomfortably crowded: visit on a weekday, if possible. To get to Gosudonggil from Danyang cross the bridge, pass the tourist office, and continue until you see the souvenir shops on the left-hand side. The road beyond forks to give access to two further caves, both only a couple of kilometres further away. **Cheondonggul** is highly beautiful, but its tight tunnels make it unsuitable for claustrophobes. **Nodongdonggul** is a smaller, far less-visited version of Gosudonggul; buses to this cave are extremely rare so it's better to take a taxi, which should only cost about W5000 one-way. One other cave system, **Ondaldonggul**, can be found on the way to the temple of Guinsa, and forms part of a slightly tacky theme park centred around **Ondal**, the town mascot – you'll see him, and his huge eyebrows, on everything from restaurant signs to toilet doors. According to local legend, he was the town fool until wooing a local princess to these caves for an underground tryst; after their subsequent marriage, Ondal became a soldier of such skill that he eventually found himself promoted to general, fighting fierce battles at the **fortress** up the hill. The extremely Korean moral of the story seems to be that anything is possible with a good woman at your side.

Practicalities

Danyang's **train** station is inconveniently located a few kilometres west of the centre; the intercity **bus terminal** is much more central, and can be found near the western end of the bridge crossing the Chungjuho. A little further south is a small **ferry terminal**, from where ferries head most days west along the lake towards Chungju. Schedules are rather erratic and vary depending on finance, the season and the height of the water, so get up-to-date information from the **tourist office**, which stands at the opposite end of the bridge from the bus terminal (daily 9am–6pm; ⓣ043/422-1146). English-speaking staff are not always available, but with prior notice they can sometimes organize **paragliding** or **rafting** trips in the area. The most consistent English-language information can be found near the town end of the bridge at the *Rivertel* (ⓣ043/421-5600; ❸), which is run by a friendly local and home to most of Danyang's backpackers; the rooms are, however, a little poky for the price. Better **motels** can be found along the waterfront; it's hard to miss the eight-floor *Sky Napoli* (❹), which provides great views of the lake from some rooms, or the Roman facade of the slightly seamy *Opera House* (ⓣ043/423-5751; ❷) further along. Just behind the *Rivertel* is the *Hoseong Yeoinsuk* whose tiny rooms contain nothing more than a television and a few blankets to sleep on, and has somewhat grubby shared facilities, but is extremely cheap at just W10,000. Away from the centre, near the train station, is *Danyang Tourist Hotel* (ⓣ043/423-9911, ⓦwww.danyanghotel.com; ❺), an upmarket place with a sauna and the cushiest rooms in town.

Biwon, near the ferry terminal, is a good **restaurant** – try the *sanchae bibimbap*, made entirely from local ingredients, or *olgaeng-i haejangguk*, a vegetable soup filled with tiny snails from the lake outside. For a meat feast head directly south from the bridge, and up and over the main road on the left-hand side is *Jeon-won Hoe-gwan*, a *galbi* den with large and plentiful side dishes. Also popular is *Jangdarisikdang* behind the *Rivertel*, which cooks some decent but slightly expensive hotpots, as well as *ondal* – garlic rice served with a multitude of side dishes. Danyang is famed for its **garlic**, which often fills the **market** in the town centre; there's even a festival related to the bulbs each July, which features a **Miss Garlic contest**. A word of warning: Danyang lacks decent **banking facilities**, so it's wise to stock up on cash before you get here.

Guinsa

Shoehorned into a tranquil valley northeast of Danyang is **GUINSA** (24hr; free), one of Korea's more remarkable **temple** complexes. A great divider among Koreans, many view it as the most un-Korean temple, which is emphatically true – the colours and building styles are hard to find anywhere else in the country, and the usual elegant restraint of the traditional layouts has been replaced by a desire to show off. On the other hand, numbers alone bear witness to its importance – up to 10,000 monks live here at any one time, and the kitchens can dish up food for twice that number on any given day. Guinsa is the headquarters of the Buddhist **Cheontae sect** (see box, p.344): once the most powerful in the country, it declined to near-extinction by the 1940s, but was given a second lease of life in 1945 by Songwol Wongak, a monk who put his overseas studies to good use by creating an altogether different temple. Here, the usual black slate of Korean temple roofing has occasionally been eschewed for a glazed orange finish reminiscent of that in Beijing's Forbidden City, and some buildings show hints of

▲ Guinsa temple

The Cheontae sect

Cheontae is a Buddhist sect whose Korean followers number almost two million, making it one of the biggest in the country. As with other Korean sects, the school descended from China, where it was created in the sixth century and known as *Tiantai*. On crossing the West Sea the sect's beliefs were polished into a local form deemed more logical, consistent and holistic than its Chinese predecessor; after wrestling with competitors during Unified Silla rule, the school became fully established in the eleventh century.

Lhasa's Potala Palace with their use of height and vertical lines. Buildings swarm up the valley and connect in unlikely ways, with alleys and bridges crisscrossing like the dragons depicted around the complex; you'll often wander up a path, and on looking back discover three or four routes that could have brought you to the same place. Despite being infested with an almost plague-like number of dragonflies in late summer, it's one of the most scenic places in the country.

Entry to the main body of the complex is through the **Gate of Four Heavenly Kings**, from where you'll head up to the five-storey **law hall**; this is one of the largest such facilities in Korea, and like many other buildings on the complex is elaborate both in terms of painting and structural design. Inside you'll find a golden Shakyamuni Buddha and two attendants – tempting as it may be, you are not allowed to take photos in this building. Further along the maze of paths is a courtyard, sometimes barely visible under the masses of *kimchi* pots used for making dinner, which is cooked up in colossal kitchens and served in the huge **cafeteria** (11.30am–1.30pm; voluntary donation). Close by are several buildings which serve as **living quarters**; the one with the sheer vertical face is the newest and largest structure in the still-growing complex. Heading up alongside this on a wonderful pine-covered path you come to the **Great Teacher Hall**, the achingly gorgeous golden crown of the complex, and a gleaming shrine to its creator, whose statue stands proud at the centre of the hall. Continuing on the uphill path will bring you to his well-tended gravesite, while further on are the western slopes of **Sobaeksan National Park** (see below for details).

Practicalities

Guinsa is one of the most interesting places in Korea to embark on a **temple-stay** programme, though the sheer number of people here on a typical day will dash any thoughts of Zen (the sect is, in fact, opposed to the *Seon* school which approximates Japanese Zen). It's not always possible and is best arranged through a tourist office; the nearest is in Danyang. Failing that, there are **minbak** at the foot of the complex (❶), as are plenty of **restaurants** if you miss lunch at the temple. On the way from the car park to the temple is a **bus stop**, which has hourly buses to Danyang, several every day to Seoul, and ever-changing connections to other Chungcheong cities.

Sobaeksan National Park

Far quieter than most Korean parks on account of its location, **SOBAEKSAN NATIONAL PARK** (8am–6pm; free) is an unheralded delight. It is best visited at the end of spring (around May or June), when a carpet of royal **azalea blooms** paints much of the mountainside a riot of pink, but at any time of the year the views are impressive – the park is traversed by a relatively bare ridge heading in an admirably straight line from northeast to southwest, crossing numerous high peaks. A steep three-hour uphill path runs from the main entrance at Cheondong-ri to **Birobong**, the park's highest peak at 1440m. After reaching the ridge most head straight back down, but if you follow it along in either direction you will be rewarded with a succession of amazing views. Many opt to head northeast to Gungmangbong (1421m), an hour or so away, but only the hardcore continue all the way to Hyeongjebong. Southwest of Birobong are three peaks, confusingly all named Yeonhwabong; on the central crest, taking advantage of the park's clean air and lofty elevation, is Korea's main **astronomical observatory**, though unfortunately it is closed to visitors. From here it's possible to exit the park to the south through the Huibang park entrance, the two-hour walk mopping up small waterfalls and a secluded temple on the way.

Practicalities

The **Cheondong entrance** is close to Danyang – just beyond Cheondonggul cave – and is therefore best reached by taxi (W6000), though there are local buses every hour or so from the main road outside the town's bus terminal. The park has other entrances but few are easily accessible without your own transport. The **Huibang entrance** is a 2km walk from Huibangsa train station; those travelling here on the rails from Danyang should note that the track at one point dives into the mountain, and makes a 360-degree turn before coming out again much further down.

Minbak rooms are easy to find by the Cheondong entrance, although the price goes down and the quality up the further away you get from the park entrance. However, the best rooms are about a kilometre down the road in *Carpe Diem* (Ⓣ043/421-2155, Ⓕ043/421-2187; ❺), a chic pension with a café and art gallery, whose rooms are filled with modern art and plastic fruit strewn about the place (and Marilyn Monroe at the entrance). Both park entrances have **camping grounds**, and park **maps** are available for the usual W1000.

Travel details

Trains

Cheonan to: Daejeon (regularly; 20min); Seoul (regularly; 35min).
Daecheon to: Seoul (hourly; 2hr 30min).
Daejeon to: Busan (regularly; 1hr 50min); Cheonan (regularly; 20min); Daegu (regularly; 45min); Gwangju (regularly; 1hr 45min); Jeonju (hourly; 1hr 20min); Seoul (regularly; 50min).

Buses

Buyeo to: Cheongju (10 daily; 1hr 40min); Daecheon (11 daily; 1hr); Daejeon (regularly; 1hr 30min); Gongju (regularly; 1hr); Seoul (regularly; 3hr 30min).
Cheonan to: Cheongju (regularly; 50min); Chungju (regularly; 1hr 40min); Daecheon (regularly; 2hr 40min); Daejeon (regularly; 1hr); Gongju (regularly; 1hr 10min); Jeonju (8 daily; 2hr 30min); Seoul (regularly; 1hr).
Cheongju to: Buyeo (10 daily; 1hr 40min); Chungju (regularly; 1hr 30min); Daejeon (every 5min; 1hr); Gongju (regularly; 1hr); Seoul (regularly; 1hr 20min); Songnisan (regularly; 1hr 50min).
Chungju to: Andong (7 daily; 3hr); Busan (5 daily; 4hr 30min); Cheongju (regularly; 1hr 30min); Daejeon (regularly; 1hr 30min); Seoul (regularly; 1hr 40min).
Daecheon to: Cheonan (regularly; 2hr 40min); Daejeon (regularly; 2hr 50min); Seoul (regularly; 2hr).
Daejeon Express terminal to: Busan (hourly; 3hr 10min); Cheonan (regularly; 1hr); Daegu (every 30min; 2hr 20min); Gwangju (every 30min; 2hr 30min); Gyeongju (4 daily; 2hr 40min); Jeonju (every 20min; 1hr 20min); Seoul (regularly; 1hr 50min).

Dongbu terminal to: Andong (16 daily; 2hr 40min); Cheongju (every 10min; 1hr); Chungju (regularly; 1hr 40min); Gongju (regularly; 1hr 10min); Muju (regularly; 1hr); Songnisan (regularly; 1hr 40min).
Seobu terminal to: Buyeo (every 20min; 1hr 20min); Daecheon (regularly; 1hr 50min); Gongju (regularly; 1hr).

Danyang to: Busan (1 daily; 5hr); Cheongju (regularly; 3hr 30min); Chungju (5 daily; 1hr 30min); Guinsa (13 daily; 30min); Seoul (regularly; 2hr 10min).
Gongju to: Buyeo (regularly; 1hr); Cheonan (regularly; 1hr 10min); Daecheon (regularly; 1hr 40min); Daejeon (every 5min; 50min); Seoul (regularly; 2hr).

6

Jeju

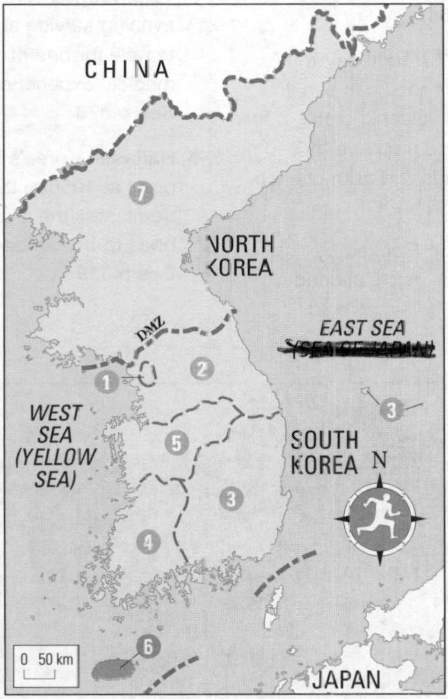
CHINA
7
NORTH KOREA
DMZ
EAST SEA
[redacted]
1
2
3
WEST SEA (YELLOW SEA)
5
SOUTH KOREA
N
3
4
6
0 50 km
JAPAN

CHAPTER 6

Highlights

* **Seongsan** Catch the sunrise from a peak above this charming town, then take a ferry to the nearby island of Udo. See p.362
* **Manjanggul** Live out your Indiana Jones fantasies at Jeju's underground lava tube, one of the world's longest. See p.364
* **Route 97** A rural day-trip along this road can see you take in a volcanic crater, a folk village and a culture museum, before finishing at the beach. See p.365
* **Seogwipo** Flanked by waterfalls, Jeju's second largest city is a relaxed base for tours of the sunny southern coast. See p.367
* **Teddy Bear Museum** The moon landings and the fall of the Berlin Wall are just some of the events to be given the teddy treatment at this shrine to high kitsch. See p.371
* **Yakcheonsa** Turn up for the evening service at this remote temple for one of Jeju's most magical experiences. See p.373
* **Hallasan** Korea's highest point at 1950m, this mountain dominates the island and just begs to be climbed. See p.379

▲ Jeongbang waterfall, Seogwipo

6

Jeju

The mass of islands draping off Korea's southern coast fades into the Pacific, before coming to an enigmatic conclusion in the crater-pocked isle of **JEJU**, known locally as Jejudo. This tectonic pimple in the South Sea is the country's number one holiday destination, particularly for Korean honeymooners, and it's easy to see why – the island's volcanic crags, innumerable beaches and colourful rural life draw comparisons with Hawaii and Bali, a fact not lost on the local tourist authorities. This very hype puts many foreign travellers off, but while the five-star hotels and tour buses can detract from Jeju's natural appeal, the island makes for a superb visit if taken on its own terms; indeed those who travel into Jeju's more remote areas may come away with the impression that little has changed here for decades. In many ways it's as if regular Korea has been given a makeover – splashes of tropical green fringe fields topped off with palm trees and tangerine groves, and while Jeju's **weather** may be breezier and damper than the mainland, its winter is eaten into by lengthier springs and autumns, allowing oranges, pineapples and dragon fruit to grow.

Around the island, you'll see much evidence of a rich local culture quite distinct from the mainland, most notably in the form of the **hareubang** – these cute, grandfatherly statues of volcanic rock were made for reasons as yet unexplained, and pop up all over the island (see box, p.378). Similarly ubiquitous are the **batdam**, walls of hand-stacked volcanic rock that separate the farmers' fields: like the drystone walls found across Britain, these were built without any bonding agents, the resulting gaps letting through the strong winds that often whip the island. Harder to spot are the *haenyeo*, **female divers** who plunge without breathing apparatus into Jeju's often treacherous waters in search of shellfish and sea urchins (see box, p.363). Although once a hard-as-nails embodiment of the island's matriarchal culture, their dwindling numbers mean that this occupation is in danger of petering out. Still in abundance though are Jeju's distinctive **thatch-roofed houses**, and a breed of miniature horse; these are of particular interest to Koreans due to the near-total dearth of equine activity on the mainland.

Jeju City is the largest settlement, and whether you arrive by plane or ferry, this will be your entry point to the island. You'll find the greatest choice of accommodation and restaurants here and most visitors choose to hole up in the city for the duration of their stay, as the rest of the island is within day-trip territory. Although there are a few sights in the city itself, getting out of town is essential if you're to make the most of your trip to Jeju. On the east coast is **Seongsan**, a sumptuously rural hideaway crowned by the dawn people-magnet of Ilchulbong, a green caldera that translates as "Sunrise Peak"; ferries run from

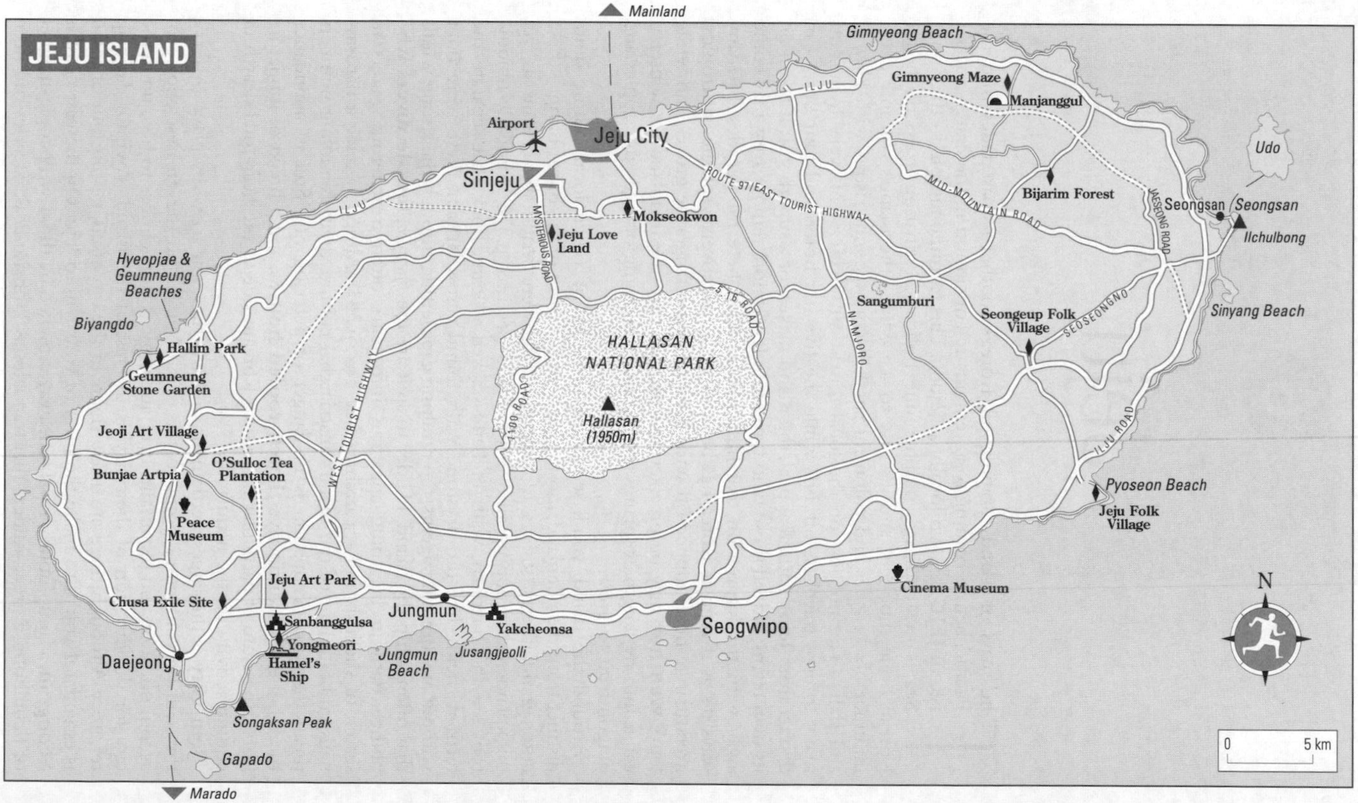
JEJU ISLAND
Mainland
Marado
Gimnyeong Beach
Gimnyeong Maze
Manjanggul
Bijarim Forest
Udo
Seongsan
Seongsan
Ilchulbong
Sinyang Beach
Airport
Jeju City
Sinjeju
Mokseokwon
Jeju Love Land
ILJU
ROUTE 97/EAST TOURIST HIGHWAY
MID-MOUNTAIN ROAD
JAESEONG ROAD
MYSTERIOUS ROAD
5.16 ROAD
NAMJORO
SEOSEONGNO
ILJU ROAD
1100 ROAD
WEST TOURIST HIGHWAY
Sangumburi
Seongeup Folk Village
Hyeopjae & Geumneung Beaches
Biyangdo
Hallim Park
Geumneung Stone Garden
HALLASAN NATIONAL PARK
Hallasan (1950m)
Jeoji Art Village
O'Sulloc Tea Plantation
Bunjae Artpia
Peace Museum
Pyoseon Beach
Jeju Folk Village
Jeju Art Park
Chusa Exile Site
Jungmun
Yakcheonsa
Sanbanggulsa
Yongmeori
Hamel's Ship
Seogwipo
Cinema Museum
Daejeong
Jungmun Beach
Jusangjeolli
Songaksan Peak
Gapado
N
0
5 km

here to **Udo**, a tiny islet which somehow manages to be yet even more bucolic. Inland are the **Manjanggul lava tubes**, one of the longest such systems in the world, and **Sangumburi**, the largest and most accessible of Jeju's many craters. All roads eventually lead to **Seogwipo** on the south coast; this relaxed, waterfall-flanked city is Jeju's second-largest settlement, and sits next to the five-star resort of **Jungmun**. Sights in Jeju's west are a little harder to access, but this makes a trip all the more worthwhile – the countryside you'll have to plough through is some of the best on the island, with the fields yellow with rapeseed in spring, and carpeted from summer to autumn with the pink-white-purple tricolour of cosmos flowers. Those with an interest in calligraphy may want to seek out the remote former home of Chusa, one of the country's most famed exponents of the art. In the very centre of the island is **Hallasan**, an extinct volcano and the country's highest point at 1950m, visible from much of the island, though often obscured by Jeju's fickle weather.

Jeju is one of the few places in Korea where renting a car or bicycle isn't tantamount to suicide (see p.361 for listings). Outside Jeju City, roads are generally empty and the scenery is almost always stunning, particularly in the inland areas, where you'll find tiny communities, some of which will never have seen a foreigner. Bicycle trips around the perimeter of the island are becoming ever more popular, with riders usually taking four days to complete the circuit – Seongsan, Seogwipo and Daecheong make sensible overnight stops.

Some history

Jejudo burst into being around two million years ago in a series of volcanic eruptions, but prior to an annexation by the mainland Goryeo dynasty in 1105 its history is sketchy and unknown. While the mainland was being ruled by the famed Three Kingdoms of Silla, Baekje and Goguryeo, Jeju was governed by the mysterious **Tamna kingdom**, though with no historical record of Tamna's founding, it is left to Jeju myth to fill in the gaps: according to legend, the three founders of the country – Go, Bu and Yang – rose from the ground at a spot now marked by **Samseonghyeol** shrine in Jeju City, and went on to populate the entire island with the help of three maidens. The *Samguk Sagi* – Korea's main historical account of the Three Kingdoms period – states that Tamna in the fifth century became a tributary state to the Baekje kingdom on the mainland's southwest, then hurriedly switched allegiance before the rival Silla kingdom swallowed Baekje whole in 660. Silla itself was consumed in 918 by the Goryeo dynasty, which set about reining in the island province; Jeju gradually relinquished autonomy before a full takeover in 1105. The inevitable **Mongol** invasion came in the mid-thirteenth century, with the marauding Khaans controlling the island for almost a hundred years. The horses bred here to support Mongol attacks on Japan fostered a local tradition of horsemanship that continues to this day – Jeju is the only place in Korea with significant equine numbers – while the visitors also left an audible legacy in the Jejanese dialect.

In 1404, with Korea finally free of Mongol control, Jeju was eventually brought under control by an embryonic **Joseon dynasty**. Its location made it the ideal place for Seoul to exile radicals. Two of the most famed of these were **King Gwanghaegun**, the victim of a coup in 1623, and **Chusa**, an esteemed calligrapher whose exile site can be found on the west of the island (see p.376). It was just after this time that the West got its first reports about Korea, from **Hendrick Hamel**, a crewman on a Dutch trading ship that crashed off the Jeju coast in 1653 (see box, p.375).

With Jeju continually held at arm's length by the central government, a long-standing feeling of resentment against the mainland was a major factor in the

Jeju Massacre of 1948. With Japanese occupation having recently ended with Japan's surrender at the end of World War II, the Korean–American coalition sought to tear out the country's communist roots, which were strong on Jejudo. Jejanese guerilla forces, provoked by regular brutality, staged a simultaneous attack on the island's police stations. A retaliation was inevitable, and the rebels and government forces continued to trade blows years after the official end of the **Korean War** in 1953, by which time this largely ignored conflict had resulted in up to 30,000 deaths, the overwhelming majority on the rebel side.

Things have since calmed down significantly. Jeju returned to its roots as a rural backwater with little bar fishing and farming to sustain its population, but its popularity with mainland tourists grew and grew after Korea's took off as an economic power, with the island becoming known for the *samda*, or three bounties – rock, wind and women. Recently tourist numbers have been decreasing slightly, with richer and more cosmopolitan Koreans increasingly choosing to spend their holidays abroad, though Jeju still remains the country's top holiday spot.

Jeju City

As the only place on Jejudo with transport connections to the mainland, it's impossible to avoid **JEJU CITY**, the capital of the province and home to more than half of its population. Markedly relaxed and low-rise for a Korean city, and loomed over by the extinct volcanic cone of Hallasan, it has a few sights of its own to explore, though the palm trees, beaches, tectonic peaks and rocky crags of Jeju are just a bus-ride away, thus making it a convenient base for the vast majority of the island's visitors.

Jeju City was, according to local folklore, the place where the island's progenitors sprung out of the ground (you can still see the holes at **Samseonghyeol**), and while there are few concrete details of the city's history up until Joseon times, the traditional buildings of **Mokgwanaji**, a governmental office located near the present centre of the city, shows that it has long been a seat of regional power. Other interesting sights include **Yongduam** ("Dragon Head Rock"), a basalt formation rising from the often fierce sea, and **Jeju Hyanggyo**, a Confucian academy. There are also a couple of vaguely interesting **museums**, best reserved as shelter on one of Jeju's many rainy days. South of the centre along the **Mysterious Road**, where objects appear to roll uphill, is the entertaining **Love Land**, a theme park filled with all manner of racy exhibits.

The term "Jeju" is part of geographic nomenclature and can cause some confusion: Jeju City – known as "Jeju-si" in Korean – is the capital of Jeju-do province, as well as the principal city of Jejudo, the island. The city in turn is split into two more Jejus – **Gujeju**, the main chunk of the city, and **Sinjeju** ("New" Jeju), a smaller and less interesting lattice of streets a few kilometres to the west. Sinjeju has some good hotels and restaurants, but no actual sights as such – the aforementioned attractions are all located in Gujeju, which also provides an atmosphere more characteristic of the island.

Arrival

Internal flights from several mainland destinations arrive every few minutes, landing at the island's **airport** a few kilometres west of the city centre. Six **bus** routes make the short run to Gujeju, the city centre, the most useful of which is #100 (W850), which heads east every fifteen minutes or so to the bus

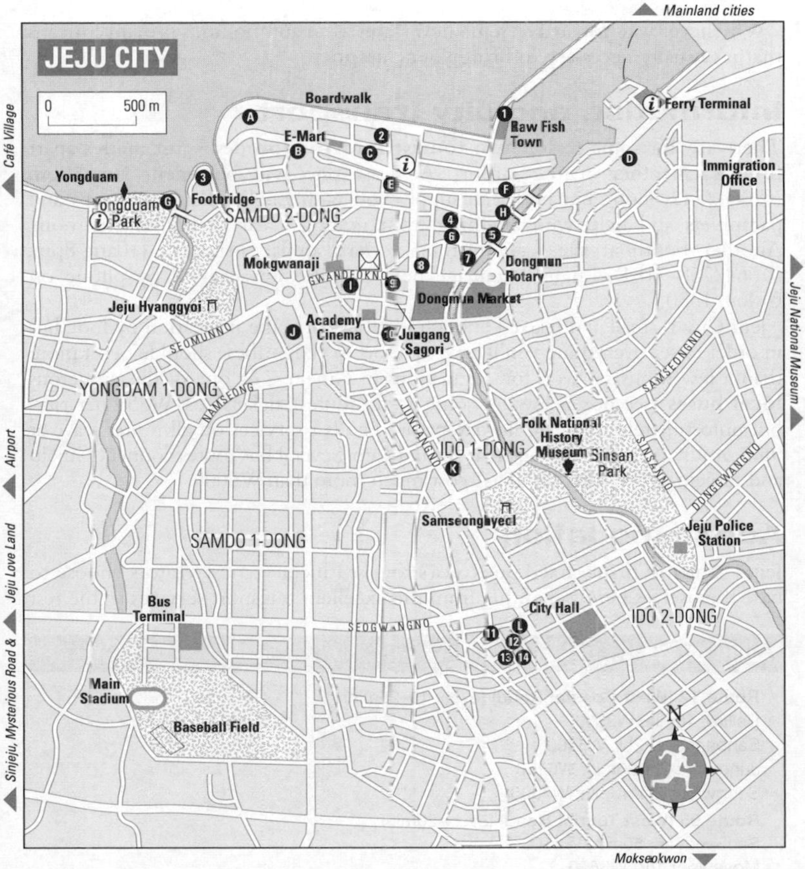

ACCOMMODATION	
Chinjeol Minbak	D
Geumseongjang Yeogwan	H
Hotel Robero	I
Jeju Pacific Hotel	J
Jeju Oriental Hotel	B
Jinyeong Motel	L
Jjimjilbang	C
KAL Hotel	K
Motel Bobos	F
Palace Hotel	E
Ramada Plaza	A
Yongoreum Minbak	G

RESTAURANTS	
Botong Saramdeul	4
Daejin Hoetjip	1
Dunkin Donuts	8
Florish Hill	10
Hwang-eum Dak-galbi	6
Jeongda-eun	3
Lotteria	2
Segeomjeongsut Bulgalbi	7
Tam	11

BARS	
Anglels Sin	13
Blue Agave	9
Dekoboko	5
Led Zeppelin	12
Makkeolli	14

terminal, then on to Dongmun Rotary in the city centre, or south to Sinjeju. Bus #600 runs at similar intervals to the top hotels in Jungmun (W3900) and Seogwipo (W5000), south of the island. At the eastern edge of the city is the **ferry terminal**, with connections from several mainland cities; decreasing flight prices mean that ferry schedules have long been in a state of flux, but at the time of writing there were daily ferries from Mokpo (see p.274) and Wando (see p.280), as well as a few overnight journeys per week from Busan (see p.241). Some ferries connecting Wando and Jeju stop at **Chujado** on their way across; this is an extremely quiet and small group of islands, but several foreigners have mistakenly alighted here, believing it to be their final destination. A couple of other companies use the **International Ferry Terminal**, a kilometre further east on the same road; despite the name there are no regular international connections, though cruise ships occasionally dock here.

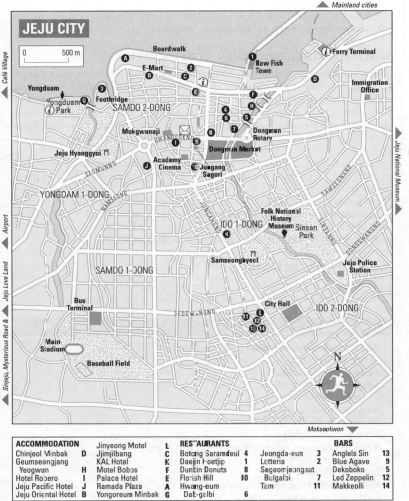

Whichever way you arrive, Jeju's new status as an autonomous province means that it's usually necessary to bring your **passport**.

Information and city transport

There are, for some reason, two **tourist information** desks just metres apart from each other at the airport. At least one will be open 8am–10pm (Ⓣ064/742-8866), but both can supply you with English-language maps and pamphlets and help with anything from renting a car to booking a room. Another booth at the ferry terminal offers similar assistance (10am–8pm; Ⓣ064/758-7181). English-language help can also be accessed by phone on Ⓣ064/1330.

Jeju City is small and relaxed enough to allow for some navigation by foot, but in order to see everything you'll have to resort to taxis – these shouldn't cost more than a few thousand won for destinations in Gujeju – or one of the numerous **local buses** (see box below for some useful routes); tickets cost W850 per ride, but unfortunately there are no day-passes. The last services on all routes leave at 9pm or just after, and start again at around 6am. Several bus routes connect Gujeju and Sinjeju, while taxis shouldn't cost much more than W6000.

Accommodation

Jeju's capital is firmly fixed on Korea's tourist itinerary; most visitors choose to base themselves here, benefiting from the excellent transport services to the rest

Jeju buses

Route 12 (West Coastal Road) (every 15–25min)
Hallim; 40min; W2300
Sanbangsan; 2hr; W5400
Jungmun; 2hr 20min; W6200
Seogwipo; 2hr 40min; W7300

Route 95 (West Tourist Road) (every 20min)
Sanbangsan; 50min; W3500
Moseulpo; 1hr; W3600

Route 95 (Jungmun Express Road) (every 10–12min)
Jungmun; 1hr; W3300
Seogwipo; 1hr 10min; W3600

Route 99 (1100 road) (every 60–90min)
1100m rest area; 40min; W2700
Jungmun; 1hr 20min; W5100

Route 11 – 5.16 road (every 12–15min)
Seongpanak; 35min; W1700
Seogwipo; 1hr 10min; W3600

Route 97 – East tourist road (every 20–60min)
Sangumburi; 25min; W1800
Seong-eup Folk Village; 45min; W2300
Pyoseon; 1hr; W3400
Jeju Folk Village; 1hr 5min; W3600

Route 12 – East coastal road (every 15–25min)
Gimnyeong; 50min; W1900
Seongsan; 1hr 30min; W3800
Pyoseon; 1hr 55min; W5100
Seogwipo; 1hr 40min; W7500

of the island, and the number of upper-class **hotels**. However, many establishments were built when Korea's economy was going great guns in the 1980s, and are now beginning to show their age. All higher-end hotels slash their rates by up to fifty percent outside July and August, so be sure to ask about **discounts**. Often you'll be asked whether you'd like a "Sea View" room facing north, or a "Mountain View" facing Hallasan; the latter is usually a little cheaper, and may be more appealing to some. If you're looking for something lower down the price scale you'll find plenty of choice in **Gujeju**, especially the more rustic area surrounding the stream that spills into the sea between Dongmun Rotary and the ferry terminal. **Sinjeju** has a greater concentration of hotels and motels, though you'll be paying more than in Gujeju – often for less quality – and it's further from the sights and transport links.

Gujeju

Chinjeol Minbak Geonip-dong ⓣ064/755-5132. One of the cheapest places to stay in the city, the friendly owners usually try to lure foreign travellers emerging from the ferry terminal, just a short walk away. The atmosphere is pleasant and can feel like a youth hostel at times; try to get a room with a private toilet and TV. ❶

Geumseongjang Yeogwan Ido 1-dong ⓣ064/757-1614. Clean rooms with cable TV and decent private facilities come at rock-bottom prices at this guesthouse, located on the left-hand side of the stream heading down from the Dongmun Rotary and market. In the summer, the stream's bank is a great place to meet locals. ❷

Jeju Oriental Hotel Samdo 2-dong ⓣ064/752-8222, ⓦwww.oriental.co.kr. Upper rooms have great sea views; few live up to the promise of the large reception area, but you'll be paying for the facilities anyway – a casino and four restaurants, Internet connections in every room, and courteous staff. Serious competition from the new *Ramada Plaza* across the road means that discounts of fifty percent are not uncommon. ❼

Jeju Pacific Hotel Yongdam 1-dong ⓣ064/758-2500, ⓕ064/758-2521. Set a bit away from things, though just a 10min walk from the sea, this hotel caters mainly to Japanese visitors, and is accordingly surrounded by sushi restaurants and karaoke rooms. All rooms have Internet connections, and from some Hallasan and the ocean may be seen from the same window. Rates are slashed off-season. ❼

Jinyeong Motel Ido 2-dong ⓣ064/752-7007. On a side street opposite city hall, this cheap motel is perfect to stumble home to after a hard night's boozing in the student area. Rooms are much as you'd expect at this price level, and come with private bathrooms. ❷

KAL Hotel Ido 2-dong ⓣ064/724-2001, ⓦwww.kalhotel.co.kr. An immaculate hotel and Jeju's tallest building at 21 floors; friendly, white-suited staff buzz about the place though the rooms lack character and are small for the price. There's a funky cocktail bar on the top floor, though budget cuts mean that, sadly, it no longer revolves. ❽

Motel Bobos Geonip-dong ⓣ064/727-7200 or 1. Don't be put off by the rather dingy reception area – the wood-floored rooms here are large and airy, and you'll get a free coffee in the morning. The motel is also within walking distance of the ferry terminal and seaside promenade, as well as some of the city sights. ❸

Palace Hotel Samdo 2-dong ⓣ064/753-8811 to 8, ⓕ064/753-8820. One of several similar hotels on the waterfront, all of which are showing their age and provide rather austere rooms bettered by many motels. The cocktail bar, sauna and two restaurants found on the premises put it above the competition nearby. ❺

Ramada Plaza Samdo 2-dong ⓣ064/729-8100, ⓦwww.ramadajeju.co.kr. A modern and cavernous hotel – it's even bigger than it appears from outside. Vertigo-inducing interior views, plush interiors and some of Jeju's best food make it the hotel of choice for those who can afford it, though some may find the atmosphere a little mall-like, especially if their stay coincides with a convention. ❾

Hotel Robero Samdo 2-dong ⓣ064/757-7111, ⓦwww.roberohotel.com. The modern art strewn about the place fails to disguise the fact that a renovation is overdue, though the rooms themselves are cosy and as good as you'd expect at this price level. Criminally, few have decent views of pretty Mokgwanaji across the road. ❺

Yongoreum Minbak Yongdam 2-dong ⓣ064/742-9051. A real bargain if you're in a group and are able to find this two-room-only *minbak*, hidden away among seaside fish restaurants near Yongduam – the price of a cheap motel gets you a whole apartment with a kitchen, lounge and two bedrooms, though it's Korean-style floor-sleeping only. ❷

Sinjeju

Aroma Tourist Hotel Yeon-dong Ⓣ064/743-8000, Ⓕ064/749-6300. Under new management at time of writing, the sleek black and gold of the reception area gives way to disappointing rooms – time will tell if things can be turned around. ❺

Cheju Grand Yeon-dong Ⓣ064/747-5000, Ⓦwww.chejugrand.com. The *Grand* rakes in the yen, the preferred currency of its guests, but its popularity is well deserved – cosy, nicely designed rooms with super comfy beds and night-time views of Sinjeju's twinkling lights, at a price undercutting most other top hotels. Golf enthusiasts will be pleased to know there's a free shuttle bus to a local course. ❼

Crowne Plaza Yeon-dong Ⓣ064/741-8000, Ⓦwww.ichotelsgroup.com. Clad in rich honey tones from lobby to roof, the *Crowne Plaza* offers homely rooms with plush beds, marble bathrooms, and tea- and coffee-making facilities. Amenities such as restaurants and sauna are also as you'd expect at this price range. ❼

Jeju Sunland Hotel Yeon-dong Ⓣ064/744-1601. Peter Falk would have felt quite at home in this hotel, whose slightly sinister decor makes it almost fit for a 1970s detective drama. Cheaper than neighbouring establishments that are fading with less grace, it's good value; all rooms are carpeted, and some have an ocean view. ❹

Wind & Sand Yeon-dong Ⓣ064/742-5001 to 7, Ⓕ064/742-0993. Nowhere near as rugged as the name suggests, this is a clean place with a friendly, English-speaking manager, tucked into a quiet street near the *Crowne Plaza*. The rooms – bright and fresh, with wood floors and cable TV – are about as cheap as you'll get in Sinjeju. ❸

The City

The capital's sights aren't a patch on those found elsewhere on the island, but some are still worthy of a visit. **Sinjeju**, the modern half of the city, can be safely ignored, as all places of note are located in salty **Gujeju**, including the "Dragon Head Rock" of Yongduam and the shrine at Samseonghyeol, which owe their popularity to the fact that Korean tourists are almost obliged to pay both a visit and show photographic evidence to friends and family. Between these, in the very centre of town, lies the former seat of Jejanese government known as Mokgwanaji, a relaxing place to take a stroll around genteel oriental buildings. A day should be enough to knock off most of the highlights, more if you choose to succumb to the city's shopping and culinary temptations.

Near the seafront

Who'd have thought that basalt could be so romantic. The knobbly seaside formation of **Yongduam**, or "Dragon Head Rock" (24hr; free), usually appears in the honeymoon albums of any Korean couple worth their salt – or, at least, the ones who don't celebrate their nuptials overseas – and is the defining symbol of the city. From the shore, and in a certain light, the crag does indeed resemble a dragon, though from the higher of two viewing platforms a similar formation to the right appears more deserving of the title. According to Jeju legend, these are the petrified remains of a regal servant who, after scouring Hallasan for magical mushrooms, was turned into a dragon by the offended mountain spirits. Strategically positioned lights illuminate the formation at night, and with fewer people around, this may be the best time to visit. On the way back east towards the city centre, you may be tempted to take one of the gorgeous paths that crisscross into and over tiny, tree-filled Hancheon creek, eventually leading to **Jeju Hyanggyo**, a Confucian shrine and school built at the very dawn of the Joseon dynasty in the late fourteenth century. Though not quite as attractive as other such facilities around the country, this academy is still active, and hosts age-old ancestral rite ceremonies in spring and autumn.

In the centre of the city are the elegant, traditional buildings of **Mokgwanaji** (Mok Office; daily 8am–7pm; W1500), a recently restored site that was Jeju's political and administrative centre during the Joseon dynasty; it's a relaxing place that makes for a satisfying meander. Outside the entrance you'll see a

Jeju City

Jeju City	제주시
Folklore and Natural History Museum	민속 자연사 박물관
Jeju Hyanggyo	제주 향교
Jeju Love Land	제주 러브 랜드
Jeju National Museum	제주 국립 박물관
Mokgwanaji	목관아지
Mokseokwon	목석원
Mysterious Road	도깨비도로
Samseonghyeol	삼성혈
Sinjeju	신제주
Yongduam	용두암
Accommodation	
Aroma Tourist Hotel	아로마 관광 호텔
Cheju Grand	제주 그랜드
Chinjeol Minbak	친절 민박
Crowne Plaza	크라운 프라자
Geumseongjang Yeogwan	금성장 여관
Hotel Robero	호텔 로베로
Jeju Oriental Hotel	제주 오리엔탈 호텔
Jeju Pacific Hotel	제주 파시픽 호텔
Jeju Sunland Hotel	제주 선랜드 호텔
Jinyeong Motel	진영 모텔
Jjimjilbang	찜질방
KAL Hotel KAL	KAL 호텔
Motel Bobos	모텔 보보스
Palace Hotel	팰레스 호텔
Ramada Plaza	라마다 플라자
Wind & Sand	윈드 안드 샌드
Yongoreum Minbak	용오름 민박
Restaurants	
Botong Saramdeul	보통 사람들
Daejin Hoetjip	대진 횟집
Dunkin Donuts	던킨 도나츠
Flourish Hill	후러리시 힐
Hwang-geum Dak-galbi	황금 닭갈비
Jeongda-eun	정다은
Lotteria	롯데리아
Segeomjeong Sutbulgalbi	세검정숯불갈비
Tam	탐

couple of authentic *hareubang* and the colourful **Gwangdeokjeong** pavilion (24hr; free), once used for banquets and military training, now somewhat choked by the large road running past it. Inside the complex, information boards detail the histories of the various buildings; refreshingly, some actually state that records give no clue as to when or why certain structures went up. Honghwagak, to the back of the complex, was a military officials' office established in 1435 during the rule of King Sejong – the creator of *hangeul*, Korea's written text, featured on the W10,000 note – and since rebuilt and repaired countless times. Several buildings once housed **concubines**, entertainment girls, and "female government slaves", while the pond-side banquet site near the site entrance was repossessed due to "noisy frogs".

There's a pleasant walking route along the **seafront promenade**, a few hundred metres north of Mokgwanaji, which curls around the *Ramada Plaza* hotel and east to a large bank of seafood restaurants that marks the beginning of the harbour. In bad weather the waves scud in to bash the rocks beneath the boardwalk, producing tall and impressive jets of spray; sea breaks are in place, but you should exercise caution all the same.

Samseonghyeol and the museums

Jeju's spiritual home, **Samseonghyeol** (daily 8am–6.30pm; W2500), is a shrine that attracts a fair number of Korean tourists year-round. Local legend has it that the island was originally populated by Go, Bu and Yang, three local demigods that rose from the ground here. On a hunting trip shortly after this curious birth, they found three maidens who had washed up on a nearby shore armed with grain and a few animals; the three fellows married the girls and using the material and livestock set up agricultural communities, each man kicking off his own clan. Descendants of these three families conduct twice-yearly – in spring and autumn – ceremonies to worship their ancestors. The glorified divots that Go, Bu and Yang are said to have sprung from are visible in a small, grassy enclosure at the centre of the park, though it's hard to spend more than a few seconds looking at what are, in effect, little more than holes in the ground. The pleasant wooded walking trails that line the complex will occupy more of your time, plus there are a few buildings to peek into, as well as an authentic *hareubang* outside the entrance.

Heading east along Samseongno you'll come across the **Folklore and Natural History Museum** (daily 8.30am–6pm; W1100). Local animals in stuffed and skeletal form populate the first rooms, before the diorama overload of the folklore exhibition, where the ceremonies, dwellings and practices of the old-time Jejuite are brought to plastic life. Unless you're planning to visit the two folk villages on Route 97 (see p.366), there are few better ways to get a grip on the island's history.

A taxi-ride (W3000) further east is **Jeju National Museum** (Tues–Fri 9am–6pm, Sat & Sun 9am–7pm; W1000). As with all other "national" museums around the country, it focuses almost exclusively on regional finds, but as this particular institution – despite its size – has surprisingly little to see, the free hour before closing time is enough for many visitors. The highlights of the museum are some early painted maps, a collection of celadon pottery dating from the twelfth century, and a small but excellent display of calligraphy – be sure to take a look at the original **Sehando**, a letter-cum-painting created by Chusa, one of Korea's most revered calligraphers (see p.376). The upper floor is not open so you'll have to make do with staring up at the sprawling stained-glass ceiling from the lobby.

South of the city

It may seem a little cheeky to have a dedicated rock-and-tree park on an island that's filled with little else, but many visitors to **Meokseokwon** (daily 8am–9pm; winter until 8pm; W2000) come away happy. Just a few kilometres south of Jeju City lies this artily arranged collection of assorted pieces of stone and wood found around the island, exhibits which provoke a range of feelings from triumph to contemplation. While none is astonishing individually, a lot of thought has gone into the park as a whole: on one side of the complex, a romantic story is played out in rock form; though cheesy, the contorted shapes of stones in love do their best to fire your imagination. The site itself is just a little too far south of the city to be overrun with visitors, but is easy to get to; bus #500 (25min; W850) runs from various places in Jeju City.

▲ Jeju Love Land

A few kilometres south of Sinjeju, and best accessed by taxi, are a couple of intriguing sights. One short section of Route 99, christened the **Mysterious Road**, has achieved national fame, and though no scheduled buses run to this famed stretch of tarmac, there's always plenty of traffic – cars and tour buses, or indeed pencils, cans of beer or anything else capable of rolling down a hill, are said to roll upwards here. Needless to say, it's a visual illusion created by the angles of the road and the lay of the land. Some people think it looks convincing, while others wonder why people are staring with such wonder at objects rolling down a slight incline, but it makes for a surreal pit stop. Right next door is another place where the tourists themselves constitute part of the attraction – **Jeju Love Land** (daily 9am–midnight; W7000) is Korea's recent sexual revolution contextualized in a theme park. This odd collection of risqué sculpture, photography and art has been immensely popular with the Koreans, now free to have a good laugh at what, for so long, was high taboo. There are statues with which you can be pictured kissing or otherwise engaging with a gallery of sexual positions (in Korean text only, but the pictures need little explanation), several erotic water features, and what may be the most bizarre of Korea's many dioramas – a grunting plastic couple in a parked car. You may never be able to look at a *hareubang* in the same way, or see regal tombs as simple mounds of earth – maybe this park is the continuation of a long-running trend. **Taxis** from Jeju City's Sinjeju district (to which plenty of buses run from the city centre) cost around W4000 or so, nearer W10,000 from Gujeju. To get back, flag down another cab or ask around for a lift.

Eating

Jeju prides itself on its **seafood**, and accordingly much of the city's seafront is taken up by fish restaurants. These congregate in groups, with two of the main clusters being the large, ferry-like complex at the eastern end of the seafront promenade, and another near Yongduam rock. West of here is the coastal road **café village**, a collection of overpriced cafés and restaurants stretching west along the coast. There's plenty of non-fishy choice away from the water – the two best areas are the shopping district around Jungang Sagori, which contains some excellent chicken *galbi* restaurants, and the trendy **student** mecca opposite City Hall. Those with a bit more cash to splash can sample the dishes laid on at the **top hotels**, but try to avoid the area around the bus station: restaurants here are dingy and the food second-rate, so if you're about to head across the island try to eat before you hit the terminal.

Botong Saramdeul Ildo 1-dong. Simple Korean mains go for W4000 and under at this friendly little lair, with daily specials bringing the price down further. Chicken cutlet (*donkass*) is a good filler and the cold buckwheat noodle dishes (*naeng-myeon*) provide relief from the summer heat. The restaurant is a little hard to find – look for the pink sign.

Daejin Hoetjip Ildo 1-dong. Located on the lower deck of the ferry-like "Raw Fish Town" complex, the *Daejin* has an English-language menu, and a decent choice for sushi experts. A huge W80,000 mixed sashimi meal could feed four, or try the delicious broiled sea bream with tofu for W10,000.

Dunkin' Donuts Jungang Sagori. If you're sick to the stomach of Korean food, try these sugary antidotes from W700 per dose. Not traditional or nutritious, but popular with locals; as is Red Mango, the healthy yoghurt shop next door.

Flourish Hill Ido 1-dong. A fresh escape from the city's traffic, near the *Blue Agave* bar. Unfortunately there's no English-language menu, but the *o-gyeopsal* is a speciality – five-layered pork belly, as opposed to the usual three – as is the *sogogi beoseot jeon-gol*, enough beef and mushroom soup to feed three or four.

Hwang-geum Dak-galbi Near Dongmun Rotary. *Dak-galbi* is a raw chicken kebab cooked at your table in a hot metal tray, which is then boiled up with a load of veggies. It costs around W7000 per portion (there's usually a minimum of two people). When it's nearly finished, you should then add some rice, noodles (or both) to the scraps for yet another meal.

Jeongda-eun Sikdang Yongdam 1-dong. Watch Jeju's air traffic glide over the sea at this fish restaurant, which occupies a great location at the tip of a small peninsula between Yongduam and the Ramada Plaza. Most dishes are for groups of three or four (W10,000 to W15,000 per person); solo eaters may have to content themselves with the *hoe dop-bap* – raw fish in spicy sauce on a bed of rice.

Lotteria Samdo 2-dong. Possibly the country's emptiest branch of this fast-food chain, which is good news for customers as it means that their burgers will be freshly made for you. If you insist on something at least a little Korean, try the *galbi* or *kimchi* burgers.

Segeomjeong Sutbulgalbi Dongmun Rotary. Low, low prices mean that this meat restaurant is almost permanently full. The menu is little more than a list of flesh to barbeque, including *saeng galbi* and the saucier *yangnyeom galbi*.

Tam Ido 2-dong; look for the Chinese sign. *Soju* flows freely into the early hours at this stylish, wood-panelled restaurant as students set fire to, then eat, a variety of meats from the menu. *Samgyeopsal* (pork belly) goes for W8000 per portion, with *kimchi* fried rice a cheap extra.

Drinking and nightlife

Most of the city's drinking takes place in a busy area across the main road, Jungangno, from City Hall in Gujeju, which has enough bars, restaurants, baseball batting cages and *noraebang* singing rooms to keep its predominantly student population entertained. *Cheongsongeoleumgol Makkeolli* has a long name and longer hours, a busy den serving up W3000 pots of *makkeolli* – a milky rice hooch – with cheap but filling snacks, under manga decorations that seem to be obligatory in such places. A stone's throw away is *Angels Sin*, a more Western-style bar with a pool table and a healthy mix of Korean and foreign boozers, or try *Led Zeppelin*, a handsome lair with a collection of over 2000 records – there's bound to be something you like, so write your request down and hand it to a member of staff. A taxi ride away near the large church in **Ido 1-dong** is expat watering hole *Blue Agave*; cooler and more loungey than *Angels Sin*, staff can be slightly frosty and there's no draught beer – bottles only – though it claws back a few points for having nachos and BLTs on the menu, a pool table and occasional live music. High-rollers, real or pretend, can sink ten-dollar cocktails in the bars of the five-star hotels, most notably the smart one on the top floor of the *KAL*. For more earthly delights head to quirky *Dekoboko* on the west side of the small stream heading towards the sea from Dongmun Rotary. This small, trinket-filled bar has a babyfoot table (table football) and a Japanese side-dish menu – *yakisoba* and *teriyaki* are also available for reasonable prices.

Listings

Banks You should have no problem exchanging cash or traveller's cheques at banks found all over the city. You may be able to use foreign cards at ATMs in convenience stores such as 7-Eleven and Family Mart.
Bike rental The Lespo Mart, just town-side of *Chinjeol Minbak* on the same side of the road, rents out decent bikes for W7000 per day; you'll need your passport to leave behind as security. The *Ramada Plaza* hotel also has a few bikes for hire, though prices are higher at W13,000 per day.
Car rental Several companies have counters at the city airport – prices can be compared with a few sideways steps. Rates vary but usually start at around W35,000 per day; to book in advance try Avis (Ⓣ064/749-3773, Ⓦwww.avis.co.kr), which is most likely to have an English-speaker at the desk.
Cinema The Academy Cinema, in a large complex a short walk south of Meokseokwon, is the best place to catch a film; tickets cost W7000.
Hiking equipment Stores can be found all over the city, with the greatest concentration in Sinjeju and the shopping area around Jungang Sagori. Prices are higher than you might expect, but Treksta is a fairly safe choice.
Hospital The best place for foreigners to head is the Jeju University hospital (Ⓣ064/750-1234); call Ⓣ119 in an emergency.
Internet Cafés are dotted all around the city – look for upper floor signs saying "PC" – and charge a uniform W1000 per hour. There are also free booths in the ferry and bus terminals.
Motorbike rental Jeju Bike, near the bus station, has motorcycles and scooters to hire or sell, and an English-speaking owner (Ⓣ064/758-5296).
Police The most convenient police station for travellers to use is at the junction of Sinsanno and Donggwangno, near the Folklore and Natural History Museum (Ⓣ064/758-8602).
Post Office Post offices across the island are open weekdays from 9am–5pm, with the central post office (Ⓣ064/758-8602) situated near Mokgwanaji also open on Saturdays until 1pm.

Eastern Jeju

The eastern half of Jeju is wonderfully unspoilt, and offers visitors an opportunity to find the true essence of the island – the coast is dotted with unhurried fishing villages, while inland you can see evidence of Jeju's turbulent creation in the form of lava tubes and volcanic craters. Buses to the region leave Jeju City with merciful swiftness, passing between the sea and lush green fields, the latter bordered by stacks of *batdam*. **Seongsan**, situated on the island's most easterly tip, is the most attractive of Jeju's many small villages, crowned by the majestic caldera of **Ilchulbong**.

Just offshore is the island **Udo**, where the female divers of bygone maritime Korea can still be seen. The sedentary pace of both places puts paid to the notion that Jeju is a purely tourist-centred destination – real life goes on here at a leisurely pace, and after spending a few days in the region you're sure to find yourself winding down a notch or two. A cluster of nature-based attractions can be found south of the port village of Gimnyeong, most notably **Manjanggul**, which are some of the world's longest underground lava tubes. Further south again, **Route 97** heads southeast from Jeju City across the island's interior, running past **Sangumburi**, a large, forested volcanic crater, and two rewarding **folk villages**: one a working community with a patchwork of traditional thatch-roofed houses, the other an open-air museum which – though devoid of Yi-Yi inhabitants – provides a little more instruction on traditional Jeju life.

Eastern Jeju

Jeju Folk Village	제주 민속마을
Manjanggul	만장굴
Sangumburi	산굼부리
Seong-eup Folk Village	성읍 민속마을
Seongsan	성산
Udo	우도

Seongsan

As long as Jeju's notoriously indecisive weather holds up, you're unlikely to be disappointed by **SEONGSAN**, an endearing rural town with one very apparent tourist draw looming over it: **Ilchulbong**, or "Sunrise Peak", is so named as it's the first place on the island to be lit up by the orange fires of dawn. The town can easily be visited as a day-trip from Jeju City but many visitors choose to spend a night here, beating the sun out of bed to clamber up the graceful, green slope to the rim of Ilchulbong's crown-shaped caldera (24hr; W2000). It's an especially popular place for Koreans to ring in the New Year – a small **festival** celebrates the changing of the digits. From the town it's a twenty-minute or so walk to the summit; a steep set of steps leads up to a 182-metre-high **viewing platform** at the top, and although the island's fickle weather and morning mists usually conspire to block the actual emergence of the sun from the sea, it's a splendid spot nonetheless. Powerful bulbs from local squid boats dot the nearby waters; as the morning light takes over, the caldera below reveals itself as green and verdant, its far side plunging sheer into the sea – unfortunately, it's not possible to hike around the rim. Turning to face west, Seongsan is visible below, and the topography of the surrounding area – hard to judge from ground level – reveals itself.

Besides the conquest of Ilchulbong, there's little to do in Seongsan bar strolling around the neighbouring fields and tucking into a fish supper, though the waters off the coast do offer some fantastic diving opportunities. South of town is **Sinyang Beach**, whose water depth and incessant wind make it a good place to windsurf; equipment is available to rent.

Practicalities

Minbak and **fish restaurants** can be found in abundance, but anybody wanting higher-end accommodation, or meat not culled from the sea, may have a hard time. Simple rooms are easy to find – alternatively, hang around and wait for the *ajummas* to find you – and are split into two main areas: those peak-side of the main road, which tend to be tiny and bunched in tight clusters, or those in the fields facing Hallasan, which are generally located in family homes, and are slightly cleaner. A bit of haggling should see the prices drop to W15,000–20,000. Comfier rooms can be found at the *Kondohyeong Minbak* (ⓣ064/784-8940; ❸), a big blue building at the southern edge of town, situated above a ground-floor restaurant. Rooms here are adequate, and some have Internet access; try to nab one with a balcony facing Ilchulbong. Sinyang beach, a few kilometres to the south, also has plenty of rooms for rent, though prices rise sharply during the summer holidays. Coffee and snacks are available from a 24-hour **convenience store** near the Ilchulbong ticket booth.

Sealife Scuba (ⓣ064/782-1150), near *Kondohyeon Minbak*, offers spectacular **diving** trips for around W150,000 per person, equipment included.

Udo

Visible from Ilchulbong is the tiny rural island **UDO**, whose stacked-stone walls and rich grassy hills give it the air of a Scottish isle transported to warmer climes. Occasionally, the nomenclature of Korea's various peaks and stony bits reaches near-Dadaist extremes; "Cow Island" is one of the best examples, its contours apparently resembling the shape of resting bovine. This sparsely populated dollop of land is one of the best places to spot two of Jeju's big draws – the stone *batdam* walls that line the island's fields and narrow roads, and the **haenyeo**, female divers long famed for their endurance (see box below). *Haenyeo* do not dive year-round here, and even in summer can be hard to spot. The most likely places to see them are by the beaches just south of the ferry terminal, or the cove under the lighthouse on the south of the island, both of which are a short distance away on the **tour buses** (W5000) that meet the ferries. Unless you have your own bicycle – at the time of writing the nearest rental shops were in Jeju City – you'll find these buses by far the easiest way of getting around the island; usually under the direction of charismatic local drivers, they first stop at a black-sand beach for half an hour or so, which allows just enough time to get up the hill to the lighthouse for amazing views that show just how rural Udo really is. The buses then stop at a small natural history **museum** (9am–5pm; closed Mon; W2000, or free entry with bus ticket), whose second-floor is home to some interesting *haenyeo* paraphernalia; it then continues past Sanhosa beach before returning to the ferry terminal.

Udo is reached on regular ferries (W5500 return) from Seongsan port, which is within walking distance of the town itself. Cars and bikes are allowed onto the ferries and at peak times they can clog up Udo's narrow lanes. There are small **restaurants** near the first and final tour-bus stops; take a note of the time the bus dropped you off, as the next one will be along an hour or so after that.

Jeju's diving grannies

It may be hard to believe in a place that once was, and in many ways still is, the most Confucian country on earth, but for a time areas of Jeju had **matriarchal** social systems. This role reversal is said to have begun in the nineteenth century as a form of tax evasion, when male divers found a loophole in the law that exempted them from tax if their wives did the work. So were born the *haenyeo*, literally "**sea women**"; while their husbands cared for the kids and did the shopping, the females often became the family breadwinners, diving without breathing apparatus for minutes at a time in search of shellfish and sea urchins. With women traditionally seen as inferior, this curious emancipation offended the country's leaders, who sent delegates from Seoul in an attempt to ban the practice. It didn't help matters that the *haenyeo* performed their duties clad only in loose white cotton, and it was made illegal for men to lay eyes on them as they worked.

Today, the *haenyeo* are one of Jeju's most famous sights. Folk songs have been written about them, their statues dot the shores, and one can buy postcards, mugs and plates decorated with dripping sea sirens rising from the sea. This romantic vision, however, is not entirely current; the old costumes have now given way to black wetsuits, and the *haenyeo* have grown older: even tougher than your average *ajumma*, many have continued to dive into their 70s. Modern life is depleting their numbers – there are easier ways to make money now, and few families are willing to encourage their daughters into what is still a dangerous profession. The figures peaked in the 1950s at around 30,000, but at the last count there were just 4300 women registered as divers, of whom ninety percent were aged over 50. Before long, the tradition may well become one of Jeju's hard-to-believe myths.

Minbak are readily available, though the rural ambience comes at a slightly higher price than you'd pay in Seongsan; prices are around W30,000 per night.

Manjanggul

A short distance east of Jeju City lies a group of natural attractions that provide an enjoyable day-trip from Jeju City. Foremost among these is **Manjanggul**

▲ Manjanggul

(daily 9am–6pm; Nov–March until 5pm; W2000), a long underground cave formed by old pyroclastic flows. Underwater eruptions millions of years ago caused channels of surface lava to crust over or burrow into the soft ground, resulting in subterranean tunnels of flowing lava. Once the flow finally stopped, these so-called "**lava tubes**" remained. Stretching for at least nine kilometres under the fields and forests south of the small port of Gimnyeong, Manjanggul is one of the longest such systems in the world, though only one kilometre or so is open to the public. This dingy and damp "tube" contains a number of hardened, lava features including balls, bridges, and an eight-metre-high pillar at the end of the course.

Just north of the cave system is the network of hedge that forms **Gimnyeong Maze** (daily 8.30am–6.30pm; winter until 6pm; W3300), designed and built by Fred Dustin, an affable Korean War veteran who enjoys having a coffee and a chat with his foreign guests. The maze was the first of its kind to be constructed in Korea (although there are now inferior copies on Jeju's south coast) and it's slightly more popular with local than foreign tourists, though few who get to ring the bell at the end of the course – without cheating – will regret the opportunity to bring out their inner child for a short time. Real kids, of course, will love it. The maze is a fifteen-minute walk down the road from the Manjanggul cave; there's no path, but traffic is usually light. Buses run between Gimnyeong – on Route 12 – and both sights every hour or so, continuing south past the cave to **Bijarim Forest**, a family-friendly network of trails and tall trees. Heading the other way, north of the cave and maze, small but busy **Gimnyeong Beach** has the area's greatest concentration of restaurants and accommodation, and is accessible on the buses that run along the coastal road.

Route 97

With a volcanic crater to see and two folk villages to explore, rural **Route 97** – also known as the East Tourist Road – is a delightful way to cut through Jeju's interior. All three attractions can be visited on a day-trip from Jeju City, or as part of a journey between the capital and Seogwipo on the south coast, though it pays to start reasonably early.

Sangumburi

Heading south from Jeju City on Route 97, the first place worth stopping at is **Sangumburi** (daily 9am–7pm; W3000), one of Jeju's many **volcanic craters**; possibly its most impressive, certainly its most accessible, though currently the only one you have to pay to visit. Hole lovers should note that this particular type is known as a Marr crater, as it was produced by an explosion in a generally flat area. One can only imagine how big an explosion it must have been – the crater, two kilometres in circumference and 132m deep, is larger than Hallasan's (see p.379). A short climb to the top affords sweeping views of some very unspoilt Jejanese terrain; peaks rise in all directions, with Hallasan 20km to the southwest, though not always visible The two obvious temptations are to walk into or around the rim, but you must refrain from doing so in order to protect the crater's wildlife – deer and badgers are among the species that live in Sangumburi. Consequently there's not an awful lot to do here, though there's a small art gallery on site. Buses (W1800) take around 25 minutes to get here from the terminal in Jeju City; note that most East Tourist Road buses miss Sangumburi, with only one an hour coming here. If you're continuing south the next bus will arrive approximately an hour after your arrival – stand on the main road to flag it down, but keep an eye out as it'll come by in a flash.

Seong-eup Folk Village

A twenty-minute bus ride south of Sangumburi will bring you to dusty **Seong-eup Folk Village**, a functioning community living in traditional Jeju-style housing, where you're free to wander among the thatch-roofed houses at will; the residents, given financial assistance by the government, are long used to curious visitors nosing around their yards. **Buses** (45min from Jeju City; W2300) usually stop near the post office, but because dwellings in the immediate area primarily function as tea showrooms for Japanese tourists or educational tools for busloads of Korean schoolchildren, it's more rewarding to move on – the street heading south from the Post Office has the most to see, with the best patch probably the area across the road from the barren, sorry-looking temple. Here you'll see life carrying on as if nothing had changed in decades – farmers going about their business and children playing while crops sway in the breeze. Most visitors spend a couple of pleasant hours here, and if you're lucky you'll run into one of the few English-speaking villagers, who act as guides. Many locals still wear the traditional Jejanese **costumes** of apricot-dyed material, which are also available to buy, though none now use the *dotongsi*, traditional open-air Jeju toilets that were usually located next to the pig enclosures (some things are best left in the past). There are a few restaurants on and around the village's main road, but at the time of writing the single *minbak* guesthouse was closed – a shame, as only in the evenings will you see the settlement devoid of tourists. You'll notice that many dwellings have near-identical gates consisting of three wooden bars poked through holes in two stone side-columns. This is a quaint local **communication system** known as *jeongnang*, unique to Jeju and still used today – when all bars are up, the owner of the house is not home, one bar up means that they'll be back soon, and if all three are down, you're free to walk on in.

Jeju Folk Village

Route 97 buses terminate near the coast at the **Jeju Folk Village** (daily 8.30am–6pm; Oct–March until 5pm; W6000). This coastal clutch of traditional Jeju buildings may be artificial, but provides an excellent complement to the Seong-eup village to its north. Information boards explain the layout and structures of the buildings, as well as telling you what the townsfolk used to get up to before selling tea and baggy orange pants to tourists. The differences between dwellings on different parts of the island are subtle but interesting – the island's southerners, for example, entwined ropes outside their door with red peppers if a boy had been born into their house. However, the buildings may all start to look a little samey without the help of an English-language **audio guide** (W2000; available from a hidden office behind the ticket booth). There's a cluster of **restaurants** near the exit, though for accommodation you'll have to take a short walk to the nearby coastal town of **Pyoseon**. The best place to stay is the *Beach Park Motel* (Ⓣ064/7877-9556; ❷), on the junction of Route 12 and the folk village access road, which has decent new rooms, though few face the large beach that sits across the road. **Buses** from Pyoseon to Seogwipo run from a road a few blocks further uphill – ask for directions. En route, near the town of Namwon, is the recently opened **Shinyoung Cinema Museum** (9am–6.30pm; closed Mon; W6000), set in a highly distinctive building whose whitewashed walls and coastal setting carry faint Mediterranean echoes. Its contents are mildly diverting – old projectors and the like – though perhaps more appealing are its surrounding gardens.

Seogwipo and Jungmun

The settlements of **Seogwipo** and **Jungmun** sit sunny-side up on Jeju's fair southern coast: whereas days in Jeju City and on the northern coast are curtailed when the sun drops beneath Hallasan's lofty horizon, the south coast has no such impediment. Proof of this extra light can be seen in the tangerine groves that surround Seogwipo, a city that manages to retain a relaxed air despite its status as the second biggest settlement on the island. There's enough to see here and around the nearby resort of Jungmun to keep you occupied for a few days at least, though the real attraction is the chance to kick back and unwind.

Seogwipo

Much like the waterfalls that flank this city, **SEOGWIPO** tumbles down Hallasan's southern foothills into the sea; though officially covering the whole southern half of the island, the city itself is small and possesses a town-like air – relaxed and pleasantly gritty, it makes a better base than the capital for those who want to chill out. For those who prefer a faster pace, there are a number of water-related activities on offer, ranging from diving to submarine tours of the coast.

Arrival, orientation and information

A roundabout at the top end of Jungangno, the north–south spine road, acts as the city centre, with the sights and accommodation lying to the south. At the time

Seogwipo and Jungmun	
Seogwipo	서귀포
Cheonjiyeon waterfalls	천지연 폭포
Jeongbangwaterfalls	정방 폭포
Lee Joong-Seop Gallery	이중섭 갤러리
Oedolgae	외돌개
Accommodation	
Jeju Hiking Inn	제주 하이킹인
Jjimjilbang	찜질방
KAL Hotel KAL	KAL 호텔
Little France	리틀 프랑스
Paradise Hotel	파라다이스 호텔
Sun Beach	선 비치 호텔
Jungmun	중문
African Art Gallery	아프리카 박물관
Jungmun Beach	중문 해수욕장
Jusangjeolli	주상절리
Teddy Bear Museum	테디베어 뮤지엄
Yakcheonsa	약천사
Accommodation	
Hotel Hana	호텔 하나
Hyatt Regency	하얏
Lotte Hotel	롯데 호텔
The Shilla	신라 호텔
The Suites	더스위트 호텔

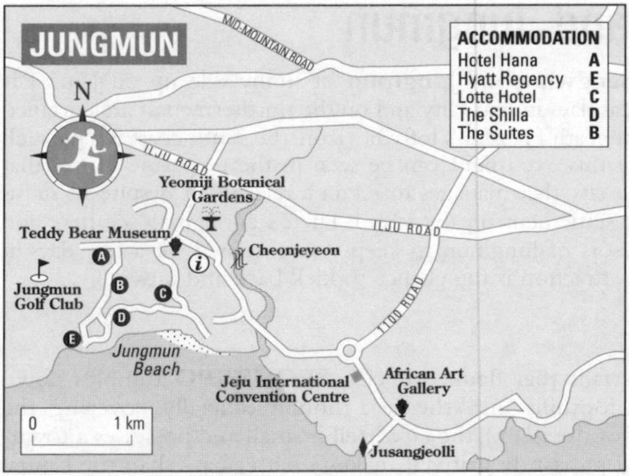

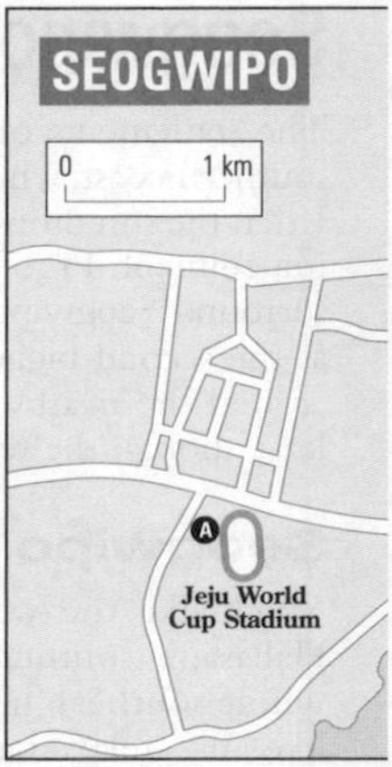

of writing, a new city **bus station** was being built near the World Cup Stadium to the west, and should be open by the time you read this, with regular shuttle buses connecting it to the city centre. The old one is located next to Jungangno. There are several bus routes across the island from Jeju City (see box, p.354).

The main **tourist information office** (daily 9am–6pm; ⓣ064/732-1330) can be found at the entrance to Cheonjiyeon, a waterfall just west of the centre. Follow the stream out towards the sea, on the same side as the ticket booth, and before long you'll come to the launch point for a **submarine tour**. Trips run every 45 minutes, and at W50,000 for an adult ticket (discounts for children and students), don't come cheap, though subs dive up to 35m and allow passengers the chance to glimpse colourful coral and marine life, including octopus, clownfish and the less familiar "stripey footballer". Those content with staying above the water may prefer to take advantage of **boat trips** around the coast and offshore islets; check with the tourist office for details. **Diving** around the same islands is also popular; Big Blue, a German-run operator (ⓣ064/733-1733; ⓦwww.bigblue33.co.kr), offers a range of courses starting at W95,000 per person.

Accommodation

Whatever your budget, you should sleep well in Seogwipo. The city's old top-end **hotels** – situated close to Cheonjiyeon waterfall – are poor value for money, and have now been trumped by a spanking new pair of excellent hotels to the east of the city. Moving down the price scale, there are plenty of motels; **camping** by Oedolgae rock is another possibility, or for a cheap and slightly bizarre place to stay, there's a **jjimjilbang** in the World Cup Stadium to the west of the city (see box, p.370).

Jeju Hiking Inn Seogwi-dong ⓣ064/763-2380. This quasi-hostel gets rave reviews from budget travellers, despite the often smelly corridors and the incredible number of mosquitoes that haunt the free Internet room in the summer. The rooms are comfy enough, with passable bathrooms. Kevin, the owner, speaks English and will be more than willing to help organize diving trips and the like; you can also rent bicycles for W5000 per day. ❶

KAL Hotel Topyeong-dong ⓣ064/733-2001, ⓦwww.kalhotel.co.kr. As with its sister hotel in Jeju City, this is a very businesslike tower that stands proudly over its surroundings. It's immaculate but a little too clinical for some, though the grounds are beautiful. There's also a tennis court, a jogging track, and a varied selection of on-site restaurants and cafés. ❼

Little France Seogwi-dong ⓣ064/732-4552,

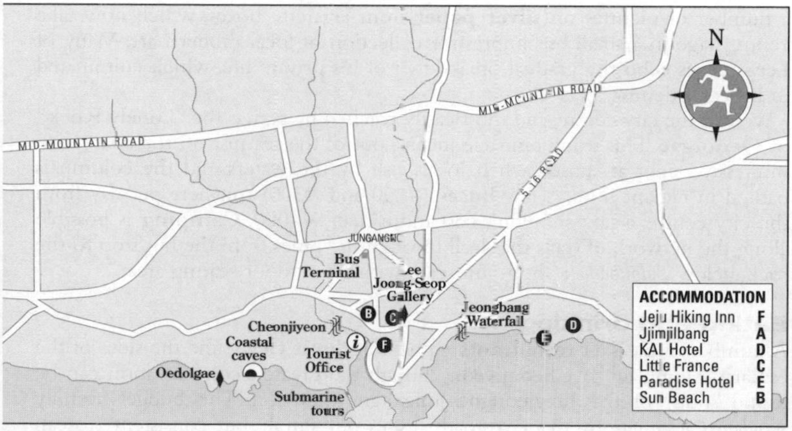

Ⓦ www.littlefrancehotel.co.kr. Vaguely European in feel, this chic hotel is a real find. Views aren't amazing but the rooms are bright and fresh, created with a warmth rarely evident in Korean accommodation. The owners speak some English, and a café and restaurant with a similar air can be found on the ground floor. ④

Paradise Topyeong-dong Ⓣ 064/763-2100, Ⓦ www.paradisehotel.co.kr. More down-to-earth than the nearby *KAL Hotel* in almost every way, this is a rustic, friendly warren with a variety of rooms that manage to be characterful and interesting without feeling over the top. Kept low-rise to augment its surrounding grounds – which make for a pleasant stroll even if you're not staying here – the cave-like interior was clearly designed with Gaudí and Picasso in mind, and leads down to a health club and outdoor swimming pool. ⑧

Sun Beach Seogwi-dong Ⓣ 064/732-5678, Ⓦ www.hotelsunbeach.co.kr. The better of two shabby hotels uphill from Cheonjiyeon waterfall. Six floors of mostly stained red carpet lead to rooms that are only good value for money when off-season discounts of up to fifty percent kick in. ⑥

The waterfalls

Most of Jeju's rainfall is swallowed up by the porous volcanic rock that forms much of the island, but a couple of **waterfalls** spill into the sea either side of Seogwipo city centre. To the east is **Jeongbang** (7.30am–6pm; W2000), a 23m-high cascade claimed to be the only one in Asia to fall directly into the ocean. Unique or not, once you've clambered down to ground level it's an impressive sight, especially when streams are swollen by the summer monsoon, at which time it's impossible to get close to the falls without being drenched by spray. Look for some Chinese characters on the right-hand side of the falls – their meaning is explained by an unintentionally comical English-language cartoon in an otherwise dull exhibition hall above the falls.

The western fall, **Cheonjiyeon** (daily 8am–11pm; Nov–March until 10pm; W2000), is shorter but wider than Jeongbang, and sits at the end of a pleasant gorge that leads from the ticket office, downhill from the city centre: take the path starting opposite *Jeju Hiking Inn*. With the long opening hours, many prefer to visit at night, when there are fewer visitors and the paths up to the gorge are bathed in dim light.

Other sights

In the centre is an interesting **gallery** (July–Sept 9am–8pm; Oct–June until 6pm; W1000) devoted to the works of **Lee Joong-Seop** (1916–56), who used to live in what are now the gallery's grounds. During the Korean War, he made a number of pictures on **silver paper** from cigarette boxes, which now take centre stage in a small but impressive collection of local modern art. Many of Lee's pieces echo the gradual breakdown of his private life, which culminated in his early demise.

West of the city centre, and most easily reached by taxi, is the "Lonely Rock" of **Oedolgae**. This stone pinnacle jutting out of the sea just off the coast is an impressive sight at sunset, when locals fish by the waters and the column is bathed in radiant hues. A few **buses** (#200 and #300) run here per day from the city centre; a taxi shouldn't cost more than W4000. **Camping** is possible along the network of trails that lead through the pines from the bus stop to the rock, below *Solbitbada*, a shop-cum-café with an outdoor seating area.

Eating and drinking

A number of pleasant **restaurants**, some with great views, line the sides of the estuary leading up to Cheonjiyeon, though the greatest concentration can be found south of the Jungjeongno-Jungangno junction. The budget-friendly *Kimbap Cheon-guk* by this crossroads dishes out simple but consistent Korean staples at low prices. A little further towards the sea is *Best Beans*, a café serving all your favourite coffee styles and more – they can even whip up a sweet potato latte. Nearby is *Gureum-e Dalgadeushi*, both restaurant and bar, catering for lovers of *makkeolli*, a milky Korean rice wine that's dangerously easy to quaff; you can sober up with *haemul pajeon*, a kind of seafood pancake. Those seeking something

Seogwipo's World Cup

Of the ten stadiums built in Korea for the 2002 **World Cup**, Jeju's was probably the most eye-catching, and has certainly proved the most controversial. Situated just west of Seogwipo, its design – said to represent a traditional sailing mast hanging over a volcanic cone – combines Jeju's tectonic and naval motifs in one fell swoop. To complete the iconography, a whole team of *hareubang* line the route to the main entrance.

Korea had originally hoped to host the tournament alone, but due to their relative infancy as a footballing nation they were eventually forced to co-host with **Japan**, who had also promised ten cities as sporting venues; this meant that twenty grounds were used for just 64 games, with the one in Seogwipo used to host only three matches. After all that planning, Jeju's World Cup was over in less than a week. By building a 42,000-seater stadium in a hard-to-reach town of just 90,000, the authorities were overoptimistic to say the least, and despite the fact that both Brazil and Germany – the eventual finalists – came to Jeju, acres of empty seats were on show. The decision to play the first knockout game here was particularly calamitous – players and fans were given the shortest amount of notice to get to the most remote ground, so it was no surprise that the ground was only half-full for Germany's win over Paraguay, deemed by many to be the poorest game of the tournament.

Things took a turn for the worse when the ground was hit by two **typhoons** in the space of a month: parts of the roof cladding were ripped off by powerful winds, and with no resident team to call it home, Jeju's stadium became a white elephant of dazzling luminescence. A reversal of fortune occurred in 2006, when the owners of **Bucheon SK**, Korean champions in 1989, suddenly upped sticks and moved the club to Jejudo; with their club suddenly no more, Bucheon's supporters were understandably furious. Nowadays you can watch the newly formed **Jeju United** here (March–Oct; tickets cost W10,000) while hardcore football fans (or travellers on a budget) can get a night's sleep for W6000 at the *jjimjilbang* inside the ground, from which it's even possible to duck out for a midnight stroll around the pitch.

more Western should head to *Jeju Naruter* near the *KAL* and *Paradise* hotels, where the menu includes spaghetti and steak, as well as some Korean dishes. There are a couple of arty **cafés** around the Lee Joong-Seop Gallery, though their opening times are somewhat capricious.

Jungmun and around

Korea's most **exclusive resort** curls along a beautiful beach west of Seogwipo, a place where expense-account tourists come from the mainland and abroad to play a few rounds of golf, shop for designer bags or relax in five-star pools in between business conventions. However, to write off **JUNGMUN** on account of its popularity with the prosperous would be a mistake – the surrounding area has the island's greatest and most varied concentration of sights, accessible on any budget, and can even credibly claim to possess the most distinctive temple, gallery and museum of Korea's inexhaustible collection, all this shoehorned amid beaches, gardens and waterfalls.

Limousine bus #600 (every 15min; 50min; W3900) runs directly from the airport to outside the top hotels listed below, though many people choose to splash out on a cab. There are also a few routes here from Jeju City's bus terminal, see the box on p.354 for details.

Accommodation

Jungmun's **accommodation** caters almost exclusively to the well-heeled, especially in the resort area, where the *Hyatt*, *Shilla* and *Lotte* all have presidential suites for the über-rich with rack rates of W5,000,000. More affordable rooms are, of course, available, and standards are among the highest in the country. These big-shot lodgings jostle for space along **Jungmun Beach**, while travellers on smaller budgets are advised to stay in nearby Seogwipo. There are also a few poor-value motels outside the resort on the main road.

Hana Jungmun Resort, next to the *Shilla* ⓣ064/738-7001. Primarily for convention-attending businessfolk, guests here are given scant attention for the price, which drops considerably outside summer months. ❻

Hyatt Regency Jungmun Resort ⓣ064/733-1234, ⓦwww.hyattcheju.com. The most relaxed of the three major hotels, whose attention to detail is much as you'd expect of this chain; a leaf-filled atrium leads to ample, muted-tone rooms, and the on-site bars and restaurants are top-notch. A health club, spa and nine-hole putting green can also be found on site, and there's a walking trail down to the beach. ❽

Lotte Jungmun Resort ⓣ064/731-1000, ⓦwww.lottehotel.com. The *Lotte* prides itself on being the "finest resort hotel in the world", but can be a little overblown for some. Aimed squarely at Louis Vuitton-clad guests from Japan and Hong Kong, the busy interior resembles a shopping mall, with the outside a theme park where every evening is celebrated with a Vegas-style volcano show; though the rooms are excellent, the outside bustle can often be hard to escape. ❾

The Shilla Jungmun Resort ⓣ064/738-4466, ⓦwww.shilla.net/jeju. Immaculately designed, *The Shilla* is the hotel of choice for Western tourists. Soft music tinkles through the lobby and plush corridors, and it's a big place – though it may look low-rise from the outside, there are seven large floors and 429 fresh yet soothing rooms. ❾

The Suites Jungmun Resort ⓣ064/738-3800, ⓦwww.suites.co.kr. This hotel is less busy and more minimalist in style than its nearby competition, but the lack of clutter and less starchy attitude of the staff may come as something of a relief. Hefty discounts can usually be clawed from the rack rate. ❼

On the resort

Although it may sound like the epitome of Jeju tack, the **Teddy Bear Museum** (daily 9am–7pm; winter until 6pm; W6000) often impresses even its most sceptical visitors. The main building is filled with floors of bears, but

▲ Jungmun Beach

the diorama room is the museum highlight, with furry depictions of historical events – one for every decade of the twentieth century. Moving backwards in time, you'll see teddies bashing down the Berlin Wall and fighting in World War II. Then following on from the battle, what appears to be a roller-skating teddy Hitler races into view, though it is soon revealed to be Charlie Chaplin. Other delights include a Teddy Elvis, a "Teddycotta" Army, and a bear-filled vision of what teddies may be up to in the year 2050, as well as a shop and outdoor garden. The museum is on the entrance road to the resort area, close to shops and restaurants.

A short walk east of the teddy museum you can stretch your legs on the paths around Cheonjeyeon (daily 8am–6pm; W2500), a string of three small **waterfalls** (not to be confused with the similar-sounding Cheonjiyeon falls in Seogwipo). Note the seven white nymphs painted onto the vermillion humpback bridge – these fairies were said to bathe in the falls in the moonlight; a performance in their honour is put on by the falls every May. The uppermost fall gushes into a pool of almost unnatural sapphire, from which emanate paths heading through subtropical flora. More leafy things can be found nearby at Yeomiji **botanical gardens** (daily 8.30am–6pm; W6000), an expansive collection of themed gardens presided over by a gigantic greenhouse.

Summer crowds throng to **Jungmun Beach**, said to be the best in Korea. Despite its popularity, though, the waves rolling in from the Pacific can often be fierce, and this short stretch of sand claims at least one victim every year. Every August it's the starting point for the Ironman Korea Triathlon when competitors thrash out a few kilometres in the ocean, followed by a 180km bike ride across the island, and a 42km marathon for dessert.

East of the resort

East of the beach, waves smash against the hexagonal basalt columns of **Jusangjeolli** (daily 10am–6pm; W2000), which rise in angular beauty from the sea in formations similar to the Giant's Causeway in Ireland. These strange creations were created when lava from one of Jeju's many volcanic explosions came in contact with sea water, and can be viewed from a loop platform that runs along the coast. The columns are about 2km from the resort – just about within walking distance, or a short taxi ride away – and can be combined with a visit to the **African Art Gallery** (daily 9am–7pm; W6000) a stone's throw away. This was the brainchild of Mr Han, a traveller and interior designer who developed his collection into a museum. The collection was moved in 2004 from Seoul to a larger and more interesting building – a large faux-dirt structure peppered with logs on the outside, built to resemble the world's largest adobe building, the spectacular Grand Mosque in Djenné, Mali. Inside there's an interesting display of African photography on the ground floor, while the upper levels are mostly filled with sub-Saharan carved wood. Make sure your visit coincides with one of the entertaining **musical performances** (Tues–Sun 11.30am, 2.30pm & 5.30pm); the groups are usually sourced from the musical hotbeds of Ghana, Nigeria and Senegal. Near the museum is the Jeju International Convention Centre, an ultramodern seven-storey cylinder of glass overlooking the Pacific that is likely to feature on the schedules of visiting business people.

Yakcheonsa temple

A few kilometres east of Jungmun, and best reached by taxi or bike, is the stunning temple of **Yakcheonsa** (24hr; free). Built in the 1990s, what it lacks in historical value it more than makes up for with its main building, a feast of intricate decoration despite its colossal size – the cavernous four-storey main hall is claimed to be the biggest in Asia, and is one of the most impressive in the country. The huge golden Buddha at the centre is best viewed from the encircling upper levels, which are themselves crowded with thousands of Buddhist figurines. Yet more (over five hundred, and all individually crafted) can be found in an exterior hall to the front of the complex; most are jovial (cheer up, no. 184) and many are individually interesting, but take a look at no. 145's disturbing party trick. The best time to visit the temple is undoubtedly 7pm on a summer evening, when worshipping locals **chant** under the interior glow with their backs to the sunset. Insect and bird calls add extra resonance to the bell rings that mark the beginning of the service, while squid boats out at sea shine like fallen stars on the horizon.

Taxis to the temple are affordable from Jungmun or even Seogwipo, or it's a beautiful half-hour **walk** on quiet farmland roads from the nearest bus stops – the route is a little circuitous, so you'll have to ask for directions, basically you want to be heading north to the main road. Few pedestrians use these paths, so the local farmers occasionally neglect to chain up their dogs; an attack is unlikely, and crouching to pick up a rock (real or imaginary) should be enough to scare away any that come too close.

Western Jeju

Jeju's western side, though strikingly beautiful, is somewhat wilder and less hospitable than east of Hallasan, with its sights even harder to reach – those without their **own transport** may have to resort to the occasional stretch of hitchhiking. However, this remoteness is very much part of the appeal, and those who've been drawn to the island by promises of empty roads, bucolic villages and unspoilt terrain should look no further – to many, this is quintessential Jeju.

The sights are grouped into three main clusters; it's possible to complete any of these within a day, even after factoring in transport to and from Jeju City (commuting from Seogwipo is also possible, but will require a little extra patience).

Jeju's windswept southwestern corner boasts a collection of sights, three of them within walking distance of each other around the mountain of Sangbangsan and accessible on a single ticket. **Sangbanggulsa** is a temple hewn out of the peak itself, which looks down on **Yongmeori**, a jagged and highly photogenic coastline pounded mercilessly by waves; adjacent to this sits a replica of a Dutch vessel which came a cropper near these crags. In the distance lie the wind- and wave-punished islets of **Gapado** and **Marado**, the latter being Korea's southernmost point.

Just north of Sangbangsan are a couple of arty attractions – contemporary fans may appreciate the large outdoor **sculpture park**, while traditionalists should head to the former exile site of **Chusa**, one of Korea's foremost calligraphers. Further inland, in a remote area hard to penetrate without your own transport but well worth the effort, are a **tea plantation**, a **bonsai park** and the underground tunnels and rusty munitions of a **peace museum**.

Sanbangsan and around

Jeju's far southwest is one of its most scenic locales, presided over by the mountain of **SANBANGSAN**, which rises crown-like from the surrounding terrain. According to local folklore, this mountain once lay in what is now Hallasan's crater area, and was blasted to the edge of the island when the mountain erupted. Although the sharp cliffs that separate Sanbangsan's lower regions from its tree-flecked summit would make rock climbers go weak at the knees, the mountain has long been considered holy, and the highest you're allowed to go is the cave temple of **Sanbanggulsa**, about halfway up (there are, however, some challenging rock trails lower down). The holy grotto (daily 8.30am–7pm; W2500), created by a monk in Goryeo times, is bare but for a Buddha on its rear wall, while fresh, drinkable mountain water drips unceasingly from the ceiling near the entrance; slow as the flow is, try to catch the drops directly in one of the plastic cups provided, as the pool that they land in is hardly ever cleaned. The cave constitutes one of Jeju's official "ten grand sights", but after sweating up the hundreds of steps that lead here you're more likely to be impressed by the superlative view of the ocean and the area's surrounding communities than the cave itself. This view is partially obscured by some ugly metal mesh at the top of the grotto opening, which provides important protection from falling rocks, a fact hammered home by several large indentations.

Western Jeju	
Bunjae Artpia	분재 아트피아
Chusa's Exile Site	추사 적거리
Geumneung Stone Garden	금능 석물원
Hallasan National Park	한라산 국립 공원
Hallim Park	할림 공원
Jeju Art Park	제주 소각 공원
O'Sulloc tea plantation	오술럭차
Sanbanggulsa	산방굴사
The Peace Museum	피스 박물관
Yongmeori	용머리

A peek inside the "Hermit Kingdom"

In 1653 a **Dutch trading ship** bound for Nagasaki in Japan encountered a fierce typhoon south of the Korean peninsula and ran aground on the tiny island of Gapado. Just half of its crew of 64 survived the shipwreck, but despite their obvious status as victims rather than aggressors, they had entered the "Hermit Kingdom" and found themselves treated with scant respect – Joseon-era Korea was a highly isolationist land, whose policy (one rarely triggered) was to bar any foreigners who washed ashore from returning to their homeland. Forced into servitude, they made repeated attempts to escape, but it was not until 1666 that a group of eight managed to flee to Japan from Yeosu, a port city in what is now Jeonnam province. Unfortunately, they found Japan little more welcoming but one year later a second escape took them back to The Netherlands. The accounts of survivor **Hendrick Hamel** became a bestseller in his homeland, and gave the West its first real portrayal of the Korean peninsula; English copies of *Hamel's Journal: A Description of the Kingdom of Korea 1653–1666* have been published, but are hard to track down.

From Sanbangsan's slopes you should be able to make out what appears to be a marooned **ship** just inland from the coast. This is a replica of a Dutch trading ship that crashed off Jeju's shores in 1653, with important consequences for Korea and its relationship with the West – see box above. An account of the ship and her crew's story is provided in an **exhibition** inside the vessel (same times as Sanbanggulsa, and accessible on the same ticket); some of this has, rather tenuously, been devoted to a more recent Dutch connection – South Korea's 2002 World Cup manager Guus Hiddink. In case you're wondering, the statue fighting the dinosaur outside the ship is also Guus, even if it does look more like Bill Clinton.

Yongmeori

The dramatic, wind-swept cliffs of **Yongmeori** stretch into the sea just past the ship, and are accessible on the same ticket (same times too). A fissure-filled walkway curls around the rocks, but be warned it may be closed if the waves are coming in with a lot of force: the seas in this unsheltered corner of Jeju are notoriously unpredictable, so don't venture too near the edge. The rock formations are stunning, their beauty somehow heightened by the strong winds that usually race in from the South Sea, and once around the outermost tip the contrast between the golden horizontal strata of the cliffside and the vertical grey crags of Sanbangsan become apparent. Keep an eye out for naturally made water paths that surge through the rock, where small fish peek out and dash between the crevices. *Ajummas* sometimes set up little stalls along here to sell freshly caught fish. The community settled along this stretch of the coast is **HWASUN**, situated at what would be an idyllic place if it weren't for the ugly power station that was built by the shore to supply much of Jeju's energy. If this blight wasn't enough, now the depth of the bay (and its convenient location, as far as possible from Pyongyang) has attracted the **South Korean navy**, which plans to move a number of destroyers into a purpose-built naval port by 2020. The residents' regular protests are doing little to block a deal apparently set in stone, which makes a mockery of Jeju's designation as the "Island of World Peace". For now, though, nearby **Hwasun beach** is a scenic place to relax.

Offshore lie the islets of **GAPADO** and **MARADO**, home to tiny communities of just a few dozen people who somehow manage to eke out a living here from land and sea. Low-lying Gapado was the unlikely conduit for the West's first contact with Korea, as it was where Hamel's ship ran aground. Marado is smaller, loftier and more popular, attracting fans of geographical extremities who come to stand at Korea's southernmost speck of land. Marado recently achieved national fame as part of a popular television commercial, in which a parachutist floated onto the island asking who had ordered the *jjajang-myeon*, a Chinese noodle dish; now an essential part of any Korean tourist's visit, the island's restaurants serve little else. From the ferry, you may notice caves in the cliffs – these were military storage cavities made by the Japanese during their occupation of Korea, in anticipation of American attacks on strategically important Jeju.

Practicalities

Despite sharing the same coast as Seogwipo, this southwestern region is much more easily visited from Jeju City; **buses** run every 20 minutes from the island's capital (W3500), usually arriving at Sanbangsan within an hour. A similarly frequent bus runs along the coast, though this takes more than twice as long to arrive. Those seeking to travel from Seogwipo or Jungmun may have to change once or twice but services are frustratingly irregular; the drivers should be able to drop you off in the right places, and have even been known to telephone their colleagues to make doubly sure that foreign guests are picked up. If you fancy the "remote Jeju" experience, you may find **staying overnight** rather appealing, and there are a few acceptable places in the area; one of these, nestling between Sanbangsan and the sea (and easy to find), is *Ocean House Jeju* (❹), a wood cabin with cooking facilities in every room.

Twice-daily **ferries** to Gapado and Marado run from Daejeong harbour, which can be reached via West Coastal Road buses from Jeju City. However, a number of factors can wreak havoc on the schedule so call ⓣ064/794-3500 to check if it's running, or pop into any tourist information booth on the island. Ferries also run to Marado from Songaksan on Jeju; there are currently four per day, though again it's wise to call for up-to-date information (ⓣ064/794-6661). Marado also features on a number of tours run by hotels and travel agencies in Jeju City.

Jeju Art Park and Chusa's Exile Site

A few kilometres north of Sangbangsan – off Route 95 – is **Jeju Art Park** (daily 8am–7.30pm; W4500), a large, open-air exhibition of contemporary sculpture from around the world. If you can imagine Copenhagen's Little Mermaid having a garden party with a bunch of oddly shaped friends, you're on the right track, but though metal statues are the predominant features around the park's grassy confines, there are several themed areas to poke around too, as well as a couple of indoor painting exhibitions. Buses run to a stop near the park fairly regularly from Jeju City, but whether it's worth the trawl is questionable. Those wanting to make a day of it can try to track down the exile site of a calligrapher named **Chusa** (daily 9am–6pm; W500), which sits a couple of kilometres west in the midst of some of Jeju's most beautiful farmland. Kim Chun-hee, better known by his pen name, was exiled here in 1840 for his involvement in a political plot. Like a naughty boy sent to a far-off room to consider his actions, he took to drawing on the walls, eventually honing his brushstrokes to such a degree that he is now revered as one of Korea's greatest artists and calligraphers. A letter-cum-painting named **Sehando** is his most famous piece, though the one on display is a replica, the original having been moved to Jeju National Museum (p.358). The exhibition room is small with few actual articles, and there's no English-language information. After you've seen the art you can wander around the nearby traditional buildings that Chusa once called home. While there's little here to detain all but ardent devotees of his work, the surrounding area – particularly that leading up to the distinctive mountain to the south – contains some achingly bucolic farming communities, a timeless land where elderly ladies sow grain, beasts plough the fields and mainland Korea feels a lifetime away.

O'Sulloc tea plantation and around

Heading further north from the two art sites the countryside feels ever more remote; covered with the purples, pinks and whites of cosmos bloom from summer to autumn, this is Jeju at its rural best. It's a fantastic area to explore by bicycle, but without wheels of some kind it can be tough to get around. Somewhat paradoxically, Jeju's lack of traffic means that it's the best place in Korea to hitchhike – even though there are few vehicles on the road, you'd be unfortunate to have more than two or three turn you down. That said, there are one or two busy areas, and tour buses descend en masse to the open plan **O'Sulloc tea plantation**, which serves as a pleasant pit stop for groups touring the west of the island. A café in the visitor centre (daily 10am–6pm; Oct–March until 5pm; free) serves a whole stash of green-tea-related goods: try *nok-cha* tiramisu, cookies, ice cream – or even have a cup of tea – before visiting the viewing deck on the top level. The big building on view is the factory itself, one of two that the company uses to make the nation's favourite tea (though to keep costs down, much of it is now grown in China). The real attraction here is the opportunity to walk through the **tea fields**. If you've been to Boseong in Jeolla-do you'll know what to expect, though the fields here are flatter, and despite the plantation's popularity with Korean tourists, a little walk will find you alone among the leaves.

Bunjae Artpia

Greenery of a tinier kind can be found at the **Bunjae Artpia** (daily 8.30am–6pm; W7000), a highly picturesque bonsai garden that's hard to reach on public transport. Not so long ago the site on which the park now sits was wild, uncultivated land; nowadays, thanks primarily to the efforts of a lone botanist, this site claims to be the largest bonsai exhibition in the world. Though the English language uses the Japanese word, bonsai culture actually originated in China, where it was known as *penjing*, and hit Korea (known here as *bunjae*), before finally making it to Japan. There's lots of English information (and Russian too) to read as you take a sweet-smelling walk around the gentle mounds of earth that make up the complex. A five-hundred-year-old juniper stands in tiny pride as the star of the show, a mushroom-shaped mini-tree with a two-tone trunk – the light wood is dead, the dark still going strong. A more dynamic exhibit is a Korean elm that has wedged open the rock beside it, in a manner similar to the Angkor temple of Ta Prohm in Cambodia. Capsules of fish food can be bought to feed the **koi carp** that swim in a nearby pond, some of which are over twenty years old. For food, there's a **buffet** in the dining room (11.20am–2pm; W6500), or try the delicious red snapper set menu in the afternoon (2.30–5pm; W8000).

The Peace Museum

Tucked away in countryside near the tea plantation is the **Peace Museum** (daily 8.30am–6pm; W5000), one of many such places in Korea. Like the others, it's entirely devoted to Japan's occupation of the Korean peninsula, and not so peaceful at all when groups of school kids are having nationalistic rhetoric barked at them through megaphones. If you're lucky enough to avoid these, you'll be rewarded with a modest but absorbing exhibition set in an extremely tranquil area. Deeming Jeju a strategically important hub between China, Korea and the Japanese mainland, Japanese forces established headquarters on the site of the museum during their occupation of Korea, and at one point planned to station up to 70,000 soldiers on the island. Korean slaves were used to dig the two kilometres of **tunnels** that still snake underfoot; at the time of writing only one was open to the public – cool, squat and dark, it's not for claustrophobes – though a further three were being primed. There are relics from the occupation period on show in the main building (guns and grenades, and the like), where staff will be pleased to show you an English-language film. This contains interviews with survivors from the camp, and explains the site with a refreshing lack of vitriol, though as there are a few gory pictures, it's not really for kids. Also in the area is **Jeoji Artists Village**, which wasn't open at the time of research, although this large rural site may be full of creative endeavour by the time you read this. Across the road is a **botanical garden** (daily 9am–5pm; W1000), which is a great place to reward your endeavours for getting this far with a cup of herbal tea.

The northwestern coast

Hareubang are all over Jeju – and Korea, in fact – so you may question the need for gathering together a whole park full of them. However, **Geumneung Stone Garden** (daily 8am–7pm; W1000) is an absorbing sight nonetheless since it houses Jeju's famed stone grandfathers in substantial numbers. Many of these are in the regular *hareubang* shape, though most have been pushed and pulled into unconventional forms by young local artists. Big, small, wonky or squat, they make for some great photo opportunities, as do the statues with Buddhist and local themes. Abandon hope all ye who enter the **Hell Path** – a crying child points the way to a narrow, snaking trail of ghoulish stone misshapes that, in true hellish fashion, seems to go on without end. There's also a collection of small *hareubang* presented to – and presumably given back by – some of Jeju's most luminous international guests.

If you're travelling with children or your time on Jeju is short, a visit to **Hallim Park** (daily 8.30am–6pm; W6000) makes a worthwhile trip as it

Grandfathers of rock

What is it with Pacific islands and **statues**? The *moai* of Easter Island are the most famous, but similar relics have been found on Fiji, Tahiti and Okinawa, among other places. Jeju's own version is the *dolhareubang*, or **"stone grandfather"**. Commonly abbreviated to *hareubang*, they can be found all over Korea – nowadays usually outside restaurants that wish to drum up custom. Bulgy-eyed and often quite cheerful-looking, they differ from their Polynesian counterparts by being quite expressive. Their hands rest on their tummies as if full of food; those with left above right are said to be military, as opposed to the more scholarly right-above-left brigade.

Like the *moai*, the origin and purpose of the statues remain shrouded in mystery, though it seems likely that they were placed at village entrances as a means of protection. Another theory, and one supported by their extremely **phallic appearance**, is that they served as sources of fertility – today, miniature versions are sold to women who are having trouble getting pregnant, as well as tourists wanting a souvenir of their trip to Jeju.

Today, only a few dozen **authentic** *hareubang* remain; the most accessible can be found in Jeju City, at the entrance to the Folklore and Natural History Museum, and outside Samseonghyeol.

▲ Hareubang

groups some of Jeju's principal attractions into one easy-to-swallow site; caves, stone sculptures, traditional Jeju houses or bonsai gardens – they're all here. Two good **beaches** (Hyeopjae and Geumneung) stretch from the park entrance, the palm trees fringing shallow, turquoise water lending the scene an almost Caribbean air. Across the sea is the beautiful nearby islet of **BIYANGDO**, accessible by ferry. **Minbak** accommodation is plentiful in this area, and there's also a fragrant camping ground among the pine trees; the *Hallim Geumneung Motel* (☎064/796-0015; ⑤) offers spacious and well-appointed rooms, some with a decent view of the beach. Regular **buses** head down the West Coastal Road from Jeju City (see box, p.354).

Hallasan National Park

Arriving by ferry on a clear day, you can see the whole of Jeju tapering slowly to Mount Halla, known locally as **HALLASAN**, a dormant volcano at the centre of the island, and Korea's highest point at 1950m. Blanketed with pink azalea, in the springs and snow in the winter, the centre of the island has long been a **national park**, with four well-trodden hikes heading to Hallasan's crater, a grassy bowl pocked with grey volcanic rocks, and home to a couple of small lakes. As long as the weather cooperates, a climb up Hallasan is one of the main goals for adventurous visitors from the mainland. The four main routes, starting from the north and heading clockwise, are Gwanamsa, Seongpanak, Yeongsil and Eorimok.

Hiking Hallasan

Jeju's porous volcanic rock means that Hallasan's climbing trails provide more grip than your average Korean national park, even in wet weather. Though the climb is not a terribly difficult walk, hikers should take certain **precautions** if attempting to reach the summit. In order to stop lots of feet stomping indelible lines into the mountain, trail sections – or even whole routes – are regularly **closed off**; your first point of call should be one of Jeju's many tourist offices, or telephone the tourist information line on ⓣ064/1330 for up-to-date information. To make sure that everyone gets down in time, routes may close earlier than expected, sometimes even at 9am. This also reduces the chance of getting wet, which becomes increasingly higher towards evening as the air cools, though bear in mind that even a sunny morning may degenerate rapidly into thick fog and zero visibility at higher elevations – **bad weather** is the number one cause of most failed attempts to the summit. Even if you avoid the rain, strong winds can bite – bring at least a few layers of decent clothing. Also remember to take enough **water** with you – Halla's rock absorbs most of the rainwater, so there are very few springs on the trails. With the longer walks some

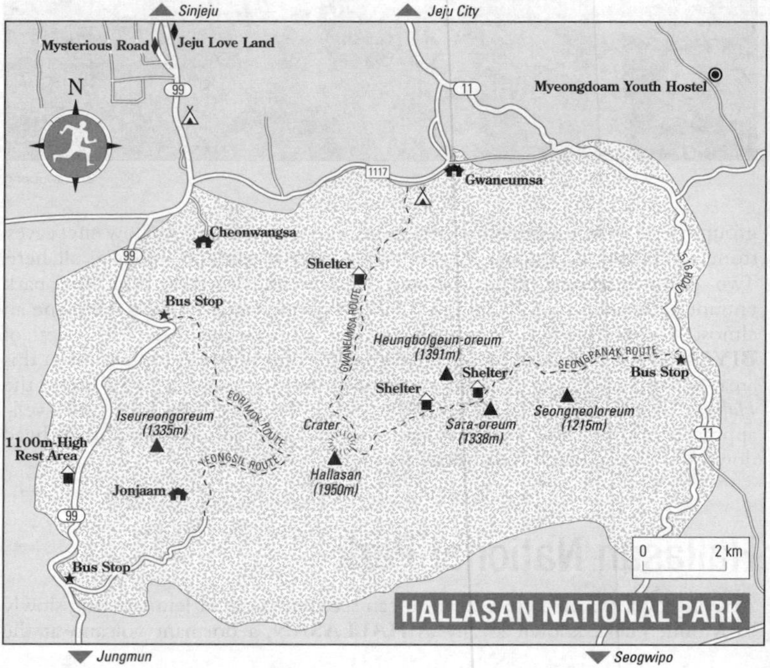

▲ Hallasan National Park

energy-giving **snacks** are a must; cooking and camping are prohibited, though the usual snack shops can be found at the trailheads.

Gwanamsa route

This route, heading to the peak from the north, is the best to take if you'd like to tackle the peak without the crowds. Comparatively few hikers use this path, as it's longer, more challenging and **less accessible** than others – there are no public buses here, and though it's only an 11km taxi ride from Jeju City, you may have to pay almost double for the trip, as the driver will have next to no chance of picking someone up for the return leg. The most important advice is to get to the entrance early – it opens at 6am (5am in the summer) but is already closed at 10am between May and August, and 9am at other times. From here, most hikers take around four hours to walk the 8.3km to the summit, but as there are a lot of steps on this route, many opt to use it for their **downhill** run. Initially, it's easy going, but things soon get steeper. The park's only **campsite** is located near the start of the trail – book from one of Jeju's tourist offices.

Seongpanak route

This popular route also heads to the summit, this time from the east. At 9.6km, it's longer than the Gwanamsa trail, but the gradient is gentle and makes for a much **easier climb** – it's possible to complete it in a moderately sturdy pair of trainers, as long as the weather agrees. The **entrance** can be reached by bus from Jeju City's bus terminal; it's a 35min ride on the 5.16 Road bus, which leaves every fifteen minutes or so, and the entrance hours are the same as for the Gwanamsa route. The walk takes four to five hours and is especially popular in the spring, when the path is surrounded by pink azaleas and other flowers.

Yeongsil route

This is the easiest and **shortest** route up the mountain, although at the time of writing the final burst to the **summit** was closed – this will no doubt change at some point, so ask staff at a tourist office for advice. The picturesque course starts off higher up the mountain than other routes, heading past some impressive rock scenery on the way to the top. There's currently no **public transport** to the park entrance, and it's a fair walk uphill from the "Yeongsil" bus stop on the 1100 Road bus route, with annoyingly irregular buses every hour or so – get hold of an up-to-date schedule at a tourist office, or the Jeju City bus terminal. Alternatively you could try flagging down a car heading up from the main road. The entrance **closes** at 2pm from May to August, at noon November to February, and at 1pm the rest of the year.

Eorimok route

At the time of writing, this route also terminated before the summit, coming to an end at the same point as the **Yeongsil** route. It's a trail of **moderate** difficulty, approaching the park from the northwest; the 1100 Road buses (details above) take half an hour to get from Jeju City to the park entrance, which has the same opening hours as Yeongsil. Passing through lush forest at the beginning before heading into bamboo, it's a three-hour walk to the end of the course. Many Koreans believe this to be the most beautiful of the park's paths.

Travel details

Ferries

Daejeong to: Gapado (2 daily; 15min); Marado (3 daily; 30min).
Jeju City to: Busan (7 daily except Sun; 11hr); Incheon (7 Tues, Thurs, Sat; 13hr); Mokpo (2–3 daily; 3hr 10min–4hr 30min); Wando (daily; 4hr 30min).
Sanseong to: Udo (hourly; 10min).

Buses

Jeju is not connected to the mainland by road, but a number of bus routes spread out across the island from Jeju City; see box, p.354 for details.

Flights

Jeju City to: Busan (9 daily; 55min); Cheongju (hourly; 1hr); Gunsan (2 daily; 50min); Gwangju (9 daily; 45min); Incheon (at least 1 weekly; 1hr 5min); Jinju (at least 2 weekly; 50min); Seoul Gimpo (every 15min; 1hr 5min); Ulsan (2–7 weekly; 1hr); Wonju (daily; 1hr 10min); Yeosu (at least 2 weekly; 45min).

North Korea Basics

North Korea Basics

Getting there

First things first: yes, it is possible to enter North Korea. However, you can't just pop in on a whim, and those permitted entry will only be able to visit government-approved sights, and even then only in the company of a local guide. The process is often lengthy and never cheap, but it can be surprisingly simple: a travel agency usually does all the hard work with visas, permits and suchlike. The price of your tour will include pretty much everything: transport (most commonly a flight from Beijing to Pyongyang and an overnight train back out, as well as all internal travel), accommodation, meals and entry fees. Citizens of certain countries – most pertinently the USA and Israel – will find their opportunities limited, but are occasionally allowed in.

Note that you can actually enter the country **from South Korea** in two ways – one for a few seconds, one for a couple of nights: some of the DMZ tours from Seoul allow you to take a few highly guarded steps across the border in the Joint Security Area (see p.160), while buses dash across the border for visits to the wonderful Kumgang Mountains (p.413). Though extremely enjoyable, neither of these offers a true taste of the DPRK – for this, you'll just have to head to Pyongyang.

From China

While several routes into North Korea exist – there's even a direct train from Moscow – almost all Western travellers start their journey in **Beijing**. From here you can either take a weekly flight on Air Koryo, or an overnight train; which one you use will depend on the tour operator that you go through, and the cost will be factored into your tour price. Most tour groups fly into Pyongyang and take the train out, the latter leg giving a warts-and-all view of the North Korean countryside. But you're advised not to be too trigger-happy on the camera: some tourists have got into trouble after being reported as spies by local farmers (see p.392 for more on photography restrictions).

The **flight** (around 2hr from Beijing to Pyongyang) is interesting to say the least. Air Koryo's planes are Soviet relics from the 1970s and 1980s which take off very slowly, but then drop like a sack of flour into Pyongyang airport while throughout the flight, cabin pressure can yo-yo quite uncomfortably. Air Koryo has actually been **banned from flying** into the EU, and in 2007 was the only carrier worldwide to be given a one-star seal of disapproval by Skytrax, but many passengers find this a highly interesting reprise of air travel in the 1970s.

Train journeys take around 24 hours from Beijing, though with the permission of your tour company you'll also be able to get on in Dandong, a Chinese city near the North Korean border; from here it's only a seven-hour trip. Carriages are split into four-bed berths, with foreigners usually grouped together in the same carriage. There's also a restaurant car. Note that if crossing the border by train, the **toilets** are often locked for hours – go before you reach Dandong on the way to North Korea, and before arriving at Sinuiju, a city just a few kilometres from the Chinese border, on the way out. At Sinuiju station you'll be allowed off the train to stretch your legs; don't miss the opportunity to take a look out over the town square.

Customs inspections are usually thorough, whether at the airport or at Sinuiju, so expect to be questioned (see box on p.386 for information on what not to bring).

Tours and packages

A surprising number of travel operators offer **tours** into North Korea (see the list on p.386 for a few of the best), most lasting for four to seven days. All visit the same core of Pyongyang-based sights, though some of the more expensive ones head to locations around the country. Group tours are cheapest – the size of the party can be anything from four to forty – but some also offer **individual packages**. These may sound appealing, but ironically you get more freedom on group trips – it's simply a lot harder for the two guides to keep tabs on twenty people than one or two, so those on group tours get a bit more leeway when walking around, such as more picture-taking opportunities, the occasional chance to wander off by yourself for a few minutes, and less official spiel. Many is the tale of woe from an individual traveller who has been marched around the same sights as group tourists, had no foreign company to bounce ideas, questions or frustrations off, and paid twice the price for the privilege.

While all tours are pretty dear, it's possible to save a lot of money by going through a **Chinese operator** in Beijing; the drawbacks are that these tours are hard to arrange, conducted in Mandarin only, and tend to revolve more around food than sightseeing.

To travel with the following operators, try to apply at least four weeks in advance.

Tour operators

Explore Nelson House, 55 Victoria Road, Farnborough GU14 7PA, UK ⓣ 0870/333 4001, ⓦ www.explore.co.uk. This UK-based operator offers occasional twelve-day tours from London, which include four nights in Pyongyang, two at other DPRK destinations and a few in Beijing, from £1949 per person.

Geographic Expeditions 1008 General Kennedy Av, PO Box 29902, San Francisco, USA ⓣ 415/922-0448, ⓦ www.geoex.com. This group's action-packed all-inclusive ten-day tours head from San Francisco to north and south Korea – four nights in the South, three in the North and one in Beijing – but are expensive at $6895 per person and up.

Koryo Tours Near Yashow Market, Sanlitun, Beijing, China ⓣ 10/6416 7544, ⓦ www.koryogroup.com. This company takes more than half of the DPRK's foreign tourists, and its success is fully deserved – the tours are the best-informed and most enjoyable to go on; so good are Nick Bonner's contacts within North Korea that he's been allowed to co-produce three documentaries in this highly secretive nation: see **p.439** for more information. All tours head off from Beijing, and range from four nights (€990) to seven-days (from €1690). Individual tours are available from €1790 per person for a three-day tour, and they even offer a golfing holiday option.

Regent Holidays Froomsgate House, Rupert St, Bristol, UK ⓣ 0845/277 3317, ⓦ www.regent-holidays.co.uk. Has over two decades of experience of sending travellers to North Korea and other far-out destinations. A standard tour gives seven nights in the DPRK for £1220, though three-night "long weekend" trips can be half this price if travelling in a pair: all tours tend to include one day in Beijing. Also of interest is an "Alternative Trans-Siberian" tour, which takes travellers from Beijing to Moscow via Pyongyang.

Ryohaengsa Room 401, Building 9, Xinglongjiauwen, Jianguolu 29, Chaoyang District, Beijing, China ⓣ 86/13381 119247 (mobile). All tours to the DPRK have to go through the rather frosty Ryohaengsa, a state organization which basically fulfils the same function as Intourist once did in the Soviet Union; tour groups will deal with them on your behalf, but going directly can save you a whole heap of money – prices can be as low as $450 for three-day tours. The disadvantage is that tours with Ryohaengsa are impossible to arrange outside China, and if they don't feel like taking you in (some get offered a tour, others nothing more than foul-mouthed abuse in Korean and/or Mandarin) you'll be left with little recourse other than to wait weeks or months to join a "real" tour.

How to get deported

Be careful when **packing your bags** for North Korea – with your trip likely to cost a pretty penny, it would be a shame to have to end it at **customs control**. In addition to the regular contraband – drugs, weapons, pornography and the like – you should be careful about taking in electronic equipment. Most cameras are fine (lenses larger than 150mm are not allowed), though video recorders may be confiscated on entry, as will any **mobile phones** or other communications equipment – these will be given back to you as you leave. Beware of taking anything that's very obviously American or South Korean – while K-pop on your music player is unlikely to be picked up, any clothing emblazoned with the stars and stripes surely will. Literature deemed to be of a subversive nature (which may include this guidebook) will also be frowned upon.

Getting around

Once inside North Korea you'll have precious little say in your day-to-day travels – all transportation requirements will be arranged before you set foot inside the country, the cost factored in as part of the tour price, and you'll be obliged to stick to the schedule.

Most travel is done by **tour bus** if you're in a group, and **taxi** on independent tours, both within Pyongyang and for most trips to nearby destinations. You'll notice that the roads are quiet in the capital, and almost deserted outside. Contrary to popular belief, the countryside around the highways hasn't been overhauled to present a false face to foreign tourists, and you'll see a great deal of poverty. The main highways themselves however, are almost exclusively for foreign tour groups and military vehicles – they pass small villages, but there are almost no exits (hardly surprising given that almost no rural civilians own a car). There's a **subway system** in Pyongyang, which figures on most tour schedules – see p.407 for details – though the city's trams and buses are off-limits on all but the most expensive tours. **Internal flights** also exist, and those heading to Paekdusan or other more remote locations will find themselves taking one.

Accommodation

As with transportation, all of your accommodation requirements will be taken care of and paid for prior to your arrival.

Most travellers spend every night of their tour in **Pyongyang**, where there are a few excellent hotels – see p.402 for more information – but some tours include a night or two outside the capital; the two most common provincial bases are **Kaesong**, near the DMZ (p.411), and **Paekdusan**, a mountain straddling the Chinese border (p.415). Those on Kumgangsan tours from South Korea will also spend at least one night in the DPRK (p.413).

Food and drink

Food has long been in scarce supply in North Korea. While the country has occasional – and often severe – problems sourcing food, and leans heavily on the outside world for aid, try not to feel too guilty about eating here: the money you're paying is more than enough to cover what you eat, and at least part of it will be used to help feed the locals.

The quality of your own **food** will vary according to financial, political and climatic conditions at the time of your visit, but most visitors emerge well fed. You're unlikely to have much say over where and what you eat – if you have special dietary requirements you should make them clear to your tour company on application. Local specialities include *naengmyeon* (a buckwheat noodle dish similar to Japanese *soba*, but served in a spicy cold soup) and barbecued duck. See p.409 for information on a few of the best restaurants in Pyongyang.

There's more choice with local **drink**, as it's one of the only things that you'll have to pay for once inside the country; many travellers buy a few bottles of grog to take home (perhaps more for the bragging rights than the taste). There are an assortment of local hooches to choose from, including some curious mushroom, ginseng and berry concoctions, and the **beers** are great value at around €0.50 per bottle – Taedong-gang is the most popular, but try to hunt down Ryongsong, which has a distinctive hoppy taste.

The media

While locals subsist on the Nodong Shinmun ("Workers' Daily"), North Korea also produces a surprising amount of English-language printed material, and is more than happy to offload it to foreign visitors.

In addition to the **books** written by Kim Jong-il – he's said to have authored well over a thousand, and many have been translated into various languages for foreign consumption – there are a few interesting **newspapers** and periodicals, some of which may be dropped into your lap on the flight from Beijing. Once you get to your hotel, you'll be able to tune into **KCTV**, the state television channel – for locals, this is off-air for much of the day, but foreign visitors get a full 24 hours of looped North Korean news and period drama. The latter is mainly made up of patriotic heroes refusing to capitulate to foreign forces, the themes a mix of Japanese occupation period, Korean War times, and not much else. In addition, there's Ⓦwww.kcna.co.jp, the official news website of the DPRK; the near-daily stories (some real, some not) of South Korean unrest against American military presence bring to mind the news reports about Eurasian and Eastasian activity in Orwell's *Nineteen Eighty-Four*.

Titles to look out for include *Korea Pictorial* – look for a colourful A3 magazine with the word "Korea" on the front – a glossy monthly publication that focuses more on photography than reportage, though some of the stories are rather absorbing. *Korea Today* is a smaller, far wordier version of *Korea*

Pictorial, with a songsheet reading of the "Song of General Kim Il-Sung" on the inside cover. The articles are rather insipid, but for the odd gem. The weekly newspaper, the *Pyongyang Times*, is not always easy to find inside the country, though its stories are fascinating ("School performs well"; "Factory increases shoe production"), and inevitably Kims-obsessed. Hang on to your copy should you be given one on the plane.

Festivals

There's only one event on the North Korean travel calendar, but what an event it is.

The **Mass Games** (see box, p.401 for more on this event) must count as one of the world's great spectacles, but contrary to popular belief, this colourful feast of song and dance is not aimed at tourists – almost all of the spectators are North Korean, and almost all citizens aim to see it at least once in their life: a kind of Juche rite of passage (see p.406 for more on Juche).

The timing of the games has been erratic of late, but the authorities are trying to make it a yearly celebration taking place in **July and August**. Festival season normally lasts three or four weeks, during which time there's usually a performance every evening, lasting around ninety minutes, with tickets costing €50.

Special events are held on important anniversaries, and the 100th anniversary of the birth of Kim Il-sung in April 2012 promises to be one hell of a bash, perhaps the biggest ever seen in the DPRK – apply for your trip well in advance.

Culture and etiquette

The first rule you need to remember when travelling through North Korea is this: do not disrespect the Kims. Disobeying this could lead to dramatic consequences.

However, the sheer madness of the place makes acquiescence a hard line to toe – it's difficult not to pass comment on something that is likely to run contrary to your own upbringing. While the **propaganda** stuffed down your throat may be hard to stomach, it's unwise to react to it – asking questions or making accusations is not going to change the way that anybody thinks, much less the running of the country, and can only lead to trouble. You'd be foolish to travel to North Korea with the intention of creating a stink, even after your visit: while a critical blog or travel article will not be of any danger to its author, the North Korean guides tarnished by association may get into a lot of trouble, and travel agencies have been known to lose their licences.

Good behaviour is required in private as well as public places – rumours abound of hotel rooms being **bugged**, and these cannot be wholly discounted; it's also claimed that some in the *Koryo* have hidden cameras. Even seemingly innocent activity is not above suspicion – there's one oft-quoted tale of a traveller who got into serious trouble after stubbing out his cigarette on a newspaper, inadvertently desecrating the holy face of Kim Jong-il.

However frightening all of this may seem, the vast majority of travellers encounter no problems whatsoever, and most have a fantastic time. Simply do as you're told, don't go running off, don't take pictures when you've been told not to, and keep any frustrations bottled up until you're back in Beijing. The local **guides** are usually amiable folk; getting into their good books at the beginning of the tour by behaving yourself and asking permission to take pictures is likely to result in your gaining greater leeway as you make your way around. Neither should you fear the local North Korean people, who end up being the highlight of many a journey. Repeated contact with Western tour groups has convinced many Pyongyangites that foreigners are not to be feared; acting in a courteous manner will continue the trend.

Shopping

While staunchly anti-capitalist North Korea isn't exactly renowned for its shopping possibilities, there are a number of interesting things to buy once inside the country; most of these are impossible to get anywhere else, and make fantastic souvenirs.

The race to stock up on as much North Korean material as possible often starts on the plane – wet-wipe packets, tissues, cutlery sleeves and even sick bags can be sold for a quick buck on the Internet, though most people choose to hang on to these little mementoes. You may also be handed propaganda-filled North Korean periodicals during your flight – see p.388.

The larger tourist hotels have shops in which local goods can be purchased. Among the more appealing buys are **pin-badges**, which come in a variety of styles from national flags to commemorations of judo events; **postcards**, which render the beautiful DPRK in both photographic and socialist realist fashions; and a range of **alcoholic drinks**, usually including beer, mulberry wine and some acrid mushroom concoctions. Of interest to some are the **tailored suits** made in room #301 on the third floor of the *Yanggakdo*; note that, for whatever reason, there are two rooms with this number. Most customers are looking for Kim Jong-il's distinctive buttoned-up-to-the-collar chic, affectionately known to DPRK veterans as the "Kim-suit". Prices vary – and on big occasions the tailors are booked solid with work – but for just over €100 you can usually get a made-to-measure bargain. Unfortunately, the sale to foreigners of one of the other great DPRK purchases – **socialist realist prints** and paintings – was recently made illegal, ostensibly because the espoused Juche philosophy is for North Korean consumption only. Those still interested can head to a shop near the Koryo Tours office in Beijing (see p.386), though the convenient near-monopoly has pushed prices up considerably.

You're likely to be shown around a few shops on your travels around Pyongyang. The **stamp shop** is a popular stop that will delight philatelists and novices alike. If you're staying in the *Koryo* and ask your guide nicely you may even be able to pop there on your own, as it's just down the road from the hotel's main entrance. There's also the **foreign language bookshop**, which stocks translated works from the pens of Kim & Kim, as well as a range of absorbing booklets about the country and a few of its more minor heroes. In Pyongyang there are also a couple of department stores, though you're unlikely to be allowed to visit them.

Travel essentials

Children's Korea

It's quite possible to travel to North Korea with your **children**, but there are two points to consider. First, the sight-packed days can be hard even on adults – you'll spend a lot of time in a tour bus or taxi, and yet more standing at sights while being bombarded with the greatness of the Kims. Second, there are precious few facilities for children, either in the hotels or around the country – bring everything that your child will need. That said, every housing block in Pyongyang has a small playground area; while tightly planned group tours are unlikely to squeeze this in, independent tours should be able to work a quick play into the schedule.

Communication and mail

It's possible to make **international calls** or send **faxes** from all major hotels, but the prices are guaranteed to be high – unless you're happy with paying €15 for a minute-long telephone call or €20 for a one-sheet fax, it's best to assume that you'll be incommunicado with the outside world for the duration of your stay in North Korea. Also note that your mobile phone will not work thanks to interference devices placed around the border (you'll even experience this if visiting Panmunjeom from South Korea), and it will in any case have been confiscated on your arrival.

In the major hotels you'll find a computer terminal, from which you can send **emails**; this can only be done on the hotel's account, and it's not possible to receive replies. Also bear in mind that whatever you say or send is likely to be monitored. This also applies to **post**, which will be read and understood, whatever the language; anything that seems cryptic will be thrown away, and may also be used as evidence of espionage.

Costs and money

All accommodation and transport will be included in your tour fee, as well as two or three meals per day, but for drinks, snacks and souvenirs you'll have to use hard currency, as there are no ATMs or banks accessible to foreigners. Most prices for tourist goods are quoted in **euros**, though American dollars and Chinese yuan are just as widely accepted. Those in North Korea for the Mass Games (see p.401) will have to pay €50 for a ticket, which is quite a bargain for such a stupendous event.

The official currency of the DPRK is the **North Korean won**, but you're unlikely to have too much contact with it as foreigners aren't allowed to use local money; for what it's worth, the exchange rates at the time of writing were W290 to £1, W145 to US$1, W125 to A$1 and W200 to €1. There was a time when the won was pegged at 2.16 to the dollar, a fiscally ridiculous nod to Kim Jong-il's birthday on February 16, but this policy was abandoned in 2001.

Note that it's illegal to export **North Korean currency** out of the country – if you do manage to get hold of some, keep your cache of cash well hidden when leaving. The easiest approach is to ask at your hotel reception; usually they won't mind if you say that you're collecting money from around the world. The notes that they dole out are suspiciously clean, but while they make for good souvenirs they're nothing like the dirty, tattered, falling-to-bits rags that ordinary North Koreans use; to get your

> It's also a good idea to bring **gifts**, not just for your guides and driver but for the locals who you're likely to run into along the way. Make sure that they're appropriate – nothing overtly capitalist, American or South Korean in origin. Western cigarettes go down well with local men and postcards from home with everyone, while balloons and small toys are always popular with children; try to ask a parent's permission before handing anything over.

hands on one of these, you'll have to use a bit of initiative. One good source are the tiny ice-cream stands that you'll see around Pyongyang in warmer months – you don't have any local money, the ice-cream women will only have local change and will be glad for foreign currency, so everyone's a winner. As long as your guide doesn't notice, you should be able to walk away with a fistful of genuine notes.

Tipping is not a Korean custom, but will obviously be appreciated in a country as poor as this. A representative from most tour groups will usually pass the hat around on your final day, then split the pooled money between the various guides and drivers, who are not well paid despite their regular contact with foreigners – North Korean convention tends to reward work on the basis of danger, so guiding tourists is not high on the list. In larger groups, €5 per person usually adds up to a sizeable donation, while those travelling individually are advised to give around €20 to each guide and driver.

Disabled travellers

Travellers with **disabilities** can travel to North Korea, but there are next to no access facilities laid on for wheelchairs, and there are far easier countries to visit, a North Korean trip is not out of the question. It's interesting to note that disabled locals are highly revered in North Korea, a country where brave resistance is the theme of most songs, films and television dramas; many women, indeed, consider it their duty to marry injured soldiers.

Entry requirements

Everyone needs a **visa** to enter North Korea, and though the process of obtaining one is lengthy, as long as you've got money and make your plans a couple of months in advance you should find it pretty easy to get in. Those from the "wrong countries" (ie USA and Israel) are allowed in occasionally, most often during the Mass Games period – ask one of the travel agencies listed on p.386 for the latest details. **Journalists** can also find it hard to get in, though again it's not impossible – it's the travel agency's responsibility to vet applicants, so if you say that you're a circus freak and they believe you, you're in. Many try to avoid fraud by asking for signed confirmation from your employer.

Your visa is organized prior to arrival by the travel agency and forms part of your tour price. It comes on a slip of paper (not as an insert in your passport) that you'll only possess for a short time on entry to North Korea. You won't receive a stamp, so there'll be no evidence of your visit in your passport.

It's wise to have **travel insurance** wherever you go, and North Korea is no exception. Most travel policies cover North Korea, but do check by making a quick call to your company; if they won't cover you, find one that will.

Photography

In terms of pictures per traveller, North Korea must be one of the most photographed nations on Earth, a hugely ironic fact given that most of it is closed off, and even official sights are subject to **photographic restriction**. This is a nation where even the mundane is incredible, and even on the shortest trips some travellers end up with over a thousand images.

Some of the photographic **rules** are those that apply worldwide: don't take pictures of military installations or soldiers (unless you're in the DMZ, where it is almost expected), and ask permission if taking any photographs of people. Others are a little harder to guess, many of them surrounding **the Kims** – if you're taking a picture of a statue, mural or painting of the great men, try to get the whole body into your shot, as anything else may be viewed as disrespectful. (This can be quite a feat at the huge bronze statue of Kim Il-sung at Mansudae; see p.404.) It's also risky to photograph anything that might be taken as a **criticism of the country**: a picture of a peasant sitting by the roadside could be construed as a deliberate attempt to smear North Korea's stellar reputation (something which may also see you hauled in and accused of being a spy). In practice, though, these rules are hard to police, and customs officials simply can't sift through each and every picture.

7 North Korea

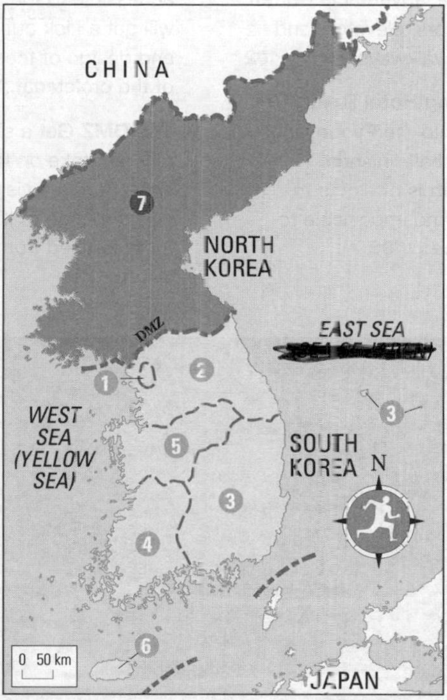

CHAPTER 7 Highlights

* **The Mass Games** Unquestionably one of the most spectacular events you'll ever see – try to time your visit to coincide with it if at all possible. See box, p.401

* **Kumsusan Memorial Palace** Pay a visit to the father of the nation, who lies in state beyond a labyrinthine warren of corridors, elevators and moving walkways. See p.402

* **Ryugyong Hotel** Rising 105 stories into the Pyongyang sky, this half-finished mammoth is off-limits to tourists and impossible to miss. See p.403

* **Monumental Pyongyang** The largest granite tower in the world and a colossal bronze effigy of the "Great Leader" are just a few of the capital's larger-than-life sights. See p.406

* **Pyongyang Subway** Though only two stations are accessible to foreigners, most will get a kick out of the depth and design of these palaces of the proletariat. See p.407

* **The DMZ** Get a slightly different take on the Korean crisis during a visit to the northern side of the world's most fortified frontier. See p.412

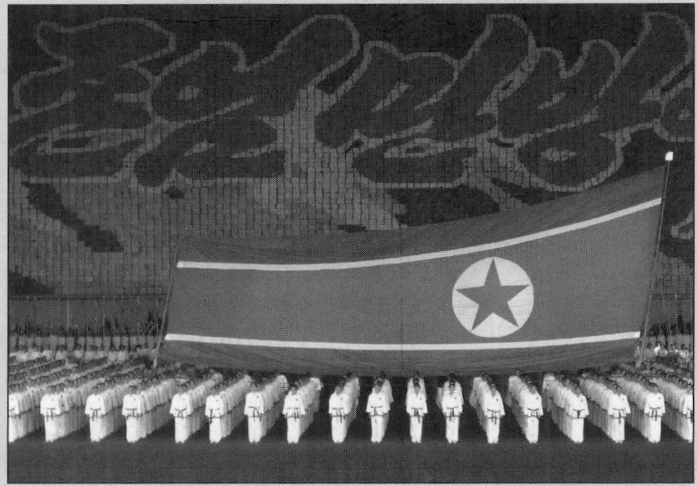

▲ The Mass Games, Pyongyang

7

North Korea

Espionage, famine and nuclear brinkmanship; perpetrator-in-chief of an international axis of evil; a rigidly controlled population under the shadowy rule of a President long deceased... you've heard it all before, but North Korea's dubious charms make it the Holy Grail for hard-bitten travellers. A trip to this tightly-controlled Communist society is only possible as part of an expensive package, but a high proportion of those fortunate and intrepid enough to visit rank it their most interesting travel experience.

North Korea is officially known as the **Democratic People's Republic of Korea**, or the DPRK. However, real democracy is thin on the ground, and comparisons with the police state in Orwell's *Nineteen Eighty-Four* are impossible to avoid: in addition to a regime that acts as a single source of information, residents of Pyongyang, and many other cities, do indeed wake up to government-sent messages and songs broadcast through speakers in their apartments, which can be turned down but never off – the fact that this is often the cue for callisthenic exercises further strengthens associations with the book. Other Big Brother similarities include verified claims that the country is crawling with informants, each seeking to further his or her own existence by denouncing friends, neighbours or even family for such crimes as letting their portrait of the Great Leader gather dust, singing unenthusiastically during a march, or simply

Busting myths

Much has been said and written about the current situation in North Korea, much of it true. These crazy truths, however, make it awfully easy to paint **rumours**, assumptions and hearsay as cast-iron fact. Political falsehoods have been detailed by excellent authors such as Cumings, Winchester and Oberdorfer, who take both sides' views into account (see p.442 for some recommended reading), but a few of the more straightforward rumours can be easily debunked.

The first great untruth to put to bed is that North Koreans are intrinsically **evil**; whatever their leader's state of mind, remember that the large majority of the population have no choice whatsoever in the running of the country or even their own lives, much less than other populations that have found themselves under authoritarian rule. Another myth is that you'll be escorted around by a **gun-wielding soldier**; it's true that you'll have guides with you whenever you're outside the hotel, but they're generally very nice people and it's occasionally possible to slip away for a few minutes.

Sometimes even the myths are myths: the tale of Kim Jong-il hitting **eleven holes in one** on his first ever round of golf is bandied about as evidence of mindless indoctrination in the West, but actually unheard of in North Korea.

being related to the wrong person. Also true is the rumour that locals have to wear a **pin-badge** portraying at least one of the leaders – **Kim Il-sung**, the country's inaugurator and "Great Leader", and the "Dear Leader", his eldest son **Kim Jong-il**. Interestingly, Kim Il-sung remains the country's official president, despite having died in 1994. Both Kims are revered almost as gods, by a people with precious little choice in the matter.

For all this, North Korea exerts a **unique appeal** for those willing and able to visit. Whether you're looking out over Pyongyang's oddly barren cityscape or eating a bowl of rice in your hotel restaurant, the simple fact that you're in one of the world's most inaccessible countries will bring an epic feel to everything you do. It's also important to note the human aspect of the North Korean machine. Behind the Kims and the carefully managed stage curtain live real people leading real lives, under severe financial, nutritional, political and personal restrictions unimaginable in the West. Thousands upon thousands have found conditions so bad that they've risked imprisonment or even death to escape North Korea's state-imposed straightjacket. All the more surprising, then, that it's often the locals who provide the highlight of a visit to the DPRK – many, especially in Pyongyang, are extremely happy to see foreigners visiting their country, and you're likely to meet at least a couple of people on your way around, whether it's sharing an outdoor *galbi* meal with a local family, chatting with the staff at your hotel, or saluting back to a marching gaggle of schoolchildren. This fascinating society functions in front of an equally absorbing backdrop of brutalist architecture, bronze statues, red stars and colossal murals, a scene just as distinctive for its lack of traffic, advertising or Western influence.

A visit to North Korea will confirm some of the things you've heard about the country, while destroying other preconceptions. One guarantee is that you'll leave with more questions than answers.

Some history

The Democratic Republic of Korea was created in 1948 as a result of global shifts in power following the Japanese defeat in World War II and the **Korean War** that followed (see p.428 for more information on these events). The Korean War, which ended in 1953, left much of the DPRK in tatters; led by **Kim Il-sung**, a young, ambitious resistance fighter from Japanese annexation days, the DPRK busied itself with efforts to haul its standard of life and productive capacity back to pre-war levels. Kim himself purged his "democratic" party of any policies or people that he deemed a threat to his leadership – effectively achieving the same ends throughout the country – and fostering a personality cult that lasts to this day. Before long, he was being referred to by his people as *Suryong*, meaning "Great Leader", and *Tongji*, a somewhat paradoxical term describing a higher class of comrade (in North Korea, some comrades are evidently more equal than others). He also did away with the elements of Marxist, Leninist or Maoist thought that did not appeal to him, preferring instead to follow "**Juche**", a Korean brand of Communism that focused on national self-sufficiency (see box, p.406). For a time, his policies were not without success – levels of education, healthcare, employment and production went up, and North Korea's development was second only to Japan in the East Asian area. Its GDP-per-head rate actually remained above that of South Korea until the mid-1970s.

The **American threat** never went away, and North Koreans were constantly drilled to expect an attack at any time. The US Army had, in fact, reneged on a 1953 armistice agreement by re-introducing **nuclear weapons** into South Korea, and went against an international pact by threatening to use such arms against a country that did not possess any; North Korea duly got to work on a reactor of their own at Yongbyon.

There were regular skirmishes both around the **DMZ** and beyond, including an attack on the USS *Pueblo* in 1968 (see p.408), assassination attempts on Kim Il-sung and South Korean president Park Chung-hee around the same time, and the famed "Axe Murder Incident" that took place in the Joint Security Area in 1976 (p.164). During the 1970s at least three tunnels were discovered heading under the DMZ (see p.162 & p.171), which undetected could have seen KPA forces in Seoul within hours.

Decline to crisis

Then came the inevitable **decline** – *Juche* was simply not malleable enough as a concept to cope with external prodding or poor internal decision-making. Having developed into a pariah state without parallel, North Korea was forced to rely on the help of fellow communist states – the Soviet Union and China, which was busy solving problems of its own under the leadership of Chairman Mao. The economy ground almost to a halt during the 1970s, while in the face of a American–South Korean threat that never diminished, military spending remained high. It was around this time that **Kim Jong-il**

Nuclear brinkmanship

Say this about North Korea's leaders: they may be Stalinist fanatics, they may be terrorists, they may be building nuclear bombs, but they are not without subtlety. They have mastered the art of dangling Washington on a string.

David Sanger, *New York Times,* March 20, 1994

Since the opening of a reactor at **Yongbyon** in 1987, North Korea has kept the outside world guessing as to its **nuclear capabilities**, playing a continued game of bluff and brinkmanship to achieve its aims of self-preservation and eventual reunification with the South. The folding of the Soviet Union in 1991 choked off much of the DPRK's energy supply; with few resources of their own, increasing importance was placed on nuclear energy, but the refusal to allow international inspectors in strengthened rumours that they were also using the facilities to create weapons-grade plutonium. **Hans Blix** and his crew at the International Atomic Energy Agency (IAEA) were finally permitted entry in 1992, but were refused access to two suspected waste disposal sites, which would have provided strong evidence about whether processed plutonium was being created or not; Blix was, however, shown around a couple of huge underground facilities that no one on the outside even knew about. North Korea was unhappy with the sharing of information between American intelligence (the CIA) and the independent IAEA, but after threatening to withdraw from the **Nuclear Nonproliferation Treaty** (NPT) they agreed in 1994 to freeze their programme in exchange for fuel. This only happened after an election within the White House – Bill Clinton was more willing to compromise than his predecessor George Bush Senior. North Korea continued to do itself no favours, at one point launching a missile into the Sea of Japan in 1993 (though this was actually a failed attempt at launching a satellite, it was seen by many as practice for a future attack).

The second part of the crisis erupted more suddenly. In 2002, after making veiled threats about a possible resumption of their nuclear programme, North Korea abruptly booted out IAEA inspectors. Coming at the start of the war in Afghanistan, the timing was risky to say the least, but Pyongyang skated even closer to the line by admitting not only to having **nuclear devices** (and claiming that it did not know how to dismantle them), but also to being willing to sell them on the world market. All of these were bargaining ploys aimed at getting George W. Bush's administration to follow the "Sunshine Policy" pursued by Clinton and Kim Dae-jung. Regular six-party talks between China, Russia, Japan, the US and the two Koreas achieved little, and in 2006 North Korea conducted its **first nuclear test**, and sent another missile into the Sea of Japan. North Korea had shown it had yet another card up its sleeve, and talks continued with greater candour. In July 2007 Pyongyang finally announced that it was shutting down its Yongbyon reactor in exchange for aid, and its permanent disability was confirmed by international inspectors two months later.

was being groomed as the next leader of the DPRK – the communist world's first dynastic succession.

During the 1990s North Korea experienced alienation, famine, nuclear threats and the death of its beloved leader. The break-up of the **Soviet Union** in 1991 nullified North Korea's greatest source of funds, and a country officially extolling self-sufficiency increasingly found itself unable to feed its own people. Despite the **nuclear crisis** with the US (see box above) the DPRK was making a few tentative moves towards peace with the South; indeed, it was just after examining accommodation facilities prepared for the first-ever North–South presidential summit that Kim Il-sung suffered a heart attack and died. This day in July 1994 was followed by a long period of intense public mourning – hundreds of thousands attended his funeral, in Pyongyang, and millions more paid their respects around the country – after which came a terrible **famine**, a period known as the "Arduous March". Despite being dead, Kim Il-sung was elected "Eternal President", though his son, Kim Jong-il, eventually assumed most of the duties that require the authorization of a living body, and was made Supreme Commander of the army.

The Sunshine Policy

The year 1998 brought great changes to North–South relations. **Kim Dae-jung** was elected president of South Korea, and immediately started his "**Sunshine Policy**" of reconciliation with the North, which aimed for integration without absorption (assimilation having been the main goal of both sides up until this point). With US president **Bill Clinton** echoing these desires in the White House, all three sides seemed to be pulling the same way for the first time since the Korean War. The two Kims held an historic Pyongyang summit in 2000, the same year in which Kim Dae-jung was awarded the Nobel Peace Prize. The southern premier revealed to the Western media that Kim Jong-il actually wanted the American army to remain in the south (to keep the peace on the peninsula, as well as for protection from powerful China and an ever more militarist Japan), as long as Washington accepted North Korea as a state and pursued reconciliation over confrontation. Clinton was actually set for a summit of his own in Pyongyang, but the election of **George W. Bush** in 2000 put paid to that. Bush undid many of the inroads that had been made, and antagonized the DPRK, famously labelling it part of an "Axis of Evil" in 2002.

The **second nuclear crisis**, in 2002 (see box opposite), brought about a surprise admission from the North – Japanese prime minister **Junichiro Koizumi** went across for a summit expecting to be forced into saying sorry for Japanese atrocities during occupation. Instead it was Kim Jong-il who did the apologizing, astonishingly admitting to a long-suspected series of **kidnappings** on the Japanese coast in the late 1970s and early 1980s, ostensibly as a rather convoluted way of teaching his secret service personnel Japanese. Though the number of abductions was probably higher, Kim admitted to having taken thirteen people, of whom eight had died; one of the survivors had married **Charles Robert Jenkins**, an American defector from the post-Korean War period. The belief that more hostages were unaccounted for – and possibly still alive – made it impossible for Koizumi to continue his policy of engagement with the DPRK.

In 2002 **Roh Moo-hyun** was elected South Korean president, and adhered to the precepts of the Sunshine Policy. While the course under his tenure was far from smooth – the US and the DPRK continued to make things difficult for each other, South Korean youth turned massively **against reunification**, and Roh himself suffered impeachment for an unrelated issue – there was some movement, notably the symbolic re-opening of train lines across the DMZ in 2007, and after a peace pact later in the year, the world's most intractable conflict looked as close as ever to being solved.

Pyongyang

The North Korean capital of **PYONGYANG** could credibly claim to be the most distinctly unique city on the face of the Earth. This city of empty streets, lined with huge grey monuments and buildings, and studded with bronze

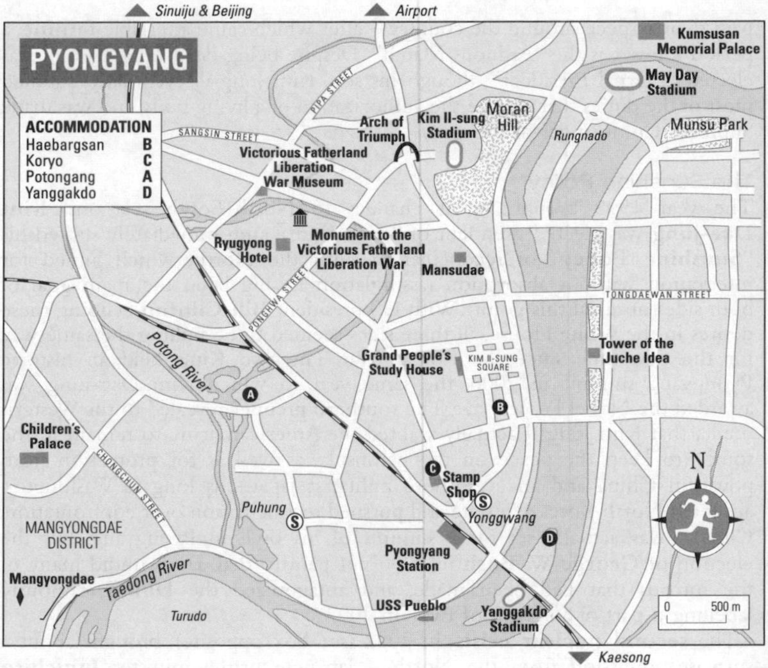

statues and murals in honour of its idolized leaders, is a strange concrete and marble experiment in socialist realism. It stands as a showcase of North Korean might, with its skyscrapers and wide boulevards giving a feint echo of Le Corbusier's visions of brutalist urban utopia: every street, rooftop, doorway and windowsill has been designed in keeping with a single grand vision. On closer inspection, however, you'll notice that the buildings are dirty and crumbling, and the people under very apparent control.

Every single one of Pyongyang's near three million inhabitants has been vetted and approved by the government, and regards living in the capital as an immense privilege. Life here is far better than in the countryside, though you'll still see signs of poverty: power cuts are commonplace, and each evening the city tumbles into a quiet darkness hard to fathom in a capital city. There's also next to no visible commerce – the city is entirely devoid of the billboards and flashy lights commonplace in a metropolis of this size; instead socialist-realist murals form the only advertising, and vie for attention with the communist slogans screamed in red from the tallest buildings. You'll be taken by bus around a selection of officially sanctioned sights. These include **Kumsusan Memorial Palace**, where the body of Kim Il-sung lies in state, and **Mansudae**, his colossal statue; the distinctive granite **Juche Tower** overlooking the river Taedong River; and the **Pyongyang metro**, one of the world's most intriguingly secretive subway systems. Pyongyang is also the venue for the amazing **Mass Games** (see box opposite), which take place at the May Day Stadium. However, regardless of whether you're eating at a restaurant or relaxing in your hotel, you'll be experiencing the city's unmistakably unique feel – Pyongyang is simply fascinating.

Arrival, information and city transport

Most visitors to Pyongyang are here to start a guided excursion of some kind, so whether you **arrive** by plane or train – your only two options – a bus or private car will be waiting, ready to whisk you to your hotel. Though short, the twenty-minute journey from the airport to central Pyongyang is a fascinating one for first-time visitors, displaying an impoverishment that the authorities have made surprisingly little effort to conceal. The road is in good condition but usually empty, save for occasional pedestrians on their way to or from work, and the countryside rather barren. Those disembarking at the far more central train station will have to settle for urban views. Given the tightness of the average itinerary, you're actually likely to visit at least one sight before checking in at your hotel.

There's no such thing as a tourist **information** office in North Korea, but your **guide** will be on hand to answer any questions. Most topics are fine, but asking questions that could be construed as disparaging of the regime could land you or your host in hot water. The guides are usually amiable folk, though at some sights you'll be in the hands of specialists employed to bark out nationalistic vitriol (which, you'll notice, increases in force and volume when either of the Kims are mentioned).

Getting around the city is usually as simple as waking up in time to catch your tour bus (those left behind will be stuck in the hotel until their group returns). Pyongyang's crammed **public buses** and **trams** are for locals only, and your guides would think you crazy to want to use them when you already have paid-for private transport, but if you have any say in the workings of your schedule be sure to ask for a ride on the **Pyongyang metro** – see p.407 for further details. The public buses themselves are highly photogenic Hungarian relics from the 1950s; keep an eye out for the stars on their sides, as each one represents 5000 accident-free kilometres from the bus and its crew.

The Mass Games

The spectacular **Mass Games** is one of the world's must-see events. Also known as the "Arirang Games", it takes place in Pyongyang's 150,000-seater **May Day Stadium**, which is always full to bursting. Unbelievably, though, there are always more performers than there are spectators. Wildly popular with foreign tourists, the show is actually created for local consumption – this is a propaganda exercise extraordinaire, one used by the West as evidence of a rigidly controlled population in thrall to the Kim dynasty.

Even the warm-up will fill you with wonder, awe and trepidation. Your entry to the stadium is serenaded by upwards of 20,000 schoolchildren; filling the opposite stand, they scream out in perfect unison while flashing up the names of their schools on large **coloured flipbooks**, effectively forming human pixels on a giant television screen that remains an ever-changing backdrop throughout the show. The performers themselves come out in wave after wave, relaying stories about the hardships under Japanese occupation, the **creation of the DPRK**, and the bravery in the face of American aggression, as well as less bombastic parables about farming life or how to be safe at the seaside. Among the cast will be thousands-strong teams of *chosonbok*-wearing dancers, ball-hurling schoolkids and miniskirt-wearing female "soldiers" wielding rifles and swords, their every move choreographed to a colourful perfection. The form of the displays changes throughout the course of the event – military-style marches give way to performances of gymnastics or traditional dance, and the cast are at one point illuminated in brilliant blue, forming a rippling sea. Visitors are often left speechless – you'll just have to see for yourself. See p.389 for more details.

Traffic ladies

While Pyongyang does have a few traffic lights dotted around its rather empty streets, these eat up energy in a country not blessed with a surplus of power – step forward the **traffic ladies**. Chosen for their beauty by the powers-that-be, and evidently well schooled, they direct the traffic with super-fast precision, in the middle of some of the busier intersections, and sport distinctive blue (sometimes white) jackets, hats and skirts, as well as regulation white socks. The traffic ladies are rather popular with some visitors, and one or two tour-groups have persuaded their guides to stop by for a brief photo-shoot.

Accommodation

Despite there being fewer than a dozen hotels designated for foreigners, finding **accommodation** doesn't present a problem in Pyongyang as all will be organized in advance by your tour operator. Most tour groups stay at Pyongyang's **top hotels**, the *Koryo* and *Yanggakdo*; there's little to choose between them in terms of service and quality. Both provide a memorable experience and count as tourist draws in their own right, which is a good thing, considering the amount of time you'll be spending there – in the evening, when your daily schedule is completed, there's not really anywhere else to go. Independent travellers who have opted to save money by staying at **cheaper places** – such as the *Haebangsan* or *Potonggang* – usually end up wishing they'd paid the extra to stay somewhere livelier.

Haebangsan This is the cheapest hotel for foreigners and the rooms are just about acceptable, but it's generally agreed that the savings don't make up for the near-total lack of atmosphere or on-site activities.

Koryo Hotel The rooms at this 40-storey hotel are well kept and the on-site restaurants passable, while the ground-floor mini-market – stocked with foreign drinks, biscuits and other comestibles – is the best place in the city to sate any Western sugar cravings. The salmon-pink twin towers of the *Koryo* sit on a main thoroughfare, making for a much better appreciation of local life than is possible in the *Yanggakdo*, and those on independent tours can request trips to nearby restaurants, or the Swiss co-venture bakery-cum-café across the road.

Potonggang Just west of central Pyongyang, in an uninteresting part of town, the *Potonggang* is the only country to feed a couple of American television channels into the rooms. Despite the acceptable facilities, few Westerners end up staying here; if you do, you'll find it hard to miss the huge Kim mural in the lobby.

Yanggakdo This 47-storey hotel sits on an islet in the Taedong, and commands superb views of both the river and the city from its clean, spacious rooms. The isolated location means that you'll be able to wander around outside without provoking the ire of guides or guards, though to be honest there's precious little to do. The on-site restaurants are excellent, with one that revolves slowly at the top of the tower, which is a great place for a nightcap. The ground-floor bar brews its own beer, which is quite delicious after a hard day slogging around sights. Also on site are a bowling alley, a karaoke room and a tailor (see p.390).

Kumsusan Memorial Palace

The huge **Kumsusan Memorial Palace** is a North Korean cathedral, labyrinth, palace and Mecca all rolled into one, and the single most important place in the country. It's here that the body of **Kim Il-sung** lies in state, though this is an opportunity only afforded to invitees – you'll see a lot of high-ranking military proudly wearing their medals and stripes. The official residence of Kim Il-sung until his death in 1994, it was transformed into his final resting place under the orders of his son and heir to the throne, Kim Jong-il. While perceived disrespect to the Great Leader isn't advisable anywhere in the country, it will

The world's largest shell

The Ministry of Truth – Minitrue, in Newspeak – was startlingly different from any other object in sight. It was an enormous pyramidal structure of glittering white concrete, soaring up, terrace after terrace, three hundred metres into the air... the Ministry of Truth contained, it was said, three thousand rooms above ground level, and corresponding ramifications below.

Nineteen Eighty-Four

In a Pyongyang skyline dominated by rectangular apartment blocks, one particular building is the undisputed king of the hill – the **Ryugyong Hotel** looms over the city, a bizarre triangular fusion of Dracula's castle and the Empire State building. Despite the fact that it sticks out like a sore and rather weathered thumb, no locals seem to want to talk about it – this is something that can't be painted over with the regular whitewash of propaganda.

Construction of the pyramidal 105-floor structure started in 1987, a mammoth project intended to showcase North Korean might. The central peak was to be topped with a revolving restaurant, while the two lower cones may have held smaller versions of the same. For a time, Pyongyang was one of only three cities in the world that could boast a hundred-storey-plus building, the others being New York and Chicago. Kim Il-sung had expected the *Ryugyong* to become one of the world's most admired hotels, its near-3000 rooms filled with awestruck tourists. But no sooner had the concrete casing been completed than the funding fell through, and the project was put on indefinite hold. It was left empty, a mere skeleton devoid of electricity, carpeting and windows.

The *Ryugyong* is visible from all across the city, though you're not allowed to enter its immediate area – those who have the Victorious Fatherland Liberation War Square on their schedules will get quite near. Up close and personal, the hulking frame is rather beautiful; creamy, crumbling and peppered with holes like Swiss cheese, it looks like one of Turkey's Cappadocian cave-towers. Given time the *Ryugyong* may one day blossom into one of the world's largest hotels; until then, the building crane that remains stranded atop the structure's highest turret maintains its lonely vigil.

not be tolerated here – be on your best behaviour, dress smartly and keep any conversation hushed.

The walk around the palace and past Kim Il-Sung is a long, slow experience, one that usually takes well over an hour. **Security** is understandably tight – you'll be searched at the entrance and told to leave cameras, coats and bags at reception. Then starts the long haul through corridor after marble corridor, some of which are hundreds of metres long; thankfully, moving walkways are in place, but stand on them, rather than walk – it's an experience to be savoured, and you're likely to see several locals in tears, even the butchest of soldiers. After accessing an upper floor by elevator, your proximity to Kim's body will be made clear by a piped rendition of the "Song of General Kim Il-sung", composed after his death (see box, p.404). Absolute silence is expected as visitors pass into the main room, bathed in a dim red light. A queue circles around the illuminated body – follow the North Korean lead, and take a deep bow on each side.

After paying your respects, you'll be ushered through more corridors. In one room are Kim's many medals, prizes, doctorates and awards that were given throughout his eventful life – note that a few of the universities on his dozens of diplomas have never existed. Another room is filled with reliefs and friezes of the Korean people mourning the loss of their leader; here you'll be handed a Dictaphone for an **English-language lecture**, one delivered in a posh, quavering voice and as bombastic as they come – "just as the sun destroys itself

The Song of General Kim Il-sung

Bright traces of blood on the crags of Changbaek still gleam,
Still the Amnok carries along signs of blood in its stream,
Still do those hallowed faces shine resplendently,
Over Korea ever flourishing and free!

Tell, blizzards that rage in the wild Manchurian plains,
Tell, you nights in forests deep where silence reigns,
Who is the partisan whose deeds are unsurpassed?
Who is the patriot whose fame shall ever last?

He severed the chains of the masses, brought them liberty,
The sun of Korea today, democratic and free.
For the Twenty Points united we stand fast,
Over our fair homeland, spring has come at last!

Refrain
So dear to all our hearts is our General's glorious name,
Our beloved Kim Il-sung of undying fame!

to nourish our world with light, Kim Il-sung threw himself headlong into serving his people". Then it's past a wall-map of the world showing the countries that Kim visited, and the train carriage and car that he did some of his travelling in. After collecting your things you'll usually be allowed out onto the main square for a much-needed stroll.

Mansudae Grand Monument

At **Mansudae**, west of the river, a huge **bronze statue** of Kim Il-sung stands in triumph, backed by a mural of Mount Paekdu – spiritual home of the Korean nation, see p.415 – and lifting a benevolent arm to his people. Unlike the mausoleum, this is not actually a memorial, but was cast when Kim was still alive: a sixtieth birthday present to himself, paid for by the people and monies donated by the Chinese government (Beijing was said to be unhappy with the unnecessary extravagance of the original gold coating, and it was soon removed). So important is the statue that, despite its size, it's given a thorough scrub at least once a week. The respect given by North Korean visitors to the statue is also expected of foreigners: each individual, or every second or third person if it's a large tour party, will have to **lay flowers** at the divine metal feet (these will be bought on the walk towards the monument, and you may be asked to chip in). Each group must also line up and perform a simultaneous bow – stay down for at least a few seconds. Note that taking any pictures that might be deemed "offensive", which includes those cutting part of the statue off or pretending to support Kim as you might the Leaning Tower of Pisa, may result in your camera being confiscated.

Sloping up from the monument is **Moran Hill**, a small park crisscrossed with pleasant paths, and used by city-dwellers as a place to kick back and relax. While there's nothing specific to see, those who visit on a busy day will get a chance to see North Korean life at first hand – this is one of the best places in the country to make a few temporary friends. A simple smile, wave or "*annyeong haseyo*" has seen travellers invited to scoff *bulgogi* at a picnic or dance along to traditional tunes with a clutch of chuckling grannies.

The Arch of Triumph

The huge white granite **Arch of Triumph**, residing at the bottom of Moran Hill, is on almost every tourist itinerary; you may even be taken here before checking in to your hotel. Modelled on the Arc de Triomphe in Paris, but deliberately built a little higher than its French counterpart, it's the largest such structure in the world. The arch was completed in 1982 to commemorate Korea's resistance to Japan, whose occupation ended in 1945. Despite the fact that it was actually Soviet forces that liberated the city, the on-site guide will tell you that **Kim Il-sung** did all the hard work. Though these erroneous contentions are rather absorbing, if you're part of a larger group you may prefer to sidestep the spiel for a stroll around the area. Just a minute's walk away, and easily visible from the arch, is a tremendous **mural** of the Great Leader receiving the adulation of his public, while set further back is the 100,000-seater **Kim Il-sung Stadium**; don't venture too close to the latter, lest you want to receive reprimanding whistles from folk in uniforms. There's also a small **theme park** nearby, which features on some itineraries; the rides are fun, if a little rickety.

Kim Il-sung Square and around

West of the Taedong River is **Kim Il-sung Square**, a huge paved area where the sense of space is heightened by its near-total lack of people. First-time visitors may also get a sense of *déjà vu* – this is the site of the stock North Korean footage of goose-stepping soldiers which is shown whenever the country finds itself in the news (incidentally this act is far from a daily event,

A resident's view of life in Pyongyang

"We in Pyongyang are pretty lucky – life here is much better than in the countryside. As elsewhere, our apartments are provided to us by the government, and we don't pay rent. Most people have a TV and a refrigerator, some have a washing machine, and quite a few now have a computer; these are usually second-hand units from Europe or China. Actually, kids have been getting into chatting on the Internet, but it's not possible to contact people outside the country, and sometimes the whole network goes down for weeks or even years at a time, the same as for our mobile telephones. We all hate it when that happens.

"I guess our educational system is pretty similar to other countries. We have club activities after lessons, usually sports, and we can study foreign languages at school – English is the most popular, followed by Russian. One thing people won't get outside our country is teachings on the 'Three Revolutions': these are ideology – that's the most important one – culture and technology. Kim Jong-il says that technology is important if we are to progress so lots of people want to study it at university now. Kim Il-sung University is the biggest, with maybe 12,000 students, but there are other ones around the country; the one in Wonsan, for example, is pretty famous for economics. Military service is compulsory for boys, who have to do three years, and girls can join as volunteers.

"In my free time I like to listen to music, and sing it too, of course. Like lots of people I go to a sports club – football, basketball and fishing are popular, but I like volleyball more, so that's what I do. It's also pretty common to rent movies; we can get American films from the rental store as well as local ones, but nothing really political. Men like to drink beer – they get five litres per month from the government in vouchers, and often go to the bar straight after work. This makes them drunk before they come home for dinner, which makes a lot of our women really angry."

Anon

and not even an annual one – it's only performed on important military anniversaries). State propaganda peers down into the square from all sides in the form of oversized pictures and slogans. The message on the party headquarters on the north side of the square reads "Long live the Democratic People's Republic of Choson!" Others say "With the Revolutionary Spirit of Paekdu Mountain!" and "Follow the Three Revolutionary Flags!" – the red flags in question read "history", "skill" and "culture", and are being reared away from by Chollima, a winged horse of Korean legend. Visible to the east across the river is the soaring flame-like tip of the Juche Tower (see below). At the west of the square is the **Grand People's Study House**, effectively an oversized library and one of few buildings in the city to be built with anything approaching a traditional style, a little ironic, considering its status as a vault of re-written history. This isn't on all tour itineraries, but those given the chance to enter will doubtless be impressed by the super-modern filing system.

Tower of the Juche Idea

While the Mansudae Grand Monument was Kim Il-Sung's 60th birthday gift to himself, the **Tower of the Juche Idea** is what he unwrapped when he turned 70 in 1982, a giant, 150-metre-high candle topped with a 20-metre red flame, rising up from its site on the banks of the Taedong River. Named after the North Korean take on communist theory (see box below) it's the tallest granite tower in the world, and one of the few points of light in Pyongyang's

The Juche idea

A local take on Marxist–Leninist theory, **Juche** is the official state ideology of the DPRK, and a system that informs the decision-making of each and every one of its inhabitants. Though Kim Il-sung claims the credit for its invention the basic precepts were formed by *yangban* scholars in the early twentieth century, created as a means of asserting Korean identity during the Japanese occupation. The basic principle is one of **self-reliance** – both nation and individual are intended to be responsible for their own destiny. Kim Il-sung introduced Juche as the official ideology in the early 1970s, and the doctrines were put to paper in 1982 by his son Kim Jong-il in a book entitled *On the Juche Idea*. Foreign-language editions are available at hotels in Pyongyang, though the core principle of the treatise is as follows:

...man is a social being with independence, creativity and consciousness, which are his social attributes formed and developed in the course of social life and through the historic process of development; these essential qualities enable man to take a position and play a role as master of the world.

As one local puts it, "Juche is more centred around human benefit than material gain relative to the theories of Marx or Lenin. There's no time for asking why we don't have something, or excusing yourself because of this absence... if the state doesn't provide something, make it yourself!" In spite of this apparent confidence, there are some pretty serious flaws and contradictions evident in the DPRK's pursuit of its own creed – the country preaches self-reliance but has long been heavily dependent on the international community for aid, and though Juche Man is said to be free to make his own decisions, **democracy** remains little more than a component part of the state's official title.

Despite the all-too-apparent failings of North Korea's interpretation of the theory, Juche managed to sow seeds abroad – Pol Pot and Ceaucescu borrowed heavily from the philosophy, though neither achieved much success, a lesson for Kim Jong-il, perhaps.

dim night sky. A kind of socialist version of Cheomseongdae in the South (see p.208), but without the astrological capabilities, it is made out of 25,550 granite slabs – one for each day of Kim's 70 years.

It's possible to take a **lift** to the torch-level for stupendous views over Pyongyang. You could choose to stay behind, citing a fear of heights, for a guide-free walk around the area: the two guides will have to go up with your group, leaving you alone to wander the riverside park; given the slug-like speed of the lift, this may be some time.

The Children's Palace

Behind their strained faces, you sense all the concentration that goes into playing the music, and especially into trying to keep up those Miss World smiles...It's all so cold and sad. I could cry.

Guy Delisle, *Pyongyang*

The **Children's Palace** showcases the impressive talents of some of the most gifted youths in the country – you'll be escorted from room to room, taking in displays of everything from volleyball and gymnastics to embroidery and song. For some visitors, this by-product of Kim Il-sung's contention that "children are the treasure of the nation" is a sweet and pleasant part of the tour, for others the atmosphere can be more than a little depressing – while there's no denying the abilities of the young performers, it's hard to dispel the level of intensity required in their training. At the end of the tour is an impressive but brutally regimental **performance** of song and dance in the large auditorium, showcasing North Korean expertise to foreign guests, but many leave wondering what the country would be like if similar efforts were put into more productive educational pursuits.

Pyongyang subway

Many visitors find it incredible that a country as poor as North Korea has something as decadent as a functioning **subway system**, one that even has two lines; in fact, there are likely to be several more for government-only use, though details are kept well under wraps. Only two of the sixteen known stations – **Puhung** and **Yonggwang** – are open to foreign visitors, a fact that has led some reporters to declare that no more exist. Some even claim that North Korean passengers on the line are nothing more than actors who shuffle onto the trains, only to reappear minutes later on the other platform, but a visit of your own should put paid to these notions.

The first thing you'll notice is the length of the escalator; Pyongyang has some of the world's **deepest** subway platforms, said to be reinforced and deep enough to provide protection to the Pyongyang masses in the event of a military attack. Marble-floored, with sculpted columns and bathed in the dull glow of low-wattage chandelier lights, these platforms maintain a surprisingly opulent appearance, and are backed by large socialist realist mosaics. The trains themselves are a mix of Chinese rejects and relics of the Berlin U-Bahn, the latter evident in the occasional bit of ageing German graffiti, and all feature the obligatory Kim pictures at the end of each train carriage.

The journey between stations doesn't last long, but will give you the chance to make a little contact with the locals: a smile or an "*annyeong-haseyo*" won't go amiss. Photos of the subway or the boards that mark it from the outside – "*ji*" in Korean text, short for *jihacheol* – go down particularly well with South Koreans, most of whom are totally unaware that such a facility exists in the North. Visit Ⓦ www.pyongyang-metro.com for more information on the line.

▲ Pyongyang subway

USS Pueblo

A piece of history floating on the Taedong River, the **USS Pueblo** would count as a Pyongyang must-see if it weren't for the fact that you'll probably have to see it anyway. On January 23, 1968, this small American research ship was boarded and captured by KPA forces in the East Sea – whether it was in North Korean or international waters at the time depends on whom you ask. The reasons for the attack, in which one crew-member was killed, also vary from one side to the other – the North Koreans made accusations of espionage, the Americans contend that Stalin wanted an on-board encryptor – as do accounts of what happened to the 83 captured crew during their enforced stay in the DPRK; the misty cloak of propaganda makes it hard to verify tales of torture, but they're equally difficult to reject. What's known for sure is that Pyongyang spent months waiting for an **apology** which the Americans deferred for months, and it was only on December 23 that the crew finally crossed to safety over Panmunjom's "Bridge of No Return" (p.161).

During your visit you'll be ushered into the ship, part of which has been converted into a tiny cinema, and shown a short **documentary**. This is utterly fascinating, and states the North Korean position on the matter in no ambiguous terms, showing how well the prisoners were kept, then reprimanding these "brazen-faced American aggressors" for failing to turn around to salute their captors on crossing at Panmunjom. A uniformed "soldier" will then escort you through the rest of the ship, pointing out bullet holes and the like, before escorting you back onto dry land.

The museums

North Korean tours once revolved around Pyongyang's surprisingly large number of **museums**. Tour companies have mercifully wised up to the fact that most travellers would prefer simply to stroll down a city street than be bombarded with hours of national triumph and foreign aggression, and consequently the average number of museum visits has been pared down to two or three. There are few better windows into the "official" national mentality, or what's taught at school across the land.

If you have any say in your daily schedule, make sure that it includes a visit to the **Victorious Fatherland Liberation War Museum**. Right from the huge, cheery mural at the entrance, you'll be subjected to the most fervent America-bashing that you're likely to hear in North Korea; the terms "aggressors", "imperialists" and "imperialist aggressors" are used avidly. Inside you'll be escorted through rooms filled with photographs and documents relating to atrocities said to have been inflicted on Korea by the Americans, many of which were apparently seized after the liberation of Seoul during the Korean War. The important bits on the documents are underlined, which helps to steer the eye away from some suspiciously shoddy English – however obvious forgeries may be (and there are some), don't go making any claims, and just treat it as part of the game. The tour then continues to the basement, which is full of war machinery including several bullet-ravaged planes, a torpedo ship and some captured guns and trucks. Of most interest is a **helicopter** shot down over North Korean territory; next to the vehicle's carcass is an extraordinary photograph of the pilot surrendering next to his dead buddy. From here you then move on to the **panorama room**, a relatively new addition where the scenery slowly revolves around a central platform. This depiction of a battle in the Daejeon area is spectacular, having been rendered on an apparently seamless 15m x 132m length of canvas.

Mangyongdae

A visit to **Mangyongdae** – the purported **birthplace** of Kim Il-sung on April 15, 1912 – is almost guaranteed to feature on your itinerary. Despite the lack of things to see, the park-like area is pretty in a dull sort of way, and kept as modest as possible, its wooden buildings surrounded by greenery and meandering paths providing a nod to Kim's peasant upbringing. You'll likely be offered spring water from the on-site well, which supposedly gets visitors "into the revolutionary spirit of things". The nearby funfair is marginally more interesting, and features a coconut shy where you can hurl projectiles at, as the guide puts it, "imperialist American swine".

Eating and drinking

As with accommodation, all your **dining** requirements will be sorted out in advance. North Koreans seem to think that foreigners will only enjoy their meal if they're rotating slowly – both the *Koryo* and *Yanggakdo* hotels have revolving restaurants.

You usually have breakfast in your hotel, and on some days will also have lunch or dinner there. Both the volume and the quality of food will depend on the prevailing food situation at the time of your visit – experienced diplomats suggest that the fare seems to improve when big groups or important folk are in town.

Most meals are served at your hotel, but contrary to reports other **restaurants** do exist in Pyongyang; in fact, there's one on almost every block, but many are camouflaged by their lack of signage and rather hard to spot (the locals know where to go and almost all are off-limits to outsiders, so there's no need for a sign). The best restaurants are closed to all but foreigners and the party elite, and you'll probably get to see a different one on each day of your stay: two of the most popular are *Pyongyang Best Barbequed Duck*, which serves this and not much else, and the *Chongnyu*, which specializes in Korean hotpot. Those staying

▲ Victorious Fatherland Liberation War memorial

at the *Koyro* should ask to be taken to *Byolmori*, a nearby café-cum-bakery part-owned by a Swiss group – in addition to some tasty snacks, they serve what's undoubtedly the best coffee in the country. Those visiting in warmer months may spot ladies selling **ice cream** from tiny booths. There's usually only one variety – a creamy stick-bar called an Eskimo – but the real appeal for many is the opportunity to get some North Korean money as change (see p.392).

Drinking can be one of Pyongyang's most unexpected delights – while you won't exactly be painting the town red, many travellers stagger to bed from the hotel bar absolutely sozzled every single night of their stay (and then have to get up at 7am to catch the tour bus). The two most interesting bars in terms of clientele – the *Diplo* and the *Random Access Club* – are in the diplomatic district and therefore off-limits to most tourists, but the *Koryo* and *Yanggakdo* offer a surprising range of drinking options. Both are topped with revolving restaurants that become bars of an evening – perfect for a nightcap with a view of Pyongyang's galaxy of faint lights. The ground-floor bar in the *Yanggakdo* churns out draught beer and stout from an on-site microbrewery – try to avoid the pitiful sight of Lewis, the unfortunate trapped turtle at the entrance. The nightclubs found in the bowels of most hotels are usually dead, though you may strike it lucky if there's a big Russian or Chinese group in town; usually more lively are the hotel karaoke rooms, the terminus of many an evening.

Other sights in the DPRK

Most of the country is totally closed off to foreign visitors, but even the shortest tour itinerary is likely to contain at least one sight outside Pyongyang. The most common trip is to **Panmunjom** in the DMZ, via **Kaesong**, the closest city to the border, but there are other popular excursions to **Paekdusan**, the mythical birthplace of the Korean nation and its highest peak, and the wonderful "Diamond Mountains" of **Kumgangsan** near the South Korean border. If you do venture further than Pyongyang, you'll witness poverty-stricken North Korea at first hand – in the capital there's little to remind you of its Third World status, but outside things are extremely different, and this is only the poverty you're allowed to see. You'll also notice a notable change in the locals' reaction to your presence: whereas a smile or wave may be reciprocated in Pyongyang, elsewhere you may invoke trepidation.

Kaesong

Other than Pyongyang, **KAESONG** is usually the only North Korean city that foreign travellers get to see. From the capital, it's an easy ninety-minute trip south along the traffic-free **Reunification Highway**; the road actually continues all the way to Seoul, just 80km away, though it's blocked by the DMZ a few kilometres south of Kaesong. Its proximity to the border means the surrounding area is armed to bursting and crawling with soldiers, and it's hardly surprising that Kaesong's long-suffering citizens often come across as a little edgy. The city itself is drab and grimy in comparison with Pyongyang, but offers a far more accurate reflection of "typical" North Korean life.

Despite the palpable tension, Kaesong – romanized as "Gaeseong" in the South – is actually a place of considerable history: this was once the capital of the **Goryeo dynasty**, which ruled over the peninsula from 936 to 1392, though thanks to wholesale destruction in the Korean War, you'll see precious little evidence of this today. One exception is **Sonjuk Bridge**, which was built in the early thirteenth century; it was here that an eponymous Goryeo loyalist was assassinated as his dynasty fell. The one sight guaranteed to catch the eye is somewhat more modern – a huge **statue of Kim Il-sung**. One of the most prominent such statues in the country, and even visible from the Reunification Highway on the way to Panmunjom, it's illuminated at night come what may owing to its own generator, which enables it to surf the crest of any power shortages that afflict the rest of the city.

There are a few officially sanctioned sights in Kaesong's surrounding countryside. West of the city on the road to Pyongyang is the tomb of the unfortunately named **Wang Kon**, the first leader of Goryeo and the man responsible for moving the dynasty's capital to Kaesong, his home town. In the South, he's more commonly known as King Taejo and his decorated grass-mound tomb is

▲ Kaesong

similar to those that can be found in Seoul (see p.114). Further west is another tomb, this one belonging to **Wang Jon**. Also known as King Kongmin, he ruled (1351–74) during Mongol domination of the continent; in keeping with the traditions of the time, he married a Mongol princess and was buried alongside her – the tiger statues surrounding the tomb represent the Goryeo dynasty, while the sheep are a nod to the Mongol influence. North of Wang Kon's tomb is **Pakyon**, a forest waterfall whose surrounding include a fortress gate and a beautiful temple.

Groups heading to or from Panmunjom often have a **lunch** stop in Kaesong; the unnamed restaurant favoured by most tour leaders lays on a superb spread, apportioned into little golden bowls. It's also possible to **stay** overnight in Kaesong, and this is highly recommended – the *Kaesong Folk Hotel* is a parade of traditional rooms running off a courtyard, the complex dotted with swaying trees and bisected by a peaceful stream. The rooms are basic, and sometimes fall victim to power outages, but it's a unique experience with an entirely different vibe from the big hotels in Pyongyang.

Panmunjom

Do I hate Americans? Not really – I don't like the policies of their government or military, but that's no reason to hate the people. Our Dear Leader himself has American friends – have you heard of Billy Graham? We don't have many Americans on this tour, but I always make a special effort to please them; in fact, I stay in touch with a couple as pen-pals. One of my dreams is that Korea will re-unify, and then I can meet them again, either here or in their own country.

North Korean soldier, Joint Security Area

The village of **PANMUNJOM** sits bang in the middle of the **Demilitarized Zone** that separates North and South Korea (see p.159 for more information on how it can be reached from the south, where it's referred to as Panmunjeom). You'll see much the same from the north, but with the propaganda reversed – all of a sudden it was the US Army that started the Korean War and Kim Il-sung who won it. Interestingly, many visitors note that the cant is just as strong on the American side (though usually more balanced).

The route to Panmunjom follows the Reunification Highway from Kaesong. Your first stop will be at the **KPA guardpost**, which sits just outside the northern barrier of the DMZ; the southern flank and the democracy beyond are just 4km away, though it feels far further than that. Here you'll see a wonderful hand-painted picture of a boy and girl from each side savouring unification, but for some reason the guards aren't keen on people taking photos of it. After being given a short presentation of the site by a local soldier, it's back onto your bus for the ride to the DMZ itself – note the huge slabs of concrete at the sides of the road, ready to be dropped to block the way of any invading tanks (this same system is in place on the other side). A short way into the DMZ is the **Armistice Hall**, which was cobbled together at incredible speed by North Korean soldiers to provide a suitable venue for the signing of the Korean Armistice Agreement, a document which brought about a ceasefire to the Korean War on July 27, 1953. Tucked away in a corner is what is said to be the weapon from the famed "Axe Murder Incident", an incident for which North Korea claims little responsibility (see box, p.164).

From the Armistice Hall you are taken to the **Joint Security Area** (see p.160), where Panmun Hall – which, whatever the American soldiers on the other side might say, is a real, multi-level building of more than a couple of yards in depth – looks across the border at a South Korean building of similar size. You may even see a few tourists being escorted around. From here, you are taken into one of the halls that straddle the official line of control, and are permitted to take a few heavily guarded steps into South Korean territory. The whole experience is bizarre, but utterly fascinating, and an oddly tranquil place, despite its status as one of the world's most dangerous border points.

Many of the same **DMZ rules** apply, whichever side you're coming from – dress smartly, refrain from gesticulating to the other side, and don't go off on your own. It's possible to pop briefly across the official border, but it almost goes without saying that you won't be allowed to go any further. If you time it right, you could even hit the border from both sides within a few days, and stand in almost exactly the same square yard without having had any hope of crossing immediately to the other side: such is the nature of the Korean conflict.

Kumgangsan

Before partition, the **KUMGANGSAN** mountain range – which sits just north of the DMZ on Korea's east coast – was widely considered to be the most beautiful on the peninsula. The DPRK's relative inaccessibility has ensured that this remains the case. Spectacular crags and spires of rock tower over a skirt of pine-clad foothills, its pristine lakes and waterfalls adding to a richly forested beauty rivalled only by Seoraksan just across the border (see p.178). There are said to be over twelve thousand pinnacles, though the principal peak is Birobong, which rises to 1638m above sea level.

Kumgangsan can be visited as part of a North Korean tour, though the overwhelming majority visit on **a trip from South Korea** (where it's spelt "Geumgangsan", but pronounced the same); other than the few steps across the border allowed at the DMZ, this is your only opportunity to get into North Korean territory from the South, and visa restrictions mean that it's usually the only way in for Americans and South Koreans. Tours aren't cheap, and they don't provide as great a window into North Korean life as might be expected – while locals act as guards, guides and hotel employees, the area can almost be viewed as the "Republic of Hyundai", having been leased for controlled tourism by the South Korean business behemoth (see box, p.414). Security is tight, and though most visitors enjoy themselves, some come away feeling that

The Hyundai Asan scandal

In 1998 a section of the Kumgangsan mountains in North Korea was bought on a long-term lease by **Hyundai Asan**, a wing of the gigantic Hyundai corporation which was in charge of various cross-border business ventures. Its head, **Chung Mong-hun** – the son of tycoon Chung Ju-yung, Hyundai's founder – found himself accused of illegally shifting hundreds of millions of dollars to Kim Jong-il's coffers. The secret payments centred around the first summit between the leaders of North and South Korea, which took place in 2000 and eventually landed the South Korean president, Kim Dae-jung, the Nobel Peace Prize; it didn't help that the North seemed to be using at least some of these funds to recommence work on their Yongbyon nuclear reactors. Chung Mong-hun was eventually indicted in what became known as the "Cash-for-summit" scandal; disgraced and heading for prison, he leapt to his death from his high-level office on August 4, 2003.

they've received poor value for money, and little sense that they've just been inside one of the world's most curious countries. Most groups take the stunning hike up to **Sangpaldam**, a collection of lofty pools with astonishingly pure water. It's possible to race up and down in under two hours, but there's precious little reason to do so; on your way up the stream you'll pass waterfall after waterfall, and stop off for traditional North Korean food at *Mongnangwan*, a restaurant surrounded by magnolia trees. Another hike heads up to the cliffs of **Cheonseondae** and **Mangyangdae**, with the former possibly the most scenic point in the whole park.

Most guests stay at the *Hotel Haegeumgang*, though some tours include a few nights at a village with hot springs; regardless of the DPRK's own situation, all visitors pay a lot and are accordingly well fed. **Package tours** can be booked on the main Korean tourist website – go to ⓦenglish.tour2korea.com, then click on "Sightseeing", followed by "North Korea tours". Tours leave most days from Seoul – check the online calendar to be sure – and should be booked at least two weeks in advance; all trips last two nights and three days, though note that on cheaper schedules only one night will be in North Korea. Whereas tourists once boarded a ferry from Sokcho, groups now pierce the DMZ by **bus** on a little-used highway. Tour **prices** vary according to season, with the December–March low around W280,000 rising to over W500,000 during the main Korean holiday windows in July, August and September; at other times of year, figure on around W400,000.

Myohyangsan

Many North Korean package tours include a visit to this pristine area of hills, lakes and waterfalls, located around 150km north of Pyongyang, and about as close as the DPRK comes to a mountain resort. However, the reason for coming here isn't to walk the delightful hiking trails, but to visit the **International Friendship Exhibition** – a colossal display showing the array of presents given to the Kims by overseas well-wishers. After the exhibition you're likely to be taken to see **Pohyonsa**, an eleventh-century temple just a short walk away, and **Ryongmun**, a stalactite-filled limestone cave that burrows for a number of kilometres under the surrounding mountains.

Should your schedule allow for an overnight stay, you're likely to find yourself spending the night at the pyramidal *Hyangsan Hotel*; note that though there's the obligatory top-floor revolving restaurant, the quality of the food is otherwise not quite as high as that in Pyongyang.

The International Friendship Exhibition

The halls of the **International Friendship Exhibition** burrow deep into a mountainside – insurance against any nuclear attacks that come the DPRK's way. Indeed, such is the emphasis on preservation that you'll be forced to don a pair of comically oversized slippers before you enter the halls. The combination of highly polished granite floors and friction-lite footwear makes it incredibly tempting to take off down the corridors like a speed skater, but this would be looked on as a sign of immense disrespect and is therefore cautioned against. Inside the exhibition hall, gifts numbering 200,000 and rising have been arranged in order of country of origin, the evident intention being to convince visitors that Kim Senior and Kim Junior command immense respect all over the world – this is not the place to air any painful truths. Mercifully, you won't have to see all of the presents, though even the officially edited highlights can become a drag.

The first rooms you come to are those dedicated to **Kim Il-sung**. For a time, gifts were pouring in from all over the communist world, including a limousine from Stalin and an armoured train carriage from Chairman Mao. There are also a number of medals, tea sets, pots, cutlery and military arms, as well as more incongruous offerings such as fishing rods and a refrigerator. Next you'll be ushered into a room featuring a life-size **wax statue** of the great man; local visitors bestow on this exhibit all the respect they would on Kim himself, and you'll be required to bow in front of the figure – with piped music echoing all over the room it's a truly surreal experience. The **Kim Jong-il** rooms are less stacked with goodies, and instead feature heavily corporate treats and electronic gadgets. Perhaps most interesting is the **basketball** donated by former American Secretary of State Madeleine Albright, signed by Michael Jordan, of whom Kim is apparently a big fan; on receiving the ball he was said to have been eager to get outside for a quick jam.

Paekdusan

The highest peak on the Korean peninsula at 2744m, the extinct volcano of **PAEKDUSAN** straddles the border between North Korea and China, and is the source of the Tuman and Amnok rivers (Tumen and Yalu in Mandarin) that separate the countries. Within its caldera is a vibrant blue **crater lake** surrounded by a ring of jagged peaks, it's a beguiling place steeped in myth and legend. This was said to be the landing point for **Dangun**, the divine creator of Korea, after his journey from heaven in 2333 BC (see p.420); more recently, it was also the apparent birthplace of **Kim Jong-il**, an event said to have been accompanied by flying white horses, rainbows and the emergence of a new star in the sky. Records seem to suggest that he was born in Soviet Siberia, but who needs history when the myth is so expressive. In fact, "new" history is discovered here from time to time in the form of slogans etched into the mountain's trees, apparently carved during Kim Il-sung's time here as a resistance fighter, and somehow always in keeping with the political beliefs prevailing during their time of discovery. Emblazoned on one of the slopes surrounding the crater lake is the slogan, "Mount Paekdu, sacred mountain of the revolution".

Even with so much historical significance, it's the natural beauty of the place that attracts foreign visitors to Paekdusan. The ring of mountains is cloaked with lush forest, with some pines rising up to over fifty metres in height, and bears, wolves, boar and deer inhabiting the area; it's even home to a small population of **Siberian tigers**, though you're highly unlikely to see any. As long as the weather holds – and at this height, it often doesn't – you may be able to climb

North Korea from the outside

If budgetary constraints or possession of the wrong kind of passport make a trip to North Korea impossible, there are a number of ways to peer into the country from outside.

From South Korea

The two Koreas share a 250km-long border, and though the area around the Demilitarized Zone that separates them is largely off limits, there are a number of vantage points from which you can look across. **DMZ tours from Seoul** are highly popular (see p.160). Itineraries vary, but can include views of the North from an observatory, a trip inside tunnels dug by North Koreans in preparation for an attack on Seoul, as well as the chance to step onto **DPRK territory** in the Joint Security Area. While these excursions are good value for money, you can visit a similar observatory and tunnel for free on a guided tour from the remote town of **Cheorwon** (p.169), and there's another observatory just north of **Sokcho** on the east coast (p.176). It's even possible to take an expensive tour across the border to the gorgeous mountains of **Kumgangsan**; see p.413 for details.

From China

Two Chinese provinces border North Korea. Over one million ethnic Koreans live in Jilin (a city as well as a province) and another 250,000 in Liaoning – the latter even contains an autonomous Korean prefecture, where the mix of communism and poverty make some towns fairly similar in feel to the DPRK.

The large city of **Dandong** is right on the North Korean border, with only the Yalu river ("Amnok" in Korean) separating it from Sinuiju on the other side; those entering North Korea by train will pass through Dandong, and some choose to stop off on their return leg. The two cities offer a rather incredible contrast, with the tall, neon-seared skyscrapers on the Chinese side overlooking poor, low-rise Sinuiju across the river. On Dandong's riverside promenade you'll be able to buy (mostly counterfeit) North Korean banknotes and pin-badges, and protruding from this is the Old Yalu bridge, which comes to an abrupt halt in the middle of the river, its North Korean half having been dismantled. From the promenade, you can also take a boat trip to within a single yard of the North Korean shore, and get just as close from Tiger Mountain, 25km east of the city and the easternmost section of China's famed Great Wall. Although jumping across for a quick picture may appear tempting, note that one foreign traveller foolish enough to do this spent months in a DPRK *gulag* after being snatched by hidden guards.

With the mountain and its crater lake straddling the border, it's also possible to visit **Paekdusan** (p.415) from the Chinese side, a trip highly popular with South Koreans. The simplest approach is to join a tour from Jilin city; this will include all accommodation, entrance fees and transport, though it's possible to chalk much of the distance off on an overnight train from Beijing to Baihe, a village close to the mountain.

to the top of the Korean peninsula by taking a hike to **Jong-il peak**. A cable car also whisks guests down to the lakeside, where you can have a splash in the inviting waters in warmer months.

With Paekdusan being a place of such importance, every person in the country is expected to make the pilgrimage at some point; the journey is usually paid for in full by the government, even though it's well over a day by train from Pyongyang. Foreign tourists wishing to visit must take a **chartered flight** from Pyongyang, and then a car the rest of the way, though due to weather conditions the journey from the capital is usually only possible during warmer months. It's also possible to visit from the Chinese side, as thousands of South Koreans do each year (see box above).

Contexts

Contexts

History

With its two-millennium-long chain of **unbroken regal rule** interspersed by regular fisticuffs the Korean peninsula offers plenty for history buffs to get their teeth into. The country's early beginnings are shrouded in mystery, though events have been well documented since before the birth of Christ, a period when famed **Three Kingdoms** were springing into existence. Replacing Gojoseon – the first known Korean kingdom – these were **Silla**, **Goguryeo** and **Baekje**, three states that jostled for peninsular power for centuries, seeing off other nascent fiefdoms while dealing with the Chinese and Japanese states of the time. Even today, tangible evidence of all three kingdoms can still be seen. It was Silla that eventually prevailed, emerging victorious from a series of battles to bring the peninsula under **unified control**. Infighting and poor governance led to its demise, the slack taken up by the **Goryeo** dynasty, which lasted for almost five hundred years before folding and being replaced by **Joseon** rule. This was to last even longer, but was snuffed out by the Japanese at a time of global turmoil, bringing to an end Korea's succession of well over one hundred kings. World War II ended **Japanese annexation**, after which Korea was split in two in the face of the looming Cold War. There then followed the brutal **Korean War**, and in 1953 the communist north and the capitalist south went their separate ways, each writing their own historical versions of the time, and in the case of North Korea, slewing historical events even prior to partition. The war was never technically brought to an end, and its resolution – either peaceable, or by force – will add the next chapter to Korea's long history.

The beginnings

Remains of *homo erectus* show that the Korean peninsula may have been home to hominids for more than half a million years. The first evidence of habitation can be found in several clusters of Neanderthal sites dating from the Middle Paleolithic period (roughly 100,000–40,000 BC). The assortment of hand axes, scrapers and other tools made of stone and bone hauled from the complexes suggest a **hunter-gatherer** existence, while fish bones, nut shells and burnt

The major historical eras

Gojoseon	*c.*2333 BC to *c.*109 BC
Three Kingdoms	*c.*57 BC to 668 AD
Silla	*c.*57 BC to 668 AD
Goguryeo	*c.*37 BC to 668 AD
Baekje	*c.*18 BC to 660 AD
Unified Silla	668–935
Goryeo	918–1392
Joseon	1392–1910
Japanese colonial period	1910–1945
Republic of Korea	1945 to present day
Democratic People's Republic of Korea	1945 to present day

rice provide further windows on the Korean caveman diet; the presence of carved tigers, leopards and bears on animal bones, as well as drawings, also shows that artistic endeavour on the peninsula goes back a long way. **Neolithic** sites (8000–3000 BC) are far more numerous than those from the Paleolithic era, and in these were found thousands of remnants from the peninsula's transition from the Stone to the Bronze Age. In addition to the use of metal tools, from 7000 BC **pottery** was being produced with distinctive comb-toothed patterns (*jeulmun*) similar to those found in Mongolia and Manchuria. Fired earth also came to play a part in death rituals, a fact made evident by small, shell-like "jars" into which the bodies were placed together with personal belongings; these were then lowered into a pit and covered with earth. An even more distinctive style of burial was to develop, with some tombs covered with large stone slabs known as **dolmen** ("*goindol*" in Korean). Korea is home to over 30,000 burial mounds. Three of the most important sites – Gochang and Hwasun in the Jeolla provinces, and Ganghwado, west of Incheon – have been proclaimed as World Heritage sites by UNESCO. The peninsula's first kingdom was known as Joseon, though is today usually referred to as **Gojoseon** ("Old Joseon") in an effort to distinguish it from the later Joseon period (1392–1910). Its origins are obscure to say the least; most experts agree that it got going in 2333 BC under the leadership of **Dangun**, who has since become the subject of one of Korea's most cherished myths (see box below). Joseon initially functioned as a loose federation of fiefdoms covering not only the Korean peninsula but large swathes of Manchuria too. By 500 BC it had become a single, highly organized dominion, even drawing praise from Confucius and other Chinese sages. Accounts of the fall of Joseon are also rather vague, but large swathes of its Manchurian population were squeezed onto the Korean peninsula during the Chinese **Warring States Period** (470–221 BC), and it seems likely to have fallen victim to a nascent Han dynasty in 109 BC. Joseon's historical name lives on: North Korea continues to refer to its land as such (and South Korea as Namjoseon, or "South Joseon"), while many South Korean tourist brochures use "The Land of Morning Calm" – a literal translation of the term – as a national motto.

The legend of Dangun

The Korean peninsula has played host to some of the world's longest-running monarchies, and such regal durability has made for comprehensive records. However, much of what's known about the years preceding the Three Kingdoms period remains obscure, and Korea has resorted to mythology to fill in the gaps of its creation – primarily the legend of **Dangun**.

The story begins with **Hwanin**, the "Lord of Heaven", whose son **Hwanung** desired to live as a mortal being on Earth. Hwanin set his son down on Mount Paekdu (located in present-day North Korea) together with an army of 3000 disciples. Hwanung and his tribe took charge of the locals, and fostered celestial ideals of law, art and social structure. Two of his pets – a bear and a tiger – prayed to Hwanung that they be made human, just as he had been; they were each given twenty cloves of garlic and a bundle of mugwort, and told to survive on nothing else for a hundred days, before being sent to a cave. The tiger failed the challenge, but the bear prevailed, and on being made human soon bore Hwanung's child, Dangun, who went on to found **Joseon** in 2333 BC.

In 1993 North Korean officials announced that they had found Dangun's tomb in a location close to Pyongyang; unfortunately, they've been unwilling to share this evidence with the rest of the world.

The Three Kingdoms period

By 109 BC, after the fall of Gojoseon, power on the peninsula was decentralized to half-a-dozen fiefdoms, the most powerful of which – **Silla**, **Goguryeo** and **Baekje** – went on to become the Three Kingdoms. Though exact details regarding their beginnings are just as sketchy as those surrounding Gojoseon – two of the inaugurators are said to have hatched from eggs – this period saw the first definitive drawing of borders in Korean history, although it must be noted that none of them became fully-fledged kingdoms for a couple of centuries, each existing initially as a loose confederation of fiefdoms. Several of those jostling for power after Gojoseon's demise are not included under the Three Kingdoms banner; most notably, these include the states of **Gaya**, which was absorbed by Silla, and **Buyeo**, parts of which were sucked up by Goguryeo and Baekje. The kingdom of **Tamna**, isolated on Jeju Island, also came under Baekje control.

Territorial borders shifted continuously as all three kingdoms jostled for power, and a number of fortresses went up across the land, many of which can still be seen today. Outside forces were occasionally roped in to help; interestingly, Baekje was closely aligned with Japan for much of its time, while Silla sided with the Chinese Tang dynasty, despite their positions on the "wrong" sides of the peninsula. Because of these close ties with China and Japan, Korea acted as a conduit for a number of customs imported from the continent: Chinese characters came to be used with the Korean language and the import and gradual flourishing of **Buddhism** saw temples popping up all over the peninsula. However, it was **Confucianism**, another Chinese import, that provided the social building blocks, with a number of educational academies supplying the *yangban* scholars at the head of the aristocracy. Great advances were made in the arts, particularly with regard to jewellery and pottery; wonderful relics of the time have been discovered in their thousands from the grassy hill-tombs of dead kings and other formerly sacred sites. After **centuries of warring** that saw the kingdoms continually changing allegiance to each other and to Chinese and Japanese dynasties, matters finally came to a head in the mid-seventh century. In 660, supplemented by Tang forces from China, Silla **triumphed in battle** against Baekje, whose people leapt to their death from a cliff in the city of Buyeo. Muyeol died just a year later, but within a decade his son King Munmu defeated Goguryeo, setting the scene for a first-ever **unified rule** on the peninsula.

Goguryeo

The kingdom of **Goguryeo** covered the whole of present-day North Korea, a large chunk of Chinese Manchuria and much of what is now Gangwon-do in the South, making it by far the largest of the Three Kingdoms by territory. Because of its location, the majority of Goguryeo's relics are a little harder to come by today than those from the Baekje or Silla kingdoms, and the history even more vague; most guesses place the inauguration of the first Goguryeo king, Dongmyeong, at 37 BC. At this point Goguryeo was still paying tax and tribute to China, but when the **Han dynasty** started to weaken in the third century, Goguryeo advanced and occupied swathes of territory; they eventually came to rule over an area (much of which is now in the Chinese region of Dongbei) almost three times the size of the present-day Korean peninsula. Baekje and Silla forces mounted sporadic attacks from the south, and the

Chinese Tang invaded from the north, squeezing Goguryeo towards the Tuman and Anmok rivers that mark North Korea's present boundary. The Tang also provided pressure from the south by allying with the Silla dynasty, and when this **Tang–Silla coalition** defeated Baekje in 660, the fall of Goguryeo was inevitable; it was finally snuffed out in 668.

Baekje

The **Baekje** dynasty, which controlled the southwest, was created as the result of great movements of people on the western side of the Korean peninsula. **Buyeo**, a smaller state not considered one of the Three Kingdoms, was pushed southward by the nascent kingdom of Goguryeo, and some elements decided to coalesce around a new leader – **Onjo**, the son of Dongmyeong, the first king of Goguryeo. Jealous of his brother's inheritance of that kingdom, Onjo proclaimed his own dynasty in 18 BC. Baekje is notable for its production of fine jewellery, which exhibited more restraint than that found in the other kingdoms, a fact often attributed to the dynasty's relatively early adoption of Buddhism as a state religion. Evidence of Baekje's close relationship with the **Japanese kingdom of Wa** can still be seen today – the lacquered boxes, folding screens, immaculate earthenware and intricate jewellery of Japan are said to derive from the influence of Baekje artisans. Unfortunately for Baekje, the Wa did not provide such protection as the Chinese Tang dynasty gave Silla, and much of its later history was spent conceding territory to Goguryeo. The capital shifted south from a location near present-day Seoul to Ungjin (now known as Gongju), then south again to Sabi (now Buyeo); after one final battle, fought in 660 against a Tang–Silla coalition, Baekje's small remaining population chose death over dishonour, and committed suicide from Sabi's riverside fortress.

Silla

Although it held the smallest territory of the Three Kingdoms, in the southeast, and was for centuries the most peaceable, it was the **Silla** dynasty that defeated Baekje and Goguryeo to rule over the whole peninsula. Unlike its competitors, it only had one dynastic capital – Gyeongju – and many of the riches accumulated in almost a millennium of power (including over two hundred years as the capital of the whole peninsula) can still be seen today.

Silla's first king – Hyeokgeose – was crowned in 57 BC, but it was not until the sixth century AD that things got interesting. At this time, Silla accepted Buddhism as its state religion (the last of the Three Kingdoms to do so), and created a Confucian "bone rank" system in which people's lives were governed largely by heredity: Buddhism was used to sate spiritual needs, and Confucianism as a regulator of society. Following threats from the Japanese kingdom of Wa, they also began a rapid build-up of military strength; under the rule of King Jinheung (540–76) they absorbed the neighbouring **Gaya** confederacy, and started to nibble away at the other neighbouring kingdoms. Initially they sided with Baekje to attack Goguryeo, a dynasty already weakened by internal strife and pressure from the Chinese Tang to the north; a century later, Silla turned the tables on Baekje by allying with the **Tang**, then used the same alliance to finish off Goguryeo to the north and bring the Korean peninsula under unified rule. See p.199 for more information about Silla times.

Unified Silla

Following the quickfire defeats of its two competitor kingdoms in the 660s, the **Silla dynasty** gave rise to the Korean peninsula's first ever unification, keeping Gyeongju as the seat of power This was, however, no easy matter: small pockets of Baekje and Goguryeo resistance lingered on, and a new (perhaps necessarily) nationalistic fervour developed by the king meant that the Chinese Tang – allies previously so crucial to Silla – had to be driven out, an action that also sent a strong "stay away" message to would-be Japanese invaders. Silla also had to contend with **Balhae** to the north; this large but unwieldy successor state to Goguryeo claimed back much of that kingdom's former territory, and set about establishing favourable relationships with nearby groups to the north.Once the dust had settled, the Chinese officially accepted the dynasty in exchange for regular tributes paid to Tang emperors; King Seongdeok (ruled 702–37) did much of the work, convincing the Tang that his kingdom would be much more useful as an ally than as a rival. Silla set about cultivating a peninsular **sense of identity**, and the pooling of ideas and talent saw the eighth century become a high-water mark of artistic development, particularly in metalwork and earthenware.This time also saw temple design reach elaborate heights, particularly at Bulguksa, built near Gyeongju in 751. Rulers stuck to a rigidly Confucian "bone rank" system, which placed strict limits on what an individual could achieve in life, based almost entirely on their genetic background. Though it largely succeeded in keeping the proletariat quiet, this highly centralized system was to lead to Silla's demise.

Decline and fall

The late eighth century and most of the ninth were characterized by **corruption and in-fighting** at the highest levels of Silla society. Kings' reigns tended to be brief and bloody – the years from 836 to 839 alone saw five kings on the throne, the result of power struggles, murder and enforced suicide. Tales of regal immorality trickled down to the peasant class, leading to a number of **rebellions**; these increased in size and number as regal power over the countryside waned, eventually enveloping Silla in a state of perpetual civil war. With the Silla king reduced to little more than a figurehead, the former kingdoms of Baekje and Goguryeo were resurrected (now known as "**Hubaekje**" and "**Taebong**" respectively). Silla shrunk back beyond its Three Kingdoms-era borders, and after a power struggle Taebong took control of the peninsula; in 935 at Gyeongju's Anapji Pond, King Gyeongsun ceded control of his empire in a peaceful transfer of power to Taebong leader **Wang Geon**, who went on to become Taejo, the first king of the Goryeo dynasty.

The Goryeo dynasty

Having grown from a mini-kingdom known as Taebong, one of the many battling for power following the collapse of Silla control, it was the name of the Goryeo dynasty that eventually gave rise to the English term "Korea". It began life in 918 under the rule of **Taejo**, a powerful leader who needed less than two decades to bring the whole peninsula under his control. One of his daughters was to marry Gyeongsun, the last king of Silla, and Taejo himself to wed a Silla queen, two telling examples of the new king's desire to cultivate a sense of national unity; he was even known to give positions of authority to known enemies. Relations with China and Japan were good, and the kingdom became ever more prosperous.

Following the fall of Silla, Taejo moved the national capital to his home town, Kaesong, a city in present-day North Korea. He and successive leaders also changed some of the bureaucratic systems that had contributed to Silla's downfall: power was centralized in the king but devolved to the furthest reaches of his domain, and even those without aristocratic backgrounds could, in theory, reach lofty governmental positions via a system of state-run examinations. Despite the Confucian social system, **Buddhism** continued to function as the state religion: the *Tripitaka Koreana* – a set of over 80,000 wooden blocks carved with doctrine – was completed in 1251, and now resides in Haeinsa temple. This was not the only remarkable example of Goryeo ingenuity: 1377 saw the creation of *Jikji*, the world's first book printed with movable metal type (now in Paris, and the subject of a tug-of-war with the French government), and repeated refinements in the pottery industry saw Korean produce attain a level of quality only bettered in China. In fact, despite great efforts, some **pottery techniques** perfected in Goryeo times remain a mystery today, perhaps never to be replicated.

The wars

Though the Goryeo borders as set out by King Taejo are almost identical to those that surround the Korean peninsula today, they were witness to numerous skirmishes and invasions. Notable among these were the **Khitan Wars** of the tenth and eleventh centuries, fought against proto-Mongol groups of the Chinese Liao dynasty. The Khitan had defeated Balhae just before the fall of Silla, and were attempting to gain control over the whole of China as well as the Korean peninsula, but three great invasions failed to take Goryeo territory, and a peace treaty was eventually signed. Two centuries later came the **Mongol hordes**; the Korean peninsula was part of the Eurasian landmass, and therefore a target for the great Khaans. Under the rule of Ögedei Khaan, the first invasion came in 1231, but it was not until the sixth campaign – which ended in 1248 – that Goryeo finally became a vassal state, a series of forced marriages effectively making its leaders part of the Mongol royal family. This lasted almost a century, before **King Gongmin** took advantage of a weakening Chinese–Mongol Yuan dynasty (founded by Kublai Khaan) to regain independence.

The Mongol annexation came at a great human cost, one echoed in a gradual worsening of Goryeo's economy and social structure. Gongmin made an attempt at reform, purging the top ranks of those he felt to be pro-Mongol, but this instilled fear of yet more change into the *yangban* elite: in conjunction with a series of decidedly non-Confucian love-triangles and affairs with young boys, this was to lead to his murder. His young and unprepared successor, King U, was pushed into battle with the Chinese Ming dynasty; Joseon's General **Yi Seong-gye** led the charge, but fearful of losing his soldiers he stopped at the border and returned to Seoul, forcing the abdication of the king, and putting U's young son Chang on the throne. The General decided that he was not yet happy with the arrangement, and had both U and Chang executed (the latter just 8 years old at the time); after one more failed attempt at putting the right puppet king on the throne, he decided to take the mantle himself, and in 1392 declared himself King Taejo, the first leader of the Joseon dynasty.

The Joseon dynasty

The **Joseon era** started off much the same as the Goryeo dynasty had almost five centuries beforehand, with a militaristic king named **Taejo** on the throne, a name that translates as "The Grand Ancestor". Joseon was to last even longer, with a full 27 kings ruling from 1392 until the Japanese annexation in 1910. Taejo moved the capital from Kaesong to **Seoul**, and immediately set about entrenching his power with a series of mammoth projects; the first few years of his reign saw the wonderful palace of Gyeongbokgung, the ancestral shrines of Jongmyo and a gate-studded city wall go up. His vision was quite astonishing – the chosen capital and its palace and shrine remain to this day, together with sections of the wall. More grand palaces would go up in due course, with another four at some point home to the royal throne. From the start of the dynasty, Buddhism declined in power, and **Confucianism** permeated society yet further in its stead. Joseon's social system became even more hierarchical in nature, with the king and other royalty at the top, and the hereditary **yangban** class of scholars and aristocrats just beneath, then various levels of employment towards the servants and slaves at the bottom of the pile. All of these social strata were governed by heredity, but the *yangban* became ever more powerful as the dynasty progressed, gradually starting to undermine the power of the king. They were viewed as a world apart by the commoners, and placed great emphasis on study and the arts. Only the *yangban* had access to such education as could foster literacy in a country that wrote with Chinese characters. In the 1440s **King Sejong** (reigned 1418–50) devised **Hangeul**, a new and simple local script that all classes could read and write; the *yangban* were not fond of this, and it was banned at the beginning of the sixteeth century, lying largely dormant until beached by waves of nationalist sentiment created by the end of Japanese annexation in 1945.

The Japanese invasions

In 1592, under the command of feared warlord **Hideyoshi**, Japan set out to conquer the Ming dynasty, with China a stepping stone towards possible domination of the whole Asian continent. The Korean peninsula had the misfortune to be both in the way and loyal to the Ming, and after King Seonjo refused to allow Japanese troops safe passage, Hideyoshi mustered all his military's power and unloaded the lot at Korea. After two relatively peaceable centuries, the Joseon dynasty was ill-prepared for such an assault, and within a month the Japanese had eaten up most of the peninsula; the advance was halted with forces from a Ming dynasty keen to defend its territory.

By the time of the second main wave of attacks in 1597, Korean **Admiral Yi Sun-shin** had been able to better prepare Korea's southern coastline, now protected by a number of fortresses. The Japanese found themselves losing battle after battle, undone by Admiral Yi's "**turtle ships**", vessels proclaimed by Koreans as the world's first armoured warships.

The "Hermit Kingdom"

The Japanese attacks – together with the dynastic transfer from Ming to Qing in China in the 1640s, which led to Joseon becoming a vassal state forced to spend substantial sums paying tribute to the emperors in Beijing – prompted Korea to turn inwards; it became known as the "**Hermit Kingdom**", one of which outsiders knew little, and saw even less. One exception was a Dutch ship which crashed off Jeju Island in 1653 en route to Japan; the survivors were kept prisoner for thirteen years but finally managed to escape; the accounts of **Hendrick Hamel** provided the western world with one of its first windows into isolationist Korea.

The Dutch prisoners had entered a land in which corruption and factionalism were rife, one that achieved little social or economic stability until the rule of **King Yeongjo** (1724–76), who authorized a purge of crooked officials. In 1767, inside the grounds of Changgyeonggung palace, he forced Sado – his son and the country's crown prince – into a rice basket, locked the flap and left him inside to starve rather than let the country fall into his hands. Sado's son **Jeongjo** came to the throne on Yeongjo's death in 1776; he went on to become one of the most revered of Korea's kings, instigating top-to-bottom reform to wrench power from the *yangban* elite, and allowing for the creation of a small middle class. The lot of the poor man gradually improved.

The end of isolation

Following Japan's **opening up** to foreign trade in the 1860s (the "Meiji Restoration"), Korea found itself under pressure to do likewise, not just from the Japanese but from the United States and the more powerful European countries – warships were sent from around the globe to ensure agreement. Much of the activity occurred on and around the island of Ganghwado, just west of Seoul: the French occupied the isle but failed with advances on the mainland in 1866, their battle fought partly as retaliation for the murder of several of their missionaries in Korea. Five years later, and in the same location, the Americans also attempted to prise the country open to trade; though they failed, the third bout of gunboat diplomacy – this time by the Japanese in 1876 – resulted in the Treaty of Ganghwa, which dragged Korea into the global marketplace on unfair terms. From this point to the present day, Korea would be a ship largely steered along by foreign powers.

Through means both political and economic, the Japanese underwent a gradual strengthening of their position in Korea. Local resentment boiled over into occasional riots and protests, and peaked in 1895 after the Japanese-orchestrated **murder of Empress Myeongseong** – "Queen Min", to the Japanese – in Gyeongbokgung palace. After this event, **King Gojong** (reigned 1863–1910) fled to the Russian embassy for protection; in 1897, when things had quietened down sufficiently, he moved into the nearby palace of Deoksugung, there to set up the short-lived **Empire of Korea**, a toothless administration under almost full Japanese control. In 1902 Japan forged an alliance with the British Empire, recognizing British interests in China in return for British acknowledgment of Japanese interests in Korea. Sensing shifts in power, Russia at this point began moving its rooks into Korea, though they ran into the Japanese on the way. To avoid confrontation, Japan suggested that the two countries carve Korea up along the **38th parallel**, a line roughly bisecting the peninsula. Russia refused to accept, the two fought the Russo-Japanese War in 1904–5, and after its surprise victory Japan was in a position to occupy the peninsula outright. They were given tacit permission to do so in 1905 by US Secretary of State and President-to-be William Taft, who agreed in a secret meeting to accept Japanese domination of Korea if Japan would accept the American occupation of the Philippines. Korea became a Japanese protectorate that year, and Japan gradually ratcheted up its power on the peninsula before a final **outright**

annexation in 1910. Joseon's kings had next to no say in the running of the country during its last quarter-century under dynastic succession, and it was with a whimper that the book closed on Korea's near two thousand years of unbroken regal rule.

The Japanese occupation

After the signing of the Annexation Treaty in 1910, Japan wasted no time in putting themselves in all the top posts in politics, banking, law and industry with its own personnel; despite the fact that they never represented more than four percent of the peninsular population, they came to control almost every sphere of its workings. Korea was but part of the Empire of Japan's dream of **continental hegemony**; being the nearest stepping stone to the motherland, it was also the most heavily trampled on. While the Japanese went on to occupy most of Southeast Asia and large swathes of China, only in Korea did they have the time and leverage necessary to attempt a total annihilation of **national identity**. Some of the most powerful insults to national pride were hammered home early. The royal palace of **Gyeongbokgung** had all the Confucian principles observed in its construction shattered by the placing of a modern Japanese structure in its first holy courtyard. Korean currency, clothing and even the language itself were placed under ever stricter control, and thousands of local "**comfort women**" were forced into sexual slavery. Korean productivity grew, but much of this was also for Japan's benefit – within ten years, more than half of the country's rice was heading across the sea.

In 1919, the **March 1st Movement** saw millions of Koreans take to the streets in a series of non-violent nationwide protests. A declaration of independence was read out in Seoul's Tapgol Park, an act followed by processions through the streets and the singing of the Korean national anthem. The Japanese police attempted to suppress the revolt through force; around 7000 died in the months of resistance demonstrations that followed. The result, however, was a marked change of Japanese policy towards Korea, with Saito Makoto (the Admiral in charge of quelling the chaos) agreeing to lift the bans on Korean radio, printed matter and the creation of organizations, and promoting harmony rather than pushing the militarist line. The pendulum swung back towards oppression on the approach to World War II – in the late 1930s, Japan began forcing Koreans to worship at Shinto shrines, speak in Japanese, and even adopt a Japanese name (a practice known as *soshi-kaimei*), all helped by local **collaborators** (*chinilpa*). Thousands of these went across to Japan, but though many were there to do business and strengthen imperial ties, most were simply squeezed out of Korea by Japanese land confiscations.

The Korean War

Known to many as the "**Forgotten War**", sandwiched as it was between World War II and the war in Vietnam, the Korean conflict was one of the twentieth century's greatest tragedies. The impoverished peninsula had already been pushed to the back of the global mind during World War II; the land was under Japanese control, but the Allied forces had developed no plans for its future should the war be won. In fact, at the close of the war American Secretary of State Edward Stettinius had to be told in a meeting where Korea actually was. It was only when the **Soviet Union** sent troops into Korea in 1945 that consideration was given to Korea's postwar life. During an emergency meeting on August 10, 1945, officials and high-rankers with no in-depth knowledge of the peninsula sat with a map and a pencil, and scratched a line across the 38th parallel – a simple solution, but one that was to have grave repercussions for Korea.

The build up to war

With World War II rapidly developing into the **Cold War**, Soviet forces occupied the northern half of the peninsula, Americans the south. Both countries imposed their own social, political and economic norms on the Koreans under their control, thereby creating two de facto states that refused to recognize each other, the two diametrically opposed in ideology. The **Republic of Korea** (now more commonly referred to as "South Korea") declared independence on August 15, 1948, exactly three years after liberation from the Japanese, and the **Democratic People's Republic of Korea** followed suit just over three weeks later. The US installed a leader favourable to them, selecting **Syngman Rhee** (ironically born in what is now North Korea), who had degrees from American universities. Stalin chose the much younger **Kim Il-sung**, who like Rhee had been in exile for much of the Japanese occupation. The foreign forces withdrew, and the two Koreas were left to their own devices, each hellbent on unifying the peninsula by absorbing the opposing half; inevitably, locals were forced into a polarization of opinion, one that split friends and even families apart. Kim wanted to wade into war immediately, and Stalin turned down two requests for approval of such an action. The third time, for reasons that remain open to conjecture, he gave the nod.

The war

On June 25, 1950, troops from the northern **Korean People's Army** (KPA) burst across the 38th parallel, then little more than a roll of tape. The DPRK itself claims that it was the south that started the war, and indeed both sides had started smaller conflicts along the line on several occasions, but declassified Soviet information shows that the main battle was kicked off by the north. With the southern forces substantially ill-equipped in comparison, Seoul fell just three days later, but they were soon aided by a sixteen-nation coalition fighting under the **United Nations** banner – the vast majority of troops were from the United States, but additional forces arrived from Britain, Canada, Australia, the Philippines, Turkey, the Netherlands, France, New Zealand, Thailand, Ethiopia, Greece, Colombia, Belgium, South Africa and Luxembourg; other countries provided non-combative support.

Within three months, the KPA had hemmed the United Nations Command (UNC) into the far southeast of the country, behind a short line of control that became known as the **Pusan Perimeter**, a boundary surrounding the newly romanized city of Busan. Though the KPA held most of the peninsula, American general Douglas MacArthur identified a weak logistical spine and poor supply lines as their Achilles heel, and ordered amphibious landings behind enemy lines at **Incheon**, just west of Seoul, in an attempt to cut off their enemy. The ambitious plan worked to perfection, and UNC forces pushed north way beyond the 38th parallel, reaching sections of the Chinese border within six weeks. At this stage, with the battle seemingly won, the **Chinese** entered the fight and ordered almost a million troops into North Korea; with their help, the KPA were able to push back past the 38th parallel. The UNC made one more thrust north in early 1951, and after six months the two sides ended up pretty much where they started. The lines of the conflict settled around the 38th Parallel, near what was to become the **Demilitarized Zone**, but the fighting did not end for well over two years, until the signing of an **armistice agreement** on July 27, 1953. In effect, both sides lost, as neither had achieved the aims espoused at the outset. Seoul had fallen four times – twice to each side – and Korea's population was literally decimated, with over 3 million killed, wounded or missing over the course of the war; to this can be added around half a million UNC troops, and what may well be over a million Chinese. Had the war been "contained" and brought to an end when the line of control stabilized in early 1951, these figures would have been far lower. The war split thousands of families; in addition to the confusion created by a front line that yo-yoed up and down the land, people were forced to switch sides to avoid starvation or torture, or to stay in contact with family members. Though the course of the battle and its aftermath were fairly straightforward, propaganda clouded many of the more basic details, and the war was largely forgotten by the west. For all the coverage of Vietnam, few know that a far greater amount of **napalm** fell on North Korea, a much more "suitable" target for the material thanks to its greater number of large urban areas; also kept quiet is how close **nuclear weapons** were to being used in the conflict. In his excellent book *North Korea*, Bruce Cumings quotes General MacArthur as saying after the war: "I would have dropped between 30 and 50 atomic bombs... strung across the neck of Manchuria." Since the end of the war there have been innumerable accounts of atrocities committed by both sides, many detailing beatings, torture and the unlawful murder of prisoners of war, others documenting the slaughter of entire villages. Korea lay in ruins, yet two countries were slowly able to emerge from the ashes.

To the present day

Considering its state after the war, South Korea's transformation is nothing short of astonishing. What's often referred to as the "**Economic Miracle**" saw the country become one of Asia's most ferocious tiger economies; in Seoul, it also owns one of the world's largest and most dynamic cities. The country's GDP-per-head shot up from under US$100 in 1963 to well over US$24,000 in 2007; thanks in large part to the bullishness of large *jaebeol* such as Samsung, Hyundai and LG, it now sits proudly on the cusp of the world's ten most powerful economies. Since flinging off its autocratic straight-jacket in the 1980s, it developed sufficiently to be selected as host of two of the world's most high-profile events – the **Olympics** in 1988, and football's **World Cup** in 2002.

The following information refers to South Korean history after the Korean War. For details on North Korean events and information on North–South relations since the conflict, see p.397.

Problematic beginnings

The **post-war period** proved extremely difficult for South Korea: cities had been laid to waste and families torn apart, accusations and recriminations were rife, and everyone knew that hostilities with the North could resume at any moment. **Syngman Rhee**, who had been selected as president before the war, ruled in an increasingly autocratic manner, making constitutional amendments to stay in power and purging parliament of those against his policies. In 1960 disgruntled students led the **April 19 Movement** against his rule, and after being toppled in a coup he was forced into exile, choosing Hawaii as his new home. He was succeeded by military general **Park Chung-hee**, a man whose name became equally synonymous with corruption, dictatorship and the flouting of human rights – thousands were jailed merely for daring to criticize his rule. To his credit, Park introduced the economic reforms that allowed his country to push forward – until the mid-1970s, the South Korean economy actually lagged behind that of North Korea – and the country made great advances in automotive, electronic, heavy and chemical industries. He also set about renovating places of national pride, notably in Gyeongju, a city close to his home town in the southeastern province of Gyeongbuk. Park's authoritarian rule continued to ruffle feathers around the country, and the danger from the North had far from subsided – Park was the subject of two failed **assassination** attempts by North Korean agents. It was, however, members of his own intelligence service who gunned him down in 1979, claiming that he was "an insurmountable obstacle to democratic reform". Those responsible were hanged the following year. Park's eventual successor, **Chun Doo-hwan**, was also from the southeast of the country, and the resultant Seoul–Gyeongsang tangent of power saw those parts of the country developing rapidly, while others languished far behind. The arrest of liberal southwestern politician **Kim Dae-jung**, as well as the botched trials following the assassination of Park Chung-hee, was a catalyst for mass uprisings across the land, though mainly concentrated in Jeju Island and the Jeolla provinces. These culminated in the **Gwangju Massacre** of May 1980, where over two hundred civilians died after their protest was crushed by the military.

The Olympic legacy

Rather incredibly, just one year after the massacre, Seoul was given the rights to host the **1988 Summer Olympics**. Originally the brainchild of Park Chung-hee, Chun Doo-hwan had followed through on the plan in an apparent attempt to seek international recognition of his authoritarian rule. Though he may have regarded the winning of the 1981 Olympic vote as a tacit global nod, the strategy backfired somewhat when the country was thrust into the spotlight; as a result of this increased attention, the country's first ever free elections were held in 1987, all of this coming as Korean conglomerates known as the *jaebeol* were spreading their financial arms around the world. In 1998 once-condemned Kim Dae-jung completed a remarkable turnaround by being appointed president himself. The first South Korean leader to favour a peaceable reunification of the peninsula, he wasted no time in kicking off his "**Sunshine Policy**" of reconciliation with the north, and in 2000 – after an historic Pyongyang summit with North Korean leader Kim Jong-il – he was awarded the **Nobel Peace Prize**. The country's international reputation was further enhanced by the hugely successful co-hosting of the **2002 World Cup** with Japan. In 2006 the feeling of international acceptance jumped up another notch, when South Korean **Ban Ki-moon** succeeded Kofi Annan as Secretary-General of the United Nations.

Religion

Korea has a long and fascinating religious history, one that has continued to inform local life to the present day. With the land strewn with temples, **Buddhism** is the religion most closely identified with Korea, though **Christianity** now has a greater number of followers. The rise of the latter is particularly interesting when laid over Korea's largely **Confucian** mindset, which is often diametrically opposed to Christian ideals. Religion is anathema in **North Korea**, where a communist government has been in place since the Korean War. Buddhist, Confucianist and even Christian groups do exist, but only under the close scrutiny of a government that will tolerate no freedom of expression resulting from ideological theorizing. For information about **Juche**, the DPRK's own stylized brand of communism, see p.406

Buddhism

An import from China (who pinched it from the Indian subcontinent), **Buddhism** arrived in Korea at the beginning of the Three Kingdoms period. **Goguryeo** and **Baekje** both adopted it at around the same time, in the last decades of the fourth century: Goguryeo king Sosurim accepted Buddhism almost as soon as the first Chinese monks touched down in 372, while Baekje king Chimnyu adopted it after taking the throne in 384. The **Silla** kings were less impressed by the creed but their resistance crumbled in 527 after an interesting episode involving an official who had decided to switch to Buddhism. He was to be beheaded for his beliefs, and with his final few gasps swore to the king that his blood would not be red, but a milky white; his promise rang true, and the king soon chose Buddhism as his state religion.

Even in China, Buddhism was at this point in something of an embryonic phase, and Korean monks took the opportunity to develop the **Mahayana** style by ironing out what they saw to be inconsistencies in the doctrine; disagreements were to lead to the creation of several **sects**, of which the **Jogye** order is by far the largest, covering about ninety percent of Korea's Buddhists; other notable sects include **Seon**, largely known in the west as Zen, the Japanese translation, and **Cheontae**, which is likewise better known under its Chinese name of Tiantai.

Ornate **temples** sprang up all over the peninsula during the **Unified Silla** period, but though Buddhism remained the state religion throughout the **Goryeo** era, it was given the squeeze by Confucianism during **Joseon** times. Monks were treated with scant respect and temples were largely removed from the main cities (one reason why there are relatively few in Seoul, the Joseon capital), but though the religion was repressed, it never came close to evaporating entirely. Further troubles were to come during the **Japanese occupation period**, during the latter years of which many Koreans were forced to worship at Shinto shrines. Mercifully, although many of the temples that weren't closed by the Japanese were burnt down in the Korean War that followed the Japanese occupation, reconstruction programmes have been so comprehensive that you will seldom be more than a walk away from the nearest temple; all are still active places of worship, the number of monks in residence anything from one (mountain hermitages) to hundreds (Guinsa).

Temples

Korea's many **temples** are some of the most visually appealing places in the country – even in little-visited city suburbs, you'll see them being repainted with an almost painful care to attention. The end result is nothing short of jaw-dropping; most agree that **Bulguksa**, just east of Gyeongju, is the most intricately painted, but others of note are **Beopjusa**, with its enormous golden Buddha, and historic **Hwa-eomsa** on the west of Jirisan National Park. It's not only the older temples that are worth tracking down – **Yakcheonsa** is large and modern but has a sea view to die for, while **Guinsa** is a traditionalist's nightmare but there is still plenty to see.

On entry to the temple complex you'll pass through the *ilchumun*, or "first gate", then the *jeonwangmun*. The latter almost always contains **four large guardians**, two menacing figures towering on each side of the dividing walkway (Seonamsa in **Jeollanam-do** is one notable exception); these control the four heavens and provide guidance to those with a righteous heart. The central building of a Korean temple is the **main hall**, or *daeungjeon*. Initially, it was only Sakyamuni – the historical Buddha – who was enshrined here, but this was soon flanked on left and right by bodhisattvas. Most of these halls have doors at the front, which are usually only for elder monks; novices (and visiting foreigners) use side-entrances. Among the many other halls that you may find on the complex are the *daecheokgwangjeon*, the hall of the Vairocana Buddha; *gwaneumjeon*, a hall for the Bodhisattva of Compassion; *geungnakjeon*, the Nirvana Hall and home to the celestial Amitabha Buddha; *mireukjeon*, the hall of the future Maitreya Buddha; and *nahanjeon*, the hall of disciples. Some also feature the *palsangjeon*, a hall featuring **eight paintings** detailing the life of the Sakyamuni Buddha, though these are more often found on the outside of another hall.

Somewhere on the complex you'll find the *beomjonggak*, a "**bell pavilion**" containing instruments to awaken the four sentient beings – a drum for land animals, a wooden fish for the water-borne, a bronze gong for creatures of the air, and a large bell for monks who have slept in. The bell itself can sometimes weigh upwards of twenty tonnes; certain bell-casting techniques reached an apex of design in Silla times, and the best will have an information board telling you how far away it can be heard if you were to strike it lightly with your fist. Needless to say, you shouldn't test these contentions.

Confucianism

Like Buddhism, **Confucian thought** made its way across the sea from China – the exact date remains a mystery, but it seems that it first spread to Korea at the beginning of the Three Kingdoms era. For centuries it co-existed with the state religion, informing not only political thought but national ethics, and in many ways it still governs the Korean way of life today. Central to the concept are the **Five Moral Disciplines** of human-to-human conduct, namely ruler to subject, father to son, husband to wife, elder to younger and friend to friend. Although it can't be classified as a religion – there's no central figure of worship, or concept of an afterlife – it is used a means of self-cultivation, and a guide to "proper" conduct, particularly the showing of respect for those higher up the social hierarchy.

During the Three Kingdoms period, the concepts described above of filial piety began to permeate Korean life, with adherence to the rules gradually taking the form of ceremonial rites; in the Silla kingdom there developed a "bone rank" system used to segregate social strata, one that was to increase in rigidity until the **Joseon era** in which Korean Confucianism really took hold. At the very dawn of the dynasty in 1392, King Taejo had the **Jongmyo shrines** built in central Seoul; for centuries afterwards, ruling kings would venerate their ancestors here in regular ceremonies. Numerous academies (*hyanggyo*) were also built around the country, at which students from the elite *yangban* classes would wade through wave after wave of punishing examinations on their way to senior governmental posts. Buddhism had been on the decline for some time; Confucian scholars argued that making appeals to gods unseen had a detrimental effect on the national psyche, and that the building of ornate temples absorbed funds too readily. Some, in fact, began to clamour for the burning of those temples, as well as the murder of monks. As with other beliefs, some followers violated the core principles for their own ends and, despite the birth of great neo-Confucian philosophers such as **Yi-Yi** and **Toegye**, enforced slavery and servitude meant that the lot of those at the lower levels changed little over the centuries.

Confucianism today

In addition to several remaining academies and shrines – there are wonderful examples near Gyeongju and Andong – colourful ancestral ceremonies take place each year at Jongmyo in Seoul. It's often said that Korea remains the **most Confucian** of all the world's societies – on getting to know a local, you'll generally be asked a series of questions both direct and indirect (particularly with regard to age, marriage, education and employment), the answers to which will be used to file you into mental pigeonholes. Though foreigners are treated somewhat differently, this is the main reason why locals see nothing wrong in barging strangers out of the way in bank queues or showing no mercy on the road – no introduction has been made, and without knowledge of the behaviour "proper" to such a situation no moves are made towards showing respect. Among those who do know each other, it's easy to find **Confucian traits** – women are still seen as inferior to men (their salary continues to lag far behind, and they're usually expected to quit their job on having a child, never to return to the workplace); the boss or highest earner will usually pay after a group meal; family values remain high; and paper qualifications from reputable universities carry more weight than actual intelligence. Also notable is **bungsu**, a concept which involves the moving of ancestral grave sites. Perhaps the most high-profile examples of corpse-shifting have been before general elections – Kim Dae-jung lost the elections in 1987 and 1992 before deciding to move the graves of his ancestors to more auspicious locations; he duly won the next one in 1998. Confucian ideas are slowly being eroded as Westernization continues to eat into the country, particularly the ever-growing number of Christians.

Christianity

Christianity is now Korea's leading religion by number of worshippers (making up well over a quarter of the country), having surpassed Buddhism just after the turn of the century. Surprisingly the religion has been on the peninsula since the end of the eighteenth century. The Confucian *yangban* in charge at

Village practices

Mountain rites

By far the most common form of spirit worship in Korea, the *sansinje* remains a part of annual village festivals all across the country. The Dano festival in Gangneung – the biggest traditional event in the land – actually starts off with one of these in honour of General Kim Yu-sin, spearhead of the Silla campaigns that resulted in the unification of the country. Near Samcheok, just down the way, groups head to the hills for shamanistic *gut* ceremonies and animal exorcisms.

Rites to sea spirits

Though these rites are held at points all along Korea's coastline, they are most numerous in Gangwon province on the east, particularly around the city of Gangneung. The spirit is often the ghost of a local female who perished tragically, often without having married (see "Phallicism" below); when finally placated by ceremonies and sacrifices, she becomes a patron of the village in question. One popular Gangwon tale regards a man who was prompted in a dream to rescue a travelling woman from a nearby islet; all he found on arrival was a basket containing the woman's portrait, and after carrying it home his village was blessed with a bumper crop. Villagers continue to pay respects to this day.

Rites to tree spirits

Korea has many trees dating back five centuries or more, so it's understandable that many local Korean myths – including the Tangun legend, which details Korea's creation – include a sacred tree somewhere along the way. Trees of such repute are treated with enormous respect, as even to snap a twig is said to invoke a punishment of some kind from the spirit that lives within.

Rites to rock spirits

As you make your way around Korea, you'll see English-language pamphlets pointing you towards rocks that are said to resemble turtles, tigers, sea dragons and the like. While some require an almost superhuman stretch of the imagination, many of these are still the subject of regular ceremonies for the spirits that are said to reside within the rock. You'll also see man-made stone mounds in and around certain temples, most notably wonderful Tapsa in Maisan Provincial Park, which is surrounded by spires of rock, all of which were stacked by just one man.

Jangseung

You'll see these carved wooden sticks at the entrance to traditional villages, where they have long served a range of purposes from protector to boundary marker. Some have jovial faces, others snarling mouths full of blocky, painted teeth, but these days you're more likely to find a replica outside a traditional restaurant than a bona fide one in the countryside.

Phallicism

Anyone who has seen the mysterious but rather phallic *hareubang* statues on beautiful Jeju Island will know that willy worship has long been popular in Korea. This usually takes the form of fertility rites, but the reasoning for some ceremonies is not so predictable: on a village south of Samcheok in Gangwon province once lived a young bride-to-be who was swept from the shore in a powerful storm. Her enraged spirit chased the fish from the seas until it was placated by a carved wooden penis; hundreds of the things now rise from the ground in a nearby park.

the time were fearful of change, hardly surprising considering how far apart the fundamental beliefs of the two creeds are. The Christian refusal to perform ancestral rites eventually led to forceful repression, and hundreds were **martyred** in the 1870s and 1880s, most notably in Jeonju. A number of French missionaries were also murdered in this period, before Korea was forcefully opened up for trade. The numbers have been growing ever since, the majority now belonging to the Presbyterian, Catholic or Methodist churches. Before the Korean War, **Pyongyang** had by far the highest number of Christians in the land – estimated at around 300,000, over a quarter of its population at the time – but they were forced to flee south or face persecution when a communist government rolled into power.

Churches tend to be monstrous concrete edifices (sporting the red neon crosses), and some are huge, with room for thousands of worshippers; the island of Yeouido, near Seoul, officially has the largest church in the world, with 170 pastors and over 100,000 registered deacons.

Film

For all of its efforts in finance, electronics and promoting its food and tradition, it's Korea's film industry that has had the most success in pushing the country as a global brand. While Korean horror flicks have developed an international cult following, and a number of esteemed directors have set international film festivals abuzz, special mention must be made of the locally produced television **dramas** that have caught on like wildfire across Asia. Like many of the movies, these are highly melodramatic offerings that don't seek to play on the heartstrings so much as power-chord the merry hell out of them. All of these form part of the **Hallyeo movement**, a "New Wave" of Korean production that has been in motion since cinematic restrictions were lifted in the 1980s.

Film was first introduced to Korea at the very end of the **nineteenth century**; in 1899, just after making Korea's first ever telephone call, King Gojong was shown a short documentary about the country put together by American traveller Burton Holmes, and Seoul's first cinema was opened shortly afterwards. Unfortunately, few examples from the pre-war **silent era** have made it onto the international market; Korean produce was also scaled down, and at one point cut off entirely, during the Japanese occupation period (1910–45). After **World War II**, and the end of annexation, there followed a short burst of films – many of which, understandably, had freedom as a central concept – but this was brought to an abrupt halt by the outbreak of the **Korean War** in 1950.

Following the war, the film industries of the two Koreas developed separately; leaders on both sides saw movies as a hugely useful **propaganda tool**, and made immediate efforts to revive local cinema – see opposite for the continuation of the North Korean story. In the south, President Syngman Rhee conferred tax-exempt status on moviemakers, who got busy with works looking back at the misery of wartime and the occupation period, and forward to a rosy future for non-communist Korea. By the end of the 1950s, annual movie output had reached triple figures, the most popular being watched by millions, but the accession of **Park Chung-hee** to president in 1961 brought an end to what passed for cinematic freedom. In addition to the censorship and hard-fisted control over local produce, foreign films were vetted for approval and placed under a strict quota system, elements of which remained until 2006. As Park's rule grew ever more dictatorial, he inaugurated a short-lived era of **"governmental policy" films**; these were hugely unpopular, and cinema attendance dropped sharply. After Park's death, democratization and the gradual relaxation of restrictions gave rise to the Hallyeo movement.

The Hallyeo "New Wave"

Throughout the periods of governmental suppression, a clutch of talented directors were forced to keep their best ideas under wraps, or else be very clever about putting them forward. As the loosening of the lid in the 1980s slowly started to give them free rein, the most highly skilled came to the fore and finally gave Korea exposure in the West; foremost among these was **Im Kwon-taek**, a maverick who shrugged off his role as a creator of commercial quota-fillers to unleash striking new works on the global community. The South Korean government continued to provide funding for films until the

1992 release of *Swiri*, the country's first fully independent film. Since then the industry has moved forward in leaps and bounds, reaching an ever-greater international audience. Evidence of cinematic immaturity still remains – almost every film will feature at least one overlong shot of a pretty girl's face, during which time the viewer is expected to assess her beauty and nothing more – but a number of Korean directors such as **Kim Ki-duk** and **Park Chan-wook** are now globally acclaimed.

Korean success has not been limited to the silver screen; in fact, the country's **dramas** have arguably been even more successful than its movies, though with an appeal largely limited to the Asian continent. Foremost among these was *Winter Sonata*, a series whose appeal became almost religious in Japan (see p.170).

North Korean cinema

Cinema is surprisingly big business in **North Korea** – Kim Jong-il was pouring funds into the industry for decades before he became leader of the country, and in 1978 even went so far as to organize the kidnapping of **Shin Sang-ok** – a prominent South Korean director – in an effort to improve the quality of local produce. North Korea produces some of the world's most distinctive films; unfortunately, this niche in global cinema has remained

Dan Gordon's documentaries

The DPRK has kept a tight lid on foreign production within the country, but after years of cajoling British director Daniel Gordon was allowed in to shoot a documentary about survivors of the country's 1966 football team. Together with his two follow-up efforts, they represent some of the best windows into contemporary North Korean society.

The Game of Their Lives (2002)
In 1966 North Korea's football team had gone into the World Cup Finals in England as rank underdogs, but a stirring victory over Italy sent them through to the quarter-finals, where they lost 5–3 in an amazing game against Portugal; incredibly, they were 3–0 up at one point and heading for the semi-finals. The team returned home as international heroes, but little more was heard of them until the screening of this revealing documentary.

A State of Mind (2004)
On the surface, this is a documentary about two young girls training for the Arirang Mass Games in Pyongyang, but it amounts to a first-ever stab at genuinely portraying the average life of today's North Koreans. It was evidently a success: after the film was shown on DPRK state television, locals complained that it was "dull", having merely filmed them going about their daily lives; little did they know how compelling such reportage is to the average foreign viewer.

Crossing The Line (2006)
James Joseph Dresnok is a movie-maker's delight, but this fascinating documentary is the world's only peek inside the mind of "Comrade Joe", one of four American soldiers known to have defected to North Korea after the Korean War. With a candour that shows a genuine love of his new country, Dresnok tells of his journey from a troubled adolescence to old age in Pyongyang, including his crossing of the treacherous DMZ, a failed attempt at escape, and his stint as a star on the North Korean silver screen.

almost entirely unexplored by the outside world. A few films have recently started to trickle onto the **international market**; to buy, go to Ⓦwww.north-korea-books.com. The themes stick rigidly to brave North Korean resistance during the Korean War and the Japanese occupation period, depicting Americans as unspeakably evil and South Koreans as their puppets. Highlights include *Nameless Heroes* (a twenty-part series produced at immense cost while the country was gripped by famine), *Sea of Blood*, *Duty of a Generation*, *We Love Our Soldiers* and the surprisingly comical *Family Basketball Team*.

Kim Ki-duk

3-Iron (2004) Korean movies about eccentric loners are ten a penny. Here, the protagonist is a delivery boy who breaks into and then polishes up the houses that he knows to be empty. When he happens across one that's still home to a lonely girl, the couple begin a strange kind of silent relationship. Superbly acted, and an interesting take on the traditional love story.

Bad Guy (2001) A sadomasochistic thread runs through Kim Ki-duk's films, and is no more resonant than in *Bad Guy*, where a mute thug falls in love with a young beauty and tricks her into becoming a prostitute. This disturbing study of small-time gangsters and sexual slavery tells painful truths about Korean society, and though clichéd is thoroughly absorbing in more than a voyeuristic sense.

Samaritan Girl (2004) A storyline that's less explicit and far deeper than may seem the case on the outside. Two teenage girls looking to save up for a trip to Europe enter the murky world of prostitution, one sleeping with the clients, the other managing the affairs while keeping an eye out for the cops. Inevitably, things don't quite go according to plan.

Spring, Summer, Fall, Winter... and Spring (2003) With just one set – a monastery in the middle of a remote lake – and a small cast, Kim Ki-duk somehow spins together a necessarily slow but undeniably beautiful allegory of human nature, one that relays the life of a boy nurtured to manhood by a reclusive monk.

The Isle (2001) In the middle of a lake, a mute woman rents out small floating huts to men looking to escape city life for a while, sometimes selling herself to them, sometimes murdering them. This was the film that pushed Kim Ki-duk's unique style onto the world stage, a dark love story with a couple of nasty surprises.

War and history

Chihwaseon (2002) Sometimes going under the title *Painted Fire*, this beautifully shot tale of Jang Seung-eop – a nineteenth-century painter best known by his pen name Owon – won the Best Director award at Cannes for Im Kwon-taek, a maverick who had been around for decades but was previously ignored on the international stage.

Joint Security Area (2000) Any Korean film about the DMZ is worth a look, as is anything by acclaimed director Park Chan-wook. Here, two North Korean soldiers are killed in the DMZ; like *Memento* (which, incidentally, came out the following year), the story plays backwards, revealing the lead up piece by piece.

Shiri (1999) Also known as *Swiri*, this was a landmark film in Korean cinema, marking the dawn of a Hollywood-style long suppressed by government. The mix of explosions and loud music is not of as much interest to foreigners as it is to Koreans, but the plot – South Korean cops hunt down a North Korean sniper girl – is interesting enough. The girl was played by Yunjin Kim, who later found fame on the American TV series *Lost*.

Silmido (2003) Loosely based on events in the 1960s, which saw South Korean operatives receive secret training on the island of Silmido to assassinate North Korean leader Kim Il-sung. The film broke Korean ticket records, and provides a fascinating depiction of the tensions of the time.

Taegukgi (2004) Though it suffers from the occasional bit of shoddy acting, and the sense of history is unconvincing, this is an enjoyable war film, following the fate of two brothers as they battle through the horrors and in-fighting of the Korean War.

The King and the Clown (2005) A period drama with homosexual undercurrents, this was an unexpected smash hit at the box office. Set during the reign of King Yeonsan – whose short rule began in 1494 – it tells of a pair of street entertainers who find themselves in the royal court. One of them fosters an ever-closer relationship with the king.

Welcome to Dongmakgol (2005) Too twee for some, but heart-warming to others and beautifully shot to boot, this tells of a motley assortment of American, South Korean and North Korean combatants from the Korean War who somehow end up in the same village, among people unaware not only of the conflict raging around them but of warfare in general.

Park Chan-wook's "Vengeance Trilogy"

Sympathy for Mr Vengeance (2002)
Acclaimed director Park Chan-wook kicked off a trio of films about revenge with this tale of a deaf-mute man who hatches a plot to find a kidney for his ailing sister, inadvertently kicking off a series of revenge-fuelled murders.

Oldboy (2003)
Oldboy was the first Korean film to win big at Cannes, a dark and violent tale of a businessman mysteriously arrested after a night out, imprisoned for years then suddenly given three days to discover why he was put away and to hunt down those responsible. Though lead man Choi Min-sik has an unfortunate habit of looking like an actor, even when he's not acting, most will find this riveting.

Sympathy for Lady Vengeance (2005)
A teenage girl gets framed and sent down for killing a young boy, and spends her time in jail plotting revenge. On her release she's offered a plate of metaphorically cleansing white tofu by a Christian group; the tofu ends up on the floor and our heroine sets about getting back at the man to blame for her imprisonment.

Drama

A Tale of Two Sisters (2003) In a manner similar to *The Shining*, this chiller seeks to petrify viewers not with lashings of ultra-violence but with that which cannot be seen. This adaptation of a Joseon-era folk story keeps its audience guessing, and most will find it Korea's best take on the horror genre.

Chingu (2001) This is a semi-autobiographical account of the director Kwak Kyung-taek's boyhood in Busan, looking at the lives of four boys on their journey from carefree childhood to Korea's gangster underworld. There exists no better primer on the staccato accent of Korea's southeast corner; watch this after visiting Busan and you'll be able to relive your time in Korea's most characterful city.

The Host (2006) The tranquil lives of a riverside merchant are blown to smithereens when the formaldehyde disposed into the river by the American military create a ferocious underwater creature. This comic thriller smashed box office records in Korea, but even though its international reception was nowhere near as fervent, it's worth watching.

Comedy

200 Pounds Beauty (2006) An overweight girl with a fantastic voice does lip-sync work for a famous singer, while moonlighting as a phone sex employee. One of her customers offers her a way out, but even though she goes on to become a pop star, she finds that being thin and beautiful is no picnic either. Lead actress Kim Ajoong is hot property in Korea, and has been the face of countless advertising campaigns.

My Sassy Girl (2001) A mega hit from Tokyo to Taipei, this tale doesn't add too much to the romcom genre, but one scene was almost entirely responsible for a spate of high-school-themed club nights. It's worth watching, as is *My Tutor Friend*, a follow-up that hits most of the same buttons.

Save the Green Planet! (2003) A social recluse and his tightrope-walker girlfriend endeavour to save the earth by hunting down the aliens that they believe to have infiltrated mankind; once captured, the extraterrestrials can only be destroyed by applying menthol rub to their groin and feet. Enough said.

Sex is Zero (2002) Fans of *American Pie* may care to hunt down this Korean take on the gross-out comedy.

The President's Last Bang (2005) Korea has long been crying out for some satire, particularly something able to inject a little fun into its turgid political reportage, and this hits the nail squarely on the head (as proven by the lawsuit that followed). It's based on a true story, namely the assassination of president Park Chung-hee in 1979; the portrayal of Park as something of a Japanese-sympathetic playboy certainly ruffled a few feathers.

Books

Despite Korea's long and interesting history, the East Asian sections in most bookstores largely remain the domain of books about China and Japan. The majority of books that are devoted to Korea cover **North Korea** or the **Korean War**; far less biased than most newspaper or television reports, these are the best form of reportage about the world's most curious state and how it was created Also notable is the range of fascinating English-language North Korean **propaganda material**, which though churned out in surprisingly large amounts is hard to get hold of unless you're booked on a tour to Pyongyang; see p.388 for a little more info.

Historical

Bruce Cumings *Korea's Place in the Sun: A Modern History*. The Korean peninsula went through myriad changes in the twentieth century, and this weighty tome analyses the effects of such disquiet on its population, showing that the South's seemingly smooth trajectory towards democracy and capitalism masked a great suffering of the national psyche.

Kim Dong-uk *Palaces of Korea*. A photo-filled hardcover detailing not only the minutae of Seoul's wonderful palaces, but how they vary in style and form fromthose found elsewhere in Asia.

Korean Cultural Heritage *Korecna*. A compendium of articles written about Korean culture, mainly with reference to religious and shamanistic practices. Much of the detal overlaps, but it's worth tracking down.

Keith Pratt *Everlasting Flower: A History of Korea*. This thoroughly readable book provides a chronicle of Korean goings-on from the very first kingdoms to the modern day, its text broken up with interesting illustrated features on the arts and customs prevalent at the time.

Korean society

Michael Breen *The Koreans: Who they Are, What they Want, Where their Future Lies*. Although the four main sections of this book – society, history, economy and politics – may seem awfully dry, the accounts are relayed with warmth and a pleasing depth of knowledge.

Min Byoung-chul *Ugly Koreans, Ugly Americans*. It's getting harder to find with each passing year, but this is an entertaining and informative guide to the differences between Koreans and Americans, with text in both languages and cartoon-like illustrations.

Rhee Won-sok *Korea Unmasked: In Search of the Country, the Society and the People*. The peculiarities of Korean society are relayed here in an easy-to-read comic strip. While it could be said that it makes light of some serious problems, it's an excellent primer on the local psyche for those looking to spend some time in the country.

Simon Winchester *Korea: A Walk Through the Land of*

Miracles. This highly entertaining book details Winchester's walk from southern Jeju to the North Korean border. Written in the 1980s, it's now an extremely dated snapshot of Korean society; those familiar with the country today will be amazed at how much it has changed in such a short time.

North Korea and the Korean War

Jasper Becker *Rogue Regime: Kim Jong Il and the Looming Threat of North Korea*. Despite Becker's view of North Korea being thoroughly one-sided, it often lends itself to easy sensationalism. A meaty fleshing-out of how the Western world sees Kim Jong-il.

Erik Cornell *North Korea Under Communism – Report of a Special Envoy to Paradise*. Sweden was the first Western country to open up diplomatic connections to the DPRK, and Cornell spent three years as the head of its embassy in Pyongyang. His book is rather political in nature, but nevertheless provides a unique insight into life in North Korea.

Bruce Cumings *North Korea: Another Country*. The American–North Korean dispute is far more complex than Western media would have you imagine, and this book provides a revealing – if slightly hard to digest – glance at the flipside. Cumings' meticulous research is without parallel, and the accounts of American atrocities and cover-ups both in the "Forgotten War" and during the nuclear crisis offer plenty of food for thought.

Guy Delisle *Pyongyang*. A comic strip relaying of his time as a cartoonist in Pyongyang, Delisle's well-observed and frequently hilarious book is a North Korean rarity – one that merely tells it like it is, and doesn't seek to make political or ideological statements. His illustrations are eerily accurate, and for anyone with even a passing interest in North Korean life, this is a must-read.

Max Hastings *The Korean War*. A conflict is not quite a war until it has been given the treatment by acclaimed historian Max Hastings. With his book on the Korean War, he has provided more than his usual mix of fascinating, balanced and well-researched material. The account of the stand of the Glousesters on the Imjin is particularly absorbing.

Kang Chol-Hwan *The Aquariums of Pyongyang*. Having fled his homeland after spending time in a North Korean gulag, Kang's harrowing accounts of squalor, starvation and brutality represent one of the only windows into the world's most fenced-off social systems. He's not an author, however, and the confused sermonizing at the end of the book rather dilutes its appeal.

Bradley K. Martin *Under the Loving Care of the Fatherly Leader*. At almost 900 pages in length – 200 of which are references – this isn't one to carry around in your backpack, but for an in-depth look at the Kims and the perpetration of their personality cult, it's hard to beat.

Don Oberdorfer *The Two Koreas: A Contemporary History*. Lengthy, but engaging and surprisingly easy to read, this book traces the various occurrences in post-war Korea, as well as examining how they were affected by the actions and policies of China, Russia, Japan and the US. You'd be hard pressed to find a book about North Korea more neutral in tone.

Language

Peter Constantine *Making Out in Korean*. This cheap, slim-line series covers the more amorous aspects of Asian languages. The Korean edition is just as useful for swearing, colloquialisms and street-speech as it is for romance – great for impressing (or offending) Korean friends.

Andrew Inseok-Kim *Colloquial Korean*. Part of a mammoth series covering languages from all around the world. Despite a few flaws, the vocabulary and sentence structure here is not quite as formal as in most Korean study books, and it's well worth a look.

Jaehoon Yeon and Mark Vincent *Teach Yourself Korean*. With a confusing mix of retired transliteratary systems and an awful dictionary section, this is nowhere near the usual excellent standards of the *Teach Yourself* series, but with such a dearth of Korean language titles it's still the best to go for.

Recipe books

Cecilia Hae-Jin Lee *Eating Korean: From Barbeque to Kimchi, Recipes from My Home*. Easy-to-follow instructions to over a hundred Korean dishes. The more predictable rice and noodle dishes are supplemented with side dishes, soups, teas and desserts.

Young Jin Song *Korean Cooking: Traditions, Ingredients, Flavours, Techniques, Recipes*. As the sweeping subtitle suggests, this is not so much a recipe book as an all-encompassing guide to Korean cuisine.

A–Z of contemporary Korea

A: Ajumma Power

An **ajumma** is a Korean woman, though the term is something of a grey area: it encompasses old age and anything approaching it, but can also be used to describe a married female, or one with children. However, with women understandably reluctant to be tarred with the term, it's usually reserved for Korean grandmothers. In a country where women are still not regarded as equals – they've fought their way through war and poverty to provide a tough-as-nails embodiment of harder times, many regarding old age as a liberation of a kind from chauvinistic yokes – to do something with strength, purpose and resilience is to do it with "Ajumma Power". Note that almost every single old-age *ajumma* has exactly the same hairstyle – a bubble-perm affectionately known as a *bbogeul-bbogeul* (pronounced "boggle-boggle"). Although it may seem mandatory, it's a matter of choice – foreign women with even a slight natural curl to their hair may well be asked where they go to get it permed.

B: Burberry Man

What's generally known as a "flasher" in English is referred to as a **Burberry Man** in Korea. These gents – dressed in a three-quarter-length jacket and little else – hang around universities in order to expose themselves to female students, most commonly when large crowds are gathered in the front enclosures of the country's educational establishments. They're surprisingly common – most Korean girls will have seen at least one, and many schools see a Burberry Man show up regularly. Korea's love of conformity means that even these sex pests have a uniform of sorts: while the Burberry label is not essential, most of their jackets are brown, and for some reason knee-length grey socks seem almost mandatory.

C: Clones and couple-look

The subject of **cloning** has long been controversial, but in Korea questions of morality come with a tinge of scandal. In 2005 a team of scientists from Seoul National University created an Afghan Hound named "Snuppy" – a combination of "puppy" and the initials of the university – and the world's first cloned human embryo, both to tumultuous acclaim from the world scientific community. Shortly afterwards, the team leader – Dr Hwang Woo-suk – was revealed to have fabricated much of his evidence; surrounded by inconsolable team members, Dr Hwang issued a profuse apology on live television. While the human embryo had been bluffed, the dog was later found to be a bona fide clone.

Identical appearances are nothing new in Korea – newlyweds have long worn matching clothes for the duration of their honeymoon, a concept known as "**couple-look**". The preponderance of pinks and pastels shows which half of the pair usually makes the decisions, though it's becoming increasingly common for men to sport clothes that complement, rather than match, those of their bride. The best places to see the trend in action are Seoul's Myeong-dong district, and the "honeymoon island" of Jeju-do.

D: Daeri-unjeon

In Korea, businessmen inevitably find themselves having to drink an awful lot as "social" job obligations, even if travelling with a car. To get round this situation Korea has **daeri-unjeon**, a network of drivers who drive both the customer and his car home, and who can be called from most bars; the telephone numbers usually end with 2882, digits whose pronunciation is almost identical to the Korean for "hurry, hurry!"

E: Eyelids

In a country where appearance is not quite everything but pretty damn close, beauty is big business. The large and thriving plastic surgery industry that vanity has inspired sees women – and more than a few men – get all sorts from nose-jobs to a nip and tuck, but the most popular alteration by far is **eyelid surgery**. This involves the creation of a crease in the upper eyelid, the results being apparently more beautiful to Koreans, but distinctly non-oriental.

F: Fighting and "fan Death"

With taekwondo – the national sport – not only a compulsory subject at schools, but forming part of mandatory national service for men, it's little wonder that **fights** in Korea can become huge, movie-like affairs. The expertise has even been taken overseas: *taekwondo* is now one of the world's biggest martial arts by participation, a Korean sumo wrestler named Kasugao has been a regular top-division competitor in Japan, while man-mountain Choi Hong-man – all seven-foot-two of him – has become a celebrity on the international K1 circuit.

"**Fan death**" is a truly curious phenomenon – whereas around the world people fall asleep with a fan or the air-conditioning left on, only in Korea does such folly regularly seem to result in fatalities. The reasons given include air currents starving the victim of air, reduced room temperatures inducing hypothermia, or even fan blades actually cutting the oxygen molecules in two. This is enough to convince most Koreans that the humble electric fan is an instrument to be feared – even broadsheet newspapers run fan-death stories, and the Korean government has issued warnings against using fans at night. Such beliefs are of much amusement to Korea's expat population (unless they find themselves sharing a room with a Korean in the summer).

G: Golf and the gyopo

Despite its mountainous countryside and crowded, sprawling cities, **golf** has become one of the most popular sports in Korea. Daejeon's Se Ri Pak is perhaps the best known, having won three of the four majors on the women's circuit and found her way onto the World Golf Hall of Fame; Grace Park and Jeong Jang have also won major titles. The men have fared less well, but K. J. Choi broke into the world's top 10 in 2007. Michelle Wie, a child prodigy dubbed the "female Tiger Woods" and competing in male events when barely into her teens, was born in Hawaii to Korean parents.

Wie is one of the most famous **gyopo**; this is a term used to refer to ethnic Koreans who live outside Korea, especially those who have become citizens of another country. Other famous *gyopo* include Yunjin Kim of *Lost* fame; Joe Hahn from nu-metal band Linkin Park; *ESPN* anchor Michael Kim; and Woody Allen's wife Soon-yi Previn. "Oddjob", the Korean villain of Bond fame, was actually played by a Japanese-American wrestler.

H: Hompy and Harisu

Koreans don't tend to follow worldwide Internet trends, they're usually one step ahead. Most Koreans have for years had a **hompy** (a Korean bastardization of the world "homepage"), onto which they load countless photographs, musings, journal entries, songs and any other digitizable part of their lives. Foreigners living in Korea will often be asked to create a local hompy by Korean friends – if you don't exist online, you don't exist at all – and some have found them a great way to expand their social network.

Harisu didn't need the Internet to find fame, just a sex change. Born male, she underwent sexual reassignment surgery, and flew in the face of a conservative society to become the country's first celebrity transsexual; she was also one of the first in the queue to change gender when it became legal to do so. Harisu's big break was a cosmetics commercial, in which the camera focused on her Adam's apple; her fame and voice were enough to propel several albums into the chart, and she has appeared in a number of films.

I: Internet deaths

Koreans are famed for their use of computers, most notably the amount of time they spend playing online games. In fact, there is a growing backlash among the non-Korean gaming community: such is their domination that the country's gamers are accused of taking over international gaming sites and tournaments. They even hit the international headlines with occasional **Internet deaths**: stories of gamers making mammoth stints (one was measured at 92 hours) at one of the ubiquitous PC bars have become less common since the government ordered tighter controls, but there's still the occasional death behind closed doors.

J: Jaebeol and jeonse

Korean business is dominated by a troupe of gigantic business conglomerates known as **jaebeol**. A few of these organizations have achieved fame around the world, though most foreigners probably wouldn't know that the company is Korean even if the name is familiar to them. Some of the largest and most renowned *jaebeol* include Samsung, LG, Hyundai, SK, Lotte, Daewoo and Kumho Asiana. Most are still family-controlled, leading to enormous riches for the man at the helm; their power was a driving force behind Korea's "Economic Miracle". Times have changed; after the Asian Financial Crisis and the resultant reforms, many chose (or were forced) to break up into smaller units.

Foreigners who choose to live in Korea full-time may well come into contact with **jeonse**, the country's unique system of property rental. Instead of paying a monthly rent, tenants slam down a huge "key money" deposit, which in most cases is over half of the property's value; the landlord earns off the interest, and refunds the deposit at the end of the contract. This is one reason why most Koreans live with their parents until marriage – youngsters are usually only able to pay the lump sum with family help. It's also quite risky – many families have lost everything after their landlord did a runner. This system is slowly giving way to a more international rental style, prompted in part by much lower interest rates.

L: Louis Vuitton

Though the numbers are gradually starting to decline, patterned brown handbags from French designer **Louis Vuitton** have long been standard issue on female Korean arms. However, high prices – and increased expertise of counterfeiting in China – force many to invest in a fake bag. Watch what happens if it starts to rain.

M: Missionaries and military service

Many visitors to Korea are surprised to learn that Buddhism, the state religion for centuries, was surpassed as the most common religion by Christianity. Koreans assume most foreigners to be Christian, and some of the most actively religious will stop you in the street for a chat about joining their church – expats soon learn to steer clear of those approaching with a pamphlet or book. Korean Christianity made world news in 2007, when a group of 23 **missionaries** was abducted by the Taliban in Afghanistan; two were executed before a deal could be struck, and the rest had to suffer for over a month before their release.

South Korea still has compulsory **military service** for its young men. This was once 36 months, but is now around 24 months it's likely to decrease further in decades to come. Conscientious objectors will be jailed, but there are ways around the rule – many students manage to tie their service into university courses such as logistics and electronic engineering. Military service is also mandatory for men in North Korea, and women are actively encouraged to enrol as volunteers.

N: Nocheonnyu

A **nocheonnyu** is an "over-the-hill spinster", a woman who has gone past the perceived outer boundary of marriageable age; 30 has long been the feared number, though the Korean age-counting system (whereby children are born aged 1 and become 2 on the date of the next Lunar New Year) makes this 28 or 29 in international terms. While it remains much harder for a woman to marry after achieving *nocheonnyu* status, societal shifts (notably an increase in divorce rates, and the slow decline of resign-after-marriage path for females) mean that it's by no means impossible.

O: Ohmy News

In a country whose news output generally ranges from insipid to downright corrupt, **Ohmy News** has ruffled feathers by providing a much-needed independent voice. In operation since 2000, this online newspaper may not be written by journalists (their motto is "Every Citizen is a Reporter", and around eighty percent of their content comes from the public), but regular scoops have made them a big part of the news scene. They've even made a name for themselves abroad – the *New York Times* of March 6, 2003, ran with the headline "Online Newspaper Shakes Up Korean Politics", a reference to the popular belief that *Ohmy* influenced the outcome of the 2002 presidential election by prompting protests against the American army presence.

P: Private tutoring

With Korea's mix of generous salaries and relatively poor foreign language rates, there's a large and growing market for English teachers. Most head across – at least initially – to teach children at after-school **private tutoring** institutes known as *hagwon*. These are not just for English lessons – the huge pressures inherent in Korea's educational system prompt an extremely high proportion of parents to push their kids into extra-curricular classes from ages as young as 5. In addition to language classes and "regular" school, the little mites may have violin lessons, computer training, art classes, dance groups and piano recitals crammed into their weekly schedule.

Q: Questionable English

Anyone spending a bit of time in Korea will note that expats employed as translators are having a good laugh. T-shirts splashed with **questionable English** are all over the place – "Skinny Bitch" got to be popular with young girls, though "Hey Guy! Lay Me" was a mercifully short-lived fad; some have more surreal slogans such as "Is Your Barn Insured?", and others simply have random cuttings from foreign newspapers. The mirth is not restricted to clothing – *Kiss* and *Asse* are two of the biggest brands of toilet paper, there's an energy drink called *Coolpis*, a bakery chain called *Gout*, children's clothing shops called *Hunt Kids* and *Baby Hunt*, and bars with such names as *Super Excellent Big Boy Club*. Some questionable names, however, are purely down to the Koreans. There are spelling mistakes galore: "crab" is spelt with a "p" on a surprising number of the country's menus, and a certain hamburger chain is often spelt "Bugger King" on English-language maps. There's also the legacy of football hero Ahn Jung-hwan, who celebrated his two goals in the 2002 World Cup by kissing then holding aloft his wedding ring; within days, hundreds of bars and restaurants across the land had changed their name to "Kiss Ring".

R: Red Devils

Having casually pinched their nickname from England's Manchester United, the South Korean national football team is often referred to as the "**Red Devils**", as are their main supporters' group. A noisy but friendly bunch, the latter were one of the highlights of the 2002 World Cup, an event half-hosted in Korea; wearing standard-issue red T-shirts, their chant of "*Dae-Han-Min-Guk!*" – the country's name in Korean – pushed the team on to the semi-finals of the competition. Most wore a T-shirt emblazoned with "Be The Reds!", perhaps the best-known example of "Konglish" (a hybrid of Korean and English which makes little sense in either language). The inventors of the logo initially neglected to copyright it, and it was eventually superseded by the official slogan of the supporters' club, the more grammatically correct "Reds Go Together".

S: Sexy bars and sogaeting

Sexy bars are one of Korea's many takes on the hostess theme. Drinks at these places are served by scantily clad women to male customers who are expected to pay not just for their own drinks, but for the expensive ones selected by the woman or women. Those who just want a beer or two will be tolerated, but it's rich, whisky-quaffing regulars who get the preferential treatment. Though this doesn't always lead to sex – there are plenty of dedicated brothels around, and many customers head to sexy bars for nothing more than an ego-boosting chat – it does happen. This line of work has become popular with university students seeking to top up their funds, but many girls are trafficked in from Southeast Asia or former Soviet states, and have little more freedom than the Korean "comfort women" from the Japanese annexation period.

One thing a sexy bar certainly won't play host to is a blind date, or "**sogaeting**". Until recently, these were usually arranged by parents in anticipation of a happy marriage between friendly families, but in an increasingly liberal Korea sogaeting is now more common as a way for boys and girls to find their own partners.

T: Tongil and table gifts

Ever since the cleaving apart of the Korean peninsula, both sides have held a strong desire for reunification. "**Tongil**", the local word for the concept, forms part of the names of parks, monuments, roads, bars, restaurants, hairdressers and countless more besides, but its popularity has been noticeably declining with the South Korean youth: in an all-pervasive manner of which the North would be quite proud, almost everyone born after 1980 will push exactly the same counter-argument, claiming that the absorption of such a poor country would play havoc on their own economy, and pointing to Germany's fiscal woes after the fall of the Berlin Wall.

A first birthday party is a pretty special event wherever you are in the world, but Korea has added its own distinctive twist to proceedings – **table gifts**. At some point in the proceedings, the baby will be seated on or dangled over a table laid out with money, rice, thread and a pencil, and pushed to make a selection that, it is said, will influence their future path. Money speaks for itself, but the selection of rice is said to lead to a comfortable life, thread to a long one, and a pencil to a scholarly career. Of course, this is not enough to satisfy many modern parents, who throw contemporary choices such as golf balls, footballs, DVDs or microphones onto the table too, often giving their young one precious little choice in the selection. Also interesting are the parties thrown to celebrate the hundredth day of a child's life – in times of high infant mortality, this was when the child was said to have "made it", and the special day continues to be celebrated with a feast of colourful rice-cake.

U: Unconstitutional law and US Forces

Koreans were, until recently, banned from marrying anyone of the same clan. This may have sounded like an extremely severe rule in a country with so few family names (around one-quarter of Koreans are named Kim, another fifteen percent Lee, and almost ten percent Park), but the ruling only in fact covered those who had both the same name and the same ancestral clan; some of these subdivisions, however, were over a million-strong in number. Same-clan marriages were termed incestuous, even if the pair were a dozen generations apart, but this law was found **unconstitutional** by the Korean court in 1997, and thousands have since taken advantage of this ruling.

US forces arrived back on Korean soil at the beginning of the Korean War in 1950, only years after leaving the area following Japan's defeat in World War II; they have remained on the peninsula ever since in their tens of thousands. Their presence is largely unpopular in Korea, with regular protests taking place in Seoul. Successive Korean leaders have been forced to walk a political tightrope, telling locals that the American presence would be scaled down, but simultaneously begging them to stay. The mini-cities of good-time girls that have developed outside the major bases would also be short of custom.

V: Vanity mirrors

Korean girls are famed throughout East Asia for being a little vain. A **vanity mirror** is an almost essential part of every girl's armament; these are used at what can be disturbingly regular intervals to make sure that every single eyelash is in perfect position, and are usually kept in outer pockets – for some, the inside of a handbag is just too far away. Some companies sensed an opportunity to mix vanity mirrors with implements of equal importance, and many Korean girls now have mirrored screens on their mobile phones.

W: Westernization

Though it remains one of the most unique societies on earth, Korea certainly doesn't suffer from a lack of **Western influence**. The once-traditional *hanbok* suits and horsehair hats gave way decades ago to T-shirts and jeans, the former almost always adorned by an English-language logo or slogan. Innumerable Western loan-words have entered the Korean lexicon, albeit altered to fit the local tongue; foreign fast-food chains are everywhere; and American shows such as *CSI*, *Lost* and *Prison Break* are among the most popular on television.

X: Xenophobia

Koreans tend to make foreigners feel very welcome in their country, but this friendliness conceals a rampant **xenophobia**. Though an established part of the world community, Korea remains one of the most homogenous societies on earth, and traces of the "Hermit Kingdom" remain, mainly thanks to history lessons that paint the motherland in virginal white while detailing every single injustice inflicted on her; most of the official ire is reserved for the Japanese, but anti-Americanism is also rife. It must be said that this very rarely results in anything approaching violence – Korea is simply seen as a world apart, where foreigners will always be viewed as such, even if they were born in Korea and speak the language fluently. People are likewise seen as nationals first and human beings second, which leads to some blanket stereotyping; the rationale for many local deeds will be "because I'm Korean". It also explains the surprise that many Koreans will show to Westerners able to use chopsticks – no matter how close you live to a Chinatown, it's simply not in your DNA.

Y: Yuhaeng and Yes!!

Yuhaeng is a Korean word meaning "in vogue", and one trend among the innumerable fads to have benefitted from such a description has been the desire for fancy underwear. After years of beige-coloured bras, Korean women (and their men, of course) needed something different, and one of the biggest and most innovative movers was **Yes!!**, a nationwide lingerie chain. One notable piece of marketing genius was seen on a bra-and-knickers set which had the word "No" plastered all over it; with the aid of glow-in-the-dark printing, this magically changed to "Yes!!" when the lights were off.

Z: Zodiac

Koreans are a superstitious bunch, and you'll see small tent-like fortune-telling booths in every city, most often attended by young couples looking for celestial approval of their relationship, or workers thinking about changing jobs. People's place in the **zodiac** may also be supplemented by palm-reading, teacup-gazing, craniology or Tarot cards.

Language

Korean language

Korean language

The sole official tongue of both North and South Korea, the **Korean** language is used by upwards of seventy million people, making it by some estimates the eleventh most spoken in the world. While it's a highly tricky language to pick up, it's not just regular foreign students who have problems with it – much to the chagrin of linguists, it remains stubbornly "unclassified" on the global language tree, its very origins something of a mystery. Some lump it in with the **Altaic** group (itself rather vague), which would put it on the same branch as Turkish and Mongolian, though many view it as a **language isolate**. Korean is therefore in the same boat as Japanese, its closest linguistic brother; both share a **subject-object-verb** syntax and similar grammar, though well over half of the Korean words themselves actually originate from China. Korea also used Chinese text for centuries, even after creating its own characters – known as **Hangeul** – in the 1440s, but now almost exclusively uses the local system for everyday functions.

Native speakers of European languages will encounter some highly significant **grammatical differences** when attempting to get a handle on the Korean tongue. Korean **nouns** remain unaffected whether they refer to singular or plural words, very little use is made of **articles**, and **verbs** do not change case according to who or what they're referring to – *gayo* can mean "I go", "he/she/it goes" or "we/they go", the meaning made clear by the context. Verbs do, however, alter depending on which **level of politeness** the speaker desires to use – the country's Confucian legacy is still evident; the conversation will sound quite different depending on whether it's between a child and a mother, a boss and an employee, or even good friends of slightly different age. In general, it's pretty safe to stick to verbs with the polite **–yo** ending. See p.443 for a couple of recommended Korean language study books.

Korean characters

An almost child-like scrawl of circles and Tetris shapes, many foreigners find Korean text surprisingly **easy to learn**. Koreans tend to assume that foreigners don't have the inclination or mental capability to decipher *Hangeul*, so your efforts will not go unappreciated. Koreans are immensely proud of *Hangeul*, which they see as the world's most logical written system. While this is no great exaggeration, the efficiency also has a downside – user-friendly it may well be,

English–Korean language boxes

To make getting around the country that little bit easier, we've included language boxes in chapters 1–6, giving the Korean Hangeul of sights, hotels and restaurants next to their English name.

Hangeul

ㄱ	g (k)	ㅎ	h	ㅔ	e
ㄴ	n	ㅇ	ng	ㅐ	ae
ㄷ	d (t)	ㅏ	a	ㅖ	ye
ㄹ	r/l	ㅑ	ya	ㅒ	yae
ㅁ	m	ㅓ	eo	ㅟ	wi
ㅂ	b (p)	ㅕ	yeo	ㅞ	we
ㅅ	s (t)	ㅗ	o	ㅙ	wae
ㅈ	j (t)	ㅛ	yo	ㅘ	wa
ㅊ	ch (t)	ㅜ	u	ㅚ	oe
ㅋ	k	ㅠ	yu	ㅢ	ui
ㅌ	t	ㅡ	eu	ㅝ	wo
ㅍ	p	ㅣ	i		

but in reality *Hangeul* is a very narrow system that cannot cope with sounds not found in the Korean language, a fact that partially explains the Korean people's generally poor grasp of foreign tongues.

Though it may seem surprising, *Hangeul* was actually a royal creation, having been the brainchild of **King Sejong** in the 1440s. Up until then, his Joseon kingdom and the dynasties that went before had been using Chinese characters, but seeing that most of his citizens were illiterate and denied education, the king devised a system that would be easier for the common man to learn. The king was forced to do much of his work in secret, as the change did not go down well with the Confucian *yangban* scholars, some of whom were almost king-like in their power at the time; as the only members of society to receive an education strong enough to make reading Chinese characters a possibility, they argued against the change in an effort to maintain their privileged access to historical texts and the like. *Hangeul* experienced periodic bursts of popularity, but was kept down first by the *yangban*, and then almost erased entirely by the Japanese during their occupation of the peninsula (1910–45), but it's now the **official writing system** of both North and South Korea, as well as a small autonomous Korean pocket in the Chinese province of Jilin. Students in Korea study at least 2000 Chinese characters at school, and some of the simpler ones are still used in daily life.

Korean characters are grouped into **syllabic boxes** of more-or-less equal size, and generally arranged left-to-right – if you see a line of text made up of eighteen of these character-chunks, it will have eighteen syllables when spoken. The way in which the **characters** fall into the boxes is rather unique and takes a bit of figuring out – some have two characters in the top half and one at the bottom (the top two are read left-to-right, followed by the bottom one, so 한 makes *han*), while others have two or three characters arranged vertically (these are read downwards, so 국 makes *guk*). Thus put together, we have 한국 – *hanguk*, meaning "Korea". The basic building blocks are listed in the box above, though note that some of these symbols **change sounds** depending on whether they're at the beginning or end of a syllable or word (syllable-ending sounds are bracketed in the boxed text), and that "ng" is used as an initial null consonant for syllables that start with a vowel. Guides to pronouncing the **vowel clusters** are given in the next section; there also exist consonantal clusters, though these are beyond the scope of this book.

Pronunciation

Pronouncing Korean words is a tough task – some sounds simply do not have English-language equivalents. You'll see from the *Hangeul* box that there's only one character for "l" and "r", with its actual sound some way in between the two – try saying both phonemes at the same time. The letters "k", "d", "b" and "j" are often written "k", "t", "p" and "ch", and are pronounced approximately half-way towards those Roman equivalents; unfortunately, the second set also have their place in the official system, and are usually referred to as **aspirated consonants**, accompanied as they are by a puff of air. Consonants are fairly easy to master – note that some are doubled up, and spoken more forcefully – but pronunciation guides to some of the tricky **vowels** and **dipthongs** are as follows (British English readings offer the closest equivalents):

a	as in "car"	yu	pronounced "you"
ya	as in "Jan"	eu	like the *e* in "bitten"; grimace and make a quick "uhh" sound of disgust
eo	as in "hot"	i	as in "pea"
yeo	as in "yob"	e	as in "bed"
o	pronounced "ore"		
yo	pronounced "your"		
u	as in "Jew"		

Transliteratary troubles

Rendering the Korean language in Roman text is, simply, a battle that can never be won – a classic problem of square pegs and round holes. Numerous systems have been employed down the years, perhaps best exemplified in the Korean family name now usually romanized as "Lee": this has also been written as Rhee, Li, Ri, Lih, Rhi, Ree, Yi, Rii and more besides. Under the current system it would be "I", but the actual pronunciation is simply "ee" – it's amazing how much trouble a simple vowel can cause (especially when almost a fifth of the country has this name).

A Korean's age, schooling, family and even lifestyle influence the way that they'll romanize a given word, but official standards have long been in place. The **Yale** and **McCune–Reischauer** systems became widely accepted in the 1940s, and the latter is still much in evidence today; under its rules, aspirated consonants are marked with apostrophes, and certain vowels with breves. One problem – other than looking ugly – was that these punctuation markings are often neglected, even in language study books; though it remains the official system in North Korea, the South formulated its own system of **Revised Romanization** in the year 2000. While this is far from perfect, it's the official standard, and has been used throughout this book; exceptions include names of the many hotels, restaurants, universities and individuals who cling to the old ways. One other issue is the Korean syllable *shi*; this is now romanized as *si*, a rather ridiculous change since it takes Koreans years of language classes before they can pronounce the syllable without palatalizing it – "six" and "sister" will be pronounced "shix" and "shister". We've written it as *shi* in the language listings to help you achieve the correct pronunciation, but obeyed the official system in the rest of the book – Sinchon is pronounced "Shinchon", Sapsido as "Sapshido", and so on.

Koreans themselves find it hard to render **foreign words** in *Hangeul* as there are many sounds that don't fit into the system – the difficulties with "l" and "r" sharing the same character being an obvious example – but even when parallels exist they are sometimes distorted. The letter "a" is usually written as an "e" or "ae" in an unsuccessful effort to Americanize the pronunciation – "hat", for example, will be pronounced "het" by the majority of the population.

ae	as in "air"	wa	as in "wag"
ye	as in "yet"	oe	as in the beginning of "way"
yae	as in "yeah"	ui	no English equivalent; add an "ee" sound to *eu* above
wi	as in "window"	wo	as in "wad"
we	as in "wedding"		
wae	as the beginning of "where"		

Useful words and phrases

Basics

Yes	*ye/ne*	예/네
No	*aniyo*	아니요
Please (asking for something)	*...juseyo*	...주세요
Excuse me	*shillye hamnida*	실례 합니다
I'm sorry	*mian hamnida*	미안 합니다
Thank you	*gamsa hamnida*	감사 합니다
You're welcome	*gwaenchan-ayo*	괜찮아요
What?	*muot?*	무엇?
When?	*eonje?*	언제?
Where?	*eodi?*	어디?
Who?	*nugu?*	누구?
How?	*eotteokke?*	어떻게?
How much?	*eolma-eyo?*	얼마에요?
How many?	*myeokke-eyo?*	몇게에요?
I want...	*...hago-shipeoyo*	...하고 싶어요
Please help me	*dowa-juseyo*	도와주세요

Communicating

I can't speak Korean	*jeo-neun hangugeo-reul mot haeyo*	저는 한국어를 못 해요
I can't read Korean	*jeo-neun hangugeo-reul mok ilgeoyo*	저는 한국어를 못 읽어요
Do you speak English?	*yeongeo halsu-isseoyo?*	영어 할수 있어요?
Is there someone who can speak English?	*yeongeo-reul haljul a-neun bun isseoyo?*	영어를 할줄아는분있어요?
Can you please speak slowly?	*jom cheoncheonhi mal haejuseyo?*	좀 천천히 말 해주세요?
Please say that again	*dashi han-beon mal haejuseyo*	다시 한번말 해주세요
I understand/I see	*alasseoyo*	알았어요
I (really) don't understand	*(jal) mollayo*	(잘) 몰라요
What does this mean?	*i-geot museun ddeushi-eyo?*	이것 무슨 뜻이에요?
How do you say (x) in Korean?	*(x) eul/reul hanguk-eoro eotteoke mal haeyo?*	(x) 을/를 한국어로 어떻게 말해요?
Please write in English	*yeongeo-ro jegeo jushillaeyo*	영어로 적어 주실래요

Please wait (a moment)	*(jamggan) gidariseyo*	(잠깐) 기다리세요
Just a minute	*jamggan manyo*	잠깐 만요

Meetings and greetings

Hello; Good morning/ afternoon/evening	*annyeong haseyo*	안녕 하세요
Hello (polite)	*annyeong hashimnikka*	안녕 하십니까
How are you?	*jal jinaesseoyo?*	잘 지냈어요?
I'm fine	*jal jinaesseoyo/jo-ayo*	잘 지냈어요 / 좋아요
Nice to meet you	*bangapseumnida*	반갑습니다
Goodbye (when staying)	*annyeong-hi gaseyo*	안녕히 가세요
Goodbye (when leaving)	*annyeong-hi gyeseyo*	안녕히 계세요
What's your name?	*ireum-i eotteokke doeshimnikka?*	이름이 어떻게 되십니까?
My name is…	*ireum-i … imnida*	이름이 … 입니다
Where are you from?	*eodi-eso wasseoyo?*	어디에서 왔어요?
I'm from…	*…eso wasseoyo*	…에서 왔어요
Korea	*han-guk*	한국
Britain	*yeong-guk*	영국
Ireland	*aillaendeu*	아일랜드
America	*mi-guk*	미국
Australia	*oseuteureillia/hoju*	오스트레일리아 / 호주
Canada	*kae-nada*	캐나다
New Zealand	*nyu jillaendeu*	뉴질랜드
South Africa	*nam apeurika*	남 아프리카
How old are you?	*myeot-sal ieyo?*	몇살이에요?
I am (age)	*(age)-sal ieyo*	(age)살이에요
Do you like…?	*…jo-a haeyo?*	…좋아 해요?
I like…	*jo-a haeyo*	좋아 해요
I don't like…	*an jo-a haeyo*	안 좋아 해요
Do you have (free) time?	*shigan-i isseoyo?*	시간이 있어요?

Numbers

Rather confusingly, the Korean language has two separate number systems operating in parallel – a **native Korean** system, and a **Sino-Korean** system of Chinese origin – and you'll have to learn according to the situation which one to use. To tell the time, you'll actually need both – amazingly, minutes and hours run on different systems! The native Korean system only goes up to 99, and has been placed on the right-hand side of the readings. Dates and months use the Sino-Korean system alone, with *il* (sun) used as a suffix for days, and *wol* (moon) for months: June 7 is simply *yuk-wol chil-il*.

Zero	*yeong/gong*	영/공	**Five**	*o/daseot*	오/다섯
One	*il/hana*	일/하나	**Six**	*yuk/yeoseot*	육/여섯
Two	*i (pronounced "ee")/dul*	이/둘	**Seven**	*chil/ilgop*	칠/일곱
			Eight	*pal/yeodeol*	팔/여덟
Three	*sam/set*	삼/셋	**Nine**	*gu/ahop*	구/아홉
Four	*sa/net*	사/넷	**Ten**	*ship/yeol*	십/열

Eleven	*shib-il/ yeol-hana*	십일/열하나
Twelve	*shib-I/ yeol-dul*	십이/열둘
Twenty	*i-shib/ seumul*	이십/스물
Thirty	*sam-shib/ seoreun*	삼십/서른
One hundred	*baek*	백
Two hundred	*i-baek*	이백
Thousand	*cheon*	천
Ten thousand	*man*	만
One hundred thousand	*sim-man*	십만
One million	*baeng-man*	백만
One hundred million	*eok*	억

Time and dates

Now	*jigeum*	지금
Today	*o-neul*	오늘
Morning	*achim*	아침
Afternoon	*ohu*	오후
Evening	*jeonyok*	저녁
Night	*bam*	밤
Tomorrow	*nae-il*	내일
Yesterday	*eoje*	어제
Week	*ju*	주
Month	*wol/dal*	월/달
Year	*nyeon*	년
Monday	*wolyo-il*	월요일
Tuesday	*hwayo-il*	화요일
Wednesday	*suyo-il*	수요일
Thursday	*mogyo-il*	목요일
Friday	*geumyo-il*	금요일
Saturday	*toyo-il*	토요일
Sunday	*ilyo-il*	일요일
What time is it?	*myo-shi-eyo?*	몇시에요?
It's 10 o'clock	*yeol-shi-eyo*	열시에요
10.20	*yeol-shi i-ship-bun*	열시 이십분
10.30	*yeol-shi sam-ship-bun*	열시 삼십분
10.50	*yeol-shi o-ship-bun*	열시 오십분

Transport and travel

Aeroplane	*bihaenggi*	비행기
Airport	*gonghang*	공항
Bus	*beoseu*	버스
Express bus (terminal)	*gosok beoseu (teominal)*	고속 버스 (터미널)
Intercity bus (terminal)	*shi-oe beoseu (teominal)*	시외 버스 (터미널)
City bus	*shinae beoseu*	시내 버스
Airport bus	*gonghang beoseu*	공항 버스
City bus stop	*jeong-ryu-jang*	정류장
Train	*gicha*	기차
Train station	*yeok*	역
Subway	*jihacheol*	지하철
Ferry	*yeogaek-seon*	여객선
Ferry terminal	*yeogaek teominal*	여객 터미널
Left-luggage office	*jimbogwanso*	짐보관소
Ticket office	*maepyoso*	매표소
Ticket	*pyo*	표
Platform	*seunggangjang*	승강장
Bicycle	*jajeon-geo*	자전거
Taxi	*taek-shi*	택시

Directions and general places

Where is (x)?	*-i/ga eodi-eyo?*	-이/가 어디에요?
Straight ahead	*jikjin*	직진
Left	*oen-jjok (pronounced "wen-chok")*	왼쪽
Right	*oreun-jjok*	오른쪽
Behind	*dwi-e*	뒤에
In front of	*ap-e*	앞에
North	*buk*	북
South	*nam*	남
East	*dong*	동

West	*seo*	서
Map	*maep/jido*	맵/지도
Entrance	*ip-gu*	입구
Exit	*chul-gu*	출구
Art gallery	*misulgwan*	미술관
Bank	*eunhaeng*	은행
Beach	*haebyeon*	해변
Department store	*baekhwajeom*	백화점

Embassy	*daesagwan*	대사관
Hot spring spa	*oncheon*	온천
Museum	*bangmulgwan*	박물관
Park	*gongwon*	공원
Sea	*haean/bada*	해안/바다
Temple	*Jeol/sachal*	절/사찰
Toilet	*hwajang-shil*	화장실
Tourist office	*gwan-gwang annaeso*	관광 안내소

Accommodation

Hotel	*hotel*	호텔
Motel	*motel*	모텔
Guesthouse	*yeogwan*	여관
Budget guesthouse	*yeoinsuk*	여인숙
Rented room	*minbak*	민박
Youth hostel	*yuseu hoseutel*	유스 호스텔
Korean-style room	*ondol-bang*	온돌방
Western-style room	*chimdae-bang*	침대방
Single room	*shinggeul chimdae*	싱글 침대
Double room	*deobeul chimdae*	더블 침대
Twin room	*chimdae dugae*	침대 두개
En-suite room	*yokshil-ddallin bang*	욕실딸린방
Shower	*syaweo*	샤워
Bath	*yokjo*	욕조

Key	*ki*	키
Passport	*yeogwon*	여권
Do you have any vacancies?	*bang isseoyo?*	방 있어요?
I have a reservation	*jeo-neun yeyak haesseoyo*	저는 예약 했어요
I don't have a reservation	*jeo-neun yeyak anhaesseoyo*	저는 예약 안했어요
How much is the room?	*bang-i eolma -eyo?*	방이 얼마에요?
Does that include breakfast?	*gagyeok-e achim-shiksa pcham-dwae isseoyo?*	가격에 아침식사 포함돼 있어요?
One/two/ three nights	*haruppam/ i-bak/ sam-bak*	하룻밤/ 이박/삼박
One week	*il-ju-il*	일주일
May I see the room?	*bang jom bolsu-isseoyo?*	방 좀 볼수 있어요?

Shopping, money and banks

Bank	*eunhaeng*	은행
Foreign exchange	*woe-hwan*	외환
Won	*won*	원
Pounds	*pa-un-deu*	파운드
Dollars	*dalleo*	달러
Cash	*don*	돈
Travellers' cheque	*yeohaengja supyo*	여행자 수표
How much is it?	*eolma-eyo?*	얼마에요?
It's too expensive	*neomu bissayo*	너무 비싸요
Please make it a little cheaper	*jom kkakka-juseyo*	좀 깎아주세요
Do you accept credit cards?	*keureditеu kadeu gyesan dwaeyo?*	크레디트 카드 계산 돼요?

Post and telephones

Post office	*uche-guk*	우체국
Envelope	*bongtu*	봉투
Letter	*pyeonji*	편지
Postcard	*yeopseo*	엽서
Stamp	*u-pyo*	우표
Airmail	*hanggong u-pyeon*	항공 우편
Surface mail	*seonbak u-pyeon*	선박 우편
Telephone	*jeon-hwa*	전화
Fax	*paekseu*	팩스
Telephone card	*jeonhwa kadeu*	전화 카드
Internet café	*PC-bang*	PC방
I would like to call...	*...hante jeonhwa hago-shipeoyo*	...한테 전화 하고 싶어요
May I speak to...	*...jom baggwo juseyo*	...좀 바꿔주세요
Hello?	*yeoboseyo?*	여보세요?

Health

Hospital	*byeongwon*	병원
Pharmacy	*yak-guk*	약국
Medicine	*yak*	약
Doctor	*uisa*	의사
Dentist	*chigwa-uisa*	치과의사
Diarrhoea	*seolsa*	설사
Nausea	*meseukkeo-um*	메스꺼움
Fever	*yeol*	열
Food poisoning	*shikjungdok*	식중독
Antibiotics	*hangsaengje*	항생제
Antiseptic	*sodok-yak*	소독약
Condom	*kondom*	콘돔
Penicillin	*penishillin*	페니실린
Tampons	*tampon*	탐폰
I'm ill	*jeo-neun apayo*	저는 아파요
I have a cold	*gamgi geoll-yeosseoyo*	감기 걸렸어요
I'm allergic to...	*...allereugi-ga isseoyo*	...알레르기가 있어요
It hurts here	*yeogi-ga apayo*	여기가 아파요
Please call a doctor	*uisa-reul bulleo juseyo*	의사를 불러 주세요

Food and drink

Places

Restaurant	*sikdang*	식당
Korean barbeque restaurant	*galbi-jip*	갈비집
Korean staples (fast food) restaurant	*gimbap-cheonguk*	김밥천국
Seafood restaurant	*hoet-jip*	횟집
Western-style restaurant	*reseutorang*	레스토랑
Italian restaurant	*itallian reseutorang*	이탈리안 레스토랑
Chinese restaurant	*jungguk-jip*	중국집
Japanese restaurant	*ilshik-jip*	일식집
Burger bar	*paeseuteu-pudeu-jeom*	패스트푸드점

Convenience store	*pyeonui-jeom*	편의점
Market	*shijang*	시장
Café	*kape*	카페
Bar	*ba/suljip*	바/술집
Club	*naiteu-keulleob*	나이트클럽
Expat bar	*woeguk-in ba (pronounced "way-guk-in ba")*	외국인 바
Makkeolli bar	*makkeolli-jip*	막걸리집
Soju tent	*pojangmacha*	포장마차
Where's (a) ... ?	*...eodi isseoyo?*	...어디 있어요?

Ordering

Waiter/Waitress (lit. "Here!")	*yeogiyo!*	여기요!
How much is that?	*eolma-eyo?*	얼마에요?
I would like...	*...hago shipeoyo*	...하고 싶어요
May I have the bill?	*gyesanseo juseyo?*	계산서 주세요?
I'm a vegetarian	*jeo-neun chaeshikju uija-eyo*	저는 채식주의자에요
Can I have this without meat?	*gogi bbaego haejushilsu isseoyo?*	고기 빼고 해주실수 있어요?
I can't eat spicy food	*maeun-geot mot meogeoyo*	매운것 못 먹어요
Delicious!	*mashisseoyo!*	맛있어요!
Chopsticks	*jeot-garak*	젓가락
Fork	*po-keu*	포크
Knife	*nai-peu/kal*	나이프/칼
Spoon	*sut-garak*	숟가락
Menu	*menyu*	메뉴

Staple ingredients

Beef	*so-gogi*	소고기
Chicken	*dak-gogi*	닭고기
Duck meat	*ori-gogi*	오리고기
Gimchi	*gimchi*	김치
Fish	*saengsun/ hoe (raw fish)*	생선/회
Ham	*haem*	햄
Meat	*gogi*	고기
Noodles	*myeon*	면
Pork	*dwaeji-gogi*	돼지고기
Red pepper paste	*gochu-jang*	고추장
Rice	*bap*	밥
Rice-cake	*ddeok*	떡
Seaweed laver	*gim*	김
Shrimp	*sae-u*	새우
Squid	*ojing-eo*	오징어
Tuna	*chamchi*	참치
Vegetables	*yachae*	야채

Rice dishes

Bibimbap	*bibimbap*	비빔밥
Fried rice (usually with egg and vegetables)	*bokkeumbap*	볶음밥
Marinaded beef on rice	*bulgogi (deop-bap)*	불고기 (덮밥)
Rice rolls	*gimbap*	김밥

Meat dishes

Barbequed ribs	*galbi*	갈비
Boiled beef rolls	*syabu-syabu*	샤부샤부
Dog-meat soup	*boshintang/yeongyangtang*	보신탕/영양탕
Marinaded beef	*bulgogi*	불고기
Pork belly slices	*samgyeopsal*	삼겹살
Spicy squid on rice	*ojingeo deop-bap*	오징어 덮밥
Steamed ribs	*galbi-jjim*	갈비찜

Stews and soups

Beef and noodle soup	*seolleong-tang*	설렁탕
Beef rib soup	*galbi-tang*	갈비탕
Cold buckwheat noodle soup	*naengmyeon*	냉면
Dumpling soup	*mandu-guk*	만두국
Gimchi broth	*gimchi jjigae*	김치 찌개
Ginseng-stuffed chicken soup	*samgye-tang*	삼계탕
Noodles with vegetables and meat	*makguksu*	막국수
Soybean broth (miso)	*doenjang jjigae*	된장 찌개
Spicy fish soup	*maeun-tang*	매운탕
Spicy noodle soup	*ramyeon*	라면
Spicy tofu soup	*sundubu*	순두부
Tuna broth	*chamchi jjigae*	참치 찌개

Snacks and Korean fast food

Battered flash-fried snacks (tempura)	*twigim*	튀김
Breaded pork cutlet	*donkkaseu*	돈까스
Dumplings	*mandu*	만두
Fried dumplings	*gun-mandu*	군만두
Rice wrapped in omelette	*omeuraiseu*	오므라이스
Rice-cake in red pepper paste	*ddeokbokki*	떡볶이
Savoury pancake with vegetables	*pajeon*	파전
Steamed dumplings	*jjin-mandu*	찐만두
Stuffed sausage	*sundae*	순대

Seafood

Broiled fish	*saengseon-gu-i*	생선구이
Fried baby octopus	*nakji bokkeum*	낙지 볶음
Raw fish platter	*modeum-hoe*	모듬회
Sliced raw fish	*saengseon-hoe*	생선회

Western food

Bread	*bbang*	빵	**Fruit**	*gwa-il*	과일
Cereal	*shiri-eol*	시리얼	**Pizza**	*pija*	피자
Cheese	*chi-jeu*	치즈	**Spaghetti**	*seupageti*	스파게티
Chocolate	*chokollit*	초콜릿	**Steak**	*seuteikeu*	스테이크
Eggs	*gyeran*	계란			

Tea

Black tea (lit. "red tea")	*hong-cha*	홍차	**Ginseng tea**	*insam-cha*	인삼차
Chrysanthemum tea	*gukhwa-cha*	국화차	**Green tea**	*nok-cha*	녹차
Cinnamon tea	*gyepi-cha*	계피차	**Honey ginseng tea**	*gyulsam-cha*	귤삼차
Citron tea	*yuja-cha*	유자차	**"Job's Tears" tea**	*yulmu-cha*	율무차
"Five flavours" tea	*omija-cha*	오미자차	**Jujube tea**	*daechu-cha*	대추차
Ginger tea	*saenggang -cha*	생강차	**Medicinal herb tea**	*yak-cha*	약차
			Plum tea	*maeshil-cha*	매실차
			Wild herb tea	*ma-cha*	마차

Alcoholic drinks

Baekseju	*baekseju*	백세주	**Ginseng wine**	*insamju*	인삼주
Beer	*maekju*	객주	**Makkeolli**	*makkeolli*	막걸리
Blackberry wine	*bokbunja*	복분자	**Plum brandy**	*maeshilju*	매실주
Bottled beer	*byeong maekju*	병 맥주	**Soju**	*soju*	소주
Cocktail	*kakteil*	칵테일	**Wine**	*wain*	와인
Dongdongju	*dongdongju*	동동주	**Whisky**	*wiseuki*	위스키
Draught beer	*saeng maekju*	생맥주			

Other drinks

Coffee	*keopi*	커피	**Milk**	*uyu*	우유
Orange juice	*orenji jyuseu*	오렌지 쥬스	**Mineral water**	*saengsu*	생수
Fruit juice	*gwa-il jyuseu*	과일 쥬스	**Water**	*mul*	물

Glossary

ajeossi an older or married man.

ajumma an older or married woman; see p.444.

-am hermitage.

anju bar snacks.

-bang room.

-bawi boulder or large rock.

-bong mountain peak. The highest peak in a park is often referred to as *ilchulbong* ("Number One Peak").

buk- north.

buncheong a Korean style of pottery that became popular in Joseon times. The end product is often bluish-green in colour.

celadon a Korean style of pottery (also common in China and Japan), used since the Three Kingdoms period but largely overtaken by *buncheong* in Joseon times. The end product is often pale green in colour, with a cracked glaze.

cha tea.

-cheon stream or river of less than 100km in length.

Chuseok Korean Thanksgiving.

dae- big, large, great.

daeri-unjeon a network of taxi drivers without taxis; see p.445.

Dangun mythical founder of Korea.

DMZ the Demilitarized Zone that separates North and South Korea.

-do island.

-do province.

-dong city neighbourhood; part of a *–gu*.

dong- east.

dongdongju a milky rice wine much favoured by Korean students; very similar to *makkeolli*.

DPRK Democratic People's Republic of Korea.

-eup town.

-ga section of a major street.

-gang river of over 100km in length.

geobukseon the "turtle ships" as used by Admiral Yi in the late sixteenth century; see p.289.

-gil street.

-gu district of a city, subdivided into *–dong* neighbourhoods.

-gul cave.

-gun county.

-gung palace.

gwageo civil service examinations in the Joseon era.

Gyopo Koreans, or people of Korean descent, living overseas.

hae sea. Korea's East, West and South seas are referred to as *Donghae*, *Seohae* and *Namhae* respectively, though the international nomenclature of the first two (more readily referred to as the "Sea of Japan" and the "Yellow Sea" abroad) is a touchy subject with Koreans.

haenyeo diving ladies, a few of whom can still be found on Jeju Island (see p.363).

hagwon private academy for after-school study. Many expats in Korea are working at an English academy (*yeongeo hagwon*).

hallyu the "Korean New Wave" of pop culture, most specifically cinematic produce.

hanbok traditional Korean clothing.

-hang harbour.

Hangeul the Korean alphabet.

hanja Chinese characters, which are still sometimes used in Korea.

hanji traditional handmade paper.

hanok a style of traditional, tile-roofed wooden housing.

hareubang the famed "grandfather statues" of Jeju Island (see p.378).

-ho lake; also used for those artificially created after the construction of a dam.

hof a Korean-style bar.

Hompy personal homepage.

insam ginseng.

jaebeol major Korean corporation; see p.446.

-jeon temple hall.

jeonse Korean system of property rental; see p.446.

jjimjilbang Korean spa-cum-sauna facilities, often used by families, youth groups and the occasional budget traveller (see p.41).

Juche North Korea's state-sanctioned "religion", a take on Marxist–Leninist theory developed during the Japanese occupation period.

KNTO Korea National Tourism Organization.

KTX the fastest class of Korean train.

makkeolli a milky rice wine much favoured by Korean students; very similar to *dongdongju*.

minbak rented rooms in a private house or building, most commonly found near beaches and national park entrances.

mudang shamanist practitioner; usually female.

mugunghwa Korea's third-highest level of train, one below a *saemaeul*. Named after Korea's national flower, a variety of hibiscus; also known as the "Flower of Sharon", it arrives punctually each year.

-mun city or fortress gate.

-myo Confucian shrine.

nam- south.

-ni village; sometimes pronounced *–ri*.

-no large street; sometimes pronounced *–ro*.

nocheonnyu an "over-the-hill" female; see p.447.

noraebang a "singing room" often the venue of choice for the end of a night out.

oncheon hot spring bath or spa.

ondol traditional underfloor system of heating, made by wood fires underneath traditional buildings, but replaced with gas-fired systems in Korean apartments and modern houses.

pansori Korean opera derived from shamanistic songs, sung by female vocalists to minimalist musical accompaniment.

-pokpo waterfalls.

pyeong Korean unit of measurement equivalent to approximately 3.3 square metres; still commonly used to measure the floorspace of housing or offices.

Red Devils a nickname for the South Korean national football team, or their noisy supporters.

-ri village; sometimes pronounced *–ni*.

-ro large street; sometimes pronounced *–no*.

ROK Republic of Korea.

-sa temple.

Saemaeul Korea's second-highest level of train, one faster than a *mugunghwa* but slower than a KTX. Also the name of the "New Community Movement" inaugurated by Korean president Park Chung-hee in the 1970s.

-san mountain; often used to describe an entire range.

sanseong mountain fortress.

seo- west.

Seon Korean Buddhist sect proximate to Zen in Japan.

seonsaengnim title for a teacher, which goes before the family name, or before the given name in the case of most expat teachers in Korea. Hence, a teacher named Martin will be referred to as "Martin *seonsaengnim*". It's also used as a version of "Mister".

seowon Confucian academy, most prevalent in Joseon times.

-si city, subdivided into *–gu* districts.

sijang market.

soju clear alcoholic drink (around 25 percent alcohol by volume) which is often compared to vodka, and usually cheaper than water at convenience stores up and down the land.

ssireum a Korean wrestling style inevitably compared to sumo, but far closer in form to Mongolian or Greco–Roman styles.

taekwondo Korean martial art; now practised around the world.

tap Pagoda.

tongil unification, a highly important concept on the divided Korean peninsula.

tongmu "comrade", especially useful in communist North Korea.

trot a highly distinctive style of Korean music much favoured by older generations.

woeguk-in foreigner; pronounced "way-goog-in". *Woeguk-saram* is also used.

yangban the scholarly "upper class" in Joseon-era Korea.

yeogwan Korean form of accommodation, similar to a motel but privately run and almost always older.

yeoinsuk Korean form of accommodation, similar to a *yeogwan* but with communal toilets and showers.

South Africa, Lesotho & Swaziland
Syria
Tanzania
Tunisia
West Africa
Zanzibar

Travel Specials
First-Time Africa
First-Time Around the World
First-Time Asia
First-Time Europe
First-Time Latin America
Travel Health
Travel Online
Travel Survival
Walks in London & SE England
Women Travel
World Party

Maps
Algarve
Amsterdam
Andalucia & Costa del Sol
Argentina
Athens
Australia
Barcelona
Berlin
Boston & Cambridge
Brittany
Brussels
California
Chicago
Chile
Corsica
Costa Rica & Panama
Crete
Croatia
Cuba
Cyprus
Czech Republic
Dominican Republic
Dubai & UAE
Dublin
Egypt
France
Frankfurt
Germany
Greece
Guatemala & Belize
Iceland
India
Ireland
Italy
Kenya & Northern Tanzania
Lisbon
London
Los Angeles
Madrid
Malaysia
Mallorca
Marrakesh
Mexico
Miami & Key West
Morocco
New England
New York City
New Zealand
Northern Spain
Paris
Peru
Portugal
Prague
Pyrenees & Andorra
Rome
San Francisco
Sicily
South Africa
South India
Spain & Portugal
Sri Lanka
Tenerife
Thailand
Toronto
Trinidad & Tobago
Tunisia
Turkey
Tuscany
Venice
Vietnam, Laos & Cambodia
Washington DC
Yucatán Peninsula

Phrasebooks
Croatian
Czech
Dutch
Egyptian Arabic
French
German
Greek
Hindi & Urdu
Italian
Japanese
Latin American Spanish
Mandarin Chinese
Mexican Spanish
Polish
Portuguese
Russian
Spanish
Swahili
Thai
Turkish
Vietnamese

Computers
Blogging
eBay
iPhone
iPods, iTunes & music online
The Internet
Macs & OS X
MySpace
PCs and Windows
PlayStation Portable
Website Directory

Film & TV
American Independent Film
British Cult Comedy
Chick Flicks
Comedy Movies
Cult Movies
Film
Film Musicals
Film Noir
Gangster Movies
Horror Movies
Kids' Movies
Sci-Fi Movies
Westerns

Lifestyle
Babies
Ethical Living
Pregnancy & Birth
Running

Music Guides
The Beatles
Blues
Bob Dylan
Book of Playlists
Classical Music
Elvis
Frank Sinatra
Heavy Metal
Hip-Hop
Jazz
Led Zeppelin
Opera
Pink Floyd
Punk
Reggae
Rock
The Rolling Stones
Soul and R&B
Velvet Underground
World Music (2 vols)

Popular Culture
Books for Teenagers
Children's Books, 5-11
Conspiracy Theories
Crime Fiction
Cult Fiction
The Da Vinci Code
His Dark Materials
Lord of the Rings
Shakespeare
Superheroes
The Templars
Unexplained Phenomena

Science
The Brain
Climate Change
The Earth
Genes & Cloning
The Universe
Weather

NOTES

NOTES

NOTES

NOTES

Small print and

Index

A Rough Guide to Rough Guides

Published in 1982, the first Rough Guide – to Greece – was a student scheme that became a publishing phenomenon. Mark Ellingham, a recent graduate in English from Bristol University, had been travelling in Greece the previous summer and couldn't find the right guidebook. With a small group of friends he wrote his own guide, combining a highly contemporary, journalistic style with a thoroughly practical approach to travellers' needs.

The immediate success of the book spawned a series that rapidly covered dozens of destinations. And, in addition to impecunious backpackers, Rough Guides soon acquired a much broader and older readership that relished the guides' wit and inquisitiveness as much as their enthusiastic, critical approach and value-for-money ethos.

These days, Rough Guides include recommendations from shoestring to luxury and cover more than 200 destinations around the globe, including almost every country in the Americas and Europe, more than half of Africa and most of Asia and Australasia. Our ever-growing team of authors and photographers is spread all over the world, particularly in Europe, the USA and Australia.

In the early 1990s, Rough Guides branched out of travel, with the publication of Rough Guides to World Music, Classical Music and the Internet. All three have become benchmark titles in their fields, spearheading the publication of a wide range of books under the Rough Guide name.

Including the travel series, Rough Guides now number more than 350 titles, covering: phrasebooks, waterproof maps, music guides from Opera to Heavy Metal, reference works as diverse as Conspiracy Theories and Shakespeare, and popular culture books from iPods to Poker. Rough Guides also produce a series of more than 120 World Music CDs in partnership with World Music Network.

Visit www.roughguides.com to see our latest publications.

Rough Guide travel images are available for commercial licensing at www.roughguidespictures.com

Rough Guide credits

Text editor: Karoline Thomas
Layout: Jessica Subramanian
Cartography: Animesh Pathak
Picture editor: Mark Thomas
Production: Rebecca Short
Proofreaders: Susannah Wight and Joohee Hahm
Cover design: Chloë Roberts
Photographer: Tim Draper
Editorial: London Ruth Blackmore, Alison Murchie, Andy Turner, Keith Drew, Edward Aves, Alice Park, Lucy White, Jo Kirby, James Smart, Natasha Foges, Róisín Cameron, Emma Traynor, Emma Gibbs, James Rice, Kathryn Lane, Christina Valhouli, Monica Woods, Mani Ramaswamy, Joe Staines, Peter Buckley, Matthew Milton, Tracy Hopkins, Ruth Tidball; **New York** Andrew Rosenberg, Steven Horak, AnneLise Sorensen, April Isaacs, Ella Steim, Anna Owens, Sean Mahoney, Paula Neudorf, Courtney Miller; **Delhi** Madhavi Singh, Karen D'Souza
Design & Pictures: London Scott Stickland, Dan May, Diana Jarvis, Nicole Newman, Sarah Cummins, Emily Taylor; **Delhi** Umesh Aggarwal, Ajay Verma, Ankur Guha, Pradeep Thapliyal, Sachin Tanwar, Anita Singh, Nikhil Agarwal
Production: Vicky Baldwin
Cartography: London Maxine Repath, Ed Wright, Katie Lloyd-Jones; **Delhi** Jai Prakash Mishra, Rajesh Chhibber, Ashutosh Bharti, Rajesh Mishra, Amod Singh, Jasbir Sandhu, Karobi Gogoi, Alakananda Bhattacharya, Swati Handoo
Online: Narender Kumar, Rakesh Kumar, Amit Verma, Rahul Kumar, Ganesh Sharma, Debojit Borah, Saurabh Sati, Ravi Yadav
Marketing & Publicity: London Liz Statham, Niki Hanmer, Louise Maher, Jess Carter, Vanessa Godden, Vivienne Watton, Anna Paynton, Rachel Sprackett, Libby Jellie, Jayne McPherson, Holly Dudley; **New York** Geoff Colquitt, Katy Ball; **Delhi** Ragini Govind
Manager India: Punita Singh
Reference Director: Andrew Lockett
Operations Manager: Helen Phillips
PA to Publishing Director: Nicola Henderson
Publishing Director: Martin Dunford
Commercial Manager: Gino Magnotta
Managing Director: John Duhigg

Publishing information

This first edition published August 2008 by
Rough Guides Ltd,
80 Strand, London WC2R 0RL
345 Hudson St, 4th Floor,
New York, NY 10014, USA
14 Local Shopping Centre, Panchsheel Park,
New Delhi 110017, India
Distributed by the Penguin Group
Penguin Books Ltd,
80 Strand, London WC2R 0RL
Penguin Group (USA)
375 Hudson Street, NY 10014, USA
Penguin Group (Australia)
250 Camberwell Road, Camberwell,
Victoria 3124, Australia
Penguin Books Canada Ltd,
10 Alcorn Avenue, Toronto, Ontario,
Canada M4V 1E4
Penguin Group (NZ)
67 Apollo Drive, Mairangi Bay, Auckland 1310,
New Zealand

Cover concept by Peter Dyer.

Typeset in Bembo and Helvetica to an original design by Henry Iles.

Printed and bound in China

488pp includes index

A catalogue record for this book is available from the British Library

ISBN: 978-1-84353-810-3

1 3 5 7 9 8 6 4 2

Help us update

We've gone to a lot of effort to ensure that the first edition of **The Rough Guide to Korea** is accurate and up to date. However, things change – places get "discovered", opening hours are notoriously fickle, restaurants and rooms raise prices or lower standards. If you feel we've got it wrong or left something out, we'd like to know, and if you can remember the address, the price, the hours, the phone number, so much the better.

Please send your comments with the subject line "**Rough Guide Korea Update**" to ©mail@roughguides.com. We'll credit all contributions and send a copy of the next edition (or any other Rough Guide if you prefer) for the very best emails.

Have your questions answered and tell others about your trip at
@community.roughguides.com

Acknowledgements

Norbert Paxton Every page, every word in this book is dedicated to my mother, Teresa, who passed away between my first and second research trips and remains sorely missed. A thousand thank yous to those who gave me shelter in times of need: Matt Baldwin in Daejeon, Jee in Gwangju, Chris Bemrose in Gunsan, Aram in Aeogae and Christine in Daehangno. Thanks also to Mike Spavor and Jiin for being fantastic travel buddies, James Mullarkey and Darryl Sheepwash for being most excellent partners in crime, Joohee Hahm for all kinds of help (and Nick and cohorts for rather more specific assistance), Daisy for reminding me of the Burberry Man, Najee for the Zorba thing, and Penny Wang for being Penny Wang (and being damn good at it). My blessings on Daejeon for providing such a perfect introduction to the peninsula, and the hundreds of Koreans on both sides of the border who made the creation of my guide seem more of a pleasure than a mode of employment.

Photo credits

All photos © Rough Guides except the following:

Introduction
Mural in Pyongyang © Martin Zatko

Things not to miss
05 Clubbing in Hongdae © Jenny Acheson/Axiom
22 Paekdusan © JTB/Alamy

Colour section: Korean cuisine
Street food © Jenny Acheson/Axiom

Colour section: Hiking in Korea
Ulleungdo © Travel Pix/Alamy

Black and white pictures
p.394 The Mass Games © Martin Zatko
p.408 Pyongyang subway © Martin Zatko
p.410 Victorious Fatherland Liberation War Memorial © Martin Zatko
p.412 Kaesong © Martin Zatko

Index

Map entries are in colour.

INDEX

T

U

V

W

Y

NOTES

Map symbols

maps are listed in the full index using coloured text

- --- Chapter division boundary
- International boundary
- Regional boundary
- Motorway
- Major road
- Minor road
- Pedestrianized street
- Railway
- •----• Cable Car
- ----- Footpath
- River
- Ferry
- ■ ■ ■ Wall/fortification
- ⊠ Gate
-)(Bridge
- Cliff
- Mountain range
- ▲ Mountain peak
- Mountain pass
- Rocks
- Cave
- Spring
- Mountain Lodge
- Lighthouse
- ✈ Airport
- Ⓢ Subway
- Museum
- ★ Bus stop
- ♦ Point of interest
- Observatory
- Monument
- ⓘ Tourist office/information point
- ✉ Post office
- Golf Course
- ∩ Arch
- ◉ Accommodation
- Skiing
- Campsite
- Border Crossing
- Fortress
- Shrine
- Buddhist Temple
- ⊙ Statue/memorial
- Temple
- Pagoda
- □ Market
- ■ Building
- Church
- Stadium
- Park
- Beach

MAP SYMBOLS

Travel store